COMMANDER-IN-CHIEF
GENERAL VÕ NGUYÊN GIÁP

Trần Trọng Trung

COMMANDER-IN-CHIEF
GENERAL VÕ NGUYÊN GIÁP

Thế Giới Publishers

© Thế Giới Publishers 2014
English translation
First edition 2014
Printed in Việt Nam
VN-TG - 05-48-1
ISBN: 978-604-77-0975-5

All rights reserved. No part of this publication may be reproduced, stored in or introduced into a retrieval system, or transmitted, in any form, or by any means (electronic, mechanical, photocopying, recording or otherwise) without the prior written permission of the publisher.

National Library of Vietnam Cataloguing in Publication Data

Tran Trong Trung

Commander in chief General Võ Nguyên Giáp = Tổng tư lệnh Đại tướng Võ Nguyên Giáp / Tran Trong Trung. - H. : The gioi,. - 843 p. : phot. ; 21 cm

1. Vo Nguyen Giap, General, 1911-2013, Vietnam 2. History 3. French resistance war

959.704092 - dc23

TGK0038p-CIP

Trần Trọng Trung

COMMANDER-IN-CHIEF
GENERAL VÕ NGUYÊN GIÁP

Thế Giới Publishers

© Thế Giới Publishers 2014
English translation
First edition 2014
Printed in Việt Nam
VN-TG - 05-48-1
ISBN: 978-604-77-0975-5

All rights reserved. No part of this publication may be reproduced, stored in or introduced into a retrieval system, or transmitted, in any form, or by any means (electronic, mechanical, photocopying, recording or otherwise) without the prior written permission of the publisher.

National Library of Vietnam Cataloguing in Publication Data

Tran Trong Trung

Commander in chief General Võ Nguyên Giáp = Tổng tư lệnh Đại tướng Võ Nguyên Giáp / Tran Trong Trung. - H. : The gioi,. - 843 p. : phot. ; 21 cm

1. Vo Nguyen Giap, General, 1911-2013, Vietnam 2. History 3. French resistance war

959.704092 - dc23

TGK0038p-CIP

GENERAL VÕ NGUYÊN GIÁP
(1911–2013)

TABLE OF CONTENTS

Opening Chapter:
Defeating Ten Generals in an Odyssey 9

Chapter One:
The Path to a Military Career 60
    From a Schoolboy to a Politician 60
    From the Meeting with Nguyễn Ái Quốc to the First Lessons on the Revolution 70
    From a Pathfinder to a Military Commander 82
    When the Opportunity Came 98
    From Tân Trào to Hà Nội 111

Chapter Two:
Sixteen Months in the Capital City 121
    Meeting Uninvited Guests 121
    A Snow-covered Volcano 146
    "... We Have Old Huỳnh and Young Giáp" 160
    "A French Attack will Only Be a Matter of Time..." 170
    When the Enemy was Bent on War 184
    The Day Before the War Began 193

Chapter Three:
Early Challenges 207
    Keeping Abreast of the Developments
    in the Main Battlefields 207
    Transferring the Capital 227
    Entering the Dry Season 242
    Turning the Tables 267
    Celebrating Victory 282

Chapter Four:
Advance to a Strange Turning Point 301
    Launching "Flexible Strategic Counter-attacks"
    on the Enemy's Temporarily-occupied Areas 301
    Practising Mobile War—The Firm Steps 308
    Creating Factors for Victory in the
    First Large-scale Campaign 330
    The Combat of Wits on the 4th Route 360

Chapter Five:
On the Way to Promote the War of Movement ... 397
    General de Lattre—The Fifth Opponent 397
    The Midlands—A Sensitive Battlefield 402
    In the Forum of the National Party Congress 423
    Heavy Impressions on the 18th Route 439
    In the Battlefield in the Flooded Rice Area 459

Chapter Six:
Determination to Hold the Offensive 485
    Crushing de Lattre's Plot to Gain the Initiative 485
    Maintaining the Struggle in Areas Behind
    the Enemy Lines 527

Changing the Attack Direction to the Northwest
Mountainous Battlefield 561

In the Lao Battlefield 616

Chapter Seven:
The Final Efforts of France and the United States 647

The Seventh Commander-in-chief
of the French Expeditionary Army 647

The First Strategic Moves on the Threshold
of the Dry Season 661

To the Front with the Whole Nation 681

Twelve Unforgettable Days 703

Chapter Eight:
The Final Strategic Move 726

Preparation for a Decisive Battle 726

"Peeling" 744

April—The Touchstone 766

Time for Action 788

Concluding Chapter:
Portrait of a General 813

A Politician First, a Military Officer Later 817

The "Ego" in the Relation with the Collective 827

"A Great Commander-in-chief" 833

A Man of Humanism 836

Opening Chapter

DEFEATING TEN GENERALS IN AN ODYSSEY

Hà Nội—the capital city of Việt Nam, 26 years after the liberation of the South

Never had there been more articles written on Võ Nguyên Giáp than during the closing months of 2001, when General Giáp was nearing his 90th birthday anniversary. He is affectionately called the "Big Brother" of the Vietnamese People's Army, and is a Vietnamese commander-in-chief who wins the hearts of not only his men and military colleagues but also the general public as a whole.

Authors of those articles come from diverse backgrounds, ranging from scholars to military figures, from his childhood classmates to his comrades in the 30-year struggle, from his family relatives to people of much younger generations. Although they addressed the same topic and talked about the same man, these articles had extremely diverse contents. All of them attempted to portray what they believed, from their field or perspective, as the most outstanding features of General Giáp's while his childhood classmates and former students recalled their numerous memories with

"Teacher Võ–Brother Văn." Historians, meanwhile, wrote about Giáp's relations with Hồ Chí Minh, who had a great impact on his military career, both technically and ethically. Military analysts described him as a visionary strategist with outstanding combat mettle—one of Việt Nam's military geniuses of the Hồ Chí Minh epoch who commanded his people's army to victory over ten generals of two imperialist superpowers. Medical caregivers recollected the memories they had with General Giáp while security officers recounted their missions to protect the general during his foreign visits. One of his family relatives even went extra length to search far and wide to gather distant memories of him and pieced them together in a book titled *Võ Nguyên Giáp—Quê hương, gia đình, tuổi thơ* (literally: Võ Nguyên Giáp—Hometown, Family and Childhood). There was also one journalist who chose to look at him from a different perspective, depicting him in his daily life as a 90-year-old man of razor-sharp mind who practiced Zen every morning; jogged every afternoon in his garden; worked three to four hours; ate five meals (for easy digestion, as he explains); and spent the rest of the day reading book, watching TV, playing the piano and with his grandchildren.

The *Quân đội nhân dân* (literally: **People's Army**) daily chose August 25—Giáp's birthday—to publish an article about his longevity anniversary. It reads:

> Days before the General's birthday anniversary, his house had already been full of visitors, including government leaders, military officers, leaders of mass organizations, the elderly and the young alike, families living in the wartime revolutionary military bases, and family relatives. The whole house was filled with bunches of flowers. Some of these were sent from his former military men and comrades; some were

presents from Pác Bó while others came from overseas. The warm feelings he received were indicative of the reverence and adoration people reserved for the first General of our army—an excellent student of our beloved Uncle Hô.

Many researchers took this occasion to re-read General Giáp's military writings or books that foreign authors wrote about him, be it a simple chronological biography or a thorough work about one of the most prominent figures of Việt Nam's modern revolutionary military history.

Earlier some foreign historians or statesmen had expressed their doubts as to when Võ Nguyên Giáp was born—was it in 1910, 1911, or 1912? A historian by the name of James Fox even insisted in his article published on *The Sunday Times* magazine (November 5–12, 1972) that he had accidentally came across Giáp's certificate of birth in Paris which showed that he was born on September 1, 1910. His exact date of birth had seemed a secret to international biographers when somehow on this year birthday anniversary, an article quoted Giáp's wife Đặng Bích Hà as saying that she ascertained, relying on her mother-in-law's words and on comparison between Western solar calendar and Vietnamese lunar calendar, that he was born on August 25, 1911. It was also in this year that Hô Chí Minh started his odyssey in search of a path to regain independence for Việt Nam. When he set foot on the Port of Dunkirk (French: *Dunkerque*), he couldn't have imagined that a man born in his country on the same day would become his right-hand aid and confidant 30 years later. Many researchers take a keen interest in this numerical permutation: Võ Nguyên Giáp was born on August 25 (25/8) and 37 years later, on May 28 (28/5), he was named General by Hô Chí Minh.

The four silver stars conferred to him in 1948 by President Hồ Chí Minh on behalf of the entire people were born on Giáp's shoulder-straps for the remaining years of his military life, even until his longevity birthday celebration, when his hair had turned cloud-white.

To use a military term, the event on May 28, 1948 was just a "regularization" of a decision Hồ Chí Minh made three years before when he "assigned Brother Văn—Giáp's nickname—with the task of forming a liberation army" by the end of 1944. That time, along with the decision to entrust the national army to Giáp came guiding instructions for that army to survive, develop, and champion—Party guidance, popular support, and discipline and solidarity. Bearing in mind those teachings, Giáp led his men, whom Hồ Chí Minh affectionately called "the fledgling army," to maturity and repeated victories over the course of the nation's three stages of glorious struggle: military preparation and uprising to gain authority, resistance war against the French colonizers, and resistance war against the American imperialists. During that long march of 30 years (1945–1975), the revolutionary army, who started with bare-footed men armed with nothing more than rifles, forced the defeat of ten generals (seven were French and three were American) on this land under Giáp's talented command.

During the 1945 August Revolution, the day Giáp deployed the troops from Tân Trào to liberate Thái Nguyên coincided with the day when President Charles de Gaulle sent the four-star general Philippe Leclerc and the French expeditionary army under the latter's command to reoccupy Indochina. From that September onwards, Leclerc became the first adversary of Giáp, who was then the Chairman of the Military Committee and the Minister of Interiors of the newly-established revolutionary government.

Given the Vietnamese army's unsophisticated weaponry and lack of military experience at the initial stage of the war, it was no surprise that the French troops soon managed to expand their scope of occupation in the South. At the end of February 1946, Leclerc, the commander-in-chief of the French army, was quick to declare an end to the occupation stage and a switch to a northward advance for pacification. One crucial thing that none of the French generals at that time and later American counterparts were able to gauge appropriately on multiple occasions was that loss of land in one place does not mean defeat. It was the support of the local people that made the decisive factor.

Immediately after fighting broke out in Sài Gòn (present-day Hồ Chí Minh City), Chairman of the Military Committee Võ Nguyên Giáp instructed Chief of the General Staff Hoàng Văn Thái to deploy troops to the South in support of the battlefront there. On September 26, just three days after the French provoked hostilities in the South, the first train carrying the best soldiers and weaponry departed from Hàng Cỏ Railway Station (present-day Hà Nội Railway Station) heading for the South. The soldiers on the train sang in unison a song General Thái composed at the suggestion of General Giáp. Here are two lines of the song: "Raising high our liberating flag, we march forward./ Our compatriots are longing."

The Lunar New Year of 1946, the first *Tết* after independence, General Giáp went on an inspection tour to the South. Seeing the Vietnamese troops at a disadvantaged position, he instructed the commanders of Central Highlands and Southern Central Coast fronts not to deploy huge forces of troops against the advance of the enemy but to send small and medium-sized units infiltrating the French-controlled areas to reinstall political bases, organize guerrilla-style war, and mobilized the locals to join the widespread war of attrition against the enemy with any kind of weapon they had in hand. It was thanks to this strategic switch in operation that political and military bases[1] began to make their presence in the South as the March-6 Preliminary Accords (commonly referred to in Western scholarly works as the Hồ-Sainteny Agreement) and the Franco-Vietnamese Modus Vivendi of September 14, 1946 were signed, giving the Vietnamese army a better strategic position in many parts of the South to "stage a renewed uprising." As a result, the revolutionary forces in the South were relatively well-prepared when the popular resistance erupted.

In July 1946, General Leclerc was summoned back to France, not only because of his failure to realize his pledged intention of "conquering Cochinchina within matters of weeks" when he set foot on Sài Gòn but also because the French government cabinet had then been led by Georges Bidault, who was determined to accelerate the war. Leclerc was the only commander-in-chief who, basing on his on-the-spot judgement of the battle situations, did not believe in the possibility of conquering Indochina by use of military might. He therefore acceded to negotiations with the Việt Minh, a move that irritated the war-like faction in France, including High Commissioner Georges Thierry d'Argenlieu and even

---

1. Small and large areas where revolutionary forces were able to install political or military, covert or overt bases operating right within enemy-controlled regions.

those who had earlier served as Governor-General of French Indochina like Albert Sarraut, or those whose political influence remained high although they were no longer in office like De Gaulle. In the wake of General Leclerc's departure, Etienne Valluy, who was seen as "competent enough to shoulder the extremely difficult task of defeating General Giáp and his Việt Minh troops," held the post of Commander of the French army and became Giáp's second adversary. Unlike Leclerc, this general was intent on the use of force, as evidenced in his policy to resort to military might to "finish quickly any battle." In the middle of April 1946, only one month after the French army entered Hà Nội as a result of the Preliminary Accords, Valluy—in the role of Commander of the French army in the north of Indochina—instructed his subordinates to develop a combat plan in such a way that it could transform an aggression totally military in nature into simply "a coup d'état." While this new commander, after assuming his post, was "successful" in using military action to provoke, encroach, and finally erupt the war throughout the country, he had to concede defeat in two battles against Giáp, mentally and militarily. In July 1946, as soon as he assumed office, Valluy and his lackeys and subordinates intended to stage a coup d'état right in Hà Nội in order to overthrow the revolutionary government while the Vietnamese delegation headed by Hồ Chí Minh was in France for negotiations. Approved by General Secretary Trường Chinh and Acting President Huỳnh Thúc Kháng, General Giáp directed security officers and militiamen to capture all the lackeys together with evidence of their subversive plot, thwarting Valluy's coup d'état attempt right from its seminal stage. The second strategically significant "defeat" for Valluy was his failure to wipe out the small-sized revolutionary army right in the heart of Hà Nội after December 19, 1946. The unpredictability of guerrilla tactics employed by these bare-footed militiamen, armed with nothing but rifles, enabled them to withstand French attack for as long as two months right in the heart of the capital city, exceeding substantially the expectation of the Việt Minh leaders in terms of both their ability to hold up French army and the number of enemy troops they killed. They subsequently withdrew from the city to the safety zone and later became the key elements of the future regular army.

In the summer of 1947, there started to be anxiety among the authorities in Paris regarding the prolonged and costly war they had waged. As a result, it was decided that Valluy would be aided by Raoul Salan—a cunning and "old-hand" colonial officer who was reputed to know Indochina, particularly the Tonkinese highlands, as thoroughly as he knew the back of his hand, having served as a chief of the Đình Lập Post in Lạng Sơn between 1925 and 1930, speaking the local Tày and Nùng languages, drinking *rượu cần* (wine drunk out of a jar through pipes), and inhaling opium. Throughout the summer and autumn of 1947, thanks to Salan's familiarity with the region, the French Command decided to fight a decisive battle in the dry season. It was in this period that General Giáp and his associates in the military headquarters withdrew from the suburbs of Hà Nội to retreat to Việt Bắc.[1] He convened, on each phase of the retreat, several military meetings in the attendance of officers from different levels. These meetings, which were actually short-term training sessions, aimed to provide heads of military units at both central and local levels with a guideline

---

1. Việt Bắc is a mountainous region of Việt Nam north of Hà Nội that served as the Việt Minh's base of support during the First Indochina War (1946–1954).

as to how to "respond" to hot, and sometimes urgent, military issues that arose in the battlefield. General Giáp is known for his thorough and detailed instructions to military cadres, especially those whose skills and awareness remained limited at the inception of the Franco-Vietnamese war.

The first "dry season" of the resistance war came, when the French Military Command was intent on launching a decisive battle. On October 7, 1947, approximately 20,000 French troops formed two huge pincer attacks, one to the East against Hà Nội-Lạng Sơn-Cao Bằng extending about 400 kilometers and another to the West against Hà Nội-Tuyên Quang-Chiêm Hóa, about 250 kilometers, encircling the Việt Minh resistance military base. Here, they combined with paratroops who landed directly onto the heart of Việt Bắc (i.e. Bắc Cạn Town, wrongly believed by the French as the Resistance Capital as they thought Hồ Chí Minh was working there), intending to capture the whole cabinet of the Hồ Chí Minh government and eliminate the Việt Minh regular forces. This sudden attack came at a wrong time for the Việt Minh as it happened while General Giáp was on an inspection tour to Chiêm Hóa District in Tuyên Quang Province.

As soon as he was back to the Headquarters, Giáp was informed of the French attack and immediately spotted the enemy's dead-wrong move of deploying too many troops on a vast hilly locality, far from the lowland bases, which made supply and enforcements difficult. He then reported the situation to the Central Committee and Hồ Chí Minh, and suggested a tactical change in fighting back the French. Specifically, Giáp suggested that as the enemy resorted to infantry, paratroops, tanks, and artillery to launch a massive attack, the Việt Minh should not stick to its original plan of using its major regular army from regional and central levels to fight against. Rather, they should send small- and medium-sized units to ambush the enemy mainly on land and on waterway while sending some companies of regular soldiers to operate independently in different districts tasked mainly with waging a war of attrition against the enemy, assisting the local armed forces in launching an extensive guerrilla war, and encouraging the local people to "leave their houses and gardens empty," hide away the food sources, and destroy local infrastructure like bridges and roads. Only several weeks after the deployment of forces in three directions, the 3rd and 4th Routes and the Lô River (the 2nd Route), tens of thousands of enemy troops were confronted with increasingly difficult situations due to the debilitating extreme highland weather and shortage of reinforcements and supplies. They also constantly faced up with unpredictable attacks by what they called *"armée fantôme"* (literally: "ghost army") who took advantage of the dense forests and towering mountains to launch daily ambushes in a war of attrition which forced them to flee out of Việt Bắc after 75 days. The strategically important victory in the first dry season of the resistance war could be directly attributed to the well-chosen combat tactics and the prompt decision to change fighting tactics to suit the on-the-spot situations at the battlefield.

In early 1948, President Hồ Chí Minh and the Central Committee of the Communist Party of Việt Nam (Party Central Committee for short) advocated a nation-wide guerrilla war, calling upon the whole nation to engage in a war of attrition against the enemy, forcing them to split their own troops into different fronts, and limiting their ability to occupy and pacify the temporarily conquered areas, especially those in the midland and lowland of the North. This strategic policy was carried out in a most creative way. With his newly gained experience in commanding the companies operating independently in different districts throughout the Việt Bắc campaign and in mobilizing popular support during the preparation for the military upheaval, Giáp proposed that the Central Party Committee split up one third of the core forces into several independent companies to provide backing for the armed propaganda units when they infiltrated into the temporarily occupied regions to re-establish grassroots political bases and assist the local cadres in forming clandestine armed forces, building fighting villages, launching guerrilla war, and protecting the hamlets. Through this method of operation, the political and military organizations (known among the enemy as "red spots") began to mushroom on the battlefield map of the enemy rear regions. The small yet increasingly omnipresent battles waged by the on-the-spot armed forces were successful in fatiguing a major portion of the enemy's regular army, forcing them to disperse their troops into smaller units thereby confronting the French Command with a critical numerical shortage of troops. The other two thirds of the Việt Minh's core soldiers were divided into different concentrated battalions who gradually became more seasoned through small-scale operations that involved two to three battalions, concentrating on killing and fatiguing the enemy while drawing out their own lessons and gathering increased experience in reality. The developments in the battlefields between 1948 and 1950 showed that General Giáp accorded utmost attention to the strategic importance of guerrilla war. He however did not equate guerrilla warfare with small, sporadic, and spontaneous clashes. Instead, he increasingly combined guerrilla wars with regular wars from a lower to a higher level.[1] The "independent company-concentrated battalion" model of troop development was unheard of in any military annals east or west, old or new. It was a unique invention of Võ Nguyên Giáp so as to give his army a firm "tripod-like footing," consisting of regular troops, local troops, and militia and guerrillas. It was thanks to this tactics that he was able to carry out the policy of the Party Central Committee on waging guerrilla warfare while maintaining a close and constant link between two strategic operational methods: guerrilla warfare and regular warfare—a Vietnamese style of warfare that begins with concentrated battles of small and medium scales.

Failure to control the highland, midland, and lowland regions resulted in General Valluy's being recalled and replaced by General Roger Blaizot, who became Giáp's third adversary. It was on this very occasion that Võ Nguyên Giáp, then aged 37, was named "General" by President Hồ Chí Minh on behalf of the Government and the people. This was the first and also the only time he had a military rank conferred upon.

---

1. Refer to the following military directives: *"Về sự cần thiết phải chuyển sang du kích vận động chiến"* (literally: "On the Need to Switch to Guerrilla Battles") (March 6, 1947), *"Chuyển từ tiêu hao chiến sang tiêu diệt chiến"* (literally: "Switching from War of Attrition to War of Decimation") (August 1947), *"Phát động chiến tranh du kích—Nhiệm vụ quân sự căn bản trong giai đoạn này"* (literally: "Waging Guerrilla Wars—A Fundamental Military Task in the Meantime") (November 14, 1947), in *Những tài liệu chỉ đạo cuộc đấu tranh vũ trang của Trung ương Đảng và Tổng Quân ủy* (literally: *Collection of Military Directives on Armed Struggle Issued by the Party Central Committee and its Central Military Commission*), published by the General Staff Command, Hà Nội, 1964, vol. 1, pp. 141, 205 & 163.

The regular troops, after engaging in over 20 small-scale campaigns, now became more mature and skilled, evidenced in the coming into existence of two first major brigades (the 308th and 304th Brigades in August 1949 and March 1950 respectively). France, in the meantime, was confronted with mounting heaps of challenges. Twelve different cabinets had been changed within the course of only four years since the war began. Unable to pursue a prolonged war that wreaked havoc with national budget, Paris decided in May 1949 to send Chief of Staff General Georges Revers to Việt Nam to make a plan to gradually place the first Indochina War into the orbit of the United States while revoking General Blaizot to be replaced by General Marcel Carpentier as Commander-in-chief, who would take entire responsibility for the implementation of the Revers Strategy.[1] Carpentier became Giáp's fourth adversary, at the time when the very first American ships dispatched by the White House and the Pentagon that carried military assistance reached the harbours of Sài Gòn and Hải Phòng. Within the space of only one year, with the first large-scale attack (involving two brigades) in the dry season of 1950 on the Northeastern battlefield that killed approximately ten battalions of French and Afro-European army, General Giáp forced General Carpentier to admit what the French side bitterly referred to as "the Cao Bằng catastrophe," which

---

1. The Revers Strategy included: 1- Making use of American aid to reinforce the expeditionary army; 2- Applying the policy "Using war to feed war—Using Vietnamese to fight against Vietnamese" (all-out war); 3- Upholding a pro-French government to attract the anti-revolutionary forces; 4- Reducing the Northeastern frontier defense line to Lạng Sơn, strengthening the temporarily occupied zones in the midland and mid-Red River Delta; 5- Developing mercenary army along with establishing a bigger Euro-African mobile task force.

resulted in the latter being recalled to his home country. In December of the same year, Paris had to send another general, aged 60, with five silver stars on his shoulder strap insignia to command the expeditionary army. He was tasked with an extremely important mission of "saving the Indochina from slipping out of the French Union". This well-known veteran general, who was of noble extraction, belonged to the older generation among the French top-flight military officers thanks to his remarkable achievements and deeds during the Second World War. He was Jean de Lattre de Tassigny, Giáp's fifth and also seen as most worthy adversary. In addition, he received the highest trust and privilege from Governor-General Sarraut.

De Lattre arrived in Sàigon on December 17, 1950, accompanied by a completely new command made up of high-ranking officers whom he gave utmost trust as they used to serve under him in the 1st Corps. This corps was known for their successful liberation of Paris in the autumn of 1944, with the aid of the Allied army. In this new commanding team, again, was Salan, this time in the new position as de Lattre's deputy. To demonstrate their determination in protecting what the colonialists in Paris called "the most beautiful flower in the garden of French colonies," especially in order to exert full and real control over the Red River Delta, which the military people in France praised as a useful plain, de Lattre mapped out a crucial strategic plan with the ambition of regaining the upper-hand position from General Giáp. The most salient component of this plan, which rested on increasing American aid, was the ambition to establish a concrete defense line encompassing the northern Red River Delta and build the mercenary army to an unprecedented scale since the inception of the war, with a view to remedying the worsening shortage of military force. The new feature of the de Lattre plan, however, was the first appearance of the term "Vietnamization" which implied the conscription of increasingly large local mercenary army, backed by the United States of America. de Lattre was the one who took the initiative to give the American imperialists favourable conditions to intervene more deeply into the Indochina War. Linking what de Lattre did at the beginning of the 1950s to the war of invasion that the Americans waged against Việt Nam tem years later, General Giáp later remarked in a memoir titled *"Đường tới Điện Biên Phủ"* (literally: "Road to Điện Biên Phủ") that, "By opening the door to welcome in the new colonialists, de Lattre brought a long-term threat to our nation."

One of the favourable conditions for de Lattre was that from as early as the Second World War, he had developed close relations with many of the highest-ranking generals in the Allied forces like American General Dwight Eisenhower and British General Bernard Montgomery, who were ready to pressure their governments into providing France with assistance during the Indochina War. It was because of this "heartfelt" support and assistance from the United States of America and Britain that de Lattre was able to carry out his above-mentioned plan in a fairly easy manner. During the autumn months of 1951, however, the implementation of the de Lattre plan was seriously challenged by the Việt Minh's three successive offensives on the battlefields in the midland and the Red River Delta. In these three campaigns, the Commander-in-chief of the French army had to rely on the favourable geographical conditions conducive to relief troops and reinforcements and the use of mighty weaponry to elevate the demoralized army after heavy defeats in the frontier the previous dry season.

The first major battle was when Giáp launched an offensive on the land of Vĩnh Yên (known as the Trần Hưng Đạo campaign, January 1951). De Lattre and Salan took turns to embark on shuttle flights to and fro between Vĩnh Yên and Hà Nội, almost on a daily basis. There were occasions, such as January 15, when the two generals made three return flights in one single day. Before de Lattre, few top commanders would be physically present right in the battlefield where gunfire roared; it was really a rare sight. In addition, tens of battalions were speedily dispatched to provide aid and reinforcements. General Baillif, deputy commander of the Southern battlefield, was given order to immediately go north to conduct the war in Vĩnh Yên directly. The French in fact conducted as many as 250 air raids on such a small land as Vĩnh Yên; there were days when as many as 80 fighting aircraft were involved and French artillery fired up to 50 thousand 105-mm cannon bullets and 200 thousand 75-mm ones. It was also during this period that napalm bombs were used for the first time. However, as General Salan later recounted in his memoir, de Lattre had to admit that he was worried about the huge casualties suffered by the French and the Afro-European troops in Vĩnh Yên, and that the Vĩnh Yên battle taught him many vital lessons. For his part, the Vĩnh Yên incident, according to General Salan, showed that "the Việt Minh army represented a military might that we, the French, could not afford to disrespect. All their warriors were so well-educated and trained that they demonstrated exceptional morale. That profoundly impressed and enormously affected the fighting spirit of the North African troops. It was General de Lattre himself who was agitated by the enthusiasm and intelligence that the Việt Minh soldier demonstrated in the battlefield day and night."

The second clash took place two months later on Road 18 and the Northeastern coastal region. General Giáp launched the Hoàng Hoa Thám campaign at the time when de Lattre was back in France requesting reinforcements and aids. Having heard of "the bursting mine," de Lattre hastily left Paris for Hà Nội on the evening of March 26 and then travelled to Hải Phòng to directly lead the army against the spreading offensive by the opposing side. Admiral Paul Ortoli was immediately summoned and every means of fire-power, including naval artillery, was mobilized to save Mạo Khê, Bí Chợ, and Tràng Bạch. Another development that took de Lattre by surprise happened two months later: General Giáp opened another campaign, i.e. Quang Trung campaign, this time in the direction of Hà Nam Ninh. It was in this third major battle that General de Lattre suffered an unimaginable pain: his only son and the last descendent of the family, Bernard de Lattre, aged 23, lost his life in the battle of Gối Hạc on May 30. Salan noted that after the death of his son, the Commander-in-chief was so grief-laden that he became emaciated.

By the end of 1951, the physical component of the de Lattre strategic plan had been basically completed. Twenty-eight out of 45 battalions of mercenary troops had been created and were initially organized into four divisions, under the command of French officers. On the other hand, the French and Afro-European troops were gradually developed into seven mobile regiments which later became the core forces deployed by de Lattre to confront the spring-summer offensives launched by the Việt Minh. The bunker defense line had basically taken shape with over 80 posts (around 800 blockhouses), stretching from the northeastern region to the northwestern midland of Hà Nội before reaching out to the Red River Delta to the south of Hà Nội. Twenty-five Afro-European battalions were bogged down here, together with a huge amount of military supplies for the defense line. A series of large-scale mopping-up operations took place on a frequent basis inside the defense line to wipe out the "red spots" and pacify the rear. French troops stopped at nothing, resorting to even the most brutal and barbaric acts like setting fire to rice granaries, killing cattle, destroying farm tools, massacring civilians, and especially conscripting local men to supplement their mercenary army.

At the beginning of November 1951, although their plan had not been totally completed, the French administration urged General de Lattre to deploy troops to regain the strategic initiative from General Giáp. Under that pressure, General de Lattre decided to deploy over 30 battalions out of the bunker defense line to conquer Hòa Bình Town, the 6th Route, and the Đà River route, with the intention of "breaking the Việt Minh into halves." On November 15, after the operation finished, General de Lattre declared in a press conference that he had "captured the enemy." The next day, he personally came to Hòa Bình Town to encourage his men to "strengthen fortifications and wait for the Việt Minh to come." Four days later, he left Sài Gòn for France on a medical leave, having passed the command of the army to General Salan.

In a letter to Vietnamese cadres, military officers, militiamen, and guerillas involved in the Hòa Bình campaign, President Hồ Chí Minh wrote, "Formerly we had to lure them out. Now they've presented themselves for us to strike. It's a good chance for us."[1] In fact, General de Lattre had hoped that General Giáp would use all forces in hand to attack the entrenched fortifications (with six élite battalions well equipped with weapons and machines) that he had built in Hòa Bình Town. These fortifications were built for the purpose of "breaking the Việt Minh in halves." However, as historian Bernard Fall noted, General Giáp had his own strategy. He would not engage his army immediately into a battle if it was not in an advantageous position over the enemy. Only after the enemy had invested all their energy and strength in attacking an unmanned battlefield in the mountainous area, which meant giving Giáp an opportunity to score a victory like that on the 4th Route in 1950, did Giáp deploy most of his regular army into the battlefield of Hòa Bình at such an unprecedented and unimagined speed. When assigning tasks to brigade commanders, Giáp, in his capacity as Commander-in-chief, encouraged them to turn the Đà River into the Lô River, and the 6th Route into the 4th Route.[2]

Giáp's commanding manner and genius was beyond the anticipation of General de Lattre and his French colleagues. By estimating the limited power of his troops, Giáp instructed them to stay away from the enemy stronghold in Hòa Bình and attack ferociously on land and on waterway instead, aiming particularly at French transportation vans on the 6th

---

1. *Hồ Chí Minh toàn tập* (literally: Hồ Chí Minh's Complete Works), National Political Publishing House, Hà Nội, 2002, pp. 6 & 341.
2. It means to force the French to suffer the same defeat as that on the Lô River and the 4th Route in the Việt Bắc campaign during the dry season of 1947.

Route (dubbed "the dry gullet") and on the Đà River ("the wet gullet"), which were the two vital reinforcement channels feeding the whole French army at the Hòa Bình front. It was also in this situation that General Giáp demonstrated another aspect of his commanding talent. Envisioning the paucity and laxity of defense at the enemy's rear after they had moved their major forces to the front, he ordered two brigades to edge their way through the bunker defense line to penetrate further into the midland and the Red River Delta, combining with the local armed forces to destroy scores of French outposts and liberating approximately two million civilians in an area of 4,000 square kilometres within the enemy rear. Fiercely attacked on both fronts, General Salan sent the 1st, 3rd, 4th, and 7th Mobile Regiments moving like shuttles and spinners in and out of the defense line, yet his attempts were of little or no avail. He was unable to reverse the situation. With the two "gullets" being strictly blocked and even totally severed, the "stomach" of Hòa Bình gradually shrank. It was in these anxious moments that the French suffered another severe setback as the thunderbolt news came from Paris informing them of General de Lattre's decease on January 11, 1952. Salan immediately decided to withdraw from the Hòa Bình front on February 22. Bernard Fall underscored a remarkable detail: in order to guarantee safe withdrawal for an about-20,000-troop army within the course of three successive days, the French had to fire over 30,000 cannon bullets all the way from Hòa Bình to Xuân Mai, along the 6th Route. General Salan later confessed in his memoir that it was not until 6 am on February 25, after the last unit managed to withdraw past the Xuân Mai crossroads, that he could breathe a sigh of relief, as if he had been stripped of a burden.

This was a "sincere" admission of the failure of the general offensive to conquer Hòa Bình, and ultimately the failed intention of regaining the strategic initiative. Bernard Fall quoted a high-ranking officer in the French army as saying that General de Lattre seemed to have timed his demise properly, so that he would not have to witness his humiliating defeat with his own eyes and himself being given the sack.

Being entrusted with the commanding position, first temporarily since January 1952 and then officially since April of the same year, General Salan became General Giáp's sixth adversary. His constant worry was how to prevent the Red River Delta from further "decay." Never had there been such brutal and ferocious mopping and raid as what was seen in the spring and summer of 1952, which inflicted heavy losses on the Vietnamese part. In anticipation of the difficulties which might occur at the enemy rear when they had withdrawn from Hòa Bình to the lowland, Giáp instructed different agencies of the Ministry of National Defense to coordinate with relevant responsible sectors to make concerted efforts to firmly maintain the position and status of the revolutionary army inside the areas under the enemy's temporary control. During the course of seven years, never had there been such elaborate, detailed, and immediate orders from the Commander-in-chief. The "pace of guerrillas" needed to match and support the "pace of the regular army."

As the dry season approached, Commander-in-chief Võ Nguyên Giáp had to find the answer to a big question: In which strategic direction should the core troops advance? With six strategic substitute brigades under his command, which direction would engender a change or development of strategic significance? He ruled out the possibility and suggestion to engage in "small-scale battles." After examining the difficulties encountered on the midland and lowland battlefields during the spring and summer of 1951 and the advantages gained from the recent battlefield in the mountainous Hòa Bình, he came to a strategically important decision, asking the Party Central Committee for permission to change the direction of the core army to the mountainous battlefield of the West. With that strategic change, the Northwest campaign at the end of 1952 and another campaign launched in coordination with the Pathet Lao army in the Upper Laos in the summer of 1953 constituted not only two major offensives that helped to liberate the people and the land and laid the foundation for the establishment of a spacious military base in the Northwestern region of the country, but also gave the Laotian revolution a firm foothold in the north of Laos and, more importantly, an advantageous position in the battlefield conducive for the implementation of the Việt Minh's subsequent strategic plans, including the Điện Biên Phủ campaign.

It was during the days when General Giáp was instructing his men in pursuit of the enemy on a 270-km route during the Sam Neua campaign in Upper Laos that the French administration decided once again to change horse in midstream. Raoul Salan was replaced by Henri Navarre, a young general who started his career as an intelligence officer and who was known for his strategic vision. He was not only recommended by Marshal Alphonse Juin himself but also received congratulations from American President Eisenhower on the occasion. On May 7, 1953, during an audience with French Prime Minister René Mayer, Navarre was charged with a general task of "bringing the war to an honourable end for the French government." What that way could be and how it could be in honour was for Navarre himself to decide. From that memorable day, May 7, Commander-in-chief, General Henri Navarre became the seventh and also the last French adversary of Commander-in-chief, General Võ Nguyên Giáp.

General Navarre appeared on the battlefield of Indochina with remarkable figures and events. Only after one month examining, the strategic 18-month plan was formulated and approved by the French National Defense Committee (French: *Commité de la Défense Nationale de France*).[1] The prerequisite for the implementation of the plan remained American aid, and for the first time, Washington was generous enough to sponsor up to 78 percent of France's war expenses in Indochina. Therefore, only after more than six months, French military power had risen to 480,000 troops, with 286 battalions of different types, of which the strategic mobile strike forces (dubbed by Western press as "the strategic fist") amounted to as many as 50 battalions, most of which were deployed in the Red River Delta. It was no surprise why General Navarre declared eloquently to "play with Giáp in a card game of absolute pink."

Never had Commander-in-chief Võ Nguyên Giáp been confronted with an adversary with so much wealth, troops, and weapons. The question then was how to neutralize those huge mobile strike forces of Navarre. President Hồ Chí

---

1. The Navarre Plan consists of two major phases: the first phase—building a defense line south of the 16th parallel to concentrate on the establishment of a strong strategic mobile strike force, which served as a means to the second phase—launching a large-scale offensive to score an important victory of strategic importance to bring the war to an honorable end.

Minh instructed Giáp to launch the campaign in different strategic directions, forcing the enemy to disperse their army in confrontation. At the beginning of the dry season of 1953-1954, after eight to nine years of war, for the first time General Giáp deployed core regular brigades to strike in five different directions simultaneously. These five brigades were to provide mutual support for one another between the five strategic directions on the mountainous battlefields of Northwestern Việt Nam, Middle Laos, Lower Laos, Central Highlands, and Upper Laos while instructing the militiamen at the enemy rear across the nation to intensify their attacks on the enemy to hold them back and provide necessary support for the advancement of other campaigns. For every move General Giáp made, the whole French Command had to send huge numbers of troops in response, making the "strategic mobile budget" that Navarre painstakingly gathered became increasingly smaller. The very first phase of the spring 1953-autumn 1954 war against the new French commander-in-chief saw Giáp forcing over 40 battalions of General Navarre, who had earlier concentrated densely in a key battlefield of the Red River Delta, to spread thinly into the quagmire of the mountainous battlefields across Indochina. Prior to the Điện Biên Phủ campaign, Navarre was left with no more than 20 substitute battalions who, despite their concentration in the lowland, were no longer able to engage effectively in battles because they were thinned out and overstretched in dealing with the Việt Minh's guerrilla warfare, especially along the 5th Route. Reinforcements for all the directions were reduced, even when Điện Biên Phủ was identified as the pivotal point of the Navarre Plan. As such, in the first phase of the war, the dry season of 1953-1954, Navarre made a strategically wrong decision. He then decided to invest all what he had into the next crucial move. What transpired later in the Mường Thanh valley became the decisive moments that thwarted the strategic plan of General Giáp's final French adversary.

When General Giáp launched the campaign to liberate Lai Châu, General Navarre hastily deployed six battalions into the Mường Thanh valley (in Điện Biên Phủ) with the declared aim of preventing the Việt Minh core forces from marching to Upper Laos "to lock the door to Laos." About half a month later, Navarre came up with another new plan, an intention of strategic significance unheard of in the original plan, which is to establish right in the field of Mường Thanh what was believed to be the most impregnable fortified outpost of Indochina. It served dual purposes of easing the pressure on the French troops in the lowland and provoking and decimating the Việt Minh core army if they attacked. Navarre strongly believed in the feasibility of this plan as General Giáp, according to his evaluation, lacked experience in commanding attacks on a remote outpost, especially a well-built one. Back to the battle in Hòa Bình, General Giáp tried to avoid the first fortified outpost that appeared. Back to the Northwest campaign at the end of 1952, after several attempts on the outer outposts of the Nà Sản fortified stronghold, where his side was not 100 percent certain of victory, Giáp decided not to continue attacking. In the summer of 1953, he was determined to annihilate the Sam Neua fortified outpost. However, when the brigades were only about ten kilometers from the target, the French troops fled. Giáp ordered his men to chase the enemy for the whole seven days and nights, even until they reached the Plain of Jars. While vast majority of the enemy troops who fled Sam Neua were killed, Giáp's intention to attack the fortified outpost remained unfulfilled.

Navarre's strategic move, which was conceived at the beginning of December 1953, made the French determined to establish a French garrison in Điện Biên Phủ. This garrison consisted of 49 firm outposts equipped with state-of-the-art readily available machinery and weaponry. It could mobilize as many as 16,000 elite troops, manifold stronger than those bases in Hòa Bình, Nà Sản, and Sam Neua previously. The garrison was so strong that all French and American military officers who saw it personally concluded that it constituted "an impregnable fortress" and "a grinding machine" which could grind the opposing troops to pulp if they dared to launch an attack. Military experts of all kinds who were close to General Navarre also concurred that it would be impossible for Giáp to transport a considerable mass of heavy artillery pieces across towering mountain ranges around the Mường Thanh valley, and that simple means of transportation would be unable to provide the necessary supplies for tens of thousands of troops in a protracted battle.

On the Vietnamese part, the original plan laid out by the Advisory Board was to send one brigade to the west and two others to the east of the Mường Thanh valley. These brigades were to stage combined attack in order to resolutely annihilate all the enemy troops in the fortified outpost within only several days and nights, under the slogan "strike quickly, finish quickly." This plan had been disseminated to officers of all levels and every necessary preparation had been made in that direction. However, after watching closely how the enemy reacted in the valley, and after taking everything into account, General Giáp decided that, as the situations had changed, the "human-sea attack" strategy would not guarantee total and complete victory. Bearing in mind what President told him before they parted, Giáp made "one of the most difficult decisions" in his military career, which was to cancel the attack and switch his slogan from "strike quickly and finish quickly" to "strike surely and advance cautiously." The following morning, after hours of discussion and persuasion, Giáp and other members of the Party Committee of the Battlefield decided to change the attack strategy. Given the fact that every mental and material preparation had been made and every soldier was ready for engagement, it was by no means an easy decision to make to order the brigades to leave the battlefield and pull their artillery back to the assembly point. In these crucial moments of the campaign, with events of paramount importance, the Commander-in-chief had to demonstrate utmost responsibility to the Party and the people and must have been highly confident and decisive to lead the whole army to such a victory.

Only after spending nearly 50 days and nights making speedy preparation and amassing all the necessary factors to guarantee victory did Commander-in-chief Võ Nguyên Giáp give out orders for his men to start the campaign on March 13, 1954. The 56 days of the Điện Biên Phủ campaign witnessed General Giáp and his comrades in the Party Committee of the Battlefield applying all the most creative and active methods to contain and neutralize the material superiority of the French weaponry and technology. They were able to destabilize the modern fortified outpost, limit and cut off the only sources of reinforcements by air, and foil all their plans to flee. Commanding his men to score a resounding victory in the battle of Điện Biên Phủ, his most profound pride was that he had appreciated fully the advice and instructions from Hồ Chí Minh Minh before he parted for the battlefield: nothing but victory would be accepted.

Several decades later, this was reaffirmed in scientific seminars and personal memoirs of heads of the brigades who participated in the Điện Biên Phủ campaign. According to General Vương Thừa Vũ, if they had stuck rigidly to the original tactics of "strike quickly, finish quickly," the war could have dragged on for ten years more. For his part, General Lê Trọng Tấn remarked that if it had not been for the decision to change the war tactics, most of them would not have had the luck to join the anti-American resistance, hinting that they could have all been perished on the field of Mường Thanh. Twenty-nine years later, on April 8, 1983, two French journalists, Georges Boudarel and François Caviglioli, published an article titled *"Comment Giáp a failli perdre la bataille de Dien Bien Phu"* (literally: "How Giáp Almost Lost the Battle of Điện Biên Phủ") on the French newspaper *Le Nouvel Observateur* (literally: The New Observer), elaborating on the developments of the battle and the switch in the Vietnamese tactics. They concluded:

> Giáp is both a military and a political genius as he dared to acknowledge shortcomings of his strategy instead of sticking slavishly to a fixed theory by abandoning the original "human-sea attack" tactics which proved inappropriate in the Vietnamese context.

A rare and striking coincidence was the fact that the victory day of Võ Nguyên Giáp on May 7, 1954, was also the day one year before when General Henri Navarre received orders to take charge of the First Indochina War. The defeat of the French army at Điện Biên Phủ entailed the collapse of the entire strategic plan intended for 18 months, smashing the hope of not only Paris but also Washington. Two months later, a peace accord was signed, putting an end to the long struggle in which General Giáp, mentally and materially, defeated seven French generals, one after another, during the course of nine years, including five years when both Paris and Sài Gòn administrations were given full backing and assistance by Washington.

Cecil Currey, author of *Victory at any Cost*[1] on one occasion asked Giáp about which military theory he adopted to push back the French Expeditionary Corps. Giáp replied briefly that the only military "institute" that he studied in was the jungle itself. It was in this "jungle institute" that he and his comrades revised the lessons of military geniuses of Việt Nam in the past, combining with orthodoxical Marxist military principles and applying them into the reality of the war to gain victory.

After the victory of Điện Biên Phủ, in the South began a process popularly known as "Diệm's return and the American arrival before the French withdrawal" with a wicked scheme of partitioning our country for good and turning the South into a new-styled colony and an American military base. The people in the South did not enjoy a single day of real peace. Hardly had the Geneva Accords been inked when it was seriously violated. Bloody terrorist retaliative attack against people who participated in the resistance war escalated day in day out. Ngô Đình Diệm publicly refused to enter into talks about a general election to reunify the country, knowing that the United States of America was giving the Sài

---

1. *Victory at any Cost*, Brassley's Inc, New York, 1997.

Gòn administration full backing in developing a large-scale army. To prepare for the worst, as early as 1957, following the 12th Resolution on major military issues passed by the Party Central Committee, Võ Nguyên Giáp in his capacity as Commander-in-chief attempted to develop the army and consolidate national defense capabilities, along with his colleagues in the Central Military Commission. Two years later, when the Diệm administration, backed by the United States of America, overtly indicated their scheme to invade and partition the country, the Party Central Committee convened its 15th Plenum, affirming that the tasks of the revolutionary cause in the South included overthrowing the ruling regime of Ngô Đình Diệm—lackeys and puppets of the United States of America, by use of force. Together with the 15th Resolution, the strategic 559th Route also took shape. In a later interview with a female British writer,[1] General Giáp said:

> We decided to build the Hồ Chí Minh Trail because we were attacked by the Americans.... We anticipated right from the beginning that the Americans, with their flexible responses, would intervene and escalate the war. So we needed to make long-term preparations. I myself understood that should we be able to regain the South, where guerrilla warfare was being conducted, we would have to expand our battlefront and engage ourselves in large-scale campaigns. Therefore, in May 1959, we ordered the construction of the Hồ Chí Minh Trail.

Before American troops got directly involved into the war, the people of the South had undergone nine years

---

1. Virginia Louisse Morris, *A History of the Ho Chi Minh Trail: The Road to Freedom*, Orchid Press, London, 2005.

tempered in the resistance war against the French. After that, buoyed by patriotic heroism and outstanding creativity in opposing ruthless terrorist raids by the government of Ngô Đình Diệm, the people of the South, under the leadership of the Central Office for South Việt Nam, switched from legal political struggle to avoid human losses to combining political struggle with armed struggle, thereby gradually moving from armed uprising to revolutionary war. By 1964, when Maxwell Taylor, considered to be American number-one general, was chosen to replace Henri Cabot Lodge as American ambassador to South Việt Nam and General William Westmoreland replaced General Paul Harkins as the Commander-in-chief in preparation for a switch to "localized war," the situations in the South had witnessed changes in favour of the revolutionary forces, which was unlike the first years after the Geneva Accords.

In the spring of 1965, the White House made public President Lyndon B. Johnson's decision to get the American troops directly involved in South Việt Nam. It was also during this time that the strategic route—Hồ Chí Minh Trail—witnessed a huge deployment of soldiers from the north to the south, about 14 times greater in terms of the number of core army, ten times greater in terms of combat gears and machinery. The battlefields of Cochinchina (South Việt Nam), the 5th Zone, and the Central Highlands had been established. Three types of troops, with the core combatants being organized in terms of divisions, had been deployed on major strategic localities.

The improved strength and position of the Việt Minh army on the Southern battlefield was for an important part due to the smooth functioning of the military machine operated by General Giáp and his colleagues at the Central Military Commission in light of the new situations. The whole army bore deeply in mind the words of President Hồ Chí Minh when he addressed the Sixth Plenum of the Party Central Committee: "We must always remain well-prepared, by predicting any moves the enemy may make, be it in war time or in peace time." After ten years of development, nine of which were tested in the resistance war, the Vietnamese People's Army had become a mature force both in terms of organization, equipment, and combat experience. Many of the cadres who previously had only low and patchy level of education now became tacticians and skilled commanders of major campaigns.

Some of the generals who were trained and tested in the first resistance war such as Hoàng Văn Thái, Chu Huy Mân, Lê Trọng Tấn, Trần Độ, Hoàng Cầm, and Nguyễn Hòa had been sent by the Party Central Committee to the battlefield to coordinate with the Regional Command to conduct the war. One of the members of the Politburo, Deputy Secretary of the Central Military Commission, General Nguyễn Chí Thanh was sent by President Hồ Chí Minh and the Politburo to the Central Office for South Việt Nam to directly conduct the war against a new enemy. In terms of leadership, given the maturity of military officers and generals, as well as the establishment of the Central Office for South Việt Nam, Regional Command, and Campaign Command, the instructions from the Supreme Command and the Central Military Commission in general and the Command-in-Chief in particular were different from those in the first resistance war. With the exception of some overall strategic decisions co-made with other members of the Politburo, Party Central

Committee, and Central Military Commission, General Giáp did not issue direct instructions and commands as he had done during the nine-year resistance war. The development of the revolutionary war in the South coincided with his efforts to instruct the agencies from Ministry of National Defense to organize forces and coordinate with ministries and sectors to provide supplies and aids to meet the growing demand of the front line in the South in terms of both human resources and material supplies. He also directed the arms and services to fight and protect the North from destructive war waged by the United States of America, and personally directed the operations of the Trị Thiên battlefield following the establishment of the Trị Thiên Front (B5) to the south of the "big rear."

It was clear that in 1965, the General Headquarters, General Võ Nguyên Giáp, and the entire army and militiamen confronted directly with the American expeditionary army in a context totally different from that 20 years earlier, when the anti-French resistance war began. The key issue was how to apply the newly-acquired knowledge and experience in formal schools inside and outside the country into the context of a new and different enemy—the most powerful nation in the world in terms of weaponry and technology.

In the spring of 1965, when American troops made a massive landfall in the battlefield of South Việt Nam, the newly-approved strategic plan for the 1965–1967 period mapped out by General Westmoreland also began to take effect. American generals and troops, aided by their mercenaries and lackeys, entered the war. Hundreds of thousands of American troops and mercenaries, together with half a million Sài Gòn troops, were placed under the command of the so-called United States Military Assistance Command in Việt Nam (MACV), headed by General Westmoreland. If we do not take into account American generals like John W. O'Daniel and Paul Harkins, who operated the United States Military Advisory and Assistance Group (MAAG) when the American troops had not intervened directly into the war in Việt Nam, then the four-star General Westmoreland was in fact General Giáp's eighth adversary and the first one to be American.

One of the pivotal problems acknowledged several years earlier by the Supreme Command and military officers from both the North and the South of Việt Nam in general and by Giáp himself in particular, that is how to strike and defeat the American imperialists, now became increasingly urgent and needed to be resolved. At a congress honouring war heroes and military men of remarkable service of the South held in May 1965, General Nguyễn Chí Thanh concluded, "We will know how to defeat the Americans once we have engaged ourselves in direct battles against them." It was also during this occasion that the commanders of the 5th Zone decided to focus on annihilating one of the American units to lower their fighting spirit and aggressive mentality, as well as to gain experience for the whole zone. The Núi Thành Battle on May 27, 1965, went down in history as the first victory against Americans in a direct battle. From that battle onwards, there appeared a slogan "Search, strike, and kill Americans." Half a year later, in November 1965, General Chu Huy Mân commanded the first anti-American campaign—Playme campaign—which consisted of a battle described in the *Pentagon Papers* as "bloody fighting at Ia Drang Valley, the first battle." Even from those early years, Western journalists in general and American journalists in particular already paid special attention to this battle. The *New York Times* commented that Ia Drang was one of the places where the American combatants were thrown into ultimate challenge and ordeals, and where American military officers had to fight in the Việt Cộng (Vietnamese communist) way.

By the middle of 1966, the establishment of the Trị Thiên Front was perceived by many experts as a "deadly move" by the Vietnamese Supreme Command. It was known that before deploying his army, Giáp would normally force his enemy to spread their forces out first. This time, his move was seen as "deadly" because it could well push the American military officers into a strategically disadvantageous position, forcing Westmoreland to dispatch two American divisions to the mountainous and remote battlefields in the Central Coast region of Việt Nam before the second dry season began. Experts believed that one of the most salient features in the material and mental war between these two warring sides during the first two years of American direct engagement in the war was that the Vietnamese generals, during the strategic counter-attacks of the two dry seasons of 196–1966 and 1967–1968, were able to "bankrupt" the "search and destroy" strategy, which had been carefully drafted, revised, and approved by the Pentagon prior to Westmoreland's deployment of troops. A lot had been said about the failure of the Operation Junction City, which lasted from February to April of 1967 and was seen as one of the largest "search and destroy" operations throughout the Việt Nam War, with the involvement of 45,000 troops, aiming to break the Việt Cộng spine. That explained why on December 8, when the second dry season ended, Secretary of State Dean Rusk complained

43

that 1967 was the hardest and most miserable year for the American army in the Việt Nam War.

Defeats in two successive dry seasons led to disorder and division among the American officials themselves. Cabot Lodge returned to replace Maxwell Taylor as the American ambassador to Sài Gòn. More than a year later, he himself was replaced by Ellsworth Bunker. This was followed by Secretary of Robert McNamara's decision to exit from the Pentagon. Then the Tết Offensive launched by the people and armed forces of in the South broke out even before the new American secretary of defense took office. An irony was that the offensive took place at a time when the presence of the American army was at its peak with over 540,000 combatants. Washington could not understand why it took Commander-in-chief Westmoreland half a month to send an official report about that ground-shaking incident, which happened at the end of January 1968. According to the report, five major cities, 34 provinces, 64 districts, and all the towns had come under the Việt Cộng attack. It was such a resounding event that many years later, it still attracted the attention of many American and Western military officers and researchers who discussed the event in a wide range of books, newspapers, and journals.

Once again, the command of the American expeditionary troops underwent a major reshuffle in the wake of the first phase of the Tết Offensive. Both Commander-in-chief Westmoreland and Commander of the United States Pacific Fleet Grant Sharp were dismissed. American Secretary of Defense McNamara officially left office, handing the post over to Clark Clifford. The first phase of this offensive also forced President Johnson to make an important concession, which was to stop bombing North Việt Nam and send a delegation to Paris to negotiate with the opposing side. In a speech delivered on March 31, 1968, he announced that he would not run for office again in the subsequent presidential election. When the Tết Offensive began, few would expect that it would exert such a huge effect on the top-flight war commanders of the United States. On May 4, 1968, at the inception of the second phase of the Tết Offensive, Creighton Abrams officially succeeded Westmoreland as Commander-in-chief and became General Giáp's ninth adversary. To create favourable conditions for the new commander to carry out the plan of Vietnamizing the war, President Johnson called on the Congress to spend another 6.3 billion dollars, but the proposal was dismissed, though not totally, by the House of Representatives. Only one twentieth of this amount was approved, which was around 300 million dollars. Even with such a small sum, General Abrams had to implement two tasks simultaneously: gradually withdrawing American troops according to a process instructed by the Pentagon and trying out the ability of the Sài Gòn army to fight independently so that they would become less dependent on American-supported fire-power.

For his part, General Giáp did not pay particular attention to repetitive declarations by the newly-elected American President Richard Nixon and the new American Secretary of Defense Melvin Laird regarding the withdrawal of American troops. Yet he was concerned about the moves of the new commander-in-chief. Giáp anticipated that Abrams would focus on Northeastern Cambodia and Mid and Lower Laos so as to block the Vietnamese traffic routes and deprive the Vietnamese troops of a foothold on their friendly neighbouring countries. He learnt from a report by the Advisory Board of the General Headquarters that in June 1969 Abrams declared that if American troops could destroy the holy land of Việt Cộng in Cambodia, they could end the war in South Việt Nam within a year.

At the order of the Central Military Commission and Commander-in-chief Võ Nguyên Giáp, preparations for battlefields along the 9th Route were quickly made. Corps 70 was established, standing ready to serve as a strategic mobile force. On the American part, it was not until the beginning of February 1971 that the strategic plan was approved by the White House and the Pentagon. Therefore, before Abrams actually initiated the "Vietnamization of the war" strategy, Giáp had been able to make important moves and preparations. According to the American plan, General Abrams and the Staff of Nguyễn Văn Thiệu, who was then President of the Republic of Việt Nam, would throw the Sài Gòn army into three attacks: one to the 9th Route-Southern Laos (known as the 719th Lam Sơn operation), one to Northeastern Cambodia (Toàn Thắng operation), and one to the frontier of the Central Highlands (the 4th Quang Trung operation). While Commander-in-chief Võ Nguyên Giáp instructed his colleagues on all the battlefields to "brace themselves up" for the Toàn Thắng and 4th Quang Trung operations, Lê Trọng Tấn and Lê Quang Đạo, according to the common plan formulated by the Headquarters, received orders to organize and conduct the the 9th Route-Southern Laos Front, so as to defeat the 719th Lam Sơn operation, a major march of the American army targeting Bản Đông-Sepon in Laos, aiming to sever the strategic 559th Route.

On February 8, 1971, the United States and Sài Gòn deployed their troops. Abrams reported to President Nixon that he would conquer Sepon within no more than 13 days. One thing he had not expected was the speed with which General Giáp sent his army, beyond the expectation of the United States-Sài Gòn alliance. Later, in his memoir titled *A Soldier Reports*,[1] the retired general Westmoreland recounted that when the North Vietnamese troops began their counter-attacks, the American troops and their Sài Gòn counterparts had to make one of the most difficult moves of all military activities, which was to withdraw under the offensive might of the opposing side, such that the Sài Gòn troops had to immediately cross the river to retreat even though they were only about one kilometres from Sepon. Moreover, the author of *Victory at Any Cost* recounted that American TV viewers, who watched the evening news, witnessed South Vietnamese soldiers clinging on to the landing skids of the helicopters, their faces being filled with horror. He then concluded that this march put an end to the American plan of Vietnamizing the war.

On the battlefields of Central Highlands and Cambodia, Operations Toàn Thắng 1/71 and Quang Trung 4 also suffered the same defeat as Operation Lam Sơn 719. From that time to the end of 1972, the Regional Command, following strategic plans and directions from the Politburo and the Central Military Commission, continued to conduct the battlefields in the South and scored numerous victories in successive campaigns. At the end of such operations as North Central Highlands and Trị Thiên, which lasted from March to June

---

1. William Westmoreland: *A Soldier Reports*, Double and Company, New York, 1976.

1972, Washington had to replace their top commanders. From the middle of 1972, when the commanding post of American expeditionary troops was handed from General Abrams to General Frederick C. Weyand, who became Giáp's tenth adversary and the third one to be American, General Giáp was working in Hà Nội with Chief of the General Staff Văn Tiến Dũng to instruct agencies from the Headquarters and Air Defense-Air Force Service Command to find out feasible methods to strike American B52s. The White House's recent foreign policies and activities in some superpowers during the months of spring and summer indicated a high possibility of an American B52 attack against North Việt Nam.

The B52 attacks on Hà Nội and Hải Phòng had been anticipated very early on by President Hồ Chí Minh. Yet what remained unknown was how the Vietnamese army could confront and defeat such powerful attacks by American air force. In August 1967, when a missile regiment was reported to have been sent to Vĩnh Linh to figure out a way to strike B52s, President Hồ Chí Minh commended the effort and said metaphorically that if they wished to catch the tiger, they needed to enter the tiger's den. The praise became a guiding principle for the Headquarters and the leadership of the Air Defense Service. The remaining concern among North Vietnamese generals was "the how." Talking to the commander of the Air Defense-Air Force Service, General Giáp encouraged the Service to try and find out how they could strike the Americans in the air, even if the latter resorted to B52 bombers, given the former's success in fighting the latter on land. A group of cadres in the Service was tasked with composing a set of guidelines to combat B52s. At the beginning of 1971, the Commander-in-chief gave permission for some of the pilots who had recently graduated from training courses in the Union of Soviet Socialist Republics (USSR) to join forces in Trường Sơn Trail to "identify B52s." At the same time, some Mig jet fighter aircraft were embedded into some of the airports in the locality of the 4th Zone. Some flights took turns to carry out sorties while some radar stations were erected along the left bank of the Mekong River in the Laos territory to practice detecting B52s in jamming conditions, under such slogans as "Overcoming jamming to unmask the enemy" and "Determined to defeat American electronic jamming." Every time a B52 was gunned down,[1] the Command-in-Chief asked the Service to draw out useful lessons in a timely manner. Based on daily experience, the guidelines on how to strike B52s were finally completed after ample revision, discussion, and research, and was finally introduced during a meeting at the end of October 1972 where the Commander-in-chief instructed participants to discuss and agree on how missile service could strike B52s. One important conclusion at the meeting was that, "We can shoot down American B52s on the spot." This was a scientifically grounded belief, and after the meeting, a booklet titled "How Missile Forces can Strike B52s" was published and became popularly known among the Service as the "Red-covered Guidelines." It was thanks to this set of guidelines that the H63 missile team in Nghệ An was able to score the first victory after the meeting in October. The regiment had been able to neutralize the jamming and for the first time

---

1. For example in September 1967 in Vĩnh Linh, in March 1971 during the 9th Route-Southern Laos Campaign, in April 1972 during the Quảng Trị Campaign, and so on.

managed to shoot down a B52 to the north of the 17th parallel in broad daylight. The vivid reality of the soldiers' creativity was summarized and theorized to become guidelines, which in turns, were passed on again to soldiers. These wobbly first steps ultimately contributed to the resounding victory at the end of December 1972, popularly known as "Điện Biên Phủ in the air."

General Võ Nguyên Giáp was extremely appreciative of the intelligence and creativity of the people who later made history with what he called "taking the Americans by absolute surprise." Immediately after the victory over American B52s, in a meeting held in the convention hall of the Service, he lifted up the "Red-covered Guidelines" to which he attributed as one of the most important reasons for the B52 victory.

Following the failure of the B52 strategic raid, less than ten months after General Westmoreland took over the commanding authority, the American Command in Sài Gòn lowered and rolled up their flags to pull out of Việt Nam on March 29, 1973, two months after the Paris Agreement was signed. Commander-in-chief Weyand and his 2,501 soldiers were the "final military men" of the American air force to leave South Việt Nam, marking the end of successive defeats of three American generals during seven years conducting the expeditionary troops to combat directly in Việt Nam.

After the Paris Agreement was concluded, General Võ Nguyên Giáp and his colleagues at the Central Military Commission, acting by strategic directions from the Politburo and observations of the war against pacification and encroachment to maintain and enhance the position and strength of the revolution in the South, were bent on making proposals about the next steps to liberate the South completely and reunify the country. Based on ideas amassed from discussions during meetings in 1974, especially the open meetings of the Politburo and the Central Military Commission, which convened from December 18, 1974, to January 8, 1975, Giáp and his coordinates identified major issues that needed to be applied into instructing the Key Team of the General Headquarters to examine and finalize the strategic plan for the liberation of the South. Eventually, after eight revisions, the plan was adopted by the Politburo. According to the plan, Buôn Ma Thuột was chosen as the place to open the 1975 Spring Strategic Offensive.

In this final strategic stage of the anti-American resistance war, Commander-in-chief Võ Nguyên Giáp had one of his most helpful aides, General Văn Tiến Dũng—a member of the Politburo cum Chief of the General Staff—who was sent by the Party Central Committee to directly conduct and instruct the strategic attack. General Giáp continued to take responsibility for the functioning of the Central Military Commission, aided by First Deputy Minister of Defense Hoàng Văn Thái and other deputy chiefs of the General Staff to follow closely the movement of regiments, making sure that they abided by the strategic principles mapped out by the Politburo in each decisive moment. Since February 5, 1975, when General Văn Tiến Dũng began journeying to the Central Highlands battlefield, contact between the two generals Giáp and Dũng, who were then working under the code names of Chiến and Tuấn respectively, was made on daily basis.

Subsequent to the Central Highlands victory, which inspired the strategic offensive, General Võ Nguyễn Giáp, in his capacity as Secretary of the Central Military Commission and Commander-in-chief, was well-aware of the favourable developments of the regiments. He therefore proposed some strategic ideas that received unanimous approval from the Politburo and the Central Military Commission, as these ideas were expected to accelerate the advancement of the regiments. What was originally intended to be only a strategic attack soon became a general strategic offensive, shortening the expected time in the plan for the liberation of the South from two years (1975–1976) to one year (1975) while switching from the original limited plan of liberating Sài Gòn before the rainy season to a determination to gain complete victory within April 1975. The slogan "velocity–boldness–unpredictability–certainty," regularly repeated in Giáp's telegrams sent to the regiments who were marching in different directions, was a major source of inspiration and guidance for every cadre and soldier in the spring days of 1975. Giáp also proposed the establishment of Quảng Nam-Đà Nẵng Campaign Command, under the supervision of General Lê Trọng Tấn and General Chu Huy Mân. The Command was tasked with an ambitious plan of annihilating and killing the 100,000 Sài Gòn troops and, within a record time of three days, thwarting their plot to stand their grounds in Đà Nẵng. After Đà Nẵng was liberated, he again decided to establish the East-oriented Regiment, commanded by generals Lê Trọng Tấn and Lê Quang Hòa, asking them to "kill the enemy to march forth and pave the way to advance" and march with lightning speed to approach Sài Gòn as close as possible from the East. One particularly important decision was that Giáp ordered the 5th Zone and the Navy to grab the opportunity to liberate some of the islands on the Trường Sa (Spratly) Archipelago.

In April 1975, Giáp left his house to stay in the "Dragon House" of the Headquarters so as to give prompt instructions to the whole army to liberate Sài Gòn. It was here that he had frequent exchanges of ideas, sometimes even on hourly basis, with his comrades, including Tuấn, Phạm Hùng, Lê Đức Thọ, Trần Văn Trà, and Đinh Đức Thiện, who worked in the Hồ Chí Minh Campaign Command. Apart from the scheduled briefings, he also had separate discussions with the First Secretary of the Party Central Committee, Lê Duẩn, about matters of urgency and importance. After April 26, when the East-oriented Regiment, under the command of General Lê Trọng Tấn and General Lê Quang Hòa, opened fire to start the campaign, Giáp kept frequent contact with his colleagues from the operational and intelligence offices to follow closely the developments of the war and the advancement of his army toward Sài Gòn from different directions, so that he could make prompt proposals to the Hồ Chí Minh Campaign Command to take necessary resulting steps, which included the incorporation of Tân Sơn Nhất Airport in the upcoming plan, the take-over of Sài Gòn-Chợ Lớn after liberation, and the termination of battles on the remaining localities across the Mekong River Delta and islands such Phú Quốc and Côn Sơn.

At around noon of April 30, after receiving reports of our troops advancing into the Independence Palace, General Giáp sent an urgent telegram to the South, providing instructions from the Politburo and the Central Military Commission. The telegram read, "It may be necessary to ask Dương Văn Minh to call on the Sài Gòn army to drop weapons, not as President but as an ordinary man who has decided to side with his people." Shortly after that, a subsequent congratulatory telegram from the Secretary of the Central Military Commission was sent to the commanding generals in the battlefields. It read:

> The Headquarters received news of our troops flying our flags on the Independence Palace at 11 am. We at the Central Military Commission wish to congratulate you on your great victory. Our comrades at the Politburo were all extremely delighted.
>
> (Signed)
>
> Văn

That was also the last telegram sent by the Headquarters to the frontline on the historic day of April 30, 1975.

That night, under a fireworks-lit sky, the people of Hà Nội rushed onto the streets, their faces beaming with delight as they shared the happiness of reunification with their Southern fellowmen who "started first but arrived later." None of those in that huge influx of people, however, was aware of the presence of a man who followed President Hồ Chí Minh's instructions to take command of the army throughout more than 30 years. It was thanks to his command and endeavour that the Vietnamese Party, people, and army could reach the destination mapped out by Hồ Chí Minh: "Driving out the Americans and overthrowing their South Vietnamese government."

As the author of this book, I believe that it was completed at a very meaningful moment.

By 2006, General Giáp will have been 95 years old. The 30-year war of 1944–1975 in which he played essential part as commander-in-chief already concluded 30 years ago. A large volume of scholarly works and articles have been written about the holy war of national salvation and unification of the Vietnamese people. Among the factors attributed to the victory over the French and the Americans, some deserve greater scholarly examination, such as the commanding talent of Việt Nam's number-one general, Võ Nguyên Giáp, who was directly responsible for developing an empty-handed and fledgling army, bare-footed and armed with nothing but rifles, into a powerful army and who defeated ten commanding generals of the seasoned expeditionary troops of two superpowers.

He has moved from a young compatriot into a real communist, from a history teacher who was untrained in any military institution to a well-known general. The success of his military career was closely linked to the guidance and support of Hồ Chí Minh from early years.

Some people believe that foreigners speak and know more about Võ Nguyên Giáp than the Vietnamese people themselves. This observation is correct to some extent. It should be added that the foreign academic circle who understand Giáp includes not only historians and journalists but also military officers, American and French alike, who were once his adversaries in the battlefield.

A case in point was General Westmoreland, Võ Nguyên Giáp's first American adversary. During the seven years of American direct involvement in South Việt Nam, he was commander-in-chief for four years and two months and as such, witnessed more important military events than any other Americans when the United States escalated the war in the increased size and scale of their marches, as well as their airborne and on-land military activities both in the South and in the North of Việt Nam. In the final years of the

55

war, as in his capacity as Chief of Staff of American Army, Westmoreland still followed closely the developments in the battlefields. In *A Soldier Reports* he made some justifications, but in the end he had to commend his own adversary. Peter Mac Donald, author of *Giap—An Assessment*,[1] wrote that General Westmoreland had to acknowledge that Giáp had all the qualities of a great military marshal—decisiveness, resilience, mental capabilities, and concentration of the mind.

Giáp's name is highlighted in the encyclopaedias of the two countries that once invaded Việt Nam, and the evaluations are non-biased. The French encyclopaedia published in 1987 wrote:

> As the organizer of the Vietnamese People's Army, Võ Nguyên Giáp successfully created a symbiosis between Marxist military doctrines and the long-established tradition of resistance against foreign invasion and aggression, and applied it tactfully into the conditions of a fairly small and narrow country. In Giáp, the politician outpaces the military officer. His ideology and actions are not restricted rigidly within military principles. Rather, they are based on a steady political precondition—the massive participation of the people into the resistance war, an inherent characteristic of guerrilla warfare. Rather than being merely a general whose role is only important in a short period of time, Võ Nguyên Giáp provides an example of how military ideas could be used to achieve political purposes. He proves lucidly the feasibility of resistance wars and the specific methods that help the resistance movements to defeat "mighty superpowers" despite being weaker in appearance.

---

1. Peter Mac Donald: *Giap—Une evaluation* (Jean Clem & Frank Straschitz, Trans.), Perrin Publishing House, Paris, 1992.

According to the *Encyclopaedia of the American Military* published in 1993, Giáp's commanding talent in terms of tactics, strategy, and logistics is combined flexibly with political and diplomatic endeavours to help Asian people, specifically the Vietnamese and Indochinese, defeat Western generals and their doctrines to emerge as victors in the second Indochinese War. His determination and his men's selflessness enables the socialist forces in Third World countries to outwit the Western superpowers and their allies. The economic and technological superiority, added by the military might and fire-power, of Western countries had to bow to the commanding talent of a history teacher turned general. Although some commentators refuse to acknowledge his military genius by underscoring the huge losses that his nation had to suffer, the personal military and political achievements of General Giáp, which are closely linked to those of his nation, will prevail forever.

Since the late 1970s, many Western journalists have been researching about the daily life of Võ Nguyên Giáp, whom they consider as "the only outstanding war figure still living." Given a rare chance in 2000 to interview the legendary general of Việt Nam, journalist Greg Myre of the *Associated Press* later wrote a long article about Giáp, in which he admitted that he had been trying to understand Giáp's thinking about the war and about his former adversaries. Myre recollected how for centuries both friends and foes have underestimated the power and will of the Vietnamese people. In the middle of 1997, he once observed to former American Secretary of Defense Robert McNamara that the Americans failed to appreciate the most important determinant of the Vietnamese people's victory—their patriotic spirit. He also affirmed that

Việt Nam would have been doomed to failure had it decided to engage in head-to-head battles with the United States and their endless B52 air raids. He himself once remarked to USSR Premier Alexei Kosygin that Việt Nam would not have won the war if they had fought against the United States in the Soviet Union way. In response to questions about his former foe, Myre replied that while the Vietnamese people can put behind the bitterness of the past, the Americans cannot. In a personal meeting with Admiral Elmo Zumwalt, Giáp said:

When you came with a Thompson submachine gun, you were not welcomed, but now that you've come back as a tourist, you are bound to be greeted differently. The Americans will find themselves more than welcome when they come back to help Việt Nam repair the terrible effects of the war and contribute to the fight against the ongoing poverty and backwardness.

At the beginning of Chapter 26 (the conclusion chapter), the author of *Giap—An Assessment*, recounted in verbatim Giáp's well-meaning words: "We want to live peacefully with other nations in the world." It was also in this conclusion chapter that the author recapitulated his views on the Vietnamese people's armed struggle to regain independence and the general's talent behind this war. According to him, the Vietnamese people, men and women alike, were the real victors of the war. They were resilient, disciplined, dogged, optimistic, and selfless. They also had exceptional leaders. Hồ Chí Minh was at the helm and Võ Nguyên Giáp was the commander of the armed forces. Between 1944 and 1975, Giáp's life was closely attached to battles and victories, which made him one of the greatest commanders-in-chief of all times. Within 30 years as commander-in-chief and almost

50 years at the highest level of the Vietnamese political hierarchy, he proved to be a man of exceptional qualities. In all aspects of the war, he was hardly matched in the ability to combine guerrilla warfare with regular warfare at a high level. This combination was unprecedented. In terms of strategy, he was a man of vision who quickly captured the pivotal issues. In terms of tactics, he was a master of guerrilla warfare. In terms of regular warfare, more than anyone else, he knew how to make his men understand the importance of grabbing opportunities, the significance of unpredictability, and the effect of camouflage and of deploying coy army. In terms of logistics, he proved to be outstanding throughout the Indochina War, from the reinforcement route for Điện Biên Phủ to the Hồ Chí Minh Trail.

Hà Nội, Spring 2005

Chapter One

THE PATH TO A MILITARY CAREER

From a Schoolboy to a Politician

Võ Nguyên Giáp was the fifth child in a large but poor peasant family in An Xá Village, Lệ Thủy Commune, in the central province of Quảng Bình. When he was born, his father Võ Quang Nghiêm, a Confucian scholar of high local reputation, gave the boy a name that several dozen years later brought pride to his family, hometown, and the whole country.

At that time, children whose fathers were Confucian scholars normally started their first lessons with primers written in Chinese classical characters. Mr. Nghiêm taught village kids and his own son. Giáp's mother, Nguyễn Thị Kiên, recounted that even in his early years, Giáp demonstrated an exceptional talent and had an elephant memory. Much later in his life, he still remembered all the stories told by his mother whom he resembled not only the short build and the round face but also the white complexion and especially the bright eyes that brimmed with intelligence. Many a night, she would tell her son the stories of how the Cần Vương (Aid the King) movement, of which her father was a member, fought against the French right on the land of Quảng Bình. Giáp himself was taken many times by his mother to his maternal hometown where his grandfather would hold him in his lap and answer his many innocent questions. His grandfather was not aware that in so doing, he had instilled the very first light into the mind of one of the world's most brilliant generals.

By the time he was seven, Võ Nguyên Giáp was sent to the canton[1] school in a neighbouring village. Two years later, he left home to study in a boarding school in the district. He recalled that, "the first days without the loving company of my mother were a huge problem for a 9-year-old boy like me." Later in his old age, during one of the interviews with historian Cecil Currey, author of *Victory at Any Cost*, Giáp retold this story and how he felt at that time. He was even willing to disclose a childhood secret that he cried at the news of having to be away from home for schooling. Comforted by his parents, however, he agreed to be taken to the district school by ferry. One year later, he soon became used to living away from home when he moved to the provincial school in the town of Đồng Hới. At the district school, Giáp had always been the best student in the class and in the very first year at the provincial school, his academic performance drew attention from headmaster Phạm Phú Lượng and particularly Đào Duy Anh, a teacher of the school and also a well-known scholar nationwide. After three years, his family, friends and relatives, and especially the school board of management were all very proud and happy when Giáp came first in the primary school graduation examination.

---

1. Under French colonialism, "canton" (Vietnamese: "*tổng*") was an administrative unit larger than "commune" but smaller than "district."

Entering 1925–1926 school-year, Võ Nguyên Giáp left home to study at the prestigious Huế National School. The whole family was excited at the news, although they were aware that in the immediate future they would have to work hard, trying to earn enough money to finance his schooling. None of them had any idea that entry to Huế National School marked not only a move from primary to secondary school but also one of the most important turning points in the life of a man who later became a remarkable talent of the country.

Võ Nguyên Giáp, together with four or five other students, took up private lodging near the school and started his study with great enthusiasm and avidity. One of his classmates by the name of Lê Sĩ Ngọc, who shared the rented room with Giáp, later recounted, "We soon found in him a good and polite friend, a smart and exceptional student.... Apart from natural sciences, Giáp also took unusual interest in history as a subject...."

An event then accidentally drew Giáp's attention to, and later involvement in, the revolutionary movement—the presence of Phan Bội Châu, a patriotic scholar who was being put under house arrest and surveillance in Huế by the French colonialist authorities.

Phan Bội Châu lived not far away from Huế National School. So Giáp and his friends had opportunities to talk to him. Phan Bội Châu's ideas, which aimed mainly to alert the "young politicians" to the humiliation of losing the country, soon became popular and influential among students at Huế National School. His advice on the motives of study touched deeply on the sensitive hearts and souls of young people like Giáp.

Totally by chance, Giáp became the core of the "young politicians" group and served as a bridge between them and Phan Bội Châu. Many of his friends later recollected that his political awareness soon became sharpened, and they all concurred that Huế National School would be a real cradle for the students' patriotic movement in the central region of Việt Nam.

In his second year at Huế National School, an important event took place and marked a major change in the political awareness of Võ Nguyên Giáp. One of his close friends by the name of Nguyễn Khoa Văn (Hải Triều) lent him *Le Procès de la colonisation française* (literally: The Trial of French Colonialism), camouflaged under the title of *Arabic Letters*, written by Nguyễn Ái Quốc, who later became internationally known as Hồ Chí Minh. He passed the book among his friends and discussed with them its contents and ideas. They all acknowledged that the book had blown in a fresh revolutionary wind for them all students. Listening to what Phan Bội Châu said and linking it to the contents of the book, they were all happy to realize that everyone was of the same mind on one of the most fundamental views: the young must be responsible for the future of the country. That was how Giáp became familiar with the great ideals of the revolution. And as many of his friends later recalled, the young Giáp was obviously waiting for an opportunity to do something big.

That opportunity finally came. It was at the end of March 1926, when the whole country was in mourning for the veteran revolutionary Phan Chu Trinh. The students at Huế National School strongly protested against a decision from the board of management that prevented them from holding a funeral for Phan Chu Trinh. A strike then broke out, not only in Huế National School but also in Đồng Khánh School, a school for girls, and other Christian schools in Huế and other central provinces of Việt Nam. Võ Nguyên Giáp and Nguyễn Chí Diểu, together with several other students, had their names put on a blacklist and were finally expelled from the school on charge of "causing troubles and disorder."

With his expulsion from Huế National School and his debut article titled *"À bas le tyranneau de Quoc hoc!"* (literally: "Down with the Tyrant of the National School!") published on *L'Annam*,[1] Võ Nguyên Giáp entered the revolutionary press circle at the age of 16, overtly confronting the colonial authorities. The year of 1927 became a significant milestone in the life of the young revolutionary.

One day, Nguyễn Chí Diểu came to see Võ Nguyên Giáp and gave him some articles written in French by Nguyễn Ái Quốc. He also told Giáp about a newly established revolutionary organization, by the name of Tân Việt (literally New Vietnamese Revolutionary Party). Võ Nguyên Giáp immediately took keen interest in this organization and soon became aware that although it was not a communist organization, it had Marxist political leanings to certain extent and its slogan was "domestic revolution takes precedence over international revolution."

After becoming a member of the Tân Việt Party, Võ Nguyên Giáp remained in Huế and worked as an editor for the *Tiếng dân* (literally: People's Voice). It was one of the leading newspapers with progressive tendency and as such, it was naturally under close French scrutiny and censorship.

---

1. The only French newspaper published in Sài Gòn which overtly criticized French colonial policies.

Despite knowledge that he was working under constant surveillance of the Second Bureau of the General Staff (French: *Deuxième Bureau de l'État-major general*), France's external military intelligence agency from 1871 to 1940, Giáp strongly held on to his belief that he would use the press as a sharp weapon in semi-legal conditions. To keep the police at bay, he wrote many of the articles under assumed names. However, his articles remained under close scrutiny by the French censorship and many a time what was left of his article was only three words "omitted by censorship."

Events that took place inside and outside the country since the beginning of 1930[1] which led to French widespread white terrorism from north to south made it increasingly hard for Giáp to continue his press activities. The 19-year-old member of the Tân Việt Party had to work fully stretched in the editorial board of the *Tiếng dân* while participating in practical political activities held by the intellectual circles, including the vocal support for the protest against French execution of the people who masterminded the Yên Bái uprising. The multiple activities that Giáp participated in during the last couple of years, which the French authorities called "troublesome," were under the close surveillance of the Second Bureau of the General Staff. By the end of 1930, Võ Nguyên Giáp and his younger brother Võ Thuần Nho were arrested together with several other intellectuals, including Đặng Thai Mai—a member of the Tân Việt Party and a teacher of literature at Huế National School, and Nguyễn Thị Quang Thái—a student at Đồng Khánh School. All of them

---

1. Particularly the Yên Bái uprising organized by the Việt Nam Nationalist Party and the Soviet-Nghệ Tĩnh movement following the advent of the Indochinese Communist Party.

were detained in the Thừa Phủ Prison in Huế. More than a year later, by a directive of the protectorate government, the political prisoners who were to serve less than four years in prisons had their terms commuted before being released. They were not totally free, however, as they remained under the supervision of local authorities in their hometowns. One day in the beginning month of 1932, Võ Nguyên Giáp and other comrade inmates, including Đặng Thái Mai and Nguyễn Thị Quang Thái, were released from prison.

Giáp was intent on remaining in Huế to continue writing revolutionary newspaper articles, but the French authorities was determined to expel him to his native hometown. After several days sojourning in An Xá, he secretly left for Vinh, a central province about 350 kilometers north of Huế. Đặng Thai Mai, Giáp's teacher at Huế National School, comrade in the Tân Việt Party, and prison mate in Thừa Phủ, arranged for him to become a family tutor, teaching mathematics and French. What Giáp had never expected was that Nguyễn Thị Quang Thái, his prison friend who was four years younger than him, also became one of his students. Having known and admired each other during their detention, the two comrades Giáp and Thái, first as tutor and tutee, gradually became lovers.

In 1933, Võ Nguyên Giáp followed Đặng Thai Mai to Hà Nội and got admitted to Albert Sarraut[1] Secondary School. One year later, at the age of 23, he was awarded full baccalaureate. To compensate for the time he lost several years earlier, Giáp worked as a history teacher at Thăng Long School while pursuing a tertiary course at the University

---

1. Albert Pierre Sarraut (1872–1962) served two terms as Governor-General of Indochina during the 1911–1914 and 1917–1919 periods.

of Law. The academic environment at the private school of Thăng Long was conducive to the revolutionary activities of the young teacher.[1] His activities in the youth movement then involved a new task. Taking advantage of his position as a history teacher, he worked to instil patriotic and democratic ideas into the mind of his students while equipping himself with different types of knowledge necessary for his future revolutionary activities. Under the guise of lectures on the French Revolution and on the world-famous general Napoleon, Võ Nguyên Giáp was able to transfer to his students what he wanted to say beyond the suspicious eyes of the authorities.

In 1936, when he learnt that the French Popular Front was established and the leftist government of Léon Blum assumed power, Giáp believed that this important event would exert direct effect on the political stage of Indochina. This was the main reason why he decided to part with academic learning and discontinue his doctoral course in politico-economic studies. In addition, he also declined an offer by Gaëtan Pirou, who was then envoy of the French Ministry of Education, to go to Paris to pursue further studies. With his particularly acute political awareness, he believed that the event that had just taken place in Paris was an excellent opportunity to overtly publish a newspaper. Given support and green light from the teachers at Thăng Long School, Giáp worked with some of his friends to bring a new journal tiled *Hồn trẻ* (literally:

---

1. During a meeting in November 1985, Hoàng Minh Giám, former Headmaster of Thăng Long School, recounted, "At the beginning of the 1930s, Thăng Long became one of the real cores of the youth movement in Hà Nội. The school activities were secretly guided by the Party. Patriotic and revolutionary political activities in the school were like undercurrents that became increasingly strong among both teachers and students. . ."

The Youthful Soul) to the public on June 6, 1936. It was the first Vietnamese newspaper which publicly aired its support for the French Popular Front and the leftist government in Paris while demanding democracy and amnesty for political prisoners in Indochina. That explained why French colonial authorities quickly banned the journal after its sixth issue. But the ban could not dishearten Võ Nguyên Giáp and his friends. As the journal was banned because it was published in Vietnamese, they switched to a French-language version and changed the name to *Le Travail* (literally: Labour) on September 16 of the same year, citing the provisions in the Press Law of the colonialist regime. After seven months of existence with 30 issues, however, *Le Travail* suffered the same fate as the *Hồn trẻ* when it was closed down by the French authorities.

An event in 1937 that had a great influence on the political life of Võ Nguyên Giáp was the appearance of two people in Hà Nội: Đặng Xuân Khu, who later became known as Trường Chinh, and Phạm Văn Đồng. The former was arrested by the French in 1930 and sentenced to 12 years' imprisonment in Sơn La. He was released before his imprisonment expired thanks to the combined effect of the Vietnamese people's movement that demanded the emancipation of political prisoners and the victory of the French Popular Front. The latter, in the wake of the academic strike in Huế National School in mourning for Phan Chu Trinh, escaped to China where he attended a political class held by Nguyễn Ái Quốc. After returning to the country, he was also arrested by the French colonial authorities and exiled to Côn Đảo to serve a ten-year sentence. He was freed after the victory of the movement demanding the release of Indochinese political prisoners.

Chapter One: THE PATH TO A MILITARY CAREER

The trio of Đặng Xuân Khu, Phạm Văn Đồng, and Võ Nguyên Giáp soon became close comrades, taking advantage of the legal loopholes to actively participate in the press front in Hà Nội.[1] Working with two senior comrades, Giáp had his mind broadened and political awareness raised. Đặng Xuân Khu and Phạm Văn Đồng told him many captivating stories about the Indochinese Communist Party and its founder, Nguyễn Ái Quốc, and helped him later to become one of its members in 1937. It was also during this period of time that Võ Nguyên Giáp and Đặng Xuân Khu, pen-named Vân Đình and Qua Ninh respectively, co-authored a book titled *Vấn đề dân cày* (literally: On the Issue of the Tiller) which, together with other legal newspapers of the time, contributed to the dissemination and popularization of the Indochinese Communist Party's policies on peasants and rural areas in Việt Nam.

Throughout the democratic movement, especially during the 1938–1939 period, Nguyễn Ái Quốc, whose pen-name was P. C. Line, sent many articles from China to be published on the *Notre Voix* (literally: Our Voice). Having listened to the stories Phạm Văn Đồng told him about Nguyễn Ái Quốc, Giáp felt that he could not wait to meet the leader of the Vietnamese revolutionary movement in person.

Since the beginning of 1939, after getting married with Nguyễn Thị Quang Thái and settling down in Hà Nội, Võ

---

1. After the *Le Travail* was closed down, there remained several French newspapers in Hà Nội and Sài Gòn, such as the *Rassemblement* (literally: Gathering), the *En Avant* (literally: Forward), the *Notre Voix* (literally: Our Voice), the *Avant-garde* (literally: Vanguard), and the *Le Peuple* (literally: People), in addition to the many Vietnamese newspapers. Võ Nguyên Giáp was a contributor for many of these newspapers, but mainly for the several French newspapers in the North.

Nguyên Giáp continued to contribute actively to the press front and teach at Thăng Long School. Toward the end of the 1930s, however, there were significant changes. A series of major events that took place in the world, one after another, especially in France itself had quick and strong effects on the political scenario of Indochina. These changes heralded a new turning point in the revolutionary life of the young intellectual Võ Nguyên Giáp.

From the Meeting with Nguyễn Ái Quốc to the First Lessons on the Revolution

After the collapse of the Léon Blum cabinet, Édouard Daladier took office in April 1938 in Paris. Alarmed by the increasingly complicated political situations in France, Indochinese Governor-General Joseph Jules Brévié and the French colonizers started a crackdown on the revolutionary movement. In Hà Nội, many of the Communist Party cadres were expelled from the city. One newspaper after another was closed down and more and more journalists were arrested. Since September 1939, semi-legal working conditions ceased, especially in the wake of the German Nazi attack on Poland that triggered the Second World War. Next came the decision of the colonial authorities to outlaw the Communist Party. The trio of Trường Chinh, Phạm Văn Đồng, and Võ Nguyên Giáp therefore had to switch to clandestine activities, and on many occasions they had to leave the city, each taking temporary lodging in one of the revolutionary grassroots bases in the suburbs of Hà Nội.

One day in the summer of 1940, Phạm Văn Đồng and Võ Nguyên Giáp were asked by Hoàng Văn Thụ, Secretary of the Northern Regional Party Committee, to come for a clandestine appointment in Chèm in the suburbs of Hà Nội. It was here that they learnt about the Party Central Committee's new directives which instructed a switch from continued struggle for democracy and livelihood to making preparations for an overthrow of the government of the colonialist regime and their puppets and lackeys. Specifically, this meant moving from legal and semi-legal activities to illegal and clandestine activities, preparing political and armed forces, and waiting for an opportunity to carry out an armed uprising to regain government. Finally, Hoàng Văn Thụ added that by a decision of the Party, Phạm Văn Đồng and Võ Nguyên Giáp were to be sent to Huanan (China) to be given new tasks by Nguyễn Ái Quốc.

Four months after Nguyễn Thị Quang Thái gave birth to a girl, named Hồng Anh, Giáp had to hit the road.

That afternoon, Thái stood on Cổ Ngư Street (present-day Thanh Niên Street in Hà Nội), holding the baby in her arms, to see off her husband. To the superficial passers-by, the young couple and their baby seemed to be enjoying fresh air by the side of West Lake. Neither Giáp nor Thái knew that they would never meet again!

On the train all the way from Hà Nội to Lào Cai, Phạm Văn Đồng and Võ Nguyên Giáp did not sit next to each other, but both of them were extremely anxious, putting themselves on high alert for the French spies. When the train stopped, the two blended into the crowd of passengers and then followed the liaison to a quiet forest before crossing the Nậm Ty River that flows between Lào Cai and the Chinese province of Yunnan. Then they took the Hukou-Kunming train and again had to watch out carefully for not only Chiang Kai-shek's spies but also fare and identity inspectors. However, the most nerve-racking moments when they found themselves in a totally different place with language barriers were finally over and they were able to meet the contact person when the train reached the Station of Kunming—the chief city of Yunnan Province.

Nguyễn Ái Quốc, under the pseudonym of Wang, was away on business. The two made use of the waiting time to acquire some Chinese. One day early in June, Giáp and Đông were invited by Phùng Chí Kiên to take a promenade by the side of Green Lake (Chinese: *Cuihu*), a popular tourist attraction in Kunming. On the way, Kiên told them that comrade Wang had returned and asked to have an appointment with them. Giáp was filled with some anxiety at the news. A quarter of century later, he recounted those memorable moments of his life:

> When we reached Green Lake, I saw Vũ Anh sitting in a boat with a thin, middle-aged man with bright eyes wearing a grey Sun Yatsen-style outfit and a felt hat. I immediately recognized that he was comrade Nguyễn Ái Quốc. Compared with a photo of him I had seen earlier, he seemed a lot quicker and more acute in real life. Before I met him, I had thought that he must look different from ordinary people, but I seemed to have mistaken. What struck me most at that time was that during our conversation, he sometimes spoke with the central Vietnamese accent. I was surprised that having been away for so long, he could still speak such authentic Vietnamese...

It had been 15 years from the time Giáp first read *Le Procès de la colonisation française* while at Huế National School, and had some superficial knowledge of its author, to the moment he realized that the man in the boat was the very person he had been longing to meet. That 15 years led him to commit his whole life to the Vietnamese revolution and to Nguyễn Ái Quốc.

After listening to Phạm Văn Đồng and Võ Nguyên Giáp's report on the domestic revolutionary movement, Nguyễn Ái Quốc told them about the possibility of Japanese troops entering Indochina and having their interest in conflict with the French. He also analysed in great detail Chiang Kai-shek's plot to invade Việt Nam under the guise of the so-called "Chinese troops entering Việt Nam" plan, and warned that some Vietnamese-formed political parties abroad were also intent on tail-gating the Chiang Kai-shek army to infiltrate the country.

Several days later, Nguyễn Ái Quốc decided to send Phạm Văn Đồng and Võ Nguyên Giáp to a course at Yan'an Politico-military Institute founded by the Chinese Communist Party. During their stopover in Guiyang to catch a coach to Yan'an, they learnt that the German Nazi troops had entered Paris. Nguyễn Ái Quốc asked the two to immediately return to Guilin. When they met again and evaluated the situations, Nguyễn Ái Quốc said that the defeat of France by the Nazi presented a wonderful opportunity for the Vietnamese revolution. They concurred that they should return to Việt Nam as soon as possible to grab the opportunity. During the discussion on the potentials and preparations for the uprising, there were concerns about the feasibility of overthrowing the colonialist regime with no weapons in hand. Nguyễn Ái Quốc said while he agreed that no uprising could be carried out without guns, a more important factor was the quality of the people who would use those guns. According to him, there was no point preparing weapons when they were not even sure about who would use them. It made more sense that they returned first to the country and then mobilized the participation of the mass. Once the people had grown alive to the ideals of the revolution, they would automatically have weapons.

By the end of November 1940, Võ Nguyên Giáp, together with Cao Hồng Lĩnh and Vũ Anh, reached Jingxi, a small town in Guangxi, which borders the two Vietnamese provinces of Cao Bằng and Lạng Sơn. They learnt that over forty young Vietnamese had just crossed the border to China due to the increased French suppression in Cao Bằng and Lạng Sơn. After listening to reports, Nguyễn Ái Quốc remarked that this presented a good opportunity to establish a link with the people inside Việt Nam, through Cao Bằng. Therefore, he instructed that a training class be immediately organized for these young people before sending them back to consolidate the existing revolutionary bases and expanding the movement in Cao Bằng to serve dual role as a foothold for the revolutionary forces and a launching pad to advance toward the plains.

The political training course was opened in January 1941 in two villages in Jingxi, under the supervision of Phùng Chí Kiên, Phạm Văn Đồng, and Võ Nguyên Giáp. The main content of the course was to make these youngsters better aware of the new tasks of the Vietnamese revolution, its current situation, as well as methods to establish political mass organizations and map out action plans that suited the new situation. Nguyễn Ái Quốc set concrete requirements for the training program. Specifically, the political content must be appropriate; its wording must be clear, succinct, and accessible to the learners, whose general knowledge and academic level remained limited as most of them were of ethnic minority backgrounds.

Although he had significant pedagogic experience working for many years as a teacher at Thăng Long School, Võ Nguyên Giáp found these textbook requirements new and useful in organizing a training course on mass mobilization for young cadres. In terms of methodology, he always bore in mind Nguyễn Ái Quốc's request that the course should be conducted in such a way that upon completion, trainees knew "the what" and "the how" when they returned to Việt Nam. What this actually meant was that "theory and practice must go hand in hand." One of the most important goals that Nguyễn Ái Quốc set out for the trainees was what he called "Five dos and don'ts."[1] After three weeks training, the course ended. The 43 young men crossed the border again to return to their original political bases, mainly in the two districts of Hà Quảng and Hòa An in Cao Bằng to develop the mass political movement. Before they departed, Nguyễn Ái Quốc told them to keep in mind that the first priority was to find and gain a foothold, first in one small area, then in many larger regions which were connected to form an entire and spacious revolutionary base. That "foothold" had to be understood as a firm place in the heart and mind of the

---

1. The five dos include: 1- Help the local people in most essential daily work; 2- Understand the local practices and customs; respect the local people's cultural taboos; 3- Learn the language of the locals and teach them to sing and read to win their popularity; 4- Choose the right time and place to carry out revolutionary propaganda; 5- Give the people the impression that revolutionary people are disciplined, hardworking, and reliable so as to win their trust and support. The five don'ts include: 1- Cause damage to the local people's assets, deface or ruin their houses and crops; 2- Insist on buying or borrowing something; 3- Break promises; 4- Infringe upon local practices, customs, and beliefs; 5- Disclose secrets.

people, as "the greatest threats do not come from the enemy, but from the lack of popular support."

In fact, the development of the movement between the end of 1941 and the beginning of 1942 showed that the 43 young cadres were the first seeds carefully nurtured and sowed by Nguyễn Ái Quốc on a land plot he chose as the revolutionary base. These seeds soon took roots and spread quickly and extensively to every hamlet and village in many districts of Cao Bằng. It was them who helped to lay a firm political foundation for the establishment of the Unified National Front in particular, and for the political movement across Việt Bắc in general, during the long process of preparing for an armed uprising. Among these 43 cadres were the likes of Lê Quang Ba, Hoàng Sâm, and Bằng Giang, who later became high-ranking officers in the armed forces and assumed important positions throughout the armed uprising and the revolutionary war.

By the end of January 1941, when Nguyễn Ái Quốc and several other cadres crossed the Sino-Vietnamese border and made their return in the direction of Cao Bằng, he asked Võ Nguyên Giáp, Phạm Văn Đồng, and Hoàng Văn Hoan to stay behind and, on behalf of the Việt Nam Liberation Allied League,[1] persuade the local Chiang Kai-shek authorities to help organize a military training course. Trainees included cadres from Việt Nam, selected by Hoàng Văn Thụ and sent to China around 1941. Chiang Kai-shek's representative in Guilin, Li Jishen, agreed to help open a training course on military issues in Tiandong, one on sabotage in Jingxi, and

---

1. A Vietnamese political organization once linked to Chiang Kai-shek's administration in Huanan.

one on radio communications in Liuzhou. The reason why the Chinese was ready to help was probably because they hoped these training courses later would be of great use for Chiang Kai-shek's "Chinese troops entering Việt Nam" plan.

Among the cadres sent by Hoàng Văn Thụ to attend the military training course in Tiandong in the middle of 1941 was Hoàng Văn Thái, a 26-year-old man who had participated in the combat in Võ Nhai-Tràng Xá (Thái Nguyên) after the Bắc Sơn uprising in September 1940. The relationship between Võ Nguyên Giáp and Hoàng Văn Thái began since then, and the latter, who were four years younger than Giáp, later became one of his closest aides throughout the two national liberation wars.

During their stay in Jingxi, Phạm Văn Đồng, Hoàng Văn Hoan, and Võ Nguyên Giáp normally took turns to go to Cao Bằng to report the situations to Nguyễn Ái Quốc. Around the end of May 1941, Giáp crossed the border to return to Việt Nam for the first time, after having made every necessary preparation for the military training course. To mark the first time returning to the motherland on the day he turned 30 years old, Giáp decided to assume the new pseudonym *"Văn"* (literally "literature"). This name had been with him throughout his military career ever since. Even when he already became old, he was still affectionately called "Brother Văn."

The contact man escorted Võ Nguyên Giáp to the lodging place of Nguyễn Ái Quốc, who was then known under the name of Hồ Chí Minh. His headquarters was in the cave of Cốc Bó (which means "upstream" in the local language), situated in Pác Bó Village, Trường Hà Commune, Hà Quảng District, Cao Bằng Province, adjacent to the Sino-Vietnamese border.

77

In this return to the country, Võ Nguyên Giáp had a chance to listen to Hồ Chí Minh's brief explanation of the resolution of the Eighth Plenum of the Party Central Committee, which had convened in the middle of May. The main contents of the resolution discussed how the domestic and global situations might influence the success of the Vietnamese revolution; identified struggle for national liberation as the main task of the revolution; advocated the establishment of the Unified National Front (Vietnamese: *Mặt trận dân tộc thống* nhất), which was also known as the Việt Nam Independence League (Vietnamese: *Việt Nam độc lập đồng minh*) or Việt Minh for short; and quickly prepared for an armed uprising. At the Plenum, Trường Chinh was elected as the Party General Secretary. Hồ Chí Minh asked Võ Nguyên Giáp to spend time examining the resolution of the Eighth Plenum of the Party Central Committee and the Việt Minh Program, particularly the sections on preparations for a guerrilla war, a part-by-part armed uprising, the seizure of power in each locality toward the seizure of power on a nationwide scale, and the resolution on the organization of a self-defense team.

What Võ Nguyên Giáp regretted was his failure to meet Trường Chinh to ask after the situations in Hanoi and news of his family. For more than a year, he had not heard from his wife and daughter.

On another return trip around July 1941, Hồ Chí Minh told Giáp not to return to Jingxi any more and put him in charge of the Việt Minh's newspaper *Việt Lập* (literally: Independent Việt Nam)—the mouthpiece of the Việt Minh Front that served to mobilize the mass for revolutionary activities. This time, working conditions were far different from what he experienced in Huế or Hà Nội. The local people helped collect paper for printing, piece by piece, in market sessions. Newspapers were printed on only two small-sized pages while the letters had to be large enough to make it easier for the people to read, according to a requirement from Hồ Chí Minh. This meant the passages had to be short, no more than a hundred words each, as there was not enough space for lengthy articles. The wording must be simple and accessible to the general public. Giáp later recalled it was the first time in his position as a journalist that he "found writing difficult."

The newspaper made its debut on August 1, 1941. In the first place, it was published every month and had only several dozen two-paged copies. Soon after that, it came out two or three times a month, with hundreds of copies and more pages. On some occasions, the newspaper was printed in as many as four hundred copies and on up to four pages. Hồ Chí Minh was the biggest and most regular contributor for the *Việt Lập*.

When the newspaper had obtained a smooth operation, Hồ Chí Minh tasked Võ Nguyên Giáp with organizing mobile political training courses in different localities across districts in Cao Bằng. By this time, the revolutionary movement had developed extensively and intensively in many cantons, although not yet equally and steadily, especially in mountainous areas. The situations called for not only continued reinforcement but also immediate expansion of mass movements across all the bases in Cao Bằng, thus creating political foundations for an increasingly firm foothold. That was the most important pre-condition for the advance toward mass armed struggle, the launching of limited guerrilla warfare and part-by-part uprising, and the seizure of power in each locality in line with the resolution of the Party Central Committee's Eighth Plenum in May 1941.

Titled "*Con đường giải phóng*" (literally: "Road to Liberation"), the materials intended for this political training course were the same documents prepared for the one in Jingxi, with some additions and amendments to make them more suitable for the current situations. Additions included commentary on the latest developments inside and outside the country, the method of organizing self-defense units, and the preparations for an armed uprising.

Political training classes were successively opened, one after another across the province of Cao Bằng. This was probably the most active but also hardest period of time for Võ Nguyên Giáp since his return to the country. Together with Lê Thiết Hùng, he crossed mountains and rivers to reach minority people living even in some of the highest mountains, carrying out "three-together" policy, which included eating together, living together, and working together, so that he could approach them and introduce to them the Việt Minh policies and lines. Initially with only a handful of cadres and a unique foothold in one hamlet, the movement quickly expanded like a "ripple effect." At the commencement of each training course, there were normally around ten participants. Language barriers were also one of the biggest challenges for Giáp, especially when it came to conveying political concepts, as very few ethnic minority people at that time could speak the Kinh majority language (general Vietnamese). One of the greatest achievements of Võ Nguyên Giáp during this period of time was his ability to learn the local languages, including Dao, Nùng, and Tày, to converse more effectively with the locals. Having spent years with the locals in different districts and localities across Cao Bằng, speaking their languages, living in their community, and patiently educating them, Võ Nguyên Giáp and his comrades were able to establish many strong political bases to serve dual role as footholds for the revolution and a springboard for gradual southward progress in the direction of Bắc Cạn. As a result, Giáp himself was affectionately called "teacher of the highland people" by the locals who dozens of years later still remembered him, a reliable cadre who had been sent by the revolution and stood side by side with them in the biggest ordeals of the initial days of the national liberation war.

During those years, Võ Nguyên Giáp not only contributed an essential part to the expansion and consolidation of the revolutionary bases in the lowland and highland of Cao Bằng but also more importantly was able to draw out fundamental conclusions that testified Hồ Chí Minh's views on the role of the populace in the revolutionary cause and in building base networks. Twenty years later, Giáp wrote in his memoir:

> Experience at the training courses showed that it would be easier to get revolutionary ideas across to the local people if we were able to relate them to their daily needs and aspirations. The mass mobilization process would then be a great deal more attractive and encourage people to advance in their struggle. Another valuable lesson that I learnt was that, once the revolution had been able to win the heart of the innocent and pure-minded people in the highland, their belief in the revolution would be immutable and unshakable.

The many years he spent mobilizing the minority people gave Giáp certain fundamental qualities—love for his countrymen, political responsibility for the mass, and familiarity with the life of people in different localities.

These qualities deepened his view on the power of the people and enabled him to command successfully a people's army throughout the 30-year-long war. The core principle, according to him, was to rely on the might of the whole people for the victory of the army.

From a Pathfinder to a Military Commander

Since its Eighth Plenum in May 1941, the Party Central Committee operated in two separate regions, physically distant from each other, and communication was extremely limited. While Hồ Chí Minh's headquarters was situated in Cao Bằng, General Secretary Trường Chinh's area of operation was in the vicinity of Hà Nội. It was therefore very difficult to evaluate the situations together and agree upon the course of actions to take. As a result, establishing a communication channel between Cao Bằng and the lowland became one of the most urgent issues.

Toward the middle of 1942, based on evaluation that the foothold in Cao Bằng had been expanded and fortified, Hồ Chí Minh decided to develop the movement across the three provinces of Cao Bằng, Bắc Cạn, and Lạng Sơn before gradually moving southward. Võ Nguyên Giáp and Lê Thiết Hùng were asked by Hồ Chí Minh to build a political corridor conducive to the movement toward the provinces of Thái Nguyên and Tuyên Quang. Imminently, the movement would be gradually developed from the launching pad of Nguyên Bình (Cao Bằng Province) to Ngân Sơn District, Chợ Rã Town, and then Chợ Đồn District (Bắc Cạn Province) before it was linked to the Bắc Sơn-Vũ Nhai base. From here linkage with the Central units in the lowland would be gradually established. Movement was not only made southward but also eastward from Đông Khê Town (Cao Bằng Province) down to Lạng Sơn Province and Đình Cả Town (Thái Nguyên Province), and westward (to Hà Giang Province) in the charge of Hoàng Văn Hoan and Phạm Văn Đồng respectively. It was also on this occasion that Chu Văn Tấn and several other members of the National Salvation Army[1] departed from Tràng Xá Commune, Võ Nhai District, Thái Nguyên Province, to move northward in the direction of Chợ Chu Town (Thái Nguyên Province) and Chợ Đồn District (Bắc Cạn Province).

Establishing a political corridor was in essence expanding the grassroots political bases in the form of a "ripple effect" on a larger scale, from Cao Bằng Province southward. Giáp was totally aware of the importance of the task he was given, one of long-term strategic significance. He also anticipated the hardship and challenges involved. More than a hundred young and fit cadres were rigorously selected and staffed into a new organization by the name of "Southward Voluntary Teams" (Vietnamese: *Đội Xung phong Nam tiến*). Successive training courses were quickly set up in order to pass down to the southward volunteers the ample experience garnered for years in the area of mass mobilization, including from methods of political education to best practices in the application of the "Five dos and don'ts" under the new circumstances. Võ Nguyên Giáp shared with his young colleagues specific experience in how to respect the local mores and customs, reverence to the old, appropriate treatment of local children

---

1. The National Salvation Army (Vietnamese: *Cứu quốc quân*) was the common name of all anti-French guerrilla teams that operated in the Bắc Sơn base during the 1941–1945 period. This armed force was tasked to fight against terrorism, build and safeguard the Việt Minh's revolutionary bases. It was the precursor of the Vietnamese People's Army.

and women, as well as the importance of keeping one's promise in maintaining people's trust. Other issues like daily hygiene and physical exercise to be fit enough for a protracted mission under extreme weather conditions also needed to be taken into serious consideration. Of paramount importance was the need to keep a secret of movement directions and destinations, and what to do in accidental encounter with the enemy on the road.

In the middle of August 1942, nineteen Southward Voluntary Teams departed, one after another, in the respective directions they had been given using what was dubbed the "inchworm method."[1]

As the Southward Voluntary Teams worked to develop mass organizations, Giáp usually chose to stop and help those hamlets where development was difficult, pointing for the team members why the problems occurred and how to solve them.

One year of hard work by nearly a hundred volunteers helped to materialize Hồ Chí Minh's idea of a political corridor. In the middle of August 1943, while Giáp's southward units

---

1. On each direction, the Southward Voluntary Teams were divided into two smaller units. One would go on probing and inspection trip to their assigned localities, finding local sympathizers and carrying out propaganda for Việt Minh to win popular support in each family, each hamlet. The other who came later would choose areas with the highest number of Việt Minh sympathizers to carry out further propaganda to attract more members for the mass organizations associated with Việt Minh Front. They also opened political training courses for members of these mass organizations, screened for the most active and able participants, and gave them added training to turn them into core and regular cadres who would serve to maintain and develop the local movements. Once all these jobs had been completed and done in a locality, the teams moved southward to another area and repeated the process, hence the name "inchworm method."

were on their way from Cao Bằng Province to Nghĩa Tá Commune (Chợ Đồn District, Bắc Cạn Province), young soldiers of the National Salvation Army under the supervision of Chu Văn Tấn were moving in the opposite direction from Bắc Sơn District. When they met, Võ Nguyên Giáp and Chu Văn Tấn agreed to give the commune the new name *"Thắng Lợi"* (literally: "Victory") to mark the place where the two newly-opened routes converged.

The two commanders exchanged ideas and evaluated the developments of the movements in their respective revolutionary bases and in the whole country. That a lot of change had taken place after only one year spoke volumes about the rise and popularity of the revolution. The movement in Bắc Sơn-Vũ Nhai had been consolidated and expanded to the districts of Chợ Chu and Đại Từ (Thái Nguyên Province) and Yên Thế District (Bắc Giang Province). Chu Văn Tấn had an especially good piece of news to inform: communication with the Party Central Committee had been established. And according to news received, despite the French and Japanese heightened terrorist policy, the national salvation associations in the Việt Minh Front continued to expand, right in the heart of the Red River Delta and in the suburbs of Hà Nội.

On returning to Cao Bằng, Võ Nguyên Giáp learnt that Phạm Văn Đồng and Vũ Anh were waiting for him to come back to discuss the ongoing situations and make plans for the future. In their exchanges, Giáp and his colleagues shared a common concern over Hồ Chí Minh's capture by the Chinese Guomintang (literally Chinese Nationalist Party) when he was on a business trip abroad. Scouts had been sent to China to sound out the situation, but nothing new had been heard. They discussed and agreed that the victorious counter-attack by the Soviet Red Army in the Winter 1943–Spring 1943 on the Stalingrad Front had created a crucial turning point in the Soviet-Nazi War in particular and wars in Europe and the Asia-Pacific region in general. The latest developments of the Second World War proved to be advantageous for the Vietnamese revolution. Domestically, the Việt Minh movement was spreading quickly and strongly in many lowland provinces. Giáp and his colleague, however, also anticipated that the Japanese would take advantage of the situation and collude with the French to increase their repressive activities so as to prevent the revolutionary movement from further expansion and at the same time establish "a safe rear" in case of major incidents. Latest news showed that the enemy was carrying out another terrorist attack on the revolutionary bases, and that the popular movements in Cao Bằng were likely to face difficulties, or even contraction. The emergency nature of the situation required urgent instructions for revolutionary forces in each locality as to how to confront the enemy and maintain and strengthen the grassroots bases. Giáp and his two comrades underscored the protection of the "political corridor" that linked Cao Bằng and Bắc Sơn-Nhai as a task of paramount importance.

So amidst the very first days of the Lunar New Year of 1944, Võ Nguyên Giáp, Hoàng Sâm, and some Southward units hit the road again. This time, the journey proved a lot more challenging right from the very first miles, as the enemy's mopping-up operations had intensified immediately after its inception. The more they moved southward, the more worrying the situation became. Enemy troops were stationed

Chapter One: THE PATH TO A MILITARY CAREER

along some of the most crucial routes and many hamlets had become their garrisons. The "popular road" opened just several months earlier then became disrupted in many sections. There were roads which were flanked by villages torn apart by the enemy's attack. Many of the most candid cadres were arrested and killed; scores of local houses were set on fire while the local people, especially those who failed to flee into the jungle, were caged into the enemy's concentration camps. Many areas, once very active in revolutionary movements just a few months before, became almost empty both in the fields and in the milpas. While in their previous campaigns, the enemy used a mixture of threat and persuasion of the members to submit themselves, this time, apart from coaxing, they also resorted to force, brutal suppression, and crackdown. Many people of the populace were so scared that they had to surrender to the enemy. During the daytime, the cadres had to move to the forest and one of the most difficult tasks for them was at nightfall, when they moved back again to the villages to comfort and assure the locals, they were evaded. The locals were too afraid of the enemy to let them in. Many of these cadres also grew disheartened by the surveillance of the enemy and lost their belief in the ability of the movement to bounce back. There were even cases of cadres submitting and surrendering themselves to the enemy in the wrong belief that this could save the local people from torture and repression by the enemy.

Being aware of the ongoing and spreading complicated situations, Võ Nguyên Giáp, Hoàng Sâm, and other Southward cadres discussed from the very early stages how to boost the morale of the local cadres, revitalize the local movements, and maintain the political bases along the North-

South route. Having finished discussing and identified the appropriate measures, Giáp repeated Hồ Chí Minh's advice: to every challenge and ordeal, the most reliable and stable backing came from the trust and support of the people. The more challenging the situation became, the more patient the cadres should be, so that they could gradually restore the people's belief in the future of the revolution. Having identified intimacy to the people as the key to success to restoring grassroots bases, each of the units continued with their respective given tasks, joining hands to reinvigorate the movements while standing ready to confront all the new challenges and hardship.

After nearly ten months of intense and fierce fighting against enemy suppression and protecting the people while gradually restoring the local movements, the popular road that connected Cao Bằng-Lạng Sơn with Bắc Cạn-Thái Nguyên had basically been opened, although the grassroots bases in some places had not completely regained its original strength and stability.

On September 20, 1944, Hồ Chí Minh returned from China and set foot on Cao Bằng. Several days later, Vũ Anh and Võ Nguyên Giáp came to see him to report on the operation of all the political bases across Cao Bằng and briefed him on the recent struggle against French repressive attacks. As for the Southward route, Hồ Chí Minh learnt from his two comrades that some sections remained disrupted, which meant communication with Bắc Sơn had not been totally restored. He paid special attention as he listened to a report on a recent resolution issued in July by the Interprovincial Party Committee of Cao Bằng-Bắc Cạn-Lạng Sơn (known collectively as Cao-Bắc-Lạng) which advocated calling on the masses to stage an armed uprising to take control of the mountainous areas. Specifically, the resolution advocated launching a localized guerrilla war, or a part-by-part uprising, to seize power in some places along the line of the resolution issued in May 1941 by the Party Central Committee. The above-mentioned policy was grounded on the evaluation that the situation of the mass movement in Cao-Bắc-Lạng had become stable and conditions were ripe for an armed uprising. In addition, leaders of the Interprovincial Party Committee believed that the policy was well-suited to the aspirations of the people who were feeling utmost hatred against the terrorist acts of the enemy.

After asking some additional questions about the preparations and the planned time of the uprising, Hồ Chí Minh pondered for a while and then started to analyze the policy, noting that it had only based on the specific situations of the locality and had not taken into account the overall situation of the revolution nationwide. He explained that at the moment, no place had enough conditions to launch a guerrilla war to respond to and join hands with the base. If we urged the local people to stage an uprising, it was likely that the uprising would be isolated and repressed by the French, which put the movement into a worse-than-ever situation.

Analyzing the sensitivity and vulnerability of the current situation, Hồ Chí Minh remarked that the period of peaceful development for the revolution had gone, but an armed uprising then would be immature. This meant that if the same form of political activities was repeated, it would not push the movement forward. But if an armed uprising was staged immediately, the enemy would muster their forces in response. Therefore, another form of struggle which could protect the grassroots political bases while continuing to push the movement forward was needed. It was armed propaganda, which used armed activities to exert intensive and extensive political influence on the general public, laying the foundation for the gradual transference from political activities to armed activities. Hồ Chí Minh emphasized that in the short term, "political measures must take precedence over military actions."

With that evaluation in mind, the remaining issue was to organize a concentrated armed group, an armed propaganda brigade whose main function was in political mass mobilization. At that time there were several cadres in Cao-Bắc-Lạng who had certain knowledge and experience in carrying out military activities. For example, Lê Thiết Hùng had once been sent by the Party to work in the strategic advisory board of the Chiang Kai-shek army. Lê Quảng Ba and Hoàng Sâm had been sent across the border to work with the guerrilla forces of the Chinese Communist Party in the 1937–1938 period, and they also had a thorough understanding of military forces in the Cao-Bắc-Lạng base. However, apparently having considered carefully about these options before, Hồ Chí Minh decided to choose Võ Nguyên Giáp to take charge of organizing and commanding the concentrated armed brigade, which later came to be known as the first major core brigade of the revolutionary armed forces nationwide.[1]

Before Võ Nguyên Giáp departed for the new task, Hồ Chí Minh reminded him of some fundamental issues, basic

---

1. Hồ Chí Minh's decision to name Võ Nguyên Giáp, a history teacher who had not attended any military training course, as commander-in-chief of the army was deemed a mystery that attracted the attention and examination of many people in both academic and military circles.

knowledge about the Vietnamese revolutionary military philosophy, such as organizational skills and operational guidelines. Hồ Chí Minh underlined some vital factors that would guarantee the maturity and invincibility of the liberation army: 1- The role of the Communist Party cell as the core leader; 2- Reliance on the people, a warranty for victory over any enemy no matter how mighty it is; 3- The foothold must be a place conducive for both attack and defense.

Having reviewed all the guerrilla units in the whole base and considered the ability of each person, Võ Nguyên Giáp and Lê Quảng Ba agreed to propose the formation of only one platoon, called "Liberation Army," which in the first place consisted of only 34 soldiers of four ethnicities.[1] In terms of equipment and machinery, despite efforts to prepare the best weapons, there were only enough to equip each soldier with one type of weapon, mainly rifles (17 were made in France and China). The remaining were matchlocks.[2] Hoàng Sâm and Dương Mạc Thạch (i.e. Xích Thắng—Secretary of Nguyên Bình District Party Cell) were appointed respectively as leader and commissar of the Liberation Army while Hoàng Văn Thái was put in charge of intelligence and combat. Thái had just returned to the country after the completion of the military training course in Tiandong in Huanan.

Having approved of the organizational and personnel plan, Hồ Chí Minh gave additional instructions on the development and operation of the army.

---

1. They included 19 Tày, 9 Nùng, 4 Kinh, and 1 Dao. Of these 34 soldiers, 28 were natives of Cao Bằng.
2. The matchlock was a kind of simple gun made by the ethnic minority people of the highland of Việt Bắc, mainly for hunting purposes.

Firstly, regarding the name of the platoon, it was deemed necessary to add the word "propaganda" to better reflect the functions of the platoon, which was also suitable with the current maxim of "political measures taking precedence over military actions." The official name, therefore, would be "Việt Nam Propaganda and Liberation Army" (Vietnamese: *"Việt Nam tuyên truyền giải phóng quân"*).

Secondly, two months after coming into being, the army would have to be put into action. "Confidentiality" and "secret" would be a top priority and principle. The army should "come and go without leaving any traces" and its location should always remain unknown to the enemy, say, making them believe that the army was in the west while in fact it was in the east. "The first battle must be victorious" to boost the morale and bolster the strength of the army, as well as creating a good start for the whole army later on.

Finally, regarding the relations between the core army and the guerrilla units in districts and the militia forces in villages, Hồ Chí Minh clearly defined that the Việt Nam Propaganda and Liberation Army Brigade was the leading army, but all the three forces mentioned above were important in combat. Local armed forces should work closely with the core army and provide necessary additions for the core army. In returns, the core army needed to be responsible for helping the local militia forces to grow in both size and experience.

Hồ Chí Minh's clear and succinct instructions later became the guidelines for Võ Nguyên Giáp throughout his military life. And in the history of the Vietnamese People's Army, be it during wartime or peacetime, the existence, maturity, and invincibility of the whole army were all grounded on these fundamental principles and instructions by Hồ Chí Minh.

One urgent issue at the moment was to hold an official ceremony to mark the foundation of the liberation army and get prepared for the first battle.

As the day neared, Võ Nguyên Giáp received an official directive from Hồ Chí Minh in which he recapitulated, in written from, what he had said several months earlier about the army's name, functions, roles, tasks, organizational principles, and relation with the local militia forces, as well as the forms and principles of its operation. At the end of the directive, Hồ Chí Minh wrote:

> The Việt Nam Propaganda and Liberation Army Brigade is an eldest brother, and hopefully it will have more siblings. Although it is now small in size, its future is bright . . . . It is the starting point of the Liberation Army and can march the length of Việt Nam, from north to south.

The foundation ceremony was solemnly organized on the afternoon of December 22, 1944, in a forest situated between the two cantons named after two Vietnamese heroes, Trần Hưng Đạo and Hoàng Hoa Thám. In attendance were representatives of Cao-Bắc-Lạng Interprovincial Party Committee and ethnic minorities living in Cao Bằng and Bắc Cạn. In a speech delivered at the ceremony, Võ Nguyên Giáp stated the major tasks and motto of the Brigade and highlighted the revolutionary nature of the liberation army soldier. Before the ceremony ended, the 34 soldiers stood solemnly under the flag, reciting in one voice the Brigade's "Ten Pledges of Honor" composed by Võ Nguyên Giáp. These pledges were the quintessence of the soldiers' revolutionary qualities and served as guiding stars for everything they did in their later tasks, be it in learning or in combat.

When he recalled this historic moment 20 years later, Võ Nguyên Giáp wrote, "In my mind at that time were images of the glorious future of the revolutionary army and what I wanted to do was to materialize those images so that they would not only a product of imagination..."

Giáp paid special attention to the choice of target for attack and method of combat in the first battle, bearing in mind Hồ Chí Minh's requirement of "putting the army into action after one month." The overall principle was to choose as the target of attack any enemy military post which was well-known to the local people, whose support was crucial for a guaranteed victory in the first battle. All the plans were brought into thorough discussion, such as whether to choose a target near or far away from the villages and whether to use ambush or direct attack. Finally, Võ Nguyên Giáp and the other commanders of the Brigade concurred that the two posts of Phai Khắt and Nà Ngần in Nguyên Bình District, Cao Bằng Province, would be singled out as the first two targets for attack. And the method of combat was "surprise attack."[1] The combat plan and other logistics for combat were revised carefully for the last time before the army was deployed.

The two battles of Phai Khắt and Nà Ngần, which took place on December 25–26, 1944—the first victories of the revolutionary army of Việt Nam under the command of Võ Nguyên Giáp, were described in great detail in various historical research projects and war memoirs. What is worthy of further scholarly examination was how Hồ Chí

---

1. "Surprise attack" relies on the surprise element for success and victory.

Minh's military philosophy influenced Giáp's military style and helped him scored the first two victories. This is important if we are to explain why such a fledgling army founded only several days earlier could emerge as a victor in its very first battles.

First of all, it is obvious that Võ Nguyên Giáp held in specially high regards the leadership role of the Party, in this case the Party cell. Although there was a big gap in the military awareness and knowledge of the Party members, Võ Nguyên Giáp still decided to bring the commanding of the battle to open discussion so that everyone could raise their own voice. Everyone agreed that the target chosen should be commensurate with their capability, one that would guarantee a military victory and would not cause any political losses or subject the grassroots bases to any repressive and retaliative actions from the French. Next, on the afternoon of December 25, before the whole Brigade marched back to Phai Khắt, the cadres and Party members went to meet the soldiers personally, gave them meticulous advice, and encouraged them to try their best to fulfil the given task in their very first real battle.

Hồ Chí Minh reminded the Brigade, on repeated occasions, to rely on the local people and tactfully combine the core army with local militia forces. In the two battles of Phai Khắt and Nà Ngần, that advice was well heeded. The local people, guerrilla units, and self-defense units really became a vital factor for the victory, especially in the battle of Phai Khắt. The cadres at the base and the local villagers (notably the family of Mr. Nông Văn Lạc) provided the Brigade with detailed and reliable information about the conditions of the enemy in the post. They tried every way to find enough partisan outfits for the Brigade's men to put on and disguise themselves as enemy soldiers to infiltrate the post. They also made sure that there were sufficient foods and supplies for the army from its foundation day to its first battle, which ended in victory, while guaranteeing that its operation was kept a top secret. They knew how to make up stories to respond to the enemy's interrogation when they brought their army back to the village following the loss of their post, thereby keeping a secret of the whereabouts of the Brigade. The local armed forces not only joined the core army in direct combat against the enemy but also showed the army the directions and camouflaged their steps and traces when they marched through the village. They also successfully overpowered the lackeys of the enemy in the locality before and after the battle.[1] The above-mentioned activities, albeit small and initial, were early signs of what later became known as the "people's war."

Only with two first battles, Giáp demonstrated successfully in practice Hồ Chí Minh's instructions on the military art, as evidenced above all by his strategy to proactively search and kill the enemy, irrespective of whether the enemy post was located within a place with strong grassroots political bases like Phai Khắt or in a remote, separate, and inaccessible area like Nà Ngần. The fledgling army confronted the enemy for the first time when the enemy was largely in a dominating

---

1. In an article published in the *Tạp chí Lịch sử quân sự* (literally: Military History Journal) in December 1984, General Hoàng Văn Thái revealed that in the battle of Phai Khắt, some of the Việt Minh cadres in Tam Kim Commune, aided by the local guerrilla soldiers, worked to block information sources, stayed on watch in the outer circle, and guarded and blocked all the routes around the area where the Liberation Army was stationed before departure. The total number of people who participated in the battle amounted to 50.

Chapter One: THE PATH TO A MILITARY CAREER

position, but Giáp managed to promote the spiritual strength of an army which otherwise was inferior to the enemy in terms of equipment to gain victory. That was the art of choosing a suitable target for attack to guarantee victory based on careful analysis of the balance of power between the two sides; the art of choosing the propitious time for an attack when the enemy was taken by the biggest surprise (5 pm in the Phai Khắt battle when the enemy was having dinner and their guns were resting on racks or 7 am in the Nà Ngần battle when the enemy had hardly got out of bed) and conducive for an immediate withdraw of the army after the surprise attack; the art of building on the creativity and the cleverness of the army to take full advantage of the surprise element. It was also the flexibility, resoluteness, and responsiveness with which the army fought and which resulted in their taking control of the battle, capture of the enemy as soldiers, and confiscation of weaponry. Guided by the principle of "using the enemy's own weapons to attack them and equipping themselves with the weapons taken on the spot," the army set out from the very beginning the goal of collecting war booties to improve their own sources of equipment. While the booties collected after the Phai Khắt battle were only enough to arm half of the platoon, the weapons confiscated after the Nà Ngần battle were so remarkable that the army was able to develop itself into a company prior to the Đồng Mu battle. It was obvious that with the first two battles, the Brigade successfully established for itself, and for the whole army later on, a tradition of gaining victory right from the beginning and growing stronger after each battle. Another secret was the Brigade's sensible combination of fighting militarily with the enemy and encouraging the local people spiritually. On the one hand, the enemy was killed and their weapons were confiscated; on the other hand, the Brigade's reputation was boosted and had far-reaching political influence over a spacious region.

When the Opportunity Came

After the two battles of Phai Khắt and Nà Ngần, the Việt Nam Propaganda and Liberation Army Brigade developed into a company while the armed forces in the districts, motivated by the victory, also grew in size. At the beginning of March 1945, Phạm Văn Đồng and Vũ Anh came to see Võ Nguyên Giáp and the Brigade. They passed the news that the Japanese fascists in Indochina had staged a coup d'état to overthrow the French colonial government and emphasized that there were initial opportunities to implement the policy of "widening the pond for the fish to swim freely"[1] advocated by the Việt Minh Headquarters. From this moment onward, the Brigade's activities took a completely new turning point, operating overtly in a new political environment. At that time, on the whole Indochina Peninsula, most of the French troops were either captured or killed by the Japanese. The remainder were busy fleeing across the border. While the French colonial regime had been ousted, a new pro-Japan government had not taken shape. The Vietnamese puppet authorities from provincial to grassroots levels became extremely puzzled because they had lost their backing. The time was propitious for the mass organizations in the Việt

---

1. Meaning that popular political bases were to be quickly expanded to create favorable conditions for the development and operation of the armed forces, making preparations and practicing part-by-part uprising in the localities and getting ready to seize the opportunity to stage a general uprising nationwide. The time between March and August 1945 was referred to by the mainstream publications as the "pre-uprising period."

Minh Front to call upon the populace to rise and stage a localized guerrilla war to seize power in each locality.

From this moment onward, the mass political movements, backed by the on-the-spot armed forces, rose to overthrow the lackey government to seize power in villages, communes, and districts, first in the mountainous areas.

While Hoàng Sâm, Quang Trung, Hoàng Văn Thái, Lê Thiết Hùng, and Lê Quảng Ba made their ways in different directions to instruct the localities on how to organize an uprising, Võ Nguyên Giáp and the core army marched straight forward to Chợ Rã and Chợ Chu to overthrow the local colonial authorities. In April 1945, Giáp went to Hiệp Hòa District, Bắc Giang Province, to attend the North Việt Nam Military Meeting, convened by Secretary General Trường Chinh. At the meeting, it was decided that opportunities should be created and seized to switch from part-by-part uprising to a national general uprising. It was also on this occasion that Trường Chinh condoled Giáp on his wife's arrest in 1941, adding that she died in the Hỏa Lò (French: *Maison Centrale*) Prison, Hà Nội, in the middle of February 1944, upholding her revolutionary dignity. To Trường Chinh's amazement, Giáp had never heard of the news before and it hit him like a thunderbolt; he was overcome with grief.

As the situation was changing rapidly, Giáp had to repress the grief of his bereavement to continue his work.

When the military meeting concluded, Võ Nguyên Giáp returned immediately to Chợ Chu to prepare for the amalgamation of the armed forces, slated for May 15, 1945, in Định Biên Thượng in Chợ Chu Town, Thái Nguyên Province. Thirteen companies, including the Việt Nam Propaganda and

Liberation Army Brigade units and the National Salvation forces under the command of Chu Văn Tấn, were merged together to become one unique core force called "Việt Nam Liberation Army" under the leadership of the Northern Command, which consisted of Võ Nguyên Giáp, Trần Đăng Ninh, and Chu Văn Tấn. At local level, however, the armed forces were unanimously referred to as "Liberation Army." So, after only half a year, the small army Giáp was tasked with had become a major force, the leading bird of the nationwide armed forces, as Hồ Chí Minh anticipated in a directive he had issued at the end of the previous year.

That night Giáp could hardly sleep. He lay in bed meditating about the heavy duty of the Việt Nam Liberation Army as the core force of the whole nation in the upcoming general uprising. Early next morning, he received an urgent letter from the Interprovincial Party Committee saying that Hồ Chí Minh had begun to travel to the lowland. Predicting that by then Hồ Chí Minh would have passed Chợ Đồn, Võ Nguyên Giáp quickly hit the road, heading in the direction of Bản Coóc (or Thành Cóc) to meet him.

On May 17, when he reached Nà Kiến in Nghĩa Tá Commune, he saw Hồ Chí Minh with an envoy of more than 20 people, including some foreigners, with a cumbersome communication machine carried on horseback. It was the first time he met his old teacher and comrade since Giáp took charge of the army eight months ealier. Hồ Chí Minh seemed emaciated and tired after ten days on a long journey, but his bright eyes were brimming with joy. After listening to Giáp report on the overall situations, and especially on the outcome of the Military Meeting in Hiệp Hòa, Hồ Chí Minh instructed everyone to immediately choose a locality which had strong grassroots bases and was convenient in terms of travelling to serve as the main headquarters of the movement.

From Nghĩa Tá, Giáp returned to Kim Quan Thượng to discuss with Song Hào and the leadership of Nguyễn Huệ Zone.[1] Everyone concurred to propose to Hồ Chí Minh to choose Tân Trào (i.e. Tân Lập Village, Sơn Dương District, Tuyên Quang Province), a vast forest area situated between the provinces of Tuyên Quang and Thái Nguyên, far from the main road. After accompanying Song Hào, Tạ Xuân Thu, and Lê Trung Đình to Tân Trào for news of the latest development and the plan for accommodation and work, Võ Nguyên Giáp returned to Bản Coóc to pick up Hồ Chí Minh. On the afternoon of May 21, having arrived in Tân Trào, Giáp arranged for Hồ Chí Minh and two telegraphists[2] to stay at Mr. Nguyễn Tiến Sự's house and asked Đinh Đại Toàn to take care of their daily needs. Several days later, Hồ Chí Minh and Nguyễn Tiến Sự went into the forest of Nà Lừa, about one kilometer from the village, to find a suitable place to build a shack which was later called "Nà Lừa Shack." At the end of May 1945, Nà Lừa Shack became the General Headquarters of the Supreme Commander of

---

1. According to a directive by the North Việt Nam Regional Party Committee, Nguyễn Huệ Military Zone (commonly known as Zone B) was built on the right bank of the Cầu River, including part of Thái Nguyên and Bắc Cạn and the whole provinces of Tuyên Quang and Hà Giang. Song Hào was Secretary of Nguyễn Huệ Zone Party Committee.
2. They were Frank Tann and Mac Shin, two American Chinese telegraphists who were working for the Office of Strategic Services (OSS)—an American intelligence agency. They accompanied Hồ Chí Minh on his way back to Việt Nam from Huanan to work as liaison officers between the Vietnamese Headquarters and the American Command in China's Kunming. During their stay in Tân Trào, they helped train telegraphists for an intelligence course held on Nà Lừa Hill, near the lodging place of Hồ Chí Minh.

the national army. It was from here that the most important decisions that led to the victory of the General Uprising to seize power nationwide were made. From this moment onward, Nà Lừa Shack and many other geographical names started to go down into the history of the armed uprising and revolutionary war of Việt Nam.

On June 4, Hồ Chí Minh convened the first cadres meeting in Tân Trào. Among the participants were Trường Chinh and Nguyễn Lương Bằng, who came from the lowlands, and Hoàng Quốc Việt, who had returned from Huanan. At the beginning of the meeting, General Secretary Trường Chinh delivered a report on the policies and strategies of the Party Central Committee, including the directive "Franco-Japanese War and Our Actions (dated March 12, 1945), and the overall situations of the revolution across the country. On his part, Võ Nguyên Giáp briefed the audience about the results of the North Vietnam Military Meeting and the specific situations in the two revolutionary bases in Việt Bắc. Hồ Chí Minh showed his approval of the policies practiced by the Party Central Committee, as they were "commensurate with the realities of Việt Nam." He commended the directed dated March 12, 1945, as "propitiously timed" and offered feedback on some issues in the Resolution of the North Việt Nam Military Meeting. He advocated the amalgamation of the two bases in Việt Bắc to become one unique military base to fight against the Japanese. The liberated area at that time was already an enormous region, consisting of many mountainous areas in the provinces of Cao Bằng, Bắc Cạn, Lạng Sơn, Hà Giang, Tuyên Quang, and Thái Nguyên, and several areas in Bắc Giang, Vĩnh Yên, Phú Thọ, and Yên Bái. Therefore, it was necessary to establish a larger revolutionary military base under the name of "Liberated Zone" to call for a nationwide anti-Japanese movement.

To materialize the resolution of the June 4 meeting and the Ten Major Policies of the Việt Minh Front, the Liberated Zone came into being and was quickly developed into a fortified military base in political, military, economic, and cultural terms. Tân Trào became the capital of the Liberated Zone and a connecting point between Hồ Chí Minh and the Party Central Committee in the lowland, the military zones nationwide, and the American mission in Kunming. The Provisional Command Committee of the Liberated Zone, which oversaw military issues, was established with Võ Nguyên Giáp appointed as its head. Giáp's main responsibilities at that time focused on making preparations for the armed forces to stand ready to stage an all-people general uprising when opportunities matured. He instructed the immediate development and realignment of both the core troops and the local militia. He attached special importance to the training of grassroots cadres, the establishment of Party cells, and the elevation of political awareness among the Liberation Army. Under the Resolution of the North Việt Nam Military Meeting, he and Hoàng Văn Thái, alias Khang, were directors of the Anti-Japanese Politico-military School. The first organization was opened in the middle of June 1945 in Khuổi Kịch, about three kilometers from Tân Trào. This was the first institution of the Vietnamese revolutionary army that trained beginning politico-military officers in a fairly systematic manner and provided core support for the activities of the Liberation Army at the peak of the forthcoming General Uprising. Trainees at this school included mainly young cadres selected for training by the localities. Although it was called a politico-military school, training was more political than military. Lectures given by Giáp and other members of the Party Central Committee on the Việt Minh Program, the Ten Major Policies of the Việt Minh Front, preparations for the general popular uprising, the best practices in mass mobilization, the experience from the first battles, and some other issues made up a larger portion of the training time than those on basic combat gestures. Giáp was constantly present at the training sessions, giving students careful instructions on every specific issue.

On July 17, according to an agreed-upon plan between Hồ Chí Minh in Tân Trào and the American Command in Kunming, the OSS Deer Team including some American intelligence officers headed by Major Allison Thomas, parachuted onto Tân Trào to help train the Liberation Army. The same day, Lê Giản detected and reported to Võ Nguyên Giáp that in the first batch of parachuters, apart from Thomas and two other Americans, there was also a French lieutenant by the name of Montfort and two Vietnamese junior lieutenants, who were staffed with the 5th Mission, a French intelligence agency in Huanan. Võ Nguyên Giáp again reported to Hồ Chí Minh and frankly requested Thomas to return these three men to Kunming. In the ensuing days, Giáp worked normally with Thomas to reach an agreement on the locations where the Deer Team could operate, the collection of weapons dropped by the American parachutes,[1]

---

1. The weapons dropped by parachuters to train the Liberation Army were later reused by the Vietnamese-American Company in the Thái Nguyên battle. They included one machine-gun, two 60-mm mortars, eight Brenn light machine-guns, twenty Thompson submachine guns, sixty carbines, eight automatic rifles, and twenty pistols.

Chapter One: THE PATH TO A MILITARY CAREER

and the training plan for the Liberation Army soldiers. On July 21, the Quang Trung Company (known at that time as the Vietnamese-American Company) was formed and made up of 200 Liberation Army soldiers with Đàm Quang Trung as group leader and Thomas as chief-of-staff. Immediately after that, the training commenced and lasted until August 15 with the students using mainly new weapons provided by the American officers.

As Thomas' working team usually travelled to and from the area of Chợ Chu–Sơn Dương, some students at the Anti-Japanese Politico-military School who could speak English were sent to accompany them as interpreters, guards, and liaisons between them and the locals. Giáp was careful and considerate in giving assignments to young cadres who had had no experience working with foreign military officers. He asked them not only to promise secrecy, but also to demonstrate proper manners toward these Western friends, who were fighting the Japanese alongside the Việt Minh. The cadres were asked to bear in mind that they were hosts and these foreigners were guests. Therefore, in daily contact, they should be courteous, but frank.

What concerned Giáp most at that time was Hồ Chí Minh's health, who frequently had high fever and delirium but kept working hard whenever he felt a little better. Giáp later recalled that one night, seeing that Hồ Chí Minh was not feeling well, he decided to remain with him in the shack of Nà Lừa. As soon as Hồ Chí Minh finished a bowl of porridge prepared and taken to him from the village by Ms Minh Châu, Secretary of the Liberated Zone's Office, he asked Giáp to immediately discuss military issues. It was on this occasion that he told Giáp the historic saying: "Propitious time has come. We must at any cost regain independence, whatever the sacrifice. Even if that means we have to set the whole Trường Sơn Range on fire."

Hồ Chí Minh's assertion of the strategic opportunity urged Giáp to quickly commence the second cohort of anti-Japanese politico-military training and make preparations for the armed forces not only in Tân Trào but also in other localities in the entire Liberated Zone. The core army was then organized into the size of a battalion headed by Lâm Cẩm Như (or Lâm Kính) and consisted of several companies headed by Vi Dân, Đàm Quang Trung, and Đàm Quốc Chủng. Particularly, the company under the command of Đàm Quang Trung was stationed in the heart of the Tân Trào base.

From the beginning of August, the overall global situations witnessed rapid changes. The Việt Minh learnt from foreign media sources that the Potsdam Conference between superpowers had concluded on August 2. The outcomes of the conference included, apart from post-war policies toward Germany and Europe, a declaration "demanding the Japanese government to order its armed forces to surrender unconditionally." Then came the news of the United States dropping two atomic bombs onto Hiroshima and Nagasaki and the Soviet Union's declaration of war with Japan. Given those rapid changes, Hồ Chí Minh instructed Võ Nguyên Giáp to write urgent letters urging delegates from all bases to quickly come and participate in the National Party Congress and the National Delegates Meeting. He said, "The meetings should be held soon but briefly. We must not waste even a second or a minute. The overall situations will change very quickly, and we cannot afford to miss this golden opportunity." During the days of August 12 and 13, after learning about

Chapter One: THE PATH TO A MILITARY CAREER

Japan's diplomatic note to the Big Four saying they accepted the Declaration of the Potsdam Conference, Hồ Chí Minh decided, as had been agreed upon with the Standing Commission of the Central Committee of the Communist Party of Việt Nam (or Standing Central Committee for short) earlier, to launch a nationwide general armed uprising to seize power and establish a provisional government.

Initially the National Party Congress was expected to be delayed, as some delegates who were based in remote areas could not make it on time. However, anticipating the imminent surrender of the then Japanese King to the Allied forces, Hồ Chí Minh instructed the Congress to commence immediately on August 13 although there were at that time only about 30 delegates altogether, including cadres from central and local levels, and some who were based overseas but were then present in Tân Trào.[1] As his health conditions had not improved, Hồ Chí Minh was not able to be present at the opening session of the National Party Congress and the meeting went ahead under the chairmanship of General Secretary Trường Chinh. Võ Nguyên Giáp and Phạm Văn Đồng served as members of the secretariat. In his report, Trường Chinh emphasized the urgency of the situation that necessitated prompt actions to call on the whole people to rise

---

1. Participants included Hồ Chí Minh, Trường Chinh, Hoàng Quốc Việt, Nguyễn Lương Bằng, Võ Nguyên Giáp, Phạm Văn Đồng, Trần Huy Liệu, Trần Đăng Ninh, Lê Đức Thọ, Tố Hữu, Chu Văn Tấn, Hoàng Văn Hoan, Nguyễn Văn Trân, Trần Quốc Hoàn, Lê Thanh Nghị, Hà Thị Quế, Vũ Thị Khôi, Nguyễn Chí Thanh, Trần Quý Hai, Lê Hữu Kiều, Ung Văn Khiêm, Hà Huy Giáp, and some delegates who were based abroad. Ms Nguyễn Thị Thập, who was from the South, could only arrive when the Congress had concluded and hence was only able to attend the National Delegates Meeting on August 16, 1945.

and seize power before the Allied forces entered Việt Nam. He said that it was the only possible way for Việt Nam to regain independence. The Congress spent three days listening to reports, holding discussions, ratifying resolutions, and electing four extra members, one of whom was Võ Nguyên Giáp, for the Standing Central Committee. On the morning of August 15, after listening to the Tokyo radio station broadcasting the then Japanese King's "official acceptance of the July 26 Potsdam Declaration," Hồ Chí Minh requested the National Delegates Meeting should finish quickly so that the delegates could return to their respective localities to lead popular uprisings and ensure the seize of power. In the afternoon, when the meeting concluded, Hồ Chí Minh tried to be present and talk to the participants although he was still unwell. He emphasized the important role of enhanced national unity as an unrivalled source of power in regaining independence.

On August 13, under the leadership of Hồ Chí Minh, the National Uprising Committee was founded and approved the "First Military Order" prepared by Trần Huy Liệu. At 11 pm that day, the National Uprising Committee issued the "First Military Order," thereby officially staging a general uprising nationwide.

Two days later, through the radio station of the Deer Team, Hồ Chí Minh on behalf of the National Liberation Committee of the Việt Minh Front requested the American administration to announce to the United Nations that, the Vietnamese people had sided with the United Nations to uphold the solemn principle of respecting every nation's democracy and independence. If the United Nations refused to respect the independence of the whole Indochina

Chapter One: THE PATH TO A MILITARY CAREER

Peninsula, the Vietnamese people would fight to the end until final and entire independence was obtained.

One day after the conclusion of the National Party Congress, the National Delegates Meeting was held in the Communal House of Tân Trào on August 16. Over 60 delegates from the three regions of Việt Nam, representatives of mass organizations, and overseas Vietnamese gathered together in the meeting. In an article titled *"Khu giải phóng"* (literally: "The Liberated Zone") published in the *Cứu quốc* (literally: National Salvation) newspaper in 1946, Giáp remarked that, "Never has there been such a solemn meeting in the revolutionary history of Việt Nam." Among the 60 delegates attending the meeting, many scholars and friends were glad to see Giáp "after 'vanishing' from Hà Nội for five years."

After indicating their consent and approval of the Việt Minh Front's policies,[1] the meeting elected the Vietnamese National Liberation Committee, known as the Provisional Government, with Hồ Chí Minh as its President.[2] The official choice of the national flag and national anthem was also made.

On the afternoon of the same day, before the meeting came to an end, the delegates gathered under the Tân Trào banyan tree to see off the soldiers. At exactly 14:30 pm, under a large-sized red flag with a yellow star, a company of Liberation Army troops stood solemnly under the supervision of Đàm Quang

---

1. The Việt Minh Front's policies included calling upon the whole nation to launch an uprising to seize power, carrying out the Ten Major Policies of the Việt Minh Front, and, as the owners of the country, welcoming the Allied forces into the country to disarm the Japanese troops.
2. The standing members of the National Liberation Committee were Hồ Chí Minh, Trần Huy Liệu, Phạm Văn Đồng, Nguyễn Lương Bằng, and Dương Đức Hiền.

Trung, listening to Võ Nguyên Giáp reading the 1st Combat Order on behalf of the National Uprising Committee. After that, he tasked the soldiers with the liberation of Thái Nguyên Province, which was an important position to southern Việt Bắc Interzone. He also informed the soldiers that during the last few days, the people in many localities nationwide had succeeded in seizing power in their respective areas. In the mountainous area of Việt Bắc alone, the Liberation Army managed to destroy the remaining Japanese military posts in Cao Bằng, Bắc Cạn, Tuyên Quang, and Yên Bái. In the solemn atmosphere of the deployment ceremony, Đàm Quang Trung, on behalf of the army, promised the delegates that with the support of the whole people, the army would fight with the greatest enthusiasm and courage to regain independence for the motherland. They departed shortly after that. All the delegates stood waving goodbye and remained there until the last soldier was out of sight.

On the morning of August 17, the National Liberation Committee was introduced to the whole nation and organized an oath-taking ceremony in front of the Tân Trào Communal House. On behalf of the Committee, Hồ Chí Minh saluted the national flag flying on top of the communal house and read the pledge. In Nguyễn Lương Bằng's recollection, the pledge was more or less as follows:

> We, members of the National Liberation Committee, elected by the national delegates to lead the revolution of our people, pledge, in front of the sacred flag of our nation, to lead the whole nation forward, fight the enemy with all our hearts and minds, and restore the independence for our nation until our final drop of blood!

All the delegates swore in unison while one of the armed units fired a salute to the National Liberation Committee.

On the August 18, via the American radio station in Tân Trào and the American mission in Kunming, Hồ Chí Minh sent a message to the French government. On behalf of the National Liberation Committee of Việt Nam, he made a five-point proposal regarding the Franco-Vietnamese relations in the new situation.[1] According to Robert Shaplen, author of *The Enigma of Ho Chi Minh*, the message did reach the hand of the French representatives Léon Pignon and Jean Sainteny, who were then in Kunming, but it went unheeded and was never replied.

The meeting concluded at the peak of the General Uprising and victories were reported from all over the country. From Tân Trào, Võ Nguyên Giáp and his entourage hit the road quickly to catch up with the soldiers marching forward to liberate Thái Nguyên.

From Tân Trào to Hà Nội

Võ Nguyên Giáp did not know that as the General Uprising in Việt Nam was reaching its peak, President of the French Provisional Government Charles de Gaulle had appointed Admiral Georges Thierry d'Argenlieu as high commissioner and the four-star general Philippe Leclerc as commander-in-chief, and ordered them to bring the French

---

1. According to King C. Chen in *Vietnam and China 1938–1945* (Princeton University Press, Princeton, New York, 1969, p. 107), the five points were: 1- The French government recognized the Việt Minh government; 2- The Việt Minh government acknowledged the French rights in Việt Nam within from five to ten years, after which France would return independence to Việt Nam; 3- Within those five or ten years, Việt Nam was to enjoy autonomy in terms of internal affairs; 4- The French government was given preferential treatment in trade and commerce in Việt Nam; 5- The French could serve as advisors in foreign affairs.

Expeditionary Army "back to Indochina." This appeared to be a striking coincidence as on the same day, two contending armies were dispatched. One fought for the just cause of national liberation while the other aimed to invade another country out of no justifiable reason. Võ Nguyên Giáp's 25 years of military life started on that unforgettable day of August 16, as he was ten days shy of his 34th birthday.

On the afternoon of August 19, when the company commanded by Đàm Quang Trung arrived in Thịnh Đán, adjacent to Thái Nguyên Town, Vi Dân's company from Đại Từ and Đàm Quốc Trung's company from Chợ Chu also arrived in the same place. The three companies merged under the command of Lâm Kính. One of the Liberation Army unit in Bắc Giang also regrouped in Gia Sàng, taking responsibility for blocking the reinforcements of the enemy from Hà Nội. Võ Nguyên Giáp commanded the army in the battle liberating Thái Nguyên. The Provisional Provincial Party Committee of Thái Nguyên were also present at the headquarters of the Liberation Army, which was situated at the post office of Thái Nguyên Town.

The Japanese army and its peace-keeping troops[1] in Thái Nguyên Town were garrisoned in two clusters. The first cluster was made up of about 120 soldiers concentrating in the former camp of local guardsmen and in the Resident Palace high on the hill. There were also scattered groups of Japanese soldiers stationed in some key traffic posts in the town. The second cluster had about 400 peace-keeping soldiers concentrating in French former military camps.

---

1. Peace-keeping troops in this case refer to the Vietnamese who were used and organized by the Japanese and served as a tool to crack down on the revolution.

Chapter One: THE PATH TO A MILITARY CAREER

During the process of making preparations for the battle, the Liberation Army was provided with fairly detailed administrative maps of the town by the officials of the Thái Nguyên Department of Civil Engineering. The young locals, in the meantime, volunteered to serve as pathfinders for the Liberation Army. At 4 am on the morning of August 20, 1945, all the Liberation Army soldiers had been deployed in their positions. One hour and a half later, the Command of the General Uprising sent an ultimatum to the provincial chief Bùi Huy Lượng, who quickly transferred the government to the National Uprising Committee. At the same time, supervisor Khiêm, who was also head of the peace-keeping troops of the town, also handed the post and all the weapons to the revolutionary forces. Phan Mỹ, special envoy of the Command of the Liberation Army, instructed the young men to put together the 600 booty guns to be carried south of the town. With the confiscated weapons, Võ Nguyên Giáp permitted the formation of another unit, called the "Fourth Unit," which consisted of five major forces: the company of Đàm Quang Trung, the Bắc Giang soldiers who had just arrived, the self-defense units of Thái Nguyên, the new young recruits, and even some of the peace-keeping soldiers who had joined the revolution. Đàm Quang Trung was nominated as head of the 4th Unit. As the local provisional authorities had then been established and begun to operate, the law and order in the town was guaranteed, and the people's life remained stable.

At 8 am on August 20, when all the Japanese positions had been besieged, the Liberation Army Command sent the provincial chief Bùi Huy Lượng and several cadres to carry an ultimatum to meet the Japanese lieutenant in his camp. The

113

ultimatum, undersigned by Võ Nguyên Giáp on behalf of the National Uprising Committee and Việt Nam Liberation Army, stated clearly that the then Japanese King had surrendered to the Allies, and that the Vietnamese revolutionaries had no grudge against the Japanese people, thus calling upon the Japanese troops not to force the Vietnamese side to cause any bloodshed. The Liberation Army requested that the Japanese troops in Thái Nguyên to hand in their weapons. The former also undertook to treat the latter well and arrange for them to go home if the request was met. If not, the former would have no choice but to open fire, as they did not wish to see the latter's weapons fall into the hands of another force or another country's army. The first negotiation ended without success, so the Liberation Army decided to send a second ultimatum, this time in English, prepared by Thomas on behalf of both the Liberation Army and the Vietnamese-American soldiers, demanding that the Japanese submit their weapons. The Japanese side, on the excuse that weapons had to be handed in to the Allies, only accepted to take no further action and maintain the status quo. The Liberation Army therefore had to issue a final warning: if the weapons were not handed in by 2 pm, they would attack. During this time, the units were given orders to open fire on the Japanese soldiers in scattered locations in the town. As for the main target, there was no reply from the Japanese Command even when the deadline had been extended another hour (3 pm), so the forces began to attack. Being placed under close siege and having reinforcements severed, the Japanese lieutenant appealed for a resumption of negotiation, but only agreed to hand in weapons in some suburban locations of Thái Nguyên, such as Đại Từ, Phấn Mễ, Giang Tiên, and Đá Gân.

As the Liberation Army troops were attacking the Japanese camp, General Secretary Trường Chinh dropped by Thái Nguyên on his way to the lowland from Tân Trào. He entered the post office, which housed the Liberation Army Command to see Võ Nguyên Giáp. Shortly after that, three cadres sent by Nguyễn Khang from Hà Nội came to report to the General Secretary that the people of Hà Nội had successfully seized power and many urgent matters had arisen, so the top leaders were required to return to Hà Nội immediately.

Trường Chinh asked Giáp to send someone to Tân Trào to report the situations to Hồ Chí Minh and accompany him to Hà Nội. As for the battle in Thái Nguyên, it was only necessary to leave one part of the Liberation Army to continue the siege; Giáp and the core forces were required to quickly return to Hà Nội to welcome the Provisional Government, leaving the provincial authorities to deal with the remaining issues. Right on the afternoon of August 20, after bidding farewell to Trường Chinh, Võ Nguyên Giáp went to the municipal stadium. Addressing the huge audience attending the rally organized by the Việt Minh at the stadium, Giáp declared on behalf of the National Uprising Committee the removal of the Japanese authorities and their lackeys and the establishment of the new provisional revolutionary government in Thái Nguyên Province. The following day, after dispatching a unit to Tân Trào to escort Hồ Chí Minh to the lowland, Giáp instructed Quang Trung and Lâm Kính to send the majority of the 3rd and 4th Units marching down to Hà Nội. On August 21, he and his entourage also travelled to Hà Nội along the 3rd Route. Due to a dam disruption and the consequent inundation, they had to switch to using boats when they reached Thị Cầu. On August 22, as they passed Gia Lâm and witnessed the rising alluvial water of the Red River, Giáp stood silently on the bridge looking toward the city center, where waves of red flags were flying, feeling extremely moved. Five years had swiftly gone by since the day he and Phạm Văn Đồng left this beloved land. As he recalled the memorable moment of setting foot on the land of Hà Nội again, Giáp later wrote:

> Looking at the changes taking place in the motherland and witnessing the countrymen, who had been emancipated from a hundred years of colonial domination, eagerly waiting for the independence day of the nation, all of us were so happy that we were near tears.

On the afternoon of August 24, Giáp felt really relieved knowing that Hồ Chí Minh had finally arrived safe and sound at Gạ Village (present-day Phú Gia Village, Phú Thượng Commune, Từ Liêm District, Hà Nội). Shortly after that, Trần Đăng Ninh and Võ Nguyên Giáp came to see Hồ Chí Minh and report to him on the successful seizure of power in different localities. Hồ Chí Minh listened attentively to the situations in Hà Nội. He was happy to know that the leaders of the General Uprising had flexibly and creatively translated the Party's policies into the real situations in the city, grabbed the opportunities, carefully analysed the balance of power, and built on the overwhelming political strength of the people to force the Japanese to meet their requirements. The General Uprising ended quickly with no bloodshed. After its successful seizure of power, Hà Nội established the Provisional Revolutionary People's Committee. An important piece of news was that on August 22, three days after the people of Hà Nội seized power, an American aircraft landed in Gia Lâm. It was noteworthy that apart from a group of American officers headed by Lieutenant Colonel Archimedes Patti, there was also a group of French officers headed by Lieutenant Colonel Jean Sainteny. These men were no strangers to Hồ Chí Minh, who told Võ Nguyên Giáp and Trần Đăng Ninh that he met them in Kunming. Hồ Chí Minh then asked Giáp and Ninh to remind the Hà Nội authorities to be cautious and to start talking as soon as possible with the group of American officers to sound out the attitude of the Allies toward the French impending "return" to Indochina.

The following afternoon, General Secretary Trường Chinh went to Gạ Village to accompany Hồ Chí Minh to the city center. The latter was glad to see the former and listen to further reports on the current situations. The car took Hồ Chí Minh past the streets of Nhật Tân, Yên Phụ, Hàng Đậu, Hàng Giấy, and Hàng Đường, and finally stopped at number 48 Hàng Ngang Street, which housed the family of Trịnh Văn Bô, a national bourgeois who traded in silk. This house was also one of the long-established revolutionary bases in the city center. Seeing the cityscape of Hà Nội overshadowed by a sea of red flags, Hồ Chí Minh was extremely moved. It was the first time he set foot in Hà Nội—the land of thousand-year-old traditions which only a few days later would become the capital city of the independent Việt Nam.

On the morning of August 26, Võ Nguyên Giáp and some other members of the Party Central Committee and the Việt Minh General Command attended a meeting of the Standing Central Committee chaired by Hồ Chí Minh. The agenda of the meeting had been drafted earlier by the General Secretary and his colleagues in the Standing Central Committee. Hồ Chí Minh approved the policies raised by the

Standing Central Committee regarding internal and external affairs in the new context and underlined the importance of upholding widened national solidarity. The expansion of the Provisional Government was a necessary condition, but for it to be sufficient, further expansion was needed to incorporate representatives from other patriotic parties, and members of the intellectual circle who were not affiliated with any political associations and who were not driven by fame or benefit. Hồ Chí Minh made a proposal, which was consented by the whole meeting, that a mass rally be held in Hà Nội so that the Provisional Government could present itself to the general public across the country. It was also on that day that Việt Nam would officially declare its independence and start building a republic democratic regime. When it came to appointing positions in the new government, everyone voted unanimously for Hồ Chí Minh to become President. Nguyễn Lương Bằng and several other members of the National Liberation Committee voluntarily withdrew to leave room for other patriotic intellects who had not participated in the Việt Minh Front. Their self-denying gesture was welcomed and appreciated by Hồ Chí Minh and every other participant at the meeting.

After Hồ Chí Minh had spoken with some of the intellects who were invited into the Provisional Government, including even the doctor who had been invited to the position of the Chairman of the People's Committee of Hà Nội,[1] the list of Provisional Government members was announced publicly

---

1. After the General Uprising, Trần Quang Huy was assigned with the governance of Hà Nội. Then the Standing Central Committee and Hồ Chí Minh himself felt it necessary to invite some member of the intellectual circle to the position, and they finally sought the assistance of doctor Trần Duy Hưng.

Chapter One: THE PATH TO A MILITARY CAREER

on mass media on August 28. Võ Nguyên Giáp was put in charge of the Ministry of Interior Affairs. From then onward, for the next 16 months of sojourn in the capital city, he assumed dual responsibilities for national defense and public security to protect Việt Nam against the plots and schemes of anti-revolutionary forces inside and outside the country, a position the Standing Central Committee and Hồ Chí Minh entrusted him with.[1]

On the afternoon of September 2, 1945, in a big rally at Ba Đình Square in Hà Nội, Hồ Chí Minh read the Declaration of Independence before Minister of Interior Affairs Võ Nguyên Giáp briefed the whole nation about the current situations and the Provisional Government's policies. Then, on behalf of the Provisional Government, he appealed to the whole people to stay alert to the impending enemy's threat of overthrowing the fledgling government.[2] He said, "The French will never

---

1. Regarding Party issues, in January 1946, the Central Military Commission was officially founded to help the Party Central Committee develop the armed forces and other military-related issues. Võ Nguyên Giáp was appointed Secretary of the Central Military Commission. In terms of governance, early in March 1946, the National Assembly decided to establish the National Resistance Committee, and Giáp was elected Deputy Chairman of the Committee. In May 1946, when the National Resistance Committee was renamed "Military Association," Giáp became the Chairman of the Association, which existed in parallel with the Ministry of National Defense, then headed by a member of the intelligentsia. The Association operated under the tutelage and aegis of the Ministry of National Defense. In the wake of the National Military Conference in October 1946, the Ministry of National Defense was amalgamated with the Military Association to become the Ministry of National Defense–General Command, with Giáp as Minister of National Defense cum Commander-in-Chief.

2. At that time, Võ Nguyên Giáp had a chance to meet with both Archimedes Patti and Jean Sainteny. By the way the French lieutenant spoke, he saw through the dark scheme of the then French President Charles de Gaulle and his administration of restoring colonial regime in the Indochina Peninsula.

119

abandon their wicked ambition of invading our country, but with the solidarity and sacrifice of our whole people, we will eventually win. We will never let them yoke us like cattle again . . ." He warned Paris to "be wise and acknowledge the total independence of Việt Nam. Should they resort to violence to invade our country again, we will fight to the last breath in self-defense. And they will be bitterly annihilated . . ." At the end of the speech, he said, "Following the bright examples our predecessors, we will fight a final victory to guarantee that our children and grandchildren can have an independent, free, and happy life."

Chapter Two

SIXTEEN MONTHS IN THE CAPITAL CITY

Meeting Uninvited Guests

On August 22, 1945, the day when Võ Nguyên Giáp returned to Hà Nội from Thái Nguyên coincided with the day when the negotiation between American President Harry Truman and his French counterpart Charles de Gaulle came to an end. The American side agreed to let Paris bring their expeditionary army "back to" Indochina. On the same day, a C47 aircraft carrying the American mission headed by Archimedes Patti landed on Gia Lâm Airport, where they met a group of French military officers headed by Jean Sainteny. Both groups were authorized by the Japanese to enter the city, staying at the Metropole Hotel. At the sight of the Western soldiers, the people of Hà Nội, without prior arrangement, assembled in growing number to voice their protest. The Japanese troops, even with bayonets on their rifles, had a really hard time preventing the crowd from storming into the hotel.

About an hour later, Lê Trọng Nghĩa, who represented the Provisional Government of Hà Nội, came to see Patti to sound out the attitude of the Allies and the overall global situation. In response to his American interlocutor's question about the crowd in front of the hotel, Lê Trọng Nghĩa explained that the people of Hà Nội were protesting against the presence of the French military officers who accompanied the American mission to the city, and not against the presence of the representative Allies. He added that if the French did not use force to intervene with the affairs of the Provisional Government, their safety would be warranted. Patti told Nghĩa that the American mission came to Hà Nội with two tasks: 1- Looking after the Allied soldiers who were captured and imprisoned by the Japanese and repatriating them; 2- Preparing the dossiers for the reception of Japanese army's surrender to the Allies in the North of Indochina.

He gladly informed Nghĩa that he had just met Hồ Chí Minh in Kunming at the end of April when the latter was there to meet General Claire Lee Chennault, Commander of the 14th American Air Force in China. Patti reassured that the Americans did not pave the way for the French arrival, and that there was no question of the United States supporting colonialism. According to him, the French who accompanied him merely came on the "humanitarian purposes" of looking after the French prisoners in the Citadel of Hà Nội.

After listening to Lê Trọng Nghĩa reporting on the first contact between him and the American team, Võ Nguyên Giáp instructed the municipal authorities to organize an official meeting with Patti's mission to sound out the attitudes of the Americans, the French, and Chiang Kai-shek's Kuomintang. Khuất Duy Tiến was entrusted by the Provisional Committee of Hà Nội City with the task of "initiating a close relationship with the Allies." Patti spent a lot of time trying to sound Tiến

Chapter Two: SIXTEEN MONTHS IN THE CAPITAL CITY

out about the "bloodshed-free power-seizing uprising" staged by the people of Hà Nội. Later in his book *Why Vietnam?*,[1] the American officer commented that with only one blow and no gunfire, the whole colonialist regime became disintegrated and the puppet government of Bảo Đại overthrown. Hà Nội, France's central seat of power in Indochina Peninsula, was able to liberate itself and set a precedent and a model for the remaining parts of the country.

As he was having an audience with representatives of the municipal authorities of Hà Nội, Patti was informed by Lieutenant Colonel Yuitsu Tsuchihashi[2] that three armies of the People's Republic of China had crossed the border in Lào Cai, Hà Giang, and Cao Bằng, and were marching southward. The Japanese general also briefed Patti on what the French team had been up to in the Governor-General's Palace. They demanded the release of the French prisoners in the Citadel of Hà Nội and a French rally to welcome the French who had accompanied the American mission to Hà Nội from Kunming.

The first news of the foreigners who had been arriving in Hà Nội drew special attention from President Hồ Chí Minh and the Standing Central Committee. According to Hồ Chí Minh's directive, Võ Nguyên Giáp, as Minister of Interior Affairs of the Provisional Government, headed a delegation to pay "a visit" and sound out their intention, especially that of Major Sainteny, member of the French intelligence agency

---

1. Archimedes L. A. Patti: *Tại sao Việt Nam?* (Lê Trọng Nghĩa, Trans.), Đà Nẵng Publishing House, Đà Nẵng, 1995.
2. Yuitsu Tsuchihashi was Commander of the 38th Japanese Imperial Army, which was then headquartered in the Louis Finot Museum (present-day Museum of Vietnamese History) in Hà Nội.

General Directorate for Studies and Research (French: *Direction Générale des Études et Recherces*), head of the Fifth Mission, and Charles de Gaulle's loyal disciple, who played a key role in an anti-Vietnamese campaign in Huanan in the dying years of the Second World War.

Võ Nguyên Giáp, together with Minister of Youth Dương Đức Hiền and Khuất Duy Tiến, representative of the local authorities of Hà Nội, came to see Patti on the morning of August 26. After delivering some welcoming words and pleasantries, Giáp frankly questioned Patti on the presence of the French military officers who accompanied the American mission. Why did the Americans bring this French team to Hà Nội at such an early stage? Was it because there were changes in the plan of the Allies? What did the French come here for? Was it because the Allies gave them carte blanche in making preparations for a comeback to Indochina? According to initial report sent to the Provisional Government, these French officers harboured overtly aggressive attitudes toward Việt Nam.

The American interlocutor reluctantly explained that the Americans certainly had no intention of backing up a French return. He added that while they were not supportive of the French colonialist policies, they could not bring themselves to decline their ally's request to accompany them to Việt Nam, on condition that the latter would only be limited to humanitarian work in service of the French military prisoners and nationals, which they were not even allowed to do for the time being. At the Potsdam Conference, it was agreed that the Chinese were to enter Indochina from the 16th parallel northward to accept the surrender of the Japanese and repatriate the defeated Japanese troops. The French army in

Huanan[1] were permitted to move part by part to the South of Việt Nam only when Japanese surrender had been accepted by the Allies. Patti reasserted that in his understanding, neither the Chinese nor the Americans harboured any intention of helping the French to return to Indochina by force.

Giáp made it clear to Patti that the Vietnamese government knew exactly who Sainteny was and what role he played in the anti-Vietnamese campaign in China during the last few years. The French came back to Việt Nam definitely not for "humanitarian work in service of the prisoners." Finally, Giáp reasserted that the French should not harbour any illusion that they could halt the historic advancement of the Vietnamese people.

The exchanges took place in an open yet friendly manner, and ended with a salutation in front of the hotel. A Liberation Army unit, a military music band, and scores of Hanoians gathered under the flagpoles flying the national colours of the five countries namely the United States of America, Britain, the Soviet Union, the People's Republic of China, and the Democratic Republic of Việt Nam. As the flag salutation ceremony commenced, the military music band played each country's national anthem when the corresponding flag was hoisted. This was followed by a public parade, with the military music band at the front. The parade brought along the national flags of the five countries and banners welcoming the Allies mission. Patti had a chance to meet Hồ Chí Minh again. Also in attendance at the luncheon that day were Trường Chinh, Võ Nguyên Giáp, Nguyên Khang, and

---

1. Referring to the several thousand French troops under the command of Marcel Alessandri who fled to China in the wake of the Japanese coup d'état on March 9, 1945.

so on. After the meal, Hồ Chí Minh insisted on Patti staying behind for a face-to-face discussion of the current affairs. He reminded the latter of what had happened since their first meeting in Kunming about four or five months earlier. He also missed no chance to alert Patti to all the complications that were likely to befall Việt Nam due to the schemes harboured by the French team who had just arrived in Hà Nội and the fact that the operations of Britain, France, and Chinese Chiang Kai-shek would cause a lot of difficulties to the national liberation of Việt Nam.

At the end of the talk, Patti said he hoped that the United States would reconsider the situations in Indochina in light of the new developments. As he left afterward, Patti could feel Hồ Chí Minh's strong determination and optimistic attitude "to free his country from foreign domination."

That evening, Sainteny expressed his interest in seeing Hồ, Chí Minh, with Patti as an intermediary. Hồ Chí Minh said he would send Võ Nguyên Giáp to meet Sainteny if Patti was also present. The meeting took place at 10 am the following day, August 27, between Võ Nguyên Giáp and Dương Đức Hiền on the Vietnamese side and Sainteny, accompanied by Patti, on the other side. This meeting was later recounted in greater detail by Patti in his book.

Right from the beginning of the talk, Patti immediately realized that the French diplomatic tradition was surely on a mediocre decline. Although he pretended to be courteous, Sainteny could not help making a pre-emptive move with a "condescending speech" criticizing the behaviour of the Annamese which, according to him, led the world to believe that the French presence in Indochina was no longer welcomed. Sainteny also warned the Vietnamese side that he would keep a vigilant eye on the activities of the so-called Provisional Government and assess the contributions of each of its members in governing Indochina after the war.

Patti was extremely surprised by Giáp's composure and restraints. With Sainteny's provocative and humiliating words, Giáp could at any time leave the conversation, but he did not react that way. In a perfect French, Giáp said he came neither to listen to pontification nor to justify the course of actions the Vietnamese people were taking. Rather, he came at the invitation of a person who represented the new French government. Therefore, he was willing to engage in a friendly exchange of views. Witnessing the conversation with his own eyes, Patti remarked that for the first time in his life, Sainteny had to face an intrepid Vietnamese who was bold enough to challenge the French. With a less hostile attitude and even a reconciliatory smile, Sainteny began to make vague promises about freedom for "the Annamese," a fairly generous policy for Indochina. Unmoved by the vague promises from his French interlocutor, Võ Nguyên Giáp demanded for specific and concrete promises. Sainteny on his part made more similarly vague pledges. As the atmosphere of the conversation gradually returned to a state of increased tension and distrust, when Sainteny resorted to the tough line, both Giáp and Hiền seemed resolute not to make any concession to give the French any voice in the future of Việt Nam.

The Franco-Vietnamese meeting ended when Giáp said it was time he reviewed the Liberation Army units who had just returned from the military base. Giáp and Hiền left the Governor-General's Palace after a cold handshake and farewell from both sides, as Patti later remarked. Recalling Sainteny's complacency after the talk, Patti assessed that he was not sensitive enough to realize that he had just confronted a man who would later be put down in history as the mastermind of the radical disintegration of the French colonialism in the Far East. The Giáp he talked to that evening was simply an envoy sent by Hồ Chí Minh to "work with the French representative to declare Việt Nam's refusal of their generous invitations of great freedom."

In the following days, Giáp instructed his men to keep an eye on the French moves and he was fairly well-informed about the French plot, from Sainteny and Mordant[1] in Hà Nội to Jean Cédile in Sài Gòn, as well as news about the bargain between France and Chiang Kai-shek which was taking place in Chongqing.

During the last ten days of August, while the first expeditionary units commanded by General Leclerc had not arrived in South Việt Nam, Jean Cédile, who was captured by the Japanese after parachuting onto Tây Ninh but later released in Sài Gòn, hastily tried to contact the old fox colonizer Bazé, the ruling mandarins, and French prisoners who had been captivated since March 9, 1945, in order to make urgent preparations for their reconquering of South Việt Nam. However, before they were able to do anything, the people of Sài Gòn and the whole region of Cochinchina had successfully seized power. Cédile was left with no choice but to meet with the representative of the provisional revolutionary government, yet he pressured the Việt Minh into accepting the political regime stipulated

---

1. Eugène Mordant, Chief of Staff of the French troops in Indochina, who was being imprisoned by the Japanese in the Citadel in the wake of the coup d'état on March 9, 1945.

in De Gaulle's declaration on March 24, 1945.[1] The first meeting was unfruitful, as Cédile relied on the protection of the Japanese troops to make rapid preparations and instruct the French nationals to make provocations on the streets of Sài Gòn, including most notably the opening of fire at the Vietnamese in the Independence rally on September 2. On September 6, following General Douglas Gracey and his British mission's arrival in Sài Gòn, accompanied by a French commando company, Cédile started to make preparations, under the shield of Gracey, for Leclerc and his French expeditionary troops to carry out aggressive rebellions in the south of Việt Nam.

For their part, although the British troops were allowed to enter the south of Indochina to disarm the Japanese army under an agreement by the Allies superpowers at the Potsdam Conference in July 1945, only months later, General Gracey blatantly intervened in the internal affairs of the Vietnamese revolutionary government for a few months by creating every possible condition for the French to retake control of South Việt Nam after the Vietnamese people had seized power nationwide. On September 22, to prepare for the French aggression the following day, Gracey, under the pretext of maintaining law and order for the city, issued a ban against press and media, declared martial law, and claimed the right to control the police forces of Sài Gòn. As French General Jean-Baptiste Marchand later wrote that all those

---

1. The Declaration briefly stipulated that the three regions of Việt Nam, namely Tonkin, Annam, and Cochinchina, were to merge with Laos and Cambodia to form the Indochinese Union, also known as French Indochina, under the aegis of a French governor-general like what had happened before 1939.

acts had only served to infuriate the revolutionary elements and forced them to resort to violence.

After the night of September 23—the first night of the Southern Resistance War—in his capacity as head of military issues of the Party, Võ Nguyên Giáp instructed Chief of the General Staff Hoàng Văn Thái to prepare urgent reinforcements for the South. Only several days later, the first Southward company marched from the 5th Zone to Bình Lợi Bridge (Sài Gòn). The Chief of the General Staff himself went to many of the North Vietnamese provinces to urge the local authorities to speed up the organization of Southward forces. As early as September 26, many units left Hà Nội, Nam Định, and Thanh Hóa. Many of them were able to advance to great length by train and worked with the local military and civilian forces in the South to kill and prevent the enemy. However, in the early days, even though the French military strength was inconsiderable, they were backed by the British and the Japanese troops (under British command) and thus they enjoyed huge superiority over the Vietnamese side in the battlefield. Fighting broke out and became widespread in Cochinchina, the Central Highlands, and the South Central Coast. After only several months, the French-controlled region became much widened, putting the Vietnamese army and people into a difficult situation in terms of not only military strength but also equipment, organization, and tactics.

By the middle of January 1946, Secretary of the Central Military Commission and Minister of Interior Affairs Võ Nguyên Giáp was sent by Hồ Chí Minh to the South to inspect the situations of the battlefield. The purpose of the trip was also to carry the message of determination from the Party Central Committee to the provinces from Nghệ An southward, encourage the army and people of the South to uphold their fighting spirit, and instruct them on how to conduct guerrilla and attrition warfare to prevent the French advancement.

On January 18, 1946, Võ Nguyên Giáp left Hà Nội. For a long time, he had not returned to the Central Coast. Now he was travelling across each of the familiar places. Sweet and bitter childhood memories came back to him, one by one, interrupted by meditations about the dark scheme of the Chiang Kai-shek troops in Tonkin and the rapidly changing and deteriorating situations of the battlefield in the South. He could see with his own eyes the "looking-south" sentiment of the people in different provinces along the way. When arriving in Huế, he could see more clearly than ever that the city had become the direct rear of the Southern battlefield, as each sector, each institution, and each living quarter enthusiastically busied themselves preparing supplies and reinforcements for the front.

When he arrived in Bình Định, Võ Nguyên Giáp asked the chauffeur to make use of the time and go straight to Pleiku and Kon tum in the Central Highlands, so that he could investigate the situations along the 19th Route. Stopping at one of the units affiliated with Tây Sơn Battalion in An Khê Town, Giáp felt assured of the political situations and organization of the unit, especially after he talked to military officers and cadres working to protect the Ba River Bridge. He gave careful and detailed instructions as to what should be done immediately to get the unit ready to join any on-the-spot combat in defense this key location or to head south immediately if and when requested.

Back to Quy Nhơn in Bình Định Province, as he crossed the Cù Mông Pass that links the provinces of Bình Định and

Phú Yên and went further, Võ Nguyên Giáp witnessed the urgency with which the locals were preparing for a resistance war. Ninh Hòa became the direct rear of the Nha Trang Front—a hot spot of the Southern battlefield. The French army had marched toward Nha Trang since October, not only to release scores of French nationals held captive by the Japanese troops in the wake of the coup d'état, but also to sever our reinforcement route from north to south. Due to the crucial role of the Nha Trang Front, the armed forces of Khánh Hòa and many other Southward units were given orders to lay siege against the enemy over a period of three months so as to reduce the enemy's number, slow down their advancement, and ease the pressure on Cochinchina and the Central Highlands. It was here that, in the presence of the Southward soldiers from 19 provinces in the Central Coast and the North, Giáp named the Khánh Hòa-Nha Trang Battlefield as "the gathering place of soldiers nationwide." On their part, taking advantage of the backing from the Japanese and British troops to quickly raise the siege for Nha Trang was identified by the French as a top priority. It was here that a rare and unexpected coincidence occurred, one that went without public knowledge until much later. General Giáp arrived in Ninh Hòa on the very same day that his French adversary Leclerc was organizing the Gaur march—the biggest attack since the French reconquer of Cochinchina. More than 15,000 French troops formed two huge pincers, one moving northward from the South and one moving down from the 21st Route. These two pincers joined forces in Nha Trang to raise the siege for this crucial port city.

The car carrying Võ Nguyên Giáp travelled through Rù Rì Pass and stopped in Bóng Hamlet. At that time, the fighting was growing fiercer on the other bank of the Cái River. Giáp could hear the guns resounding ceaselessly from the southern bank and the enemy's aircraft hovering over Diên Khánh Road toward the sea and on the either side of the Cái River. After paying a visit to some of the units who had just retreated for the building of the about-18-km Cây Đa-Quán Giếng defense line, about six kilometres from the town center, Giáp returned to the ancient citadel of Diên Khánh to talk to the Chairman of the Administrative and Resistance War Committee of Khánh Hòa Province and other cadres who commanded the Nha Trang Front. He conveyed the greetings and commendations from President Hồ Chí Minh to the fellowmen and soldiers in the South Central Coast front who had successfully thwarted the enemy's strategic scheme of "rapid fight, rapid settlement," thereby creating more favourable conditions for the rear to make preparations for the resistance war. Having passed on the "Resistance War for National Salvation" directive by the Party Central Committee, Võ Nguyên Giáp, based on his observations and knowledge of the Nha Trang Front, expressed his opinions on the operational, commanding, and fighting tactics. He made it clear that while the establishment of a defense line three months ago to reduce the enemy's numerical advantage and prevent their advancement was deemed a sensible policy as the enemy had just marched to the South Central Coast and their forces remained undeveloped, it would be a blunder then, given the comparative change in the two sides, to consider the defense line as a Vietnamese Maginot,[1] no

---

1. The Maginot defense line was built to the east of France to prevent the German troops in the Second World War. It was named after the French Minister of War Affairs André Maginot (1877–1932).

matter how solid and substantial it could be. He asserted that the current defense line could not maintain the current status forever, as the Vietnamese side could not use huge numbers of soldiers to counter the artillery and air force because of the superior technology of the enemy. In the coming time, the enemy might reinforce their military power and prepare an imminent attack on the rear of Vietnamese troops. If the Vietnamese side had not taken proactive measures to change their directions, they would have been doomed to failure. He instructed clearly that it was sensible to leave a small group of soldiers to blend with the local people, survey the enemy, and inflict frequent losses on them in the city. The majority of the core army needed to retreat and organize themselves into small combat units, mostly the size of a company, which were neat and mobile, and engage themselves in extensive guerrilla and attrition wars, ambushing the enemy's mobile forces. The remainder of the troops was to be divided into platoons, squads, and even armed groups to infiltrate into the rural area immediately adjacent to the enemy-controlled areas, using armed propaganda to restore, maintain, and strengthen the grassroots political bases while preventing the loss of people and land to the enemy, developing clandestine armed groups, and building combat villages. They were also instructed to develop guerrilla warfare and build an all-people struggle to fight against the enemy. On the part of the local authorities, it was necessary to act on their own initiatives and choose a geographically favourable location that was conducive for both attack and retreat and develop it into a military base, which provided a firm foothold for the top commanders of the war in the long run. Giáp also identified the experience of Cao-Bắc-Lạng in previous years as one of the determinants of the success of guerrilla warfare, and cited Hồ Chí Minh's guiding principle of relying on popular support for ultimate victory. In the highland, guerrilla soldiers should take advantage of the forests and mountains for attack and retreat while in the plain, they must rely on the support of the ordinary people. Shielded by the people, the army would be able to launch attack in any place. Giáp later spoke personally to Political Commissar Nguyễn Mô, Commander Trần Công Khanh, and Chief of the General Staff of the Nha Trang Front Hà Văn Lâu. He instructed them to immediately disassemble the defense line, and encouraged all the people to take part in the guerrilla warfare and intensify the battle to gain an advantageous position in the upcoming negotiation with the French.

Although he had never before commanded an army, especially in a medium- or large-scale battle, Võ Nguyên Giáp quickly identified the problem and showed the cadres and commanders which tactics should be adopted to kill the enemy and reduce their march, while making the troops less vulnerable. The three-prong approach suggested by him (including the main force's tactics, the local leaders' foothold, and the popular support) later served as a decisive factor for the gradual formation of the people-based war that best suited the Vietnamese troops given the current imbalance between the two warring sides.

As he was about to continue his southward journey, Võ Nguyên Giáp received a telegram from Hồ Chí Minh asking him to come back to the North. Knowing that it was an urgent issue, Giáp quickly hit the road. Right on the New Year's Eve of 1946, he and his escort passed the Hải Vân Pass in a car. It was a pitch dark, freezing, and rainy night. He was so lost in thought about the uncertainties in the battlefields that he almost forgot that a new year had ushered in. He later recalled, perhaps only slightly, that, "We greeted the new spring in the middle of the pass, in a rainy night."

Back to Hà Nội, Võ Nguyên Giáp reported to Hồ Chí Minh and the Standing Central Committee the results of his trip and the change in operational direction in the Khánh Hòa-Nha Trang Front. The local authorities and the Command of the Front had chosen a suitable time and proactively carried out the policy to withdraw troops from the city to preserve forces and change the tactics. The withdrawal was done promptly, safely, and in a timely manner; it was a big victory, according to Võ Nguyên Giáp. President Hồ Chí Minh agreed on the change in the operational direction in the Nha Trang Front, as it suited the ongoing developments in the battlefield. It was time that the soldiers and militia in Nha Trang quickly switched to guerrilla and people-based warfare.

"In retrospect, we can see clearly now that the decision marked a breakthrough in military thinking, given the situation at that time. Had we insisted on building a defense line or stuck slavishly to the pure defense tactics, had we deployed our troops simply to counter the enemy passively, we would have suffered inevitable defeat. Our rigid and conservative mind would have been the engineer of our own downfall, a recipe for disaster."

It was part of Giáp's assessment published in the *Tạp chí Lịch sử quân sự* (literally: Military History Journal) more than 50 years later. Every success in his military career could be attributed to his painstaking accumulation of experience and resilience, as well as the result of his critical thinking and sharp analysis based on selective lessons withdrawn from the battlefield realities.

Chapter Two: SIXTEEN MONTHS IN THE CAPITAL CITY

In early February, Giáp returned to Hà Nội at a time when the situations in the North were changing and developing rapidly. In the Northwest direction, following the first units to cross the border into Việt Nam in January 1945, the French troops from Huanan continued to penetrate into Lai Châu, moving down to Tuần Giáo to occupy Điện Biên Phủ. More Vietnamese Westward units were deployed to reinforce the Sơn La Brigade in fighting against the enemy. After the successful establishment of the provisional coalition government on September 2, 1945, and the general election on January 6, 1946, the political situations continued to be extremely unpredictable. Opposition parties created by Chiang Kai-shek,[1] particularly the Việt Nam Nationalist Party and Việt Nam Revolutionary League were extremely hostile, demanding a reshuffle of the government before the Chiang Kai-shek army withdrew back to China. The struggle between the Việt Minh Front and these opposition political organizations witnessed many negotiations without agreement on the official structure of the government. Meanwhile, the diplomatic wars between Việt Nam and France, between Việt Nam and the Chiang Kai-shek government, or between France and the Chiang Kai-shek government were concurrent, rapid, and mutually affective throughout February 1946. As the Standing Central

---

1. Examples include the Greater Việt People's Party (Vietnamese: *Đại Việt dân chính*) founded by Nguyễn Tường Tam, Việt Nam Revolutionary League (Vietnamese: *Việt Nam cách mạng đồng chí hội*) by Nguyễn Hải Thần, and Việt Nam Nationalist Party or Vietnamese Kuomintang (Vietnamese: *Việt Nam quốc dân đảng*) by Vũ Hồng Khanh. These political parties, which disguised under the "nationalist" label, in fact served as hirelings of the Chiang Kai-shek regime. They followed the Chinese Chiang Kai-shek army into Việt Nam in the wake of the August Revolution and overtly opposed the revolutionary government.

Committee had already anticipated, the Franco-Chiang Kai-shek negotiation in Chongqing finally concluded with a deal: the Chongqing authorities agreed to let the French troops replace the Chiang Kai-shek troops in the North of Indochina. Confronted with this situation, and by way of critical analysis of every aspect, the March 3 meeting of the Standing Central Committee successfully found out the answer to an extremely important strategic question at this particularly sensitive moment, which was whether to make war with or make concession to the French.

"The problem now is not whether we want to fight or not, but to know ourselves and our enemy, and to evaluate the favourable and unfavourable conditions inside and outside the country before choosing what policy and tactics to adopt."[1]

The Standing Central Committee and President Hồ Chí Minh wanted a peace treaty with France. The Preliminary Accords between Việt Nam and France were inked on the afternoon of March 6, 1946, in Hà Nội. They included three main provisions as follows:

1- France would acknowledge the Democratic Republic of Việt Nam as an independent country which consisted of three regions and was part of the Indochinese Federation and the French Union.

2- Việt Nam would agree to let 15,000 French soldiers enter the North of Việt Nam to replace the Chinese army, on condition that the French army would not remain in Indochina more than five years.

---

1. Communist Party of Việt Nam: *Văn kiện Đảng toàn tập* (literally: The Complete Collection of Party Documents), vol. 8, National Political Publishing House, Hà Nội, pp. 43–44.

3- The two sides would enter into a ceasefire to open a formal negotiation, and maintain the status quo while talks were in progress.

Reflecting on this important event, Võ Nguyên Giáp wrote a quarter of a century later that:

> The enemy with a huge number of troops with numerous aircraft, fighting vessels, armoured vehicles had entered into talks with us on an equal footing. The French government was forced to acknowledge what they did not want to . . . . The first country to acknowledge the freedom of Việt Nam was the one who 60 years earlier had deprived us of all freedom...For our part, we allowed 15,000 French soldiers to enter the North of Việt Nam in a specified period of time in order to drive out the 18,000 Chiang Kai-shek troops, who had claimed that they would remain here on a non-limited basis . . . . The enemy had been forced to make one basic concession. This victory was, however, only an initial achievement for us. The shore of success remained far away.

Hồ Chí Minh and the Standing Central Committee felt the need to provide some clarification for the people to understand why the Government had to sign the Preliminary Accords on March 6, 1946. The movement of the 15,000 French troops to the North took many people by surprise. Minister of Interior Affairs Võ Nguyên Giáp was assigned by Hồ Chí Minh to explain on behalf of the Government and the Communist Party, to the people about the Party's "Conciliate to Advance" policy. On the morning of March 7, at a meeting held in the port city of Hải Phòng, where the French would make landfall right after they reached the North, Võ Nguyên Giáp explained to the people why President Hồ Chí Minh and the Government decided to enter into a negotiation with the French. He briefed them about what the Preliminary

Accords meant and called on everyone to unite, stay on alert, and abide by all the orders and policies of the Government and President Hồ Chí Minh. At 4 pm that day, he was back to the capital city to address a huge rally at the Opera House Square. The French historian Philippe Devillers' works,[1] based on articles published inside and outside the country at that time, summarized Giáp's speech. In these Accords, according to him, there were both acceptable and less acceptable provisions. Acceptable, though not totally satisfactory, provisions included, for example, the French acknowledgement that the Democratic Republic of Việt Nam was a free country. "Free" is more than "self-governing," but not as much as "independent." Once Việt Nam had been freed, they would obtain partial and then total independence.

France wanted to occupy Cochinchina, but the Government has made a strong rejection that, "If someone wants to partition the South, the Central, and the North regions of our country, we will fight till the end." Would any Vietnamese not want these three regions to belong to one and the same country?

Why did the Government allow the French to enter now? First, it was because they would still enter Việt Nam, even if they were not allowed. China had signed with France an agreement to let the French army replace the Chinese army in Việt Nam. Moreover, France had also made quite a number of concessions to Việt Nam. Had Việt Nam not allowed them to enter, Việt Nam would not have reached an agreement.

---

1. Philippe Devillers: *Histoire du Vietnam de 1940 à 1952* (literally: Vietnamese History from 1940 to 1952), Seuil, Paris, 1952; *Paris-Saigon-Hanoi*, Gallimard-Julliard, Paris, 1988.

Dissatisfied people only saw entire independence as a motto or an order, in paper or by word of mouth. They could not understand that national independence was the result of external conditions. In the struggle for independence, it is necessary to be sometimes flexible, sometimes firm. Việt Nam had chosen to negotiate in order to create more favourable conditions for their struggle for full independence and wait for the right opportunity to obtain complete independence. Việt Nam negotiated mainly to defend their political, military, and economic stance. Việt Nam was a free country, and all the rights of freedom were in their hand. Việt Nam had enough power and time to undertake autonomy, to enhance their military means, to develop their economy, and to improve their people's lives.

The guiding principle and the target of the Government were peace and progress. The Accords might open the door for their real and full independence in a near future. That was their ultimate goal.[1]

The sea of audience suddenly burst into applause. And beyond everyone's expectation, President Hồ Chí Minh appeared on the balcony of the Opera House. For many among the audience, it was the first time they had seen the leader of the nation. Hồ Chí Minh signalled silence and then talked briefly to implant trust in the mind of the people. For the whole people to understand, he analysed that although the Government had returned to the hands of the people, none of the superpowers had recognized the independence of Việt Nam. The conclusion of an agreement might instigate international recognition, giving Việt Nam an increasingly firm footing in the world

---

1. Philippe Devillers: *Paris-Saigon-Hanoi*, op cit.

stage, and that was a great political victory. The French troops would arrive, but under the agreement, they would have to withdraw gradually from the country. Choosing to negotiate instead of waging war was a sign of political sensitiveness. Hồ Chí Minh called on the whole nation to remain calm, united, and disciplined. Việt Nam had many friends in the world and was blessed with the solidarity and camaraderie of the people who also supported the Government. However, it was necessary to stay alert and prepared.

Tens of thousands of people were then moved to silence when Hồ Chí Minh ended his speech with an assertion:

> I, Hồ Chí Minh, have fought alongside my compatriots my whole life for the independence of our Fatherland. You may be well aware that I would rather die than betray my country. I swear that I have never gone against the interest of my country and fellowmen.[1]

On the afternoon of March 6, when the Franco-Vietnamese Preliminary Accords (known also as the Hồ-Sainteny Accords) were signed, the French naval fleet had already arrived in the port city of Hải Phòng. Through the French negotiation mission, General Leclerc asked to meet the representative of the Vietnamese government before his men made landfall. Hồ Chí Minh told Võ Nguyên Giáp to go and see the French general on behalf of the Government. Giáp did not really want to meet this Frenchman, but the order was given from Hồ Chí Minh at a highly sensitive time, so he could not decline. When he attempted to recommend Hoàng Hữu Nam instead, Hồ Chí Minh said, "You are a politician, and a politician does not always do only what

---

1. Ibid.

he wants. You must represent our government. Văn (Giáp's pseudonym), that saturnine look is not appropriate for a diplomatic mission. Look at yourself in the mirror and try to smile up!"

On March 8, 1946, Võ Nguyên Giáp headed for Hải Phòng, representing the Vietnamese government to meet the head of the French Expeditionary Corps who had instigated the conflict in the South and later was allowed to bring his troops to the North. It was reported that the afternoon earlier, when he met Phan Mỹ, this French general uttered these complacent and arrogant words: "Once we've begun our journey, we shall arrive in our chosen destination, whether you guys agree or not." Giáp was aware that the "Conciliate to Advance" policy required that he should stay calm and repress his anger when hearing such utterances. He also knew that the French troops could not arrive in Hải Phòng had it not been for the agreement between his government and the Command of the Chiang Kai-shek army.

A general relatively advanced in age, later became known as Jean-Étienne Valluy, went up to the pier to escort the Vietnamese representative to a canoe which took them all to the Senegale battleship being anchored in the mouth of the Gấm River. Later, Võ Nguyên Giáp recounted his conversation with General Leclerc as follows:

> After a handshake and some exchange of formalities, Leclerc spoke with a voice that implied some degree of menace. He said, "I love France, and I want its honour to be respected everywhere."
>
> I felt angered, but with self-control I tried to respond. I said, "I am a communist who fights for the independence of our

country. I believe that those who truly love their countries know how to respect other people's patriotic love."

As the atmosphere became less intense, I mentioned the extremely intrepid struggle of our nation against the Japanese fascists to free ourselves from the chains and yokes of slavery and then added, "You yourself have fought against the German fascists, so I believe we do have some room for mutual understanding."

Leclerc took me to the lounge of the vessel and introduced me to the other military officers. During our subsequent exchange, he promised to try and maintain the Franco-Vietnamese friendship. It was typical of Leclerc to always emphasize his personal role. We discussed the implementation of the Preliminary Accords in terms of military. While awaiting an official agreement between the two governments, it was important to identify where and how many French soldiers were going to station when the joint French and the Vietnamese troops monitored the Chiang Kai-shek army.

On March 15, 1946, the French soldiers made landfall onto Hải Phòng. Three days later, more than 1,000 soldiers and 200 vehicles left Hải Phòng for Hà Nội. The first thing that Leclerc did was to release and equip the French military inmates imprisoned by the Japanese in the city to supplement the French combat troops who had just arrived in Hà Nội. This indicated that they were about to go against their promises and violate the agreement. During a conversation with Võ Nguyên Giáp, this French general dropped hints that he wished to know the attitudes of the Vietnamese toward the French. Võ Nguyên Giáp asked, "We are both military officers. Do you want a straight answer?" "Yes," the French general replied. Giáp continued, "As you do not mean what you say about peace and cooperation, in the eyes of the Vietnamese you are no more than invaders and aggressors."

In a situation when the Chinese had not left while the French had already come, the need to enhance security and defense in order to protect the newly gained revolutionary achievements became ever more urgent. And it was all placed on the shoulder of Võ Nguyên Giáp who at that time served as Minister of Interior Affairs, Secretary of the Central Military Commission, and Chairman of the National Resistance Committee taking charge of military issues on behalf of the Party. A few days later, in the Resistance Coalition Government, it was decided that the National Resistance Committee would be changed into the Military Commission Association under the chairmanship of Võ Nguyên Giáp. An intellect by the name of Phan Anh assumed the role of Minister of National Defense and took charge of administrative issues of the army. The Military Commission Association was a commanding agency. Phan Anh later recalled, "Even though I assumed the position of Minister of National Defense, I did not have to worry about specialized military issues, as they were in the charge of Võ Nguyên Giáp."[1]

At this time, Võ Nguyên Giáp was constantly concerned about how he could force the French to respect and implement the Preliminary Accords. Therefore, he entrusted Chief of the General Staff Hoàng Văn Thái the task of building armed forces and making preparations for the prolonged resistance war.

---

1. See *Tạp chí Lịch sử quân sự* (literally: Military History Journal), issue 36, December 1988.

A Snow-covered Volcano

On March 17, 1946, Admiral Georges Thierry d'Argenlieu sent President Hồ Chí Minh a letter saying that he would be happy to receive the latter on March 24 at Hạ Long Bay "with all the usual pomp and circumstance." That invitation suited the Vietnamese intention of wanting to meet the highest representative of the French government in Indochina to pave the way for the formal meetings in Paris. In the March 24 midday meeting on the cruiser Émile Bertin anchored in the bay of Hạ Long, the two sides agreed on the following points:

1- In the middle of April 1946, Việt Nam would send a National Assembly delegation to France for a friendly visit.

2- A preparatory conference would be held in Đà Lạt between 12 Vietnamese delegates and 12 French counterparts.

3- At the end of May, the Vietnamese delegation would go to Paris for a formal negotiation.

The Government appointed 12 official members and 12 advisors, under the leadership of Minister of Foreign Affairs Nguyễn Tường Tam as head of the delegation and Chairman of the Military Commission Association and Minister of Interior Affairs Võ Nguyên Giáp as vice head, in the negotiation delegation to participate in the Đà Lạt Preparatory Conference.[1] On the afternoon of April

---

1. Apart from the head and deputy head of the delegation, other members included Trịnh Văn Bính, Cù Huy Cận, Hoàng Xuân Hãn, Vũ Văn Hiền, Vũ Hồng Khanh, Trần Đăng Khoa, Nguyễn Văn Luyện, Dương Bạch Mai, Phạm Ngọc Thạch, Bùi Công Trừng, and Nguyễn Mạnh Tường. Advisors included Tạ Quang Bửu, Kha Vạng Cân, Kiều Quang Cung, Phạm Khắc Hòe, Đinh Văn Hớn, Nguyễn Văn Huyên, Hồ Đắc Liên, Phan Phác, Nguyễn Duy Thanh, Nguyễn Tường Thụy, Nguyễn Văn Tình, and Hồ Hữu Tường.

15, the whole delegation met with Hồ Chí Minh and the Government members before departure. The first thing Hồ Chí Minh emphasized was that the mission had to maintain internal solidarity, both in ideas and actions. Regarding the negotiation, he said that it was only a preparatory conference and the formal talks would convene in France. Therefore, if a certain issue could not be agreed upon, the Vietnamese negotiators should recommend that it be temporarily shelved, rather than saying that the Government had to be consulted, which meant that the Government should not be tied to this preparatory conference. Hồ Chí Minh reminded the delegation to maintain their stance, and base on the main tenets of the March 6 Preliminary Accords[1] to materialize a sincere cooperation with the French. After Nguyễn Tường Tam thanked the Government for its trust and promised to fulfil their duties, Võ Nguyên Giáp reassured President Hồ

---

1. The Vietnamese stance toward some of the main provisions of the March 6 Preliminary Accords included:
   - A free state: It was necessary to determine the exact degree of freedom, especially in terms of territory; complete unification was a must.
   - Federation: The Indochinese Federation would only exist in economic terms, and no federal government would be acceptable.
   - French Union: Việt Nam would accept to liaise with the French, but the rights and obligations of Việt Nam had to be clearly specified. Việt Nam had to be given rights to discuss and vote on the issues in the Union which were related to Việt Nam. Việt Nam had to maintain minimal diplomatic relations, which meant bilateral ties with superpowers like Britain, the United States of America, Russia, and China, as well as with neighboring countries like Thailand, India, and the Philippines. It was necessary to introduce Việt Nam to the United Nations. In terms of finance, Việt Nam had to have banks and currency. In terms of economy, the economic sovereignty had to belong to the State of Việt Nam. In terms of military, Việt Nam would not accept a federal army. The number of soldiers, the types of tasks, venues, and time of French military presence in Việt Nam had to be clearly specified.

Chí Minh about the solidarity and unity among the delegates in order to accomplish the important task assigned by the Government.

With that assurance, Võ Nguyên Giáp was fully aware of the heavy task placed on his shoulder that he had to not only fight against the opponent but also maintain solidarity among the members of the delegation, which Hồ Chí Minh had strongly requested. He had reasons to make that promise to Hồ Chí Minh and the Government, as this Vietnamese delegation was "a special mission." The head of the mission, Nguyễn Tường Tam, was the leader of the opposition party, who had just been added to the Coalition Government to serve as the Minister of Foreign Affairs. Another member of the delegation was Vũ Hồng Khanh, one of the leaders of the Nationalist Party, who in the name of the "special representative of the Government" signed the Preliminary Accords right below the signature of Hồ Chí Minh. Only a short while earlier, both Nguyễn Tường Tam and Vũ Hồng Khanh had sent their subordinates to use loudspeakers to publicly denounce the revolutionary government all over the capital city of Hà Nội. With the exception of these two special figures, the large majority of the delegates were intellects aged from 35 to 40 with different socio-political statuses. Some of them were renowned writers and poets; some held two doctoral degrees in jurisprudence and philology and were extremely conversed in the French language. Some used to serve as mandarins under the Nguyễn Dynasty, while others were sent by the Government to receive the jade seal of the last emperor Bảo Đại. Some were allowed by the French to look at the Brazzaville Declaration by General De Gaulle on the French plot to return to Indochina, and had been linked to General Eugène Mordant and the French resistance faction" in Indochina between 1943 and 1944. Most of them became revolution sympathizers before and after the height of the National General Uprising, while there were others who had joined the Resistance Coalition Government only two weeks before. Some were lucky enough to talk personally to Hồ Chí Minh and tell him frankly about the relations between Việt Minh and other existing parties as competing parties,[1] but then wondered what he would think about their "straightforward and candid words." Although each of them had different understanding of the current situation, most of them shared a common concern toward the threats that were against newly obtained independence. Having heard the French return, many of them hoped that the United States and China, who had "the mission of safeguarding peace in the Far East," would prevent the French from re-establishing their rule over the Indochina Peninsula. But later they saw that the French were able to expand the controlled area in the South, and then the Sino-French Treaty (dated February 28, 1946) and the Franco-Vietnamese Preliminary Accords (dated March 6, 1946) were signed. The French marched to the North, and some people could not help feeling disappointed. They thought that their aspirations for independence and freedom, once feasible, were now beyond their reach, and the Vietnamese people were facing the impending threat of losing the country. Using scorched earth strategy was a brave attempt, but what result would it lead to? Would it be

---

1. Implying that the political motives of Việt Minh were no different from those of other parties such as Việt Nam Nationalist Party (Vietnamese: *Việt Quốc*) and *Việt Nam Revolutionary League* (Vietnamese: *Việt Cách*), who harbored contradicting ideas and were struggling with each other for influence and power, not for national interest.

as gloomy as what had befallen predecessors such as Trương Công Định, Phan Đình Phùng, and Hoàng Hoa Thám in the late 19th and early 20th centuries? Tasked by President Hồ Chí Minh and the Standing Central Committee with the co-leadership of such a negotiation delegation, Võ Nguyên Giáp found it difficult not only to talk with the representatives of the French anti-revolutionary interests, but also to capitalize on the intellectual capabilities of each of the member in the delegation so as to ensure solidarity, internal unity, and unison of action, especially with Nguyễn Tường Tam.

What were the delegation members' first impressions of Võ Nguyên Giáp? In the 23rd and 24th issues of the *Tập san Sử-Địa* (literally: Historic-geographic Journal) published in Sài Gòn in 1971, Hoàng Xuân Hãn wrote:

> It was the first time I met Võ Nguyên Giáp personally. Contrary to rumours that he was quick-tempered, Giáp proved to be courteous and full of affection, but firm in action. Having spent more than three weeks working and living together, I became better aware of the special mettle of this young revolutionary.

The cordial camaraderie among the members could be felt right on the first evening of April 16 when the delegation had to stop in Pakse (Laos) because the plane had a technical problem. Having some small talks with other members in the delegation, Giáp recounted his life in the combat zone. "The scenery was breath-taking," he said, "On our way back, I would take you all on a visit to the combat zone…" As they were talking merrily, Nguyễn Mạnh Tường suddenly digressed the topic. "Giáp, you really should get married again soon," he said. Võ Nguyên Giáp smiled and replied, "Please choose a wife for me." When Nguyễn Mạnh Tường mentioned the name of a famous contemporary female revolutionary, Giáp tried to look surprised, but then he only laughed off the matter.

Cordiality and mutual trust were also evidenced in the partition of the delegation into different committees to counter the opponent. Võ Nguyên Giáp was named Head of the Military Committee, but he simultaneously served in the Political and Economic-financial Committees of the Vietnamese side. After the committees had taken shape, the delegation adopted a fairly strict working schedule. Being members of the first diplomatic mission of the new Việt Nam, none of them had experience in negotiation skills, especially in dealing with a cunning and politically conservative opponent under the distant leadership of not only Admiral Georges Thierry d'Argenlieu in Sài Gòn, but also Foreign Minister Georges Bidault in Paris. In each of the committees, the members always tried to put themselves in the shoes of France to predict what their real intentions were, so that they could identify their own target and what their discussions were to come up with combat strategy. The Economic-financial Committee even adopted a fairly original mode called "battle rehearsal." The committee often divided itself into two sides to argue against each other on every issue and idea. The most typical of which was the debate on the evening of May 4 about monetary issue between Vũ Văn Hiền (playing the role of the French side) and doctor Nguyễn Văn Luyện (playing the role of the Vietnamese side), arbitrated by Trịnh Văn Bính. Vũ Văn Hiền, who tried to imitate the voice of the French economic-financial specialist Gonon, gave Nguyễn Văn Luyện a really hard time with his rapid-fire questions.

Finally, the two "sides" and the arbitrator could not help but burst out laughing and sat down together to find answers to each of the issues the French side was likely to challenge.

Having possibly realized the important role of Võ Nguyên Giáp, some of the members in the French delegation such as Messmer, Bousquet, and Salan "sought after" the vice head of the Vietnamese delegation. Salan had known Giáp since the initial negotiation days in Hà Nội. In this conference, whenever there was discontentment and tension between the two sides, this French general often approached Giáp to settle the dispute, but what he received was always what he later recalled "hardline argument under the guise of a courteous and tactful attitude." As for Messmer and Bousquet, although they were meeting Giáp for the first time, both tried to "put on a friendly face" with him. After each of the discussions he had with them, Giáp reported their ideas back to the delegation so that the Vietnamese side could work together to assess the intentions of the opposing side. They included even the face-to-face meeting between him and Alphonse Juin when this French general cum Chief of the General Staff returned from China and stopped in Đà Lạt on April 30. Although Juin promised to raise the idea of a cease-fire in the South of Việt Nam to General Leclerc, Giáp warned his team-mates that the promise was made totally out of lip service and shirking of responsibility. Despite this, the Vietnamese delegation was aware that the more personal exchanges were made, the better they could predict the overall intentions of the opposing side. They then concurred with the policy of enhancing personal contact and meeting between the two sides, apart from formal meetings.

Right from the beginning, the Vietnamese side more or less collected information about the background of some of the French taking part in this preparatory conference. The head of the French delegation, Max André, was a member of the Popular Republic Movement—Foreign Minister Bidault's conservative party with Christianity-based ideology. Max André was also one of Bidault's confidantes. Messmer was a notorious colonial ruler during the French colonial period who had parachuted onto the North of Việt Nam at the height of the National General Uprising and had been arrested by the security officers before being released at the Sino-Vietnamese border. Legal adviser Torel, financial adviser Gonon, and political adviser Pignon were all d'Argenlieu's "hands and feet." Salan was arguably the most senior and experienced colonialist general who was extremely knowledgeable about and "fond of Indochina." Later, thanks to an outpour of documents from abroad, the Vietnamese side knew that one day before the commencement of the Đà Lạt Conference, the French government had sent its delegation a directive dated April 14, 1946 emphasizing that the establishment of an Indochinese Federation with maximal members was in France's essential interest. This meant that the French delegation had to try everything not only to materialize the French government's plot of partitioning Indochina into five "regions" as mentioned in De Gaulle's Declaration of March 24, 1945, but also to separate from Việt Nam a "Westernized Region" with Đà Lạt as the capital city according to d'Argenlieu's plan. Therefore, whenever it came to discussing the issues of Cochinchina and a referendum to unify Việt Nam, the French side always used a tactic which Võ Nguyên Giáp described as "pouring a bucket of cold water on Việt Nam's willingness to negotiate."

As the Vietnamese delegation had expected, confronting such a French delegation was really a fierce struggle. The latter blatantly heated up the negotiation process, both inside and outside the convention hall. For example, they demanded that Tạ Quang Bửu be expelled and Phạm Ngọc Thạch arrested and transferred to Sài Gòn. They also demanded that the Vietnamese delegation ask for permission before using the radio transmitter to contact their government in Hà Nội and tried to prevent the latter from contact with the local people. More seriously, they established the "autonomous Cochinchina" before the commencement of the Conference. They resolutely refused to abide by one of the provisions of the March 6 Preliminary Accords, which stipulated a moratorium to fighting in the South to create a peaceful atmosphere for negotiations, or discuss any military issues to the south of the 16th parallel. All of these realities explained why the Đà Lạt Preparatory Conference was called off after three weeks of negotiation. The repressed feelings of the Vietnamese delegation in the plenary sessions as well as in committee meetings reached a climax in the final plenary meeting, which took place on May 11, 1946.

That day, it was Messmer's turn to chair the conference. The two sides discussed two of the many bones of contention, namely the ethnic minority issue (which was the selfsame Westernized Region proposed by the French) and the referendum issue (which in fact was the struggle to unify the country as proposed by the Vietnamese delegation). Following d'Argenlieu's directive, the French delegation demanded that the Central Highlands be separated from Việt Nam to become a region affiliated to France, so that

France could gain a footing in the Indochinese Federation. Bourgouin argued that the Central Highlands was not part of Việt Nam, and that "France takes responsibility to the world for the protection and safety of the ethnic minority groups in the Central Highlands." Confronted with such blatant arguments, Võ Nguyên Giáp immediately responded, "The issue of ethnic minorities in the Central Highlands is Việt Nam's internal affair. The Vietnamese Government has already developed a plan and is implementing it." Exchanges of blows followed, and finally the outstanding problem was shelved until the formal talks in Paris. Before discussing the referendum issue, the French announced a declaration read by Torel, with basically the following ideas:

1- Việt Nam would not have only three regions. The number of regions would depend on the national referendum.

2- The referendum, organized by the French, would only take place in the Central and South regions of Việt Nam (known as Annam and Cochinchina respectively). The Vietnamese Government were not allowed to interfere with the political situations in these two regions before the announcement of the referendum results.

3- In this preparatory conference, the Vietnamese delegation would have no right to discuss issues related to these self-governing regions.

The Vietnamese delegates were extremely incensed by the French side's arrogance, especially when a Frenchman said, "You have nothing to say on this issue" (originally: *"Vous n'avez rien a dire sur cette question"*). However, they tried their best to pocket their anger and remain calm. They understood that their ultimate goal was to make known the Vietnamese determination to reunify their country, while showing the French that they had continued to go in the wrong direction. After giving Dương Bạch Mai, the representative of the South, a chance to raise his voice, the other Vietnamese delegates made it clear that the three regions were part and parcel of Việt Nam, and that Cochinchina was an inseparable part of the country. Nguyễn Mạnh Tường said, "The South is our flesh and blood," while Nguyễn Văn Huyên said, "It's not that the South belongs to Việt Nam, but rather Việt Nam belongs to the South."

The French side had listened to Võ Nguyên Giáp's arguments many times, especially in the April 22 meeting of the Political Committee that discussed a ceasefire in the South. That day, Võ Nguyên Giáp said, "At this moment, gunfire is still roaring in the South. You French said that it is for the purpose of pushing back the bandits. If you see our troops in the South as bandits, then do you mean that the French Forces of the Interior who fought against the German Nazi fascism during the Second World War were also bandits?" Next, in the plenary meeting on May 3, which debated issues related to the South, Võ Nguyên Giáp asserted that, "People cannot resort to marches and raids to force the Southerners to lay down their arms." Also in this meeting, when denouncing the French plot about the Indochinese Federation, Võ Nguyên Giáp spoke seriously, "We solemnly declare the end of the rule of the Governors-General." In the last plenary meeting held on May 11, when the issue of Cochinchina was revisited, Võ Nguyên Giáp reaffirmed that, "Should Cochinchina be severed from Việt Nam, we, the Vietnamese, will fight with highest spirit and determination until it is regained."

Head of the Political Committee Hoàng Xuân Hãn was the last to speak. In a calm voice, he proved the patience with which the Vietnamese delegation tried to find a solution acceptable to both sides on pivotal matters related to the future of Việt Nam. He also strongly condemned the French's terrible plot of trying to partition Việt Nam.

As the tension grew in the plenary session, Võ Nguyên Giáp suddenly rose and announced candidly, "If your real intention is to spoil negotiation and continue your war of aggression against Việt Nam, our country will become a land of redemption."

Having said that, he grasped his briefcase and quickly made his way to the door to the amazement of delegates from both sides. Immediately, Hồ Hữu Tường stood up and followed him. It was the midday of May 11. After walking out of the room, Giáp slammed the door closed. The French delegation was left dumbfounded and speechless, and the most amazed was General Salan himself. Later, he associated Giáp's action with another "slamming of the door" in 1954. This time it was not in Đà Lạt, like eight years before, but in Điện Biên Phủ in northwestern Việt Nam. The "victims" of this second "slamming of the door" were no longer Mac André and Georges Thierry d'Argenlieu, but Christian de Castries and Henri Navarre, and further out, Prime Minister Joseph Laniel and Foreign Minister Georges Bidault in Paris.

In the last meeting of the delegation on the afternoon of May 11, Nguyễn Tường Tam said in a cordial voice after reviewing what had been done in the last couple of weeks:

> Although the Đà Lạt Conference could not bring about any agreement between Việt Nam and France, one good thing

is that we have been of one mind and united in our actions, as we had promised to the Government before departure. This morning, Đà Lạt has witnessed a memorable moment: despite our different political leanings, all of us, communists and nationalists alike, have shown our detest against the French's wicked plot of depriving Việt Nam of its land.

Võ Nguyên Giáp followed up:

> The Communist Party and the Việt Minh Front's consistent policy is to unite all the Vietnamese. During the past few weeks, we have been united as we had promised to our President. I believe that apart from the parties, our other brothers have also been very united. Diplomacy must start from roots.

After some other delegates had recounted stories of affection and solidarity shown in the protection of Phạm Ngọc Thạch and the caring for Nguyễn Tường Tam when he fell ill, or demonstration of mutual understanding on the May Day commemoration ceremony and during the whole three weeks working together, Hoàng Xuân Hãn repeated to some new members in the delegation Giáp's intimate words on April 28 that "Việt Minh harbours no prejudice against the intellectual circle," and that "We stand ready to cooperate with respectable nationalists like you. If only we had known you earlier."

Bringing everyone back to the missions of the delegation, delegation Nguyễn Tường Tam made the final remarks before the meeting concluded. He said, "We have acted according to the Government's request: stretch, but not break or sever the relationship with France; and reject anything that goes against the interest and will of the nation while causing no trouble to the Government."

The following morning on May 12, they headed for the airport without knowing that in the capital city, the Hà Nội-based French newspaper *L'Entente* (literally: The Agreement) had published an article summarizing the Đà Lạt Conference. The article unveiled what the Paris administration requested from the French delegation in a directive dated April 14. Accordingly, the French delegation had to try to lead the whole world to believe that the Vietnamese side was to blame for the breakdown of the Đà Lạt Conference. At the end of the article ran a commentary that the failure of the preparatory conference was essentially due to the poor management of the vice head of the Vietnamese delegation Võ Nguyên Giáp, a communist minister.

Half a century later, when reviewing the Đà Lạt Conference in his book titled *Victory at Any Cost*, the American military historian Cecil Currey revealed another detail unknown to the Vietnamese delegation at that time: Giáp's icy exterior overlaid a temper so fiery both inside and outside the Conference that the French described him as "a snow-covered volcano" (originally: *"un volcan covert de neige"*). How did the French understand that phrase? According to historian Jean Lacouture, that image was a combination of fervent enthusiasm and razor-sharp mind, which created the power of this man. Lacouture recounted that when the long interview after the Đà Lạt Conference ended, Giáp asked to read again and edit the manuscript himself. On the failure of the Đà Lạt Conference, Lacouture said, "It was Giáp who suggested that I use the French term *"désaccord cordial"* (literally: "cordial disagreement") to describe the Đà Lạt Conference." It was obvious that even in the most intense moment, the Vietnamese side did not want to sever diplomatic links with

159

France. It was a pity that until the summer of 1946, the French had not realized that goodwill.

". . . We Have Old Huỳnh and Young Giáp"

As had been agreed upon between the two sides, the Vietnamese delegation headed by Phạm Văn Đồng left for France on May 31 to begin the formal negotiation.[1] President Hồ Chí Minh, as guest of the French Government, accompanied the delegation. Gia Lâm Airport was full of red flags on that day. Hồ Chí Minh proceeded to bid farewell to the Acting President Huỳnh Thúc Kháng, members of the Cabinet, and ordinary people who came to see him off. Hồ Chí Minh held Old Huỳnh's hands and said solicitously, "I'm going away for a while to fulfil the task assigned by the nation and the people, leaving all the difficulties at home in your hands and other comrades'. Please remember to use the unchanging to deal with the constantly changing."[2]

Old Huỳnh and the Cabinet members were all moved. Before boarding the plane, Hồ Chí Minh reminded the

---

1. The delegation encompassed Hoàng Minh Giám, Phan Anh, Tạ Quang Bửu, Nguyễn Văn Huyên, Trịnh Văn Bính, and some others. Lawyer Phan Anh, Minister of National Defense, was named chief presenter, taking charge of legal issues for the delegation. Minister of Foreign Affairs Nguyễn Tường Tam stayed behind on an excuse of illness. Phan Anh later recounted that the members of the delegation regarded this withdrawal as an act of sabotage. His action was indicative of his discontent toward the Government regarding the negotiation with the French, which contradicted what he had said earlier about the solidarity among the members at the Đà Lạt Conference.
2. Phan Anh later recollected that in the understanding of the delegation members, the "unchanging" in this case referred to solidarity on the basis of independence and freedom while "the constantly changing" referred to the wicked plots and tricks of the foreign aggressors and the counter-revolutionaries inside the country.

delegates in the negotiation team to uphold solidarity and unity of mind to fulfil the heavy task given by the nation.

Hồ Chí Minh was aware of the concerns the delegates had for the situations at home, as everyone predicted that the French would continually provoke, while the President and many of the Cabinet members were away on a long trip. Hồ Chí Minh told them to set their mind at ease. "For every eventuality at home, we have old Huỳnh and young Giáp."

There was mutual care and concern for each other between the leavers and the stayers. Half a century later, Võ Nguyên Giáp recalled:

> Uncle Hồ had previously discussed with people at the Standing Central Committee whether he should leave for France at that time. He had earlier been sentenced to death by the French reactionaries. In the event of an unsuccessful negotiation, his security was likely to be jeopardized should the French go back against their words. Another unspoken worry that bothered us during that flight was the possibility of a plane crash, which was not uncommon in those days.

After Hồ Chí Minh and the Vietnamese delegation departed, the situations in the country continued to be extremely complicated and unpredictable throughout the summer and autumn months of 1946. Võ Nguyên Giáp held constant talks with General Secretary Trường Chinh and members of the Standing Central Committee in order to arrive at exact assessment of the situations and passage of policies for the whole country and especially for the capital city of Hà Nội. The enemy could take advantage of Hồ Chí Minh's absence to act more blatantly and fiercely.

From the French position in the Đà Lạt Conference, Võ Nguyên Giáp predicted that apart from the plot to separate

South Việt Nam, the French would sooner or later, under the pretext of "protecting the ethnic minorities," resort to force to take the Central Highlands to establish a foothold for the puppet government of the "Autonomous Westernized Region." The Party and Government had taken one important step ahead. The Congress of Ethnic Minorities-Congress of Solidarity against French Aggression held in Playku on April 19, 1946, under a directive issued by Hồ Chí Minh was a radical and timely preparation, mentally and politically, for the ethnic minority people in the Central Highlands in terms of orientation and direction for the war. Later through Devillers' documents which transpired in early May, d'Argenlieu already urged Leclerc to resolutely accelerate their northward advancement along the Playku-Kon Tum route, as they need to expand their power in Annam (Central Việt Nam) in the direction of the 16th parallel, especially toward the region of the Highlanders (French: *Montagnard*). Leclerc hesitated, for fear of confronting the resistance from the Vietnamese Government. So he replied, "We can do it whenever we want, but we must determine when it is most propitious." The propitious opportunity was when Hồ Chí Minh and the Vietnamese delegation were already airborne.

On the morning of June 21, Valluy came to see Giáp and handed a note addressed to the Acting President of the Democratic Republic of Việt Nam. It abruptly read, "The High Commissioner, Admiral d'Argenlieu, has ordered the French troops to occupy the Mọi Western Highlands (the Central Highlands), as he had said to Hồ Chí Minh when he was in Hà Nội."

While the General Staff sent an urgent telegram to the armed forces of the Central Highlands conveying the order of Chairman of the Military Commission Association Võ Nguyên Giáp to block all the marching directions of the French, Acting President Huỳnh Thúc Kháng sent back a note dismissing the cunning arguments of the French and resolutely denouncing their blatant encroachment. The Acting President pointed out clearly that, "Hồ Chí Minh had never been informed by the French of their imminent occupation of the Central Highlands, and under no circumstances would he agree to such an occupation."

At the end of June, when the occupation expanded in the Central Highlands battlefield with a substantial imbalance of power, Võ Nguyên Giáp instructed the Central Highlands military men and people to change their activities to feed a prolonged war. Abiding by that policy, the armed propaganda brigades tried to infiltrate into the temporarily occupied regions of Cheo Reo, M'Đrắc, Buôn Hồ, Đắc Lây, and Kom Brẫy to lay foundations for clandestine political and military bases, thereby gradually restoring authority. The Highland cadres quickly matured in mobilizing the people to fight against the enemy with every self-made rudimentary weapon available. The two difficult months had passed, and by September the situations in the Central Highlands battlefield had undergone remarkable changes. The guerrilla war had developed. The 94th and 95th Regiments and Ba Tơ Battalion had also become more effective in attacking the enemy's posts, blockhouses, and encroaching marches. Military operations had effectively supported the restoration of popular government in 53 communes of the mountainous region of An Khê and Cheo Reo. Onsite revolutionary military bases were established in Cheo Reo, M'Đrắc, and Buôn Hồ. The armed propaganda brigades and national defense guards in Củng Sơn, Buôn Hồ, Cheo Reo, and An Khê gradually expanded their scope of operation and infiltrated deep into the temporarily occupied areas of the two provinces of Gia Lai and Kon Tum.

It was thanks to the reinforcement of political armed bases that by the end of 1946 the ethnic minority peoples of the Central Highlands were well prepared to join the resistance war alongside their fellowmen all over the country. Moreover, a large proportion of the enemy's combat troops were attracted to the Central Highlands battle, thereby aggravating their personnel crisis. The number of enemy troops in South Việt Nam was thinned out and insufficient, prompting the people and army there to accelerate their activities.

Through political awareness-raising activities, the people in South Việt Nam gradually understood that the signing of the March 6 Preliminary Accords had marked a major breakthrough in the protracted war of their country, with most soldiers ready to follow President Hồ Chí Minh's appeal and remain firm at their position. At the end of May 1946, upon instructions from President Hồ Chí Minh and General Secretary Trường Chinh, Võ Nguyên Giáp and some other members of the Party Central Committee held an open conference involving the participation of commanding cadres for the Southern battlefield in order to identify the new directions for fighting under new circumstances. The realities in the battlefield during the later half of 1946 showed that the resolution of the congress[1] had paved the way for a

---

1. The resolution of the meeting between the Party Central Committee and Southern cadres at the end of May 1946 stipulated that the armed struggle at this stage was mainly for defensive purposes, and that the

"re-insurrection" in the rural area of South Việt Nam. General Võ Nguyên Giáp later remarked:

> During this period, our troops had favourable conditions to operate, as the enemy had sent a large proportion of their forces to the North under the Preliminary Accords, leaving the remainder highly dispersed and thinned out. In addition, our guerrilla warfare tactics had developed strongly in the 7th, 8th, and 9th Zones (all over South Việt Nam), and we were able to destroy the enemy's scattered groups of soldiers and military posts, while warding off their barbarous mopping-up operations and restoring our grab on power. Our armed forces, taking this opportunity, grew substantially in size, and following the Modus Vivendi of September 14, 1946, developed all the more. South Việt Nam had been able to launch a people's war.[1]

In the North, the main target of the French was the capital city of Hà Nội due to the limitations and restricted size of their combat troops. Specific examples of their

---

overarching operational principle was for political solutions to take precedence over military struggle. Therefore, it was important to: 1- Adjust and unify instructions and commands; 2- Maintain a proactive position in operations while not causing obstacles for diplomatic attempts; 3- Develop armed propaganda units in the enemy-controlled areas; 4- Trigger chaos and disorder in big cities; 5- Attack the enemy cautiously, without taking too much risk in order to preserve forces; 6- Be careful in killing Vietnamese lackeys. See *Văn kiện quân sự của Đảng* (literally: Party's Military Documents), People's Army Publishing House, Hà Nội, 1976, vol. 2, p. 49.

1. General Võ Nguyên Giáp's overall assessment in *Huấn lệnh về phương châm quân sự của ta ở Nam Bộ* (literally: Instructions on Our Military Strategies in South Việt Nam) (November 1, 1948) printed in *Những tài liệu chỉ đạo cuộc đấu tranh vũ trang của Trung ương Đảng và Tổng Quân ủy* (literally: The Party Central Committee and General Military Commission's Guiding Documents for Armed Struggle), published by the General Staff, vol. 1, p. 323.

violations and provocations included their occupation of the Ministry of Finance at the end of March and the former Governor-General's Palace at the end of June, and the opening of fire in their clashes with the Chinese Chiang Kai-shek army right in the streets of Hà Nội. The biggest plot of the French military leaders was to make use of the French military presence in Hà Nội to create all the necessary conditions to stage a coup d'état to overthrow the revolutionary government. It was known later from Western scholarly works that Leclerc had intended to "make one sweep" when he and Võ Nguyên Giáp reviewed the parade on March 22, only four days after the French troops entered the capital city. However, as revealed by Devillers, Valluy[1] himself had to admit that it was beyond their ken at that time. Throughout the summer, France failed to carry out their plan of using spies, secret agents, and commandos to nullify secretly and unpredictably the Vietnamese leaders. That Hồ Chí Minh was away presented them with a good opportunity to implement a bolder new plan.

At the end of June, when the Chiang Kai-shek army withdrew out of Hà Nội, some of their hirelings followed them, leaving behind other subordinates with a scheme of "changing masters." Since then, these subordinates had colluded with the French to overthrow the revolutionary government and establish a pro-French government. A typical example was their plot of a coup d'état at the end of July, co-staged by the

---

1. Jean-Étienne Valluy, Commander-in-Chief of the Ninth Division, the major force to be present in Hà Nội in the wake of the Preliminary Accords of March 6, 1946. He was appointed commander of the French army in North Việt Nam in March 1946, and replaced Leclerc to become Commander-in-chief of the French Expeditionary Corps in Indochina in July 1946.

Chapter Two: SIXTEEN MONTHS IN THE CAPITAL CITY

Greater Việt People's Party and Việt Nam Nationalist Party, under a plan mapped out by Valluy. On the occasion of the French National Day, July 14, the French Command proposed that the Vietnamese Government allow them to organize a parade on some of the main streets of Hà Nội. Before a reply was made, on July 11, General Director of the Northern Police Department Lê Giản reported to the Standing Central Committee and the Acting President that the Greater Việt People's Party and Việt Nam Nationalist Party were colluding with the French to oust the Vietnamese Government. Taking advantage of the French upcoming parade, their hirelings and running dogs would hide on either side of the streets, firing bullets and throwing grenades at the French soldiers, thereby creating a pretext for France to arrest the leaders of the Vietnamese Party and Government. In the meantime, their hirelings distributed political pamphlets all over, calling the Vietnamese people to rise and overthrow the Vietnamese Government. A lot of leaflets were printed in preparation for an overthrow on the French National Day. After listening to reports, Acting President Huỳnh Thúc Kháng instructed that the Government need to collect sufficient proof before taking action, or else people would think of them as fighting for political power. Having discussed matters with General Secretary Trường Chinh, Chairman of the Central Military Commission Võ Nguyên Giáp sent a reply rejecting the parade proposal of the French army, while instructing the City Protection Committee and the Public Security Service to work together to thwart the wicked plot of the reactionaries before July 13.

With secret information provided by ordinary people in the neighbourhood, at 4:30 pm on July 12, the self-defense guards and police officers all of a sudden stormed into the headquarters of the Việt Nam Nationalist Party, arresting Phan Kích Nam (i.e. Phan Xuân Thiện, one of the leaders of the Việt Nam Nationalist Party) and escorting him to the Northern Police Department. At the same time, police officers and self-defense guards raided their dens at numbers 132 Minh Khai Street and 7 Ôn Như Hầu Street (present-day Nguyễn Gia Thiều Street), confiscating many items as evidence, including for example weapons, printers, counterfeit money notes, pamphlets, and a coup d'état plan on July 14. Particularly in the house at number 7 Ôn Như Hầu Street, the self-defense guards and police officers released many people held captive for ransoms. They also discovered several makeshift burial grounds in the yard and in the garden where people, including even revolutionary cadres who had been abducted and killed, were buried. During that night and the following morning of July 13, the police officers continued to hunt for the reactionaries in their dens on such streets in Hà Nội as Quán Thánh, Đỗ Hữu Vị (present-day Cửa Bắc), Hàng Than, and Hàng Bún, catching many more red-handed.

At a press conference on the July 16, after being invited to have a look at the proof of the Việt Nam Nationalist Party's crime at number 7 Ôn Như Hau Street, Acting President Huỳnh Thúc Kháng labelled them as robbers, scoundrels, and villains in the name of "nationalists." He then added:

> Solidarity is needed to develop a democratic republic, but no one can use solidarity as a facade or a pretext for illegal actions. I call on every party and national to be united. The recent search is necessary for the sake of public security; it was not done out of political infightings between parties. We live within the same legal framework. It is also in the

interest of the nation and the respect for law that I will have to bring to justice those who acted illegally.

Also on this occasion, after discussing matters with the Acting President and the Secretary General and getting their approval, Võ Nguyên Giáp ordered his men and the local armed forces in the midland, Northwest, and Northeast of Việt Nam to work with mass organizations to proselytize the enemy to disintegrate their forces, while attacking the reactionaries who were occupying many parts of Vĩnh Yên, Phú Thọ, Yên Bái, and Lào Cai provinces, and mining areas. The revolutionary government was gradually restored on an increasingly large area, giving the people a first chance to live in freedom. As he paid an inspection trip to some of the midland provinces in early August, Võ Nguyên Giáp was extremely moved to see his countrymen living happily after being emancipated from the repression of the foreign aggressors and their Vietnamese lackeys.

The French and international progressive press spotted a striking coincidence. General Leclerc was recalled at exactly the same time with the failed coup d'état in Hà Nội, which was brought to public knowledge. As early as in those days, many of the French journalists had raised the question of whether the Commander-in-chief of the French Expeditionary Corps was dismissed and had to leave Sài Gòn on July 19 because of his failure to "pacify the South in matters of weeks" or because of Valluy's unsuccessful coup d'état in the North. Forty-two years later, this question found an answer from Philippe Devillers.[1] According to him, the abortive coup d'état should be attributed to General Valluy, author of the Contingency

---

1. Philippe Devillers: *Paris-Saigon-Hanoi*, op cit.

Plan 2 dated April 10, 1946, in which he mapped out a plan and assigned tasks to the French commanders in Tonkin (North Việt Nam). The purpose of the plan was to turn a purely normal military activity in the first place into a coup d'état. The middle of July marked a change in Valluy's military career: from the position of Commander of the French Expeditionary Corps in northern Indochina, he became the Commander-in-chief of the French Expeditionary Corps all over Indochina. Therefore, this abortive coup d'état allegedly dealt a heavy double blow to Valluy in both his previous and current positions.

The reality showed that Valluy, as a loyalist to the Paris administration's policy of "reoccupation," before becoming the Commander-in-chief, had been an effective aide of d'Argenlieu in nullifying all agreements between France and Việt Nam and rejecting all negotiations to expand the war, both covertly and overtly.

"A French Attack will Only Be a Matter of Time..."

Following their abortive coup d'état, the French continuously attempted to trigger conflicts. In August 1946 alone, they deliberately caused recurrent provocations on the Đuống Bridge and the Đuống Bridge-Bắc Ninh route, and then illegally occupied Bắc Ninh Town, about 30 kilometers to the north of Hà Nội. Next came provocations in the northeastern coastal region. In the northwestern direction, the French troops from Sơn La started a southward encroachment. Particularly perilous was their instigation of tariff-related problems in the port of Hải Phòng.

The complicated developments of the war constantly occupied Võ Nguyên Giáp's mind. Many a night he stayed up very late to examine the situations and find commensurate solutions to deal tactfully with France along the strategic line of "Conciliate to Advance." He was all the more occupied when the *Sự thật* (literally: Truth) Publishing House insisted that he try and finalize the two works synthesizing the experience of the pre-upheaval period, namely *Khu giải phóng* (literally: Liberated Zone) and *Kinh nghiệm Việt Minh ở Việt Bắc* (literally: The Việt Minh Experience in Việt Bắc) on the occasion of the first anniversary of the August Revolution. Steeped with the guiding principle suggested by President Hồ Chí Minh, Võ Nguyên Giáp tried to exert self-control and avoided making the atmosphere more intense. Furthermore, when coping with the French provocations in Bắc Ninh, he not only sent cadres to solve the problem on the spot, but also met Crépin[1] personally to talk the French out of blatant violations. During a discussion to settle the conflicts in Bắc Ninh, this French military officer not only refused to establish a reconciliation committee but also created a tense atmosphere, which prompted Võ Nguyên Giáp to give a blunt message that, "If you want peace, you'll get peace; if you want war, you'll get war." Apart from this occasion, Võ Nguyên Giáp mostly attempted to tone down his voice and show a humble attitude. Western journalists in Hà Nội noted Giáp's compromising attitude when he saw Valluy to the Commander-in-chief's office in Sài Gòn, joined Crépin in laying a wreath at the Martyrs' Monument and attended a party organized by the French to commemorate victory over German fascism, and welcomed General Louis-Constant Morlière, French Commander in North Việt Nam, to Hà Nội to replace Valluy.

---

1. Jean Albert Emile Crépin: Commander of the French army in Tonkin from July 1946.

As the first anniversary of Việt Nam's independence was nearing, Võ Nguyên Giáp called on the whole army to be on full alert and make necessary preparations to protect the revolution's results should the enemy force the Vietnamese people to rise in arms. From the experiences in the South during the past year, he had sufficient grounds to believe in the ultimate victory of the protracted war. Later Võ Nguyên Giáp wrote:

> The first birthday of the Democratic Republic of Việt Nam coincided with the first anniversary of fighting in the South. Initial difficult days have passed. We no longer had to retreat in face of the enemy massive attack. The South had grown mature after one year of fighting, readying themselves to launch staunchest counter-attack against the enemy. In the first place, the French Expeditionary Corps from Sài Gòn dispersed to urban areas and then spread to the rural areas. Now, they are being driven out of the vast rural areas back to Sài Gòn . . . . Some of the French military commanders' illusion of a quick battle and quick victory has vanished. Our people and army in the South now know how to strike the enemy, dragging the French Expeditionary Corps into the quagmire of a long war.

Reading the "Order for the Day" in a mass rally at Chí Linh Park (Hà Nội), Võ Nguyên Giáp reminded the general public of the significance of the Independence Day of September 2. He commended the armed forces across the country and emphasized that although the Vietnamese national defense guards were fledgling, they had scored glorious victory. It was because they learned not only from the experience of their contemporary comrades but also from their ancestors

Chapter Two: SIXTEEN MONTHS IN THE CAPITAL CITY

in the past. This included Trần Hưng Đạo's[1] strategy of using a small army against a huge one, Lê Lợi's[2] tactics of protracted war, Quang Trung's[3] outstanding military strategy, Hoàng Hoa Thám's[4] tactics of guerrilla warfare in mountainous areas, and Nguyễn Thiện Thuật's[5] tactics of guerrilla warfare in the lowland.

Giáp called on the entire Vietnamese army to uphold and build on the tradition of the revolutionary army by constantly learning and upgrading competence, while standing on full alert against the provocative acts of the enemy.

In the previous year's Independence Day ceremony, there was no parade because all they had was a Liberation Army unit which had been back from the military zone, with war booty being clothes confiscated from the security soldiers and machinery being rudimentary. In this year's ceremony, however, they had the service of a regiment consisting of three complete National Defense Guard battalions with improved equipment, uniforms, yellow-star-sided caps,

---

1. Born Prince Trần Quốc Tuấn, Trần Hưng Đạo (1228–1300) was the Supreme Commander of Việt Nam during the Trần Dynasty, who commanded the Vietnamese army to repel three major Yuan Mongolian invasions.
2. Lê Lợi (1384 or 1385?–1433), posthumously known with the temple name Lê Thái Tổ, was emperor of Việt Nam and founder of the Later Lê Dynasty.
3. Emperor Quang Trung (1753–1792), born Nguyễn Huệ, was the second emperor of the Tây Sơn Dynasty of Việt Nam, reigning from 1788 until 1792. He was also one of the most successful military commanders in the Vietnamese history.
4. Hoàng Hoa Thám (1858–1913), also known as Đề Thám (Colonel Thám), was the Vietnamese leader of the Yên Thế insurrection, holding out against French control in northern Việt Nam for 25 years.
5. Nguyễn Thiện Thuật (1841–1926) was a Vietnamese revolutionary leader who commanded armed forces during the anti-colonial struggle.

and leather footwear. After the parade, these battalions proudly marched past the rostrum against the background of military music. With the parade and showcase on the morning of September 2, 1946, the National Army officially made its debut in front of the Government and the general public, and demonstrated their maturity and readiness to enter a protracted war. No one could have imagined that not until nine years later, on January 1, 1955—the day when the capital city was regained, did the sons of Hà Nội and of the whole country have a chance to organize a parade to report to President Hồ Chí Minh, the Government, and the whole people their achievements in the resistance war against the French, the most resounding of which was the Điện Biên Phủ victory.

Võ Nguyên Giáp felt the need to call on the Vietnamese people in general and the Hanoians in particular to remain on full alert in the face of the increasingly blatant and wicked plots of the French. Gone were the days when the country was hanging by a thread. In the South, the developments in the battlefield had tilted in our balance. In the North, the two hundred thousand Chiang Kai-shek troops had left, famines had been reduced, and millions of poor people had become literate. Although the life of the people remained hard, their living standards had generally improved and the society had changed radically under the new democratic regime, which had been time-tested and gone through a lot of ordeals. However, the possibility of peace between the two countries was still limited, as the French remained assertive and aggressive in the Fontainebleau Conference while provocative in many local battlefields throughout Việt Nam. It was obvious that one of the most urgent tasks at this time was to put the whole people and army on full alert to ward off potential invasion by the French. Minister of Interior Affairs Võ Nguyên Giáp discussed with Minister of Information and Communication Trần Huy Liệu, and the two concurred that it was necessary to address in front of a rally as massive as possible in order to remind the countrymen, especially youngsters, of President Hồ Chí Minh's warnings on September 2, 1945: "My fellowmen, peace is not yet totally guaranteed." Upon the recommendation of Trần Huy Liệu, Võ Nguyên Giáp called to invite Trần Văn Hà[1] to the Palace of the Resident-superior in Tonkin. He said:

> The death anniversary of General Trần Hưng Đạo is coming.[2] Please make preparations for my speech at the Opera House. Could you get a copy of Trần Trọng Kim's *Việt Nam sử lược* (literally: A Brief History of Việt Nam), read carefully, and make notes on the margin of important parts in the book? Also, please prepare for me an about-two-page-long outline of main ideas, bullet points only but clearly written.

Fifty years later, Professor Trần Văn Hà recalled that meeting with General Giáp:

> As he stood in front of a map of the Trần Dynasty's anti-Mongolian war during the 13th century, Brother Văn's voice

---

1. Trần Văn Hà was then Director of Hà Nội Information and Communication Service. Although he was not a former student at Thăng Long School, he got to know the General since the days the latter was teaching in Hà Nội. This event was recounted by Professor Trần Văn Hà 55 years later in an article of the *Tiền phong* (literally: Vanguard) newspaper published at the end of August 2001.
2. Trần Hưng Đạo passed away on the 20th day of the eighth lunar month in 1300.

was eloquent, now deep with the Diên Hồng Congress[1], now enthusiastic with the Battle of Bạch Đằng.[2] The audience burst into wild and ceaseless applause. The Opera House of Hà Nội was packed with people that day.

When Võ Nguyên Giáp associated the current happenings in the country with those in the Trần Dynasty in the face of Mongolian invasion, obviously referring to the deadlocked Franco-Vietnamese talks as the French would not stop provoking and encroaching, Trần Văn Hà noticed that in the audience "many people held one another's hands firmly, their hearts burning with patriotism. All of them wanted to make concerted efforts to do something for their country."

Similar to the days he spent in the highland areas of Cao Bằng-Lạng Sơn before, Võ Nguyên Giáp tried his best to give the people as much knowledge as possible, so that the army and the locals could fight back-on-back against the enemy on the threshold of historic moments that marked the turning point. This was characteristic of a man who always put political activities before military actions.

About half a month after the Independence Day anniversary, the Standing Central Committee was well informed of the fundamental content of the Modus Vivendi of September 14, 1946 that President Hồ Chí Minh signed

---

1. The Diên Hồng Conference, convened in 1284 by Emperor Trần Thánh Tông, was an assembly of notables considering the resistance against the Yuan Mongolian invasion.
2. The Battle of Bạch Đằng took place in 938 in the Bạch Đằng River, near Hạ Long Bay in northern Việt Nam. At this battle, the Vietnamese forces, led by Ngô Quyền, defeated the invading forces of the Southern Han state of China and put an end to the centuries of Chinese imperial domination in Việt Nam.

with the representative of the French Government. In an issue published on September 20, an article on the *Sự thật* wrote:

> When he signed the Modus Vivendi, Hồ Chí Minh wanted to see the Franco-Vietnamese relations further improved compared with the March 6 Preliminary Accords and the ties between the two democracies more friendly, aiming at a higher level of solidarity. The President knew that signing an agreement with the French might help to reconcile the Franco-Vietnamese tensions and allow us to gain some more time to make necessary preparations while awaiting a better opportunity. It also aimed to show the French colonizers that our nation was keen on negotiations with the French, thus generating the support of the general public in France and in other free nations.

As early as during these days, it was understood that the September 14 Modus Vivendi served only to solve and satisfy mostly the parochial economic, financial, and cultural problems and demands of France, and failed to meet satisfactorily the basic demands of Việt Nam in terms of political independence and territorial unity.[1]

Given the virtual inevitability of war, one of the most urgent tasks was making military preparations while "awaiting a better opportunity," as had been written in the Party's newspaper.

One day at the end of September, General Secretary Trường Chinh and Secretary of the Central Military

---

1. Ministry of Foreign Affairs of Việt Nam: *Đấu tranh ngoại giao trong cách mạng dân tộc dân chủ nhân dân* (literally: Diplomatic Struggles in the National, Democratic, and Demotic Revolution), Internally circulated documents, vol. 1, p. 221.

Commission Võ Nguyên Giáp listened to Chief of the General Staff Hoàng Văn Thái report on the military preparations made during the past few months. Unlike previous briefings, Võ Nguyên Giáp instructed that the report prepared by Hoàng Văn Thái this time synthesized organizational situations and the real combat competence of the whole army on which the Standing Central Committee could base to prepare for the forthcoming national military congress.

It was also this day five years before, on September 7, 1945, only five days after the Independence Day ceremony, that Hồ Chí Minh tasked Võ Nguyên Giáp and Hoàng Văn Thái with the establishment of a general commanding body for the whole army. Hoàng Văn Thái said he did not dare to take up the position of Chief of the General Staff as he admitted having no previous experience in this area. Hồ Chí Minh said that other members of the Cabinet, including himself, had never had any experience in assuming power. He added that they currently had a government and an army, so they necessarily needed a commanding body. The President encouraged Hoàng Văn Thái to "learn as we do" and asserted that with the leadership of the Party and the support of Giáp, they could definitely build a commanding body capable of directing the revolutionary army in the face of new situations. The first Chief of the General Staff of the Vietnamese revolutionary army took the advice of President Hồ Chí Minh to "learn as we do" and spent a year acquiring from the most basic things, such as the number of every unit and arms of the enemy, the methods of organizing the commanding engine, directing the departments, and performing specific tasks like forming Southward units or keeping abreast of the situations of both their forces and those of the enemy, in the battlefields and in the rear. He also learned a great deal in negotiations with the French military officers and how to make them respect the agreements. Now sitting in front of the General Secretary and the Secretary of the Central Military Commission was a Chief of the General Staff who had had an initial understanding of strategic counselling, a modest and conscientious comrade in whom Võ Nguyên Giáp placed his whole trust.

According to the report by the Chief of the General Staff, the National Army now numbered 82,000 (a year-on-year increase of 32,000), divided into 32 regiments and 11 independent battalions. To meet continuous combat requirements, the Southern and Southern Central Coast battlefields still maintained the battalion mode. The artillery had installed their first base, which was the three artillery platoons in the capital city of Hà Nội, including five 75-mm anti-aircraft guns confiscated during the General Uprising and turned into field guns. The information and communications system in the whole army, albeit rudimentary and lacking, had functioned smoothly from the central to local levels, including the Southern battlefields. The whole country had about a million self-defense guards and guerrillas. To the north of the 16th parallel, the self-defense guards were made up of the mass armed forces who served importantly to limit many provocative acts of the French troops in the areas where they were allowed to station. The two-pronged leadership from the Central Military Commission and Ministry of National Defense to the localities had been reinforced. With around 8,000 Party members in the whole army, the Party-related and political issues among core soldiers had been completed from the central to local military commissions. Logistics, then known as supplies, with three components namely military supplies, military weaponry, and military medicine, had successfully performed its function of guaranteeing the daily life and combat material needs of the soldiers. The staff officers had become a system functioning from the ministry level to the zone and regiment levels, although their specialized experience and knowledge remained lacking and limited. The whole country was divided into 12 military zones,[1] and even those where fighting had not broken out had prepared their own separate fronts and rears once the war spread out. Answering the questions of the General Secretary about the staff, the Chief of the General Staff reported that apart from the politico-military institutes at the zone and regiment levels, which trained local staff, the Party Central Committee had already opened the Hồ Chí Minh Self-Defense Cadre Training School, Bắc Sơn Politico-military School, Trần Quốc Tuấn Military Training School, and Quảng Ngãi Infantry Secondary School. The Tông Military School of Sơn Tây, which was responsible for training battalion-level cadres, was about to conclude its first cohort and commence a second one. In terms of training content, due the paucity of well-designed materials, the schools had to resort to lectures on tactics prepared by the French, Japanese, and Chinese Chiang Kai-shek armies. However, under a directive issued by the Chairman of the Military Commission Association, all the schools had to research and teach guerrilla tactics, based

---

1. The North included the 1st, 2nd, 3rd, 10th, and 12th Zones and the 11th Special Zone (Hà Nội); the Central Coast included the 4th, 5th, and 6th Zones; the South was made up of the 7th, 8th, and 9th Zones.

on a book titled *Cách đánh du kích* (literally: Approach to Guerrilla Warfare) compiled by President Hồ Chí Minh. The last point the Chief of the General Staff reported was that the General Staff was directing the whole army to redress the shortcomings identified in the recently held Congress of Central Cadres on the preparations for military readiness.[1]

In a follow-up report, Võ Nguyên Giáp talked about the division of tasks between the Military Commission Association and the Ministry of National Defense following the establishment of the Resistance Coalition Government. The implementation of the presidential ordinances had important effect in the division of staff from central to local levels and in managing the soldiers who had step by step become regular. The recent development and maturity of the army was largely attributed to the Party Central Committee's ability to overcome budget tightness to provide the army with increasing equipment based on the support of the people. The urgent training of cadres, which resulted in thousands being promptly sent to grassroots units, had to some extent met the urgent needs of the army in its process of preparing the armed forces which would stand ready for combat.

To prepare for the upcoming military congress, General Secretary Trường Chinh and Secretary of the Central Military Commission Võ Nguyên Giáp discussed in greater detail the unity of the central-level military leadership body and tasks to be implemented, so that the armed forces could

---

1. One of the most useful lessons in the recent spring-summer campaign shared in the Congress of Central Cadres held between July 31 and August 1, 1946, was the "excessive trust in the Preliminary Accords, to the point that hindered active attacks."

be ready to switch from peacetime to wartime. An important final conclusion was that the French could well instigate an all-out war, and the ultimately crucial military task for the time being was not to put themselves in a strategically passive position.

On October 19, at number 56 Nguyễn Du Street, Hà Nội, the National Military Congress took place under the chairmanship of General Secretary Trường Chinh. This was the first ever large-scale military congress held under the new democratic regime. Apart from the central members and key cadres at the General Headquarters, commanders of zones from the 4th Zone northward were also in attendance. The Congress was held at a time when the negotiation in France had ended in failure. President Hồ Chí Minh was on his way back, while French provocative acts continued to be incessant in the North. Regarding the Modus Vivendi of September 14, the Congress concurred that commanders at all levels had to explain to the soldiers that it was only an ad hoc agreement, so it was necessary to make better preparations and be on higher alert for war. The Congress emphasized the need to be constantly vigilant so that their army would not be taken aback by any enemy's surprise attack. Their policy was to maintain friendly ties and avoid provocations, yet in the event of an enemy's attack, they would definitely fight back in self-defense, while trying to prevent conflicts from spreading. Based on the conclusion that "a French attack will only be a matter of time, and we have no choice but to fight back," the Congress decided to call on the whole army and people to make all necessary preparations in the event of a comprehensive war. With regards to internal issues of the army, the Congress decided to combine the leadership and commanding bodies into one; attach special importance to personnel issue;, improve the quality of national defense guards, militia, guerrillas, and self-protect guards; and consolidate Party cells in the army to serve as the core for higher levels of leadership. With regards to enhanced discipline, solidarity, and Party spirit, the Congress concluded that mistakes were inevitable during their cause and therefore raised the need of carrying out self-criticism and self-rectification. The Congress also mentioned the strengths and shortcomings that needed correcting. Finally, the Congress called on every participant to watch out for an "ease of mind" attitude and lack of vigilance, and encouraged the whole army to be "confident that although we were technologically inferior, we would definitely emerge as victors with our resilience and elasticity."

Hardly had the Congress concluded when there was news from Hải Phòng: the Dumont Durville battleship on which President Hồ Chí Minh and his envoy were travelling had reached Bến Ngự, Hải Phòng. Early the following morning, Võ Nguyên Giáp, on behalf of the Government, made for the port city to welcome back President Hồ Chí Minh. Then he escorted the President and his envoy on the train to Hà Nội, which departed at 10 am on October 21, 1946. At 3:15 pm that day, the special train reached Hàng Cỏ Railway Station and was greeted on the platform by a delegation of National Assembly deputies, Cabinet members, and mass organizations headed by Acting President Huỳnh Thúc Kháng. French General Louis-Constant Morliere was also present, together with an honour guard and a band of military music sent to the station by the French Command.

Before mounting the car to get back to the Palace of the Resident-superior in Tonkin, Hồ Chí Minh greeted and thanked the people who came to welcome him back. He also talked to the French soldiers in honour guard. On a later occasion, as he recalled the atmosphere with which President Hồ Chí Minh was greeted on his return from France, Võ Nguyên Giáp wrote:

> The whole country was overflowed with joy, with everyone's face beaming with happiness to see their president back safe and sound. That bliss was also radiant on his face. With him at the helm, the Boat of the Fatherland would definitely brave the winds and waves to advance.

When the Enemy was Bent on War

At its second plenum convened from October 28 to November 9, 1946, the National Assembly decided to merge the Military Commission Association and the Ministry of National Defense into the Ministry of National Defense-General Command, with Võ Nguyên Giáp as Minister.[1]

Based on the spirit and the words of the Modus Vivendi, on October 26, Commander-in-chief Võ Nguyên Giáp instructed the Vietnamese armed forces in the South to begin a ceasefire at 0:00 am on October 30 while sending a diplomatic note to the French asking them to do the same. In his reply, General Valluy said he had ordered his men

---

1. Ordinance 230 dated November 30, 1946 by President Hồ Chí Minh read, "Conferring the Commander-in-chiefship of the National Army and Ministership of National Defense on Võ Nguyên Giáp. From this moment onward, Võ Nguyên Giáp is to assume the role of Minister of National Defense cum Commander-in-chief. In Party-related issues, Võ Nguyên Giáp continues to be Secretary of the Central Military Commission."

to stop firing and sent General Nyo, who was appointed by d'Argenlieu as Head of the French Military Mission, to the North to discuss the establishment of the Joint Franco-Vietnamese Military Committee.

On November 4, General Morliere took Nyo to greet President Hồ Chí Minh. Participants at the reception also included Võ Nguyên Giáp and Deputy Minister of Interior Affairs Hoàng Hữu Nam. Three days later, in the first working session of the Joint Franco-Vietnamese Military Committee, the Vietnamese side accused the French troops in the South of not only violating the ceasefire but also widening their terrorist acts in many places. Through negotiations, many of the issues stipulated in the Modus Vivendi or agreed to between President Hồ Chí Minh and Admiral d'Argenlieu in Cam Ranh on October 18 were all rejected by the French. From the very beginning, France deliberately neutralized and nullified the Joint Franco-Vietnamese Military Committee. That explained why the Committee failed to prevent French provocations, the most typical of which were their occupation of Lạng Sơn Town and the so-called "Hải Phòng incident" on November 20. According to Lacouture and Devillers, the tariff problem in Hải Phòng Port was only a pretext that the French relied on to trigger conflicts and occupy the port city.[1] The whole story dated back long ago, from the meeting between Prime Minister Bidault and General Valluy in Paris several weeks earlier. Valluy was given the green light by the Prime Minister "to open fire." That decision suited both Valluy and d'Argenlieu, so while former directed and fabricated

---

1. Jean Lacouture: *Hồ Chí Minh*, Seuil, Paris, 1967; Philippe Devillers: *Paris-Saigon-Hanoi*, op cit.

the incident in Hải Phòng, the latter made a fuss that "Việt Minh's too insolent to be tolerated." Here is what Philippe Devillers recounted in the tenth chapter of his book *Paris-Saigon-Hanoi* about the thing he wished to say:

> The details of the Hải Phòng incident have been narrated in many works so far, and this is not the right time to recount its developments. However, it is necessary to specify stages to place it within the context of extremely sensitive ongoing political situations . . . . They (i.e. Lami and Hoàng Hữu Nam who had been sent from Hà Nội) had to negotiate and painstakingly reached a ceasefire. Signing a ceasefire is already difficult; getting it respected and implemented is another story, due to the arrogance of Colonel Pierre-Louis Debes, who was commander of the French troops garrisoned in Hải Phòng. In fact, Debes even secretly nullified and abandoned the efforts made by his senior General Morliere and his political advisor Colonel Lami. Debes had the feeling that he was protected by General Valluy, while the latter had surpassed even Morliere, who assumed highest military responsibility in the North, to make a direct phone call to Debes. He ordered Debes to firstly force the whole regular and paramilitary forces of Việt Nam to withdraw from Hải Phòng and secondly to make sure that the French troops could be freely garrisoned in the capital city. Despite Morliere's efforts to make Valluy well aware of the risks he might suffer for his requirements, the latter said, "The détente initiatives no longer work . . . . . It's time to teach Vietnamese troops a just lesson . . . . With all conditions in hand, you have to seize control of Hải Phòng . . . ."

Finally Devillers concluded that Commander-in-chief Valluy embarked on the adventure without even bothering to ask for instructions from the Government, and thus dragging the whole country with him. From this moment onward and throughout the ensuing 35 years (before the archives were deciphered and the truth was uncovered as to which side harboured ill intentions in the first place), what Valluy made up as "our enemy covertly harboured a different scheme" remained the official view of the French government with regard to the First Indochina War.[1]

Despite the numerical and technological imbalance, the armed forces of Hải Phòng were able to fight courageously for seven days in a row (November 20–26). The Battle of Hải Phòng, including a glorious victory in which the Vietnamese armed forces killed scores of enemy troops, confiscated almost all of their weapons and supplies and archives, and took control of Cát Bi Airport from November 23–26, served as a "grand rehearsal" for the protracted battle in the capital city about one month later.

Confronted with the possibility of the enemy widening their aggressive war all over the country, Võ Nguyên Giáp focused all his mind on instructing the implementation of the resolution of the recent National Military Congress. Of all the tasks that needed attending to, the most immediate and urgent issue was to find out the best way to strike the enemy inside urban areas, especially in Hà Nội, as part of efforts to switch the country and the army from peacetime to wartime. The Standing Central Committee had approved his proposal

---

1. In a report dated January 30, 1947 titled "Political and Military Incidents in Northern Indochina during the Last Quarter of 1946," General Morliere admitted that the occupation of Hải Phòng meant "a complete breakdown of the Preliminary Accords of March 6, 1946 and the Modus Vivendi of September 14, 1946," and that "the incident of Hải Phòng showed clearly that France had chosen to use force." See Georges Chaffard: *Les deux guerres du Vietnam* (literally: The Two Wars in Việt Nam), Table Ronde, Paris, 1969, p. 36.

to appoint Vương Thừa Vũ as Commander of the Hà Nội Front (or the 11th Zone) and Trần Độ as Political Commissar. By the end of October, General Secretary Trường Chinh urged Vương Thừa Vũ to fulfil the two following strategic tasks for Hà Nội: 1- Stand ready at all time to guard against surprise attacks and be prepared to strike if and when the enemy "change their faces"; 2- Hold up the enemy in the city for as long as possible, preventing them from expanding the war to external areas thus giving the whole country enough time to switch to wartime.

In the additional directive, Commander-in-chief Võ Nguyên Giáp highlighted the special importance of city-defense guards who according to him should try their best not to fall into the provocative trap of the enemy.

He was fully sympathetic to the difficulties of the Hà Nội Command. In the course of national defense globally, arguably few countries have to fight an enemy who was living among their own population in the same city like in Hà Nội and many other towns in the North. In Hà Nội and Gia Lâm alone, the enemy occupied as many as nine major locations and 43 smaller ones, thereby forming an intertwining position with the Vietnamese army and blocking off many parts of the city. Many important targets, such as the electricity and water factories, train stations, banks, and Long Biên Bridge, were under the guard of both Vietnamese and French troops. Moreover, the enemy occupied other adjacent positions, such as the Majestic Cinema (present-day August Cinema), which was opposite the Central National Defense Camp at number 40 Hàng Bài Street, and the Metropole Hotel (present-day Thống Nhất Hotel), which was opposite the Palace of the Resident-superior in Tonkin (present-day Government Guesthouse), from which they could control many of Vietnamese important targets. Given the proximity of the enemy and the urgency with which the Vietnamese side had to make preparations, sometimes on the spot, for war, it was hard to reconcile the conflict between standing ready for fighting on the one hand and trying not to be seen as being provocative on the other hand. Also given the huge gap that Võ Nguyên Giáp dubbed "an era gap" between his country's army and that of the enemy, an issue of crucial significance for the Vietnamese side was how to strike.

According to the resolution issued in the National Military Congress and the strategic outline of the Standing Central Committee, Võ Nguyên Giáp instructed Chief of the General Staff Hoàng Văn Thái and the Advisory Board to quickly finalize the combat plan on a national scale for what was later called by Giáp as an "all-out battle." The first task was to assist the Command of the 11th Zone to develop and carry out the plan of the Hà Nội Front, the key battlefield of the whole country at this time. Võ Nguyên Giáp spent a lot of time discussing with Hoàng Văn Thái and Vương Thừa Vũ all the eventualities of war in Hà Nội and their corresponding solutions. Giáp normally brought the following questions to his two associates' attention: "How will the enemy strike, even in a surprise attack?" and "How shall we respond, so that we can at the same time kill and hold up the enemy while preserving, nurturing, and developing our forces in preparation for a protracted war?"

While the operational method and plan were taking shape in the minds of Hoàng Văn Thái and Vương Thừa Vũ, Võ Nguyên Giáp suggested that they read an article by

189

General Secretary Trường Chinh on the *Sự thật* published in early December on the tactics of strike in urban areas. In this article, the author shed light on many issues, such as the policy to rely on popular support (people-based approach), preparations for war, strike tactics, sabotage, breakage of the enemy's supply route, and particularly the active-responsive-consecutive guiding principle. The author affirmed that, "The guerrillas have to fight to survive; those who remain in one place and stop fighting will only end in self-destruction." Võ Nguyên Giáp proposed that his two comrades examine the possible application of this strategy into the specific conditions of Hà Nội, especially the people-based policy and the active-responsive-consecutive principle.

After more than a month of preparation, and following repeated amendments and adjustments, the final version of the combat plan of the Hà Nội Front was approved by Minister of National Defense cum Commander-in-chief Võ Nguyên Giáp. It had the following main contents:

1- Based on the enemy's deployment, the Vietnamese side was able to predict that right from the beginning, the French would use combat troops to take control of their four most important targets: Long Biên Bridge, Palace of the Resident-superior in Tonkin, Town Hall, and Hàng Cỏ Railway Station.

2- The overarching principle was to be proactive in attack, defense, and withdrawal after the completion of fighting inside the city.

3- In order to implement the aforesaid principle, the whole city was divided into two operational zones, which fought reciprocally against the enemy from inside and outside. The 1st Zone (also known as the 1st Interzone) covered most of the area of what are now the districts of Ba Đình and Hoàn Kiếm, where geographical positions were conducive to long-day resistance within the city; the 2nd Zone included the 2nd and 3rd Interzones and the remaining land of the capital city.

4- The 1st Interzone, with two National Defense battalions (the 101st and 145th battalions), five tank-attack suicide squads, and 3,000 City Protection militiamen, was developed into a combat center, a vital battlefield of the city. It was expected that after three days of fighting and attrition against the enemy, the forces of the 1st Interzone would shrink for a long-day battle on a ready-made locality.

5- The 2nd and 3rd Interzones, with three National Protection battalions (including the 77th, 212th, and 523rd battalions), eight tank-attack suicide squads, and about 5,000 City Protection militiamen, would reach out to the main city entries after about three days of fighting and launch surprise attacks every night to disturb and disperse the enemy, forcing them to thin out their forces to respond and making it hard for them to occupy the city.

After approving the plan, Commander-in-chief Võ Nguyên Giáp instructed Chief of the General Staff Hoàng Văn Thái and Chief of the 11th Zone Vương Thừa Vũ to quickly check and review all the necessary preparations in every aspect. All such tasks as deploying forces, preparing firing targets for artillery fields, organizing command headquarters and information systems, preparing immunity points, making holes in the walls to connect houses to secretly deploy troops, preparing logistics for combat and daily activities, and researching the building of a subterranean tunnel system from the inner city areas to the outside to facilitate secret and safe withdrawal when requested were supposed to be completed by the middle of December. The erection of barricades and the preparation of equipment had to be made ready for deployment and utilization whenever the General Staff requested, especially on main routes and axes adjacent to the enemy. The launching of a substantial diversionary attack[1] would be undertaken by the two provinces abutting on Hà Nội, namely Sơn Tây and Hà Đông, under the direction of the General Staff.

On the afternoon of December 13, after chairing the Conference of Zone Chiefs, which involved the participations of the chiefs of zones from Bình Trị Thiên northward, to check preparations made by the localities, Commander-in-chief Võ Nguyên Giáp became assured of the preparations for the switch from peacetime to wartime. While in the middle of November Giáp, having been asked by Hồ Chí Minh how long the Vietnamese armed forces could keep Hà Nội, could only modestly promise to keep it at least a fortnight, now after examining the experience of Hải Phòng, he could raise his estimate of the soldiers' ability to retain the capital city. On December 17, after a meeting with the Cabinet Council, Giáp reported to Hồ Chí Minh that Hà Nội could be sustained for at least one month. The President then asked, "What about other cities?" "We can keep them longer," Giáp replied. The President continued, "What about the rural areas?" "They definitely won't be lost," Giáp answered.

---

1. About 20,000 militiamen and guerrillas from the provinces of Sơn Tây and Hà Đông were mobilized to march into the inner city area at dusk and secretly retreat at dawn in seven days in a row so as to divert the enemy's attention and wrong their estimation of Vietnamese combat troops.

Hồ Chí Minh reaffirmed an issue which had been approved by the Standing Central Committee that they would return to Tân Trào. About half a month earlier, Nguyễn Lương Bằng had been tasked by the President with making comprehensive preparations for the transference of the capital city when necessary.

Since early December, the French had conducted provocations, thus tensing the situations in Hà Nội. Meetings between representatives of the Vietnamese and French governments, including even the meeting on December 3 between the Vietnamese representative and Sainteny, who had just returned from France, had failed to bring about any significant improvements in the overall situations. The bellicose French in Indochina were trying fish in the troubled water of the French political situations to make continued encroachment. By the middle of December, many signs indicated that war was almost unavoidable. Therefore, Hà Nội was like a gunpowder store that could go off at any time.

The Day Before the War Began

Assigned by the Party Central Committee, the Government, and President Hồ Chí Minh with defense-related issues, including finding out the right answer to the military problems of overall strategic importance at a time of burning fire and boiling water, Commander-in-chief Võ Nguyên Giáp spent many a night working late with Chief of the General Staff Hoàng Văn Thái. As a 35-year-old man, highly spirited, lucid-minded, and physically fit, especially added by the regular and timely instruction from President Hồ Chí Minh and the support of the Standing Central Committee, Võ Nguyên Giáp was able to survive the hardest and most intense work throughout the week before the war officially broke out. News from Hải Phòng showed that the French military officers had just gathered in the port city to discuss an early move. This was part of Commander-in-chief Valluy's intention of "immediate strike," which had been approved by Prime Minister Bidault the previous month.

After chairing the Conference of Zone Chiefs and instructing the agencies to advise battlefields on how to finalize and expedite the combat plan, the Commander-in-chief focused on working for many days with Commander of the Hà Nội Front Vương Thừa Vũ to finalize the combat plan of the key battlefields. On some occasions, the two had to return to some certain streets to double-check the feasibility of the combat plan. On December 16, Giáp went on an inspection trip to the artillery field at Láng in order to check the possibility of turning the operation of 75-mm guns into that of field guns. Even the Láng Fortress—a battlefield nicknamed the "eldest brother" of all fortresses with the task of firing the first bullet upon order—had only two anti-aircraft guns. The Commander-in-chief encouraged the artillery soldiers not only to perform well the role of land-based guns, but also to try to investigate and make further renovation (for example, the barrels of the guns must be able to be lowered to fire straight at the enemy when necessary), while doing their best to preserve and retain weapons.

Leaving the Láng Fortress, Võ Nguyên Giáp told the chauffeur to take him to the the Voice of Việt Nam (then located in the Trầm Pagoda neighbourhood), where he checked the technical preparations and reminded the staff to ensure the safety of the people and machinery throughout the process of moving to the revolutionary military base and to maintain regular and uninterrupted service. He asked the head of the radio station to immediately make necessary technical and personnel preparations to broadcast "a special document."

On December 17, after receiving the first ultimatum of the Command of the French Expeditionary Corps, Võ Nguyên Giáp felt the need to lay bare their faces as bellicose reactionaries to the whole world and to call on the Vietnamese people and army to stand ready for war against the enemy's wicked plot. Giáp rang the editorial board of the *Cứu quốc* (National Salvation) and asked to speak to Xuân Thủy, but the latter was away on business and one of his colleagues Hoàng Hà was on the other end of the line. Giáp read to Hà the translation of the French ultimatum and asked him to publish it on the newspaper as soon as possible. Hồ Chí Minh had left the city on November 26 and sojourned in one of the bases near the Canh Crossroads. On December 3, he returned to Vạn Phúc Village near Hà Đông Town, about ten kilometers to the southwest of Hà Nội. It was in this place that on December 18 he chaired the Open Conference of the Standing Central Committee in order to assess the situations and map out new guiding principles under the new circumstances.

Võ Nguyên Giáp later retold in his book titled *Những năm tháng không thể nào quên* (literally: Unforgettable Years) that before the Conference, President Hồ Chí Minh asked about the crops, the destruction of traffic routes to prevent the enemy, and "if the soldiers have enough rice to eat should war erupt." He was glad to learn that in many places this year, the farmers were having fruitful crops and more food to eat than the previous year thanks to propitious weather. The districts in the vicinity of Hà Nội and other provinces had already gathered sufficient rice for the soldiers, and every village had set up their own supply team. During the Conference, the participants concurred that given the current situations, there was no longer any chance for peace, and that the more concession they made, the more the enemy would press on. Their people could not go back to the life of slavery again. Once the war broke out, the whole country would go through a prolonged struggle, but would eventually emerge as victors. As proposed by Hồ Chí Minh, the participants at the Conference contributed their ideas to his draft of the Appeal for National Resistance. Also, with high unanimity and determination, the Standing Central Committee approved an important decision related to the fate of the whole nation which was to launch a resistance war against the French aggressors on a national scale.

No sooner had Võ Nguyên Giáp returned to Hà Nội from Vạn Phúc than the phone rang. On the other end was a French who identified himself as Jean Julien, Head of the Franco-Vietnamese Liaison and Control Committee. He told Giáp that he had just called Hoàng Hữu Nam and Phan Mỹ, but no one was on the phone. Having heard that the French officer wanted to see him to propose some ideas about the Franco-Việt Minh relations, Võ Nguyên Giáp agreed to a personal meeting. He believed that even during these urgent moments, when the enemy had delivered an ultimatum, it was still important to learn more about their attitude. No one would have known about this conversation if French General Jean Julien Fonde himself had not recounted 25 years later in his book.[1]

---

1. Jean Julien Fonde: *Traitez à tout prix—Leclerc et le Vietnam* (literally: Treat at All Costs—Leclerc and Việt Nam), Robert Laffont, Paris, 1971; *Tạp chí Lịch sử Đảng* (literally: Journal of Party History), December 2001.

Chapter Two: SIXTEEN MONTHS IN THE CAPITAL CITY

Jean was very glad to be given a personal rendezvous with Giáp, and he was even more surprised to learn that Giáp was still in Hà Nội at that time. The Vietnamese liaison officer took the French officer to a room on the second floor, which a few minutes later Giáp entered with a guarded smile. Getting a cup of tea from his interlocutor, Jean made an excuse for his sudden arrival without prior announcement. He said, "Mr. Chairman,[1] I have not forgotten the words you told me the day I came to see you after I took office, that I could see you any time when it was necessary. Today, the urgent situations have prompted me to come here, in my capacity as Head of the Franco-Vietnamese Liaison and Control Committee, without the knowledge of even the Commander-in-chief and Republican (he implied Valluy and Sainteny) and my associates."

Giáp listened attentively, but with a straight face. The French officer began to complain about the roads being destroyed and the barricades blocking the movement and supplies of the French troops. He also mentioned what he called "the excessive actions of self-defense guards and policemen," which fuelled the hostility and suspicion between the two sides. Giáp remained silent; he still listened but no longer wore even a diplomatic smile. Jean continued, "Some days ago, I had a chance to talk to Hoàng Hữu Nam and Phan Mỹ, but there was no improvement in the situations. The tragedy is still looming. The Franco-Vietnamese Liaison and Control Committee can no longer fulfil its functions, and I think that you have not been reported the entire story."

---

1. Jean was addressing Giáp by his position as Chairman of the Military Commission Association.

"The stories I got reported to were complete and full," Giáp said in an angry low voice.

"But Mr. Chairman, our soldiers need to eat, drink, entertain, travel, and breathe. Where would we go then?"

"It's none of my concern."

"These are the most basic and vital needs. They cannot be repressed for too long, or else they will erupt."

"As you wish."

"Mr. Chairman, this situation can't go on any longer. Something must be done soon. I know what war is like, a lot of casualties and losses. Cities, industrial centres, and facilities will be destroyed. You must try to prevent these tragedies from befalling your country."

"Aren't these problems what you French want to see? We have made up our mind, and there's no way we'll make further concessions. There will definitely be destructions and losses, but our determination for national independence and unity is clear. Millions of Vietnamese may fall, but France will also lose its men. That's certain, and we're all prepared."

Võ Nguyên Giáp then stopped and was about to rise when Jean tried to make another point. He said, "France wants peace. According to the Modus Vivendi, negotiations are slated within less than a month. Việt Nam is very near independence, and the whole world is making enormous strides. What will happen in one or five years' time? Mr. Chairman, please wait for the opportunity and avoid any irreparable damage and loss."

"All of these happenings are your own wish. There have been numerous talks between France and Việt Nam, but after

South Việt Nam come the Central Highlands, Hải Phòng, and Lạng Sơn. And the repeated ultimata during the last few days. That's the end of it. We will never make any further concessions," Giáp said. Then he rose, extending his hand for a diplomatic handshake. The conversation ended.

The Commander-in-chief had demonstrated unequivocally the determination of the people and government of Việt Nam. That determination derived from the recurring provocations during these year-end days. There are Vietnamese sayings like "The tree craves calm, yet the wind keeps blowing," and "Once the water is overflowed, the river bursts its banks." Today, reading again such books as *Hồ Chí Minh—Biên niên tiểu sử* (literally: Hồ Chí Minh—A Chronological Biography) and *Thư ký Bác Hồ kể chuyện* (literally: Stories Told by Hồ Chí Minh's Personal Assistant), one can see clearly that although the Franco-Vietnamese relations were aggravated almost beyond repair following the Hải Phòng incident, Hồ Chí Minh still tried tirelessly until the early days of December to keep peace, even when there were only slight beams of hope, as he wanted to avoid an all-out war. The letter addressed to the French Government and Parliament on the December 6, the diplomatic note dated December 13 to the French Government and Admiral d'Argenlieu, the message sent to French Prime Minister on December 15, the meeting with Moffard (Director of Asian Affairs Agency under the United States Department of State), the interview with the *Paris-Saigon* on December 7, and that with the *New York Times* on December 14—all indicated the goodwill of the Vietnamese people to work with France to avoid a war, but all of the efforts from the Vietnamese Government had gone unheeded.

December 19 was the busiest day for the General Headquarters and Commander-in-chief Võ Nguyên Giáp, when the French sent its third ultimatum after three consecutive days. They demanded to disarm the self-defense guards of Hà Nội and requested a moratorium to all the preparations made on the Vietnameses part as well as the right to control the security of the whole city under the pretext that "Việt Minh police officers are helpless." In the morning, Hồ Chí Minh sent his personal assistant Vũ Kỳ to bring to Võ Nguyên Giáp a letter which he intended to ask Hoàng Minh Giám to pass on to the French representative Sainteny. At midday, Võ Nguyên Giáp received a phone call from Hồ Chí Minh asking him to come immediately to Vạn Phúc for an urgent meeting. As Giáp arrived, he saw the President and some other comrades in the Standing Central Committee talking in group. Vũ Kỳ had just returned to inform the President that Sainteny put off seeing Hoàng Minh Giám until the next day on the grounds of feeling unwell. The following day would be December 20, the time French planned to act according to what was said in their December 18 ultimatum. As it was written in Vũ Kỳ's diary, Hồ Chí Minh seemed to have uttered something like "If you want war, then as you wish." As Devillers put it, once "the machine of war was kicked start, it would work in a most barbarous way," when the last span of the peace bridge was broken by the French themselves, and it was little wonder Hồ Chí Minh made such an utterance. That spontaneous utterance by Hồ Chí Minh had gone down in history.

Leaving Vạn Phúc after the discussion of the Standing Central Committee, Võ Nguyên Giáp arrived at exactly 2 pm (six hours before the guns of war finally went off) at

Bạch Mai where the Command Headquarters of the 11th Zone was located. He and Trần Quốc Hoàn—special envoy sent by the Central Party Committee—double-checked the preparations made for war and officially assigned the armed forces of Hà Nội with combat tasks. In attendance at this historic moment of the capital city to listen to the Commander-in-chief officially issue the order of fighting were Chief of the General Staff Hoàng Văn Thái, Secretary of the 11th Zone Party Committee Nguyễn Văn Trân, and the whole Command of the Hà Nội Front. After that, from Bạch Mai, Võ Nguyên Giáp made his way back to Vạn Phúc. He felt confident to report the situations of the whole country and Hà Nội to President Hồ Chí Minh and the Standing Central Committee before the opening of fire. Then Trường Chinh, Lê Đức Thọ, and Võ Nguyên Giáp listened for the last time to the Appeal for National Resistance against the French, which President Hồ Chí Minh had made amendments based on the feedback gathered.

As Võ Nguyên Giáp came to bid farewell to Hồ Chí Minh and the Standing Central Committee to come back to the Command Headquarters, the President reminded him to make sure that the orders to the battlefields were exact, confidential, and timely. Giáp responded, "Please rest assured, Uncle. This has been taken care of by the Information and Code Department of the General Staff, under the supervision of Hoàng Văn Thái."

It was common knowledge that the General Staff at that time was only in its seminal stage, so transferring such an important telegram to the battlefields nationwide at the same time was a completely new task for the information officers, and they needed close instructions. In the Conference of

Zone Chiefs on December 13, the Commander-in-chief concurred with the zone chiefs that once the Party Central Committee had made up their mind, the Advisory Board would send telegrams to the battlefields twice. For the first time, a general announcement would be made, but no specifics were given; the second time, the exact time for the whole country to open fire, later became known as "the G hour," would be specified. The Commander-in-chief had instructed the Chief of the General Staff to personally supervise and monitor closely this most important task. The operational body of the General Staff and the chiefs of staff at zone level carried out a "rehearsal" together for subsequent smooth cooperation.

At about 9 am on December 19, the first telegram was codified and sent, with the following content:

> To zones and fronts,
>
> The French bandits have sent an ultimatum demanding to disarm us. Our Government have dismissed that ultimatum. Consequently, within no more than 24 hours, the French is bound to open fire. The Party Central Committee instructed everyone to stand ready.
>
> December 19, 1946
>
> (Signed)
>
> The Standing Central Committee

The second telegram was sent in the afternoon, when Sainteny refused to see Hoàng Minh Giám and President Chí Minh had made the final decision. The content of the second telegram was more succinct, and there was no signature at the end:

> To the 1st, 2nd, 3rd, 4th, and 11th Zones and Đà Nẵng,

The freight will arrive by 18:00 on December 21, 1946. The goods will be coded A+2 and B-2. Remember to collect them on time.[1]

In *Nhật ký một bộ trưởng* (literally: A Minister's Diary), Lê Văn Hiến wrote that after the working session around 16:00 that day, Văn (i.e. Commander-in-chief Võ Nguyên Giáp) released the final news, which was the news about the kick-off time. Only one hour later, the Commander-in-chief, accompanied by Trần Quốc Hoàn, Hoàng Văn Thái, and Vương Thừa Vũ, headed to Ô Chợ Dừa and then Khâm Thiên Street to inspect the onsite situations of a random unit before the G hour. From the moats and trenches came the sound of a mandolin, an atmosphere typical of the elegant Hà Nội. They went to even the self-defense unit stationed at the near end of Khâm Thiên Street, and then Hàng Lọng Street (present-day Lê Duẩn Street), talking to railway workers and self-defense guards and taking memory photos with them. The soldiers who were preparing for the first battle may not have known whom they were talking and taking photos with.

Saying goodbye to everyone, Võ Nguyên Giáp headed for Hà Đông.

At exactly 20:00 on December 19, the Voice of Việt Nam broadcast the order of combat issued by Minister of National Defense cum Commander-in-chief Võ Nguyên Giáp to the armed forces all over the country. The order read:

Our Fatherland is in peril!

---

1. By a convention agreed upon among the zone chiefs during the conference on December 13, 1946, "A" represented "time" and "B" was for "day," so "A+2" meant "18:00 plus 2 equaled 20:00" and "B-2" meant "21 minus 2 equaled 19." Therefore, the date for opening fire would be 20:00 hours on December 19, 1946.

The crucial hour has struck!

According to the directive issued by President Hồ Chí Minh and the Government, in the name of Minister of National Defense and Commander-in-chief, I order the whole army, national protection guards and militia from north to south to rise unanimously.

Let's march to the front, killing the bandits to save our country!

Sacrifice ourselves to fight until the last drop of blood!

Annihilate the French colonizers!

Long live our independent and unified Việt Nam!

Long live our victorious resistance war!

Fight until the end!

December 19, 1946

(Signed)

Võ Nguyên Giáp

As he recollected one of the most significant moments in his military life, Võ Nguyên Giáp wrote half a century later in his memoir:

> From Tây Mỗ[1] Village about ten kilometers from Hà Nội, I awaited anxiously for this moment. Hoàng Văn Thái was constantly sitting next to the telephone of the Ministry installed in the town of Hà Đông to keep abreast of the operational situations, and he was supposed to report to me every two hours.
>
> 20:00 hours
>
> 20:03. All the lights in Hà Nội went out. The cannons and guns roared from the Láng Fortress. Immediately

---

1. Some documents named the village as Tay Tuu.

after that, the whole Hà Nội resounded with the sound of guns.

General Secretary Trường Chinh later in his work *Kháng chiến nhất định thắng lợi* (literally: The Resistance War is Bound to Succeed) described that historic moment as "a sky-shooting strength which resulted from the long suppression in the heart of our nation."

On the morning of December 20, in the village of Tây Mỗ, through the radio, Commander-in-chief listened to the Appeal for National Resistance written by President Hồ Chí Minh to people of all the three regions of the country. The staff at the radio station had made very careful technical preparations, so the voice of the broadcaster was extremely clear:

> All compatriots,
>
> As we desire peace, we have made concessions. But the more concessions we make, the more the French colonialists press on, for they are bent on robbing our country once again. No, we would rather sacrifice all than be enslaved.
>
> My fellow countrymen, we have to stand up![1]

Some days before in Vạn Phúc, Commander-in-chief Võ Nguyên Giáp and the Standing Central Committee had had a chance to listen to President Hồ Chí Minh himself read the Appeal for National Resistance, and together they showed their unanimous determination at the historic moment of the nation. As he listened to the appeal today on the radio, however, he was still greatly moved in a way he himself found hard to explain. That feeling of extreme passion may

---

1. *Hồ Chí Minh toàn tập* (literally: Hồ Chí Minh's Complete Works), op cit., vol. 4, p. 480.

have resulted from his role as the Commander-in-chief of the whole army to the sacred call of the nation. He and his beloved soldiers were about to embark on a comprehensive all-out war with the enemy.

Chapter Three

EARLY CHALLENGES

Keeping Abreast of the Developments in the Main Battlefields

Newspapers and books published in France and elsewhere in the world later confirmed that French troops stationed in Hà Nội and other Northern cities did harbour an intention of staging a pre-emptive strike against the Vietnamese forces on December 20. According to Philippe Devillers, Sainteny and his French military colleagues in Indochina observed that given the Hải Phòng incident, the Franco-Việt Minh no longer stood any chance of reconciliation, and there could be no compromise between France's interest and the existence of the Hồ Chí Minh government. The Vietnamese side could not afford to lose Hải Phòng and Lạng Sơn to the French by making concessions. Neither could they accept France's ultimatum-like conditions. On their part, the French found it impossible to accept Việt Nam's request that they withdrew to their original place in Hải Phòng to restore the status quo before November 20. They therefore secretly made contact and agreement with local anti-governmental elements, intending to establish a pro-French government. The only outstanding issue, also a minor and simple one for the French, was to stage a coup d'état. According to their assessment, "the Việt Minh bastion remains weak and can easily collapse even after the first major defeat." At this point in time, there was news that the pro-war cabinet of Georges Bidault collapsed, and that Léon Blum formed a new government on December 16. The French in Indochina was driven into a corner by the news. They believed that this Socialist Party prime minister would be intent on making peace with the Việt Minh, and consequently they felt the need to act immediately to put the other side into a fait accompli to prevent the imminent negotiations between the two "comrades," Léon Blum and Hồ Chí Minh. They, however, did not want others to lay bare their faces as the invaders. Moreover, in early December, reliable intelligence sources indicated that the Vietnamese side was preparing for an attack, but the French, as Sainteny later admitted, did not know when the conflict would break out. The French were taken by surprise when the Việt Minh troops opened fire right before the moment the French decided to take action. The Command of the French Expeditionary Corps had never imagined that they some day would be put in a disadvantageous position and cornered by their rival.

Reports made by Chief of the General Staff Hoàng Văn Thái from an on-standby telephone station installed in Hà Đông Town served to keep Commander-in-chief Võ Nguyên Giáp abreast of the fighting in the streets of Hà Nội during the night of December 19. From their headquarters in the Citadel of Hà Nội, the French troops were deployed into different directions to counter the Việt Minh troops, and this was what had been anticipated in the combat plan of the Command of the Hà Nội Front. The Commander-in-chief paid special attention to two battles. The first one took place on Tràng

Thi Street, when the his troops took the enemy by complete surprise, appearing out of no where to throw grenades, open fire, and use bombs to kill the French and destroy their tanks at the beginning of Tràng Thi Street. In the second one, his troops pushed back the enemy from Hàng Đậu Street to Long Biên Bridge, laid ambush to destroy two armored cars, one tank, one jeep, and some dozens of French soldiers. The results from these battles soon confirmed the efficiency of what Commander of the Hà Nội Front Vương Thừa Vũ called "the bolt-drawing tactics"—stopping and killing the enemy right in the street. The first conclusion that Giáp made was that it was possible for the Vietnamese troops to lay ambush against the enemy right in the middle of the city.

The following morning, while the Chief of the General Staff went to the Láng Fortress, Commander-in-chief Võ Nguyên Giáp and Special Envoy of the Party Central Committee Trần Quốc Hoàn paid a visit to the Headquarters of the Hà Nội Front. At this time, fierce fighting was going on around the Opera House, the Palace of the Resident-superior in Tonkin, and the Post Office of Hà Nội. Accompanied by General Vương Thừa Vũ to Ô Chợ Dừa and Khâm Thiên Street, General Võ Nguyên Giáp looked carefully at some of the enemy's positions at the beginning of the street and talked to the local self-defense groups. Although he was assured by the preparations, he reminded General Vũ to instruct his men to reinforce the ramparts by adding more layers and digging more trenches to facilitate the movement of the troops during combat. He also asked them to disseminate the useful experience and good practices of Tràng Thi and Hồng Phúc Junction, so that comrades in other streets could apply and win.

What concerned the Commander-in-chief, following his observations of the developments of the battle during the night of December 19 and the realities at the Khâm Thiên front, was the huge technological and numerical difference between his army and the enemy. Neither the Hà Nội Front nor the General Command had any substitute or additional forces available in hand. Moreover, Hà Nội as a special zone needed a more stable rear which was able to provide the front with prompt reinforcements when necessary. Since it was a real concern in his mind, Giáp thought of a way out: he would propose that the Standing Central Committee should merge the Hà Nội Front with the 2nd Interzone. Accordingly, Hà Đông and Sơn Tây would serve as the direct rear zones of the Hà Nội Front, while the eight provinces of the 2nd Interzone would provide material and human reinforcements for the fronts, including not only the Hà Nội Front but also Hà Đông and Sơn Tây in the long run. In the immediate future, the Commander-in-chief decided to send two battalions of the 2nd Zone to serve as substitute forces for Hà Nội, while immediately building up a substitute regiment for the General Command. Each zone-level command also needed to have one battalion in hand. Thanks to his thorough understanding of the developments in the battlefield, Giáp managed to solve the problem at a macro level after only several days of fighting: the problem of building up the rear for the front battle and the substitute forces for both the General Headquarters and each zone, firstly the Hà Nội Front.

On the evening of December 20, Trường Chinh and Võ Nguyên Giáp listened to Hoàng Văn Thái report on the developments of the battlefields nationwide after one day of fighting. Unlike Hà Nội, many provinces failed to open fire promptly, due to not only the shortage of communication devices but also the limited organizational skill of the commanding cadres. In the case of Hà Nội, however, Giáp and his comrades believed that with the recent positive results from battles, the Vietnamese troops could withstand the enemy attack and remain in the city for a long time.

Back to the General Headquarters, the Commander-in-chief discussed his planned mergence of the 11th and 2nd Zones with the General Secretary and received the latter's agreement. Both agreed that the plan would soon be brought to the Standing Central Committee for further discussion.

On December 25, after nearly one week of fighting, Chairman of the 11th Zone Resistance Committee Nguyễn Văn Trân and the Command of the Hà Nội Front were summoned to Vạn Phúc. After listening to reports on the overall situations, Commander-in-chief Võ Nguyên Giáp announced the decision to merge the 11th Zone with the 2nd Zone to accommodate the most recent developments of the war. The 2nd Zone remained under the leadership of Hoàng Sâm and Lê Hiến Mai as its commander and political commissar respectively, but it would now have Vương Thừa Vũ and Trần Độ as its deputy commander and deputy political commissar respectively, who served dual role respectively as commander and political commissar of the Hà Nội Front. From that day onwards, the Hà Nội Front became the front of the 2nd Zone, with a spacious rear and a substantial force which could participate in alternating battles while serving as a mobile force to provide added tactical support to the soldiers protecting the capital, thereby guaranteeing enhanced combat skills and laying protracted siege against the enemy. In his recollection, Vương Thừa Vũ later reaffirmed the sensibility of this decision. And that was the reason why he and Trần Độ, when asked by the Commander-in-chief what they thought about the merging plan, replied in one voice, "We are so delighted. We vote for the plan with both hands."

Commander-in-chief Võ Nguyên Giáp alerted the Command of the Hà Nội Front to the upcoming possible scenarios of the war. Earlier there had been news of the French government sending both Minister of Overseas France Marius Moutet and General Philippe Leclerc on an inspection tour to Indochina in order to find a way out for the French. It was highly likely that they would dispatch reinforcements. And once reinforcements had arrived, the enemy would be bound to launch major attacks on the suburbs of the city. Therefore, the Vietnamese side needed to make necessary preparations if and when the battles were expanded. It was important for them to decimate the French army and prevent the latter from marching to the suburbs while trying to preserve their force and brace themselves up for a protracted war.

By the middle of January 1947, their troops had been successful in holding back the enemy for more than three weeks, far longer than the originally expected two-month period. In order to draw out useful lessons and good practices after recent battles and instruct officers on different fronts on the preparations needed to enter the next phase of the grand battle, the General Headquarters convened the First National Military Conference.[1] Participants at the meeting included commanders from the 4th Zone northward and key cadres of

---

1. The Conference was known by the staff of the General Headquarters as the Chúc Sơn Conference as it was held from January 12–16, 1947, in Chúc Sơn Town, Chương Mỹ District, Hà Đông.

the Ministry of National Defense. General Secretary Trường Chinh also attended the Conference and addressed the audience on the Party's resistance policy.

In his speech at the Conference, Commander-in-chief Võ Nguyên Giáp remarked that, it was thanks to the pre-emptive strike strategy that the Vietnamese forces were able to kill part of the enemy's forces in Bắc Ninh, Bắc Giang, Cầu Đuống, Hải Dương, Nam Định, and particularly Hà Nội, maintaining a firm foothold on the battlefield and putting the enemy under constant threat for a long time. As a result, they thwarted the enemy's scheme to stage a rear attack and preserved the intactness of their forces. However, with the exception of Hà Nội and Nam Định, all of the provinces had failed to fulfil their tasks of scoring significant victories in the recent battles. The question arising then was "Why so?" It was because the enemy had anticipated their moves and thus made necessary preparations in many places to withstand their attacks. Apart from Vinh, most other places remained under the control of the enemy, whose core forces only suffered slight casualties. The Vietnamese side, due to lack of experience, failed to map out a detailed plan, give thorough instructions to their cadres and officers, and prepare their forces and commanding apparatus (including intelligence officers, scouts, coordinators, and especially transportation and liaison officers between Bắc Ninh, Bắc Giang, and Cầu Đuống who received orders too late although they were situated near the General Headquarters). The Commander-in-chief warned that after a long period of waiting for reinforcements, the enemy would turn the tide and start their attack to create favourable conditions for the implementation of their anti-revolutionary colonial policy. Accordingly, an enemy-occupied region and a revolutionary base would be established in the North. Confronted with this new plot of the enemy, the Vietnamese army was determined to maintain their gained position by sticking to the following strategies: 1- Avoid the spearhead of the enemy's core forces to preserve the combat power of their troops; 2- Launch guerrilla warfare and try to prevent the enemy from advancing rapidly and expanding the territory under the latter's control; 3- Concentrate their forces to wage a war of attrition against the enemy, killing the latter part by part while consolidating their forces and preparing for a protracted war until final victory was warranted.

The Conference spent a large proportion of its time discussing measures to redress the recent shortcomings and weaknesses in terms of the organization, commanding, and supervision of military men during wartime. For the participants at the Conference, these were new issues posed by the reality of the war. They were related to the building up and consolidation of both the regular army and militia, personnel and organization, cadre training, political education, troop management, the safeguarding of the people, the switching of the country's activities from peacetime to wartime with the help of the local authorities, and combat-related issues (such as sabotage, the scorched-earth policy, the elimination of brigands, and the war prisoner and booty policy).

Discussions at the meeting were alternated by presentations by General Vương Thừa Vũ on the Hà Nội Front's good practices during combat and methods of building force right in the middle of the war. There were also presentations by Director of the Transport and Sapping Department Hoàng Đạo Thúy on the development of the sapper force and the enemy's sabotage on the outskirts of the city. The whole meeting was extremely moved to hear Head of the Military Weapons Department Trần Đại Nghĩa confiding his emotions at the news of the heroic sacrifice of the Vietnamese soldiers when they rushed toward trying to destroy the enemy's tanks with three-pronged bombs. Then the hall became more excited when he talked of the possibility of producing bazookas and promised the Commander-in-chief and other commanders to try by all means to finish the first bazooka as soon as possible and be capable of mass-producing them no later than one month to come.[1] The whole conference hall burst into applause when Commander-in-chief Võ Nguyên Giáp rose up to shake hands and embrace him.

When Vương Thừa Vũ mentioned the establishment of the 1st Interzone Regiment, Võ Nguyên Giáp, in his capacity as Minister of National Defense cum Commander-in-chief conferred the title of *"Trung đoàn Thủ đô"* (literally: Capital Regiment) on it.

After nearly one month fighting, the Conference realized that there had emerged early signs of weaknesses in commanding, intelligence, and communications activities, thus failing to give effective instructions and command. However, due to time constraints, which prevented detailed discussion, the Conference agreed to the Commander-in-chief's suggestion that the Chief of the General Staff should be tasked with organizing a conference to draw out useful

---

1. The Director of the Military Weapon Department kept his promise. By the end of February 1947, following two test-fires in Ứng Hòa, two bazookas and ten bullets were technically completed and were placed at the disposal of the 2nd Zone soldiers. With these new weapons, two enemy tanks were destroyed near the Trầm Pagoda on March 5.

experience and redress the shortcomings in intelligence and organization activities, as well as raising political awareness in order to match the requirements of the new situations.

After only five days of the Conference, the General Command instructed the Advisory Board of the General Headquarters to complete an enormous volume of work for a short training course, which was to disseminate the first combat experience, redress the shortcomings and weaknesses in the fronts' organizational and instructional capacity and management of soldiers, and deliver instructions on the upcoming tasks to cope up with the enemy's new plots and moves. It was obvious that from the early days of the war, Commander-in-chief Võ Nguyên Giáp had a unique and original commanding style, characterized by his training of junior cadres to quickly narrow down the gap in ability between cadres at headquarters level and their colleagues at the fronts who were a few years earlier had served only as heads of squads and battalions and had never taken any regular military training. They were consequently limited in their ability to read the war and lead the army, especially when the battlefield involved a large area covering many provinces, despite their firm belief and political awareness.

For all the participants, the five-day Conference seemed too long a period. As the battles were taking place, the physical presence of the leaders and commanders was essential. As they left the Conference, the participants felt that since the Conference of Zone Chiefs on December 13, 1946, although they had participated in the battles for only a month and had attended only several days of experience sharing, they had become much better prepared to confront the renewed challenges.

As the Lunar New Year of 1947 drew near, two envoys sent by the Party Central Committee namely Trần Quốc Hoàn and Lê Quang Đạo braved the guns and shells of the battle to pay inspectional trips to the 1st Interzone. They were moved to witness how the soldiers of Hà Nội celebrated the Lunar New Year festival. On the New Year's eve, they took turns fight in battles and make preparations for the New Year party. The sounds of guns, land mines, and grenades mingled with the sounds of the firecrackers.[1] Most of them were spending their first Lunar New Year festival away from their loving family. They were partly compensated, however, by the warm camaraderie. President Hồ Chí Minh's New Year letter brought to their hands by the two government envoys were a huge and invaluable source of encouragement.

As the threshold of the New Year came, all the combat units erected makeshift altars, above which they hung the national flag and a photo of beloved President Hồ Chí Minh. On the altars were candles, scented incense sticks, some confectionery, and a small branch of peach blossoms. This was followed by the singing of the national anthem and salutations of the national flag by soldiers standing solemnly in front of the altar who then gathered together to listen to the New Year letter by President Hồ Chí Minh. All of them were moved to their hearts when the letter read, "I and other Government members could not have the heart to celebrate the Lunar New Year festival, as we are all thinking of you

---

1. On the eve of the 1947 Lunar New Year, serial battles took place around the Long Biên Bridge, North Gate of Hà Nội Ancient Citadel, Department of Forestry and Fishery, Town Hall, Hoàn Kiếm (or Sword) Lake Lighting Factory, Tavéc Roayan Hotel, Office of Transport and Public Works, the corners of Hàng Gai and Hàng Trống Streets. Land mines went off, shaking the whole street of Hàng Gai.

and the huge challenges you are undergoing." The letter then continued with commending words, which read, "You are the Suicide Squad. You've braved death for the nation's eternity. You are the finest representations of our thousand-year-long independence spirit."[1]

Listening to Trần Quốc Hoàn and Lê Quang Đạo's reports on the situations of the soldiers in the capital city, Hồ Chí Minh and his comrades in the Standing Central Committee and the Central Military Commission felt assured about the fighting spirit of the armed forces who were fighting day and night against the enemy in the streets of the capital city. After more than a month fighting and drawing experience, the soldiers succeeded in using small yet mobile units to search and attack the enemy by surprise to reduce the latter's forces while preserving their own. The soldiers themselves were developers of a special tactics referred to as "guerrilla tactics" in the heart of the city. This tactics was deemed well-suited to the reality and the conditions of their troops and those of the enemy's in Hà Nội. Given their bulldog fighting spirit and the effectiveness of their tactics, they would be able to withstand the attack of the enemy much longer than originally expected, if they were provided with both sufficient food and ammunitions.

The two men also reported to the Party Central Committee on the difficulties encountered by soldiers in the 1st Interzone. One of the causes was that after de-obstructing the 5th Route and receiving reinforcements from Hải Phòng, the enemy formed a siege encircling the 1st Interzone. However, the major

---

1. *Hồ Chí Minh toàn tập* (literally: The Complete Works of Hồ Chí Minh), op cit., vol. 5, p. 35.

Chapter Three: EARLY CHALLENGES

sources of difficulties came not only from the reinforcements of the enemy after the Lunar New Year festival, but also mainly from logistics-related issues. On January 15, as the Vietnamese and French sides agreed on a ceasefire for some of the Chinese and Indian nationals to get out, the 1st Interzone Regiment arranged for their fellow countrymen and some of the soldiers, especially the wounded, to leave the 1st Interzone and head for the liberated zone. Many of the soldiers tried every possible way to stay behind, which meant the number of troops after January 15 was not 500 as regulated by the General Command, but 800 instead.[1] Therefore, the difficulties in supplies were almost left unresolved. On the unique supply route, to import an amount of vegetable enough only for the wounded, the Lãng Bạc female transport squad even had to shed blood. Head of the Regiment Bùi Nguyên Cát encouraged the soldiers, male and female alike, to do their best to improve their own living conditions, which actually were deteriorating when the space for combat was narrowed down into an area of about one kilometer in diameter. There were places like in Hàng Gai, the enemy was stationed only one road apart from their troops. After examining the real situations, based on the spirit and the effectiveness of the soldiers' combat skills as well as the possibilities of solving the problems of supply and improvement of soldiers' lives, the Commander-in-chief had appropriate grounds to make a proposal to President Hồ Chí Minh to let the soldiers stay as long as the conditions would allow them.

---

1. Eight hundred people was in fact only the number estimated by the Hà Nội Command and the General Command to the best of their knowledge at that time. According to a later account by Political Commissar of the Regiment Lê Trung Toản, the official number of people who stayed behind was 1,200, including 75 children and 200 women.

Since early February 1947, the French army staged large-scale attacks on the 1st Interzone, beginning with strikes on the two buildings which are now Nguyễn Huệ Secondary School and Trần Nhật Duật Secondary School on February 6 and 7 respectively. These were two riparian areas, situated near the bank of the Red River. Were they to be occupied by the enemy, the Vietnamese side would lose the unique road that connected the 1st Interzone with the external areas. Therefore, the order from the General Command was for the Front to protect the two areas at any cost. Many of the enemy's attacks were defeated and the soldiers of Hà Nội were able to hold on to the ground and protect the linking road in the northeast of the city. The French then switched their attack to the multiple targets in the Old Quarter to the southwest of the 1st Interzone. They bombed many houses to rubbles and poured petrol down to set many of the streets on fire. Fighting broke out in every house, every segment, and every corner of the streets. After their attacks from the east and southwest failed, the enemy switched to the north and attacked the Đồng Xuân Market from February 11 onwards. Only after four days of intense fighting were the enemy forces able to occupy the market, but lost the even-number houses of Hàng Chiếu Street to the Vietnamese troops. This was the longest and most intense battle since the enemy focused their forces to attack the 1st Interzone after receiving reinforcements.

Whereas in the previous two times, respectively in the middle of January and following the Lunar New Year festival, the Commander-in-chief agreed to the proposal of the Front Command to let the Regiment stay behind for some extra time, this time, after the February 14 battle in the area of

Đồng Xuân Market, the Central Military Commission convened and concurred to propose to President Hồ Chí Minh and the Standing Central Committee to allow the Regiment to retreat out of the city. Knowing that his men had already successfully accomplished their mission in holding up the enemy for an extended period of time, Hồ Chí Minh and General Secretary Trường Chinh agreed to let the Regiment withdraw from the city. Right on the evening of February 14, the Front Command passed on the order from the Commander-in-chief to the Regiment, requesting that they withdraw right on the night of February 17, 1947. The military order was accompanied with some words of encouragement: "It is already a big victory that the Regiment is able to leave the 1st Interzone safely." Commander-in-chief Võ Nguyên Giáp also instructed the Chief of the General Staff to work with the Resistance Committee and the Front Command to review the plan to mobilize people's boats to collect soldiers at Tàm Xá and transport them safely across the Red River before taking them to Long Tựu Wharf in Đông Anh District. The Chief of the General Staff concurred with the Front Command to implement a withdrawing plan dubbed by General Vũ as "powerful attack-secret withdrawal." Specifically, the 2nd and 3rd Interzones were ordered to deploy their forces into such areas as Ô Cầu Dền, Cầu Giấy, Hàng Bột, and Kim Mã streets while mobile units were infiltrated into city center areas to strike the enemy in unison in every place, on the whole day of February 15, the whole night of February 16, and the early morning of 17 February, forcing the enemy to stretch out their forces in response, thereby creating enabling space for the Regiment to retreat secretly from the 1st Interzone.

During the whole day of February 17, the Commander-in-chief kept a close eye on the developments at the 1st Interzone, feeling no less anxious than the time he had been waiting for the gunfire to start two months before. On the morning of February 18, the General Command received the second telegram from the Front Command, reporting that the last unit of the 103rd Battalion had crossed the river. At noon, the Chief of the General Staff synthesized the latest developments and reported in detail that the withdrawal of the Regiment had been completely successful and all the soldiers had crossed the river safely. The Commander-in-chief immediately sent the Regiment a commendation letter which read:

> Dear fellow commanders and soldiers of the Capital Regiment,
>
> On behalf of the entire National Army of Việt Nam, I would like to commend the bravery of the soldiers, who have fought during the last couple of months to uphold the national flag right at the center of the capital city of Hà Nội. Our soldiers have demonstrated the resilience of the Vietnamese people and the glorious reputation of the National Army of Việt Nam.
>
> You have successfully escaped from the siege of the enemy and exited intact. You will continue to fight for the Motherland. We will keep fighting for ten years, or even longer if necessary.
>
> Till the day our Motherland is independent and unified.
>
> Till the day Hà Nội becomes the capital city of an independent and unified country.
>
> We pledge to annihilate the enemy.
>
> Long live the resilient spirit of the Capital Regiment!

Long live the intrepidity of the Capital Regiment!

On February 20, Commander-in-chief Võ Nguyên Giáp and his associates Trần Quốc Hoàn, Hoàng Văn Thái, and Vương Thừa Vũ paid a visit to the Regiment which was then situated in Thượng Hội Village, Đan Phượng District, Hà Đông Province. As the Commander-in-chief and his colleagues entered the village, the soldiers had already gathered at the communal house. Everyone burst into applause when the Commander-in-chief and other comrades approached the guards of honour.

Later, in his memoir, General Giáp wrote:

> Never had I seen an army of such diverse backgrounds, including soldiers of all ages, from small children to people with greying hair. There were also quite many women, in various attires. The guards of honour stood solemnly, dressed in khaki clothes with their calots (overseas caps) attached with a red-and-yellow badge, red scarves, and submachine guns. The vast majority of the soldiers were dressed like ordinary people with blue workers' clothes, jackets, blousons, sun helmets, felt hats, and black and brown civil shoes, interspersed with the green shirts of the National Defense Guard. What they shared in common was the fact that they all brought weapons and had grenades and ammunition bags around their waists. Their faces were hardened by the smoke and fire of the battlefield, yet they still brimmed with intelligence and talent which characterized the youngsters of Hà Nội.

At the beginning of his address to the soldiers, the Commander-in-chief conveyed to them President Hồ Chí Minh's commendations. As he decided to let the Regiment withdraw the week before, Hồ Chí Minh said, "It's already a victory that you were able to hold the enemy up for up to a month. Now, as you are able to defend Hà Nội for two months, it is even a bigger victory." After praising the Regiment for having intrepidly fought against the enemy and held the latter back for an extended period of time in extremely difficult circumstances, the Commander-in-chief asserted that the Regiment's magic withdrawal this time by breaking the enemy's densely-laid siege marked another milestone for the nation's victories in the Red River. It was exemplary of the bravery, organizational capacity, and sense of discipline, aided by the support from people living in the riparian communes near the Red River. He presented a flag sewn with four golden words *"Trung đoàn Thủ đô"* (literally: "Capital Regiment") and said:

> On behalf of the Government, I'm officially presenting you with the title *"Trung đoàn Thủ đô"* (literally: "Capital Regiment"). Also on behalf of the Ministry of National Defense and the National Army, I'm presenting you with another flag embroidered with the same title to highlight your bravery and to mark this joyful day today.

The soldiers' joy and pride seemed to be doubled when the Commander-in-chief explained why President Hồ Chí Minh lauded the two recent months of fighting as "great victory." According to him, the Ministry of National Defense and the Command-in-chief originally had expected the soldiers to withstand the enemy's attack for only seven to ten days, and President Hồ Chí Minh had been informed of this estimation. Yet, as he had judged that the Regiment could hold on for a longer period of time, Hồ Chí Minh agreed to an extension of resistance time, and the fact transpired that the Regiment could hold on four times as long as had originally been anticipated. The whole Regiment, therefore, well deserved the commendations and encouragement offered by the President in his New Year letter: "You've braved death for the nation's eternity."

That night, a night of celebrations on the great deeds of Hà Nội's soldiers, the Commander-in-chief joined his men merrily singing in unison a song composed just now by one of the soldiers. Part of the song's lyrics read:

> Rồi ngày mai sẽ quay về đây / Sông Hồng reo sóng, đón mừng đoàn quân quay về
>
> (Literally: We will return to this place some day / Greeted by the Red River)

To everyone's knowledge, that "some day," as it later transpired, was October 10, 1954, when the Capital Regiment and the Great Vanguard Army, after a long march of nearly eight years, returned to Hà Nội amidst the wild applause of the people of Hà Nội who flocked the five city gates to welcome in the victors.

The following day, on his way from Thượng Hội back to Hà Đông, the Commander-in-chief confided with his colleagues Trần Quốc Hoàn, Hoàng Văn Thái, and Vương Thừa Vũ. The last 60 days, at the inception of the National Resistance War, witnessed a fierce battle between Vietnamese and French armies. Inheriting the fresh experience of Hải Phòng, coupled with the support of other fronts nationwide and particularly the prompt encouragement and instruction of the Standing Central Committee and President Hồ Chí Minh, the soldiers of Hà Nội had impressively succeeded in holding back the enemy and reducing their numbers in the urban areas of the capital city. In the history of the world military, that deed was hardly matched. Such a fledgling army as the Capital Regiment was able to confront for the entire two months against one of the world's most well-equipped and well-trained invading armies, in such a narrow expanse as the 1st Interzone. In addition, what was noteworthy was that before the battle started, the positions of the Vietnamese and French forces were always on a dovetailing sawtooth pattern in every street, every target.

The Vietnamese commanders shared with one another their own thoughts about what factors could be attributed to the fruitful results of the battle. First, as decided at the military conference in October 1946, the Vietnamese side had made proactive preparations and attacked the enemy on their own initiative. Had they failed to do that, the French army would have had the right to act, as Sainteny had warned earlier. Although the Vietnamese could have been blamed and claimed by the French that they were the ones who instigated the war, they firmly believed that the tireless, last-minute efforts made by President Hồ Chí Minh to avoid the war were all known to the progressive countries who would understand that this was a just war for the sole purpose of defense.

Second, the Vietnamese side had chosen the right tactics. Instead of being passive and waiting for the enemy to act first, their troops, be it an individual soldier or a small unit, proactively launched attacks throughout the 60 days and nights of the battle with bravery, intelligence, flexibility, and creativity, thus being able to weaken the enemy while preserving their own forces. In academic terms, Giáp and his colleagues realized the need for deeper research and concluded, that this battle could be called "guerrilla war inside the city" or "people's war inside the city." Before that, when they organized the evacuation of the urban dwellers out into the outskirts, people of all social strata and ages contributed their parts to the battle. The presence of photographers, musicians, and particularly female and under-age combatants was a clear indication of the pervasive and wide-ranging nature of the struggle.

Hoàng Văn Thái và Vương Thừa Vũ received order from the Commander-in-chief that the Operational Office of the General Staff should work with the Steering Committee of the Capital Regiment to make a summary of the newly-concluded 60-day battle, which was believed to contain an enormous source of experience which could be applied to the new and changing situations.

Transferring the Capital

From the first days of the national resistance war, one of the most central issues of the Command-in-chief was how to guarantee safety for the operations of the Government agencies, particularly President Hồ Chí Minh's activities around the southwestern and northwestern areas of Hà Nội. The French kept extremely close surveillance on the movement and the activities of the Government members, and in fact, on many occasions, they were able to gather correct information about the direction in which the Vietnamese commanders travelled.

One of the top concerns in the overall operations of the Government was to protect President Hồ Chí Minh and keep a secret of his whereabouts. By the middle of February, when the war had not widely spread out, Hồ Chí Minh decided to visit many localities, some of which were very far away, like Chi Nê, Ninh Bình, and Thanh Hóa. On some occasions, his shuttle trips made the General Headquarters really worried.

For example, only a few days after he had returned to Chi Nê from Thanh Hóa on February 21, 1947, and visited the workers and self-defense units at the note-printing factory (affiliated with the Ministry of Finance), there were reports of French air raids in Chi Nê. On an earlier occasion on December 24, no sooner had he chaired a meeting of the Cabinet Council in Hà Đông than the town was attacked by the French air force. On another occasion, hardly had the Cabinet Council finished their meeting in Chương Mỹ District on March 2 when the enemy launched an attack in the direction of Chúc Sơn-Trần Pagoda. Immediately in the afternoon of the same day, Commander-in-chief Võ Nguyên Giáp went to Viên Nội Commune, Mỹ Đức District, to brief the President on the latest developments in the battlefields and proposed that he should leave that night for Sơn Tây. Trần Đăng Ninh was tasked with accompanying the President.

In the early months of the resistance war, the Government worked with intensely-packed agendas, partly because of the need to lead the people from peacetime to wartime and to transfer gradually the leadership and the national assets to the revolutionary military base. The Cabinet Council met every fortnight, and their meetings (specifically those on January 21, February 2, February 16, and March 2, 1947) normally took place in the districts of Quốc Oai, Chương Mỹ, and Thạch Thất, which were either not very far from the battles or within bombing distance of the enemy. It was not until the first ten days of March that most of the Government agencies moved out of Hà Đông and Sơn Tây. The first meeting of the Cabinet Council was organized in the middle of March in a place relatively far away from Hà Nội, specifically in Chu Hóa Commune, Lâm Thao District, Phú Thọ Province—about 100 kilometers to the north of the capital city. During this time, the assets and materials owned by ministries and sectors were scattered along the roads or rivers of the midland areas to the north of Hà Nội. One of the most important tasks for the Vietnamese side was to protect the transference of the Government agencies and assets at a time when their front was widening and their army was confronted with a burning issue of finding an appropriate combat tactics.

After the Capital Regiment left Hà Nội, and particularly at the end of February, a new development occurred on the battlefield—the breakage of the front that affected significantly the transference of the Government agencies and facilities from the lowland to Việt Bắc. Complaints from these agencies were sometimes inevitable, especially when the front was widening. Among them were complaints from the Ministry of Finance, who were tasked with the transference of money, note-printing facilities, and rice and salt to the revolutionary military base. In a book titled *Nhật ký của một bộ trưởng* (literally: A Minister's Diary), former Minister of Finance Lê Văn Hiến wrote in the March 31, 1947 entry that:

> The situations are deteriorating. For the desire to protect the core forces, the Ministry of National Defense had a policy to withdraw and avoid mechanized attacks by the French, thus forcing many Government agencies, especially the Ministry of Finance, to move around, now here now there, in a hazardous manner…In today's meeting, there have been grievances and resentment about the army's failure to provide protection for other agencies.

Being genuinely interested in examining the combat tactics of the soldiers both when they fought in urban areas and when they withdrew from the city, Commander-in-chief Võ Nguyên Giáp was well aware of the causes for the front breakage and the difficulties encountered by soldiers in the front, the people living in fighting-affected areas, and the Government agencies situated in the vicinity. The front breakage phenomenon was totally different from the situations when the Vietnamese army intentionally and purposefully withdrew.

Why was there front breakage? Right at the military meeting in Chúc Sơn when the Vietnamese troops were still fighting in urban areas like Hà Nội, Nam Định, and Huế, the General Command had already predicted that the enemy would staged attacks and counter-attacks once they had been reinforced. As a result, he instructed the army to change the tactics, switching basically to guerrilla mobilization. The resolution of the meeting identified measures to develop forces, organize leadership, train soldiers, and prepare the people for war, creating all necessary conditions for the application of guerrilla mobilization. In the wake of the Chúc Sơn Conference, the military order on guerrilla mobilization issued on February 1 by the General Staff gave units instructions on how to better themselves in terms of information, intelligence, scouting, dispersion, concentration, and soldier mobility, thereby creating a enabling environment for the application of guerrilla mobilization tactics. Later, in the middle of February, during the Open Military Commission Conference and the National Political Commissars Conference, the issue of consolidating the Party and political organizations in the army was discussed so as to "take a firm hold on the army in any circumstances." It was during these conferences that Commander-in-chief Võ Nguyên Giáp reiterated the necessity of switching from battle-based guerrilla warfare to mobile guerrilla warfare, and requested that the national army should be consolidated as the core army and avoid being put under siege and subject to disintegration. To create favourable conditions for the application of mobile guerrilla while reducing the might of the enemy's mechanized tanks, the military report underscored the importance of mobilizing public support in destroying major traffic routes which the enemy could use, building trenches and combat villages, and observing strictly the scorched-earth policy of a resistance war.

In early March, alarmed by the sluggish switch to the above tactics in various fronts, the Commander-in-chief stopped in Thạch Thán Commune (Quốc Oai District, Sơn Tây) and composed a military directive on the necessity to switch to mobile guerrilla warfare. The directive criticized the clinging on to the battle-based guerrilla tactics where conditions for such warfare were nonexistent. Specifically, while the French side concentrated their forces, the Vietnamese side scattered their human resources and heavy weaponry; while the former laid siege, the latter established a defense line and waited passively for the enemy to come; while the former used mechanized weaponry, the latter did not make full use of their heavy weaponry and other measures such as sabotage and obstacles to reduce the power and speed of the former's tanks and mechanized vehicles. In addition, the Vietnamese side's intelligence activities were ineffective while information and communications were unstable. A major weakness of the Vietnamese side was their unpreparedness, lack of daringness, and failure to indentify correctly the purpose, intention and tactics of the enemy's attacks so that counter-attack plans could be made in response. These problems were coupled with indecisiveness and unresponsiveness. In other words, the Vietnamese commanders were not yet conversed in military tactics. The military directive issued by Giáp strongly requested that corresponding changes should be made and shortcomings redressed. All necessary preparations had to be made to switch boldly to mobile guerrilla warfare. This involved the concentration of soldiers and the elevation of their morale. Soldiers should march rapidly and secretly and attack fiercely where the enemy was weak or places they had just occupied and did not have time yet to fortify. Once attack had completed, it was necessary to withdraw immediately. Of course doing so meant land had to be abandoned in many places, so the mission would not be accomplished without decisive and bold decisions. In order for the mobile guerrilla tactics to be applied successfully, communications should be rapid and uninterrupted, intelligence should be exact and comprehensive, soldiers should be trained properly, and their equipment should be mobile and portable. The troops' activities had to be top secret and there needed to be a special task force whose job was to destroy the enemy's fighting vehicles by recourse to heavy weaponry and coordination with the local people to block rivers, destroy traffic routes, and set up obstacles to hinder the progress of the enemy's mechanized tanks. As for the orientation of activities, the directive stipulated that the deployment of some troops to assist the local militia must not affect the ability to concentrate large numbers of core soldiers for major battles. The directive concluded that:

> The strict observation of these rules plays an important part in guaranteeing the reputation of the army and the existence of the country. The immediate implementation of this directive is all the more crucial in areas where the

enemy has not occupied and especially those where the enemy's attack is imminent while our people and army were feeling confused. We cannot afford to let the enemy go rampant while our troops remain passive. It is crucial to talk to the units and gather the dispersed components, reinforce their spirit, and replace low-spirited individuals with more enthusiastic members to enhance the quality. It is important to immediately launch a major battle whose victory must be guaranteed so as to gain the momentum for the implementation of mobile guerrilla warfare.

By the middle of March, while the destruction of traffic routes, the setting up of obstacles, or the blockage of rivers had to a certain extent proved to be effective in slowing down the speed of the enemy's mechanized tanks and vessels, they also became deterrents to the movement of the Government agencies who were rapidly transferring assets to the revolutionary military base. As remarked by Minister Lê Văn Hiến, the news of these activities by the army came to him as a great shock, a "thunderbolt" to him as many of the assets and facilities of the Ministry of Finance were still left scattered along the roads and rivers. He had to seek consultation with the Ministry of National Defense and requested that they halt the destruction of traffic routes on some of the major axes from the midland to Việt Bắc.

Issues that were constantly on the mind of the Commander-in-chief included the front breakage, the limited result of the destruction and obstruction of traffic routes and the blockage of rivers, and the sluggish improvement in terms of tactics in all the fronts. Võ Nguyên Giáp thought day and night about the tactics adopted by the Vietnamese side and those of the enemy. He talked to the Chief of the General Staff about convening a meeting of zone chiefs to discuss tactical issues and asked the Operational Office to find ways to make the destruction and obstruction of traffic routes and blockage of rivers to hinder the progress of the enemy's tanks and mechanized vehicles more effective. He was also glad to learn from reports that in the first time put into use in real battles in early March, the two recently-produced bazookas successfully destroyed two enemy's tanks on the Chúc Sơn-Trầm Pagoda route. The news was greeted with a lot of joy and excitement among soldiers, technicians, and military weapon workers. Giáp, however, realized that it would be long before weapons like these could be mass-produced to meet the demand of the fronts.

As the Ministry of National Defense was moving to the revolutionary military base, Giáp stopped at Tiên Kiên Commune, Lâm Thao District, Phú Thọ Province, to organize a meeting of zone chiefs. This was the Second National Military Conference, known among the Vietnamese military advisors as the Tiên Kiên Conference, convened in two days, from March 25–26, 1947. For a fledgling army which were both poorly equipped and inexperienced, lessons drawn out after three months of fighting were many, ranging from the development of forces to match the reality of the battles to political awareness raising, and the establishment of the revolutionary military base. The most pressing issue, however, remained tactics, which consequently attracted the most heated debate in this military meeting.

The Conference realized that in the previous meeting in Chúc Sơn, despite having been able to predict correctly that the French would consolidate their occupation of cities and towns while expanding their attacks to strategic traffic routes once having been reinforced, the Vietnamese side failed to guess their method of troop advancement, the flexible tactics of their commanders, the power of their mechanized vehicles, the coordination between their infantry and military vehicles (such as tanks, mechanized vehicles, airplanes, artillery, vessels, and amphibious vehicles in aquatic environments.) The reality in the battlefields from Huế northward showed that when they deployed their troops, the enemy normally combined front attacks with seeking and returning flanks, forming huge pincers to strike their opponent troops from the back or from flanks. In addition, they also combined small-scale activities of small, mobile and secret units in small areas with large-scale marches, taking advantages of rivers and roads to attack their opponents with mechanized vehicles on a large area. In terms of defense, the enemy also proved to be a seasoned and well-trained army, as evidenced in their building of fortifications, digging of trenches, arrangement of curtain-fire, mounting of guards, and storage of materials and equipment for prolonged battles.

One important conclusion made at the Conference was that after several months fighting, the Vietnamese troops had reached a new level of maturity. Although they were inexperienced originally, they were now able to draw useful lessons, some of which cost them blood and equipment, about the reasons for their failures and the advantage of the enemy in terms of commanding and technology. It was apparent that the battlefield was the best school for their cadres and soldiers. The ones that helped them become mature in battles were their enemies themselves.

What did the Vietnamese army learn after the three months of fighting? In terms of defense, soldiers should be made mobile and placed on stand-by, and they should be trained to take advantage of geographical features, set up fortification structures, place landmines, and lay ambushes; commanding cadres should learn to make predictions as to how the enemy would strike in their attacks, so that they could make necessary corresponding responses, and use decoy troops. In terms of attacks, it was necessary to always take proactive position, using attacks as one method of defense, as rigidly sticking to the preservation of core forces to the extent that hinders attack would amount to being passive and subject to disintegration.

The most enthusiastically debated issue was measures to counter the enemy's mechanized vehicles. It was concurred by participants at the Conference that:

On the one hand, it was necessary to build more obstacles and destroy roads to slow down the progress of the enemy. In order to reduce their number, however, it was important to deploy troops near the obstacles or in key road segments that had been destroyed in order to kill the enemy straight away when they were made to stop in these areas.

On the other hand, it was vital to form teams that specialized in destroying the enemy's tanks and mechanized vehicles by using landmines, or special task forces that were equipped with bazookas or heavy machine guns to strike the enemy's mechanized vehicles while serving as supporting units to coordinate with infantry.

The Conference emphasized that it was crucial to redress the ongoing weaknesses in both attack and defense. Planning needed to be done in a careful and meticulous manner to be always proactive in every situation. Simultaneously, it was advisable to make intelligence activities more effective and maintain more stable communications and better training for the soldiers.

The resolution issued at the Conference identified clearly the measures to improve the quality of soldiers, not only in political awareness and disciplinary attitudes but also in technical and tactical competence, preventing soldiers from becoming disintegrated while reducing casualties, captures, and missing-in-action soldiers. The Conference also issued another separate resolution about raising political awareness, fortifying the revolutionary military base, developing guerrilla and militiamen, and preparing sufficient supplies.

Issues on the agenda of the Tiên Kiên Conference suggested that after three months of fighting, each and every cadre had acquired more knowledge and experience about military tactics, which now became no longer foreign to them like before the start of the national resistance war. Two military meetings held within the space of only three months were exactly like short-term training courses for cadres in military zones and advisory cadres at the General Headquarters. Recalling the issues discussed and concluded in the Tiên Kiên Conference, General Giáp later wrote:

> Learning from books and formal schooling alone is not enough. A much bigger school is the battlefield itself. We can learn even from our enemy, who could never imagine that by waging war against us, they are actually teaching patriotic Vietnamese how to defeat them.

Once again, Giáp's unique leadership skills were evident in the way he organized short-term meetings and training courses in order to bridge the gap of commanding skills between senior officers and their junior, less experienced colleagues.

After the Conference was concluded, the Chief of the General Staff, upon request by the Commander-in-chief, took charge of the examination of ways to counter the enemy's tanks and mechanized vehicles and instructed local authorities in different provinces to follow suite. In the closing days of March, as the French troops widened the scope of their attack to include cities and towns, a French radio station named *Hirondelle* (literally: Swallow) referred to the marches of their mechanized units on major routes of the Red River Delta as "military promenades in a tranquil summer." Although the General Headquarters of the Vietnamese army refused to be lured into a psychological war by these provocations, it seemed obvious that the enemy's mechanized operations were inflicting a lot of difficulties on their troops, including even units which had painstakingly built barricades or destroyed traffic roads like the 66th Regiment.

An early April afternoon, when the General Staff stopped in Đại Từ District, Thái Nguyên Province, on its way to the revolutionary military base, the Commander-in-chief and the Chief of the General Staff sat down to listen to the envoys reporting on the results of their visit to the 66th Regiment to examine the sabotage activities. Working with Chief of Regiment Phùng Thế Tài and Chief of Regiment Staff Tuấn Kiệt, the envoys were keen to know why even with those acts of sabotage they failed to slow down the progress of the enemy's mechanized vehicles. The Chief of Regiment Staff cited examples of failure in chopping down big trees and erecting mounds on the routes leading from Ngã Tư Sở (Sở Crossroads) and Văn Điển to Hà Đông Town, which took them thousands of workdays but to no avail. This also happened in the case of the Hà Nội-Sơn Tây route, even though steel fences and earthen mounds had been combined. One of the reasons was that at that time their troops were not familiar with what the Tiên Kiên Conference had pointed out: the destruction of roads and the erection of earthen mounds must be accompanied by the deployment of troops and heavy gunfire power in appropriate places to strike the enemy and prevent them from rebuilding the roads and levelling the mounds. The more important reason, however, was that the Vietnamese troops had not figured out in which ways roads should be destroyed to effectively slow down the enemy's mechanized progress. After a lot of discussion, cadres of the 66th Regiment accompanied the Ministry's envoys to the site to make an experiment: digging the road in the shape of an apricot petal. The two envoys made drawings of the experiment and reported to Generals Giáp and Thái that this method of sabotage was less expensive and more effective, forcing the enemy to spend longer time fixing the roads while not causing any hindrances to the movement of the Vietnamese troops, be it on foot, by bicycle, or on horseback. The Regiment waited for further instructions from the Ministry, and if the proposal was approved, the advisors would go to each unit and locality to disseminate the experience and know-how.

When the Commander-in-chief signalled his approval of the plan, the advisors were sent to military zones to disseminate and popularize the new method so that it could soon be piloted, firstly in provinces like Sơn Tây, Hà Đông, and several midland localities. Supported by the local authorities and people in these provinces, the new method of sabotage was soon translated into reality, not only on major national highways but also on inter-provincial routes in unoccupied areas in the midland. Pivotal segments of dykes along the Red River and the Đáy River began to feature low earthen walls built in exactly the method and size that had been unanimously agreed upon. Several months later, having witnessed the operations of the enemy, the Operational Office affiliated with the General Staff was able to draw out useful conclusions to report officially to the Commander-in-chief. Accordingly, although the apricot petal-styled destruction of roads and the construction of low earthen walls on the dykes' surfaces were not able to totally stop the operations of the enemy's tanks and mechanized vehicles, they did cause multiple difficulties for their mechanized marches. The Commander-in-chìe agreed that the method could be disseminated extensively to the provinces in the Red River Delta and the 4th Zone. During the autumn of 1947, roads destroyed with this new method effectively hindered the operations of the enemy.

After about three months, the movement of Government agencies and the leadership of the resistance war in zones and provinces to the revolutionary military base had been basically completed. Along with the movement of people, some 40,000–50,000 tonnes of materials and machinery were also transferred to the new place to serve the needs of hospitals, schools, and printing agencies. Thanks to the tactful application of the "inchworm method" between its two divisions in charge of moving and broadcasting, the Voice of Việt Nam was able to maintain regular and uninterrupted broadcasts during the spring and summer as they moved from Trầm Pagoda in Hà Đông to Ba Bể in Bắc Cạn. One of the most special assets that the Ministry of Defense-General Command had managed to transfer to

Chapter Three: EARLY CHALLENGES

Sơn Tây even before the day of national resistance war was the two airplanes donated by advisor Vĩnh Thụy (former Emperor Bảo Đại). During the Lunar New Year of 1947, for fear that fighting might be escalated and the airplanes might fall into the hands of the enemy, the General Command tasked Head of the Military Training Department Phan Phác with the gradual transference of the airplanes to Việt Bắc. And this instigated a rare scene in the history of wars: the two aircraft were disassembled into many parts and transported, sometimes by oxcarts sometimes by boats, all the way to Hang Hùm (Tiger Cave) at the T-junction of the Tuyên Quang-Đoan Hùng route and finally to the Bình Ca wharf in Sơn Dương District (Tuyên Quang Province). In those days, no one could have imagined that the two planes were the only technological means that laid the foundation for the formation of the Vietnamese People's Air Force, known humbly as the Department of Aerial Research, by the Ministry of National Defense-General Command in March 1949.

The enemy failed in their intention to "search and capture" the leadership of the resistance war during the overlapping months between the spring and summer of 1947, beginning with the large-scale march in the direction of Chúc Sơn-Trầm Pagoda early in March. While the enemy was guessing that the General Headquarters of the Vietnamese army would move along the southwest direction of Hà Nội, they were actually moving step by step to Việt Bắc along the northwest direction, passing through the five provinces of Hà Đông, Sơn Tây, Phú Thọ, Tuyên Quang, and Thái Nguyên. During the whole three months of capital transference, the Advisory Board was able to maintain contact between the Ministry of National Defense-General Command with the military zones and under the constant and close guidance of the Party Central Committee and the Central Military Commission over the operations of nationwide fronts.

Receiving popular support along the way, the process of capital transference successfully ended in early May 1947. The whole mechanism of leadership was then scattered all over the enormous area of Việt Bắc, focusing on the three provinces of Bắc Cạn, Tuyên Quang, and Thái Nguyên, more particularly in the six districts of Chiêm Hóa, Chợ Đồn, Chợ Mới, Đại Từ, Sơn Dương, and Yên Sơn, which became known as the "hexagonal zone." From the summer of 1947 until the resistance war against the French ended in victory, the area around Mount Hồng, which separated the two provinces of Thái Nguyên and Tuyên Quang, with Tân Trào-Hồng Thái (Sơn Dương District, Thái Nguyên Province) in the west and Điểm Mặc-Bảo Biên (Định Hóa District, Thái Nguyên Province) in the east, became the center of the Safety Zone, which housed the whole leadership of the resistance war.

Entering the Dry Season

The six-month pervasive war coincided with the time when France was undergoing consecutive political reshuffles. Léon Blum had taken office for nearly one month when he was replaced by Paul Ramadier. The presence of a cabinet in Paris with rightist leaning was coupled with the return to the political stage of General Charles de Gaulle with a new political organization—the Popular Republican Movement or MRP (French: *Mouvément Républicaine Populaire*). The communist ministers were one by one removed from the French Government. After repeated inspection trips to

Chapter Three: EARLY CHALLENGES

Indochina by members of the French Government such as General Philippe Leclerc, Minister of Overseas France Marius Moutet, Minister of War Paul Coste-Floret, and Minister of Navy Louis Jacquinot, the heated debate on Indochina took place in the French Parliament throughout the early months of 1947. To mitigate the resentment of the angered public, Prime Minister Ramadier falsely declared in front of the Parliament in the middle of March that the Indochina issue could not be resolved by force. He promised that he would sent someone else to replace High Commissioner d'Argenlieu to find a solution through negotiation.

With his earnest wish to avoid a prolonged and pervasive war, President Hồ Chí Minh followed every political move of France with interest. He sent repeated letters to the Parliament, Government, and people of France expressing his readiness to enter talks with them to arrive at a peaceful solution, on condition that France acknowledged the independence of Việt Nam. It transpired, however, that the French administration's real intention was to continue the war with the ambition of restoring their control over the whole Indochina, as reflected through the following consecutive events, which took place around the middle of May:

1- French envoy Paul Mus met with the representative of the Vietnamese Government to present what seemingly were conditions for peace but essentially were requests for the Vietnamese people to surrender.

2- The new High Commissioner Émile Bollaert went to Hà Nội and declared openly in his speech that France would remain in Indochina and would not enter negotiations with the Government of Hồ Chí Minh.

243

3- Paris sent General Raoul Salan to Indochina, tasking him with the deployment of French troops to the northern highland of Việt Nam to lock up the Sino-Vietnamese border before the Red Chinese army moved southward in large numbers.

4- Upon request from Paris, Washington promised to send someone to Hong Kong to persaud former Emperor Bảo Đại to return to Việt Nam "in service of his country." The Western press and media drew an early conclusion that the Salan-Bảo Đại Formula had taken shape. Along with using the former Vietnamese emperor as an ace up their sleeve, Paris poured out their pocket to send General Salan reinforcements, preparing to strike a decisive blow in the dry season.

In the early summer days of 1947, Commander-in-chief Võ Nguyên Giáp and his colleagues at the General Headquarters worked to establish a firm foothold in the vast mountainous area of Việt Bắc. He demonstrated a really keen interest in using the local dialect to address the locals whenever he was on his trips to and from the two areas of Chợ Chu and Sơn Dương on either side of Mount Hồng.

Giáp's strategic vision about the northern highland of Việt Nam covered the whole arch from the easternmost Lộc Bình-Bình Liêu to the northernmost Lũng Cú-Mèo Vạc, the westernmost A Pa Chải-Mường Nhé-Điện Biên Phủ, and the Phongsali Province of the brotherly Laos. He emphasized the strategic location of the northwestern region of North Việt Nam. It was in this direction that more than 4,000 French troops passed through, stopping over in Điện Biên Phủ, as they fled to Huanan in the wake of the Japanese coup d'état. Half a year later, after the Vietnamese people had seized power, the French troops once again crossed the Sino-Vietnamese border, also in this direction, before splitting up their forces to occupy the areas of Phong Thổ, Lai Châu Town, Tuần Giáo, and Điện Biên Phủ and then moving gradually southward to Sơn La. As early as at that time, Commander-in-chief Võ Nguyên Giáp ordered some of the National Defense Guard units to engage themselves in battles in the Northwestern battlefield.

In a letter to the Westward soldiers, dated February 1, 1947, Võ Nguyên Giáp underlined the strategic importance of the Northwestern battlefield and instructed the soldiers to accord special attention to political mobilization, taking advantage of the revolution's popular support to thwart the enemy and its lackeys' wicked plan of invasion and division of the country.

On the way to the Việt Bắc base, as the fighting had not become widespread and the Tiên Kiên Conference had just concluded, Commander-in-chief Võ Nguyên Giáp and Chief of the 10th Zone Bằng Giang immediately took the train to the Phú Thọ-Lào Cai route for an inspection trip before the railway was destroyed. The isolated town near the border reminded the Commander-in-chief of an unforgettable memory. It was also in this place that he and Phạm Văn Đồng secretly crossed the Nậm Ti River by boat seven years earlier to join Hồ Chí Minh (then Nguyễn Ái Quốc) in China. Now, the national resistance war had only begun. Lào Cai and other places he had just been to would soon become the target that his army, particularly the Westward soldiers, and the French Expeditionary Corps scrambled for. On the way, during their discussion, Võ Nguyên Giáp helped Bằng Giang realize what needed to be done and how to develop and maintain political and military bases in this vast mountainous area when fighting was imminent.

To realize President Hồ Chí Minh's policy to return to Tân Trào, Võ Nguyên Giáp knew that one issue of utmost importance was the protection of the revolutionary military base, the center of which was Tân Trào. Early in April 1947, on the way to the military base, he sent letters to the locals and militia of Việt Bắc, instructing them how to confront the enemy's impending attacks. He reiterated that Việt Bắc had an important role to play, having earlier been one of the revolutionary centers during the resistance against the French and Japanese troops and serving now as the birthplace of the new Democratic Republic of Việt Nam. As a consequence, it would be subject to large-scale, concentrated attacks by the French army. Giáp also pinpointed the enemy's possible wicked and abject acts against the local people when they launched the attack, and advised the locals on what should be done immediately in coordination with the soldiers and militiamen to cope up with the enemy's aggression.

The overlapping months of summer and autumn of 1947 saw the Party Central Committee develop and materialize President Hồ Chí Minh's Appeal For National Resistance and the Standing Central Committee's Directive of an All-people War so as to complement and finalize the Party's platform for resistance war, beginning with General Secretary Trường Chinh's articles published on the *Sự thật* (literally: The Truth). Before entering the dry season of 1947, twelve articles had been collected and published in the form of a book with an assertive titled *Kháng chiến nhất định thắng lợi* (literally: The Resistance War is Bound to Succeed). The book became one of the first main teaching materials for political education, contributing an important part to encouraging the entire Party, army, and people of Việt Nam from the very first years of the national resistance war.

For the first time, the Party's resistance war policy was disseminated and discussed in the Second Party Central Committee Congress, which took place from April 3-6, 1947. The Congress issued a resolution on the strategic policy on political, military, economic, and cultural domains of the resistance war and mapped out plans to implement the national salvation and construction policies. As Giáp later remarked, "Five months after the start of the national resistance war, the Party successfully mapped out an overall guideline for the national salvation and construction war, proposing substantial policies and developing a timeframe for victory."

Regarding military issues, in the proposal prepared for the Second Party Central Committee Congress, Võ Nguyên Giáp reiterated the importance of the all-people military approach and the strategic role of the core soldiers and the local armed forces. Based on the resistance war policy formulated by the Party Central Committee, he also envisioned the different stages of this prolonged resistance war and identified the relationship between different tactics. Not only did Giáp underline mobile guerrilla war as the fundamental tactics of the soldiers for the time being, but he also discussed other issues like the establishment of military bases and resistance villages. For immediate military tasks mentioned in the proposal, Giáp emphasized the significance of strengthening the soldiers' political awareness, organization, and training. He also stressed the need for an urgent switch to the mobile guerrilla approach and the consolidation of the local militia forces. It was in this proposal that he offered the detailed explanation of a strategic policy which had been approved by the Standing Central Committee. It stipulated that some segments of the army should be transformed into normal militiamen to provide aid and assistance to the local armed movements in the enemy-controlled areas.

To translate the resolution of the Second Party Central Committee Congress into practice, Commander-in-chief Võ Nguyên Giáp made very careful preparations for the dry season by instructing the military agencies of the General Headquarters to roll up their sleeves immediately after settling down in the area around the west of Chợ Chu Town. He talked to the Chief of the General Staff about a "seasonal war" and about his prediction that the French would concentrate their troops to intensify their activities in the upcoming dry season. Whereas some parts of the Vietnamese forces in the battlefields worked to disturb the French plans for vacation, consolidation of forces, and other preparations, the others had to complete making all their preparations for the dry season within the few months of summer, when the battlefield might be regarded as inactive or silent. This was like a race between the Vietnamese and French armies during the few months of the rainy season.

One of the tasks that attracted the Commander-in-chief's special attention was the consolidation of the Vietnamese core forces and drawing out relevant experience for the commanding of military zones and regiments. The so-called "core forces," however, were very small in size, comprising the 147th Regiment, the 165th Regiment (or the Capital Regiment), and four independent battalions (including the 11th, 80th, 160th, and 223rd battalions). Some of these units had undergone multiple ordeals to gain experience and reach maturity such as the 165th Regiment and the 11th Battalion, who fought in the battlefields of Hà Nội and Hải Phòng respectively.

Under the instruction of Commander-in-chief Võ Nguyên Giáp, Chief of the General Staff Hoàng Văn Thái organized a conference in Phú Minh Commune (Đại Từ District, Thái Nguyên Province) in May 1947 to discuss the development of the core army. Participants at the Phú Minh Conference included cadres and officers who assumed positions at company level or above in the regiments and battalions of the Ministry of National Defense-General Command. In fact, the General Staff had not had enough experience to generalize into theories about the recruitment, organization, equipment, and training of core soldiers to hand down to the units. The mode of conducting the meeting was to listen and synthesize reports by the units and single out the best practices in such domains as recruitment, organization, political education, ideal guidance, military training, the organization of provision, the rapid resumption of daily life activities, the prevention and control of diseases (particularly malaria), and the instigation of household-based production such as raising livestock and poultry to improve the quality of the meals at a time when the region of Việt Bắc was confronting economic difficulties. This was in fact a short-term training course, under the chairmanship of the Chief of the General Staff, which theorized soldiers' experience into principles before passing them again to other soldiers who would apply them into the enhancement of their own units. In his address before the closing of the Congress, Commander-in-chief Võ Nguyên Giáp underlined that the results of the Congress reasserted the appropriateness of the issues that had been discussed earlier and agreed upon, explaining the war-prolonging policy and the important role of the core soldiers. He analysed why it was necessary to quickly redress an emerging issue—the reluctance to go into a hard and prolonged war and to operate in the terrain of Việt Bắc for fear of the extreme weather, the harsh topographical conditions, and the hardship of everyday life. There were some cadres who wanted to go back to the lowland, specifically to the capital city; there were others who did not want to settle down in the Bình Ca-Đà Nẵng area simply out of fear for malaria. Some units expressed the desire to return to the 3rd Zone battlefield. What the Commander-in-chief required from his men was that with their functions and roles as the core soldiers, they should be ready to meet the strategic requirement of being able to operate on a national scale and should not be restricted to any particular battlefield, be it in the lowland or highland. The core units, according to him, were those who stood ready to attack whatever target requested by the Ministry and win whenever they strike. To guarantee victory, it was necessary to develop and consolidate these units in a multi-faceted manner. Experience should be drawn out along with each battle in order to make unceasing progress, and killing the enemy should be followed by dispossessing them of their guns to improve their own stock of weapons. "The more we strike, the better we must become."

The results of the Phú Minh Conference brought initial understanding and knowledge to the Advisory Board of the General Headquarters about the method of developing the core army during wartime. It was also during this historic meeting that for the first time the term "campaign" was raised for academic discussion.

To get the local armed forces well-prepared for entering the dry season, the Commander-in-chief approved the Advisory Board's plan to open a national militia congress while preparing a proposal to implement the strategic policy which had been agreed upon by the Standing Central Committee and approved by the Second Party Central Committee Congress. According to the policy, part of the core soldiers would be transformed into militiamen to support the local armed movement. Based on the experience of the liberation army in the past, the Commander-in-chief requested that the General Headquarters and the Militia Office, which was then affiliated with the Political Department, work together to instruct the National Defense Guard units to take responsibility for assisting and training the local militia forces and getting the locals accustomed to the gun sounds, especially in areas where fighting was going on, no matter where they were stationed. These units were also supposed to help the local authorities to build fighting villages, known at that time as "resistance villages." Regarding weapons for the militia, immediately after the Chúc Sơn Conference, Head of the Military Weapons Department Trần Đại Nghĩa keenly instructed that the role of the weapon workshops and blacksmith furnaces in communes and hamlets should be enhanced and promoted in order to produce more primitive weapons, the likes of scimitars, grenades, matchlocks, landmines, arrows, and cross-bows, for use by the militia. The Commander-in-chief's letter elevated the spirit of the military weapon workers and motivated them to make as many weapons as possible to meet the increasing demands of the guerrilla soldiers and militiamen. As Trần Đại Nghĩa put it in the third congress of the military weapons sector held in December 2, 1948, the Commander-in-chief's guiding idea of "walking with two legs" (referring to guerrilla and regular forces) had been "instilled into each cogwheel of the military weapons sector."

The First National Militia Congress took place at a time when, as requested by the Central Military Commission, the Government had decided to change the name of the Ministry of National Defense-General Command of the National Army into the Ministry of National Defense-General Command of the National Army, Militia, and Self-defense Guards of Việt Nam. Militia offices were established in different localities; the system of commanders at provincial, district, and communal levels began to take shape gradually. The Party Central Committee had issued a resolution requesting provinces to ask competent cadres to take charge of the militia. Two months earlier, a military report prepared by the General Command at the Tiên Kiên Conference showed that the awareness of the local armed forces had reached another level in making a difference between regular soldiers (core soldiers) and local guerrillas, who were divorced from production, and self-defense militia, who were still engaged in production. While self-defense militia used to be civil armed organizations established by patriotic mass organizations in the Việt Minh Front, from March 1947, in the wake of the Government's decision to have the functions of the General Command added, self-defense militia had become one of the state-run armed forces, under the leadership of the General Command and local military agencies, with the participation of the mass organizations. It was clear that since the Tiên Kiên Conference, the term "three-pronged armed force" had become familiar in the military mindset of Võ Nguyên Giáp. The First National Militia Congress was convened not only to reiterate the unity of leadership and organization from the Ministry of National Defense-General Command at central to local level, but also more importantly to redress the underestimation of the strategic role of militia and guerrillas, thus asserting the Party's all-people military policies. On May 26, 1947, in the a speech delivered at the Congress, Commander-in-chief Võ Nguyên Giáp highlighted the strategic role of local armed forces and added that in military terms, the goal was to work with core forces or fight independently to reduce the enemy's number and tire them out to protect the people's villages and crops; in political terms, it was necessary to use armed propaganda methods to annihilate the wicked enemy and uphold the people's spirit; in economic terms, the goal was to protect the people's lives and help them grow and harvest rice, while attacking the enemy's economic institutions. The independent guerrilla groups needed to have their own cattle-raising teams to be self-sufficient and self-reliant. Finally, he elaborated on President Hồ Chí Minh's letter to the Congress, which read:

> Militiamen, self-defense guards, and guerrillas are an invincible force of the country, a steel wall protecting the nation. No matter how brutal and barbaric the enemy can be, if they dare to attack head-on that wall, they will surely collapse and disintegrate.[1]

---

1. *Hồ Chí Minh toàn tập* (literally: The Complete Works of Hồ Chí Minh), op cit., vol. 5, p. 132.

In order to make the local armed forces as firm and steady as President Hồ Chí Minh's wish, Giáp tasked the Ministry of National Defense-General Command with the development of the militia and guerrilla forces, to the equal level of priority to that given to core soldiers.

To get the entire army prepared for the coming autumn and winter, Commander-in-chief Võ Nguyên Giáp suggested that the Operational Office of the General Headquarters be alert to the possibility of the enemy becoming active in the dry season, tactics the Vietnamese core troops should adopt in response, and how the local armed forces could coordinate with the core army to strike the enemy. A question emerged over what the Vietnamese army could learn from the developments in the battlefields during the early months of 1947. Fighting spread out beyond urban areas, and in many cases, the core soldiers had to make temporary retreats to preserve their forces, followed by militia who left their localities to become mobile forces. Meeting with no significant resistance, the enemy had their hands free to go on the rampage, occupy places easily, and organize numerous festivities. In the meantime, the Vietnamese troops' activities remained limited throughout the whole summer because of multiple reasons related to military power, personnel organization, and operational methods (or tactics to be more specific). This was a hard question raised by the reality of the battlefields itself, and it required that the Advisory Board of the General Headquarters find out an answer or solution before the dry season came. Reading again some of the pages of the book *De la Guerre* (literally: On Wars) by Clausewitz,[1]

---

1. The German title of the book is *Vom Kriege*. Its author was a famous Prussian general named Carl Von Clausewitz (1780–1831). The French version, titled *De la Guerre*, was translated by Denise Naville.

Chapter Three: EARLY CHALLENGES

Commander-in-chief Võ Nguyên Giáp heeded some remarks by this Prussian general on the form of armed struggle adopted by the people, especially the part that discussed what the author called "small-scale wars." According to the author, small units could be mobile everywhere and were able to deal with the problems of logistics and reinforcements when needed or keep the activities a secret, while making both attack and retreat promptly and quickly even in less complex terrains than those in battlefields or those with no roads.

The Commander-in-chief realized that the issues mentioned in this book not only reminded him of famous Vietnamese military leaders and thinkers in the past such as General Trần Hưng Đạo, who fought against the Mongols, and Nguyễn Trãi, who authored the eloquent *Bình Ngô đại cáo* (literally: Proclamation upon the Pacification of the Wu), and advocated the use of a weak and small army to fight against a stronger and bigger enemy, but also gave him answers to real problems that the battlefields posed to him in this dry season—the first dry season when, according to his anticipation in a letter to the people of Việt Bắc in April, the enemy might change their direction and attack the highland. Linking to the military proposal he had prepared (later became the resolution of the Second Party Central Committee Congress in early April), which acknowledged that the Vietnamese military bases were not as spacious and stable as those in China and therefore were all subject to the enemy's direct attacks or siege, Võ Nguyên Giáp recalled the "people mountain-people sea" strategy (relying on the people to gain a firm footing in the base) that he had once mentioned in his inspection trip to the Southern battlefields back in the Lunar New Year of 1946. What mattered now to the General Headquarters was to instruct the localities on how to establish military bases in the highland and lowland and how to open a front wherever the enemy was present, be it in its front, at its back, or in its loop. To make timely preparations for the coming dry season, discuss the best way to boost the strength of both the core troops and the local militia, and find out the appropriate tactics to thwart the enemy's marching plan, the Commander-in-chief proposed that the Standing Central Committee convene the Third National Military Conference as early as in the middle of June.

Spending abundant time discussing the direction of the enemy's strategic attack in the coming dry season, the Conference came up with three possibilities: the Red River Delta, the liberated areas of the 4th Zone (Thanh Hóa-Nghệ An) and the 5th Zone (Quảng Nam-Quảng Ngãi), or a massive march to Việc Bắc. Whatever the direction might be, the Vietnamese strategic policy was to attack the enemy in its marching direction, while expanding their operations nationwide including even attacks on the temporary enemy-controlled area by combining armed propaganda with economic sabotage and counter-attacks, with particular attention given to the destruction of the enemy's traffic routes to reduce pressure for their army in the main battlefields. It was essential to find every way to capitalize on the enemy's weakness in its main marching direction so as to gradually fail its large-scale troop deployment. As it was predicted that the enemy would attack their bases, it dawned on the participants at the Conference that the enemy would mobilize a large number of troops, including even specialized forces like paratroops and jungle-savvy troops, and march in different directions. The enemy's weakness, therefore, was that they had to operate far from their bases and large number of troops might entail difficulties in terms of transportation and supplies. In response, the Vietnamese side needed to prepare the best core soldiers and choose favourable positions to attack and decimate the enemy's wings that were heading for their bases. It was also important for the Vietnamese side to train their soldiers how to strike parachuting teams, roadway troops, and waterway troops, while building on the power of the specialized anti-tank and anti-mechanized vehicle units and combining with sabotage to decelerate the mechanized advancement of the enemy.

This Conference differed from its precursors in that for the first time participants were able to identify 11 guiding principles for operational activities,[1] the most salient of which was the first principle, as it showed their preparedness to attack the enemy proactively. What happened later in the battlefields showed that these guiding principles were only the beginning, and they needed to be supplemented and finalized constantly by the real experience throughout the two resistance wars against the French and the Americans. What was noteworthy here, however, was that Võ Nguyên Giáp was able to build on collective capabilities of the cadres attending the Conference and make an important generalization of basic issues that would serve as the guidance for both strategic

---

1. These guiding principles included: 1- Remain proactive at all times; 2- Know themselves and know the enemy; 3- Flexibly use reserve troops; 4- Concentrate combat troops when necessary and make rapid and timely deployment; 5- Conceal their forces and deviate the enemy's attention; 6- Launch surprise attacks when the enemy was least prepared, and capitalize on their pitfalls; 7- Combine strategy with tactics; 8- Combine core soldiers with militia, guerrilla fighters, and self-defense guards; 9- Focus on destructive warfare; 10- Develop practical and detailed plans; 11- March with the same pace of the enemy or better to outpace them.

and tactical operations for the entire army throughout the two wars for national liberation.

After the Third National Military Conference and the Phú Minh Conference concluded, the Cabinet Council, upon proposal by the Central Military Commission, decided to partition the supreme military body into two separate ministries, namely the Ministry of National Defense and the Ministry of General Command, early in May. Minister of National Defense Tạ Quang Bửu was in charge of military administration and production while Commander-in-chief Võ Nguyên Giáp focused only on the development and operation of the army. Throughout that summer, the advisory, political, and logistical systems from ministry to zone and regiment levels were rapidly consolidated. As for the General Staff, after receiving a number of cadres who had graduated from the Trần Quốc Tuấn Military School, Bắc Sơn Politico-military School, and Quảng Ngãi Infantry School and some of the experienced cadres, the Chief of the General Staff reported to the Commander-in-chief that the agency was well-prepared for the coming dry season, with a batch of equally experienced cadres. However, the Vietnamese scouts and liaisons still failed to match the enormous tasks they were given, technically and professionally. In addition, after a lot of changes in organization, the operations of the intelligence services at different levels had not yet returned to their normal and regular functions.

Before the advent of autumn and winter, once the second and third military training courses had completed, the entire Vietnamese army would have 600 elementary cadres added to the core forces and almost 90 cadres to local authorities. This addition was expected to remedy the shortcoming

Chapter Three: EARLY CHALLENGES

pinpointed in the Third National Military Conference in June that a significant number of cadres failed to meet the pressing demand of training soldiers for entry into the dry season. To enforce the Central Military Commission's policy, in early August, the General Staff initiated a refresher course for more than 80 cadres from battalions and regiments from the 4th Zone northward. After more than six weeks of training, they were sent back to their respective localities to make timely preparations for the upcoming autumn-winter tasks. It was also during this time that by a Government decree dated August 26, 1947, the agencies of the Ministry of National Defense and the Ministry of General Command quickly established an independent brigade, under the leadership of Chief of the General Staff Hoàng Văn Thái. This was one of the core forces affiliated with the Ministry of General Command and organized on the largest scale at that time. There was cheerful ambience at this event, not only in the brigade itself but also in all the core forces of the Ministry.

In early September, Commander-in-chief Võ Nguyên Giáp paid a working visit to Bắc Cạn and Cao Bằng, to which he had been intimately linked, to review preparations for the battles. Nearly half a century later, he recalled:

> The town of Bắc Cạn had prepared bamboo stake fields as a trap to the paratroops, yet it remained a spacious rear far away from the front . . . . After the inspection trip to Cao Bằng, I rested assured about the preparations made in the northern frontier. I was taken by surprise, however, by what was awaiting us in Bắc Cạn in the dry season.

Back to the General Headquarters, he convened the Việt Bắc Politico-military Conference for midland provinces and Việt Bắc so as to keep track of the preparations made by units and localities before the autumn-winter months. Participants at the Conference included key officers and cadres in the Ministry of General Command, representatives from the Ministry of National Defense and core units from battalion level upwards, and Party cadres and representatives of the authorities in localities where fighting was expected to spread to during the dry season. The opening of the Conference coincided with the new French High Commissioner Émile Bollaert's visit to Hà Nội to deliver a speech on France's policies toward Indochina. Based on this speech, Võ Nguyên Giáp presented his analysis of the enemy's military and political plot in the coming dry season in a report he delivered at the Conference, thereby urging the soldiers and civilians in every locality to make prompt preparations for battle once the enemy launched an attack to Việt Bắc this dry season. Thanks to his familiarity with the situations in Cao Bằng and Bắc Cạn, Giáp was able to pinpoint clearly what should be done to thwart the enemy's strategic ambition. Addressing the local authorities, he highlighted the need for the construction and operation of the militia, guerrillas, sabotage activities, and scorched-earth policy, as well as the confidentiality and alertness to the enemy's wicked tricks and deception. Speaking to the core forces, he reiterated the requirement to complete the summer's military plan, including training basic skills, raising political awareness, supervising soldiers, and assisting the militia forces nationwide in both fighting the enemy and building the country.

An event of decisive importance for the entire Vietnamese army before the dry season was the Fourth National Military Conference, which took place during the last three days of September 1947. Due to the limited capacity of their

Chapter Three: EARLY CHALLENGES

intelligence activities, organizationally and professionally, it was very difficult for every Vietnamese military meeting to predict the enemy's strategic policy and possible attacks during the dry season, and hence to thwart the marching plan. It should be noted that half a month earlier, the Standing Central Committee had decided in its directive titled *"Bôla nói gì? Ta phải làm gì?"* (literally: "What did Bollaert Say? What should We Do in Response?") dated September 15 that, it was necessary for the Vietnamese troops to get prepared for the enemy's pricking attacks, wide circle attacks, parachuting, or making landfall at their back. It was also directed that all the towns that were likely to be occupied the enemy in the coming winter should be destroyed as completely as possible.[1] It was regrettable that many of the similar issues mentioned in the Standing Central Committee's directive were not properly and promptly heeded in this Conference.

Having analysed all the developments in the enemy's forces during the summer and predicted its imminent massive attack, the Commander-in-chief remarked in a report delivered at the Conference that the purpose of the enemy's attack in this dry season would be to capture their leadership, annihilate their core forces, destroy their military bases, and make socio-political grounds and foundations for the establishment of a pro-French puppet government in Việt Nam. Having identified North Việt Nam as the major battlefield, the report raised questions such as "Which direction will be the main direction of the enemy's attack?" and "Will it be the Red River Delta, Việt Bắc, or the 4th Zone?" According to the report, "Việt Bắc is a new battlefield,

---

1. Communist Party of Việt Nam: *Văn kiện Đảng toàn tập* (literally: The Complete Collection of Party Documents), op cit, vol. 8, p. 300.

difficult to predict," and "the enemy must be very bold if they choose to attack Việt Bắc first." The Commander-in-chief's report and the discussion that followed showed that many of the problems, which had been raised and decided upon, shed a lot of light on the direction and measures of defeating the enemy's advancement. The Conference emphasized that they should avoid using big combat forces in mobile warfare. Instead, they should focus on the destruction of traffic routes, use ambushes rather than surprise attacks, develop guerrilla warfare widely, and criticize the belief that land had to be retained. Some new terms that appeared for the first time in the Conference included "popular war," which later became known as "people's war." In response to the question "What will be regarded as a victory over the enemy in the coming dry season?," the Commander-in-chief said, "If we can withstand the winter attack while being able to preserve our forces, it can be seen as already a victory for us."

The Conference concluded, yet there remained unresolved questions in the mind of the Commander-in-chief about the real power of the enemy and the military tactics his army needed to adopt in response, such as "How many troops are available for mobilization?" and "What is the enemy's possible plan of attack?" There were conflicting ideas during the Conference. While some participants believed that the enemy would not dare to parachute down onto Bắc Cạn as it was too far away from their bases in the plain, others warned that they could well be bold enough to "jump down right onto our heads." What about the Vietnamese counter-attack tactics? The discussions during the Conference directed Giáp's thought to arguments made by Friedrich Engels and Carl Von Clausewitz. The former talked about the limited capacity of the militarily weaker armed groups who had to confront directly a professional, seasoned, and well-equipped opposing army, while the latter sang the praise of small-scale wars of clandestine and mobile units. But how was that related to the situations of Việt Nam in this dry season? Based on evaluation of the situations of the Vietnamese army and the ongoing developments in the battlefields, the Commander-in-chief noticed an extremely important issue: the military directive on mobile guerrilla warfare and the resolution on the transformation of part of the soldiers into militia to launch guerrilla warfare had not incorporated specific measures, and many issues still remained in the dark and had not yet been generalized or theorized.

His thoughts reminded him of what he had heard about the operations of the armed forces in the rear of the enemy in Nha Trang and Thừa Thiên, especially the story told in the recent military conference by Nguyễn Khang, who served as Secretary of the 12th Zone.[1] The story had it that a province-level armed company (known among the locals as "Insurgent Company"), who was supposed to fight in the south of Bắc Ninh and who lost contact when the battalion retreated, secretly remained in the rear of the enemy, mingling with the locals to exist. Supported and protected by the local people, the company was able not only to maintain their long fighting right inside the loop of the enemy but also to provide active aids to the guerrilla warfare movement in the entire southern area of the province by relying on the

---

1. During the anti-French resistance war, the 12th Zone covered such provinces as Lạng Sơn, Bắc Giang, Bắc Ninh, Hải Ninh, Hòn Gai, and Quảng Yên (including Đông Triều and Chí Linh).

combat villages, by being now dispersed now concentrated, now fighting independently now cooperating with soldiers from outside the province. It was apparent that this new phenomenon opened up a new possibility of a guerrilla warfare development method. Giáp decided to go to the 12th Zone to examine for himself the ability of an independent company to exist right at the back of the enemy.

After listening to report on the operations of the Insurgent Company, the Commander-in-chief concluded that its actual operations reaffirmed the feasibility of the resolution issued during the Fourth National Military Conference, which stipulated "the use of a company-level unit to operate in the battlefield of a certain locality" and that "soldiers have to remain in the rear of the enemy." He instructed the leadership of the 12th Zone to replicate the successful story of the company to other companies, so that they could serve as the core for the development of guerrilla warfare, and simultaneously expand the scope of combat villages based on the successful experience of Đình Bảng-Từ Sơn. At that time, the transformation of part of the core regular soldiers into militia to launch the guerrilla warfare had taken shape clearly in the mind of the Commander-in-chief.

On his mount to return to the military base, the Commander-in-chief recalled the milestones in the development of the recent battle. The reality in the battlefield, especially the unsuccessful attempted attack on the town of Hà Đông by a National Defense Guard regiment in early March, gradually turned his attention to the operational scope under the current circumstances. It became increasingly clear that it was not time for the Vietnamese forces to be organized into brigades or prepare a large-scale war, given the

Chapter Three: EARLY CHALLENGES

current conditions and situations. Along with the extensive development of guerrilla warfare, it was an immediate task to train the soldiers to fight in small and medium scope—from battalion to regiment and higher levels.

After stopping over in Thái Nguyên Town, Võ Nguyên Giáp travelled along the main road, passing Đại Từ, Phú Minh, and Quảng Nạp before reaching Điềm Mặc in Chợ Chu Town, Thái Nguyên Province. President Hồ Chí Minh had moved here in the middle of May. The Commander-in-chief reported to the President about the military conference, his inspection trip to the 12th Zone, his thoughts about the organization of the combat troops, the relationship between the core army and the local armed forces in the protection and construction of the country, as well as his plans to strike the enemy in the coming dry season. He proposed that the establishment of brigades be postponed for some time to deploy the combat troops in the form of independent companies and concentrated battalions, a formula that he believed to be appropriate for the policy to accelerate mobile guerrilla warfare. After several questions about the preparations for the autumn-winter campaign, President Hồ Chí Minh accepted the Commander-in-chief's proposal and said that he would discuss further with General Secretary Trường Chinh. Launching a guerrilla war had always been one of his top concerns, right from the inception of the Liberation Army that he affectionately called the "fledgling army." Hồ Chí Minh instructed that not only was it necessary to embed independent companies into the rear of the enemy, but also to pay attention to localities to which fighting could spread in this autumn-winter campaign. The specific number of companies to be deployed would be decided after his discussion with the General Secretary and after approval by the Standing Central Committee.

In the following day's working session, Trường Chinh and Võ Nguyên Giáp were able to make concrete conclusions. About one third to half of the core soldiers stationed in Bình-Trị-Thiên northward would be partitioned into independent companies, which would then be sent to localities to become the core of the upcoming guerrilla war. In each zone, the core regiment only left behind a steering board and one to two battalions called "concentrated battalions." At central level, however, the organization of the core battalions and regiments would remain unchanged and would be tasked with fighting in the directions directly chosen by the Ministry. From the 4th Zone northward, around 70 concentrated battalions would be reinforced and established to serve as the core force in mobile guerrilla warfare. Organized this way, the army were able to "walk with both legs," implying that they could provide direct support to the guerrilla war movement while playing a decisive role in the implementation of the strategic policy by switching completely to mobile guerrilla warfare.

As he returned to his office, the Commander-in-chief had no time to make amendments to the military directive dated October 4 sent to all the zones nationwide, which he had approved before heading for the 12th Zone. The new military directive, which had been issued and sent, did not contain instructions on how to organize combat troops along the latest strategic policy agreed upon by President Hồ Chí Minh and General Secretary Trường Chinh. Having listened to the report by the General Staff that there had not been any concrete signs of the enemy's attack, the Commander-in-chief decided to go and review the war preparations in Tuyên Quang Province, one of the several most important localities within the revolutionary military base. He left the General Headquarters and departed on October 6 without a slightest idea that the following day, the enemy would launch an attack on Việt Bắc at a time when the highest leaders of the Vietnamese army, including the General Secretary, General-in-chief, and Chief of the General Staff, were all absent. Both Trường Chinh and Hoàng Văn Thái were being present at the town of Bắc Cạn, which was the first target the enemy set out to occupy.

Turning the Tables

During the early days of the French attack, the Vietnamese side fell into an extremely disadvantaged position. Due to their incorrect prediction of the enemy's mobilization of combat troops, direction of attack, and operational manoeuvres, their preparations in the Bắc Cạn-Tuyên Quang-Thái Nguyên triangular center of the military base were inadequate. Most of the core soldiers of the Ministry and the Zone were sent out to prevent the enemy from marching upwards from the midland. In the north of Tuyên Quang and Thái Nguyên, the sabotage of traffic routes and houses, the evacuation of archives and offices and hospitals, and the call upon locals to carry out the scorched-earth policy remained what General Secretary Trường Chinh later criticized as "big-rear mentality." The intensity and velocity with which the enemy was marching were indicative of the scope and significance of their attack. It was obvious that the French were intent on dealing a decisive blow right in the resistance military base of the Vietnamese troops.

On the morning of October 8, the Commander-in-chief was back to his office. Having heard of the enemy's renewed attack, he and his entourage immediately travelled all the way from Chiêm Hóa District, Tuyên Quang Province, to the General Headquarters, not by car but on horseback along the shortcut through the deep jungles. By that time, the office of the Commander-in-chief and other Government offices had been moved to as far as the flanks of Mount Hồng. When he was back, Giáp was worried to learn that his two comrades Trường Chinh and Hoàng Văn Thái remained in the fighting zone.

Head of the Operational Office Đào Văn Trường reported to the Commander-in-chief on the enemy's latest parachuting onto the towns of Bắc Cạn and Chợ Mới on October 7 and on Chợ Đồn one day later, and on the movement of the enemy's mechanized vehicles since the eve of October 7 on the 4th Route from Lạng Sơn to Thất Khê. The Chief of General Staff had ordered the deployment of the 72nd Regiment to Bắc Cạn and sent to the 1st, 10th, and 12th Zones directives on the attrition war, killing the enemy, destroying the traffic roads and drainage systems, and evacuating the people and leaving empty gardens and houses behind to sever the enemy's supplies while working with the locals to protect the Government agencies from anti-revolutionary plots.

On the afternoon of that day, the Chief of the General Staff also returned safely to his office from Bắc Cạn. In subsequent exchanges, both he and the Commander-in-chief agreed that although there was not yet enough information to make a detailed assessment of the fighting evolutions, it was possible to conclude through the news gathered during the past two days that because of the Vietnamese army's inadequate preparations and thanks to their technological and weaponry superiority, the French could make bold moves in order to realize the strategic goal of killing the Vietnamese core soldiers, capturing their leadership, and destroying their revolutionary military base whose core zone was Bắc Cạn. The French operations at the end of September in the northwestern direction only served to distract the Vietnamese troops as the former had planned to launch an attack against Việt Bắc. It was in this major strategic direction that the French were able to inflict some damage against their opponents, yet they failed in their main goal and no longer had the "surprise" element. Earlier news showed that even when the French army had tens of thousands of reinforcement troops, the Vietnamese were unable to guess how many more they would mobilize to begin a march in the dry season. The French would possibly link Cao Bằng and Bắc Cạn to form a sort of pincers embracing the revolutionary military base in the northeast before organizing mopping-up operations to the south where they believed the resistance leadership of the Vietnamese army was stationed. Võ Nguyên Giáp instructed Hoàng Văn Thái to warranty the safety of the leadership at all cost and to immediately send someone to Bắc Cạn in search of the General Secretary. He requested that in the immediate term, one of the Ministry's units be dispatched from the midland to the 3rd and 4th Routes to prevent the French troops from spreading beyond the towns and townships. The 10th Zone[1] was requested to make artillery preparations to strike the enemy's ships along the Lô River on the Đoan Hùng-Tuyên Quang route and to prevent the enemy from forming a pincer position to the west of the revolutionary

---

1. During the anti-French resistance war, the 10th Zone included the provinces of Lào Cai, Hà Giang, Yên Bái, Phú Thọ, Tuyên Quang, and Vĩnh Yên.

military base. He also instructed the Operational Office and Intelligence Office to keep a close and watchful eye on the enemy's every single move to make necessary corresponding adjustments to the combat plan. It was now imperative that the independent brigade-concentrated battalion formula be implemented as soon as possible, as this strategic policy had not been reflected in the military directive dated October 4. The Chief of the General Staff was in charge of preparing a draft of this military directive in this matter.

That night, as the Commander-in-chief was working late in the dim light of an oil-lamp, the phone suddenly rang. On the other end of the line, Hoàng Văn Thái reported that the cadre sent earlier to look for the General Secretary had met him and was being accompanied by a protection unit. They were travelling from Chợ Đồn through Thành Cóc to return to the base. Hoàng Văn Thái decided that the following day he would bring a squad to escort the General Secretary back to the base. Learning about Trường Chinh's safe return to the base, the Commander-in-chief breathed a sigh of relief, and hurriedly phoned Hoàng Quốc Việt at the Party Central Committee and asked him to report the news to Hồ Chí Minh. The following day, Hoàng Văn Thái came to see the General Secretary and the protection unit at the foot of the So Pass. On their way back, the Chief of the General Staff made use of the time to report to the General Secretary on the latest developments in the battlefields. The biggest difficulty for their army in the early days was not only being taken by surprise and failing to act in advance, but also ineffective combat skills due to lack of experience. With the exception of the Capital Regiment and Lạng Sơn Regiment, who had been more or less put to the test, all the other units had no combat experience. Their level of equipment and organization did not yet allow them to engage in large-scale battles to stop or kill the French troops in the towns which had just been occupied by the latter. Hoàng Văn Thái also mentioned the Commander-in-chief's ideas about the possible tactics for the coming battle. The exchange between the two men about how to deal with the French march went on and on all the way back to the military base.

In the ensuing days, news of victory began to emerge at the General Headquarters. The soldiers of Cao Bằng had gunned down an enemy aircraft. On the very first day, while the artillery soldiers of the 10th Zone missed the opportunity to strike the French ships due to the slow movement of the artillery, the 18th Infantry Battalion was able to use bazookas to sink one LCVP (Landing Craft, Vehicle, and Personnel) ship in the Lô River and stop the French troops from making landfall on Bình Ca, the western gate of the Safety Zone. On the early morning of October 13, the communications liaison officer of the General Staff in Quán Vuông came to report that one of the liaison officers had captured an important document of the enemy from the plane gunned down in Cao Bằng. The Chief of the Staff sent his private secretary Nguyễn Văn Ngạn to obtain the document. After four days and nights traversing forests from his unit, liaison officer Nguyễn Doanh Lộc was so tired out that he immediately fell fast asleep as soon as he handed the document, without eating even a small bowl of porridge quickly prepared by the station's cook. Glimpsing at the document Nguyễn Văn Ngạn knew immediately that it was the French plan to deploy troops to Việt Bắc, an invaluable document for the Advisory Board at this time. Upon request by the Chief of the General Staff and under the guidance of Head of Operational Office Đào Văn Trường, the captured document was immediately translated and reflected on the map to report to the Commander-in-chief, who wasted no time in reading it. Right in the briefing of that morning, October 13, Commander-in-chief Võ Nguyên Giáp, Chief of the General Staff Hoàng Văn Thái, and Head of the Political Deparment Văn Tiến Dũng asked the Operational Office to make a presentation, and together they analysed the French plan for an autumn-winter offensive. Before the briefing commenced, the Commander-in-chief reminded the Political Department to award medals to the 74th Regiment of Cao Bằng for having downed the enemy's plane and captured their crucial document, and to liaison officer Nguyễn Doanh Lộc.

The French Command's plan revealed that with an army of over 15,000 soldiers,[1] their march was to be divided into two steps:

In the first step, dubbed "Léa," the French would focus on the Bắc Cạn-Chợ Mới-Chợ Đồn triangle. According to their plan, the situations might transpire as follows:

1- On October 7–8: French paratroops would occupy Bắc Cạn, Chợ Mới, and Chợ Đồn and conducted mopping-up activities in the vicinity. On October 9, the two military wings of Bắc Cạn and Chợ Đồn would meet each other in Poi Village, about 20 kilometers from Bắc Cạn on the Bắc Cạn-Chợ Đồn route.

---

1. It included five infantry regiments, three parachute battalions, two artillery battalions, two sapper battalions, three mechanized companies, two air squadrons with about 40 craft, and three naval squadrons with about 40 ships and boats.

2- On October 10, the mechanized infantry, which departed from Lạng Sơn on the eve of October 7, would coordinate with paratroops to take control of Cao Bằng and send part of its force to Bắc Cạn, slated for October 12, to join the forces in Chợ Đồn and head for Đài Thị to merge with the western wing from Đoan Hùng who traversed through the 2nd Route, the Lô River, and the Gấm River on October 13. Đài Thị was situated about 15 kilometers from Chiêm Hóa, along the Gấm River.

3- After the completion of the defense line in Chợ Mới (slated to be ready by October 11), mopping and surveillance would be intensified on the 3rd Route and the Chợ Mới-Bình Gia route.

In the second step, dubbed "Clo Clo," the focus was place on Chợ Chu. It was scheduled that on October 14, the French would attack and occupy Định Hóa District in Chợ Chu from different directions—Bắc Cạn and Chợ Mới—in combination with parachute troops who would made landfall right on Chợ Chu. Another parachute unit would descend on the south of the district, blocking the Chợ Chu-Thái Nguyên route. They would then depend on the situations to decide how to conduct mopping-up attacks in the Bắc Cạn-Chợ Chu-Chợ Mới triangle.

After discussions, Commander-in-chief Võ Nguyên Giáp made some following conclusions, which would also be presented to to the Standing Central Committee in the upcoming meeting:

1- The French had formed two pincers on the flanks of Việt Bắc revolutionary military base: the eastern pincer was more than 400 kilometers long while the western one was more than 250 kilometers long. Although the French march covered eight provinces in the area between the midland and Việt Bắc, its focus was on the Tuyên Quang-Đài Thị-Bắc Cạn-Thái Nguyên quadrangle (about 3,600 square kilometers), with the target of their mopping-up attacks being the Bắc Cạn-Chợ Chu-Chợ Mới triangle, which stretched about 300 square kilometers.

2- The French army's strength rested with their superiority of aircraft, artillery, and mechanized vehicle. That advantage, however, was cancelled out in the mountainous battlefields, especially under winter weather conditions. Their deathly weakness, on the contrary, was the fact that they had to thin out their forces on an extremely large battlefield, far away from their rear. They therefore had to rely on the two axes of land route and river route for their reinforcements and supplies. The Vietnamese troops, as a result, had a chance to engage the French in the war of attrition, reducing the latter's numbers on both the river and the road.

3- The reality over the past week indicated that the French could not implement the plan as expected, as if everything had gone according to plan, they would have met in Đài Thị on October 13. Actually their western wing had only reached Tuyên Quang, 80 kilometers from the rendezvous, while their eastern wing marching from Chợ Đồn remained 50 kilometers of jungle road from Đài Thị. If the Vietnamese troops attacked fiercely on the Lô River and the 2nd Route, they would be able to break the western pincer and thwart the French plan of troops assembly.

4- If the second step of the plan was materialized, the French would parachute into Chợ Chu, about 20 kilometers from the General Headquarters as the crow flies, and carry out mopping-up attacks on the Quán Vuông-Quảng Nạp-Phú Minh triangle, thus jeopardizing the Vietnamese Government agencies which were being located at the feet of Mount Hồng. An urgent task for the Vietnamese army at that time was to protect these agencies during the movement process to avoid the enemy's search.

5- The deployment of combat troops as instructed in the directive dated October 4 was no longer well-suited to the realities in the battlefield during the last few days. It was not yet time for the Vietnamese army to use large-scale but poorly-equipped and inexperienced combat troops against the enemy's tanks and artillery. Rather, it was important to quickly readjust the core forces by forming three fronts, namely the Lô River and the 3rd and 4th Routes. With about 20 core battalions, it made more sense to deploy small units in combination with infantry and artillery using such main attack tactics as ambush, attrition war, and blockage of reinforcements, all aiming ultimately to break the pincers of the enemy, the first being the western one.

6- It was important for the Vietnamese army to test immediately the feasibility of the independent-company tactics, firstly in districts of the four provinces of Cao Bằng, Bắc Cạn, Thái Nguyên, and Tuyên Quang. These companies would be tasked with supporting the local armed forces in developing guerrilla warfare, fighting the enemy on an extensive area, and limiting the enemy's ability to conduct searching and destroying sprees.

7- A directive should be issued immediately to redress the shortcomings and limitations of localities to the north of Thái Nguyên and Tuyên Quang towns in making preparations for fighting. The realization of sabotage, the evacuation of people, and the implementation of the scorched-earth policy should be considered as the central tasks for the people and soldiers of Việt Bắc at this time. Weapon workshops, hospitals, storehouses, and agencies needed to be moved as far away from the main roads as possible.

That night, the General Secretary listened to reports and quickly concurred with Commander-in-chief Võ Nguyên Giáp regarding the next operational directions. He decided to convene immediately a meeting of the Standing Central Committee. The following day, October 14, the meeting approved the combat plan proposed by the Commander-in-chief. Accordingly, the whole Việt Bắc would form three battlefields, including Cao Bằng-4th Route, Bắc Cạn-3rd Route, and Lô River-2nd Route, which were directly commanded by key cadres at the General Command.[1] The meeting also approved the Standing Central Committee's directive which encouraged the whole Party, army, and people of Việt Nam to drive back the French winter offensive. As the meeting concluded, President Hồ Chí Minh said:

> The political situation in France is extremely chaotic, and the struggles in the colonies are pushing France to bring the Indochina War to an end as soon as possible. However, the French are able to launch massive attacks in the early stage. If we strike them everywhere, forcing them to thin out their forces to respond, they shall be doomed to failure.

---

1. Võ Nguyên Giáp and a small leadership would go to the 4th Route battlefield to observe and instruct the nationwide battlefields; Hoàng Văn Thái would head for the 3rd Route battlefield; Trần Tử Bình and Lê Thiết Hùng would travel in the direction of the Lô River-2nd Route; Văn Tiến Dũng and the heavy component of the General Headquarters would remain in the Mount Hồng area to follow the developments and activities in different directions and battlefields.

Chapter Three: EARLY CHALLENGES

If we can preserve our core forces beyond this winter, it is already a victory. If the enemy cannot win the battle quickly to terminate the war, the situation will take a turn for the better for us.

Before departing for the battlefield, the Commander-in-chief urged the General Staff to pass on the new tasks to the 1st Zone[1] and the 10th Zone, and immediately finalize the military directives about the change in tactics and about the independent company-concentrated battalion policy before sending them to the zones. The 101st Military Directive (dated October 15) and the 104th Military Directive (dated October 16) reiterated the determination and measures of the Vietnamese army to widen the guerrilla warfare and change the combat plan to suit the ongoing circumstances in the battlefields, and materialize the tasks outlined in the October 4 Directive. They also pinpointed the operational tasks of the locality-based soldiers (independent companies) and mobile soldiers (concentrated battalions). With those two military directives, the Commander-in-chief showed the people and army of Việt Bắc the direction and measures to reverse and counter the autumn-winter plan of the French Command, thus translating the Standing Central Committee's determination to drive back the French autumn-winter offensive into reality.

On October 17, the Commander-in-chief departed for the front.

The soldiers in different battlefields followed the new operational strategy with great enthusiasm and creativity. Drawing out useful lessons from the initial failure in

---

1. During the anti-French resistance war, the 1st Zone covered the provinces of Cao Bằng, Bắc Cạn, Thái Nguyên, and Phúc Yên.

installing artillery battlefields against the enemy on the Lô River, the artillery soldiers of the 10th Zone this time coordinated with the local militia and guerrilla fighters to use decoys to deceive the enemy, while laying artillery in secret and unpredictable riparian locations under the motto of "placing near and firing straight" and thus consecutively succeeded in sinking the enemy's vessels in Khoan Bộ (October 23) and Đoan Hùng (October 24). During this time, on the land routes, the battles at the seventh kilometer of the 2nd Route on October 22 and Bông Lau of the 4th Route on October 30 were highly efficient and perilous, taking the French by complete surprise and helping to capitalize fully on their fundamental weakness of having to send mobile reinforcements on an extremely large battlefield, far away from their rear. After three weeks of troops deployment, the French found themselves increasingly distanced from the initial goals of their offensive and their march was likely to go bankrupt. As their forces were thinned out, their intention of troops assembly could not be implemented according to plan, and the military wings on both pincers suffered heavy losses, the French began to withdraw from small places, specifically from Chợ Đồn on October 23 and Chiêm Hóa and Chợ Rã on October 25, to concentrate in the towns of Bắc Cạn and Tuyên Quang. To continue cornering the enemy, the Commander-in-chief in the 132nd Military Directive (dated October 27) highlighted the need to intensify fighting on the Lô River-4th Route front and capitalize further on the increasingly disadvantageous situation of the enemy. So as not to waste any opportunity to eliminate the enemy, especially when they embarked on mechanized marches, the 132nd Military Directive requested, based on the experience gained from the effective ambush in

Bông Lau, that the concentrated battalions remain on standby and be prepared to strike upon sight of the enemy.

One day at the end of October, on his way back from Bình Gia in Lạng Sơn Province, Commander-in-chief Võ Nguyên Giáp paid a brief visit to the General Staff, which had earlier moved to the east of the 3rd Route. Addressing the advisory cadres, who were gathering in a cave of Tràng Xá, the Commander-in-chief analyzed the French strengths and weaknesses, the Vietnamese operational tactics, and the developments in the battlefields during the last three weeks. He also asserted that the Vietnamese troops had overcome successfully initial difficult days of passiveness and unpreparedness, that they had been deployed properly, and that all the fronts were launching proactive and effective attacks on the enemy. He predicted that in less than one month, specifically in the coming November, the situations in the battlefields would change very quickly in the direction increasingly favorable for the Vietnamese troops, with the smooth operation of the concentrated battalions and the maturity of the militia and guerrilla movements of Việt Bắc, which were supported by independent companies.

As the reality later transpired, the Commander-in-chief's prediction proved correct.

In the wake of the artillery victory in the Khe Lau battle (at the junction of the Lô and the Gấm rivers) on November 10, there were many signs of the French changing their plan. Instead of moving to the second step (Clo Clo), they took another one, dubbed *"Ceinture"* (literally: "Blockade"), which aimed not to tighten the siege as the name suggested but to mop up as they fled the battle.

For the Vietnamese part, although the General Command had predicted correctly the withdrawal routes of the enemy, their attack on the enemy was not effective due to multiple reasons, including their limited communicative and organizational skills, slow responses of mobile forces, and failure to figure out the enemy's decoy troops.

On December 19, the conclusion of the Việt Bắc campaign coincided with the first anniversary of the national resistance war. Though having occupied the towns of Bắc Cạn and Cao Bằng and several locations on the 3rd and 4th Routes, the French Expeditionary Corps suffered huge human and material losses without achieving any strategic target set out originally for their first major march since their return to Việt Nam. On December 22, in commemoration of the anniversary of the Vietnamese army's establishment, Commander-in-chief Võ Nguyên Giáp left the General Headquarters for Tuyên Quang to attend the victory-celebrating ceremony of the people and soldiers of Việc Bắc. In the flamboyant light of the thousand torches in the communal stadium, and in the presence of numerous core soldiers, militiamen, and self-defense guards who had scored glorious victories, and the ethnic groups of Tuyên Quang, the Commander-in-chief read the "Order for the Day" commending the achievements of the people and soldiers of Việt Bắc and the coordinating battlefields nationwide. He reminded the whole army to examine the vital experience in the battlefield of Việt Bắc and find out ways to defeat the enemy and rectify their own shortcomings. Of utmost importance was the need to realign and train the soldiers to be quicker in intelligence activities, more familiar with the topography, more responsive in communications, more convincing in mobilization, and more prompt and decisive in commanding.

Exactly three years earlier, when he received President Hồ Chí Minh's directive on the establishment of a liberation army, Võ Nguyên Giáp told his men about what attempts should be made to accomplish the tasks. That spirit was now reflected in a new situation, when that small three-year-old army, under his command and the leadership of the Party, was able to defeat the biggest march of the French colonialists right from the early days of the resistance war. As Hồ Chí Minh put it, led by the Party and supported by the people, that army had the power of a new stream and a new fire which kept flowing and growing, moving forward without retreating.

The following day, before leaving Tuyên Quang for the General Headquarters, Võ Nguyên Giáp wrote a quick letter about the victory of the Vietnamese army in the Việt Bắc campaign, and had it sent to Hồ Đắc Di and Tôn Thất Tùng in Chiêm Hóa and Tạ Quang Bửu who was then on an inspection trip to the weapon-making workshop in Bản Thi (Chợ Đồn). The letter was not only a testimony of his personal friendships with intellectuals of the same age,[1] but also a reassurance of the army's ability to protect the military base in the face of the fierce enemy's offensive amidst doubts of such ability. About half a month later, Võ Nguyên Giáp again had a document written in French, the title of which means "The French Offensive against Việt

---

1. With the exception of Hồ Đắc Di, who was significantly more advanced in age (born 1900), the other three were roughly of the same age. Tạ Quang Bửu, Võ Nguyên Giáp, and Tôn Thất Tùng were born in 1910, 1911, and 1912 respectively.

Bắc," and sent to many members of the Cabinet Council. This document was a synthesis and reorganization in chronological order of different kinds of papers collected by the Vietnamese soldiers in the battlefields, including directives, reports, and personal letters written by French officers and soldiers. These documents bore testimony to the difficulties and losses suffered by the French army during almost three months of marching in the mountainous and tough region with exposure to extreme weather conditions, diminishing supplies, and an invisible opponent who might strike at any time—all demoralizing them seriously as the march was nearing an end. President Hồ Chí Minh asked Tạ Quang Bửu and Trần Công Trường to prepare a booklet about the enemy and had it sent to the Enemy Agitation and Propaganda Office or Agitprop, so that people at the office could apply into the reeducation of captured and surrendering Afro-European soldiers. This document was of such substantial significance in terms of political and ideological communications that seven years later, during the Điện Biên Phủ campaign, Professor Tôn Thất Tùng still associated it with a lot of unforgettable memories.

Celebrating Victory

The successful conclusion of the Việt Bắc campaign coincided with several major red-letter days: the foundation of the Vietnamese army and the inception of the national resistance war. Amidst the festive atmosphere of the whole country, Hồ Chí Minh wrote several newspaper articles about those memorable events.

In an article titled *"Lời kêu gọi nhân kỷ niệm một năm kháng chiến toàn quốc"* (literally: "Appeal on the Occasion of the First Anniversary of the National Resistance War"), he wrote:

> We knew at the start that the war would be tough and long, but would certainly end in victory. Therefore, our people braved the hardship and kept on fighting until final victory, with increasing solidarity, enthusiasm, and resilience. Our soldiers, on the other hand, became increasingly experienced and brave, forcing the enemy's humiliating and demoralizing defeats in the battles of Mỹ Tho, Hải Vân Pass, Lô River, Thất Khê, and others.[1]

On this occasion, the President also gave spiritual encouragement and commendations to military officers and personnel all over the country, specialists and workers, functionaries, the general population in the temporarily-occupied areas, as well as children and Vietnamese overseas community. At the same time, on behalf of the Vietnamese people, he thanked the people in France and elsewhere in the world for "supporting our just war and denouncing the colonialists and anti-revolutionary elements."

In another article titled *"Việt Bắc anh dũng"* (literally: "The intrepid Việt Bắc"), under the pen-name Tân Sinh, he briefly recounted the developments of the campaign and quoted letters and confessions of French military officers and soldiers about their defeat. He finally concluded that:

> Thanks to the lucid leadership of the Government, the tactful instructions of the Ministry of National Defense and the Ministry of General Command, the intrepidity of the Việt Minh generals and soldiers and the militia and guerrilla combatants, as well as the enthusiasm of

---
1. *Hồ Chí Minh toàn tập* (literally: The Complete Works of Hồ Chí Minh), op cit., vol. 5, pp. 313–314.

the whole people, we were able to annihilate the French offensive against Việt Bắc.[1]

Hồ Chi Minh, however, warned the whole army and people of Việt Nam against complacency and underestimation of the enemy's power. According to him, the Vietnamese should always stand ready and on watchful alert. He wrote:

> The colonizers have not been totally defeated. They will relaunch attacks here and there.... Our resistance war will face increasingly huge challenges.
>
> With the decline of the colonial regime and their lackeys, the lucidity of our Government, the bravery of our soldiers, the resilience of our people, and the support of the global democratic movement, however, our prolonged resistance war is bound to end in absolute victory.[2]

In another article titled *"Kỷ niệm ngày thành lập Giải phóng quân Việt Nam"* (literally: "In Commemoration of the Vietnamese Liberation Army's Foundation"), he dedicated a lot of love to the soldiers for the December 22 anniversary, highlighting the rapid maturity and glorious victory of an army founded three years earlier following his directive titled *"Từ Giải phóng quân đến Vệ quốc quân"* (literally: "From Liberation Army to National Defense Guard"). He wrote:

> The first squad of the original Liberation Army was likened to a little seed which has now grown into a big forest—the National Defense Guard. To the casual and untrained eyes, this seemed like an impossible mission. And many of them would have mocked that, "A batch of young students and tillers of different ethnic extraction like Thổ, Nùng, Trại, and Kinh, armed with nothing but some self-made rifles

---

1. Ibid., p. 367.
2. Ibid., p. 368.

and a dozen scimitars, are ridiculously calling themselves an 'army' and claiming to shoulder the task of emancipating the nation."

Yet we have managed to show how wrong they were, by developing the Liberation Army under the command of comrade Võ Nguyên Giáp.

The results have showed that our policies are appropriate, as we are all convinced that this simple and essential truth will prevail: "The Vietnamese nation will definitely be liberated."[1]

Finally, the President reminded that:

National defense guards, militia, and guerrilla fighters must always maintain the iron-like discipline, the bronze-like morale, the resilience and invincibility, the intrepidity, integrity, and loyalty of the Liberation Army.[2]

That the Vietnamese army and people scored a huge victory during the first dry season of the national resistance war made Hồ Chí Minh very happy. He discussed with the Standing Central Committee and proposed to the Party Central Committee Congress on January 15, 1948, that the soldiers' fighting spirit should be encouraged and lauded, marking a new level of maturity of the armed forces after more than two years of resistance. Two days later, he convened a meeting of the Cabinet Council. The Government members approved of the National Defense Ministry's proposal of launching a soldier-supporting movement, and concurred with the policy of granting awards and conferring military ranks on some of the high-ranking officers in the army. On January 20, 1948, President Hồ Chí Minh signed Decree

---

1. Ibid., p. 329.
2. Ibid., p. 330.

110/SL conferring the military rank "General" on Võ Nguyên Giáp as Commander-in-chief of the national army and militia, and the military rank "Lieutenant General" to Chief of the General Staff Hoàng Văn Thái, Head of the 4th Zone Nguyễn Sơn, Head of the 2nd Zone Hoàng Sâm, Head of the 1st Zone Chu Văn Tấn, Head of the Cadre Inspection Office Trần Tử Bình, Head of the Political Department Văn Tiến Dũng, and Political Commissar of the 2nd Zone Lê Hiến Mai.

Subsequently, on January 25, the President signed another decree conferring the military rank "Colonel General" on Head of the 7th Zone cum Member of the Southern Military Commission Nguyễn Bình, and the military rank "Lieutenant General" on Head of the Military Weapons Office Trần Đại Nghĩa.

The Lunar New Year drew near when feelings of happiness about the victory were still lingering. On February 6, ministers and deputy ministers whose offices were stationed in Đại Từ, Sơn Dương, and Chợ Chu received a convention order requesting that they be present at the Tân Trào Police Station at exactly 10:30 the following day "to head for a special meeting." They all wondered what that emergency and important meeting was. Later, they were told later by Minister of Finance Lê Văn Hiến that President Hồ Chí Minh had invited them over for lunch to celebrate the coming of the Lunar New Year, the first anniversary of the national resistance war, and the recent autumn-winter victory. In his *Nhật ký của một bộ trưởng* (literally: A Minister's Diary), Lê Văn Hiến recounted that:

> We had to cross mountains and rivers to reach his place. He received us heartily and cheerfully. As the roads

became muddy due to the torrential rain that day, we did not reach his place until early in the evening, only to find ourselves greeted by a fire built earlier to warm us up. The meeting was attended by as many as 20 people of all fields, creating a joyful atmosphere. Before everyone got seated for the party, President Hồ Chí Minh brought up some issues for discussion and resolution. The cordial and intimate meal in the forest entertained by the President was simple yet meaningful, leaving a deep impression on us all.

The following morning, the General Command invited us to visit Văn and have lunch with him before heading back to our respective offices. The Commander-in-chief's residence was neat and nicely decorated, which was all natural because a woman was present.

The "woman" in this dairy referred to Commander-in-chief Võ Nguyên Giáp's spouse, Đặng Bích Hà.[1]

In these days, the shared joy was accompanied by private happiness. The wedding between Trần Công Tường and Vân was held on February 17, 1948. It was followed by the wedding between Việt Châu and Diệu Hồng two months later. Võ Nguyên Giáp knew that Lê Văn Hiến himself also had already had "the apple of his eyes," who was approved by President Hồ Chí Minh, but he did not know why they hesitated in organizing a wedding. Minister Lê Văn Hiến

---

1. Võ Nguyên Giáp got married before the outburst of the national resistance war. According to his family, his wedding took place at 5 pm on November 27, 1946, at number 32 Lý Thường Kiệt Street, Hà Nội. The wedding ceremony was hosted by Nguyễn Lương Bằng. Attenders at the wedding included Trần Duy Hưng as representative of the local authorities, Đặng Thai Mai and his spouse as representatives of the bride's family, and Thục Viên.

later recalled that evening, at the end of May, when they met for a Cabinet Council meeting:

Võ Nguyên Giáp whispered a question as he lay next to me, "What's the point of putting it off? Have you two chosen a day yet?" I laughed and answered, "We're waiting for favourable conditions before reaching the decisive phase." Then both of us burst into laughter . . . . Giáp's continuous questions prevented me from sleeping and kept me thinking of X[1] while he was fast asleep.

While waiting for the "favourable conditions," Lê Văn Hiến spent his free time growing vegetables. Beds of vegetables, which had been neglected and stunted during the French attack, now became verdant again. Lê Văn Hiến got a lot of joy from growing vegetables and sharing them with his friends. On one occasion, he sent Phan Anh and his wife a basket of vegetables, some fish sauce, and some oranges. The next day, he received a reply in form of a package of cakes made in Huế, accompanied by some verses:

> Fresh vegetables and sweet oranges thoughtfully delivered
> In a vast military base, we are all like a family
> In return to your kindness, I have nothing
> But a package of cakes in lieu of a gift.

Lê Văn Hiến replied, "The cakes are tasty and the poem is delicate. It's a pity that X is not here with me to share this battlefield gift." The compliment on the nice cakes and poem only reached Phan Anh when the two met on May 28 in an important meeting where President Hồ Chí Minh conferred

---

1. "X" referred to Lê Thị Xuyến, who later became Minister Lê Văn Hiến's spouse.

Chapter Three: EARLY CHALLENGES

the military rank "General" on Commander-in-chief Võ Nguyên Giáp. The meeting was scheduled in the morning, but it was put off until the afternoon because the heavy rain and the rising water level of the streams had prevented the Government members to arrive on time.

The rank-conferring ceremony finally took place solemnly in a hillside makeshift house, hiding in the foliage of the forest trees. At the foot of the hill did a big stream snake around. The Fatherland Altar was simply but solemnly adorned, flanked by red banners carrying the two mottos in yellow letters: "The prolonged resistance war is bound to end in victory" and "The cause of national reunification and independence is bound to succeed."

President Hồ Chí Minh and Head of the Permanent Committee of the National Assembly Bùi Bằng Đoàn stood in front of the altar. In the solemnly moving atmosphere, the President uttered, "Today, on behalf of the Government and the people," then suddenly stopped for being too moved to continue. He took out a handkerchief to wipe away his tears. The whole room was filled with solemnity. It took him a while to regain his composure and continued, "In the name of President of the Democratic Republic of Việt Nam, I confer on you the military rank 'General' and hope you will fulfil your duty and live up to the people's expectation."

Commander-in-chief Võ Nguyên Giáp stepped up to receive the Decree. Bùi Bằng Đoàn, on behalf of the National Assembly, and Phan Anh, on behalf of the Government, delivered some congratulatory remarks. Tạ Quang Bửu, on behalf of the Ministry of National Defense, congratulated the Commander-in-chief and reiterated the whole army's pledge to uphold their fighting spirit under the command of the

Commander-in-chief. Recalling this unforgettable moment half a century later, Võ Nguyên Giáp wrote:

> I was so moved at that moment. I said a few words expressing my deep gratitude to heroic martyrs, as well as my sincere appreciation toward the President, National Assembly, and Government for having given me this great honor. Then I promised to fulfil my duty with highest responsibility, and contribute a modest part to the general cause of national independence and reunification.

Years later, when being asked what he was thinking about at that moment, Giáp replied that the only thing in his mind at that time were the four words *"Dĩ công vi thượng"* (literally: "Common cause takes precedence") that the President told him when he tasked Giáp with the development of the Liberation Army. He had born in mind those words throughout his entire military career. He also said that after the rank-conferring ceremony was broadcast on the Voice of Việt Nam, a Western journalist asked Hồ Chí Minh what criteria or standards he had based himself on to give the military rank "General" to his military officers. The President's answer was simple and succinct: on the fulfilment of tasks and the achievements made during the previous years. Specifically, if a commander defeated an adversary colonel, then he would be called a "Colonel"; if he defeated a lieutenant general, then he would be given the title "Lieutenant General"; if he defeated a general, then he would receive the rank "General."

Hồ Chí Minh actually pointed out a historical truth that had prevailed for many years.

It was just less than three years, from the outburst of the national resistance in South Việt Nam in September 1945 to the summer of 1948, that the Paris administration had changed three general commanders of their expeditionary corps. After Leclerc, it was Valluy who had to leave his position after failing to "shoulder the difficult task of defeating Giáp and Việt Minh" after 22 months, as France had expected. The next adversary for Giáp was the French four-star general Roger Blaizot, who came to assume office in Sài Gòn in the middle of May, at the same time with Giáp's reception of the military rank "General." From 1958 onwards, the Vietnamese army became more regular and formal, with all the soldiers bearing military ranks and wearing uniforms. It was noticed that Commander-in-chief Võ Nguyên Giáp was very fond of his military attire with the four stars on his shoulder strap insignia conferred by President Hồ Chí Minh on behalf of the Government and people of Việt Nam. That habit remained until later.

After a strategically meaningful victory in the first dry season of the national resistance war, the most special concern for Commander-in-chief Võ Nguyên Giáp was to draw out useful lessons to lead the whole army forward in the face of the new tasks.

At the Central Military Commission Conference held on January 1, 1948, Võ Nguyên Giáp analysed the recent defeat of the French Expeditionary Corps, assessed the commanding practice of the Central Military Commission, and mapped out spring-summer military tasks for the nationwide battlefields.

Reviewing the strategic goals set out by the French Command for their "daring, venture-taking, and lightning-fast" offensive, the report admitted that the French were successful in severing the Vietnamese supplies in the northeastern border, destroying some of the Vietnamese storehouses, and occupying some Vietnamese localities. Their success was attributed to their spy network, which enabled them to spot out the Vietnamese weak points. They acted boldly, parachuting right into the Vietnamese rear, and thus took the Vietnamese troops by surprise. The French troops, however, failed to capture the Vietnamese leadership and smash the core forces of Việt Minh; they also failed to deceive the Vietnamese people and mop them up. That was not to mention their heavy loss of soldiers and technological equipment. Their failure was not only due to the Vietnamese army's well-made preparations or the hatred harboured by the Vietnamese people, but also due to their own complacency which prevented them from anticipating the potential difficulties of a military march on such a vast battlefield far away from their rear. These disadvantages were coupled with unfavourable topographical conditions and the tactical changes of the Việt Minh, who gradually turned the tables. With the application of the independent brigade-concentrated battalion formula, aided by the launching of three fronts, the Vietnamese step by step capitalized on their most fundamental weakness—their reliance on the land roads and river routes to solve the problem of supplies and reinforcements. With the evacuation of the people and the implementation of the scorched-earth policy, they successfully turned a massive offensive that the French generals and troops called "a straight blow to the enemy's heart" into "a big punch, yet to an empty space."

For the Vietnamese part, before the campaign began, President Hồ Chí Minh said that it would already be a victory if they could preserve their core forces beyond that winter. However, they could do more than that. Not only did they preserve their core forces after 75 days of fighting but their soldiers also had become more mature owing to the test they were put in. In addition, the revolutionary military base remained safe and well-protected. Võ Nguyên Giáp remarked that although it was the first time they encountered the enemy in the river, the Vietnamese artillery soldiers made substantial progress and fought effectively while the infantry soldiers acquired the new tactics of surprise attacks and ambush attacks. The militia and guerrilla also underwent remarkable initial development.

Speaking about the French's impending plot, he predicted that they would possibly focus their troops for an offensive against the 4th Zone, or for mopping up the Red River Delta and expanding their rear by way of the "ripple effect," coaxing the people into urban areas and bringing them under control, firstly along the 1st and 5th Routes, to reinforce the puppet government. Finally, the report made a thorough analysis of the feasible methods to thwart the French's plot.

The resolution issued by the Central Military Commission Conference was then transferred to the localities and units, beginning with a military directive by the General Command dated February 6, 1948, on the consolidation of the army and the acquisition of useful lessons from the 1947 autumn-winter campaign. The military directive emphasized the importance of experience in making predictions on the enemy's moves (including their tactics, their strengths and weaknesses in both attack and defense, marching and retreating), as well as experience in the organization and commanding of their soldiers. The General Commander's directive wrote, "Having analysed their losses, we should not be mistaken however that we are superior. We must therefore strive to build on our strengths and remedy our weaknesses with greater determination."

The military directive also pointed out what rectifications were needed in the acquisition of tactics, realignment of discipline, enhancement of political awareness, leadership of the people, and organization-related activities (such as enemy predictions, communications, regular reporting mechanism, and the obedience and observance of orders). Particularly in the prediction of the enemy's moves, the directive wrote:

> We should know their intentions: What are their next moves? Where will they go? Only by predicting correctly their plans can we map out our own effectively. In their offensive against Việt Bắc, for example, many of our predictions were correct, but many were not.

The directive also presented an example of incorrect anticipation made by the Vietnamese side in the closing phase of the campaign as follows:

> The enemy in Bắc Cạn sent their Vietnamese lackeys all over the region to spread out rumours that they would retreat to Thái Nguyên while some mechanized vehicles would head for Cao Bằng. We guessed that the enemy actually wanted to withdraw to Cao Bằng and hence sent out news of their retreat to Thái Nguyên to deceive us. Accordingly, we deployed an ambush on the Bắc Cạn-Cao Bằng route, only to find out later that the enemy actually retreated to Thái Nguyên. As a result of our wrong prediction, we exhausted our own troops.

What can be learned from this case, according to the directive, is that if sufficient information of the enemy is not available, the Vietnamese should think of different possible situations and assume that the enemy is strong to prevent themselves from being subjective.

At the end of the directive, the Commander-in-chief wrote:

In the recent Việt Bắc campaign, although the enemy lost the battle, it is hard to claim that we have won complete victory. Many of our shortcomings remain. We have to strive to learn and grow up in the battlefields. This is a sacred task the Fatherland shoulders on us at this time. Cadres of all levels and the entire army must take this responsibility and be determined to continue the strengths and redress the weaknesses to win over the enemy in this period to uphold the traditions of the Liberation Army and achieve ultimate victory.

At strategic level, on March 20, 1948, the General Command's Summation Conference on the nullification of the enemy's offensive in Việt Bắc concluded that the Vietnamese had soon rectified their initial miscalculations of the enemy and promptly changed their deployment of combat troops and tactics to fail the enemy's intention of "dealing a decisive blow" and emerged as victors. In a speech delivered at the Conference, Commander-in-chief Võ Nguyên Giáp made analytical comparison between the directive issued on October 4, 1974, and the subsequent complementary directives on October 15 and 27. Specifically, the main tactics outlined in the October 4 Directive was that guerrilla warfare was to take precedence over mobilization, and apart from core soldiers who concentrated on mobile attacks, other soldiers in local battlefields should base themselves on companies. The Commander-in-chief remarked that the overall policy sounded all right, but not specific enough. It was only when the battle had started did the Vietnamese realize that no specific instructions were given about how to concentrate and strike. As a consequence of this vague instruction, too many Vietnamese soldiers were deployed to zone level, at the

295

expense of the rear. The enemy accordingly went rampage when few of the Vietnamese troops were in sight. In addition, as the local-level regiments were stationed on a field basis, a place became empty when a unit was deployed to another one. Such imbalance in the deployment of troops made the Vietnamese susceptible to the enemy's attack, and the abundance of soldiers was cancelled out.

These shortcomings were rectified by directives issued on October 15 and 27, with the coming into being of three fronts and the establishment of independent companies, which were tasked with the protection of localities and instigation of guerrilla warfare, and concentrated battalions, which were responsible for mobile operation without sticking to any fixed tasks. Early rectification of shortcomings and adaptations of tactics enabled the Vietnamese core soldiers and local armed forces to maximize their strength in killing the enemy and winning the battle. In a summation conference in the wake of the campaign, the Commander-in-chief had personal contacts with many of the cadres at zone and regiment levels, evaluating their activities while listening to their feedback about the instructions and orders given by the General Command in this first major campaign. He commended the cadres who had fought bravely in their units to win the battle, while standing ready to speak out the limitations of the General Command in the recent large-scale test. As this was the first time the Vietnamese confronted the French in a comprehensive operation, their coordination among the battlefields nationwide remained lax and loose. However, the French difficulties in reinforcement proved the Vietnamese battlefields' initial success in cooperating with the main one in Việt Bắc and pinning down the enemy.

It was thanks to the spirit of bravely acknowledging mistakes and shortcomings and making timely rectifications that the Vietnamese were able to win in this first battle. Exactly half a century later, speaking at a conference held in December 1997 in Bắc Cạn on the occasion of the 50th anniversary of the Việt Bắc victory, Commander-in-chief Võ Nguyên Giáp shared frankly with cadres who had earlier served at the General Headquarters that had they refused to change their plans and tactics, had their blindly deployed their regiments and even the newly-formed brigades to confront the French's tanks and artillery and tens of thousands of the latter's infantry soldiers, they would have been totally crushed.

The readiness to acknowledge and rectify mistakes and shortcomings to lead the army from one victory to another was one of the most striking qualities of Võ Nguyên Giáp as a military genius.

American military historian Cecil Currey, author of *Victory at Any Cost*, later quoted Võ Nguyên Giáp's saying that, "In a war, it is less beneficial to win many battles but withdraw few lessons than to win only one battle but learn many useful lessons."

That explained why after the Việt Bắc victory, as well as throughout the two liberation wars, Võ Nguyên Giáp accorded importance not only to his own acquisition of lessons for leadership and commanding skills, but also to his soldiers' readiness to draw out experience from the combat realities so that the whole army could make continued progress to live up to the tasks given.

As Currey put it, the autumn-winter operation in Việt Bắc in 1947 served as one of the first strategic lessons that

Giáp acquired during the years he spent at "the jungle-based military academy." With this victory, he had established for himself a commanding stature at macro level.

It was not until much later that people began to fully understand the importance of that first lesson to the whole Vietnamese army in general and the General Headquarters in particular, thanks to the scientific analyses made in a book titled *Lịch sử nghệ thuật chiến dịch Việt Nam* (literally: History of the Operational Art in Việt Nam).[1] The book specified that while before October 7, 1947, the Vietnamese leaders at strategic level made incorrect estimations of the French army's marching directions and actions and hence were taken by surprise in the first place, they were able to make timely adaptations and change their tactics thanks to exact predictions of the French plans. It was owing to the timely and brave rectification of mistakes that enabled the Vietnamese to turn the tables and win the final victory.

The Việt Bắc campaign was a special operation. It was an offensive launched by the French on a vast area that covered three zones (the 1st, 10th, and 12th zones) of the Vietnamese forces. In this campaign, tens of thousands of French soldiers were deployed, aided by state-of-the-art weaponry. In addition, they acted beyond the Vietnamese leadership's initial predictions, aiming at the strategic goal of dealing a decisive blow to quickly bring the war to an end. For the Vietnamese part, the resistance war had lasted only ten months, with a lot of limitations in terms of commanding skills both at zone and regiment levels, added by the rudimentary and

---

1. Việt Nam Institute of Military History: *Lịch sử nghệ thuật chiến dịch Việt Nam* (literally: History of the Operational Art of Việt Nam), 1994.

obsolete weapons and relative inexperience, especially when the number of combat troops mobilized for the battle was huge.[1] Under such circumstances, only leaders at macro-strategic level possessed sufficient commanding competence commensurate with a large battlefield. Only they had the power and authority to deploy the armed forces and supervise the evacuation of the civil, political, and party agencies across Việt Bắc. Only the General Headquarters had the human resources which could be sent to different directions to disseminate the policies and assist the localities and units in organizing and leading combats in urgent situations.

The Việt Bắc campaign was the first campaign of the Vietnamese people and army in their resistance war against the French. Although many of the elements of a true operation remained missing, some of the key features of the operational art had begun to take shape, laying the grounds for a full-fledged development of the operational art later on. The directive of the Standing Central Committee requested that the whole army defeat the winter offensive by the French spoke volumes about the firm and thorough target of the campaign, which was to defend the brain of the resistance war, protect the revolutionary military base, and preserve the core forces. The type of campaign was exactly chosen. It was a counter-attack campaign which appeared for the first time during the anti-French resistance war. Together with the formation of three fronts to create a favourable position for their troops, the Vietnamese leadership identified exactly the focus of the campaign—breaking the French's weakest pincer

---

1. The troops at the General Headquarters and the zones amounted to 13 core regiments and 11 core battalions, excluding the local forces throughout Việt Bắc.

in the direction of the Lô River-2nd Route and destroying their combined siege plan. To achieve this goal, the Vietnamese leadership had organized forces properly and chosen appropriate tactics for their troops given the imbalance between the two sides in the campaign. The switch to small but mobile forces to strike the enemy in all the three fronts was a lucid and sensible decision in line with the law of gradual advancement, withdrawing experience and combating the enemy at the same time. However, the small-scale tactics adopted in the Việt Bắc campaign did not simply stop at the cooperation between independent companies and the local armed forces to engage the enemy into an extensive war of attrition through the use of guerrilla warfare. Along with the dispatch of independent companies to the local districts to help launch extensive guerrilla warfare, the Commander-in-chief also accorded due importance to the application of small-scale tactics, mainly through ambush both on land and in the river. The concentrated battalions of the Vietnamese army contributed a decisive part to the exploitation of the French's most obvious weakness of being mobile and exposed to the open air in the mountainous areas which were rarely within the effective support range of the French artillery. The experience that the Vietnamese forces gained after this battle about striking the French supplies and transportation while attacking their mobile mechanized infantry offered a useful lesson for many of their later attack campaigns. The independent company-concentrated battalion model of the Vietnamese army in the Việt Bắc campaign would become the guideline of their core soldiers' activities over an extended period of time, including even during the guerrilla warfare instigation on a nationwide scale in the late 1940s.

Chapter Four

ADVANCE TO A STRATEGIC TURNING POINT

Launching "Flexible Strategic Counter-attacks" on the Enemy's Temporarily-occupied Areas

After their victory in Việt Bắc, a big question of strategic significance was raised to the General Headquarters of the Vietnamese army, "Has the resistance war moved to the second phase yet?"[1] Observing what the French side was doing

---

1. At the beginning of the anti-French war, the General Headquarters expected the war would be taking place in three phases: defense, holding out, and general counter-attack. Later, drawing from the situations in the battlefield throughout nine years, the Steering Committee for War Summarization under the Politburo redefined these three phases more specifically as follows: The first phase (September 1945–December 1947) included the tasks of combining the resistance war in the South with the construction and protection of the new regime across the country, moving up to carrying out the national resistance war, and defeating the French's "quick fight, quick win" strategy. The second phase (early 1948–late 1950) included the tasks of pushing up the national comprehensive resistance war, developing the guerrila war, step by step advancing into mobile war, and crushing the enemy's attempt to prolong and expand the war and their policy of "using the Vietnamese people to fight against themselves and using the war to feed the war." The third phase (from 1951–July 1954) included the tasks of maintaining strength and promoting the

in the battlefields in late 1947 and early 1948, Commander-in-chief Võ Nguyên Giáp judged that the situations showed signs of the second phase. However, he could only conclude with reservation that the Vietnamese victory in Việt Bắc was either close to or the last milestone of the first phase. So the question to the General Headquarters should be changed into "What should we do and how would we do to move to the second phase?"

In the middle of January 1948, the Party Central Committee held a meeting to discuss the plans and strategies for the upcoming phase. In a military report at the conference on the strategic tasks and measures to advance the war to the second phase, Võ Nguyên Giáp set forth eight strategic goals, the fifth of which stated:

> To successfully adopt the motto of "using guerrilla war as the key method and mobile war as the secondary method" by using independent companies to launch militia movements, combined with training concentrated battalions to fight the mobile war and striving to organize them into mobile corps.

As the General Headquarters officers later explained, the fifth goal showed that Võ Nguyên Giáp commanded the whole army to "walk with two legs" to the second phase. Specifically, he highly stressed the strategic role of the guerilla war but also stressed that this war should not be restricted to "guerrillaism." Instead, the Vietnamese army should step by step learn to

---

Vietnamese army's rights to gaining initiative in their strategy, pushing up their offensive and counter-attacks, spoiling the utmost efforts of the French colonialists and American imperialists, and putting an end to the old colonialism in Indochina. So, Võ Nguyên Giáp was correct in his judgment that "our victory in Việt Bắc fundamentally puts an end to the first phase."

fight a concentrated war from small scale (with a couple of battalions) to larger scale. Moreover, they should promote the close combination and mutual assistance between the two forms of operation: guerrilla and concentrated.

But how could they launch the guerilla war? This had been a thorny and tenacious question throughout the first years of the war. The General Headquarters had taken some strategic measures: organized the National Militia Conference (May 1947), issued a directive on launching the guerilla war—the Vietnamese people and army's fundamental task in this phase (November 1947), and strengthened the Militia Office under the Ministry of General Command and the militia offices in different zones. However, those measures did not prove to be very effective ways to promote the role of the local armed forces (in communes, districts, and provinces) or to rage the all-people battle against the enemy.

The lesson of experience drawn from the Việt Bắc campaign about how to organize and operate independent companies (deployed for guerilla war) and to supervise the modes of combat of concentrated battalions (in order to train the regulars in concentrated attacks from small to large scale) helped the Vietnamese army answer the question of how to bring into full play the concerted strength of the three forms of troops. This experience also paved the way for Võ Nguyên Giáp to fulfill the goal set by the Party Central Committee of trying by all means to carry out a national guerila war. Using the independent company-concentrated battalion tactic was defined as one of the strategies for the three forms of troops to enter the second phase.

Getting the approval from President Hồ Chí Minh and the Standing Central Committee, Võ Nguyên Giáp decided to divide about one third of the regulars (103 of 299 companies, mainly from the 4th Zone northward) into independent companies, armed propaganda teams, and voluntary teams.[1] These organizations were managed by those cadres who were highly competent and richly experienced in politics. They would secretly enter the enemy-occupied areas[2] to encourage and involve different strata of people into mass organizations (such as those for youth, farmers, women, and the elderly). The process of strengthening and expanding the mass political organizations coincided with that of establishing guerrilla units with scales corresponding to specific conditions in localities. In their directive, the General Headquarters emphasized the orientations for those organizations as follows: 1- Regard the building of political bases among the masses as the topmost important task; 2- Only carry out the guerilla war once the widespread and reliable political bases had been established; 3- Attach great importance to the fighting for the protection of the people while helping them improve their lives; 4- Provide support in terms of training for the local cadres, especially those in the Northeastern and Northwestern regions of Việt Nam, as well as those in the battlefields in Laos. Võ Nguyên

---

1. Independent companies assumed the task of fighting while supporting the local people with equipment and in military training, and helping them little by little in the reality of guerilla combat, whilst the armed propaganda teams and voluntary teams had the task of propagating the concept of resistance amongst the masses and building up political bases. Apart from 100 companies detached from the staff and sent to work independently in the enemy territories, the number of regular force units (about 200 companies) remained in the regular workforce of battalions and regiments to learn how to fight in a concentrated combat.
2. They included first and foremost the Northeast, Northwest, 5th Route (from Hà Nội to Hải Phòng), and Upper Laos.

Giáp also relied on the characteristics and especially the specific difficulties of each battlefield in the mountainous areas and in the plains to work out the most effective mode of combat.

Regarding the battlefields in the South, the Party Central Committee and the General Headquarters sent delegations of cadres to the southern part of Central Việt Nam and to South Việt Nam in turns. They would take the task of disseminating the Vietnamese plan and goal of striving to prepare all the necessary conditions in terms of strength and capability for the transition into the new phase in the way that is most suitable to the specific conditions of each battle. An important task that the General Headquarters stressed heavily was to make use of the independent company-concentrated battalion tactic in order to realize the goal of "turning the enemy's rear into our front" and to promote the role of the regular battalions in attacking the French outposts and narrowing their occupied areas. Specifically:

In the Southern region, in the work of mass political mobilization, the Vietnamese side should pay attention to the followers of Caodaism and Hoahaoism, Khmer people, and different strata of Chinese people while directing the movement of political struggle and protecting mass bases in urban areas. Regarding the military aspect, they should carry out the guerilla war, strengthen their armed forces at grassroots level to resist the French's mopping-up operations, protect their resistance bases, and gradually learn how to carry out concentrated small and medium attacks against the enemy, on their fortifications, against their infantry and marine troops, and on their economic businesses (especially rice and rubber plantations).

In the southern part of the Central region, after repeating the important role of the Central Highlands battlefield, Võ Nguyên Giáp emphasized the task of building up and strengthening the Vietnamese guerilla bases in both the mountainous areas and the plains, and specified three immediate strategic tasks as follows: 1- Build a foothold in Buôn Ma Thuột and Đà Lạt as a springboard to move to the east of Cambodia; 2- Expand their guerilla bases in the north of Kon Tum Province and the Attopeu-Salavan-Pakse triangle in Laos; 3- Prepare plans and troops to be ready to destroy the French once they had attacked the free zone in the 5th Interzone.

In 1948 alone, by using the initiatives that suited their conditions, the Vietnamese forces could gradually realize the Party Central Committee's strategy of carrying out a guerrilla war across the territory behind their enemy line and turning its rear into their front. The strategy created the conditions for their people to rise up bravely in arms to kill and eliminate the adversaries in many rural areas. Many guerrilla areas and bases were set up. With the backup of the network of combat villages and combat hamlets set up in many places, their armed forces behind their enemy line became strengthened and matured in combat to hold on to their position, protect the villages, and back up the people's struggle for protecting their mastership gained at different levels. Also during this period, in implementing Võ Nguyên Giáp's directive, dated March 1948, on instructions and orientations for the battlefields of Laos and Cambodia, the Vietnamese forces established some political bases and armed units in East Cambodia, Lower Laos, and especially in Upper Laos.

Chapter Four: ADVANCE TO A STRANGE TURNING POINT

In early 1949, the Sixth Central Cadres Congress (January 14-18, 1949) asserted that, "Our biggest success in 1948 was that we had turned the enemy's rear line into our frontline." At the Senior Politico-military Cadres Congress held in January 1949, after repeating the above confirmation of the Congress, Võ Nguyên Giáp added, "The French's biggest defeat is that they have not been able to pacify their controlled areas and to wage any offensive in the unoccupied zone."

Later, it was written in the sum-up documents of the Steering Committee for War Summarization under the Politburo that:

> In 1948, by launching the guerilla war behind the enemy line, turning their rear into our front, and mobilizing our military, political, and economic means altogether in the insurrection to wipe out our opponents, we had actually launched a total-force war in the enemy rear. Our army and people successfully progressed from our counter-attack in Việt Bắc and carried out a strategically unique offensive on a large scale, targeting the entire French expeditionary corps and the entire network of their henchmen all over Việt Nam.

As for the strategic demand for combining both guerrilla warfare and regular warfare, the Vietnamese forces' achievements in the guerrilla warfare in the French rear created favorable and significantly decisive conditions for Vietnamese commanders to direct troops both inside and outside the French rear to attack them on two fronts: in front of them and at their back.

About the Vietnamese resistance war in this period, French military historians noted that in 1948, the Việt Minh troops launched across Tonkin (North

Việt Nam) a series of guerrilla operations which shortly became a real offensive for their continuity. This is also Võ Nguyên Giáp's explanation of his concept of "flexible strategic counter-attack" in his later memoirs.

Practising Mobile War—The Firm Steps

Commander-in-Chief Võ Nguyên Giáp highly appreciated the strategic role of guerrilla war, but he did not restrict himself to "guerrillaism." Studying his art of commandship, one could find clearly that very soon in his military career, Giáp realized the laws of the guerilla war, and that a guerilla war would necessarily be developed into and closely combined with a regular war.

In his speech titled *"Chiến lược cầm cự và nhiệm vụ chuẩn bị tổng phản công"* (literally: "The Strategy for Contending with the Enemy and the Task of Preparing for a Counter-attack"), delivered at the Senior Politico-military Cadres Congress in January 1949, Võ Nguyên Giáp said:

> Our fundamental motto right now is using guerrilla war as the main choice and mobile warfare the second choice. In the meantime we need to push up the mobile war vigorously, so that at a right time we can raise it up to an important status.... This, however, does not mean that we will make light of guerrilla warfare. By contrast, a guerrilla war in the enemy rear is a prerequisite if we want to combine mobile war with guerrilla war.

To make his troops' operations fit with the laws of how a guerrilla war was to be turned into a regular war, Võ Nguyên Giáp instructed them to gradually push up this process of transition in accordance to the specific conditions and characteristics of the Vietnamese battlefields.

Chapter Four: ADVANCE TO A STRANGE TURNING POINT

Studying the history of Việt Nam's anti-French resistance war in its early years, one finds a scholarly term uniquely typical of Việt Nam "mobile guerrilla war." This term was first used in the *"Chỉ thị toàn dân kháng chiến"* (literally: "Directive on Calling upon All the People to Stand up in Resistance") issued by the Standing Central Committee on December 22, 1946, which wrote, "We should use the mobile guerrilla war thoroughly."[1] A few days later, on the way from Hà Nội to Việt Bắc on March 6, 1947, Võ Nguyên Giáp wrote *"Huấn lệnh về sự cần thiết phải chuyển sang du kích vận động chiến"* (literally: Directive on the Necessity to Switch to Mobile Guerrilla War").

In June 1947, in a document titled *"Cuộc chiến tranh giải phóng của chúng ta—Chiến thuật và chiến lược"* (literally: "Our Liberation War—Tactics and Strategies"), Võ Nguyên Giáp explained:

> I use the term "mobile guerrilla war" to describe our general method, and not specifically guerilla war or mobile war. The guerrilla tactic is associated with the people's war: small groups of troops will use harassment, vandalism, ambushes, and raids to wipe out or destroy the enemy. While the mobile war is the tactic of the regular army, with which we'll concentrate the best strength of our troops and use multi-battalions to fight relatively big battlefields using diversionary tactics or laying siege to wipe out the enemy. In our resistance war against the French, of course, both local guerrillas and regulars will always use the guerrilla war to wear out or annihilate the enemy. However, ours is a "half guerilla half mobile" tactic because we mobilize a large force to annihilate the enemy instead of wearing them out.

---

1. Communist Party of Việt Nam: *Văn kiện Đảng toàn tập* (literally: The Complete Collection of Party Documents), op cit., vol. 8, p. 150.

Our soldiers are poorly equipped and trained; the troops we mobilize are not independent big corps; the scope of our combat is not very large; our form of combat is sometimes siege and diversion, sometimes ambush and surprise attack, or sometimes a combination of all these forms. Throughout the war, we must ensure that the guerrilla war develops into the mobile war. The two tactics are different in their level of development. Our "guerrilla and mobile tactic" is in the middle of this process of transition.[1]

In the dry season of 1947, Võ Nguyên Giáp requested the Vietnamese battalions to focus on applying the mobile guerrilla war to the Việt Bắc battlefield, and they subsequently gained victories on the 4th and 3rd Routes and the Lô River. Following those victories, the Vietnamese troops continued to launch many ambushes and mobile ambushes not only in the North but also in the Central and Southern battlefields, including famous battles such as La Ngà battle (on the Sài Gòn-Đà Lạt route in early March 1948) and Tầm Vu battle (the 9th Zone-South Việt Nam in mid April 1948).

But guerrilla mobile war was not just limited to ambushes or mobile ambushes. The ambush tactic could wear out the enemy's war means, grind down their strength, and terminate their traffic, but it could not force them to narrow their occupied areas. This meant that the Vietnamese forces could not extend their liberated areas. That explains why the Sixth Central Cadres Congress in mid January 1948 made a strategically important request to sweep all over every of the enemy's posts and narrow their occupied areas. At that time, Võ Nguyên Giáp had to answer the question on how to apply

---

1. Army Medical Department-Ministry of National Defense: *Vui sống* (literally: Enjoying Life) Publishing House, 1947.

Chapter Four: ADVANCE TO A STRANGE TURNING POINT

mobile guerrilla war to defeat what the enemy called the "war of post" (French: *"guerre des postes"*).

In their second war of aggression in Việt Nam, French generals still followed the footsteps of their predecessors Galliéni and Lyautey[1] by using two steps: use their combat troops to attack and occupy, and use the method of building their posts to expand their occupied areas and pacify them in the fashion of an "oil spill." By using their watch-tower system, which was very soon established and became increasingly denser (eventually they numbered in the thousands) in the South,[2] the French extended its control over large areas in the Mekong River Delta. Since the summer of 1947, they had been using this form of occupation in the North and thus they built a network of small bases, both in the mountains and forests and in the Red River Delta. Compared to the watch-towers, these bases were guarded with stricter security by larger numbers of troops and with more fire-power, and whenever attacked, they could be supported by artillery firepower and easily rescued by reinforcement troops (known as interceptive troops). The French used the network of small bases as a strategic measure to achieve their purposes of taking over and pacifying the Việt Minh's lands, propping up the local puppet government, protecting their trunk roads, moving from the process of attacks into that of consolidation and expansion of their occupied areas, and changing military

---

1. Chief Marshal Joseph Simon Galliéni (1849–1916) and Louis Hubert Lyautey (1884–1934). Both of them were French Ministers of War and commanded the French Expeditionary Corps during France's first war of invasion in Việt Nam.
2. They were often referred to as "de Latour watchtowers" as they were the product of General Boyer de Latour du Moulin, commander of French troops in the South of Việt Nam.

311

control into political and economic control over the Việt Minh. They also used small groups of interceptive troops to do the rescue work and on-the-spot shock teams to open raids into the locations they suspected to be the Việt Minh's agencies, workshops, and warehouses. The directive issued by the General Headquarters on February 26, 1948, confirmed that only by destroying the French small bases could the Vietnamese army narrow their scope of occupation, blocking their oil-spill plot of expanding their controlled areas, and thereby dispossess the puppet government of a source of support and create conditions for the development of Việt Nam's guerrilla warfare.

Annihilating the French bases was a new type of fighting in which the Vietnamese troops lacked experience and the Vietnamese regulars had very little equipment,[1] especially explosives for breaking down the barriers and machine guns for storming into the French posts. So the Vietnamese forces had to go from step to step, taking action and learning from lessons at the same time. Võ Nguyên Giáp asked the Ministry of General Staff to use a battalion from the Capital Regiment to pilot both intensive-attack and surprise-attack strategies[2] to annihilate the French entrenchments. Chief of the General Staff Hoàng Văn Thái had some experience with the intensive-attack strategy in the two battles of Phay Khắt

---

1. Their national resistance having gone for over a year, the spoils they collected from the French significantly improved the supplies of their regular soldiers, but by mid 1948, just half of their regular army had a gun to fight with, while the rest fought with a spear.
2. Regarding the intensive-attack strategy, the elite troops, lightly armed combatants, secretly intrude into the French camps and fight hand to hand against their opponents. As for the surprise-attack strategy, they use the strength of fire-power to break through the French positions.

and Nà Ngần long ago but little in how to launch a surprise attack, so he assigned the 11th Battalion to study the second form first. He selected a hill near the Phú Minh junction (Đại Từ District, Thái Nguyên Province) as a training ground for the soldiers. This place was not too far from the General Staff office, facilitating the Staff envoy's travel to and fro to supervise the soldiers' training.

In this military drill, for the first time, full strength combatants were divided into two opponents and fought against each other. Chief of Battalion Vũ Yên, accompanied by a scout team, went to survey Phủ Thông post on the 3rd Route (20 kilometers north of Bắc Cạn Town). When returning, he had a post, which had the same size as that in Phủ Thông, built on Phú Minh hill with trenches, bunkers, gun emplacements, and porcupine-feather fences. After long and sweaty days of drills under scorching summer sun, the 11th Battalion's officers and soldiers initially grasped the idea of how to attack a French post. Knowledge and experience gained by the General Staff from two the small campaigns in Nghĩa Lộ (March 1948) and Yên Bình Xã (June 1948) were immediately applied to the attack on Phủ Thông post in the 3rd Route campaign in late July. The General Staff took one 75-mm mountain gun from the 10th Interzone and gave it to the 11th Battalion. Other units also supported this pilot combat by stepping up their operations on the 3rd Route throughout July in order to isolate the soldiers in Phủ Thông post.

The Vietnamese troops started the attack on Phủ Thông post on the night of July 25, 1948. Their fighting spirit overwhelmed the French company from the start, and this battle was later referred to by the French press as a "fierce hand-to-hand combat." But they had to retreat at dawn before trying to realize their ultimate goal, which was to attack an underground tunnel, by the French fire-power. The Phủ Thông pilot battle was not a complete success,[1] but it gave the officers and soldiers of the 11th Battalion and the General Headquarters staff a lot of initial experience in organizing and carrying out the so-called "post-attacking battle." Particularly, it highlighted the Vietnamese army's weaknesses in reconnaissance (the underground tunnels in this regard), as well as in the organization and commanding the coordination between the infantry and artillery. When summarizing the 3rd Route campaign and Phủ Thông battle, Võ Nguyên Giáp praised the fighting spirit of the 11th Battalion and conferred the title "Phủ Thông Battalion" on them. He analyzed the weaknesses of officers and soldiers in the battle, especially the work of spying and surveying the enemy situations before the battle, and pinpointed the measures to correct them. He also reminded the General Staff of some important experience drawn from the Phủ Thông battle. The Vietnamese troops attacked Phủ Thông on July 25, 1948; three days later, the French reinforcement troops arrived from Cao Bằng along the 3rd Route to rescue. The Vietnamese command of the campaign had made no plans to block the French reinforcements. So here again the Vietnamese learnt a very useful lesson in commanding a campaign (even a small one): it is necessary to work out a plan for attacking the relief troops. Later facts showed that a plan to attack the enemy's posts and one to destroy their relief

---

1. Although the Vietnamese force had weeded out most of the French company (killing the chief and deputy chief of the post right in the opening battle), a squad of French combatants managed to hold on to a tunnel, fighting back fiercely, and the Vietnamese soldiers were not qualified for exterminating it.

troops should be made at the same time, and in many cases, the latter was just a trigger for the primary purpose of "luring the reinforcements out to kill them.

The General Staff of the Vietnamese army reviewed the lessons of experience drawn from their besieging the French posts and destroying the French relief forces in Mộc Hoá, La Bang, and Sóc Xoài in the South, and the first small campaigns in the North (including those in Yên Bình Xã, Nghĩa Lộ, and the 3rd Route), and immediately circulated them to the key zones and main regular troops under training at that time. Following that review, the study of the post-attacking tactic became an important part of the "military training-feat achieving" movement of the Vietnamese regular army during the last days of the rainy season. The hills in Đại Từ (Thái Nguyên Province), Đoan Hùng (Phú Thọ Province), and Lập Thạch (Vĩnh Yên Province) became the training grounds for the regular battalions of the Ministry of General Staff to maneuver themselves in preparation for attacking enemy posts. Through several field trips to such maneuvers in Lập Thạch, Võ Nguyên Giáp worried most about the Vietnamese officials' poor commanding skills and the Vietnamese soldier's lack of equipment for the task of shock attack on the enemy posts. Their weapons were mainly those confiscated from the French on the frontlines. Robbing the opponents of their guns and killing them with such weapons was a basic, long-term, and traditional way to improve equipment for the Vietnamese soldiers. But they also needed to encourage and further boost up the productivity of their arms factories. In a working session with Chief of General Staff Hoàng Văn Thái and Head of Military Weapons Department Trần Đại Nghĩa, Võ Nguyên Giáp agreed with the two men that they should make use of the campaign of "record-breaking production" in the "military training-feat achieving" movement of the entire army to further boost up the production of armaments, especially weapons used for attacking enemy posts. The Phủ Thông battle showed that the spirit and the will of the Vietnamese officials and soldiers played a leading and important role, and was their absolute advantage toward a victory. But the battle also showed that if the Vietnamese soldiers were better equipped, they would be able to fight more effectively. As suggested later by Võ Nguyên Giáp, at the military weapons conference, for the first time, the issue of recoilless gun (SKZ) production was put up. Through much research and many trials done by the people and factories in the all-people patriotic movement and the "record-breaking production" movement among the national defense supply industry, the Vietnamese factories succeeded in producing many kinds of heavy weapons,[1] marking an important milestone in their improvement of equipment for the regular troops, of which the 60-mm SKZ soon became an effective weapon helping the Vietnamese troops to attack French posts.[2]

To encourage the timely efforts of the military arms industry, Võ Nguyên Giáp sent a letter to the workers at national defense factories on the International Labor Day entitled *"Huấn lệnh rèn luyện cán bộ cải tiến kỹ thuật"* (literally:

---

1. They included 81-mm, 120-mm, and 185-mm mortars, and 60-mm and 120-mm recoilless guns (SKZ).
2. Since 1949, the military industry and army of Việt Nam began to remedy the weaknesses as identified by the Party General Secretary at Fifth Central Cadres Congress (mid 1948): "We are weak at the tactic of attacking small entrenched fortifications and short of the necessary weapons, so we are helpless in attacking the enemy's strongholds."

Chapter Four: ADVANCE TO A STRANGE TURNING POINT

"Directive on Staff Training and Technical Improvement"). In this directive, after praising the achievements of the industry, Võ Nguyên Giáp commented that the cadres in the national defense industry had not been fully impregnated with the necessary strategic ideology and tactics, and that the manufacturing industry and the army had not cooperated very well. Consequently, the manufacturing industry sometimes developed at a lower, and at other times faster, speed compared to the army. He reminded those working in the military arms industry to understand well their honor in serving the soldiers. He also reminded the entire military industry to keep themselves updated and to meet the needs of the soldiers and their combat missions, both in strategic and tactical terms.

The whole Vietnamese army was to embark on the second dry season of the national resistance war. They were all ready to defeat the enemy if the enemy were to advance into their unoccupied zones, and to continue proactively to train to fight mobile combats in small campaigns of attacks.

In the two military reports entitled *"Vấn đề quân sự hiện giờ ở Việt Nam"* (literally: "The Current Military Issue in Việt Nam") and *"Kiểm thảo mùa hè, chuẩn bị thu đông"* (literally: "Making Self-criticism of Our Summer Combat and Preparing for the Autumn-winter One") delivered at the Fifth Central Cadres Congress in mid August 1948, Commander-in-chief Võ Nguyên Giáp noted that:

> Since the start of the first dry season of this second phase, we have succeeded in fighting against enemy raids in the South and Xuân Mai (Hòa Bình Province) and Ân Thi (Hưng Yên Province) in the North; launched our forces into the enemy's back, especially in the Northeast, Northwest,

and the Central Highlands; made a leap-frog ahead in the use of concentrated combat troops (one or many battalions) in our first small campaigns on mountainous battlefields, such as the battles of Đồng Dương and Cẩm Lý; and managed to penetrate into some areas that we had failed to in previous years. Regarding the advisory work, in the previous years it was only until mid summer that we could come to a blueprint for our summer plan, but this year we can release it ahead of schedule. At the beginning of the dry season, the General Headquarters anticipated the situation and directed our preparations for the combat in the enemy's potential directions of attack (Việt Bắc, the 4th Zone, and the Northern midlands). Regarding the general guidelines for the coordinated operations, the General Headquarters stressed the clear-cut requirements and gave instructions on the measures to shift from attritional attack to annihilating attack, with higher concentrations of combat troops compared to the previous dry season.

Also at the Fifth Central Cadres Congress, Võ Nguyên Giáp clearly stated the strategic tactics for the three forms of troops at the time the war was shifting to the new phase as follows:

1- To fulfill the task of continually expanding their guerrilla warfare movements, the Vietnamese should thoroughly understand their goals in this period, which were to command independent companies to fulfill their mission, promote their fighting strength, and push up the guerilla movements so as to bring back the independent companies to the regular army in order to boost up their mobile war.

2- To carry out the mobile war with small campaigns, their regular army should be fully organized with concentrated fire-power, supported by sappers and artillery, and well trained in mobile war operations. They should be cautious but at the same time bold enough to push up their mobile war, and cautious but determined in mobilizing their main forces for large-scale battles. The Party Central Committee defined the strategy for small campaigns in the dry season of 1948. Regarding attacks, they should avoid adverse battles that would cause them more damages or would cause equal losses to both sides. They should avoid those battles where they had not been well prepared or well planned and would not be certain to win. In addition, they should not let ourselves be trapped by the enemy into unfavorable battles.[1]

Right from late 1948 and early 1949, in order to lead the army in each of their firm steps on the way toward the mobile war, in the context where unit commanders in the battlefield lacked experience (from the process of preparing to that of campaigning), Võ Nguyên Giáp organized workshops and issued specific instructions for the General Headquarters offices at zone and regiment levels. At the Senior Politico-military Cadres Congress held in early 1949, he cited the orientations and measures for strengthening and building the regular army, developing the militia forces, and consolidating commanding agencies. He also suggested how to draw experience and especially how to resolve the most critical issue—staff training and drilling.

Regarding troops building, Võ Nguyên Giáp suggested they should implement the phased withdrawal of independent companies and return them back into the regular army. He pinpointed the plan for consolidating commanding agencies

---

1. Communist Party of Việt Nam: *Văn kiện Đảng toàn tập* (literally: The Complete Collection of Party Documents), op cit., vol. 9, p. 220.

by gathering all the cadres into them, and for gathering weapons and means for commanding for the main force units to fight at the mobile war. In the Directive *"Rèn luyện cán bộ, chấn chỉnh quân đội"* (literally: "Staff Training and Military Reorganization"), Võ Nguyên Giáp pinpointed that the specific contents of the campaign should include the necessary knowledge required for and the principles concerning the mode of thinking, organization, techniques, tactics, and sense of discipline suitable for the mobile war. The military personnel, troop training, and supplies for them should be implemented in the way that serves the purpose of the mobile war.

Regarding the personnel work, he said, the issue of cadres is a key issue to realize the new military mottos. If we can't address this issue properly, then surely we cannot achieve satisfactory results for our mottos or plans no mater how sound and correct they seem. The new tasks require a greater number of personnel, especially artillerymen, engineers, and communicators. A mobile war needs those people suitable for it, those who know how to command tactics flexibly, have plans, initiative, vision, and can understand and judge the enemy and respond quickly and are capable of managing a large army. So we should come up to a plan for training the specialists. The training program should be based on the current strategic idea and tactic. At present, our soldiers have improved their knowledge a lot. In the new situations, commanding officers will have to shoulder new and heavier tasks, and so should upgrade themselves rapidly to keep up with them.

Regarding the relationship between the regular army and the localities where campaigns were to be launched,

Giáp wrote about the experience he drew from the previous small campaigns in 1948 (Yên Bình Xã, the 3rd Route, and the Northeast):

> Speaking about campaigns and operations of the regular army, the necessary and sufficient conditions for us to win victory are: preparing the battlefield, establishing the guerilla bases among the masses, investigating the enemy situation, transporting supplies, make pre-combat preparations, sabotaging the enemy's facilities, cleaning up after each battle, and promoting our victories during and after combat. Can the regular army undertake all these tasks by themselves? If yes, they will not be able to do them well. Conversely, if the military, civil, and political organizations can cooperate in mobilizing local troops and militiamen, human labor and wealth, people's initiative and bravery together, they can do those tasks much more effectively.

Võ Nguyên Giáp monitored the campaigns thoroughly and, based on their advantages and disadvantages and his own experience of command, he promptly circulated the information to every unit in the form of a face-to-face meeting or a notification. He directly chaired the meeting to review the Lô River campaign and the 4th Route campaign in the summer of 1949. These campaigns brought the Vietnamese troops different experience in the method of combat. In the Lô River campaign, the Vietnamese mainly chased after the French in Bạch Lưu, Lệ Mỹ, and Tiên Du; in the 4th Route campaign, Vietnamese artillery and sappers coordinated to launch attacks on the French posts in Bản Trại and Đèo Khách; in the Lũng Phầy campaign, the Vietnamese launched a big ambush, and this campaign demonstrated their experience in preparing the battlefield; the Quảng Yên battle demonstrated their experience of launching a big attack deep into the enemy den. The meeting clarified many issues on the preparation for a campaign, the organization, mobilization, and use of military forces (including the means and techniques of combat in the context of their limited resources), the carrying out of a campaign, the type of combat and forms of tactics, the political work and logistical work, the relationship with the local people, the opportunity and art of ending the campaign and promoting campaign results, as well as the organization of campaign summarization and the dissemination of and learning from experience.

In some campaigns, they had deployed big forces but in terrain which was not favorable for the commanding officers to make decisions.[1] Therefore, in order to gain best effectiveness, a few months earlier, Võ Nguyên Giáp gave out his detailed instructions about steps for preparation, the purpose of the battle, the strategies and tactics, the use of combatants, the organization of the commanding agency, the preparation of terrain, the investigation into the enemy situation, the preparation of combatants and that for coordination between soldiers and masses, as well as the preparation of food, weapons, ammunition, military medicine, communications, armed propaganda, agitation and propaganda among the enemy, and communication and reporting to the General Headquarters. In the first phase, the Lê Lợi campaign went on very well, notably the battle using the mobile warfare tactics of the 209th Regiment on the Mỏ Hẻm-Chợ Bờ route. However, in second phase, they did not fight very efficiently, because we were too passionate about

---

1. Examples include the Lê Lợi-Chợ Bờ-Hòa Bình campaign, which involved the participation of 14 regiments and took place on the banks of the Đà River from November 23 to December 30, 1949.

attacking posts while making too light of fighting back the French reinforcement troops in Hòa Bình and the 6th Route. In the face of this situation, Võ Nguyên Giáp decided to stop the campaign, asking the soldiers to withdraw and to take a rest and ordering the 3rd Interzone High Command and the 209th Regiment to continue preparing the battlefield in the direction of Hoà Bình. Chief of Regiment Lê Trọng Tấn was requested to note down their experience from the battle where the enemy withdrew on the Mỏ Hẻm-Chợ Bờ route for later circulation to each combat unit.

In general, with the close monitoring and steering of the Ministry of High Command, from autumn 1948 to summer 1950, the Vietnamese regular army opened about 20 small campaigns in all battlefields,[1] from the Northeast to the Northwest, the south of the 4th Zone, the 5th Zone, and the South. The main purpose of these campaigns was to destroy part of the enemy's vital forces, to narrow their occupied areas, most importantly to train cadres and soldiers in the concentrated-combat method (from small to big battles), and to facilitate the development of guerilla war. The main tactic of small campaigns was to attack.[2] Combatants were mobilized from two battalions (as in the case of the 2nd Yên Bình Xã campaign) or from four regiments (as in the cases

---

1. They included ten campaigns in North Việt Nam, seven in Central Việt Nam, three in South Việt Nam, and the *Shi Wan Da Shan* (literally: One Hundred Thousand Great Mountains) campaign in Huanan. In the last campaign, the Vietnamese cooperated with the Chinese to expand the Tiangui-Yuegui border area to help the latter build a liberation zone in the Yongzhou-Longzhou-Qinzhou area, bordering on northeastern Việt Nam, to receive the liberation army from lower Southern China.
2. The Lô River campaign in May 1949 against the French Pomone operation was a counter-attack.

of the 1st Đông Bắc, Lê Lai, and Lê Lợi campaigns). The main tactic used was attacking an outpost to lure in and destroy the enemy's reinforcement troops. Along with identifying the direction of attack for each locality, Võ Nguyên Giáp often sent General Headquarters envoys to zones and regiments to help them prepare for the organization and administration of the campaign and outlined experience for them to learn from. He stressed the necessity to make review and summarize and to draw from experience after each campaign. He often emphasized that each unit should review experience after each battle so that by learning from such experience their combatants could mature more and more, and that fighting the enemy should be coupled with strengthening themselves so that they would become stronger after each battle.

The 20 months of harsh trial through small campaigns marked a big improvement by the key units of the General Headquarters and interzones. What the Vietnamese soldiers achieved was not just annihilating part of the French forces, liberating part of the lands, and supporting the guerrilla warfare. The most important thing they gained was that they had matured steadily both in personnel organization, technical equipment, and skills in small-scale concentrated warfare. Also during this period, the General Headquarters, as well as interzones and regiments, recorded remarkable achievements: they understood better how to build up troops, to organize and conduct the campaigns, and make decisive contributions to perfecting their operational art. This was one of the important achievements that demonstrated their spirit of self-reliance in the years of fighting against the French siege, when we had not yet learnt from the experience of their brotherly countries with more advanced armies.

Chapter Four: ADVANCE TO A STRANGE TURNING POINT

Võ Nguyên Giáp instructed the interzones and regiments throughout Việt Nam to organize small and medium campaigns of attack while incessantly boosting up guerrilla warfare, especially in the Red River Delta. Facing the enemy's strategic plot (Revers plan) to expand their occupation in order to seize control of the Red River Delta (which they called the plan of "rolling up the useful plains"), the High Command of the 3rd Interzone strongly boosted up the guerrilla warfare to annihilate the French on a large scale and coordinated with the other interzones' regular units in the battles in Thái Ninh, Quỳnh Côi, and Tiên Hưng in Thái Bình Province, and Ứng Hoà in Hà Đông Province. The guerrilla warfare in the Red River Delta worked in close collaboration with the small campaigns in the forested and mountainous areas.

In the gradual transition from the warfare that used dispersed guerrilla groups into one that used concentrated troops (from a small to large scale) aimed at pushing up the mobile war, the Vietnamese strategists had to win in the tenacious struggle to put into practice the key guidelines, so that their regular army could meet one of the key requirements set for them: the more they fought, the stronger they would become. Võ Nguyên Giáp stressed heavily on the necessity for the Vietnamese army to draw experience from each battle. He highlighted the experience they had gained from successful battles, those which were well-directed, well-prepared, and well-supervised. But he also criticized strictly "drawn" battles, in which gains could not make up for losses, such as the Phủ Thông, Lô River, First Lê Hồng Phong battles in 1948, 1949, and the spring of 1950 respectively.

Notably, Võ Nguyên Giáp criticized the First Lê Hồng Phong Front Command for their mistakes in the Phố Lu and Nghĩa Đô battles. It was an unforgettable lesson for the Advisory Board of the General Headquarters.

In his telegram sent on March 20, 1950, Commander-in-chief Võ Nguyên Giáp asked the First Lê Hồng Phong Front Command to make thorough self-criticism to find out the cause of their casualties in the Phố Lu battle. He repeated what the Command recounted in their report:

> In the Phố Lu battle, we destroyed a vital town of the enemy, confiscated their weapons and ammunition, and killed 100 of their combatants. However, we also suffered a big loss: 100 combatants were killed, including 11 officers at company and platoon levels, and 180 were injured, including 13 officers ...

Then he raised questions for them, "Did you estimate the death toll on our side before the battle? And if you did, and you knew that we would suffer from such a big loss if we launched the attack, would you still decide to go ahead?" He concluded that in both cases, the Command must recognize their shortcomings and find the causes for their failure. He also criticized the Command for having failed to organize self-criticism as instructed. He cited evidence as follows:

1- A letter from the Political Commissar of the First Lê Hồng Phong Front Command wrote, "We suffered quite heavy casualties in the Phố Lu battle. However, the enemy built very strong fortifications in this town, and only when we arrived there did we realize that such casualties of our forces were insignificant."

2- The letter from the Deputy Commander stated many observations and comments on Phố Lu but stated nothing

Chapter Four: ADVANCE TO A STRANGE TURNING POINT

about their losses. According to this letter, if the French had been able to uphold their fighting spirit any longer, then the Vietnamese troops would have suffered more losses.

3- The Letter from the Commander read, "Our losses were caused not by the enemy but by our vehement enthusiasm."

Võ Nguyên Giáp criticized that these self-criticisms only cited their good points but not bad points, only the losses on the French side but not on their own, and that the criticizers had only explained without admitting their mistakes.

Regarding the Nghĩa Đô battle, a report wrote:

> The enemy lost part of their troops' strength. We seized from them 20 rifles and sub-machine guns and lost 32 rifles, 4 submachine guns, and light machine guns to them. Ninty-one of our combatants were killed or missing; 202 injured. As for the 11th Battalion (Phủ Thông Battalion), all best gunners and most brave commanders were killed in the battle against the paratroops. Phủ Thông lost most of its elite troop strength because most of its excellent combatants were killed.

Võ Nguyên Giáp raised a question: Was the Phủ Thông battle a failure? And he confirmed that it was. To cause the French to retreat or to annihilate part of their strength did not mean that the Vietnamese succeeded. Therefore, Võ Nguyên Giáp opined that the Vietnamese leadership should not cause misunderstanding among the officers that the Nghĩa Đô battle was a success by rewarding some excellent individual soldiers and units at this battle. To encourage the soldiers means to not only cite examples of their victories and strong points but also their failures and defects, so that they can learn from them and correct them.

To end his telegram, Võ Nguyên Giáp wrote, "You men take the heaviest responsibilities and so you should see self-criticism the strictest discipline to tighten, especially when we win."

Although some campaigns failed to meet the requirements of the strategy, and worse, some were total failures, the over 20 small campaigns between summer 1948 and autumn 1950 proved that Võ Nguyên Giáp had asked the General Headquarters, interzones, and regiment to thoroughly grasp and creatively put into practice the laws of development of the revolutionary war. Those small campaigns gave the General Headquarters important lessons in commanding the design and implementation of the strategy.

Realities have shown that the shift from guerilla to regular warfare and from small to big warfare is the indispensable law of Việt Nam's revolutionary war. In a research project summarizing the anti-French war, Commander-in-chief Võ Nguyên Giáp wrote:

> From the strategic point of view, the guerrilla war can render many difficulties and losses to the enemy, but it can only wear them out. To grind down most of the enemy's strength and liberate the land, we should advance from guerilla war to mobile warfare and positional warfare.
>
> To implement the motto of advancing guerrilla warfare into mobile warfare, right from the beginning, we had a section of our guerrilla forces fighting in a dispersed manner and another section fighting in a concentrated manner, who were the first seeds of our mobile warfare. In 1947, by using the independent company-concentrated battalion tactics, we began to learn to shift into more concentrated battles toward mobile warfare. In 1948, we launched one or more battalions to make quite big ambushes and attacks by

surprise on the enemy. We carried out small campaigns, not only in the North but also in the other areas in the country. Since 1950, we began to launch campaigns on increasingly larger scales, mainly using mobile warfare in the Northern battlefields.[1]

To evaluate the strategic significance of the more than 20 small campaigns during the Vietnamese people and army's transition from guerrilla warfare to mobile warfare, the document titled *"Lịch sử nghệ thuật chiến dịch"* (literally: "History of the Operational Art") summed up:

> During those campaigns, we wore out part of the enemy's strength and liberated part of our land, contributing to backing up the guerrilla war movement. Throughout this process, our regular army took an important step forward in terms of personnel organization, technical supplies, and tactical level from guerrilla warfare to small-scale concentrated warfare. This was also the process of gradual development of the operational art, mainly the offensive operation of launching attacks on each of the entrenched fortifications in the enemy's defense systems and their interceptive troops.
>
> . . . On our transition from guerrilla warfare to regular warfare, our commanding officers showed many weaknesses in managing the campaign, which was shown by the rare showcases of successful commanding. But thanks to those lessons, that we had to pay for with our blood and sweat to learn in the process of development from scattered warfare to concentrated warfare in such small-scale campaigns, our commanding officers trained themselves to have the firm mettle necessary to launch the

---

1. *Những kinh nghiệm lớn của Đảng ta trong lãnh đạo đấu tranh vũ trang* (literally: Our Party's Great Experience in Its Leadership of Armed Struggle), People's Army Publishing House, Hà Nội, 1967.

first and biggest ever campaign in the early autumn and winter of 1950.[1]

Creating Factors for Victory in the First Large-scale Campaign

Despite their awkward communication technology, the General Headquarters intelligence agency tried to tap thoroughly the openly publicized information sources in order to understand and analyze the major happenings on the French side, as a basis to assess their situation and work out our steps to deal with them. The Swallow Radio of the French expeditionary force, as well as the Paris and Sài Gòn press, helped provide the Advisory Board of the General Headquarters with much important information about the French side.

After five consecutive years of pursuing the war and consecutive defeats on battlefields, the French Government was facing increasingly severe economic and financial difficulties and interminable political crises. The French people's anti-war movements were spreading widely. During the time from November 1947 (when the French launched the attack on Việt Bắc) to mid 1950, the world witnessed the establishment and dissolution of the French cabinet eight times. The anti-war movements and the government's unsteady political position made all the prime ministers too scared to dare to submit the agreements signed with Emperor Bảo Đại (in Hạ Long Bay as well as in Paris) to the French Parliament because they were sure that such deals would not be approved.

---

1. Ministry of National Defense-Việt Nam Institute of Military History: *Lịch sử nghệ thuật chiến dịch* (literally: History of the Operational Art).

In military terms, the newspapers in Paris and Sài Gòn posted battlefield commanders' complaints about the French's biggest difficulty: their lack of troops. None of the French-occupied areas had enough troops for the increasingly burdensome task of fighting against the frequent activities of the growing Việt Minh force. For example, along the 300-km coast in the central part of Central Việt Nam, France had only six battalions to cope with a very "tense" situation, and so the Vietnamese side took advantage of this state of dispersion to launch the attack. Also in the North, without reinforcements, the French troops could not clear the road toward the Northwest or lift Hà Nội from the daily siege by the local guerrillas. In the Northeast, not only in Cao Bằng but also all the way along the 4th Route to the mining areas, it was likely that military upheavals would occur at any time because the Vietnamese side always gained the initiative in combat. Most worrying was the situation in the Red River Delta, a fertile and highly-populated plain which accounted for one-fifth of the North in area but was always in chaos because of the never-ending firing from the Việt Minh guerrillas. General Charles Chanson (seen as an "expert in pacifying" in the South) was appointed to "save the useful plains from being decayed."

While the canvassing for reinforcements had seen no positive signs, Paris got the news of Phủ Thông battle.[1] The French press reflected the opinion of the politicians in Paris that the Phủ Thông battle could be a "stimulant" to push the French Government to try harder in reinforcing the French troops in Indochina to rescue the worsening situation.

---

1. Referring to the attack by the 11th Battalion on Phủ Thông on July 25, 1948.

French Commander-in-chief Blaizot, however, knew very well that requesting reinforcements was always the story of "the spirit is willing but the flesh is weak" with the French Government.

Meanwhile, in Sài Gòn, High Commissioner Léon Pignon and Commander-in-chief Blaizot had been persistently in disagreement on their strategy and policy over their lack of combat troops. Blaizot asserted that they needed to boost their military efforts on the Northern battleground, which he saw as the knot of the Indochina war, while Pignon thought that they should quickly rescue the South, "the handle of the fan" of the entire Indochina Peninsula.

The face of the battlefield became increasingly detrimental to France at a time when the Chinese Liberation Army was moving quickly to Huanan. Under this circumstance, in the summer of 1949, the Paris Government sent a delegation led by Chief of the General Staff Georges Revers on an inspection tour to Indochina. The one-month mission led to the so-called "Revers plan" with the focal points being: to focus on the Northern battlefield and on a plan to soon establish an uninterrupted and perfect defensive fighting position in the Northern battlefield; to cut off all communication links between the Việt Minh forces and the Chinese Liberation Army; to maintain their control over the North by all means and to gradually integrate the issue of defending Indochina into the framework of a strategic alliance with the United States. Specifically:

1- France would make use of the American aid to build a strong Euro-African mobile block in combination with using a synthetic strategy of "feeding the war with war" and "using the Vietnamese to fight the Vietnamese," first and foremost to urgently boost up the conscription to develop an army of henchmen to make up for the deficits.

2- France would withdraw troops from Cao Bằng and Đông Khê, the two positions that required a variety of means of transport for supply of provisions on a road axis where bloody ambushes always happened.

3- To make up for the withdrawn troops, the French will launch an invading attack on Thái Nguyên and enhance their defense line from Móng Cái to Thất Khê in order to take control of the Lạng Sơn-Thái Nguyên-Hoà Bình-Hải Phòng quadrilateral zone.

4- Once having finished these two steps, France might withdraw its troops from Thất Khê and gradually expand its control over the Red River Delta.

During the meeting between the French generals with the delegation led by Revers in Sài Gòn on June 15, 1949, a fierce debate occurred surrounding the pros and cons of shortening the defense line on the 4th Route. General Marcel Alessandri, Commander of the North Indochina battlefield was the person who opposed most vehemently the decision to withdraw troops from Cao Bằng. The delegation went back to France after the generals had only "accepted with reluctance and on principle" the opinions of the representatives of Paris. Following the departure of the delegation, no conclusion had been made on the issue of shortening the defense line on the 4th Route, and this became the subject of persistent controversy between the French commanders of the expeditionary force. The delegation went back to France and the Revers plan was not officially approved because of a deep split among the Paris politicians around the political and military strategies toward Indochina. The "scandal of the generals" (as it was called by journalists) around the newly-formed strategic plan forced Chief of General Staff Revers to retire ahead of time and General Blaizot to be recalled. Revers was replaced by the four-star General Marcel Carpentier, who became the fourth Commander-in-chief in Việt Nam. This happened almost simultaneously with the overturning of the Henri cabinet. The presence of General Carpentier in Sài Gòn made the French conflict over their strategy and policy tenser, especially after the new commander-in-chief bluntly rejected Alessandri's request. This new general in charge of the North voted for the plan to use about 30 battalions to launch a big operation into the region that he called the "Hồ Chí Minh quadrangle"[1] in an attempt to "improve the situation."

After five years of invading Indochina, the French had become mired deeply in a complete deadlock, and during this period the American Government step-by-step made known their intention to intervene in Indochina. The meeting between French Foreign Minister Robert Schuman and his American counterpart Jafferson Caffery in September 1949 ignited this plot. A few months later, the first American ship transporting weapons as aid to the French landed in Sài Gòn, marking the beginning of the more-than-a-quarter-century-long process of involvement of the White House and the Pentagon in Indochina.

On the Vietnamese side, right from early 1950, in an article titled *"Nhiệm vụ quân sự trước mắt"* (literally: "The Immediate Military Mission") published in the *Quân chính*

---

1. This refers to the Tuyên Quang-Bắc Cạn-Thái Nguyên-Phú Thọ quadrangle in Việt Bắc.

Chapter Four: ADVANCE TO A STRANGE TURNING POINT

tập san (literally: *Politico-military Journal*), Võ Nguyên Giáp affirmed that 1950 was the year of the strategic redirection of the Vietnamese army and people. His affirmation showed that he had realized some upcoming strategic opportunities, based on his analysis of important changes in the world, notably the success of the Chinese revolution that gave birth to the Republic of China. After five years, the national resistance war of the Vietnamese people and army experienced a profound change in many aspects. The spirit of self-support and self-improvement helped the Vietnamese people and army to overcome all difficulties in the process of gradual switching from dispersed guerilla war to concentrated warfare, changing dramatically the balance of power between them and the French.

The clearest evidence was their establishment of the first regular brigade. This move was one of the specific strategic guidelines for the big fight approved by the Standing Central Committee. Gone was the time when such a brigade only played the formalistic role of an organization responsible for cooperating with the French troops to do the task of supporting the defense plan according to the Preliminary Accords in summer 1946. Gone also was the time when an independent brigade was dissolved right after its establishment and replaced by small squads to fight in small skirmishes to suit the state of the battlefield like the situation in the dry season of 1947. Over years of combat in extremely difficult conditions, the Vietnamese regular battalions and regiments became "fully fledged," and it was the objective requirement of the mounting resistance war to organize the regular army into brigades. The plan made and presented by Võ Nguyên Giáp on the establishment of the first regular brigade at the meeting of the Standing Central Committee in mid August got unanimous approval.

On August 28, 1949, Trần Đăng Ninh, representative of the Vietnamese Government, and Võ Nguyên Giáp went to Đồn Đu[1] to attend the founding ceremony of the 308th Brigade, known as the "Vanguard Brigade." Standing in front of the Commander-in-chief that day were no longer several dozens of barefoot guerrilla fighters with flintlocks in their hands, like the situation of nearly five years ago when the Vietnamese army was first founded, but the all-victorious and terror-inducing battalions. Standing in front of the regular units in a trim line were Vương Thừa Vũ, Vũ Yên, Vũ Lăng, Thái Dũng, and some others, who matured from the first 60 days of the outbreak of the national resistance war in Hà Nội.

In the "Order for the Day" read to thousands of soldiers, after citing the reason for the founding of the General Staff's first regular brigade, Võ Nguyên Giáp repeated clearly and fully the most typical victories of the battalions and praised the fine traditions of the units in the cause of construction and fighting. To conclude the "Order for the Day," he emphasized the fundamental tasks of the brigade: to cooperate with other regular corps to take the pioneer role in grinding down the enemy and to strive for being gradually regularized.

The founding of the 308th Brigade helped to verify Hồ Chí Minh's prediction nearly five years earlier about the glorious future of the Liberation Army founded by him. The event also proved what he foresaw after the victory of the Việt Bắc campaign: the Vietnamese forces were like a new current

---

1. A town in Phú Lương District, north of Thái Nguyên Province, close to the 3rd Route.

of water and a newly-kindled fire which would only proceed and would not move back.

In early 1950, in his report at the Sixth Military Conference and the Administration-Resistance Conference, assessing the situation when calculating a step for a strategic shift, Commander-in-chief Võ Nguyên Giáp delivered assessments of the general situation before planning a shift in the strategic direction. In his review, after two years of implementation, the guideline for the people's war become more clarified and specified, but it had not been instilled into the military, civil, and political officers at all levels.

The motto of using guerrilla war as the primary tactic and mobile war as the secondary tactic had been applied and had led to many great victories. However, it had not yet been upheld firmly in the battlefields.

In terms of troop organization and tactical command, their level of organization and tactical standards had not met the requirements of the strategic guideline and thus had not ensure its successful implementation.

Regarding the balance of power, Võ Nguyên Giáp opined that after two years of preparation, the Vietnamese military troops had grown rapidly, but they were still weaker than the French troops, despite the latter suffering from heavy losses, both physical and mental. To overcome this situation, the Vietnamese should promote their strong points and take advantage of the French weaknesses so as to gain military advantage. They should build a powerful people's army in sufficient quantity and equipped with advanced equipment and well-qualified and competent officers capable of destroying the enemy in an important battlefield.

The report also highlighted their material difficulties with regard to completing the task of preparing for a new stage. The French were forced to withdraw from Bắc Cạn Town and many other locations along the Bắc Cạn-Cao Bằng route (such as Phủ Thông, Nà Phặc, and Ngân Sơn), but they managed to expand their occupation in the midland and lowland areas. Since mid 1949, they tightened their economic and food blockade over the Vietnamese troops, making sure no rice leaked out from their occupied areas, so the Vietnamese troops suffered a shortage of rice and salt. On the other hand, they released fake Vietnamese banknotes into their unoccupied zones, causing a sharp rise in the rice price in the North.[1]

Regarding military equipment, the arms and ammunition collected in battles and produced by themselves were not enough for the Vietnamese to meet the demands of their regular units for construction and development. They also suffered a serious shortage of fire-power for attacking enemy posts. In some regular units, soldiers still fought with shock spears. In the wake of the successful Chinese revolution, to achieve their goal of building a powerful, well-equipped, well-trained, capable, and large people's army so as to switch to an all-out counter-attack, the Vietnamese should necessarily open the door for international exchange to get aid from their brotherly countries.

---

1. In many cases, managing officers at the General Headquarters had to borrow rice from the mass organizations and agencies nearly almost every day. They had to eat sweet potato or cassava instead of rice for many meals. They recalled, "It had never been so cold as it was in the dry season of 1947, and we had never suffered such a severe famine as that in the between-crop period in 1949."

Chapter Four: ADVANCE TO A STRANGE TURNING POINT

At the Administration-Resistance Conference, Võ Nguyên Giáp quoted President Hồ Chí Minh's speech at the meeting of the Cabinet Council in late 1949 to answer the question of when they should move to a general counter-offensive. Based on the analysis of the balance of power between the two sides physically and mentally, in and outside the country, Hồ Chí Minh said that in 1950, the Vietnamese should rush to complete all preparations to move from the resistance war to the general counter-offensive, and thus their hold-out period would end and their third phase would start. One of the immediate important tasks discussed by the Standing Central Committee at the mid August 1949 meeting was to prepare in all aspects to break the French siege in the Northern border area, lift their blockade on the Việt Bắc base, and clear the way for international exchange.

Commander-in-chief Võ Nguyên Giáp spent a lot of time studying and directing the preparation for the campaign to open the border—the topmost key strategic task for 1950. In the Directive dated November 10, 1949, on battlefield preparation sent to the High Commands of the 1st and 10th Interzones and the Provincial Party Committees of Lào Cai, Hà Giang, Cao Bằng, Lạng Sơn, and Hải Ninh, as well as in the Supplementary Directive dated December 24, 1949, Võ Nguyên Giáp analyzed the French plot to collude with the remnants of the Chiang Kai-shek troops being cornered in the Sino-Vietnamese border area. He also articulated the Vietnamese policy and strategy, and clarified the question of what they should do to prepare the battlefield for border liberation.

After the restricted victory of the First Lê Hồng Phong campaign, the General Headquarters advocated the plan of continuing their operations in the Northwest, creating favorable conditions for sending in more combatants for a big skirmish there to open the border in this direction. On April 22, 1950, Võ Nguyên Giáp send an order to the Northwest Front, the 308th Brigade 308, and the 209th Regiment, requesting them to prepare for the battlefield. He anticipated that the French might enhance their troops to defend Lào Cai, but in general their biggest weakness was in the Northwest. The Ministry of General Command assigned the Northwest Front the task of continuing to prepare the battlefield, so that they could launch the campaign around mid June 1950 to liberate Lào Cai and the Lào Cai-Hà Giang sub-region, opening up the Northwest border.

Along with the founding of the first regular brigade and the planned organization of some more brigades, the General Headquarters' offices were also significantly reinforced. The departments in charge of political affairs and supplies were grouped into the General Department of Politics headed by Nguyễn Chí Thanh and the General Department of Logistics headed by Trần Đăng Ninh. In February 1950, President Hồ Chí Minh issued a decree for total mobilization of manpower and material resources for the front line. Later, on March 10, the second regular infantry brigade, the 304th Brigade, was founded. All such moves aimed at completing the task of getting ready for the general counter-offensive, with the immediate goal being to pave the way for international exchange.

Whilst they were preparing for the campaign to liberate the Northwest border area, Hồ Chí Minh returned from his working trip abroad to Việt Bắc. In a consultation, after hearing Hồ Chí Minh report the results of his talks with Stalin and Mao Zedong, the Standing Central Committee took a new approach to the project devised by the Central Military Commission for border liberation: the possibility of taking advantage of the military aid from the Soviet Union and China had become a reality. By analyzing the French plot of using the American aid to constantly expand their occupation in the midland and lowland areas, the characteristics of the battlefield in the border region, and the French situation in the Northeast and Northwest highlands, Hồ Chí Minh and the Standing Central Committee decided to change their campaign target into liberating the Northeast border region. The French troops on the 4th Route were more numerous and stronger than those on the Lào Cai-Hà Giang route, and those in Cao Bằng were much stronger than those in Lào Cai. By targeting the Cao Bằng-Lạng Sơn route, however, the Vietnamese would be able to shorten the provisions supply line for the campaign, and this would make it easier for them to launch the big campaign to destroy an important part of the French forces. On the other hand, by opening up the borders in the Cao Bằng-Lạng Sơn direction, they would have a bigger chance to exchange with their fraternal countries.

On the basis of their agreement with China, some of the Vietnamese regular regiments took turns to go to China to receive weapons and learn from its Liberation Army's experience. The most notable lessons they gained were reflected in their making a big stride in their combat skills, especially in their ability to hit the enemy in their firm fortifications. At that time, China had not been able to provide them with the anti-tank and anti-craft weapons that they desperately needed. With its help, however, the Vietnamese regulars had been equipped considerably. Many Vietnamese regular battalions could then "say goodbye to" their shock spears after many years of using them to disturb the French siege and winning resounding victories across battlefields.

Since they decided to change their target to the Northeast direction, the General Headquarters had put all their efforts into preparing the Cao Bằng-Lạng Sơn battlefield, of which the most important goal was to repair and extend hundreds of kilometers of roads connecting Thái Nguyên and Cao Bằng, Thái Nguyên and Tuyên Quang, and Tuyên Quang and Phú Thọ.

To better understand all aspects of the Northeastern battlefields, Võ Nguyên Giáp summoned the Chief of the 174th Regiment to deliver a specific report on the 4th Route over the previous four years. He particularly drew conclusions about some of the successive wins by the Vietnamese forces between late 1949 and early 1950.

A few days later, while the General Headquarters' offices were attentively monitoring the French situation and preparing an combat plan for the campaign, they heard the news that the 174th Regiment had destroyed the Đông Khê entrenched fortification on the 4th Route (from Lạng Sơn to Cao Bằng) on the night of May 25. This situation came as a surprise to the General Headquarters when they were planning to start the Border Campaign. The victory of the 174th Regiment in the Đông Khê battle might "alarm" the French on the 4th Route before the big campaign was actually started.[1] After sending a telegram to praise the 174th Regiment

---

1. The Paris press commented that the Đông Khê battle proved the Việt Minh's capability of eliminating any French position on the 4th Route, and there was no reason that they would not wipe out the Cao Bằng fort.

for their "biggest fight of annihilation since the beginning of 1950," Võ Nguyên Giáp called Chief of Regiment Đặng Văn Việt to hear him report in details about the battle. Võ Nguyên Giáp especially highlighted the regiment's experience, as well as their strong and weak points shown in this attack. He commended all the officers and soldiers of the 174th Regiment and praised their fighting spirit. He assessed Đông Khê "a good fight" because it was the first time the Vietnamese troops could destroy a fortification well entrenched by a French battalion within a single night. He did not criticize the 174th Regiment for their "unscheduled" battle.[1] In early June, through the news received from the reconnaissance team in the border area, the General Staff anticipated that the battle of the 174th Regiment could make it difficult for their troops in the upcoming campaign, since the enemy would be alerted and would continue strengthening their fortifications along the 4th Route.

In June 1950, in a preliminary plan for the Border campaign, after analyzing the situation of the Indochina battlefield in general and that of the Northeast battlefield in particular, the General Staff identified that after the Đông Khê battle, the French deployed more troops to the Northeast

---

It was because of this battle, which shook the entire border area, that shortly afterwards the French command sent parachute battalions there to recapture Đông Khê. At the same time, they summoned back their troops from the small forts in the Northeast frontier and regrouped them into a complex of forts with firm fortifications, using more fire-power and deploying two or more companies in each fortification.

1. Võ Nguyên Giáp put the question to Phan Phác, Deputy Chief of the General Staff and an envoy of the General Headquarters on the 4th Route. The latter reported that the 174th Regiment had asked for approval from the Ministry several days before they started the firing but got no reply, so he gave them his approval.

343

border area to recapture it, enhanced their troops in Cao Bằng, sent their interceptive troops to the fortifications in the north of Lạng Sơn, and launched raids around Cao Bằng to destroy the Vietnamese relief provision line.

Under this project, the General Staff proposed to use one regular brigade and two regular regiments,[1] together with two local battalions of Cao Bằng and Lạng Sơn, to conduct three campaigns with the first being to eliminate the French in Cao Bằng Town.

Based on the results of the study of the situation and the preparation of the battlefield by the General Headquarters offices, on July 7, 1950, the General Command issued the Order to start the Border campaign. The Order began with a summary of the French situation (they had expanded their occupation in the Red River Delta, and strengthened their troops along the 4th Route and the coastal areas), followed by a clearly statement of the goals of the campaign—destroying party of the French troop strength on the 4th Route and liberating the border area extending from Cao Bằng to Thất Khê to open up the Northeast border. Regarding the operational motto, the Order emphasized that the combat troops should be concentrated for continuous fighting, and that they should be ready to strike against land and air interceptive troops. The Border campaign involved the participation of the 308th Brigade, the 174th and 209th Regiments, the 426th Battalion, and two local battalions of Cao Bằng and Lạng Sơn. It was under the direct command of the Ministry of General Command. After specifying the

---

1. The regular forces then included the 308th and 304th Brigades, the 174th and 209th Regiments, and the 426th Battalion.

directions for and contents of the preparations that should be continued (including those for the battlefield and troops, political issues, and logistics), the Order defined the time for opening the campaign in mid August 1950. The campaign was expected to last for two months, but a shorter time was wished. The battlefields across Việt Nam received the order to work in collaboration, especially in the diversionary tactics in the Northwest direction.

On July 25, the Standing Central Committee decided to establish the Border Front Party Committee and a High Command for the campaign. Võ Nguyên Giáp was appointed Secretary of the Border Front Party Committee and Commander-in-chief cum Political Commissar of the campaign. The Border Front Party Committee consisted of Trần Đăng Ninh, Hoàng Văn Thái, Lê Liêm (Vice Head of the General Department of Politics), and Bùi Quang Tạo (Secretary of the 1st Interzone Party Committee). Due to the important nature of the campaign, the three heads of the general departments under the Ministry of National Defense (including Võ Nguyên Giáp) directly took charge of the advisory, political, and logistical issues.

In late July, General Võ Nguyên Giáp set off for the campaign. It was the first time he had directly commanded a big and especially important campaign that would pave the way for the national resistance war to move to a new strategic phase, since the completion of the Việt Bắc campaign three years earlier. When he came from Điểm Mặc to Tân Trào to say goodbye to President Hồ Chí Minh before setting off, the President reminded him, "This campaign is important, so you must win at any cost." Hồ Chí Minh added that he would go to the front in early September, and Giáp was overjoyed with the news. The President's presence would be an invaluable source of encouragement for the entire army. But this also gave rise to the question of what they should do to ensure the confidentiality and safety for his trip to the front. It was a rare story that a supreme leader personally went to the most dangerous position in a campaign.

On his way to the front, Võ Nguyên Giáp thought hard about the importance of the campaign, about the President's directives, and the heavy responsibility laying await for him ahead. Later, when he recalled this, he wrote:

> On my way to the front, thinking of my task, I felt something wrong. Would the goal of the campaign be beyond our soldiers' capacity? Would it be correct to select Cao Bằng as the breakthrough point to start the campaign? Would we be able to collect enough food for such a large number of soldiers and conscripted laborers for a long-term campaign?[1]

Analyzing the balance of power between the two sides on the 4th Route battlefield, Giáp found this ratio to be one to one,[2] but the French outdid the Vietnamese in terms of weapons and military vehicles. The French troops were largely warlike European and African combatants, while the Vietnamese

---

1. In this first big campaign, the Campaign Headquarters estimated that the needed about 3,000 tons of food and ammunition (including 2,700 tons of rice, and 200 tons of ammunition) for 30,000 combatants and helpers in a long engagement. What was later called the "on-the-spot ordnance" of Cao Bằng failed to meet the above demands of the Campaign. Apart from some rice that could be provided by the midlands, they had to ask for other foods from China. Approved by Beijing, the leaders of Guangxi Province enthusiastically agreed to help Việt Nam.
2. It was expected that when the Campaign started, the French might employ as many as 20 infantry battalions tantamount to the Vietnamese troop strength.

Chapter Four: ADVANCE TO A STRANGE TURNING POINT

had never encountered two Euro-African battalions in a position. What were their weaknesses? Their combat force and fire-power were deployed over a 130-km route.[1] What was important here was that the Vietnamese should try their best to make use of those disadvantages of the enemy, while at the same time make full use of their maneuverability and ability to fight in the mountains and forests.

On August 3, Võ Nguyên Giáp came to the Campaign Headquarters located in Tả Phẩy Tử (Quảng Uyên District, Cao Bằng Province). The day before, Chief of Staff Hoàng Văn Thái convened a meeting to inform all the concerned units and bodies of the preliminary combat plan, so that they would be able to make timely preparations. Right on the evening of the same day, he heard agencies report on their situations in every aspect, especially their combat plans. According to the combat plan set out by Chief of Staff Hoàng Văn Thái and offices in charge of preparing for the battlefield, they would start the campaign by concentrating their combat troops and attacking to eliminate the enemy in Cao Bằng while attacking their reinforcements. Although he sensed something wrong with the selection of the location for starting the campaign (as he thought along the way), Võ Nguyên Giáp did not hurry himself into commenting about this as he had not had any opportunities to investigate the field. Two months earlier, in the preliminary project for the Border campaign, the Ministry of General Command had planned that in the first phase they would defeat Cao Bằng and contain the enemy troops in Đông Khê và Thất Khê,

---

1. The Cao Bằng-Đông Khê route is 44 kilometers long; the Đông Khê-Thất Khê route, 23 kilometers long; the Thất Khê-Lạng Sơn route, 65 kilometers long.

and in the second phase they would lay siege to the enemy in Đông Khê, wipe them out in Thất Khê, and contain them in Lạng Sơn. The combat plan proposed by Chief of Staff was based on this initial project. But several months had passed with lots of changes found on the French side.

After listening to the report on the combat plan, Giáp became more sure about his judgment that their attack on the French well-fortified positions in Cao Bằng could be a big battle that required them to combine their infantry and artillery to fight against two Euro-African battalions, and that they had not had any experience in such a battle both in terms of scale and operational method. He put forth his initial idea before the Border Front Party Committee for its members to consider. While Trần Đăng Ninh came to Guangxi to receive the delegation of Chinese military advisers,[1] on the morning of August 5, Commander-in-chief Võ Nguyên Giáp, Head of the Military Intelligence Department Cao Pha, and some General Headquarters front officials went on a reconnaissance trip to Cao Bằng. They were accompanied by Phan Phác, envoy of the General Headquarters, and Lâm Kính, Chief of Staff of the 308th Brigade.

When the fog lifted, from the observatory tower located on an overlooking point in the east, the Vietnamese scouts saw in front of them the Hiến River in the southwest, the

---

1. Under the agreement between Chinese leaders and President Hồ Chí Minh on his working trip abroad in early 1950, in June 1950, Luo Guibo came to visit Việt Nam as Ambassador of China and later Wei Guoqing came as Head of the Military Advisors Delegation to assist the General Headquarters of the Vietnamese army. Before Wei Guoqing's arrival, some Chinese advisors to the 308th Regiment came in advance to help the Vietnamese prepare for the latter's campaign.

Chapter Four: ADVANCE TO A STRANGE TURNING POINT

Trà Lĩnh River in the east, and the Bằng Giang River in the northwest intersecting with one another in Cao Bằng. One of them adjusted the telescope to point to the center so that Commander-in-chief Võ Nguyên Giáp could observe the Nà Can airport at the hill base, a section of the 4th Route, and the Bằng Giang bridge leading to the town, an old citadel-fort,[1] and other French posts. Outside the town was a system of over ten outposts built on the surrounding hills. In reply to the Commander-in-chief on the results of their reconnaissance, especially in the airport and river banks, Leader of the Scout Team Trần Quốc Trung reported that they had seen no way to penetrate quietly into the French posts. The French patrol teams made day and night tours around the area about half kilometer from the airport. Deputy Chief of the General Staff Phan Phác reported more on the layout of the enemy in the south and the west of Cao Bằng Town. The entry was lined up by successive barren hills. There were a river, fortifications, and obstacles; steep ramparts in the south; bunkers and watch-towers on both sides; and empty ground with layers of barbed wire outside. Listening to the report while observing by himself, Võ Nguyên Giáp told his company that in such a complicated and stringently-defended terrain, the French troops would not be worried about being attacked by the

---

1. It is a fort built by the French in 1938 on a hill south of Bắc Cạn Town on an area of nearly ten hectares. Its wall is made of stone and is 1,350 m in perimeter. It is located in the middle of the 4th Route in Lạng Sơn and the 3rd Route from Bắc Cạn to Cao Bằng Town. Later when the Vietnamese conducted a field survey of this area, they found that from the fort looking down they could have a good view of the surroundings, especially in the west-northwest direction, or the center of the town. This area provided advantageous conditions for the protection of the fort: the Hiến River in the west-northwest, the Bằng River with abruptly-sloped banks and swift-flowing currents in the east, and the barren hills in the south.

Vietnamese. And it was easy to understand why the French high-ranking officers delayed their withdrawal from Cao Bằng and did not hurry to shorten their defense line on the 4th Route according to the proposal of Chief of the General Staff Revers.

Giáp and his company discussed the situation, and tried to predict the difficulties their directions of attack might encounter and the ways to address these obstacles once they had approached the target, such as getting ready to attack the French forts, organizing their men to cross rivers, and dealing with the French fire-power from their outposts on heights surrounding the town once the Vietnamese troops had launched an intensive intrusion.

While wading through many flooded road sections under the heavy rain on the way back, Giáp sank into deep thought and felt more assured about his judgment: they could not choose to start the campaign in Cao Bằng since it would be hard for them to win. It was not because of the French troop strength in this town, but it was mainly because of the uncovered and dangerous terrain, where their troops would be likely to encounter the French paratroops, aircraft, and fire-power. To start a campaign in Cao Bằng would require the resolution of many problems, for example, the tactics required to attack the enemy's center where the Vietnamese troops remained so inexperienced and those to exterminate the enemy reinforcement troops. The French named the 4th Route the "fire road." The French press named the marches of their convoys past Bông Lau and Lũng Phầy on the Thất Khê-Cao Bằng route the "suicide operations." For a long time, only supplies by air could reach Cao Bằng. It was clear that once the town came under threat, the French were very unlikely to open the "path of blood" to rescue Cao Bằng. They might "sacrifice" their two battalions in Cao Bằng, and while the Vietnamese troops would be focusing on fighting back, they would quickly and safely move all their garrisons from Đông Khê and Thất Khê to Lạng Sơn. Moreover, the plan to shorten their defense line in the Northeastern border area had been proposed by the delegation headed by Revers since early summer.

So if the Vietnamese troops did not attack Cao Bằng, how should they change their tactics to fulfill their assigned tasks—destroying an important part of the enemy's troop strength, liberating Cao Bằng, and opening up the border there? When recalling this later, Võ Nguyên Giáp wrote:

> I think that the best location to kick off the campaign would be Đông Khê, an important entrenched fortification that linked Thất Khê with Cao Bằng. The French had reinforced the Đông Khê fortification, but we could definitely destroy it. Once they lost Đông Khê, they would try either to recapture it or to withdraw their troops from Cao Bằng. Thus, we would have the chance to wipe them out outside their fortification. If they did not try to reoccupy Đông Khê, we would continue to attack them in Thất Khê. Finally, we would reorganize our troops to march into liberating Cao Bằng.

During the consultation on the morning of August 6, Võ Nguyên Giáp expressed to other Party members there his uncertainty of their success in the Cao Bằng battle, and suggested that they should ask the Standing Central Committee for a change in their combat plan.

Regarding his decision to change the target of the first combat to kick off the campaign, he wrote, "A victory requires boldness. But it does not accept any adventurous action."

It was shown in the following campaigns of the Vietnamese troops that this thought was also his motto of action during his entire career as a general.

After the consultation with the Border Front Party Committee, Giáp sent a telegram consulting Hồ Chí Minh and the Standing Central Committee. In the meantime, he directed concerned agencies and units to continue preparing for the attack in Cao Bằng. When the unit commanding officers came back from their field reconnaissance, Giáp asked them what they thought about their assigned tasks. He attentively listened to them talking about the ways to resolve tactical problems such as crossing rivers, attacking the French paratroops, and attacking the French fortifications. Only the 174th Regiment opposed the idea of targeting Cao Bằng. Instead, they boldly asked Giáp to assign them with the task of annihilating Đông Khê for the second time, while other units would focus on attacking the French standby soldiers on the ground and in the air. This meant that the 174th Regiment had not been fully aware of the changes in the French situation on the 4th Route, compared to that in May, including those in the Đông Khê fortifications.

After several days of waiting, on August 15, Võ Nguyên Giáp received a telegram from the rear announcing that President Hồ Chí Minh and the Standing Central Committee agreed on targeting Đông Khê in their first battle instead of Cao Bằng. All the members of the Border Front Party Committee were both happy and worried about this decision. They were happy because such a consensus was a very basic condition for them to win the first battle, but they were worried since the change would upset their previous preparations that had previously cost them lots of efforts. So the political task then would be to help the commanders grasp and accept the change thoroughly. Many of their combatants were eager for the first battle to liberate Cao Bằng. So Giáp found it most important to help the staff of the advisory, political, and logistical offices of the campaign thoroughly understand the necessity of the change. The following day, he convened a joint meeting between the Border Front Party Committee and High Command of the campaign. The meeting involved the attendance of several key advisory, political, and logistical officers. After hearing the Commander-in-chief explain the reason for changing the combat plan, all participants showed their agreement and voiced their opinions of the urgency of completing the preparatory work. Giáp reminded everyone that they should be aware of the difficulties of having to do all the preparations again, including investigating the terrain of Đông Khê and the Đông Khê-Thất Khê route, and especially the shift of the logistical system from Cao Bằng southward. Time was very urgent, requiring them to be both urgent and thoughtful in their preparation.

After the meeting, Võ Nguyên Giáp met for talks with the Chinese delegation of military advisers, led by Wei Guoqing, who had just arrived from Guangxi. A couple of days earlier, to quickly grasp the situation, Võ Nguyên Giáp and his team had worked with the group of Chinese advisors who came in advance. It was the first time Giáp met Wei Guoqing, Advisor to the Chinese Minister of National Defense and Commander-in-chief of the Chinese army. The friendship and comradeship between Võ Nguyên Giáp and Wei Guoqing were well maintained during the remaining years of the anti-French resistance war of the Vietnamese people, when the latter stayed in Việt Nam as a military advisor. In this first meeting, after listening to Giáp's briefing on the preparations for the campaign, Wei Guoqing suggested that they wait for a couple of days for Chen Geng to come to Việt Nam to give his ideas on the matter.[1]

Chen Geng had been a close friend of Nguyễn Ái Quốc since 1925-1926, when they were working together in the Huangpu Military School. During the third revolutionary war of the Chinese people (1946-1949), he was Deputy Commander of the Field Combat Army. At that time, Wei Guoqing was a multi-battalion commander.

After the liberation of China, Chen Geng was Deputy Commander of the Southwest Military Region cum Commander of Kunming Military Region and Alternate Member of the Central Committee of the Communist Party of China. At the request of President Hồ Chí Minh and the Standing Central Committee of the Communist Party of Việt Nam, China dispatched him to Việt Nam to help with steering the Border campaign. He traveled from Kunming to the Việt Bắc base in late July, after Giáp had arrived in Cao Bằng. Having learned about the Vietnamese plan of attacking Cao Bằng for the first battle, Chen Geng proposed that they should shift the target to Đông Khê to avoid the French's strong position and attack their most weak and

---

1. Regarding the relationship between the Vietnamese Command and the Chinese delegation of military advisors in the Border Campaign, the author refers to the notes by Hoàng Minh Phương, Võ Nguyên Giáp's assistant in charge of the affairs with China during the anti-French resistance war, and the information provided in the books "Historical Facts of the Chinese Delegation of Military Advisors to Việt Nam to Help with the Anti-French Resistance War" published by the Beijing Liberation Army in 1990 and "Nine Big Battles of the Chinese People's Liberation Army" published in 1992.

Chapter Four: ADVANCE TO A STRANGE TURNING POINT

vulnerable one, implementing the Vietnamese motto of "attacking posts and exterminating relief forces" like the Chinese Liberation Army often did. His idea coincided with Võ Nguyên Giáp's (after the latter returned from his field reconnaissance trip in Cao Bằng). The proposal was approved by President Hồ Chí Minh and the Standing Central Committee, and on August 15 Võ Nguyên Giáp received Hồ Chí Minh's reply.

After that, Chen Geng left the Việt Bắc base for the Headquarters of the Border campaign in Quảng Uyên District in mid August. There he talked with the Head of the Chinese Advisory Delegation and later met with General Giáp, and they all agreed on the combat plan for the campaign. Later, Chinese advisors were organized in teams to go to help those of the Vietnamese agencies and units involved in the campaign prepare for the new plan.

Concerned officers were summoned to a meeting held from August 24–25 where they were assigned with specific tasks and instructed to thoroughly understand the new combat plan. At the meeting, Giáp explained clearly the policy of the Border Front Party Committee. He said:

> After receiving the Party Central Committee's decision to launch the Second Lê Hồng Phong campaign, we proposed a preliminary combat plan as a guideline for the battlefield investigation. According to this plan, we would target Cao Bằng first and then advance from victory to victory to target Đông Khê and, if possible, Thất Khê.
>
> After the commanding officers had finished their field survey of the enemy's situation and reported their findings, the Border Front Party Committee decided on the combat plan as follows:

355

1- We shall start to concentrate our forces in destroying the enemy troops in Đông Khê and their relief forces, especially the paratroops.

2- After exterminating the enemy troops in Đông Khê and wearing out their relief forces, in the wake of this victory, we shall muster all of our troops to eliminate the enemy troops in Thất Khê.

3- If the enemy send more troops from Lạng Sơn, we shall depend on the specific situation to decide whether to attack the reinforcements or not.

4- After wiping out the enemy troops in Đông Khê and Thất Khê and part of their reinforcement troops, we shall give our troops some rest to reorganize them, review experience, and mobilize them for the attack on Cao Bằng.

According to this explanation, the Border Front Party Committee proposed such a plan to make sure that they would win in the first battle of the campaign. This win would exert a great impact on the entire campaign.

After answering all the questions raised at the meeting, Giáp emphasized several principles of the combat plan such as launching an annihilating attack, gathering all troops and fire-power to attack small fortifications before going ahead with big ones, and combining operations in the first large-scale campaign of its kind. Finally, Giáp pointed out the conditions for a sure victory, the difficulties they would encounter in the campaign, the directions and remedies for them, and that the preparations should be hastened if we were to gain a sure victory.

The 174th and 209th Regiments were given the task of launching an attack on Đông Khê (with the former playing the main role); the 308th Brigade, the task of intercepting the

Chapter Four: ADVANCE TO A STRANGE TURNING POINT

French reinforcements. The command of the Đông Khê battle included Hoàng Văn Thái as commander, Lê Liêm as political commissar, and Lê Trọng Tấn as deputy commander. On September 14, all the concerned units would gather in their positions ready for the battle.

In the directive dated September 3, Võ Nguyên Giáp announced what had happened on the French side while they were preparing for the campaign: the French had brought more troops to the North, further strengthened the Northwest and Northeast border areas, and launched an operation to occupy Phú Thọ with a view to pulling the Vietnamese forces out of the Northwest area and blocking the roads between Việt Bắc and the 3rd Interzone. The directive clearly stated that the French had not figured out the Vietnamese forces' activities on the 4th Route, and concluded that the chance had come and the Vietnamese commanding officers should grasp it and complete all necessary preparations quickly and secretly.

On September 9, officers from the regimental level above were summoned to the meeting to make a last report on their preparations for the battle. At the meeting, Võ Nguyên Giáp presented his analysis of the order dated September 8, predicting the French's possible responses to their attack on Đông Khê and stating their tasks of "attacking posts and annihilating relief forces."

He said:

> Once we have surrounded and attacked Đông Khê, the French in Thất Khê may get there for rescue. But from our experience from the previous battle in Đông Khê,[1] I think

---

1. Referring to the 174th Regiment's attack on the French fortification in Đông Khê in late May 1950.

that with only a battalion in Thất Khê, the French will not dare to do it but wait for their troops from Lạng Sơn. In case the French troops in Thất Khê coordinate with those from Lạng Sơn to rescue Đông Khê, our interceptive troops have to determinedly destroy all of them, or at least most of them.

Once we have finished the battle in Đông Khê, the French in Thất Khê will learn that our forces are able to block their reinforcements. So they may not dare to send more reinforcements but wait for their troops from Lạng Sơn before launching an attack on Đông Khê. After we have occupied Đông Khê and isolated Cao Bằng, the French may leave Cao Bằng, shorten their defense line, gather their troops, and combine with the troops from Thất Khê to counter-attack us in Đông Khê. Then we must block the French troops from Thất Khê. First we shall gather our men to lay siege on the French troops from Cao Bằng and then return to Thất Khê to destroy their reinforcements, using the tactic of killing them part by part.

Many officers at the meeting knew that Giáp had come back from his field trip to Cao Bằng before making such a change to the combat plan. In a talk to officers of the 308th Brigade, Chief of Brigade Vương Thừa Vũ said:

He (Võ Nguyên Giáp) is not only an example of the willingness to learn for self-improvement that we should follow, but he is also an example of the military thinking, wide vision, and courage of a commander. He not only ventured himself on the field trips to fully understand the on-the-spot situation and collect facts as grounds for his consideration, but he also dared to change the combat plan to fit the objective reality and ensure victory for the campaign, first and foremost its first battle, though the change would result in lots of time and effort required for the preparations.

Chapter Four: ADVANCE TO A STRANGE TURNING POINT

Then Vương Thừa Vũ called upon the 308th Brigade to learn from the example of Võ Nguyên Giáp. In the Northwest campaign later, he himself took his men to reach as far as the French's barbed wire entanglement for field reconnaissance.

When the Border Campaign Cadres Conference was going on, the Campaign Headquarters received the news that Hồ Chí Minh had arrived in Tả Phẩy Tử. Võ Nguyên Giáp immediately rode a horse there to receive him. That afternoon, after listening to Võ Nguyên Giáp's report on the new combat plan, Hồ Chí Minh nodded his head and said with his fingers up, one after the other:

> First, attack Đông Khê; second, attack the reinforcement troops; third, attack Thất Khê; fourth, attack Cao Bằng; four steps in all.... Đông Khê is not so vast. The French troops in Đông Khê are rather weak, though it is a very important position on the Cao Bằng-Lạng Sơn route. Once we have taken Đông Khê, Cao Bằng will be isolated. Then the French will be forced to send more troops there to rescue it and we will have a good chance of killing them in mobile warfare. Once their relief force has been destroyed, the French will hardly be able to defend Cao Bằng and will withdraw from it. Then, we can defeat them more easily.

The following afternoon, Hồ Chí Minh paid a visit to inquire after the attendees. His presence at the conference was a big surprise and an invaluable source of encouragement to them. In a very simple way of speech, he repeated the reason why they had to change their combat plan. "In military affairs, we must be very determined and bold. Neither boldness nor bravery means adventurousness. Adventurousness is unwise, while bravery is wise."

Before leaving, he said:

> Your assigned tasks have been described in details, so I don't need to say any more about that. I only note you that time is very valuable now and so we must take the most of our time to prepare well for combat. Only if we can prepare well for it can we gain a big victory with few casualties. The Cao-Bắc-Lạng campaign is extremely important, and we must try all the best to win it.

In brief words, he made the campaign commanding officers and all the cadres present at the conference feel assured and truly believe in their victory. A few days later, he sent a letter of encouragement to the combatants before the battle. His very thoughtful reminders not only made each officer and soldier see the special importance of the campaign but also served as a strong driving force that encouraged them to try to overcome all the challenges to fulfill their tasks. His words were repeated by every team of three people and every battalion in their determination oath letters. From the unforgettable dry season in 1950, Hồ Chí Minh's presence at the front line has become the subject of many literary and art works in and outside the military circle. Such famous articles as *"Hồ Chí Minh đi chiến dịch"* (literally: "Hồ Chí Minh Goes to the Campaign") or the song *"Bác đang cùng chúng cháu hành quân"* (literally: "The Uncle is Marching with Us") were inspired by the images of Hồ Chí Minh on the 4th Route—the route that had gone down in the history of national liberation of Việt Nam.

The Combat of Wits on the 4th Route

A strange coincidence happened: General Võ Nguyên Giáp and General Michel Carpentier met on September 16.

From this date, they both had to solve their problems in order to win.

That day, when the news of the Vietnamese attack on Đông Khê had not been spread, Commander-in-chief Carpentier ordered Lieutenant Colonel Charton to prepare for the French withdrawal from Cao Bằng as they planned the previous summer. To ensure a safe march, he took three moves almost simultaneously: 1- Issue the order to open a march into Thái Nguyên to make up for the withdrawal from Cao Bằng; 2- Send one more black-skinned battalion to Cao Bằng to reinforce the French troops there during their withdrawal; 3- Send troops from Thất Khê to Đông Khê to support Charton's troops from Cao Bằng.

The same day, according to the plan, Commander-in-chief Võ Nguyên Giáp ordered to start the Vietnamese attack on Đông Khê while arranging troops to be ready to fight the French outdoors. He believed that once Đông Khê was lost, the the French would definitely act in response. Thus, any soldier that showed up on the 4th Route could possibly be part of the French relief forces from Thất Khê or Cao Bằng, or one of the French paratroops who had just landed.

In a letter to encourage the Vietnamese soldiers before they were going into battle, Võ Nguyên Giáp wrote:

> Once we have won this battle, we will not only annihilate the enemy's strength, but also open the way for traffic, expand our revolutionary base, discourage the enemy soldiers, spoil their autumn and winter plans, exert a direct impact on the Northeast and the midlands, create favorable conditions for the changing of the situation in the North, and heighten the morale of the soldiers and people nationwide. This is an intensive campaign. By wining this battle, we will have

recorded a big victory, while our solders will have moved from guerilla war to mobile warfare and attacks on fortified positions, learnt numerous lessons, and established a firm tradition as the foundation for the later build-up of forces.

Finally, he encouraged the whole army to compete with one another to achieve more feats and to win a complete victory for the campaign.

Early on September 16, President Hồ Chí Minh and Commander-in-chief Võ Nguyên Giáp climbed up the observatory stationed on a mountain peak in Nà Lạn Village, about ten kilometers from Đông Khê. On the observatory were a direct line of communication with the Đông Khê Front Command and big zoom binoculars for monitoring the development of the battle.

As an important link on the 4th Route connecting Cao Bằng with Thất Khê and Lạng Sơn, the Đông Khê fortification complex covered almost the entire town with Đồn To post as its most important and solid fort. The central area is surrounded by seven peripheral fortifications built on heights that make up a belt, serving as a guarding position and a shield to protect the central area. After the battle launched by the 174th Regiment on May 25, the French strengthened their troops but mainly their fortifications. At the time the Vietnamese opened the campaign, the French deployed in Đông Khê two companies of the Legionary Battalion, one company of puppet troops, and one artillery division with five 57-mm and 105-mm cannons.

The attack on Đông Khê started at 6 am on September 16, 1950. In the south, a number of units of the 209th Regiment got lost and could not completely control the battlefield, while the 174th Regiment in the north—the main direction—still fired as planned. After annihilating a number of peripheral fortifications such as Yên Ngựa, Phìa Khoá, and Cẩm Phẩy, the 174th Regiment attacked Đồn To but failed to occupy it. In all of their three attempts to penetrate through, the 174th Regiment was knocked out and could not hold on to the bridgehead. They proposed a surprise attack on the northeast of Đồn To, in combination with the 209th Regiment from the south. The proposal was approved by Commander of the Battle Hoàng Văn Thái. In the south, although the 209th Regiment did not open fire until 6 pm and was not supported by artillery, the managed to annihilate some peripheral fortifications such as Pò Hầu and Pò Đỉnh. At midnight, having attacked and took control of Phù Thiện, they received an order to send a breakthrough team to move northward to combine with the 174th Regiment to attack Đồn To. By this time, however, both regiments had not been well-prepared or closely coordinated to fulfill the task. Commander-in-chief Võ Nguyên Giáp instructed the Đông Khê Front Command to suspend firing and spend some time on reorganizing troops, drawing experience from previous battles, and preparing well for coordinated operation to ensure a complete win on the night of September 17. On the early morning of September 17, the French took advantage of the ceasefire to open drastic counter-attacks from the underground trenches, pushing the Vietnamese forces out of some of their occupied positions and thus causing some more casualties to the Vietnamese side.

On the afternoon of September 17, after having consolidated troops, found out the causes for their technical and tactical shortcomings and ways to remedy them, and made thoughtful plans for coordinated operation, the two Vietnamese regiments received the order to launch a general offensive. After more than a day of continuous fighting, the battle ended at 10 am on September 1. After the breakthrough team from the north gained the upper hand, the 209th Regiment in the south sent its reserve troops into the battle. These troops demolished the underground trench with a big explosive charge, paving the way for the others to make a fierce attack on the French headquarters and taking alive the French Command, including Captain Alioux as commanding officer of the post. About 300 French combatants were killed and captured, and a small number escaped toward Thất Khê. The Vietnamese army confiscated all the French weapons and equipment. The kick-off battle, which was also the first key battle of the campaign, was successful. The Vietnamese soldiers successfully realized Hồ Chí Minh's determination: they must definitely win the first battle however hard it might be. The battle lasted twice the expected time.[1] The Vietnamese suffered more casualties than they had previously expected, mainly due to the French fire-power from the underground trench in Đồn To.

After the victory of the kick-off battle, Commander-in-chief Võ Nguyên Giáp ordered the troops to prepare the battlefield ready for the attack on the French reinforcements. Then the 130-km Cao Bằng-Lạng Sơn route witnessed the most exciting and urgent situations of the Border campaign, as well as the combat of wits between the two commanders-in-chief of the two warring parties.

It was the fight between two generals. The French general was in a neat suit, with four silver stars on his shoulder

---

1. The battle was scheduled to last for 24 hours, but it actually took 50 hours to end it.

Chapter Four: ADVANCE TO A STRANGE TURNING POINT

straps and numerous medals on his chest. He often sat in a luxurious air-conditioned room in Norodom Palace, used the most state-of-the-art means of communication, and commanded about 300,000 modernly-equipped regulars in Indochina. Meanwhile, the Vietnamese general wore booty shoes and coat with no rank. His headquarters was located in a house-on-stilts, his observatory was a thatched hut built on a hill, and he commanded a force of primitively-equipped battalions and regiments born out of guerillas units.

On the night of September 16, after receiving the news that the Vietnamese had launched an attack on Đông Khê, Commander-in-chief Carpentier was confronted with a thorny problem of how to make sure that his troops could make a safe retreat from Cao Bằng without being destroyed. On September 17, he flew to Hà Nội and then to Lạng Sơn. A series of orders were issued. A battalion was ordered to parachute into Cao Bằng and then prepare for their retreat toward Thất Khê. A corps led by Le Page was ordered to depart from Thất Khê on September 19, but it was not until September 30 that they started leaving Lạng Sơn to welcome the corps led by Charton—a delay that made the Vietnamese troops anxious. The French operation to attack and occupy Thái Nguyên did not start until September 29.[1] Commander-in-chief Carpentier had completed the three moves of "his game." As it was revealed by the Western press later, the

---

1. The operation, coded *Phoque* (Seal) involved about 10,000 combatants, including nearly ten infantry battalions, two tank companies, four 105-mm gun companies, one squadron, eight hundred vehicles of different types, and all the aircraft that could be gathered. The operation was under the command of Colonel Gambier. After the two corps were annihilated on October 10 on the 4th Route, Gambier withdrew his troops from Thái Nguyên.

French general believed that after seeing the French parachute battalion in Cao Bằng, the Vietnamese would be persuaded that the French would stay there for a long time and thus would be unable to send troops there to cope with the French retreat. He also believed that after hearing of the coming of Le Page's troops from Lạng Sơn, the Vietnamese would think that the French were sending reinforcement troops to rescue Thất Khê and would retake it as they had done in May. And once the Việt Minh's Headquarters had been misled and thus had taken an erroneous step (such as sending troops to Thái Nguyên to rescue their "resistance capital"), the French Headquarters would "show their hands": their troops in Cao Bằng would secretly slip away along the 4th Route and meet an arm awaiting to together move to Thất Khê safely before the Vietnamese troops could come to understand and take action accordingly.

How was everything going with the Vietnamese side? The Vietnamese troops had been waiting in vain for a week for the French reinforcements to show up, and they had run out of rice in stock. Then came rapid-fire news such as the French coming attack on Thái Nguyên and the nearly simultaneous appearance of two French battalions (one withdrawing from the north and the other coming from the south) on an over-30-km road section linking Nậm Nàng and Lũng Phầy. In this situation, the Vietnamese had to solve the question of what they should do to prevent the two French arms from joining together against them before making an escape to Thất Khê. Commander-in-chief Võ Nguyên Giáp decided to focus on defeating the southern army before annihilating the northern one in order to win a complete victory for the campaign.

Chapter Four: ADVANCE TO A STRANGE TURNING POINT

It is necessary to understand why Võ Nguyên Giáp had been so assured of their success in Thái Nguyên.

Before the start of the dry season, the Vietnamese High Command had predicted the possibility of the French troops attacking to occupy Thái Nguyên. In mid March 1950, in *"Huấn luyện về nhiệm vụ quân sự năm 1950 của Liên khu Việt Bắc"* (literally: "Instructions on Việt Bắc Interzone's Military Tasks for 1950"), Commander-in-chief Võ Nguyên Giáp predicted that the French might venture to send infantry and paratroops to penetrate deep into their base to kill their soldiers, destroy their commanding agencies, demolish their warehouses and factories, and occupy Thái Nguyên and Tuyên Quang. He emphasized that one of the tasks was to watch out for the French adventurous attacks on their base. Particularly, they should pay special attention to security, reconnaissance, diversionary tactics, and secrecy; organize maneuvers to enhance the coordination between regulars and local troops; alert the people to get themselves ready and prevent them from being subjective and underestimating the enemy or being pessimistic and confused when being attacked; and disperse their offices and factories in anticipation of any attack by French bombers or paratroops.

At the news that the French were likely to attack Thái Nguyên, the Border Campaign Headquarters judged that the French attack on Thái Nguyên aimed to attract the Vietnamese regulars there so that they could reoccupy Đông Khê. The situation in Thái Nguyên was not alarming for the Vietnamese as they had prepared a plan for the local armed forces to protect their base. Võ Nguyên Giáp was still determined to patiently wait for the French reinforcement force and implement the plan for border liberation.

On the French side, through the Western publications, the reason for the late arrival of the French troops from Thất Khê was later revealed to the public.

Lieutenant Colonel Le Page received an order to lead a corps departing from Lạng Sơn on September 19. After receiving a parachute battalion, a very famous one of the French Expeditionary Corps named *"Bataillon Étranger de Parachutistes"* (literally: "Foreign Parachute Battalion"), in Thất Khê, the corps was codenamed "Bayard." In over one week starting from September 20, the entire corps, which consisted of four Euro-African battalions, only conducted small operations around Thất Khê. It was not until September 30 that they received an order from Constans, Commander of the Northeast Border Zone with its headquarters based in Lạng Sơn, to launch an attack on Đông Khê at noon on October 2. Le Page saw it "a fatal challenge," so he asked to delay the plan for 24 hours to investigate the situation and make more preparations. However, his request was turned down.

The Bayard Corps headed by Le Page set off on the night of September 30 with the paratroops taking the lead. The French troops were surprised and could not help feeling worried as their march was "so smooth," even when they passed the Lũng Phầy Pass, which was called the "bloody pass" by the French troops on the 4th Route. The following morning, there was still no glimpse of a single Vietnamese combatant in sight and the French troops entered Nà Pá with care. There they encountered a team of Vietnamese patrol men, and after hearing several gunshots, they ran toward Đông Khê. Le Page ordered his troops to cautiously march northward.

Chapter Four: ADVANCE TO A STRANGE TURNING POINT

How could Le Page's troops reach as far as Đông Khê without the knowledge of the Vietnamese ambush? It was not because the French were so smart in launching a secret operation, but it was the Vietnamese fault.

After Đông Khê was liberated, in the 4th Combat Order (dated September 21), Võ Nguyên Giáp presented his estimations of the situation. According to him, the French would send two or three more infantry battalions from Thất Khê who would march along the 4th Route and the Pò Mã-Bố Trạch route and join a parachute battalion to recapture Đông Khê. The Border Campaign Headquarters set the goal of destroying a large part of the French force (including about two battalions) in the key area from southern Đông Khê to Lũng Phẩy. The 308th Brigade was entrusted with the task of crushing the French reinforcements from the south, specifically deploying troops in mobile locations in the the Lũng Chà-Bình Xiến-Nà Pá triangle and wiping out the French in Nà Pá, Khâu Luông, and Lũng Phẩy. The 174th Regiment based in the northeast and north of Đông Khê was assigned to annihilate the French paratroops landing in Đông Khê and the vicinity. The 209th Regiment was tasked to stay in Bố Trạch as a reserve force for the campaign.

The units were then quickly deployed to attack French reinforcements according to the order. Nearly a week had passed without any single French soldier in sight. They had nearly run out of rice. Advisor Chen Geng suggested an withdrawal, because the French reinforcements had not come while their soldiers had not been strong enough to defeat the French in Thất Khê or Cao Bằng.

Commander-in-chief Võ Nguyên Giáp raised the question of how the campaign would end if they just stopped

369

halfway with their victory in Đông Khê. He held on to the idea of patiently waiting for the French reinforcements. In the 5th Combat Order (dated September 25), he said, "If our troops stay idle for a long time, the enemy may launch an operation to regain their initiative and undermine our preparations." Therefore, he sent a small part of the troops to the south to continue their missions, preparing favorable conditions and creating a good opportunity to destroy the French in Thất Khê, while the rest kept on waiting for the French reinforcements. General Giáp later recalled:

> We could not anticipate that after those many days of waiting, our officers and soldiers almost forgot their task of continuing to wait for the French reinforcement troops and were only eager to attack Thất Khê. The units of the 308th Brigade sent two-thirds of their troops to go fetching rice, leaving only exhausted and weak soldiers behind to look after the weapons and leaving no alert units to fight against the French relief troops. In the meantime, Le Page's corps were able to easily pass the forest and avoid the ambush battle prepared by the 308th Brigade.

On the evening of October 1, Chief of the 209th Regiment Lê Trọng Tấn was the first to report on the appearance of French troops, including paratroops, near Đông Khê. Estimating that they wanted to reoccupy Đông Khê, the 209th Regiment opened fire to block the French advance to Đông Khê.

Võ Nguyên Giáp asked Chief of the 308th Brigade Vương Thừa Vũ for details about the situation. Having understood why the French could easily march through Lũng Phầy, the Commander-in-chief gently said, "So the 308th Brigade let the enemy through the battlefield without the ability to fight them."

Then he ordered Vương Thừa Vũ to immediately summon back the soldiers who was on the way to the rice depot[1] back to their combat positions. While waiting for them, he gathered all those among the rest who could fight, regardless how many there were, into an army for a march towards Đông Khê. They were warned to stay alert in Khâu Luông, Cốc Xá. If the French troops fail to reach Đông Khê, they were likely to stay there. It was assumed to be a good chance for the Vietnamese troops to annihilate the French reinforcements there.

Regarding this unforgettable event, in his memoir *"Trưởng thành trong chiến đấu"* (literally: "Getting Matured in Combat") Vương Thừa Vũ wrote:

> I thought, "We must admit our failure and rise up from it." The cause of our failure was not found anywhere else but right in our management. The general instructions were good, but we did not do a good job when it came to giving specific instructions and supervising their implementation. The biggest cause of the failure was the order requesting units to send two-thirds of their troops to the depot to collect rice. After receiving the order, all units, from squad to regiment level, sent two-thirds of their most able men for that job. A squad was comprised of ten men. When seven of them had gone for rice collection, the rest could hardly manage the task of taking care of weapons, let alone tracking the enemy and fighting against them. The whole brigade was in a disorder with none of its units was in full strength and ready to fight. To reserve one-third of the force to get ready to fight, we should have give specific instructions; for example, the 1st Regiment should detain

---

1. The rice depot was located in Tà Lùng, close to the border. It took two days to get there and back.

Battalion A and the 2nd Regiment should detain Battalion B or C. Only by this way could we have a fully-organized unit, with a commanding officer and information scouts, to cope with the enemy.

Having heard that a French army was coming from Thất Khê, the Border Campaign Headquarters found it an advantage for the Vietnamese, whether this army intended to reoccupy Đông Khê or meet the troops fleeing from Cao Bằng. The chance for the Vietnamese to annihilate the enemy's troop strength finally came. Present at the Headquarters at that time, Hồ Chí Minh said to Võ Nguyên Giáp, "A very good opportunity has come. You must not miss it . . ."

In the 6th Combat Order (released at 5 pm on October 1), Võ Nguyên Giáp announced the steps of Le Page's corps, predicted possible situations, and entrusted the 209th Regiment with the task of blocking the French from entering into Đông Khê and the 308th Brigade with that of annihilating the French in Keo Ái, Khâu Luông, and crushing their paratroopers who had been expected to land in the area from Nà Pá to Pò Hầu. He stressed, "The enemy's advance into Đông Khê at this time gives us a very good opportunity to annihilate them. The commanders of the 308th Brigade and the 209th Regiment should make firm plans and be determined to destroy the enemy."[1]

On the evening of October 1, it was reported that Le Page ordered his troops to stop at the heights along the nearly-

---

1. According to the plan of promoting small operations in the south to create favorable conditions for an attack on Thất Khê, Regimen 174 was assigned to stay in Thất Khê, Na Sầm. Thus, only the 308th Brigade and the 209th Regiment were stationed in the mountainous area to the west of Đông Khê.

10-km road section from southern Đông Khê to Lũng Phầy, to the west of the 4th Route. Meantime, the Commander of Bayard Corps sent a telegram asking Lạng Sơn to parachute two cannons, so that they could launch an attack on Đông Khê Town the following day.

On the early morning of October 2, Le Page's corps left the 4th Route with the two cannons and organized themselves into two pincers, one in the east and the other in the west. They were marching along the mountain slopes to find the way down into the Đông Khê interval when they were unexpectedly stopped by the Vietnamese army. As Le Page recalled it later, no sooner had he judged that there would be no chance that they would recapture Đông Khê by force than the French Headquarters in Lạng Sơn commanded his Bayard Corps to go and meet Charton's corps marching from Cao Bằng along the 4th Route at Nậm Nàng. He ordered his entire corps to shift westbound along the 4th Route. At about 3 pm, Le Page's corps marched into a strange mountainous area and found there only vague traces of a path leading northward and seemingly running parallel with the 4th Route as shown on the map. Just then Vietnamese troops crowded in. As Lucien Bodart, the then war correspondent, put it, Vietnamese soldiers had spent long days waiting in anxiety because of the ambiguity of the situation, and so it was time for them to take action. Obeying Vương Thừa Vũ's order, the 29th Battalion (of the 88th Regiment) and the 18th Battalion (of the 102nd Regiment) joined the 36th Regiment to make an urgent deployment of troops to start fighting the French in Tróc Ngà. They wiped out one of the French companies in Tróc Ngà and pushed them out of Khâu Luông.

In the 7th Combat Order (issued on the morning of October 3), the Border Campaign Headquarters summarized that the French troops had been divided into two parts, and that the Vietnamese forces had not fulfilled all their assignments but succeeded in surrounding and kicking the French out of Khâu Áng, Nà Kiêu, and one of the mountain peaks in Khâu Luông. The Border Campaign Headquarters assumed that the French Headquarters in Lạng Sơn and Hà Nội had paid much attention to this operation of Le Page's corps, so they might reinforce their troops with paratroops or infantry troops from Thất Khê or troops withdrew from Cao Bằng.[1]

The Vietnamese Headquarters ordered the 308th Brigade to destroy the major part of the French troops in Nà Pá, Keo Ái, and Khâu Luông mountains, and sent the 88th Regiment to Cốc Tồn, Nà Kao, to join the 209th Regiment to take control of Nà Cúm and Nà Kiêu to break the contact between the two parts of Le Page's corps. The Headquarters emphasized that thy should take the opportunity to quickly destroy the French forces. Later, in an encouragement letter sent to soldiers at noon on October 3, Võ Nguyên Giáp wrote:

> Killing them (French reinforcements) means wining a big battle. It is such a rare chance for us to annihilate the French élite forces. At present, the French troops are suffering fatigue and lack of ammunition, and part of them have been killed or injured. So all soldiers, try to overcome all

---

1. Due to the shortage of means of communication and the ineffective operation of their scouts, the Border Campaign Headquarters did not receive the news of the French withdrawal from Cao Bằng until noon on October 4, thirty-six hours after the departure of Charton's corps. The Vietnamese army intelligence in Cao Bằng had to ask the local post office to send the news by phone.

difficulties, tighten the stranglehold, and promote your vanguard spirit and bravery in the fight against the enemy to annihilate and take them alive.

At noon on October 4, the Vietnamese Headquarters got the news that the leading squad of Charton's corps had arrived in Nậm Nàng and was heading Quang Liệt by order of the French Headquarters in Lạng Sơn. Võ Nguyên Giáp was determined not to let the two French corps meet. So he order his soldiers to annihilate Le Page's corps and later Charton's one. Specifically, the 209th Regiment was ordered to launch an urgent march to Quang Liệt to intercept, annihilate, and slow down the French advance from Cao Bằng; the 308th Brigade was ordered to accelerate their attack to wipe out the remaining part of Le Page's corps being crammed in Cốc Xá. According to the telegram from Lạng Sơn, the French Border Commander ordered the two corps to meet in the area known as "*Ouest calcaire*" (literally: "western karst mountain range"). The map indicates that Cốc Xá is a large karst mountain slope. About three kilometers from western Cốc Xá must be the 477th height. After locating the meeting place of the two French Corps, Võ Nguyên Giáp assigned the 308th Brigade to prevent Le Page's corps from moving to western Cốc Xá. To appeal to his soldiers to be determined to destroy Le Page's corps, Võ Nguyên Giáp wrote:

> You comrades have firmly protected our positions, seized many high points from the enemy such as Khâu Xiêm and Khâu Áng, and braved yourselves to kill and capture enemy troops and seize their weapons. Those are very commendable feats. Le Page's corps is getting exhausted and in lack of ammunition and food, and many parts of it have fled in confusion when confronting with us. Their only hope is the support from Charton's corps in Cao Bằng,

so they're trying to contact this corps. Our mission now is to promptly destroy Le Page's corps and simultaneously annihilate part of Charton's corps, creating favorable conditions for our forces to besiege and kill the remaining part of the French troops. Time is valuable now. If we take action one minute early, we'll save many lives, achieve big feats, and win victory.

With a firm determination to destroy Le Page's corps and slow down Charton's corps, thwarting the French intention of uniting their two corps, Võ Nguyên Giáp made "the first move of the game" that would decide the fate of the two corps. Under the command of Deputy Chief of the 308th Brigade Cao Văn Khánh, nine Vietnamese battalions from three directions laid a siege to Le Page's units in Cốc Xá. Despite repeated efforts, Le Page failed to lead his troops through the siege to the 477th height to meet Charton's corps.

As French war correspondents guessed, the French generals in Sài Gòn must have anticipated that Charton's corps would be undergoing fierce challenges in its retreat and so it was named *"Orage"* (literally: "Storm") and its operation, *"Thérèse"* (Saint Thérèse was born on October 3—the day of the its departure). Its retreat from Cao Bằng to Thất Khê was so important that General Carpentier said that the success or failure of the plan to shorten the defense line on the 4th Route would depend on Thérèse. French generals trusted Charton very well for his commanding ability and this lieutenant colonel was dubbed "Saint of the Legion." But having heard that Đông Khê was "overwhelmed," even Charton thought that his corps could hardly flee back to Thất Khê safely. He said to war correspondents that it was a crazy idea to take the French troops from Cao Bằng to Thất Khê when they did not have a single post along the road, while Vietnamese soldiers could be seen everywhere. He was sure that the plan would drive them to death.

But from Sài Gòn, Carpentier cheered up the "Saint of the Legion" while emphasizing that "Mandate is mandate."

After receiving the order from Lạng Sơn asking them to turn into Quang Liệt, Charton's corps, the "giant python" as called by Western journalists, threw away most heavy equipment, but it still took them almost three days and nights to "creep" to the 477th height. It was a difficult retreat not only because there was only one way through the jungle which they had to continuously check for it with a map, but also because their advance was slowed down by the nearly 500 Vietnamese civilians who were forced to leave Cao Bằng. Being intercepted and attacked all the time was the most scaring thing and a direct threat to them, because this would cause them damages and disorder among their ranks. In Sài Gòn, Hà Nội, and even in Lạng Sơn, the French high commanders were unaware of the plight of the Charton's corps. On the afternoon of October 4, the Vietnamese radio got Colonel Constant's telegram from Lạng Sơn. It wrote, "Go fast, in several hours, tonight, come and rescue Le Page." Three days later, similar radiograms were sent from Hà Nội and Sài Gòn. On the evening of October 5, the French Headquarters finally managed to contact Le Page. The latter asked Charton to move on for another three kilometers to rescue him. Charton ordered the 3rd Battalion to go ahead, trying to find the way to the 447th height. As French journalists put it figuratively, no sooner had Charton's battalion arrived at the 477th height than "they bumped into a catastrophe, like a mountain avalanche, and then was swept away into nowhere." Storm actually came to the Orage Corps.

Every step of the two French corps was closely followed by the staff of the Vietnamese Headquarters through radiograms and reports from their messengers. It was claimed that the two corps were being besieged and disheartened though they were still in full numbers. This evaluation was especially true to Le Page's corps. The French troops in Cao Bằng were worn out after several days of marching under harsh conditions and only wished to flee to Thất Khê.

Võ Nguyên Giáp learnt the situation from the messengers going to and fro between their units and the Headquarters. According to their reports, the Vietnamese troops were gaining the initiative over the French and many of them were longing to confront the enemy and achieve feats. Having spent several consecutive days fighting in severe conditions such as heavy rain, thick fog, high passes, and deep abysses, they were getting fatigued. They had to simultaneously find the way and watch out for the enemy, so some nights they could move only one kilometer. Võ Nguyên Giáp told Head of the General Department of Politics Lê Liêm to remind the units to hold on to President Hồ Chí Minh's instruction: "Once we get tired, the enemy will get ten times as exhausted. So we must try our best to find out and kill the enemy to win a complete victory."

In the 8th Combat Order sent to the units on the midnight of October 5, Võ Nguyên Giáp stressed that they should take the chance to annihilate Le Page's corps before Charton's corps could get into contact with them. After exterminating Le Page's corps, they would gather their troop strength and annihilate the rest of the French force. Võ Nguyên Giáp instructed the Vietnamese units to pay special attention to maintaining communication and making timely reports of the situations.

Chapter Four: ADVANCE TO A STRANGE TURNING POINT

The battle took place in the 40-km road section west of the 4th Route, from northwestern Đông Khê to northern Thất Khê. The 308th Brigade sent two thirds of its troops to besiege Charton's corps when the latter arrived at the 477th height. One of the three remaining battalions of the 308th Brigade were lying in wait along the path from Cốc Xá to the 477th height. The 154th Battalion of the 209th Regiment and the 89th Battalion of the 36th Regiment, led by the Chief of the 36th Regiment, managed to tighten their siege to and annihilate the North African troops and the remaining paratroops of Le Page's corps in Cốc Xá. At that time, the Cốc Xá-477th height area, the center of the battlefield, was being besieged by the 308th Brigade, reinforced by the 209th Regiment in the north and the 174th Regiment in the south (particularly the Khâu Phia-Cốc Tôn area). To encourage the units before they entered into a large attack on the Cốc Xá-477th height, Võ Nguyên Giáp made an appeal which was conveyed to combatants at 3 am on October 7. The appeal reads:

> You comrades have destroyed a vital part of Le Page's Corps. Part of its remnants are likely in a panic and are possibly running away to join Charton's corps. However, instead of strengthening the corps, they will dampen the latter's spirit with their defeats and load the latter with their wounded soldiers.
>
> Our mission therefore is to continue destroying Le Page's troops being besieged while promptly attacking Charton's corps by waylaying them, intensely outflanking them, cutting off them by parts, and besieging and destroying them.
>
> It's raining tonight and you're getting wet and tired, but as National Defense Army soldiers and revolutionary fighters, you are boiling with the fire of hatred for the enemy, patriotism, and the spirit of storming ahead.

The French troops are surely more hungry, and suffer from more deaths and wounds than we do. Moreover, they have the spirit of defeated invaders. So we should try more to kill as many of them as we can.

The fight had been taking place most fiercely in Cốc Xá and the area of the 477th height for seven consecutive days, and at around 5 pm, Charton found that they were mired in a desperate situation. He was found to have many times asked the French Headquarters in Lạng Sơn to parachute a battalion into Bản Ca (in the middle of the 477th height area and Thất Khê) to back their withdrawal to Thất Khê. Constant did not accept this request for the thought that parachuting a battalion at that time was like dropping a thing into a whirlpool to see it engulfed later, as well as expanding the scope of the Vietnamese victory. He repeated that the only way out for Charton's corps was to thread their way into the forest and quickly arrive in Nà Cạo, where they would be picked up by four companies headed by De la Beaume from Thất Khê. Having received this news, Lieutenant Colonel Charton did not think any more about his three battalions being shattered at the 477th height. He gathered a few staff officers, Chief of Cao Bằng Province Hai Thu, and a small number of soldiers to join him. Then they used a map to find their way across the forest southward. But Vietnamese soldiers and militiamen rushed after them following their footsteps and cornered them into the battlefield prepared by the 18th Battalion of the 102nd Regiment. Failing to resist the Vietnamese force, Le Page's troops surrendered at 6:30 pm on October 7. At first, the Vietnamese mistook the commanding officer for Le Page. Then Charton confessed that he had not heard of Le Page or De la Beaume's army.

Chapter Four: ADVANCE TO A STRANGE TURNING POINT

In the meantime, odd events were happening on the 4th Route battlefield. Le Page's force, the first target of the Vietnamese attack, had been basically destroyed, but the commander was fleeing. By the contrast, Charton's corps in Cao Bằng were in greater strength, but its commander had been captured and was being taken to a prison camp. The four French rescue companies, led by De la Beaume, were being intercepted and attacked vehemently by the 174th Regiment in Lũng Phầy.

On the afternoon of October 7, the fighting was going on very fiercely in the Cốc Xá-477th height area when the Vietnamese Headquarters staff heard a special dialogue between Commander-in-chief Võ Nguyên Giáp and Chief of the 308th Brigade Vương Thừa Vũ.

It was revealed later that when the Brigade was overcoming all difficulties and challenges to realize their determination to capture alive both Le Page and Charton, their commander, Vương Thừa Vũ, suffered from stomach bleeding. He asked his guards to make a stretcher to carry him so that he could be with his soldiers, but doctor Minh Tâm persuaded and nearly forced him to stay motionless. While he was listening to his assistant's report on their fighting situation in Cốc Xá, Vương Thừa Vũ received a phone call from the Headquarters. He picked up the phone and recognized the voice of Võ Nguyên Giáp on the other side of the line. Their dialogue lasted several minutes.

"How's everything going, Vũ?" Giáp asked.

"We've nearly eliminated Le Page's corps in Cốc Xá," Vũ said.

"But we haven't captured Le Page, have we?"

381

"No, sir. Some of their troops, including Le Page, have fled."

"Capture them all. How about the 477th height?"

"Yes, sir. We'll try our best to complete the task. The 102nd Regiment is outflanking Charton's corps at the 477th Height; the 88th Regiment has encircled Bản Ca south of the 477th Height, preventing them from running away.

"Try to arrange for Charton and Le Page to meet."

"Yes, sir. We promise we'll try our best."

Then both of them laughed at their joke. The battle was developing severely and Vũ did not tell anyone except the medical staff about the recurring of his stomachache. But in the dialogue with Giáp that day, he failed to hide it from Giáp since the latter could something unusual in the former's voice. Not until much later did Vũ admit that Giáp had been very sensitive when he suddenly asked, "Why is your voice so hoarse?"

"My stomach is bleeding and I'm receiving a blood transfusion," Vũ replied.

Giáp interrupted, "Try to lie down for treatment until you fully recover. Fighting is a long story. Tell the Brigade staff to notify Cao Văn Khánh that the French had sent De la Baume's corps from Thất Khê to Lũng Phầy to meet Le Page and Charton. The 308th Brigade will continue to destroy this corps."

"Yes, sir. We promise to execute the order by all means."

"But you should take a rest to recover, Vũ. You should listen to the medical staff."

Chapter Four: ADVANCE TO A STRANGE TURNING POINT

On the afternoon of October 8, the units were excited to receive Hồ Chí Minh's encouragement letter. The letter reads:

> Our beloved soldiers,
>
> Since the outbreak of our resistance war, this is the first time we've conducted mobile warfare for several consecutive days. It is a big challenge to us.
>
> Despite fatigue, hunger and cold, you've exerted yourselves to kill the enemy and succeeded in exterminating their most élite corps.
>
> You've overcome seven-tenths of the ordeal. Try to eliminate Charton's corps.
>
> The Commander-in-chief and I have ordered to prepare a meal with beef to treat you.
>
> Kiss you all.[1]

At 2 pm the following day, the Border Campaign Headquarters released an order. In this order, Võ Nguyên Giáp wrote:

> Yesterday the French High Commissioner announced that Le Page and Charton were all right. Today when they know that both of their élite corps have been destroyed, they will surely be horrified. However, we should not be subjective and underestimate the enemy or be too satisfied with the victory to be lazy.
>
> We haven't completely destroyed the remnants of Charton's corps, so we must save time and do it as soon as possible.

This order was the final verdict for Le Page and the remnants of both French corps.

---

1. *Hồ Chí Minh toàn tập* (literally: Hồ Chí Minh's Complete Works), op cit., vol. 6, p. 103.

The night before, having been informed by the French Headquarters in Lạng Sơn about De la Beaume's corps, Le Page collected some of his remnant troops and divided them into small groups to grope their way in darkness toward the south in search of De la Beaume. Then they had to stop briefly because they always faced the risk of being detected by Vietnamese soldiers. Two days and nights had passed without Le Page receiving any information of Charton's corps in Cao Bằng for he had lost contact with this lieutenant colonel. Between midnight and dawn on October 9, Le Page and his entourage continued their desperate journey, but they moved very slowly for they had to occasionally stop to hide themselves every time they heard any strange noise. On the afternoon of October 9, they had just got out of a dense forest when they were detected by the troops of the 88th Regiment. All their intentions to fight or flee were made useless. Those captured included Le Page and many French staff officers. Not until then did Le Page know that Charton had reached the "destination" long before him! But the prison camp was not the place the two French commanders had chosen to assemble their troops. The French press called their meeting "a weird date."

It was told later that on the morning of October 10, General Carpentier's office was closed. It was announced that he would not receive guests that day. The journalists had patiently waited outside Norodom Palace to see Carpentier and his press assistant before they were informed that there would be no regular press conference to announce the combat situation. The following day, they all flew to the North where they eye-witnessed the French troops escaping in panic from Thất Khê, Lạng Sơn, southward. It was said to be a dramatic, strange, and unexplainable escape.

Chapter Four: ADVANCE TO A STRANGE TURNING POINT

On the Vietnamese side, on October 9, when Hồ Chí Minh and Võ Nguyên Giáp had gone to visit the staff of the 88th Regiment, who had captured Le Page, the Headquarters received the news that the situation of the area from Thất Khê to the south of the 4th Route was developing swiftly. Across the battlefield, except for a few units who continued to chase and kill the enemy remnants, all the battalions and regiments were promptly consolidating their organizations in order to achieve victory in the south with the immediate target being Thất Khê. At that time, the French combat troops there rose to 1,500 including De la Beaume's troops, who had just arrived from the north, and a battalion of reinforcement paratroops. The French troops who had escaped from Cốc Xá and the 477th height struck their comrades there with consternation.

The following morning, the Border Combat Headquarter received unexpected news: the French were withdrawing from Thất Khê. It turned out that they had sent a parachute battalion there to prepare for their retreat. Some battalions of the 308th Brigade and the 209th and 174th Regiments were ordered to rush after the French toward Na Sầm. But they were too slow. The French made a series of successive escapes after the one in Thất Khê.[1] As a result, the Vietnamese forces missed many opportunities to destroy the French along their way of retreat. Not until much

---

1. The French withdrew from Thất Khê (and from Thái Nguyên simultaneously) on October 10, from Na Sầm on October 13, from Đồng Đăng on October 17, from Lạng Sơn and Lạng Giai on October 18, from Lộc Bình and Đình Lập on October 20, and from An Châu on October 23. Within about two weeks, the French defense line on the 4th Route was shortened by over 120 kilometers. Their retreat from their strongholds in Lạng Sơn southward was totally out of their plan.

later did they know that they had missed such a typical opportunity: on the morning of October 10, when they had just left Thất Khê for a couple of kilometers, thousands of French soldiers were crammed into the northern bank of the Kỳ Cùng River for several hours because the sappers of the 308th Brigade had destroyed the Bản Trại bridge over it the night before. Different from the retreat from Cao Bằng, which was well prepared, those occurring from October 10 onward were made in a hurry, so the French had no time to destroy their facilities, including their ammunition in the depot. On the Vietnamese side, after nearly half a month of conducting mobile warfare in harsh weather conditions and complex terrain, the troops were too tired to keep chasing the French. So Võ Nguyên Giáp canceled their pursuit of the French toward Tiên Yên and ordered to end the campaign after the ambush of the 174th Regiment in the north of Na Sầm.

After his field trip to the newly-liberated town of Thất Khê, Võ Nguyên Giáp returned to the Headquarters in Nà Lạng. There he listened to the units reviewing the situations on the border front and the coordination of battlefields nationwide. The Vietnamese army achieved far beyond the initial goal of border liberation in terms of enemy elimination and land liberation. In the Northeast battlefield, the French defense line on the 4th Route was shortened by nearly 200 kilometers or three times as much as the expected length; 8,000 French troops were killed and captured alive, including eight élite Euro-African battalions and two puppet ones. It was the first time in their anti-French resistance war they had eliminated approximately half of the French mobile forces just in one campaign. It was also the first time the Vietnamese troops across Việt Nam, thanks to the unprecedented human and material contributions of Vietnamese people in the rear, especially those in Cao Bằng and Lạng Sơn,[1] and Chinese people, won a victory of great strategic significance[2] just in a dry season.

Võ Nguyên Giáp suggested the Vietnamese Staff should find out why the French had made such a hasty retreat from their series of important positions on such a sensitive battlefield as their defense line on the 4th Route. Obviously, it was the French mistake that led to their two corps being dismantled just in a single week. Their confusion after losing two corps drove them into committing other mistakes and finally the disintegration of the entire border zone. It was also clear that the Vietnamese successes unexpectedly shook the spirit and thinking of the French Command. The French generals were subjective and underestimated the Vietnamese, so after each of their failures, they became increasingly confused and got stuck in more mistakes and failures. Not to mention Lạng Sơn, where the French Border Headquarters was located and where

---

1. In the Border Campaign, the people of Cao Bằng and Lạng Sơn contributed several hundred tons of rice and 73 tons of corn, and nearly 1.6 million workdays. Three-fourths of cadres of Cao Bằng, from provincial to grassroots level, participated in the campaign.
2. In the dry season of 1950, the Vietnamese forces across the battlefields nationwide killed about 10,000 French troops, destroyed 217 fortifications, and liberated 17 commune-level towns and 5 district-level towns of different strategic significance (including Cao Bằng, Lạng Sơn, Thái Nguyên, Lào Cai, and Hòa Bình). Those in the Northern mountainous and forested battlefield alone exterminated 110 fortifications of different sizes, and liberated two-thirds of the Sino-Vietnamese border which covered an area of 4,000 square kilometers. As a result, the Vietnamese resistance base was expanded and linked with the big rear of brotherly countries. The period of fighting within the French siege came to an end.

their huge stockpile of armaments was left,[1] the French escape from Đồng Đăng made Võ Nguyên Giáp ponder about the mood and thought of the French Command. Later he wrote:

> I was most impressed by the French fortifications in Đồng Đăng. They were much stronger than those in Đông Khê and Thất Khê. Their fire-power system was very dense. So I wonder why the French abandoned such an ideal place. If they had held their ground here, they would have created not few difficulties to our soldiers. Besides, if they had not withdrawn from Đồng Đăng in Lạng Sơn, we would have had to launch the 3rd Lê Hồng Phong campaign.[2] What lesson could we learn from their previous chain of reactions?

A few days later, at the Open Campaign Party Committee Conference, General Võ Nguyên Giáp gave further explanation of his thought. He said:

> We've won a complete victory at this campaign, gained a lot of experience from it, and made a lot of progress. But we should be specially aware that this time we fought against an opponent who showed no zeal for attack and tried to avoid face-to-face fighting (Le Page's corps) and a retreating one (Charton's corps), and all the conditions were in our favor. So we should not be subjective and underestimate the enemy.

---

1. According to the French source of information, the French military goods left in Lạng Sơn was enough to equip eight regiments, including 4,000 submachine guns, 10,000 artillery shells, 150 tons of medicine, 2,000 tons of provisions, and 1,500 tons of other supplies. These supplies were preserved until the Điện Biên Phủ Campaign in 1954, when they were used by the Vietnamese. According to the book titled *La Guerre d'Indochine* (literally: History of the Indochina War) by Lucien Bodard, the French left in Lạng Sơn 11,000 tons of ammunition, including 10,000 tons of 75-mm bullets, 4,000 new submachine guns, 600,000 liters of petrol, and others.
2. He meant that another Border Campaign should be held. The previous campaign was known as the Second Lê Hồng Phong Campaign.

Võ Nguyên Giáp had a good reason to think about the mentality of the French army and about the conditions for the Vietnamese victory that went beyond their expectation. This victory was the consequence of the domino panic—the phenomenon of rapidly-widespread demoralization—among not only the French troops in the Northeast border but also the French highest leadership in Indochina. A deeper insight into those dark days of the Command of the French Expeditionary Corps, especially their retreat from Thất Khê and Lạng Sơn, was gained from the memoirs and historical chronicles by French journalists, historians, and generals later.

No sooner had the French Headquarters on the 4th Route heard that Le Page's and Charton's corps were both destroyed than they thought of withdrawing and evacuating their troops, first and foremost those in Thất Khê. Their retreat from Thất Khê on October 10 was a "stampede retreat." Disaster struck them shortly after the legionaries got out of Thất Khê and crossed the Kỳ Cùng River. There began the tragedy. The war correspondents cited a typical example: an entire parachute battalion was sent there on the afternoon of October 9, but only five paratroops survived and managed to arrive in Lạng Sơn the following day.

In Hà Nội and Sài Gòn, the public seemed to have a different attitude toward the North African soldiers and the legionaries, who had been said to know nothing but victory. The French generals had thought that the white-skinned would never be engulfed by the yellow-skinned. But when the gun shoots were silenced in the border battlefield, this thought was changed. For the first time in Indochina, the yellow-skinned not only smashed but also destroyed corps of white-skinned troops. From being so confident, these white-skinned men became terrified and wanted to give up everything in the wake of rapid-fire occurrences. Moreover, their commanders repeatedly pushed them with words like "The Vietnamese troops are getting close, so leave before it is too late." Therefore, successive escapes of French troops from Lạng Sơn to Chũ, An Châu, and as far as the south of the 4th Route were seen during two weeks.

During the last days of October, the Vietnamese Campaign Headquarters had many tasks to do after fighting stopped in the 4th Route battlefield, the most difficult of which was the logistical one. They needed to arrange and reorganize a whole system of depots and stations after the campaign ended. The war booties collected from the French depots, especially their base depot in Lạng Sơn, went beyond all their expectations in terms of variety and quantity. Although the selection of model individuals and units would be conducted later when they returned to the base, the Campaign Headquarters instructed the political agencies on the fronts to immediately reward extraordinary individuals such as La Văn Cầu, Lý Văn Mưu (the 174th Regiment), Trần Cừ (the 209th Regiment), militiawoman Đinh Thị Dậu, and doctor Phạm Gia Triệu. One of the immediate important things that should be done by the advisory and political staff of the Campaign Headquarters was to choose a person to accompany Hồ Chí Minh to Thất Khê to visit the 308th Brigade and some units of soldiers and conscripted laboreres who had achieved excellent feats. Hồ Chí Minh also intended to meet those French officers who had been captured. Some Vietnamese Headquarters officers were prepared to join Võ Nguyên Giáp on a trip to the positions where the pivotal battles of the campaign had taken place. They wanted to gather more facts for their later summarization of the campaign to be more accurate.

In Đông Khê, Võ Nguyên Giáp had a better understanding of the reason why the fighting lasted longer and the Vietnamese side suffered more casualties than they had expected. The French forces comprised only two Euro-African companies and one puppet company, but they were stationed in a solid fortification complex, which was much different from a battalion in a single fort. More importantly, the Vietnamese attacked the French where the latter were strongest (the French underground fire-power that was not detected by the Vietnamese during their preparation for the battle). After the Đông Khê battle, while Le Page made a serious mistake by leading his whole corps to the "deadly valley" of Cốc Xá, the Vietnamese forces confronted a big difficult: they launched mobile warfare on a rocky mountain with deep abysses and abrupt slopes where they would fight barefoot. An obvious contradiction can easily be found between the battle in Đông Khê and that in the Cốc Xá-477th height area. In the first battle, the French with their fortifications and fire-power could hold on for more than two days and nights in the fight against the Vietnamese forces, who were eight or nine times as strong as they were. In the second battle, on the contrary, two French corps comprising seven battalions (the corps in Cao Bằng was nearly in full numbers) were exterminated by the nine Vietnamese battalions which had become more or less worn-out. What matters here is not the place where the battle took place (inside or outside the fortifications), but the mental balance between those who wished to make more attacks in the wake of their previous successes and those

391

who tried not to encounter their opponents for a safe escape toward the south.

After his visit to Lạng Sơn, Võ Nguyên Giáp went back to Cao Bằng. No sooner had he passed Thất Khê than he heard that 800 wounded soldiers out of 3,500 French prisoners were being returned to France. Vietnamese sappers were repairing the Thất Khê airport so that French aircraft could land. Colonel and military doctor Huyard, representative of the French Red Cross, came to receive the wounded soldiers. At that time, no one could imagine that it was this doctor who, three years later, would appear in Điện Biên Phủ to collect much more French wounded soldiers.

On the way back to Lam Sơn, Võ Nguyên Giáp told his entourage to stop at Đông Khê to look for a house to stay overnight before setting off again the following morning. He had spent three months commanding the preparation and implementation of the campaign in extremely urgent conditions, especially since the beginning of October when a French corps had arrived from the south, followed by another one from the north. During the last ten days, he almost did not sleep but frequent the Headquarters to supervise the whole battlefield awaiting the seven French battalions. Now when the battlefield had become quiet, the nearly-40-year-old commander was found, for the first time, to be in a state of exhaustion by his inferiors in the Headquarters. He said he felt a slight headache. It was right then that an unexpected and interesting event occurred. From a house on stilts in the remote and deserted hamlet came the sound of some musical instrument. In his memoirs, he wrote:

> The abrupt sound was like a magic remedy that drove away my tiredness after the battles. I felt astonished as if I had

Chapter Four: ADVANCE TO A STRANGE TURNING POINT

not ever heard any sound like it before. How strange it was! All the fatigue was immediately dissipated. I felt as if I was climbing a very steep mountain from Khuôn Chu to the Tam Đảo peak when I was suddenly bathed in very cool mist and a refreshing breeze.

The music suddenly ceased. Giáp was so fascinated by it that he had the player invited to the house on stilts he was staying in. The young musician and soldier played his guitar for about one hour without knowing who his "audience" in this simple house were or that with his humble guitar, he had brought very soothing moments to the Commander-in-chief of the Vietnamese army after his long and stressful days.

Moments of entertainment were over and the escort saw their superior lie down for a sound sleep. The following morning, along the over-40-km stretch of road, Giáp was obsessed by the question "Where will the next campaign take place?" He had raised that question when he was on the way with Deputy Chief of the General Staff Phan Phác and Deputy Chief of the Army Intelligence Cao Pha to see the French prisoners of war. What would Paris do after their defeat on the 4th Route? It had become a rule observed by French prime ministers that after each failure of strategic significance, they would change generals and increase troops. But after five years of sinking into the war, France was confronting growing difficulties in many aspects. What could Prime Minister René Pleven do in the time to come? At that time, the French reserve force in the hands of Commander-in-chief Carpentier had become exhausted. With the American aids that were being massively poured in, however, the French Headquarters could do nothing but take the immediate measures of rapidly developing their puppet troops and building up their mobile forces out of local forces to replace nearly ten thousand French élite troops that had been killed. In the conclusion made at the Open Campaign Party Committee Conference a few days later, Võ Nguyên Giáp explained more about the French plot and possibility. He said, "Once the French have been agitated, they will overestimate us and make more careful preparations for their strategic plan, application of tactics, formation and use of mobile forces and interceptive units, and reinforcing and aiding activities to cope with us."

Commander-in-chief Võ Nguyên Giáp attached much importance to the summarization of the work and he regularly conducted this as a habit during his military career. The past three months of directing the preparation for and implementation of the campaign, the first ever large-scale operation in his military career, had left him many novel impressions. There were both similarities and differences between it and its predecessors. According to Cecil Currey, author of *Victory at Any Cost*, if the Việt Bắc base were Giáp's "military school in the forest" during the anti-French resistance war, then the battle on the 4th Route would be the location for him to launch a "sudden manoeuvre" in the first year of his nine-year training course in his military career. The 2nd Lê Hồng Phong campaign was the first large-scale operation launched by Vietnamese troops, so its summarization was paid special attention to. The Ministry of National Defense instructed units from grassroots level upward to carry out this work. The Open Campaign Party Committee Conference held from October 26–29 in Cao Bằng was an important step in the preparation for the summarization conference to be held in Thái Nguyên the following month.

Chapter Four: ADVANCE TO A STRANGE TURNING POINT

In his report delivered at the Open Campaign Party Committee Conference on October 29, Võ Nguyên Giáp said:

> Our recent victory proves that we have fulfilled our tasks and known all the causes leading to this. The victory demonstrates our achievements and progress, as well as our weaknesses. We have gained some experience and so have the French. So what we should do is to promote our advantages, overcome our disadvantages, and solve our remaining problems and difficulties so that we can record more victories and fulfill our new tasks in the upcoming campaigns.
>
> Regarding the concept, we should regard the summing up as the final main task of a campaign. The campaign will remain uncompleted if this task has not been fulfilled. It should address not only minor experience but also principles, not only the completed tasks but also the upcoming ones, not only the contemporary battles but also ones in the future.

After clarifying the content, timing, and method for the summarization to be conducted by agencies and units, Võ Nguyên Giáp mentioned the new tasks. He said:

> After this campaign, the enemy will draw up new schemes, new guidelines, and new plans for their operations. So our tasks should be:
>
> 1- Strengthen our soldiers' fighting capacity;
>
> 2- Learn about the method of conducting mobile warfare (primary method) and that of attacking on strengthened fortifications (secondary method); disseminate new military tactics among troops; strengthen the regular army; develop regular and local forces;
>
> 3- Organize our soldiers into infantry brigades, artillery and sapper regiments, as well as communication, reconnaissance and transport battalions; regard the development of local forces as one of the regular forces' tasks;

4- Speed up the training, supplementation, and promotion of cadres; encourage the promotion of cadres;

5- Prepare for a new campaign; create favorable conditions for the implementation of mobile warfare.

Finally, he reminded cadres at all levels to raise high the spirit of criticism and self-criticism and promote the solidarity between them and between units while conducting the review and summarization of the campaign.

The summarization of such a large-scale campaign was completely new to the Vietnamese army, from the units to the command. It was the Commander-in-chief's custom to give specific instructions to his inferiors in every step of the implementation. The General Headquarters staff first witnessed this working style at the first military conference held in Chương Mỹ, about one month after the outbreak of the national resistance war. Over the previous five year, the cadres of the Vietnamese army had become increasingly mature, considerably thanks to the meticulous instruction of Võ Nguyên Giáp—the eldest brother of the whole army.

In late November 1950, Võ Nguyễn Giáp returned to the General Headquarters based in the Bảo Biên-Chợ Chu area. This dry season, the Vietnamese army had made a strategically significant turning-point, clearing the border and terminating the years of fighting in the French siege. Then the old question returned to the Giáp's mind: "Where will the next campaign take place?"

Chapter Five

ON THE WAY TO PROMOTE THE WAR OF MOVEMENT

General de Lattre—The Fifth Opponent

Since the end of October 1950, through newspapers sent from Vietnamese underground agents, the Advisory Board of the General Headquarters was updated on the atmosphere in Paris, Sài Gòn, and Hà Nội after "the 4th Route crisis." Alphonse Juin and Jean Letourneau were assigned to head a French mission to Việt Nam to investigate the situation. The right faction in the French Parliament demanded a general of large caliber to be dispatched to Việt Nam to save the situation. Specifically, they required General Marcel Alessandri be recalled and General Pierre Boyer de Latour du Moulin lead the French Expeditionary Corps in North Việt Nam right at the beginning of November 1950, when the battlefield was developing severely. The Vietnamese intelligence was well "acquainted" with this general, who was the author of mopping-up operations and a famous system of military posts in South Việt Nam, locally called "de Latour watchtowers," at important places which were a few kilometers apart.

It was not easy to send any French general to Indochina to lead the war here at this time. Neither General Marie-Pierre Koenig nor General Alphonse Juin was willing to command the troops on this burning peninsula. Being put in a bad fix, the French Parliament called an extraordinary meeting on November 22 to give Prime Minister René Pleven full powers to deal with the issue of Indochina. Five-star General Jean de Lattre de Tassigny, former Commander of the First Corps and famous for his hunger for success and hot temper, was the third general to be convoked. It was the first time in the Indochina War that the positions of High Commissioner and Commander-in-chief had been assumed by one person. That was the only condition set by de Lattre and accepted by the French President. It was believed that a well-known general like de Lattre could help the French Expeditionary Corps dispel the current atmosphere of defeat and "bring back its status and hope."

After ten days of preparation in Paris, on the afternoon of December 17, 1950, de Lattre and his escort set foot on the Tân Sơn Nhất airport. From this moment on, Commander-in-chief de Lattre had been known as the fifth opponent of Commander-in-chief Võ Nguyên Giáp.

When he arrived in Sài Gòn, the first news he received was that of the continuous evacuations happening in Hà Nội, especially the evacuation of French women and children to Hải Phòng as a "precaution." It was the echo of the French failure in the Border campaign. There had been more and more evacuations since the middle of December. Files were burnt by officers. The Doumer Brigde (present-day Long Biên bridge) was strictly protected because it was the only important bridge for the French to retreat to Hải Phòng if necessary. There was hot news: the Việt Minh army had got close to the north of Hà Nội.

No sooner had he arrived at Norodom Palace in Sài Gòn than the French Commander-in-chief made two orders. One the one hand, Chief of Staff Allard had to renew the French commanding apparatus—"the Cao Bằng-Lạng Sơn failure-infected apparatus." On the other hand, Second-in-command Salan got ready to accompany him to Hà Nội on the night of December 19. This news reminded the Sài Gòn press of an old memory: December 19 became a meaningful day to the French army five year ealier. They did not forget to comment that the attendance of the new French Commander-in-chief at the center of North Việt Nam on this occasion expressed his determination and challenge to the Vietnamese army.

After the review held to welcome him, de Lattre summoned all primary officers in Hà Nội that evening. In this first meeting, young officers were encouraged by inspiring words about "the glory of noble deaths." De Lattre said that he came to Việt Nam to accompany young soldiers including his son, Lieutenant Bernard de Lattre de Tassigny. He shared with them the pride this noble war would bring, and emphasized that they would fight to protect the world civilization, not for the purpose of domination. He assured that they would be well commanded and would never give up an inch of the land to the opponent. Paris was waiting for a victory, or a turning-point, from him. With an angry face, de Lattre accused the ongoing evacuations and decided that this cowardly action must be stopped.

Before leaving Hà Nội for Hải Phòng, he asked de Latour to report on their defensive plan in Hà Nội. He reminded the latter not to disregard the news that the Vietnamese army was overwhelming the city.

During his first days in Indochina, people soon noticed that he attached special importance to the journalists who kept following him closely. This was a remarkable characteristics of his working style. Through every of his actions, French and Vietnamese journalists and those from other countries, especially from the United States, all came to a comprehensive conclusion which was true to his thought and actions. In his cause in Indochina, he needed a fanatical expeditionary army and a big team of journalists who yielded to him or agreed to write what he wanted.

From the end of December 1950, General Charles Chanson, Commander in South Việt Nam, objected de Lattre's order to send reinforcement troops to the North. Salan convinced Chanson that for de Lattre, "Hà Nội is the top priority." The latter put himself into two situations, either driving his troops to the North and preparing favorable conditions to win or being annihilated for not having taken advantage of that lucky chance. No battlefield could refuse to send part of its troops to de Lattre according to his military power concentration plan after having known of his determination to urgently build seven to eight mobile regiments which would be put under the command of reliable colonels. Those responsible for important positions like Hải Phòng and Hà Nội were carefully selected. De Lattre decided to send Colonel Gambier, a level-headed and persuasive man, to the Catholic area in the south of Hà Nội to keep close control of the situation here. French mobile regiments, which were in the process of formation, were ordered to urgently deploy the area around Hà Nội, from Bắc Ninh to

Chapter Five: ON THE WAY TO PROMOTE THE WAR OF MOVEMENT

Bắc Giang, Gia Lâm, Vĩnh Phúc, Hải Dương, Phủ Lỗ, and even Đông Triều.

De Lattre often put to his assistants these question, "How shall we conduct this war?" and "Which direction is Giáp going to attack?" The answer he got from them is that there was no grounds for making any guess in this Asian land, based on their predecessors' experience. He did not believe that. He said he was waiting for a real war in which he could fight with a real strategy against an enemy in the flesh, not ghosts. He expected a regular, face-to-face war which had no place for the guerilla tactics being used by his opponent.

De Lattre went to Indochina with the great ambition of gaining the strategic initiative from his opponent and reversing the situation to keep the beautiful and resource-rich Indochina in the French Union. To reach that general strategic goal, he decided to make the most of American aids, court the sympathy of the South East Asia Treaty Organization (SEATO), and urge the Bảo Đại administration to carry out large-scale conscription for his plan of building a local army to overcome the increasing serious troop strength crisis. Psychologically, he incited his troops by repeatedly expressing his intention of retaking Lạng Sơn and taking revenge on the 4th Route, bringing honor and confidence back to the French Expeditionary Corps. De Lattre revealed his ambition of gaining the strategic initiative as early as in mid January, nearly one month after he arrived in Indochina. He entrusted Colonel Beau-Frère, who was familiar with the battlefield in the North Vietnamese highlands, with the task of leading five regiments in a surprise attack on the karst region sandwiched between the two strategic 1st and 3rd Routes, not far from Bắc Sơn and Thái Nguyên, which was considered to be the opponent's logistical center. The French Headquarters intended to launch the attack on January 14, but Giáp had taken earlier action in Vĩnh Yên. Then during the first ten months of 1951, de Lattre had to deal with successive attacks made by the Vietnamese army, build up a network of bunkers surrounding the Red River Delta, and carry out an unprecedented large-scale raid to take control of the Red River Delta. All of these acts were aimed at the initial topic: gaining the initiative.

For nearly one year of leading the French Expeditionary Corps in its invasion of Indochina, de Lattre, with his mettle, personality, and material strength, had caused Vietnamese people and army lots of difficulties, both in their operations and struggles to protect their political and armed bases in the areas temporarily occupied by the French.

In late 1950 and early 1951, the appearance of the new French Commander-in-chief, the dispatch of French reinforcement troops from Paris, and the recent deployment of French combat forces in Hà Nội were important news on which Commander-in-chief Võ Nguyên Giáp was updated by the Vietnamese intelligence as soon as the Vietnamese General Headquarters started their preparation for the next campaign in the wake of the Border campaign. Certainly at that time they had not known much about the French renewed commanding apparatus or their new strategic plot. The Vietnamese commanding apparatus was still operating according to the given plan.

The Midlands—A Sensitive Battlefield

In the second half of November 1950, Võ Nguyên Giáp was extremely busy. About ten days earlier, the Standing Central

Committee selected the midlands, specifically Vĩnh Yên, as the direction for the next campaign. Returning from the border front, Võ Nguyên Giáp summoned two conferences of the Trần Hưng Đạo Campaign[1] Party Committee on November 18 and 23 to direct the preparation for the next campaign. These two conferences was immediately followed by an official conference held on November 27 in Thái Nguyên to summarize the Border campaign. At this conference, Hồ Chí Minh instructed all attendees to "promptly take advantage of time." They intended to exploit the French troops being demoralized to attack the midlands before the latter recovered and reinforced their defense at the gateway to the delta, and simultaneously promote guerilla war in the Red River Delta and the temporarily-occupied areas nationwide. At this conference, General Secretary Trường Chinh repeated the Party's strategic guideline in early 1950 for the three areas (mountainous, midland, and lowland) of the North Vietnamese battlefield. In the mountainous area, Vietnamese soldiers completed the task of liberating the border, clearing the international communication route, breaking the strategic siege of the enemy, and cutting the beginning of their East-West corridor.[2] The two remaining tasks were supposed to be fulfilled in the midland and lowland areas.

While there were only five French battalions in the vast Việt Bắc, over half of the French army in the whole Indochina,

---

1. The code name of the Midland (Vĩnh Yên) campaign.
2. The East-West corridor was the strategic route linking Lạng Sơn, Bắc Ninh, Bắc Giang, Sơn Tây, Hòa Bình, Sơn La, and Tây Bắc. It had been formed and improved since the summer of 1949 according to the Revers plan. It not only separated the Việt Bắc revolutionary base from the Red River Delta but also served as the outer defense line of Hà Nội, preventing the Vietnamese regular forces from attacking from the North.

including the entire strategic mobile force of about 30 battalions, concentrated in the midland and lowland areas.

On the Vietnamese side, with some newly-established brigades[1] added, the Vietnamese strategic mobile infantry force in the Northern battlefield was 1.2 times as large as the French one (36 Vietnamese battalions compared to 30 French battalions), but heavy weapons were still limited. The Chinese aids in 1950 reached only 20 percent of the target. The 351st Brigade owned only old 75-mm mountain cannons.

By launching a campaign with the participation of regular forces in the midlands to annihilate an important part of the French troop strength, the Vietnamese would have conditions to expand their Việt Bắc base southward into a relatively rich and populous area with convenient transportation. However, the midland terrain was mostly featured with bare hills and short trees that made it difficult for soldiers to find shelter during the combat. Võ Nguyên Giáp soon noticed that. At the conference to summarize the Border campaign, he told the unit commanders as soon as the direction of the next campaign had been determined:

> In terms of the terrain, we've got used to fighting in the mountainous areas but haven't been accustomed to the

---

1. The 304th Brigade was established in early 1950; the 312th Brigade, in late 1950; the 320th and 325th Brigades and the 351st Engineer and Artillery Brigade, in early 1951; the 316th Brigade, in the summer of 1951. The 246th Regiment was still responsible for protecting the Central agencies in Việt Bắc. The main battlefield of the 320th Brigade was the Red River Delta; the 325th Brigade, the Bình-Trị-Thiên region. Thus, the main mobile forces of the Vietnamese General Headquarters in the North included the 308th, 304th, 312th, and 316th Infantry Brigades (comprising 36 battalions) and the 351st Brigade (comprising one engineer regiment and one artillery regiment).

Chapter Five: ON THE WAY TO PROMOTE THE WAR OF MOVEMENT

delta. However, it is easier for us to receive support from the people and get information of the enemy. If the enemy has a lot of aircraft, we'll strengthen our fortifications and made quick assaults and retreats. But we shouldn't be too excited with our victory (in the Border campaign) to become subjective and underestimate the enemy.

There emerged an important question of how to overcome terrain-caused difficulties when moving soldiers to the midlands and delta. The Chinese consultants introduced the "hit and run" tactics (to stage a forced march into a surprise attack) of their liberation army. This tactics could help soldiers limit the artillery fire-power and aircraft of the enemy, and reduce casualties when fighting in the bare terrain. According to this tactics, Vietnamese soldiers would gather about 15 kilometers out of the French artillery range and then quickly hit and ran, suddenly accessing the French at night, fighting to decimate them, cleaning up the battlefield, and then quickly leaving before dawn. In the previous small campaigns, they had decimated the French entrenched fortification in one night, so not only the French advantage of fire-power, aircraft, and artillery was limited, but also their mobile force was neutralized. The remarkable point in this campaign was that fighting would take place in the bare terrain in the midlands and delta. Besides, the gathering location would be far from the French position and thus Vietnamese soldiers would be worn out after a long way of of "hit and run" before actually entering into the combat. They had fought in a long campaign, so their health was in the process of recovery. In the demand of the new task, apart from the reinforcement of their organization and tactical and technical training, physical intensification became an important issue to be solved by the Vietnamese

405

in the remaining days before their movement of troops to the midlands.

According to the report by Head of the Intelligence Agency Lê Trọng Nghĩa at the first conference of the Midland Front Party Committee[1] on November 18, French troops retreating from Lạng Sơn, Thái Nguyên, and Hòa Bình, and one battalion from Lào Cai had gathered in the midlands and delta, so the number of French battalions in these areas had reached 65, including 30 mobile ones.[2] In the midland battlefield, French troops were divided into three subdivisions (Bắc Giang, Bắc Ninh, and Vĩnh Phúc). Most of the positions were occupied by one regiment. The French were stronger in Bắc Giang, but weaker and more dispersedly-concentrated in Bắc Ninh and Vĩnh Phúc. According to the judgment of the Intelligence Agency, they were consolidating the midlands by strengthening their combat forces (especially mobile forces) and reinforcing their fortifications.

In some books on the Indochina War, some foreign historians were reasonable to comment that the Vietnamese were "perfectionists" and their late preparation for the campaign facilitated de Lattre to deploy his troops. In fact, adversity blocked wisdom. The first cadres of the three offices of the General Headquarters had been sent to Việt Bắc to study the battlefield since late September, when the Border

---

1. The establishment of the Midland Front Party Committee was officially approved by the Standing Central Committee at the end of November. It included Võ Nguyên Giáp as Secretary cum Commander, Nguyễn Chí Thanh as Political Commissar, Chu Văn Tấn, Trần Hữu Dực, and Đào Văn Trường.
2. There were 33 battalions (including 17 mobile ones) in the north of the delta, 22 battalions (including 11 mobiles ones) in the coastal area, and 10 battalions (including 2 mobile ones) in the south of the delta.

campaign was developing promptly and the situation of the French in the North was changing dramatically. With only primitive facilities in hand, these offices had difficulties not only in mobilizing and sending food and weaponry to the midlands but also in investigating the enemy situation, preparing the battlefield, establishing logistical stations, and studying combat tactics. The Midland Front Party Committee's conference was held on November 11, nearly one month after the end of the Border campaign. The conference came to the conclusion in the light of the red-hot experience of the battle on the 4th Route that Vietnamese soldiers had encountered difficulties which affected the duration of the campaign due to insufficient supplies. Therefore, preparations for the coming campaign were required to be made promptly but still guarantee the soldiers' ability to stage long-term and continuous fighting. At this conference, the Midland Front Party Committee paid special attention to the enemy situation and their preparation for the campaign. At the end of November, the Party Committee discussed and agreed to propose the goals of the campaign both in the midlands (primary direction) and in the Northeast and the 3rd Zone (secondary direction) to the Standing Central Party as follows: 1- Decimating part of the enemy vitality; 2- Expanding the food storage; 3- Launching the guerilla war; 4- Destroying the enemy's consolidation plan, facilitating destroying more of the enemy vitality as much as possible.

The enemy situation alone was related to the goal and guideline of the campaign in both directions. Võ Nguyên Giáp commented that the enemy's mobile forces might be more densely-concentrated (including four black battalions in the coastal area and five parachute battalions in Hà Nội).

Therefore, he reminded his subordinates not to underestimate the enemy and advised them to learn more about the enemy while fighting. The Vietnamese would meet difficulties if they fought against the four black battalions and two parachute battalions all at once.

Due to fluctuations in the enemy situation,[1] in the first conference, the Midland Front Party Committee only held an initial discussion on the guideline of the campaign, firstly in the main direction. At the second meeting, held on November 23, 1950, the guideline was further discussed and then written into an instructional document to be disseminated to and thoroughly grasped by units. What was remarkable in this preparation process was that Midland Front Party Committee and the Commander had soon noticed new changes in the enemy situation and in the terrain, as well as difficulties that Vietnamese soldiers might have to overcome in the coming campaign (how it was different from the recent one) in order to prepare ideologically for the soldiers and suggest tactics that would accord with the battlefield. That guideline was not only disseminated in the conference, but also explained in written document to be thoroughly grasped and correctly applied by cadres. In the instructional document, Võ Nguyên Giáp provided a detailed analysis of the combat guideline in case the French strengthened their fortifications and concentrated their mobile forces to cope with them.

---

1. Before the beginning of the campaign, the French forces in the Vĩnh Phúc-Bắc Ninh-Bắc Giang direction comprised about 15,000 troops, two-thirds of which were Euro-African. The 3rd Mobile Regiment was stationed in the Vĩnh Yên-Việt Trì area. Other mobile regiments from Bắc Ninh, Bắc Giang, Gia Lâm, Hải Dương, and Đông Triều could be quickly mobilized for rescue.

Chapter Five: ON THE WAY TO PROMOTE THE WAR OF MOVEMENT

First of all, he warned Vietnamese forces not to be subjective and underestimate the enemy. Being subjective and underestimating the enemy meant wishing to fight a big battle and win a big victory and thus quickly switching to a general counter-offensive and unconditionally taking shortcuts. Those who might hold this completely utopian idea could not realize their limitations in troop strength which would make it hard for them to gain a combat force four or five times as big as that of the enemy; their inexperience in attacking a fortified position or launching a large-scale movement in the midlands and delta; the enemy's continuous improvement of fortifications, concentration of combat forces, and intensification of mobile forces; and that the previous failure would help the enemy heighten their alertness and become much stronger. But the Party Committee also pointed out that it would be reckless to look into the enemy's strengths and ignore their weaknesses. Because the battlefield was large and the French invasion aimed to occupy and keep land, the deeper the French went into the battlefield, the more clearly their weaknesses were revealed. Their defensive forces were thinly disposed. Most of their positions were defended by platoons; some, by companies; some others, by squads and puppet troops. Besides, they were in the process of improving their fortifications, concentrating their combat forces, strengthening their mobile forces, adjusting the battlefields, and changing their commanders.

The Midland Front Party Committee also suggested tactics suitable for the current conditions of the Vietnamese and French armies on the front—flexibly combining the dispersion of troops for small-scale battles and the quick and effective concentration of troops for mobile warfare. Troop dispersion for small guerrilla battles was only conducted in the early stage of the campaign (specifically in attacks on some fortifications defended by companies or reinforcement ones), while troop concentration for large-scale mobile warfare was carried out when the enemy's weaknesses had been revealed. This tactics required a model of organization which was flexible and suitable for the enemy situation and the terrain, and could be applied anywhere and at any time. It also required a versatile command in accordance with the general guidance. The concentration of troops for small battles does not contrast with the principle of concentrating troop strength and fire-power or hinder the implementation of mobile warfare when needed. This tactics was unique to the Vietnamese regular army in the present situation of the French. It required the combination of hit-and-run, surprise, and night warfare.[1] To apply this tactics, the soldiers should keep silent about and take advantage of night operations to be able to quickly access the enemy from a distance, surround them, launch a surprise attack on them, and decimate them all at once. Thus the enemy would not be able to respond in a timely manner.

The plan made by the Campaign Headquarters included the following points:

On the one hand, the primary direction (from Việt Trì to Bắc Giang, with the Vĩnh Yên-Phúc Yên key area being evaluated to be the place where the French forces were weak) would be undertaken by the 308th and 312th Brigades (one

---

1. Night warfare involved the swift movement of troops from a distance, the use of strong fire-power, and the launch of attack at night.

regiment missing) and four battalions of local soldiers. Regarding the secondary direction, the Northeast coastal area would be assumed by the 174th and 98th Regiments; the delta, by the 64th, 52nd, and 48th Regiments (under the 320th Brigade). To keep the directions of the campaign secret, except for some cadres coming back to prepare for the battle, the rest of the 308th and 312th Brigades remained at the border for reinforcement after the campaign on the 4th Route ended, and only appeared at the gathering position a few days before the campaign started.

On the other hand, in order to explore the French tactics and attract their reinforcements, in the first stage of the campaign, Vietnamese battalions would take turns combining hit-and-run, surprise, and night warfare to quickly decimate some French fortifications in the midlands and annihilate their reinforcements in given areas. After identifying the strong and weak points of the French forces and working out measures to cope with them, in the second stage, the Vietnamese would gather their mobile forces to launch flexible attacks, from small- to large-scale ones, on the French weak positions and their reinforcements.

In mid December, the Campaign Headquarters was based in the Quân Nhu-Cát Nê area, in the northeast of Tam Đảo, about 20 kilometers from Thái Nguyên Town as the crow flies. (It was scheduled to be moved to Tam Đảo in the second stage, so that it could monitor the development of the campaign in the south and southwest.) This location was very near the Sơn Dương-Định Hóa safety zone, so it was easy for the Campaign Headquarters to contact the safety zone. It could also communicate by phone with the Central agencies at its back.

Ten days after arriving at the Campaign Headquarters, on December 24, 1950, Võ Nguyên Giáp wrote to Hồ Chí Minh, Trường Chinh, and the Standing Central Committee to report to them on the situation.

According to his report, on December 21, the Campaign Headquarters held a conference to disseminate the combat plan to the regular units and assign tasks to local soldiers in midland provinces (for a month). After hearing the combat plan, some regular cadres were still confused about the tactics. However, after democratic analyses and discussions, all of them had a thorough grasp of the tactics, especially the hit-and-run tactics and conditions to launch a successful attack on a large scale.

After nearly two months of consolidating forces at the border and then a fortnight of operating from Cao Bằng and Lạng Sơn to the midlands, the 308th and 312th Brigades were present at the gathering position in late December. All preparations for the battle in the primary direction was completed.

According to the plan, these brigades would begin the first stage of the campaign on December 26. On the morning of December 26, however, Head of the Brigade Lê Trọng Tấn reported that three French battalions were reaching the gathering position of the brigade in Xuân Trạch in two directions.[1] The Vietnamese Campaign Headquarters

---

1. It was revealed via French documentation that it was General de Lattre who ordered the prompt launching of an exploratory operation to the unstable region. De Latour assigned this task to Colonel Muller. Muller had not known anything about the Indochinese battlefield because he had just arrived in Việt Nam to take charge of the 3rd Mobile Regiment, including three battalions which were hastily established 48 hours earlier to carry

regarded the French getting out of their fortifications and advancing toward the area of Vietnamese soldiers as a good chance to decimate them, so it allowed the 312th Brigade to fire early. The 16th Battalion was ordered to be the first to start fighting. The battle took place right on the banks of the Đáy River. The Brigade Headquarters instructed their troops to contain the French at Xuân Trạch Valley and wait until night to annihilate them. At 7:30 am the following day, the Campaign Headquarters was informed that one French battalion was completely decimated and one French parachute battalion was seriously damaged. Over 200 French troops, including Major Piscard (head of the recently-eliminated North African battalion), were captured. The 312th Brigade did not pursue the French troops for fear of letting out the directions of the campaign. Not being chased by the Vietnamese, the French troops returned to Vĩnh Yên Town. The 312th Brigade was established on December 27, and this day became the traditional day of the Brigade in the wake of its victory in the Liễn Sơn-Xuân Trạch area.

Following the 312th Brigade, other units fired according to the plan. In the midlands, Vietnamese soldiers decimated completely French positions in Đa Phúc and some positions in the north of Phúc Yên. However, the Chợ Thá and Chợ Vàng battles were not finished before dawn and had to be stopped. In the same direction, Vietnamese soldiers annihilated Bình Liêu and forced French troops to withdraw from many other

---

out the Bécassine (Snipe) Operation to raid and explore the attacking directions of Vietnamese regular forces. According to Lucien Bodard, one battalion of this French mobile regiment was completely decimated in this mopping-up operation. After the failure in the Liễn Sơn-Xuân Trạch area, General de Lattre ordered to add complements to the 3rd Mobile Regiment and put it under the command of another French colonel.

positions. But some Vietnamese units failed to fulfill the task of decimating French reinforcements and groups of French troops fleeing from their garrisons.

The first stage of the campaign lasted longer than expected. Vietnamese soldiers successfully experimented with the hit-and-run tactics, completed the task of the first stage, and decimated over one thousand enemy troops, mostly European and African, of which one battalion was entirely annihilated. The Vietnamese Headquarters found that their cadres were less worried about combating in the midlands. Nevertheless, they had not thoroughly grasped the tactics; there were still shortcomings in their command; Vietnamese soldiers had high spirits but poor health. The Vietnamese Headquarters found it necessary to make more sufficient preparations for continuous fighting, so it decided to end the first stage on December 30, allow soldiers to rest, make a preliminary summing-up of the campaign within ten days, and urgently prepare for the second stage. In his order to units, Võ Nguyên Giáp emphasized that cadres and soldiers should get ready to go into battle at any time during the preparation.

Shortly after pulling back their troops, the Vietnamese Headquarters took counsel together, made a preliminary assessment of the first stage, and anticipated the direction for the second stage.

Regarding the French army, they were still surprised and confused despite their precaution. After the first stage of the campaign, they did not leave their lost positions but intensified their mobile forces in the whole midlands, especially in Bắc Ninh and Bắc Giang. It was anticipated that the mobilization of enemy forces in the coming days would be clearer.

Regarding the Vietnamese army, they completed their task of decimating three French battalions in the first stage and improved their tactics and spirit, but not their health. There was still ambiguity in the cadres' tactical thinking and shortcomings in their command. More sufficient preparations should be made before the second stage started.

The second stage of the campaign was scheduled for January 8, 1951, by the Vietnamese Headquarters. (So Vietnamese soldiers were allowed to rest and recover their health in ten days.) The primary direction of Vĩnh Phúc was directly commanded by the Headquarters, and involved the participation of the 308th and 312th Brigades and two local battalions. The Bắc Ninh-Bắc Giang secondary direction was commanded by a steering committee including Lê Quảng Ba, Hà Kế Tấn, and Chu Huy Mân. Forces involved in this direction included the 174th and 98th Brigades and three local battalions. The 3rd Zone and battlefields nationwide were ordered to coordinate with these two directions. The 174th and 98th Brigades were ordered to move from the Northeast to Lục Nam, Bắc Giang.

On January 10, the Vietnamese intelligence informed that the enemy situation had changed. Specifically, the French had already disposed their mobile forces in the vicinity of Vĩnh Yên, Phủ Lỗ, Lục Nam, and Tiên Yên, and strengthened fortifications of the first line both in the midlands and littoral. The Vietnamese Headquarters predicted that if they decimated a relatively important position, the French would send reinforcements there to keep land. So they emphasized that the main task of Vietnamese soldiers in the second stage was to decimate the French vitality, and reminded cadres to thoroughly grasp the mentioned principles of combat, particularly in the main direction, and determine to muster combat forces to annihilate a great number of French reinforcements.

The second stage began with the assault on Bảo Chúc, about ten kilometers northwest of Vĩnh Yên Town, on the night of January 13, 1951, in the main direction; meanwhile, three regiments had deployed battlefields in Cẩm Trạch, Thanh Vân, and Đạo Tú, getting ready to fight against French reinforcements from Vĩnh Yên. Bảo Chúc was decimated. The 3rd Mobile Regiment, supported by aircraft and artillery, was sent there for rescue. One after another its battalions fell into the battlefields prepared by the 209th, 36th, and 88th Regiments; were surrounded, separated, and seriously damaged; and finally had to flee to Vĩnh Yên. French troops in a series of positions on the outside of Vĩnh Yên, including Chợ Vàng that had not been completely destroyed after being attacked twice by the 209th Regiment in the previous stage, also retreated to the town.

The French troops were in a chaos. So why did the Vietnamese troops not launch a straight attack on Vĩnh Yên Town in such a situation? French explained the situation as follows: Giáp's divisions could quickly occupy Vĩnh Yên after defeating the 3rd Mobile Regiment (but letting its commander escape), but they did not do that. Instead, they intended to use Vĩnh Yên as the bait and set traps along the 2nd Route to wait for a more important prey, which was the 1st Mobile Regiment operating from Hà Nội. In fact, the Vietnamese could not mobilize forces to operate on foot in a large area in time, so they missed the chance to attack directly the town despite the decision of the Headquarters. Commander-in-chief Võ Nguyên Giáp later wrote:

Chapter Five: ON THE WAY TO PROMOTE THE WAR OF MOVEMENT

The enemy in Vĩnh Yên Town were extremely anxious. At night, I telephoned Lê Trọng Tấn and then Vương Thừa Vũ to ask if it was possible to send a regiment to make a assault on Vĩnh Yên. However, both brigades did not know the real situation and asked to fight on the night of January 15.

On the morning of January 16, at the Campaign Headquarters based atop Tam Đảo, the advisory board of the campaign summed up the situation and reported it in the consultation of the Headquarters. In the fight against French reinforcements from Phúc Yên on January 15, Vietnamese soldiers decimated nearly 300 enemy troops but suffered heavy casualties. (Because of their slow movement, many of them were shot by the enemy aircraft before they made a sortie.) After an analysis of the general situation, the Vietnamese Headquarters noticed that the French had quickly mobilized reinforcement forces to occupy heights, creating an uninterrupted defense line outside the town. The 3rd Mobile Regiment and the North African army were attacking the 83rd, 103rd, and 210th heights, which were located between Vĩnh Yên Town and Tam Đảo. They would consolidate their defense system around the newly occupied heights. In the town, they strengthened both of their combat forces and fire-power and improved their fortifications. Finding that they no longer had any good chance to fight against French reinforcements or attack Vĩnh Yên Town, the Vietnamese Headquarters decided to change their plan. The 36th, 88th, and 209th Regiments were ordered to attack the French in Hữu Thủ while the 141st Regiment was assigned to block their reinforcements from the north. Vietnamese soldiers had gained, from their previous campaign, experience in fighting against enemies who had occupied new heights but had not had time to reinforce their defensive fortifications.

On the midday of January 16, the battles of Vietnamese regiments happened fiercely in the mountainous area to the north of the town. The French reinforcement force from Vĩnh Yên was driven back. At night, Vietnamese troops from many directions mounted an attack on heights, but till the dawn of January 17 they still failed to occupy the 210th height (or Mount Đanh).

The battles on the afternoon and evening of January 16 were so violent that 20 years later, General Salan wrote that French troops were entirely decimated in many counter-attacks. Vietnamese army, divided into sections and supported by machine-gun and mortar fire-power, gradually approached the French-occupied heights and suddenly rushed there and fought hand to hand, so the forty 105-mm guns supporting French soldiers could not identify the targets exactly. In great need, de Lattre decided to use a last fiendish card which had been prepared in advance. On the dusk of January 16, nearly 100 King Cobra aircraft and transport aircraft dropped napalm bombs on the 210th, 101st, and 47th heights, where Vietnamese and French troops absolutely alternated. According to Salan, the Vietnamese were actually taken by surprise because it was the first time they had seen that weapon. However, even French soldiers also became victims of the condensed petrol bombs dropped on their combat formation.

About the fire balls on the hills in Vĩnh Yên, war correspondent Lucien Bodard wrote:

> It is the first time I've witnessed this incendiary liquid in Indochina. So de Lattre dared to use it. Just a few weeks ago, the French were frightened when talking about this fatal product. However, de Lattre was not ashamed, but

encouraged journalists to highly appreciate the massive extermination of the 20th century incendiary substance. He clearly stated that publicity must know that the Indochina War was a real war that the French had to win at any cost.

Along with napalm bombs, French troops used machine-guns, bombs, and artillery. Nevertheless, Vietnamese troops gathered at fire-proof corners, dug tunnels, sheltered underground, and then continued to retaliate after each series of bombs. They were extraordinarily brave. Some rolled on the ground to put out the fire and then immediately returned to their combat positions. They kept on using heavy machine-guns to fire at French aircraft and downed three of them. The ground on both sides of the 2nd Route was singed. It was likely that they could not stand anymore, but they still held out. Meanwhile, no matter how many reinforcements were used, they were not enough for the French troops.

Salan had gained more experience than de Lattre had in Indochina, especially in fighting with opponents of the French, since the early days of the war, particularly in the autumn-winter of 1947. After the battle in Vĩnh Yên, he realized that the Vietnamese could mobilize a great force including up to 24 regular battalions equipped with mortars, bazookas, 75-mm guns for a real face-to-face battle.

On the dawn of January 17, having noticed that they no longer had chance to launch a surprise attack, the French mobilized all their forces in Indochina to cope with the five Vietnamese regiments in the midlands. After 22 days and nights of continuously fighting, the Vietnamese Headquarters decided to end the campaign for fear that they would meet difficulties if the battles were prolonged.

As many members of the Midland Front Party Committee and some unit cadres were going to attend the Second National Party Congress, the Campaign Headquarters summoned an early closing conference on January 23, 1951, so that all grassroots units could be updated on the latest situation before taking new tasks.

Comparing the three tasks assigned to Vietnamese soldiers by the Standing Central Committee and President Hồ Chí Minh, in the letter dated January 24, the Vietnamese Headquarters commented that the tasks of expanding the food zone and launching the guerilla war were partly done, while the task of decimating the enemy's vital forces was excellently accomplished.[1] Among the six French battalions decimated by the Vietnamese, three belonged to élite regiments. In the North Vietnamese battlefield, there were seven French regiments, each of which consisted of two or three battalions. Thus in the Midland campaign, the French forces were reduced by one regiment.

This was the first time the Vietnamese had decimated ten French positions the troop strength of which was more or less one company in a lowland campaign. It had been rare for the Vietnamese to destroy one enemy company in an entrenched fortification. It was also the first time Vietnamese soldiers annihilated over three French battalions by war of movement in a campaign. The Midland campaign marked a great progress of the Vietnamese army.

---

1. Vietnamese troops decimated 6 French battalions, including approximately 5,000 troops (2,036 prisoners); destroyed 30 French positions, including 10 positions of combat forces each of which were more or less than a company; collected over 1,000 rifles, nearly 200 submachine guns and light and heavy machine-guns, 25 mortars, 1 cannon, 38 televisions, and many military goods.

Chapter Five: ON THE WAY TO PROMOTE THE WAR OF MOVEMENT

With regard to the coming campaign, in a letter dated January 24, 1951, to President Hồ Chí Minh and the Standing Central Committee, Võ Nguyên Giáp suggested calling a meeting of the Standing Central Committee on February 3, 1951, for decision making. He repeated the Standing Central Committee's previous proposal to launch a new campaign in the 3rd Interzone in the wake of the Midland campaign, and cited the proposal made by some people that the next campaign should be launched in Lục Nam, Phủ Lạng Thương. If the second proposal was approved by the Standing Central Committee, the 304th Brigade should be arranged to move there to prepare for the campaign.

Võ Nguyên Giáp reported to Hồ Chí Minh that he would stay at the Headquarters to complete his military report before the Second National Party Congress started, and that he would go straight to Vinh Quang Commune, Chiêm Hóa District, Tuyên Quang Province, where the Congress was held, from the front line. In conclusion, he wrote that he had learnt a lot from the front, gained new experience, and had a better understanding of the enemy. He believed that the Vietnamese could gain a big win in the next campaign.

What was the new experience? Võ Nguyên Giáp later wrote:

> It was the first time Vietnamese soldiers had directly competed with French mobile forces in face-to-face battles, both during the day and at night, both in the midlands and lowlands. The French used their most élite forces and made the most of American-aided weapons.

This was the second biggest mobile campaign launched by the Vietnamese army. While Vietnamese soldiers showed their superiority in the first campaign at the border, they revealed clearly both their strengths and weaknesses in the second campaign in the midland terrain, which was not full of obstacles and difficult of access or covered with trees.

Mobility was prerequisite for the war of movement. In the race in the Cao-Bắc-Lạng mountainous and forested region, Vietnamese soldiers would cross the finish line a few hours earlier than their opponents and drive the latter into a passive position. In the midlands, the situation was reversed. Thanks to aircraft and motorized vehicles, French troops moved more quickly than Vietnamese ones. Their situation kept changing swiftly. They were completely incautious when Vietnamese soldiers attacked in the northeast, but they added two mobile regiments shortly after that. The previous night, in Vĩnh Yên Town, the 3rd Mobile Regiment had only a few hundred exhausted and hopeless Euro-African troops, but it was in full strength again after only one day.

A great quantity of ammunition would be consumed in the war of movement. A state-of-the-art gun would become useless if it ran out of bullets. The ammunition supply of Vietnamese troops was undertaken by conscripted laborers.

Vietnamese troops were in great lack of weapons for the war of movement. Their heavy weapons were insufficient to suppress their enemy's artillery-supported battlefields. They had no anti-aircraft weapons. Therefore, their attack directions and formations became the targets of enemy contour-fighters and cannons, the targets of which were pinpointed and adjusted by reconnaissance aircraft.

Vietnamese soldiers defeated the 3rd Mobile Regiment in Liễn Sơn, Xuân Trạch, Thanh Vân, and Đạo Túi; crushed the attacks of the 1st Mobile Regiment, supported by aircraft, on the Phúc Yên-Vĩnh Phúc route; and forced the French to resist for one day. However, they could not deal with the napalm bombs and shells dropped on them in the French waves of assault. The Vietnamese had not been able to overcome this weakness.

In the Forum of the National Party Congress

After hearing that the National Party Congress would be held in the middle of February, Võ Nguyên Giáp left the midland battlefield to return to his base to attend the meeting of the Cabinet Council. In his letter to Hồ Chí Minh and the Standing Central Committee the previous week, he informed them that he had nearly finished the outline of the military report for the Congress when the battles in Bình Liêu and Lập Thạch broke out one day earlier than scheduled, so he had to delay the report to keep up with the happenings. A few days later, Hồ Chí Minh wrote to him, "Give your whole mind to the battle and add details to the outline later." The Midland campaign was finished, while the report remained uncompleted. From the bottom of his heart, he wanted to make a complete report instead of an outline.

This congress was held after 21 years of interruption. The First National Party Congress took place in 1930, when the Vietnamese were still in years of slavery and did not have any inch of iron to defend themselves. For the time being, under the leadership of the Communist Party of Việt Nam, a growing army was carrying out their mission of fighting along with the Vietnamese people for national independence and unification. Born seven years earlier, the Vietnamese army had participated in the national resistance war for nearly six years. A great number of issues relating to the guideline of armed struggle and the building of armed forces in wartime needed to be discussed by the whole congress to lead the war to success.

There was not much time left to complete the military report because the meeting of the Cabinet Council would be held right in the Lunar New Year festival (or *Tết* in Vietnamese), when the conference to sum up the Midland campaign and prepare for the next campaign was underway.

Having foreseen this time limit, in its open conference held on January 24, 1951, the Midland Front Party Committee disseminated the plan of summarizing the campaign and reorganizing soldiers after it. The units at all levels, mainly those at regimental level under the direct command of brigade Party committees, had one week (from January 26 to February 1) to do the summing-up. After that, two weeks would be spent on evaluating work, rewarding, and reorganizing troops; two more weeks (from February 16 to March 1), on further training on attack techniques. The training would be organized at regimental level and would focus on issues withdrawn from the Midland campaign, both in the preparation and practice of attacks on fortified positions and mobile warfare. It mainly aimed at newly-promoted cadres and newly-recruited soldiers.

While Giáp was busy with numerous work right after the end of the campaign, a great number of representatives from central and local agencies were present at the congress location. On January 31, the preparatory conference began discussing the draft of the Political Platform of the Vietnamese Labor Party. It was told that the discussions on the Party's name, especially those on the three strategic stages of the revolution from January 31 to February 1, were pretty heated, so a subcommittee was set up to reach a final decision to be

Chapter Five: ON THE WAY TO PROMOTE THE WAR OF MOVEMENT

presented at the Second National Party Congress. While the preparatory conference was going on, some representatives had to leave the conference location to attend the meeting of the Cabinet Council.

Vietnamese Minister of National Defense Võ Nguyên Giáp tried to attend the meeting of the Cabinet Council held exactly on the morning of the Lunar New Year's Day (February 6, 1951). He arrived at the meeting place when it got dark. The New Year's Eve party was described by Minister of Finance Lê Văn Hiến as "a small *Tết*-like party." There was plenty of booty wine presented by the army. It was the second time that the Government members had celebrated the Lunar New Year festival together. The previous time, the first spring after the outbreak of the national resistance war (1947), they stopped at Quốc Oai to celebrate the festival in the enemy arc of attack. In his diary, Lê Văn Hiến described it as "a stormy Lunar New Year festival because of the enemy assault." This festival was different. In his diary, Lê Văn Hiến related a funny event that occurred on the morning of the Lunar New Year's Day of 1951. He wrote:

> Early that morning, Hồ Chí Minh got up and went to the rooms of ministers and vice ministers to wish each of them a happy New Year. At his surprise visit, some of them hastily got out of their beds, shook hands with him, and uttered some words in reply to his wishes in such a semi-conscious state that others could not help laughing.

After the breakfast, Phạm Bá Trực and Phan Kế Toại wished Hồ Chí Minh and the Government a happy New Year. Next, on behalf of the Vietnamese army, Võ Nguyên Giáp sent New Year greetings and thanks to President Hồ Chí Minh, the National Assembly, and the Government for their whole-hearted care for the soldiers. He also promised that the whole army would make every effort to gain new victories in the battlefields nationwide. The President sent his thanks and New Year greetings to everyone, and then gave each of them an orange with the message "When hardships go, happiness comes."[1] He told those with families to take it home as a gift. He also sent nice silk to cadres' children under five years old. The atmosphere was very cozy.

The meeting of the Cabinet Council started with President Hồ Chí Minh's report on the global situation, followed by Commander-in-chief Võ Nguyên Giáp's on the Midland campaign. After that, the Cabinet Council discussed and decided some immediate tasks. On the evening of the Lunar New Year's Day, they clustered round the camp-fire. Lê Văn Hiến related, "Many poems and parallel sentences were composed for Hồ Chí Minh. He asked each of us to have a performance such as reciting a poem, telling a story, or singing. He started first and then called others, one after another in alphabetical order.

One minister did not have his "self-directed" item, so he asked permission to cite Hồ Chí Minh's poem *"Xuân Tân Mão"* (literally: "Tân Mão (1951) Spring").[2] His idea was praised and considered to be wise and unique.

---

1. Hồ Chí Minh played a funny word game here. The idiom "When hardships go, happiness comes" (Vietnamese: *"Khổ tận cam lai"*) can be understood humorously as "When hardships go, oranges come," as "orange" is homonymous with "happiness" in Vietnamese.
2. Literally:
   The resistance war has gone through five springs.
   The more victorious springs, the nearer success.
   The whole people are enthusiastically and wholeheartedly
   Preparing for a timely general counter-offensive to be launched.

Chapter Five: ON THE WAY TO PROMOTE THE WAR OF MOVEMENT

On the evening of February 8, 1951 (or the third day of the Lunar New Year), all representatives gathered at the congress location. Giáp took his time to talk with military representatives at the Congress to learn more about the situation of interzones and battlefields and complete his military report before presenting it at the Congress.

The Congress opened on the morning of February 11.

The military situation at that time was so prompt that some military representatives had to leave the Congress after hearing a political report presented by President Hồ Chí Minh that night. The Congress had gone on for three days when the Standing Central Committee convened a special military conference to listen to Võ Nguyên Giáp's report on the situations of both warring sides and to discuss the guideline for the coming campaign. Hồ Chí Minh and Trường Chinh directly chaired this military conference. Lê Văn Hiến later wrote:

> After listening to the report by Võ Nguyên Giáp and complementary ideas from other representatives from North to South, President Hồ Chí Minh compared our resistance war, and especially our army, to an infant prodigy who suddenly grew up from a baby lying in his cradle and exposed his demands for clothes, food, and others. His difficulties were great, but they were only related to his process of growing up. He would be able to work and have a bright future.

On the afternoon of February 14, Võ Nguyên Giáp read his military report at the Congress. He had taken his limited time to finish an over-30-page report titled *"Xây dựng quân đội nhân dân, hoàn thành chiến tranh giải phóng"* (literally: "Building up the People's Army and Completing the War of Liberation."

As the Commander-in-chief of the Vietnamese army, Võ Nguyên Giáp had made two important summary reports titled *"Kinh nghiệm Việt Minh ở Việt Bắc"* (literally: "Việt Minh's Experience in Việt Bắc") and *"Đội quân giải phóng"* (literally: "The Liberation Army") since the end of the August Revolution. The Second National Party Congress was held when the Vietnamese resistance war was developing and when the Vietnamese army had changed from small-scale battles to large-scale ones, thus demanding more and more human and material resources and more focused and reinforced leadership from the Party. Reporting on military tasks at the Congress was an occasion for the whole Party to contribute their brain power to leading the comprehensive whole-people resistance war to victory.

In the opening of the report, Giáp said:

> This congress has been the first one of the Communist Party of Việt Nam, not only since the Party started to lead the Vietnamese army and people in the resistance war, but also since it first had its army and encouraged the Vietnamese people to carry out the armed struggle.
>
> The political line of the Party determined the line of the armed struggle.
>
> The political goal of the revolution decided the tasks of the armed struggle.
>
> In this military report, I shall present and review our Party's path of armed struggle—only focusing on the main points and the current war of liberalization—and propose the guideline of the armed struggle and tasks in army building, based on the fundamental political tasks.[1]

---

1. Communist Party of Việt Nam: *Văn kiện Đảng toàn tập* (literally: The Complete Collection of Party Documents), op cit., vol. 12, pp. 251–252.

Chapter Five: ON THE WAY TO PROMOTE THE WAR OF MOVEMENT

The military report at the Congress focused on five parts: 1- Considering the long-term armed struggle as the way to independence and democracy; 2- Thoroughly grasping the strategic guideline; 3- Building up a powerful people's army; 4- Actively assisting the Cambodians and Laos in their wars of liberation; 5- Consolidating the Party leadership in the resistance war for a complete victory.

In the first part, after reviewing the process of the Party leading the Vietnamese people to the armed struggle, Giáp said:

> Looking back to the process of the revolutionary mobilization over the last ten years, we can see that our Party has mastered the guideline of the armed struggle. Our Party has built up an army and made it stronger and stronger; the armed struggle within scattered guerilla areas has developed into a whole-people resistance war. Our Party is the first communist party that has led the armed struggle in a small and weak colonial country and led it to great victories.[1]

After a review of the six characteristics of the Vietnamese war of liberation,[2] the report came to the

---

1. Ibid., p.255.
2. 1- The Vietnamese war of liberation was a just war; 2- Việt Nam was small and weak and used to be an old French colony, but it had emerged into a nation with its army; 3- Though small and weak, Việt Nam had carried out a people's democratic revolution; 4- Việt Nam borders on Cambodia and Laos; while the Vietnamese were fighting against the French, the Laos and Cambodians rose up in arms against the French; 5- The war against the French had taken place in a country which is bounded by China and has a significantly strategic position in Southeast Asia, and in the new international situation after the Second World War; 6- The Vietnamese war of liberation was under the leadership of the working class, the Communist Party of Việt Nam, and the supreme leader Hồ Chí Minh.

conclusion that it was a long-term people's war which was bound to succeed.

Võ Nguyên Giáp said:

The war of liberation has lasted for six years.

Our regular army has trebled in quantity and made progress in quality. Regarding the armed forces, the current local forces have became stronger than those of the National Defense Army in the early resistance war. The people have become more trained and enlightened; their solidarity has become tighter and their trust has become more vehement; the vestige of the people's authorities, the Party, and President Hồ Chí Minh has been increasingly reinforced.

Six years of the resistance war has proved that the guideline of the Communist Party of Việt Nam on a long-term resistance war is right, and that although Việt Nam is a small country with limited resources and an underdeveloped economy, its people can not only continue the protracted war but also fight more strongly and gain final victory, thanks to the new domestic and international conditions.[1]

In the second part, Giáp briefly introduced three strategic stages of the resistance war to form a basis for analyzing the strengths and weaknesses of the guideline in the first stage (September 1945–December 1947) and progresses in the second stage (1948–1950). He stressed that 1945 was a successful year of the guerilla war, when the Vietnamese turned the French rear into their front, restored a lot of their bases, and established many of their revolutionary bases in the French-occupied areas in the Northwest, Red River Delta, Bình-Trị-

---

1. Communist Party of Việt Nam: *Văn kiện Đảng toàn tập* (literally: The Complete Collection of Party Documents), op cit., vol. 12, p. 264.

Thiên area, and Central Highland. The years 1949 and 1950 were the second and third years of the new stage, when the war in Việt Nam was greatly influenced by the international situation. The strategic guideline put forward the positive task of preparing for a general counter-offensive; the building of forces according to the slogan "Elite main forces, powerful reserve forces" gained many achievements; the progress of the war of movement was confirmed by the Vietnamese victorious campaigns at the fronts of Northeast, Northwest, Hòa Bình, Bình-Trị-Thiên, the 5th Interzone, and South Việt Nam (or Cochinchina). After pointing out the Vietnamese weaknesses in the preparation for the counter-offensive[1] and commenting on their great progresses in the Border campaign and Midland campaign, Giáp emphasized the importance of mobile war in the Northern battlefield, as well as the primary role of guerilla war and the secondary role of mobile war in the Central and Southern battlefields. He said:

> We should clearly consider the enemy's efforts to avoid subjectivism and their weaknesses to absolutely exploit. In order to promote our military strength and launch a general counter-offensive, we should take into consideration our new favorable conditions and rapid progresses, as well as the enemy's new efforts difficulties.[2]

Next, the report reviewed the issues of grasping the guidelines and appropriately applying them in the reality

---

1. 1- Subjectivism in assessing the French and in estimating Vietnamese difficulties in building forces as well as combating when changing from guerilla war to regular war; 2- Backwardness in directing the war of movement and unclear conception of mobile war; 3- Underestimating guerrilla war not only in the main battlefield but also in others.
2. Communist Party of Việt Nam: *Văn kiện Đảng toàn tập* (literally: The Complete Collection of Party Documents), op cit., vol. 12, p. 274.

of the battlefields, overcoming weaknesses in the attacks of attrition and having a thorough grasp of the guidelines of the attacks of annihilation, and building up revolutionary bases—an issue which was as important as and inseparable from that of building up armed forces.

In the third part on the building of a powerful people's army, after defining the concept "a people's army," analyzing the three characteristics of the Vietnamese People's Army,[1] and reviewing the three stages in the process of building up the Vietnamese People's Army,[2] Giáp said:

> Over the past ten years from the Bắc Sơn uprising and six years from the establishment of the Việt Nam Propaganda and Liberation Army Brigade, the Vietnamese People's Army has developed from nothing, then a regiment, to a strong army.
>
> That army is young and has both strengths (such as the ability to make rapid progress) and weakness (such as inexperienced cadres). It has grown up in a non-stop battle and in the condition that the enemy is much stronger than us, so it is traditionally heroic and austere. It has also grown up in a people's democratic revolution, so it has coordinated with the people to form a bloc, keeping political discipline in its relations with the people and helping and protecting them. It also keeps itself from pestering, threatening, and plundering them. Its revolutionary duty is clearly stated in the "Ten Pledges of Honor."[3]

---

1. The Vietnamese People's Army were nationalist, democratic, and modernity-oriented.
2. They included the embryonic stage (before the general uprising), the developing stage (the general uprising), and the mature stage (the resistance war).
3. Communist Party of Việt Nam: *Văn kiện Đảng toàn tập* (literally: The Complete Collection of Party Documents), op cit., vol. 12, pp. 282–283.

Chapter Five: ON THE WAY TO PROMOTE THE WAR OF MOVEMENT

After analyzing the decisive role of the regular army in the completion of the war of liberation, Giáp introduced the contents of building up the regular army in terms of organization, training, equipment, and kitchen duty.

> After the Standing Central Committee put forward the tasks of promptly preparing for and drastically changing to a general counter-offensive, the building of a regular army became a great cause. We should not only reorganize the training but also prepare for the supplementation and development the regular army; should organize not only infantry units but also specialized arms such as sappers and artillery ones in preparation for the establishment of the mechanized, air, and naval forces; and should not only solve issues concerning personnel and equipment but also introduce regulations in the army. The task of building the army should be carried out according to the slogan "Regularize the army in terms of content to avoid formalism and bureaucracy."[1]

Regarding the tasks of consolidating local soldiers and developing militiamen, after reiterating the strategic position of local armed forces and reviewing the guidance for building local armed forces in recent time, Giáp proposed some predictions. He said:

> In the coming stage, the duty of local soldiers will be hard because they will serve as the reserve forces of the regular army.... More attention should be paid to the guidance for local soldiers, because the issue of local soldiers may be disregarded once the regular army has developed.
>
> ... When our resistance war gets closer to victory, the enemy's mopping-up operations in their temporarily-

---

1. Communist Party of Việt Nam: *Văn kiện Đảng toàn tập* (literally: The Complete Collection of Party Documents), op cit., vol. 12, pp. 285–286.

occupied areas, especially those in the urban vicinities and important strategic areas along the main routes, will be more violent. In addition, the militia's work in the rear will be much harder. They will have to not only fight against unpatriotic Vietnamese but also take charge of the provision, transportation, and casualty evacuation for battlefields and large-scale campaigns. Besides, the demand for complements to the regular and local forces will be much greater.[1]

To build up the army politically, Giáp firmly stated that political work was the Party's revolutionary mobilization toward soldiers, which was educating them on the aim and nature of the warfare and the policies of the Party and Government in order to raise their awareness and fighting spirit, reinforce the army's internal and external unity, and ensure the army's implementation of the political purpose of the war.

The political work should be undertaken by the Party and based on its organization. It would not take its effect if Party organization was not consolidated. The Vietnamese had made a mistake when separating the Party work from political work. This mistake was corrected in 1949, but the issue of Party building had not been not given the top priority. It is because the Vietnamese had not considered the army as the Party's tool to carry out armed struggle or clearly understood how the Party should direct the army.

Personnel was a key issue in the building of the people's army, particularly in the transition to a general counter-offensive. During the general counter-offensive, the army should be quickly expanded and promptly regularized.

---

1. Ibid., pp. 287–288.

Chapter Five: ON THE WAY TO PROMOTE THE WAR OF MOVEMENT

To build up the regular army, the Vietnamese needed cadres for the war of movement who were able to command large corps, use specialized arms, understand both themselves and their enemy, have a flexible and planned commanding style, and become experts in the tactics of modern war. They also needed cadres for local forces who were experienced in guerilla war and able to become cadres of the regular forces in the near future.

After reviewing the strong and weak points in personnel policy, Giáp said:

> To sum up, the personnel policy should be aimed at training cadres who are good at strategies and tactics, expert in military affairs, absolutely loyal to the people's and the revolution's interests, able to keep pace with the duty and demand of a people's army which is becoming increasingly regularized, so as to lead it to fulfill the task of national liberalization assigned by the Party.[1]

In the fourth part on the active assistance to the Cambodians and Laos in their wars of liberation, Giáp provided historical evidence over the previous six years to prove that Indochina was an undivided battlefield. Simultaneously, he analyzed the characteristics of the liberation wars of Cambodia and Laos to form a basis for operational principles and to overcome shortcomings in setting up revolutionary bases, building up armed and semi-armed forces, training cadres, and applying the strategic principle of focusing on guerrilla war and facilitate the advance to mobile war. To end this part of the report, Giáp said:

> It is our duty to assist the liberation wars of Cambodia and Laos, and we must actively do it to realize President Hồ

---

1. Ibid., p. 295-296.

Chí Minh's direction in the Political Report that, "We carry out the liberation war; so do the Cambodians and Laos. French colonialists and American interventionists were the common enemies of the three peoples. Thus, we must make every effort to help the Cambodians and Laos, as well as their wars of resistance."[1]

In the opening of the fifth part on the consolidation of Party leadership during the Vietnamese resistance war for a complete victory, after reiterating President Hồ Chí Minh's words in the Political Report, Giáp said, "Our first and most urgent task at present is to lead the war of resistance to victory. Other tasks is determined by it."[2] He also emphasized that it was the Party's focal task to lead the war, both ideologically and organizationally.

Ideologically, it was necessary to give the top priority to the resistance war and consider the Party's leadership of the war as its focal task.

Organizationally, the organizational task must comply with the political one, as well as the tasks of defeating the enemy and liberating the nation. Therefore, the Party should have able cadres and encourage the excellent members of the Party, trade unions, and famers' associations to join the army.

It was required to have a thorough grasp of the Party's policy and guidance, as well as the war and military affairs, to lead the war accurately. Thus, military learning was a significant and urgent issue. Military learning should be introduced as one of the Party's learning slogans.

---

1. Ibid., p. 303.
2. Ibid., p. 304.

The over 30 pages of the report showed the crystallization of the military knowledge of the Vietnamese modern revolution and the experience in strategic guidance by a person who was entrusted by the Communist Party of Việt Nam and President Hồ Chí Minh with the heavy task of commanding the Vietnamese army during the first stage of the preparation for the armed uprising to seize power and during the first six years of the anti-French resistance war. The report drew the basic lines of the panorama of the first years of the war, in which the building of the people's armed forces under the leadership of the Party and their gradually stable growth in the reality of combat were remarkable. Recalling the atmosphere of the congress, Lê Văn Hiến later wrote that in his report, Giáp presented a clear narration of the organizing and fighting process of the Vietnamese army, from a guerilla unit to a large liberation army which was powerful and heroic.

After Giáp finished his report, the spirit of Vietnamese soldiers at the Congress was highly raised. Everyone was ebullient and energetic. Việt[1] was so deeply touched that he embraced Giáp and kissed him. At that moment, President Hồ Chí Minh said, "That is the consensus of the people and army."

While the hall was excited, President Hồ Chí Minh raised high the example of the Vietnamese People's Army in fighting, and specified the origin of such an army and the important factors that led to its gigantic growth, heroic fighting spirit, and great achievements. In such an forceful voice, he roused

---

1. Hoàng Quốc Việt (1905–1992), member of the Standing Central Committee who was then in charge of the Vietnamese Union Front.

a jubilant atmosphere among the attendees. They all gave a big round of applause. The hall overflowed with a joyful atmosphere—the atmosphere of the army's achievement-reporting ceremony before the Party.

The report was unanimously approved by the Congress.

In order to give timely directions for the preparation of the coming battle, Võ Nguyên Giáp left Chiêm Hóa when the Congress had not finished for the General Headquarters to attend a meeting with the Campaign Party Committee to discuss the implementation of the tasks. Three weeks earlier, on January 21, in the first meeting after the Midland campaign, the Central Military Commission of the Party Central Committee carefully examined the situation of the Northern battlefield to choose and suggest new directions for the next campaign. Since the Midland campaign had ended unfavorably, it was impossible for the Vietnamese to launch the next campaign in the direction of the 3rd Interzone to liberate the Red River Delta as planned by the Standing Central Committee. The 3rd Interzone battlefield was where the French had revealed weaknesses in some places, but it was also where they could make the most use of the features of their weapons and techniques, as well as their quick mobility and reinforcement. On the contrary, its uncovered terrain divided by rivers caused the Vietnamese difficulties in ammunition and food supply. It was impossible for the Vietnamese to launch the next campaign in another direction in the midlands because the French had intensified their forces and defense system there and thus ready to cope with any attack by the Vietnamese. It was also impossible to make an assault on Móng Cái to completely liberate the entire Sino-Vietnamese border area as suggested by the Chinese consultants, because Móng Cái was not only located deeply in the French-occupied area (so it would be difficult for the Vietnamese in transport) but also close to the beach (so it would be easy for Vietnamese forces to be overwhelmed by French gunboats). Even if Vietnamese forces could liberate the area, they could hardly stand firmly there. The meeting ended with a proposal for the coming campaign direction and got approval from the Standing Central Committee and President Hồ Chí Minh. Accordingly, the next campaign would be held in the Northeast battlefield, where the French were found to be weak and where the lowland terrain with alternate mountains and forests was favorable to the Vietnamese application of the fortification-attacking and reinforcement-annihilating tactics. This was an important battlefield and the campaign here was named Hoàng Hoa Thám campaign.

Heavy Impression on the 18th Route

In a meeting held on 26 February, the Hoàng Hoa Thám Campaign Party Committee[1] discussed ways of directing Vietnamese regular forces to accelerate their training in order to promptly overcome difficulties in their quality (many new troops had been recruited and many new local cadres had been promoted after the Trần Hưng Đạo campaign). In this meeting, the logistical agency was also directed to study the issue of supply, taking into consideration such factors as the long distance between the rear and the battlefield,

---

1. The Hoàng Hoa Thám Campaign Party Committee was established by the Standing Central Committee on January 31, 1951. It included Võ Nguyên Giáp as Secretary cum Commander, Nguyễn Chí Thanh, Chu Văn Tấn, Hoàng Văn Thái, and Trần Hữu Dực.

inconvenient supply route, sparse population, and poor economy. Regarding the French side, the Party Committee reminded all attendees of de Lattre's recent intensification of French mobile forces, bombardment, and fortifications. Other noteworthy issues discussed at the meeting included the route to approach the battlefield and targets of attack (there was only one path available), the long distance between the rear and the battlefield, the limited time for making preparations for the combat, and especially the collection of information about the enemy and the preparation for the battlefield. After discussing the combat plan for the coming campaign, everyone quickly approved Vĩnh Phúc and the 3rd Interzone as the secondary directions of the campaign with the coordination of battlefields nationwide. Regarding the primary direction, after considering three suggestions by the advisory board, Võ Nguyên Giáp made a preliminary conclusion to specify the directions of preparation for units and related agencies to make as follows:

1- The primary direction of the campaign would be the Bắc Giang-Lục Nam-Phả Lại-Đông Triều route.

2- In this battlefield, most of the forces would be possibly arranged in the north of the Bắc Giang-Lục Nam route or in the east of the Lục Nam-Phả Lại route. In each area, there should be enough provisions to be used by seven or eight regiments in 20 days, so that any mobilization of forces could be made flexibly under any circumstance (there should be 500 tons of food in store for combat soldiers only in each area).

3- The collection of information about the French situation should be made in this direction. However, it should be extended to the 18th Route-Tiên Yên-Móng Cái direction.

Chapter Five: ON THE WAY TO PROMOTE THE WAR OF MOVEMENT

4- It was necessary to draw lessons from the battles in Vĩnh Phúc, Bắc Ninh, and Bắc Giang in the previous campaign to make a thorough plan and actively carry it out for the launching of guerilla war.

5- In the guidance for the campaign, superiors were required to avoid French aircraft and artillery while subordinates were required to prove their bravery and make the most use of fortifications.

6- It was vital to have a thorough grasp of the situation, especially at the end of the campaign, to seize opportunities.

After carrying out a field reconnaissance and confirming the directions of the campaign, in a conference for cadres at regimental level upward held on March 4, the Party Committee explained the reason for choosing the 18th Route as the primary direction,[1] the Vĩnh Phúc-Bắc Giang route as the secondary direction, and the Sơn Tây-Hà Đông route as the coordinative direction for the purpose of decimating part of the enemy forces and developing guerilla war.

In the primary direction, a series of French entrenched fortifications were built along the 18th Route to defend the east and northeast of the 5th Route and Hải Phòng. They included such entrenched fortifications as Bãi Thảo, Đông Triều, Hà Chiếu, and Mạo Khê (in Phả Lại subdivision); Tràng Bạch and Bí Chợ (in Núi Đèo subdivision); and Lán Tháp, Uông Bí, and Yên Lập (in Quảng Yên subdivision). Before the Vietnamese assault, French infantry forces in the

---

1. The 18th Route runs from Bắc Ninh to Tiên Yên via Quế Võ, Phả Lại, Chí Linh, Đông Triều, Mạo Khê, Uông Bí, Hòn Gai, Cẩm Phả, and Mông Dương. The French had the first entrenched fortifications of their cement defense line connecting the Northeast with the midlands built here.

campaign area included six battalions and seven companies. Two 105-mm howitzer companies were stationed in Đông Triều. The French mobile force (including two battalions and one company) were stationed in Phả Lại. Meanwhile, Vietnamese forces included the 308th and 312th Brigades, the 174th and 98th Regiments, four detachments with twenty-four mountain guns, one sapper regiment, and two local companies (frequently operating in Thủy Nguyên). The Party Committee decided to apply the fortification-attacking and reinforcement-annihilating tactics in the primary direction. "Generally speaking, attacking enemy reinforcements should be paid more attention to than attacking their entrenched fortifications, but the latter could be focused in favorable and convenient conditions." The Party Committee also reminded Vietnamese forces to take precautions of the enemy's reinforced fortifications when attacking their entrenched fortifications, and take into consideration the possibility that the enemy would become more cautious, be supported by mechanized forces, and come from different directions. Vietnamese forces were assigned to decimate five enemy battalions in the primary direction.

The Vĩnh Phúc-Việt Trì-Phú Thọ direction was undertaken by the 304th Brigade and the 165th Regiment, with the coordination of local troops, under the leadership of the 304th Brigade High Command; the Bắc Giang direction, the 176th Regiment combined with the local forces of Việt Bắc Interzone; the Sơn Tây-Hà Đông direction, the 320th Brigade and local troops. Vietnamese troops in the coordinative direction was tasked to decimate part of enemy forces, attract and contain their mobile forces, and help the locals to develop guerrilla warfare. They were assigned to decimate four enemy companies.

In response to the attendees' question on the decimation target in the main direction, Võ Nguyên Giáp said:

> In this campaign, the Party Committee suggests decimating only five battalions. Is it a small target compared to those of the previous campaigns? No, it isn't. The enemy now is more difficult to defeat. This target is also to remind you not to be subjective and underestimate the enemy. It will be better if you overreach it.

He mentioned new challenges (such as newly-recruited troops and newly-promoted cadres; the enemy's intensification and reinforcement of mobile forces firepower, and fortifications; the battlefield being almost behind the enemy-occupied area; sparse population; and difficulties in supply), and proposed directions for overcome them in this campaign. He also pinpointed new advantages such as the higher concentration of Vietnamese troops, the dispersed arrangement of enemy troops, the incompletely flat terrain with alternate mountains and forests and plains, the strengthened command at various levels, and a more detailed plan of coordination with localities.

In his combat order sent to Vietnamese units in the secondary directions, Võ Nguyên Giáp reminded brigade commanders to pay attention to operational differences in each direction. Specifically, the 320th Brigade was assigned to help the 3rd Interzone High Command develop guerilla war in order to curb and attract the enemy's mobile forces and coordinate with the main battlefield, apart from the task of decimating about two enemy companies. In his combat order to the 304th Brigade and the 165th Regiment in the Vĩnh Phúc battlefield, he defined the scope of their activities being the area from Phúc Yên to Việt Trì and their tasks of annihilating two enemy companies, creating a diversion, developing guerilla war, restraining enemy forces, and coordinating with Vietnamese forces in the primary direction. Then he pointed out the operational guideline for the 304th Brigade High Command to apply in their particular difficult conditions in this campaign. These difficulties included their poorly-equipped and insufficiently-trained troops, lack of experience in concentrated combat (both in mobile war and attacking entrenched fortifications), and unfamiliar battlefield which was far away from other units.

In a letter sent to President Hồ Chí Minh, General Secretary Trường Chinh, and members of the Standing Central Committee on March 9, Võ Nguyên Giáp reported that he was trying to overcome two immediate difficulties in the primary direction—supply and secrecy (there was only one path for soldiers and conscripted laborers to travel on). The Headquarters anticipated that if the French travelled along the 13th Route to Chũ, An Châu, then the communication between the Vietnamese front and rear would be directly endangered. Võ Nguyên Giáp also reported that he would launch another campaign before the rainy season (in late April and early May) after this campaign. He asked the Standing Central Committee for their advice before taking advantage of the time to prepare for it. The field of action might be in two directions: the 3rd Interzone and Móng Cái. What mattered then was the choice of the primary direction. After discussions and analyses, the Central Military Commission decided to choose the 3rd Interzone as the primary direction.

Chapter Five: ON THE WAY TO PROMOTE THE WAR OF MOVEMENT

On March 18-19, the Party Committee had a meeting at the Headquarters based in Bãi Đá, about 15 kilometers south of Lục Ngạn. After summarizing notices from the General Headquarters, the military intelligence reported some recently emerging issues on the French side as follows:

Firstly, de Lattre was urging to accelerate the building of a powerful local army for Bảo Đại, apart from the French expeditionary army. General Georges Spillman was dispatched to Việt Nam to take charge of this. Albert Sarraut, former Governor-General of French Indochina and then Chairman of the French Union, who was having an official visit to Indochina, promised to urge Bảo Đại to "take part in." The word "Vietnamization" appeared for the first time in Western newspapers.

Secondly, the French policy of speeding up the organization of a puppet army partly resulted from General Salan's inspection tour to battlefields. A remarkable thing in his report to de Lattre was the complement crisis. It was because de Lattre had continuously ordered to excessively send French troops from the South and Central regions to the North.[1] Accordingly, the French were likely to reinforce their attacked directions in this campaign.

Lastly, the press told the news that a series of building sites were being formed all over the delta for the building of a cement defense line, called the "de Lattre defense line," around the Red River Delta. It was a significant project that

---

1. According to Salan's memoir, just within a few months in early 1951, de Lattre appointed four North African battalions, two legendary battalions, one parachute battalion, one sapper battalion, and most of the air force from the South to the North.

445

covered over 100 positions with more than 1,200 half-sinking and half-floating cement fortifications running from Hòn Gai to Đông Triều, Bắc Giang, Bắc Ninh, Sơn Tây, and Ninh Bình. Vietnamese scouts reported that in both the primary and coordinative directions of the campaign area, the first fortifications of this defense line had appeared.

In a press conference, de Lattre told journalists what he had said to convince French generals who disagreed with him for their doubt about the effectiveness of this defense line. He said:

> This is not a repetition of the Maginot line. I want to protect Hà Nội and Hải Phòng, which I shall turn into strong forts. To prevent our opponent's cannons from falling into these two centers, I shall build a defense line including cement fulcrums supported by artillery bases in the surrounding and outer circles; the distances will be covered by barbed wires and minefields, and all of the defense line will be supported by strong fire-power. At the back, combat troops hiding in strong fortifications with the support of artillerymen will be ready to fight when making an assault or when being overwhelmed by the enemy.... This is not a rigid system of defense. Moreover, it will show the presence of France here. Our three-color flag will be protected here.

On March 10, General de Lattre set off for Paris, so the French expeditionary army was put under the command of General Salan.

At the beginning of the conference in Bãi Đá, the Vietnamese Headquarters mentioned two emerging issues that should be overcome in this campaign. They were the logistics and the collection of information on the enemy side. The former was found to be harder than the latter. Despite

Chapter Five: ON THE WAY TO PROMOTE THE WAR OF MOVEMENT

the logistics' efforts in gathering rice, the collected rice was just enough for Vietnamese soldiers to use till the end of March. The Party Committee realized that such a shortage would affect the Vietnamese army's operation, tactical guideline, combat plan, and campaign's prospect. Regarding the second issue, it was reported by the rear that the French were mobilizing troops from the South, so the deployment of their defense forces had not been stabilized. As a result, Vietnamese scouts had not had a thorough grasp of the enemy situation. During their operations, Vietnamese troops were frequently disturbed by French aircraft which incessantly strafed along the way and bombed suspected stations. The 174th and 88th Regiment suffered heavy casualties because the French had bombarded their gathering position. Moreover, some Vietnamese scouts nearby had been caught by the French. The conference assumed that the French might have figured out the Vietnamese directions of attack, but they had not known the specific plan.[1] The Party Committee instructed

---

1. It was revealed later that the French had intensified their investigation of the Vietnamese directions of attack with the use of patrol squads, reconnaissance aircraft, and radios for a month. Salan was informed that his patrolmen caught the Head of the Reconnaissance Section of the 36th Regiment (under the 308th Brigade) some days earlier. However, this scout committed suicide by biting his tongue, so the French could not get any information from him. But on the night of March 19, through the radio, the French found that the 308th Brigade was moving eastwards, along the slope of Mount Đông Triều, and one unit of the 312th Brigade was discovered in Lục Nam, not in the north of Hà Nội as estimated by de Lattre. This latest news was in accordance with what Nguyễn Hữu Trí had provided. Salan hastily reported this to de Lattre in Paris and proposed moving French mobile forces to the east to deal with the pressure of the opponent. Admiral Ortoli was ordered to direct battleships and squadrons to move from estuaries to the mainland to patrol and support the French positions close to the river banks in the mining area.

the advisory board to closely follow the situation and verify the news, and decided that the core task during the campaign was to thoroughly grasp the situation to have timely and flexible guidelines. It also stressed the importance of keeping track of French reinforcements to avoid any chance to annihilate them. Besides, it reminded all Vietnamese forces to take into consideration the terrain conditions which were unsuitable for gathering and hiding soldiers or carrying out a war of movement.

The Party Committee studied and discussed two combat plans proposed by the advisory board at the conference. The question was which targets—small or large fortifications—would be chosen to facilitate the annihilation of French reinforcements. According to the first plan, Vietnamese troops would attack small fortifications (such as Lán Tháp, Lọc Nước, Máng Nước, and Sống Trâu) and get prepared to fight against French reinforcements from Quảng Yên and Uông Bí. With this plan, the Vietnamese could easily hide their forces and certainly gain victory. However, the French would rescue on a small scale. If the Vietnamese waited for large-scale reinforcements, the campaign would last long and the supply would be harder. According to the second plan, the Vietnamese would attack large fortifications (such as Uông Bí, Bí Chợ, and Tràng Bạch) and get ready to decimate French reinforcements from Phả Lại and Quảng Yên. With this plan, the Vietnamese could gain the surprise, annihilate large reinforcements, and quickly win a great victory, but they would be uncertain of victory in the first battle. As a person who had a thorough grasp of the "steady fight and assured victory" guideline, Võ Nguyên Giáp agreed with the Party Committee on the first plan. Specifically, in the first stage, the

Chapter Five: ON THE WAY TO PROMOTE THE WAR OF MOVEMENT

Vietnamese would attack four small positions in the north of Uông Bí, in the freshwater piping system from Vàng Danh to Hải Phòng, and get ready to decimate French reinforcements from Quảng Yên and Uông Bí. The target and tactics of the campaign in the second stage would be determined by the development and outcome of the first stage. Two issues were confirmed after the first plan was chosen. On the one hand, the Vietnamese should closely follow the enemy response and promptly change to the second plan when there were favorable conditions. On the other hand, they should continue to find every possible measure to overcome difficulties in supply and minimize logistical difficulties during the campaign. To assure a more thorough grasp of the French situation, the Party Committee accepted the advisory board's suggestion to spare two more days for the preparation. The campaign would start on the night of March 23.

After the Vietnamese Headquarters was moved to the foot of Mount Yên Tử, Vietnamese envoys reported that all preparations for the campaign had been basically completed. On March 23, before the time of attack, Võ Nguyên Giáp wrote to the rear. He reported to President Hồ Chí Minh and the Standing Central Committee all foreseen difficulties that might influence the development of the campaign, and anticipated that the campaign might end earlier because of logistical limitations. He also proposed the direction and area of the coming campaign, and asked the President and the Standing Central Committee for their advice before making timely preparations for its battlefield.

That night, the campaign was started with Vietnamese attacks on French positions such as Lộc Nước, Đập Nước, Sống Trâu, Lán Tháp, and Chấp Khê. Some enemy watchtowers and the Biểu Nghi bridge were also under attack. Vietnamese troops also ambushed along the Vàng Danh-Uông Bí route and waited for French reinforcements from Đông Triều. They expected that French reinforcements would come when the only freshwater source of the port city was threatened. However, three days had passed without any sight of French reinforcements. On March 27, the Vietnamese decimated two more entrenched fortifications (Bí Chợ and Tràng Bạch), but French reinforcements were still unseen. French troops had just explored the situation and strengthened their forces in positions that might be threatened.

It was not until many years later that the reason why French reinforcements did not appear in the early days of the campaign was revealed through French publications. It turned out that the French generals in Việt Nam had not figured out the Vietnamese intention, so they had to wait. Meanwhile, after reading the news of the fighting situation (which de Lattre described "as sour as vinegar"), de Lattre said to his subordinates, "I have to go back there." On March 26, de Lattre and his entourage flew back to Indochina. On the plane, he examined the map and asked other generals for their opinions on the possibilities of the battle, but they had no idea. Then de Lattre said, "It is hard to accept the Vietnamese way of fighting. It is not normal at all . . . . But don't think that they're silly. What are they trying to create?"

On arriving in Hà Nội on the night of March 28, de Lattre discovered that the section of the 18th Route in Mạo Khê was sandwiched between the upper reaches of the Đá Bạc River and the mainland. There were only several hundred troops there. After destroying Mạo Khê, Vietnamese troops would attack Đông Triều and then Phả Lại. De Lattre strongly believed that Giáp intended to clear the way to deploy forces eastwards to bully the delta. Colonel Sizaire[1] was urgently convoked and entrusted with a task of arraying every mobile force and vehicle, if necessary, to save Mạo Khê and Đông Triều. French reinforcements were scheduled to arrive in Đông Triều and Phả Lại on the afternoon of March 29, and in Mạo Khê on the evening of March 30.

Then started the race between the French expeditionary army travelling by car, canoe, and battleship and Vietnamese troops going on foot in the forests. At the French Headquarters based in Hải Phòng right after March 28, de Lattre was informed that French reconnaissance aircraft had detected "a stream of fire in the jungle" including thousands of porches on the paths to Uông Bí and Mạo Khê while Vietnamese forces were strongly operating in the 5th Route, that the Hà Nội-Hải Phòng railway had been damaged, and that many French positions in the Sơn Tây-Vĩnh Phúc direction had been attacked.

After many days waiting for French reinforcements without any sight of them, the Vietnamese Headquarters decided to attack some large fortifications around Uông Bí, including such important positions as Tràng Bạch, Bí Chợ,

---

1. Sizaire, a senior legionary officer, used to work in the Northeast coastal region after the coup d'état in March 1945. He took part in the French attack on Lạng Sơn in November 1946 and had a deep understanding of the 4th Route and the Northeast. After going back to France, he was asked by de Lattre to return to Việt Nam to take part in the French plan to regain Lạng Sơn and take revenge for the 4th Route. He had fallen into disfavor for having objected de Lattre's policy of building a bunker defense line around the Red River Delta. This time, he was allowed to use the 2nd Mobile Division, which was being built, and report directly to de Lattre in any case.

and Phán Huệ. After decimating these positions, Vietnamese troops were ordered to attack Uông Bí—an important town on the 18th Route and the center of the Vàng Danh-Tràng Bạch mining area. They were about to launch the attack when an unexpected event occurred. On March 28, French troops left Uông Bí for Quảng Yên on the 18th and 10th Routes. The Vietnamese soldiers were in such a deep sleep that they missed the chance to kill these French troops when they passed their battlefield. On March 29, the Vietnamese Headquarters decided to attack Mạo Khê, another important position on the 18th Route between Uông Bí and Đông Triều, and prepare for the assault on French reinforcements from Đông Triều, Quảng Yên, or Thủy Nguyên.

On the French side, Sizaire mustered troops in Phả Lại on the afternoon of March 29 because he guessed that Mạo Khê would be attacked. From Phả Lại, these troops had to cross 30 kilometers more in unfavorable weather. Finally, Sizaire managed to move the French Headquarters and part of his troops to Đông Triều on March 30. French naval artillery had been arranged along the Đá Bạc River. One parachute battalion and two parachute companies had moved from Đông Triều to Mạo Khê. The battlefield where Vietnamese troops ambushed to attack French reinforcements was too far away, so the French could escape easily. As the French situation in Mạo Khê had changed, the Vietnamese Headquarters ordered to stop attacking this position, but this order was sent late. Therefore, on the night of March 30, the 36th Regiment still carried out their attack on the target, which had been reinforced with four companies. The battle was very fierce. Part of the French force ran into a church where they took advantage of the high bell-tower to use fire-power to intercept Vietnamese soldiers. On the morning of March 30, Vietnamese troops had to retreat after French reinforcements were sent to Mạo Khê along the 18th Route.

In the meantime, the 209th Regiment's battle at the Mạo Khê mine was prolonged. The battle became fierce because the French land forces were supported by battleships along the Đá Bạc River. They also repeated napalm strikes as they had done in Vĩnh Yên a few months earlier.

The Vietnamese attacks on Mạo Khê, both in the streets and at the mine, were unsuccessful. When Vietnamese troops retreated because of heavy casualties, Sizaire continued to sent reinforcements, supported by aircraft and naval artillery, to launch a counter-attack. However, Vietnamese troops had disappeared before the counter-attack took place.

The first stage of the campaign ended and Vietnamese troops managed to clear nearly 30 kilometers on the Mạo Khê-Biểu Nghi route. In this stage, Vietnamese troops mainly attacked entrenched fortifications, so they suffered heavy casualties and missed many chances to annihilate French reinforcements. The policy of attacking fortifications and decimating reinforcements was not realized. The first stage went on in unfavorable conditions such as long distance, bad weather, and the frequent disturbance of French aircraft, which made it difficult for the Vietnamese in logistics. French reinforcements appeared as soon as the first stage of the campaign ended, so all French positions were immediately consolidated in terms of troop strength and fire-power.

The second stage began five days later, on the night of April 4. The Vietnamese Headquarters decided to change the direction of attack to the northeast of Phả Lại. Accordingly, Vietnamese troops were assigned to attack some French positions in the north of Đông Triều (such as Bến Tắm, Bãi Thảo, Hoàng Gián, and Hà Chiểu) and get ready to decimate French reinforcements from Phả Lại and Đông Triều. The 88th Regiment had attacked Bãi Thảo and occupied three-fourths of French fortifications here. Although Vietnamese troops were at an advantage, they were ordered to retreat the following morning since their commanders had not kept track of the situation. The 102nd Regiment mounted an assault on Bến Tắm, but they did not complete their task because they had waited for French artillery and opened fire late. They also had to withdraw the following morning. So in both battles, Vietnamese troops decimated a number of French troops but suffered heavy casualties. The French artillery from Đông Triều and the Đá Bạc River had created fire barriers deterring the Vietnamese attacks. The 209th Regiment (in charge of the attack on Hoàng Gián) and the 98th Regiment (in charge of the attack on Hà Chiểu) did not win completely. Fifteen minutes after opening fire, Vietnamese troops managed to penetrate deeply into the French area. But they were ordered to retreat at daybreak since their commanders had not fully grasped their situation. All the four battles in the second stage were unsuccessful. In the face of their disadvantageous situation,[1] the Vietnamese Headquarters decided to end the campaign on the morning of April 5.

---

1. In the primary direction, the Vietnamese side suffered heavy casualties with 495 killed (including a chief of regiment), 1,673 wounded, and 94 lost, a high rate of casualties compared to 250,000 warring soldiers and French casualties (840 killed, 350 wounded, and 119 caught). After the campaign, Vietnamese soldiers were exhausted and their combat capacity decreased.

Chapter Five: ON THE WAY TO PROMOTE THE WAR OF MOVEMENT

Vietnamese soldiers did not finish the task of the campaign: they decimated only two French battalions in the primary direction, compared to the set target of five battalions.

It is written in *"Lịch sử nghệ thuật chiến dịch Việt Nam trong 30 năm chiến tranh (1945–1975)"* (literally: History of the Vietnamese Campaign Art in Thirty Years of Warfare (1945–1975) that:

> A noticeable shortcoming in Vietnamese commanders' direction and command of the Hoàng Hoa Thám campaign was their failure to keep track of the enemy situation both in preparation and in each battle, so they dealt with some situations inappropriately. Apart from their failure to direct the military intelligence to keep track of the enemy at each specific target, they did not closely follow the development of their troops during the battle, so their inaccurate orders led to their troops' failure to decimate completely many targets and limit enemy reinforcements, and increase in casualties. Due to an inadequate understanding of the fortification-attacking and reinforcement-annihilating tactics, Vietnamese troops missed many chances to decimate French reinforcements, especially small ones.

While the campaign left a "heavy impression" on Võ Nguyên Giáp as he wrote in his memoir *"Đường tới Điện Biên Phủ"* (literally: Road to Điện Biên Phủ), it aroused controversy among French generals. Some of them proved themselves "braver than their commander-in-chief" when criticizing that de Lattre was afraid of jungles and traps and thus did not dare to counter-attack from Lục Nam and Chũ to prevent Vietnamese troops from retreating. However, de Lattre had a different opinion. He only cared about the Red River Delta. He took for granted that Giáp and Vietnamese divisions were still sheltering somewhere, and that they would attack Mạo Khê, Bến Tắm, Đông Triều, Phả Lại, and Hải Dương when having opportunity, clear the way to the delta, and attack Hải Phòng—"the lungs of the French expeditionary army." In response to opposite opinions, de Lattre said, "Giáp's divisions are still there. Yet, they are ordered to shelter in daytime and put out the light at nighttime. You're not allowed to withdraw any soldier from the 18th Route. Giáp will launch an attack."

So French troops lived in expectation the following weeks. De Lattre himself boarded a plane and flew over the mining area, while French aircraft ceaselessly bombed the edges of the jungles. From the Bạch Mai and Gia Lâm airports, French reconnaissance aircraft one after another took off and glided over the delta. A Hellcat aircraft carrying two big tanks of napalm under its wings was ready to take off. French mobile forces had not taken any action because they had not identified the Vietnamese direction of attack.

While de Lattre was confused about where Vietnamese troops had retreated and where they would attack in the coming time, on April 26, the Hoàng Hoa Thám Campaign Party Committee had ended the closing conference of the campaign at the Việt Bắc base. In his summary report presented at the conference, Võ Nguyên Giáp repeated the Politburo and President Hồ Chí Minh's comments on the Hoàng Hoa Thám campaign. In this campaign, particularly in the primary direction, Vietnamese cadres and soldiers made great efforts and heightened their sense of standing hardship. The development and outcome of the campaign revealed both their strengths and weaknesses. Vietnamese troops decimated part of French forces, promoted guerilla war, and exerted some political influence. However, they did not fully complete their tasks, so they also suffered heavy casualties. Still it would be wrong to say that the campaign was unsuccessful, because this statement would mean the unawareness of failures on the French side and difficulties on the Vietnamese side. Partial success might show some strength, while heavy losses certainly proved weaknesses.

The Party Committee's summary report pointed out the focal contents, so that units could review to learn from experience. Before the closing ceremony, Giáp invited Hồ Chí Minh to the conference. There the President talked to Vietnamese cadres about criticism and self-criticism, the execution of orders, and the relationship between cadres and soldiers and that between the army and people. Finally, he instructed Vietnamese cadres to conduct self-criticism among their units and make plans to overcome their weaknesses. Criticism and self-criticism were the weapons that helped the Vietnamese people become an army sure of victory.

Head of the 312th Brigade Lê Trọng Tấn was one of the Vietnamese high-ranking cadres who strictly executed Hồ Chí Minh's instruction on self-criticism and criticism. He was straightforward not only in telling his subordinates about shortcomings in his guidance and command in the recent campaign, but also in giving his comments to the commanders of the campaign. In his notes,[1] General Lê Trọng Tấn wrote:

> In the closing conference (of the 312th Brigade), I sincerely said to my men that in this campaign, the plan was

---

1. These notes were later arranged into his memoir titled *Từ Đồng Quan đến Điện Biên* (literally: From Đồng Quan to Điện Biên), Vietnamese People's Army Publishing House, Hà Nội, 1994.

simple and incautious because of our wrong evaluation of the enemy. In commanding, we did not realize new characteristics of the battlefield, so we rigidly applied the experience gained from the Border and Midland campaigns to the battlefield on the 18th Route, specifically in attacking entrenched fortifications and launching mobile warfare. We did not realize that any experience was only valid in a certain historical context. I take responsibility for our failure to gain complete victory and completely annihilate the enemy and for our heavy casualties.

At the ministry-level closing conference, he stated that the Hoàng Hoa Thám campaign was an unsuccessful one. The target of the campaign, whether it was to decimate the enemy or change the face of the battlefield, was unclearly stated. All the three Vietnamese brigades failed to complete their tasks. The Vietnamese opened the campaign without thorough preparations in terms of terrain and logistics. All units suffered heavy casualties and did not complete their tasks. He said that the Ministry of High Command should also take responsibility for their uncertainty in choosing the campaign's directions and defining its target. He stressed that once the Ministry had determined to launch a campaign, they should have or create elements to ensure its victory. Then he sincerely said:

> There is an opinion that if the tactics had been well applied, the face of the campaign would have been different. I don't agree with this. I think that the tactics are under the guidance of the campaign. Without a clearly-stated goal and a rightly-chosen direction, the campaign would not be successful.

That evening, after dinner, Võ Nguyên Giáp had a private talk with Lê Trọng Tấn to encourage his straightforwardness.

Tấn said, "We still learn something from an unsuccessful battle, provided that we don't give up." With that spirit, the commander dared to face the facts to further perfect himself and lead his units to the final victory.

In the Battlefield in the Flooded Rice Area

Right before launching the Hoàng Hoa Thám campaign on the 18th Route, Võ Nguyên Giáp proposed another campaign before the rainy season. The Standing Central Committee decided to open a campaign in the delta in mid April, when the campaign on the 18th Route had finished, so the preparation for it was promptly carried out. The Vietnamese had to race against nature to prevent the campaign in the flooded rice area divided by criss-cross rivers from being obstructed by the rainy season. Therefore, no sooner had the battle in the mining area ended than Võ Nguyên Giáp returned to Việt Bắc.

General Secretary Trường Chinh had received the report on the development and limited outcome of the Hoàng Hoa Thám campaign, so he understood the Commander-in-chief's unhappiness. He said:

> There are both wins and losses in fighting. We were wise; so was the enemy. We had decimated two of their corps in the borders and nearly decimated entirely the 3rd Mobile Regiment in the midlands. They had drawn some lessons, so they weren't trapped this time. We should have made some change to the fortification-attacking and reinforcement-annihilating tactics this time.

Actually, Giáp had told his subordinates about this before the campaign began. However, although they had realized changes on the French side, they were not able to predict all possibilities. Giáp later recalled that Hồ Chí Minh, Trường Chinh, and he analyzed the top leaders of the French expeditionary army at that time. De Lattre was known to be an aggressive man, but the reality of the last two campaigns showed that he was not impulsive but wise and that he had the skill and spirit of an experienced colonialist general. With his experience in Indochina, negotiating, and fighting with the Vietnamese in the beginning of the August Revolution and then in the Vietnamese national resistance, Salan was obviously a fiendish general. In the absence of de Lattre, if Salan had sent large reinforcements to rescue the mining area, Vietnamese troops would have had opportunity to decimate them and the face of the Northeast battlefield would have been different. That explained why the French mobile forces did not take any action until de Lattre was back. De Lattre and Salan started to take notice of the growth of the Vietnamese army after the two previous campaigns. After the Vĩnh Yên campaign, de Lattre told Salan that the Vietnamese army should not be underestimated. The French generals now no longer expected and challenged Vietnamese soldiers to turn up in battles of the conventional warfare to be decimated as their predecessors had. The strategic failure of the French army in the fall-winter of 1950 marked a turning-point in the French evaluation of their opponent in the battlefield. The revolutionary army equipped only with riffles and organized into brigades were active in seeking the enemy's trumps to attack, not only in the nighttime but also in the daytime, not only in the mountainous and forested area but also in the uncovered area. This change in quality forced de Lattre and Salan to think of effective ways to deal with such an army which was poorly equipped but could not be underestimated.

Chapter Five: ON THE WAY TO PROMOTE THE WAR OF MOVEMENT

On the Vietnamese side, after taking into consideration the Vietnamese human and material resources (specifically six regular infantry brigades over the population of several ten million) and analyzing the human-sea attack used by the Chinese Liberation Army in their anti-American and pro-Korea resistance, Hồ Chí Minh reminded Giáp that the Vietnamese should fight in their own way and make every effort to save their lives when launching a large-scale war of movement. He also stressed that it was not necessary to involve great numbers of troops in a battle. Việt Nam was still a poor country and thus unable to support them then.

No sooner had the Hoàng Hoa Thám campaign ended than the Intelligence Agency of the Vietnamese General Headquarters arranged forces to simultaneously carry out two tasks—preparing the battlefield and keeping track of the French implementation of de Lattre's basic strategic plan and immediate measures to cope with the Vietnamese.

De Lattre told Salan that the newly-established Henri Queueille cabinet had soon shown its wish to end the Indochina War, so the leaders of the French expeditionary army had to shoulder "the cause of safeguarding Indochina" themselves. In the short term, they had to focus on the execution of two closely-related strategic polices—setting up a defense line and building combat forces when Paris was exhausted in order to protect the Red River Delta.

With respect to combat forces, the French would muster battalions of native soldiers available and those being formed, establish for Bảo Đại four divisions to gradually replace Euro-African troops and carry out the tasks of occupying and pacifying, and withdraw expeditionary forces and organize them into divisional-scale mobile brigades which were fully-

461

fledged and able to operate in separation from localities. These were the trumps used by the French to cope with the Vietnamese, especially in the important Northern battlefield.

With the budget of three billion franc financed by Washington, the French would promptly complete a defense line around the Red River Delta as a shield to protect the delta before the dry season.

In order to execute these strategic policies, Salan suggested launching large-scale mopping-up operations in the delta, not only to eliminate the "red dots"[1] which were mushrooming on both sides of the Red River and tidy up the inner bunker defense line, but also to gather local youths into Bảo Đại's army. To develop a native army and accomplish their cause of Vietnamization, the French needed to appreciate the Trần Văn Hữu administration, achieve an order of general mobilization from Bảo Đại, and get support from the United States of America. The two leaders of the French expeditionary army set to work immediately.

On April 18, 1951, Salan was sent to Đà Lạt to deliver to Bảo Đại a letter by de Lattre. The letter was so convincing that Bảo Đại agreed to join the program of Vietnamization, the first content of which was the Vietnamization of the army. While Salan was persuading Bảo Đại in Đà Lạt, de Lattre and his escort flew to Vĩnh Yên—"the land of feats of arms"—to develop their military victory by a significant political campaign. On April 19, in the town, before a lot of French and native officials and hundreds of domestic and international reporters, de Lattre delivered an eight-page

---

1. Vietnamese political and armed bases in the French temporarily-occupied areas.

speech to persuade Prime Minister Trần Văn Hữu and other members of the Bảo Đại administration to take responsibility, as yellow-skinned allies, for a real resistance by encouraging people to follow Bảo Đại and his government.

Then the press started to mention an order of general mobilization newly released by Bảo Đại and native officer training schools to be built soon in Nam Định and Đà Lạt. A special-subject meeting on mopping-up operations was convened on the afternoon of April 28 in Hà Nội. The meeting had been waiting for an air general who was unfortunately killed on the way there from Hải Phòng, so it did not start until 8 pm that day. At the meeting, de Lattre said:

> I'm worried about the penetration of Việt Minh in this delta. As you can see, big and small red dots are everywhere on this map. That's unacceptable. You must promptly prepare necessary operations to restrict the penetration and existence of Việt Minh. You must involve all necessary means, even newly-established battalions, in these operations.

He showed his satisfaction with the outcome of the Méduse (Jellyfish) operation in mid April. With 14 battalions of different types and during a fortnight, French troops made the southwest of Hải Phòng, apart from the Hải Dương-Thái Bình area, "more comfortable" by mopping-up operations along the Hải Phòng-Ninh Giang route. In this meeting, however, de Lattre raised a higher demand as French troops had "glided too fast" in the mopping-up areas. He asked them to stay in these areas to organize civil defense units, recruit (actually force) as many local youths as possible to Bảo Đại's army, and prevent these recruits from deserting.

After the meeting, Salan was ordered to collaborate with some commanders in the delta to organize new raids. One-star General Henri de Berchoux, who had just arrived in Hà Nội to assume the post of commander in Hải Dương, was entrusted with the task of directing the Reptile operation. This operation involved the participation of four mobile regiments and four artillery battalions, and took place from May 5-8. It was assessed by Salan to be a methodically prepared and implemented operation. The Méduse and Reptile operations were later described in *Lịch sử kháng chiến chống Pháp của Liên khu 3* (literally: History of the Anti-French Resistance War of the 3rd Interzone) as follows:

> The enemy severely wiped out resistance villages, cruelly killed those suspected to be cadres and guerillas, and brutally terrorized local people . . . . Tens of thousands of youngsters were caught in these raids (over 4,000 in Hải Dương alone) . . . . In order to make Vietnamese people exhausted and surrender to them, they looted most of the local cereals. The rest was burnt down or thrown into water.

However, the French failed to reach the main target of their operations—decimating the 42nd Regiment, which was an important regiment of the 3rd Interzone and which they called the "ghost regiment." Thanks to the support of local people, the 42nd Regiment still existed, and surprisingly and successively dealt them death-blows.

While de Lattre shuttled between Malaysia and Singapore to discuss with Britain and the United States the "Southeast Asia Common Defense Plan," assigning his subordinates to launch mopping-up operations to pacify the delta, Vietnamese troops mounted an attack in the south of the Red River.

When discussing the direction of the coming campaign, the Standing Central Committee found that Vietnamese soldiers would meet difficulties in battles in the delta. At

Chapter Five: ON THE WAY TO PROMOTE THE WAR OF MOVEMENT

that time, however, there was nowhere else but the midlands and delta where French forces were such important targets that the destruction of them would bring about significant changes to the battlefield.

After Võ Nguyên Giáp reported that advisory envoys had been sent to the delta since the previous month and that the leaders of the 3rd Interzone had directed the preparation for the battlefield (soldiers could set off in the next few weeks) after thoroughly grasping the plan of the Standing Central Committee, General Secretary Trường Chinh agreed to open another campaign before the rainy season. That came up with the expectation of Vietnamese soldiers and cadres, who would like to continue the battle soon. They were not satisfied with the limited outcome of the previous campaign.

From the office of the General Secretary, Giáp went straight to the Combat Office to listen to the advisory envoys report on the situation. He asked them about the local guerrilla movement, specifically the role of local soldiers and combat villages in the anti-raid operations, and the operation of the 42nd Regiment. According to the envoys, the recent operations of the 42nd Regiment on the left bank of the Red River had attracted and controlled French mobile forces, facilitated militiamen in the delta to foil the French plan of pacification during the spring-summer months, restored many revolutionary bases, and rebuilt many guerilla zones in Hải Dương, Hưng Yên, Kiến An, and Thái Bình. The 42nd Regiment, along with local soldiers, militiamen, and guerillas, had not only rolled back French mopping-up operations but also smashed administrative-military organizations established by the French to realize their ruling policies in localities. Nevertheless, it should be noted that the French large-scale mopping-up operations in recent time had caused serious damages to some Vietnamese bases which would take a long time to recover.

On the French side, during the last summer months, most of the Euro-African units were driven to the north, so most of French forces in the south of the Red River Delta were puppet troops. Besides, mobile troops were inadequate, troops were arranged dispersedly, and fortifications had not been reinforced. French troops in Ninh Bình were found to be weaker than those in provinces in the 3rd Interzone. However, the advisory envoys also commented that it was only the immediate situation, and that the enemy could quickly muster their mobile forces to deal with Vietnamese troops once they figured out the direction of Vietnamese regular forces. Remarkably, the French succeeded in separating non-Catholics from Catholics to undermine Vietnamese forces in one of the most populous areas in the North. In addition to a network of dangerous spies, they established armed units of Catholic youngsters to cope with the Vietnamese revolution from hamlet- and commune-level bases to the large area of the self-governing Catholic province of Bùi Chu, which covered the districts of Trực Ninh, Hải Hậu, Giao Thủy, and Xuân Trường and part of Nam Trực District. They turned Bùi Chu and Phát Diệm into reactionary Catholic centers in the 3rd Interzone with 800,000 parishioners and 500 large churches, turning the holy lands into military fortifications, parishioners into cannon-fodders, and the churches' bell-towers into watch-towers and firing-posts.

After grasping the Standing Central Committee's plan, leaders of the 3rd Interzone assigned Văn Tiến Dũng to directly take charge of the preparation for the battlefield.

Chapter Five: ON THE WAY TO PROMOTE THE WAR OF MOVEMENT

The Việt Bắc-3rd Interzone route was cleared. The collection of food was satisfactory because of good crops. Nearly 200 commune- and district-level cadres attended the training course on the logistics of the campaign. Local people were enthusiastically waiting for the Vietnamese regular forces to liberate their hometowns.

At the meeting on April 20, 1951, after listening to General Giáp's report, the Standing Central Committee officially decided to open the campaign in the south of the Red River Delta in the Hà Nội-Nam Hà-Ninh Bình (or Hà-Nam-Ninh for short) area. The campaign, whose code name was Quang Trung, aimed to decimate part of French forces, develop guerrilla war, sap the puppet army, and court the people's support. Hồ Chí Minh reminded everyone to pay attention to the political aim of the campaign—courting the local people's support—because the enemy had plotted to take advantage of Catholicism to sabotage the resistance and revolution. The Standing Central Committee also established the Hà-Nam-Ninh Front Party Committee, which included some cadres from the General Headquarters and some from local authorities.[1]

Based on the General Staff's statement, the Central Military Commission considered and decided to choose the French defense line at the Đáy River, from southern Phủ Lý (Hà Nam) to Yên Mô (Ninh Bình), as the primary direction of this campaign. In the areas of Phủ Lý, Nam Định, Phát Diệm, and Ninh Bình, French forces included four battalions and twenty-seven companies (mainly

---

1. They included Võ Nguyên Giáp as Secretary cum Commander, Nguyễn Chí Thanh, Lê Thanh Nghị, Hoàng Văn Thái, Văn Tiến Dũng, and Hoàng Sâm.

Catholic puppet troops); French mobile forces included four infantry battalions (including two puppet battalions), three commando companies, one infantry company, and one marine company. According to the plan approved by the Central Military Commission, Vietnamese forces in the campaign included three brigades (the 304th, 308th, and 320th Brigades), five artillery companies, one sapper regiment, and local armed forces. They were assigned to decimate three French battalions.

Because some members of the Hà-Nam-Ninh Front Party Committee were leaders of the 3rd Interzone, Võ Nguyên Giáp and Nguyễn Chí Thanh had to set off in late April to get there in time to discuss the combat plan with them. Hoàng Văn Thái and some members of the Campaign Headquarters had started out one week earlier. It was not easy to meet leaders of the area behind enemy lines, no sooner had Võ Nguyên Giáp arrived than he spent much time working with provinces and the 42nd Regiment Command—the regular force of the 3rd Interzone—to keep track of the situation. When assigning localities in the interzone to coordinate with the primary direction of the campaign, he emphasized the tasks of developing guerrilla war, destroying roads and launching attacks on routes (such as the 5th, 1st, 6th, 10th, 21st, and 22nd Routes) and the Đại Hà dyke, stepping up mobilization among quislings, and preparing a plan to prevent French raids and protect the people's harvests. The 42nd Regiment was assigned to promptly deploy troops to the left bank to coordinate with regular forces on the right bank and promote achievements after the end of the campaign. Local troops were under the command of regular brigades.

There were early changes in the French situation, as predicted by the Front Party Committee. Part of the 4th Mobile Regiment was seen in Phủ Lý. The Party Committee also anticipated that French troops, supported by motorized vehicles, would make the most use of roads and waterways, and that the situation would change quickly once Vietnamese troops opened fire.

After the 1st Combat Order was delivered to units, at the conference held on May 24–25, Võ Nguyên Giáp analyzed the situations in the areas of Phủ Lý, Vân Đình, and Ninh Bình to confirm the primary direction of the campaign. The Vietnamese had formerly considered carefully and decided to launch the campaign in the south of Hà Đông and Hà Nam. This decision was right at that time because the French situation had not changed. In this direction, the Vietnamese would be certain of victory, decimating a great part of French forces, disintegrating part of the puppet army, and gaining great political influence. However, the situation had obviously changed for recent days. The French had sent their mobile forces to Phủ Lý and Nam Định, reinforced their defense line along the Đáy River from Phủ Lý northwards, and set up a curfew area along that defense line. In Hà Đông and Sơn Tây, they intensified fortifications and sped up patrols.

At the conference, the Front Party Committee had considered the three areas of Phủ Lý, Vân Đình, and Ninh Bình before deciding to move to the areas of Ninh Bình and Phủ Lý. French troops in Ninh Bình were relatively weaker than those in other areas along the Đáy River defense line, so Vietnamese troops could be sure of victory. Therefore, the Front Party Committee determined to muster Vietnamese combat forces primarily in Ninh Bình and secondarily in Phủ Lý.

Võ Nguyên Giáp emphasized that the directive idea of the Front Party Committee was being certain of victory. He deliberately analyzed each solution that both regular and local troops should study to overcome difficulties (such as Catholic people, flooded rice area, and changeable French situation) to win the enemy in this battlefield. He also reminded them to deal with issues related to the guidance of operational tactics in the delta and ideological orientation among troops to prevent them from being subjective and underestimating the enemy. Regarding the work plan in localities, he particularly highlighted the importance of applying the Party's policies on the Catholic community, mobilization among quislings, the development of guerrilla war, and the safeguarding of local people and crops.

The campaign began on May 28. A battalion of the 102nd Regiment of the 308th Brigade decimated entirely a naval commando company which had occupied Đại Phong Church in Ninh Bình Town. The French were alerted, but their initial resistance was weak. After the battle at Đại Phong, the 308th Regiment annihilated two French positions of Non Nước and Gối Hạc in Ninh Bình Town, which were close to the confluence of the Vân and Đáy Rivers. Lieutenant Bernard de Lattre—the only son of General de Lattre—and two other French company-level officers were killed in the battle at Gối Hạc.

After their positions in Ninh Bình Town were decimated in the first few days of the campaign, the French used both roads and waterways to muster large forces (including commandos, marines, and mobile troops) and responded violently. The 1st Mobile Regiment and marines, supported by aircraft and artillery, from Nam Định reoccupied Ninh Bình

Town and cooperated with the 4th Mobile Regiment to stop Vietnamese forces' advance in Ninh Bình and southwestern Nam Định while intensifying the important positions of Ninh Bình, Phủ Lý, and Hoàng Đan. Since Vietnamese troops had failed to decimate entirely the enemy positions of Hoàng Đan, Kỳ Cầu, and Chùa Cao, the enemy situation had quickly changed, the element of surprise had disappeared, and the balance of power had lost, the Vietnamese Headquarters found it hard to develop the campaign and thus decided to end its first stage after four days of fighting.

In the combat order for the second stage, Võ Nguyên Giáp analyzed the achievements of Vietnamese regular forces in the first stage. They decimated ten French positions (including such important ones as Ninh Bình Town) and part of French reinforcements (including nine companies). In the first stage, they suffered few casualties and remained healthy and high-spirited to continue fighting.

The Vietnamese Headquarters determined to follow two steps in the second stage. In the first step (from June 4–7), the 308th Brigade would attack Chùa Cao and French reinforcements on the waterway from Ninh Bình to Chùa Cao while positively investigating the French situation in Hoàng Đan and Ninh Bình Town and getting ready to attack when ordered. The 304th Brigade would assault French reinforcements on the river from Bến Xanh and on the road from Phát Diệm to Chùa Cao and get prepared to fight in the daytime. They would simultaneously choose and propose a plan to attack two French positions and small reinforcements. The 320th Brigade would send two battalions to Chợ Cháy (Hà Đông) and Thanh Liêm (Hà Nam), two areas behind enemy lines. Armed scouts were assigned to investigate the positions of Núi Già and Núi Bô and the French situation on the 1st Route; cadres were sent to localities to help develop the local guerrilla warfare. All brigades were responsible for equipping local soldiers involved in the campaign. In the second step, each brigade would leave one regiment in the battlefield to continue small-scale operations and withdraw the rest to the rear for consolidation and getting ready to fight. Meanwhile, local soldiers would actively implement the tasks assigned by the provincial leadership (such as eliminating reactionaries, protecting local crops, and failing French mopping-up operations).

The second stage of the campaign began on June 4, when the French kept on sending large reinforcements to their important areas. However, their forces were still dispersedly deployed and revealed weaknesses. They intensified artillery power to decimate Vietnamese troops, and their mobile forces avoided fighting with Vietnamese regular troops. During the second stage, the French continued to adjust their forces, send more troops to the Đáy River defense line, and replace troops at many positions. They used two mobile regiments to mop up Chợ Cháy in order to eliminate one unit of the 320th Brigade which had penetrated into the area behind their lines.

After one unit of the 320th Brigade had successfully crushed French mopping-up operations, killing hundreds of French troops in Chợ Cháy (Ứng Hòa District, Hà Đông Province), the Quang Trung campaign ended on June 20, 1951.

In a summary report dated June 22 on the victory of the campaign, Võ Nguyên Giáp made the following comments:

Militarily, when mounting an attack on Ninh Bình, the Vietnamese benefited from the element of surprise. The French was confused in mobilizing reinforcements. It took them three days to dispatch the 1st and 4th Mobile Regiments, who were mopping up Bình Giang and Tứ Kỳ or were going to mop up the Tiên-Hưng area, and forces from the midlands and northern Phủ Lý to Ninh Bình and Phát Diệm for rescue. Vietnamese troops gained the initiative in attack and retreat. After three weeks, Vietnamese soldiers decimated 4,050 enemies (40 percent of whom were Euro-African troops), confiscated over 1,000 guns of different types (enough to equip a strong regiment), and annihilated 30 French positions. Thanks to the military victory in the Ninh Bình-Phủ Lý-Phát Diệm battlefield, the guerrilla war started to develop on the right bank. Many local soldiers had returned to the areas behind the French lines for operation. On the left bank, the guerilla movement continued to develop, especially in the recent "Week for Crop Protection" launched among guerrillas. However, some Vietnamese units had suffered relatively heavy casualties. According to the statistics of the Advisory Board, the ratio of Vietnamese casualties to French ones (1:1.2) was unacceptable.

Politically, it was a great victory that Vietnamese soldiers had executed exactly the Party's policy on the Catholic community and puppet army, exerting a considerable impact on the attitude of part of Catholic people toward the Vietnamese resistance war and soldiers. The tolerant policy had positive impact on the spirit of puppet soldiers, initially disintegrating part of the puppet army. Riding the tide of victory, the Vietnamese restored many political bases in the areas behind the enemy lines. However, the development of this victory also depended on the following actions of localities.

Economically, the campaign broke out at the beginning of the crops in the North, when the French were going to mop up areas on both river banks and in the midlands to loot cereals and destroy crops. Vietnamese troops launched a quick attack in a direction that the French had not expected and attracted most of their mobile forces to the main battlefield, thus foiling most of their mopping-up plan and completing most of the harvest in the midlands and on the left bank. On the right bank, the local people still had difficulties in harvesting though French raids had been temporarily postponed.

In summary, the Vietnamese accomplished completely the first goal (decimating French forces) and partly the other three set by the Standing Central Committee for this campaign. They strictly followed President Hồ Chí Minh's instruction, highly appreciating both political and military victories. They were successful both militarily and politically.

In terms of guidance, the Front Party Committee showed both strengths and weaknesses in this campaign.

Regarding strengths, the Front Party Committee had made a right decision when changing the primary direction of attack from Phủ Lý to Ninh Bình, successfully instructed Vietnamese forces to simultaneously fight against the enemy and help the local people promote guerrilla warfare and protect their crops, and effectively led the execution of the Party's and Government's policies.

The Front Party Committee also revealed two main weaknesses. On the one hand, they had failed to create favorable conditions and time for Vietnamese units to complete their tasks. In many cases, it took them much time to make a decision and their decisions were inappropriate, so Vietnamese troops missed chance to annihilate the enemy. On the other hand, there had been times when they were subjective and could not anticipate all difficulties in logistics for timely measures. Võ Nguyên Giáp stressed that the Vietnamese could learn a lot from this experience. It showed that in fighting against the enemy, they would suffer a failure if they were subjective and incautious, despite all favorable conditions they might have had.

Võ Nguyên Giáp also raised high the four strong points of Vietnamese regular units. First, all the units had made progress in techniques and tactics (particularly the 308th and 304th Brigades in attacking fortified positions, and the 320th Brigade in attacking reinforcements in the daytime). Second, the cadres had made great strides in their sense of responsibility and in their spirit of overcoming difficulties. Most cadres had kept in close touch and fought heroically with soldiers. Third, the units had strictly executed policies and exerted great political influence. Last, the spirit of fighting and withstanding difficulties had been heightened among soldiers.

He also highlighted weak points that Vietnamese cadres and soldiers should overcome. Firstly cadres at all levels had not solved satisfactorily the relationship between adequate preparation and time saving to comply with each circumstance, situation, and task. Secondly, cadres were still weak in making predictions, and had not had a thorough understanding of their soldiers and the situations. Consequently, they had made mistakes in solving emerging problems and missed chances, affecting the general development of the campaign. Thirdly, they lacked flexibility in applying tactics, so they easily got puzzled, lost their temper, or turned irresolute when being put in an urgent situation. Finally, they did not make necessary predictions or continuously carry out political encouragement among soldiers, especially when some unit turned subjective after a victory or pessimistic after a failure.

To conclude the summary report, Võ Nguyên Giáp said:

> Thanks to the afore-mentioned strong points, we decimated a great part of enemy forces and gained the achievements mentioned in this report. However, due to the weaknesses mentioned above, we missed many victories which we could have achieved and the campaign was not developed according to the plan. We should recognize these points to avoid being arrogant after the victory, and try to promote the strengths and overcome the weaknesses when carrying out self-criticism and summarization. In this meeting, we should also appreciate the efforts of local soldiers in developing guerrilla war, as well as the attempts and achievements of coordinative battlefields on the left bank, in the midlands, and in the Bình-Trị-Thiên area. Particularly our soldiers on the left bank decimated the enemy and forced them to retreat from nearly 30 positions; disintegrated over 1,000 puppet troops; expanded the Tiên-Duyên-Hưng liberated area; and established new liberated areas in Tiên Lữ, Phù Cừ, Kiến Xương, and Tiên Hải. We should praise the efforts of the people in the 3rd and 4th Interzones in the preparation for the battlefield, as well as in the mobilization of human and material resources for the campaign. These efforts significantly contributed to the victory.

With respect to the guidance of the campaign, on June 25, the Front Party Committee had met for a detailed review before the Commander-in-chief and leaders of the three ministerial offices returned to Việt Bắc. They determined to address only main points because of the limited time.

In terms of the guidance for the preparation for the campaign, the Front Party Committee admitted their difficulties in preparing for the battlefield, particularly in keeping track of the enemy and logistics, due to the lack of instructions from the higher leadership. As a result, their preparations were sometimes not in accordance with the combat plan. Many prepared things were not used, and many needed things were not prepared. It was the duty of the Battlefield Preparation Board, but the Front Party Committee should be partly blamed for not sending consultants there for timely support.

Regarding the policy of launching a campaign in the rainy season, the Front Party Committee stressed the necessity of taking into consideration the mutual influence between the campaign and the matter of conscripted laborers and crops. It was inadvisable to open a campaign in the dry season in a battlefield with flooded rice fields, since it would cause Vietnamese troops difficulties in marching, sheltering, cooking, and fighting. Many Vietnamese soldiers and conscripted laborers fell ill in this campaign.

With regard to the combat policy and commanding style, it was right for the Front Party Committee to change their direction of attack from Phủ Lý to Ninh Bình. It was also right to change to launching small-scale battles and helping local soldiers develop guerrilla war after the unsuccessful Chùa Cao battle. However, they did not thoroughly grasp the situation or closely supervise the implementation of that policy. They pointed out the two specific mistakes in their command as follows:

On the first day of the campaign, the Front Party Committee took advantage of the time to keep the secret and avoid the rainy season. The time set in the order was enough for all Vietnamese units to make preparations. However, they failed to implement the plan as scheduled for their lack of frequent supervision and examination.

It was planned that after the battle in Ninh Bình, some Vietnamese units would stay there and get ready to fight against the enemy if they returned. It was a right guideline. However, the Front Party Committee had not thoroughly grasped the situation or closely supervised the implementation of assigned tasks. Consequently, they ordered most of their troops to withdraw from Ninh Bình after the battle, which enabled the enemy to reoccupy it easily.

The Front Party Committee showed both strengths and weaknesses in their working style during the campaign. The most noticeable strength was that the Front Party Committee met and discussed only major issues related to the guidelines and policies, and then gave directions to offices and units to execute. They did not hold many meetings or discuss trivial things in this campaign as in the previous ones. However, they did not closely direct the agencies in charge of consultancy, politics, and logistics. As a result, these three agencies did not cooperate with each other closely and consistently. As for the logistical agency, the Front Party Committee was so subjective that they did not realize in a timely manner their difficulties in logistics and in the evacuation of casualties, so they failed to give timely measures to overcome these difficulties. Moreover, for the lack of timely definitions of the connection between the local High Command and the 3rd Interzone Party Committee and their operations, the Front

Party Committee was confused about the arrangement of cadres and agencies there in the early days of the campaign. Regarding the 4th Interzone, the Front Party Committee had not realized the local capacity and situation, so they made localities become passive, especially in personnel appointment. The 4th Interzone Party Committee arranged personnel adequately in terms of quantity but unsuitably in terms of their fortes, so the personnel was redundant but still insufficient to undertake tasks.

In order to help the 3rd Interzone cope with French troops when Vietnamese regular soldiers had retreated, the Front Party Committee anticipated that in the coming time, the French would reinforce their occupation on the right bank in general and at the Đáy River defense line in particular, recruit more puppet soldiers, set up new garrisons, consolidate fortifications, and carry out more mopping-up operations, especially on the left bank. They would expand the Trung Hà-Ba Thá Crossroads "white zone" to Vân Đình and even farther. Vietnamese bases on the right bank were still weak in many aspects and were likely to meet difficulties. There had appeared some signs of pessimism and the quiet-seeking and difficulty-fearing spirit. The Front Party Committee found it necessary to promptly reinforce their organization and leadership. Cadres must keep in close touch with the people and strengthen the operation of local soldiers, militiamen, and guerillas. The 52nd Regiment, one battalion of the 64th Regiment, and one battalion of the 48th Regiment stayed to operate and get ready to fight against the enemy if they attacked the liberated areas and destroyed crops; however, their core and frequent task was to give reeducation to local troops and people.

Regarding the Quang Trung campaign, it is written in *Lịch sử nghệ thuật chiến dịch Việt Nam* (literally: History of the Operational Art in Việt Nam) that, it was the first time Vietnamese soldiers had decimated enemies in a delta town (Ninh Bình) and annihilated four enemy companies in entrenched fortifications after two nights and one day of the battle, setting a new record in attacking fortified positions. It was also the first time they carried out methodically the coordination between an outer line (the Đáy River defense line) and an inner line (the left bank of the Red River) in combat. This first experience showed their ability to implement the coordination between the front and the areas behind the enemy lines in the following campaigns.

A comparison of all aspects of the battlefield in the Red River Delta showed that the Quang Trung Campaign Headquarters was right in deciding to attack the Phủ Lý-Ninh Bình area, where French troops were weak, and careless. Vietnamese troops gained success thanks to this decision. Apart from decimating part of enemy forces, they also confiscated an amount of weaponry and technical equipment, initially promoted guerrilla war, and gained a new overwhelming position in the battlefield south of the Red River Delta. The French not only had to leave their large-scale raids in Bình Giang, Tứ Kỳ, and Tiên Hưng (on the left bank of the Red River) unfinished and cancel their plan of reinforcing the defense in the midlands and on the 18th Route, but they also had to send their troops to cope with Vietnamese troops in Ninh Bình and reinforce the Đáy River defense line.

However, the Quang Trung campaign failed to reach its strategic goal for several reasons. Tactically, the chosen

Chapter Five: ON THE WAY TO PROMOTE THE WAR OF MOVEMENT

direction of attack was unsuitable; the French took advantage of their artillery fire-power and mobile vehicles and favorable terrain conditions to quickly send reinforcements and thus immediately change the balance of power and the face of the battlefield. Regarding the campaign, the art of management did not enable Vietnamese soldiers to overcome the weaknesses discovered in the two previous campaigns. The weaknesses in the campaign leadership's guidance and command also had direct impact on the soldiers' fighting efficiency.

Regarding the three campaigns in the spring-summer of 1951, it is also written in *Lịch sử nghệ thuật chiến dịch Việt Nam* (literally: History of the Operational Art in Việt Nam) that, it was the first time the Vietnamese had opened three successive campaigns involving a lot of brigades attacking the enemy's defense lines in the midland and delta battlefields. Both in the primary and coordinative directions, Vietnamese troops decimated about 70 enemy positions, among which a town and some positions were each occupied by an enemy company. In fighting against enemy reinforcements, they annihilated a battalion and caused severe damages to some battalions and companies under the 1st, 3rd, and 4th Mobile Regiments. They also killed nearly 10,000 enemies (half of whom were mobile troops) and seized a considerable amount of weaponry and technical equipment.

Fighting in a new battlefield which was uncovered and under the frequent threat of enemy artillery, Vietnamese soldiers initially gained some experience in the tactics of mobile warfare, attacking enemies in stable fortifications by day and night, and attacking enemy reinforcements on the land, on the river, and in the sky. Although it was only initial experience in developing a guerrilla war into a regular one, it contributed to the improvement of the military knowledge of Vietnamese regulars. Such improvement was shown most clearly in the two battles in Xuân Trạch and Ninh Bình Town.

Unfortunately, all the three campaigns failed to fulfill their strategic tasks due to limitations in strategic guidance and in the art of campaign management.

In terms of strategic guidance, after their fall-winter victory in 1950 in the border battlefield, Vietnamese commanders made a wrong evaluation of the balance of power and failed to identify all weaknesses of their regular soldiers and the effectiveness of solutions for dealing with the enemy's strategies. Therefore, they suggested the policy of gaining a military advantage to change the face of the Northern battlefield. Specifically, they hastily launched within seven months three successive campaigns involving many brigades in the midland and delta battlefields, where the French were still strong.

It is true that the victory of the Border campaign marked the growth of Vietnamese regulars in terms of quality, organization, and military knowledge. However, it was just conditional growth. They still had some limitations such as poor equipment and low level of concentrated combat. With their facilities and fortes at that time, they were only able to combat in the mountainous and forested battlefield. In this area, they could not only limit the enemy's artillery firepower and mobility but also overcome their weaknesses in technical equipment on the mountainous terrain.

With respect to the art of campaign, in all these three campaigns, the Vietnamese Headquarters proposed the fortification-attacking and reinforcement-annihilating tactics, but they did not emphasize the importance of attacking enemy reinforcements outside their fortifications. The campaign commanders did not guarantee the victory of attacks on entrenched fortifications. They hastily ordered their troops to change the direction of attack when enemy reinforcements were not seen, or failed to give specific instructions, especially in important battles, for their lack of a thorough understanding of the enemy situation or a close supervision of their troops. In summary, although the campaign commanders put forward the policy of "attacking fortifications and decimating reinforcements," they lacked specific solutions in directing the preparation, as well as in implementing the campaign. Therefore, compared to the Border campaign, the three spring-summer campaigns in 1951 reflected a stop sign (if not a setback) in terms of the art of campaign.

Commander-in-chief Võ Nguyên Giáp had thought about these campaigns since Vietnamese regulars switched to large-scale battles involving many brigades. According to him, the four campaigns (from the Border campaign) were carried out within eight months in different battlefields, but they seemed to be a prolonged campaign for their continuity and their similar warring units, nerve centers, and tactics. The Vietnamese had changed to the period of large-scale war of movement. The battles of movement in Liễn Sơn, Xuân Trạch, Thanh Vân, and Đạo Tú (in the Trần Hưng Đạo campaign), the attack on the Bí Chợ fortification (in the Hoàng Hoa Thám campaign), and the attack on the Non Nước fortification (in the Quang Trung campaign) proved Vietnamese soldiers' progress in combat in the midland and delta areas. However, their failures in the Bãi Thảo, Bến Tắm, and Chùa Cao battles, where most of their casualties were caused by enemy artillery from a distance, should also be taken into consideration.

What he had been concerned about since the end of the Midland campaign became a great challenge to Vietnamese troops in the Hà-Nam-Ninh campaign.

De Lattre not only raised the spirit of the French expeditionary army with encouraging words, but he also earned their trust since he knew how to concentrate his troops quickly in emergencies, accepted small damages, and consistently refused to enter into face-to-face battles with Vietnamese troops when the conditions were unfavorable to the French. He managed to make the most use of modern weapons and techniques to cope with Vietnamese troops in their battles of movement as well as in their attacks on French fortifications.

The situation in the Red River Delta had turned unfavorable to the Vietnamese army. What would happen when the majority of Vietnamese regular forces had left?

The Vietnamese army was facing new challenges.

Chapter Six

DETERMINATION TO HOLD THE OFFENSIVE

Crushing de Lattre's Plot to Gain the Initiative

After several successive offensives launched by Vietnamese forces and the degradation of France's economy leading to the decrease in support from Paris, French Commander-in-chief de Lattre stressed that they would have to manage the Indochina War on their own and reaffirmed the rightness of the Vietnamization policy. In order to pursue that policy, the French expeditionary army needed more aid from the United States and the cooperation of Bảo Đại following the guideline "American guns in the hands of Vietnamese soldiers."

To promote the effectiveness of the meeting with authorities in Vĩnh Yên on April 19 and to bring Bảo Đại's order of general mobilization into force, de Lattre found it necessary to influence Vietnamese youth, who played an important role in developing a mercenary army. On July 11, he had a talk with students of Chasseloup Laubat High School in Sài Gòn. Then in the French press appeared such headlines as "The French Commander-in-chief wins the heart of Vietnamese youth."

Three days later, on July 14, de Lattre flew to the North to attend the French National Day ceremony with Bảo Đại. In order to express his gratitude to Bảo Đại for his order of general mobilization, at the solemn ceremony held in Hà Nội that day, de Lattre announced to return some sectors such as the police, post office, radio station, and treasury to the Bảo Đại government. However, there were still French advisors to this native government. This event made headlines in Sài Gòn and Hà Nội press.

One of the most pressing tasks for the French Headquarters was to promote the establishment of a native army. In retrospect, the Vietnamizaion had never taken place as quickly as it did in the summer of 1951. With the result of the conscription and the addition of ten French reinforcement battalions in 1951, the French army in Việt Nam sharply increased from 239,400 troops in late 1950 to 338,000 troops in late 1951. French ground forces were organized into 160 regular infantry, 18 artillery, 7 armored, 7 sapper, and 5 transportation battalions. To cope with the attacks by Vietnamese regular brigades, de Lattre decided to not only use seven mobile regiments and about ten parachute battalions (accounting for 18 percent of all French mobile forces in Indochina), but also establish Tonkinese (North Vietnamese) mobile divisions when the native army was strong enough to replace the French expeditionary one.

The Sài Gòn press told the news that de Lattre returned to France for medical treatment on July 17. After the death of his only son, he was stricken by another disaster: the recurrence of his cancer. Before setting off, he urged Salan to speed up the establishment of defense lines and a native army under the Bảo Đại administration, because the autumn (or

Chapter Six: DETERMINATION TO HOLD THE OFFENSIVE

"the hard time" as he called) was coming. He also reminded Salan to closely watch all Việt Minh activities, since he did not want the events at the Đáy River to be repeated.

He planned to return to Việt Nam in late October, after his trip to the United States for seeking aids.

It was during these summer days that the Vietnamese armed forces in the Central and South regions promoted their activities. In one of their mopping-up operations to the east of the 1st Route near Huế on July 26, French troops suffered heavy losses. Salan flew from Sài Gòn to Huế to order a troop withdrawal. He stayed for some days to help the French commander there limit damages to French troops in Cầu Hai and Phú Bài airport. No sooner had he arrived at the Tân Sơn Nhất airport than he heard that General Charles Chanson and Governor of South Việt Nam Thái Lập Thành had been killed in an inspection trip to Sa Đéc in South Việt Nam. Salan reported to de Lattre that French troops were continuing their mopping-up operations in the Red River Delta, that their transportation of military supplies to the Lao battlefield was being deterred, and that their troops were confronting Vietnamese sabotage in Kon Tum and thus suffering heavy damages. However, Salan informed de Lattre that he had visited Bảo Đại and that the Head of State was joining actively.

The lack of money to promote the construction of defense lines and weapons to arm thousands of new troops in the dry season were de Lattre's frequent concerns. Having heard that the battlefield was quiet, de Lattre went to the United States to seek support. Meanwhile, Bảo Đại did not miss the chance to express his gratitude to de Lattre in a lengthy letter. The letter ended with these words: "I wish you best outcomes in your noble mission, and reconfirm my loyalty to you as well as our friendship."

De Lattre achieved significant results from his trips to Washington and London but poor outcomes from that to Paris.

During his trips, he kept asking Salan about the construction of defense lines and what Giáp was doing. The answer he always got from Salan to the second question was "Giáp is preparing and our forces are ready." In fact, as Salan admitted in his memoirs, his biggest concern during those days was that he was still vague about Việt Minh brigades' direction of attack, since he was frequently informed that they were in their training season.

It was true that after Vietnamese regulars left the Hà-Nam-Ninh battlefield, Võ Nguyên Giáp got the whole Vietnamese army to take part in a basic political reeducation and military training course. Since the previous dry season, Vietnamese brigades had been involved in a long period of continuous operations from the Northeast mountainous region to the midland and plain areas, with a special level of work intensity which seemed to exceed human stamina. Six years of resistance had gone, but it was the first time Vietnamese soldiers had been enlightened to the basic issues of the Vietnamese revolution, resistance guideline, and guideline for the building of the Vietnamese People's Army. During that training period, they obtained both new and familiar things to a soldier's life. As Võ Nguyên Giáp said later, the political and military training course in the summer of 1951 marked a turning-point in the thought of Vietnamese soldiers. It was militarily different from its predecessors. It was planned to last four or five months and aimed to disseminate to newly-promoted cadres and newly-recruited soldiers fresh experience in the techniques and tactics of attacking entrenched fortifications and launching mobile battles (both in the mountainous and plain areas, on the road and river) gained from the four previous campaigns.

In order to hold their offensive in the North Vietnamese battlefield and force French troops to disperse, on September 4, the Vietnamese Politburo decided to launch the Lý Thường Kiệt campaign in the Northwest direction. The General Headquarters assigned the 312th Brigade to cooperate with the armed forces of some provinces in the Northwest and Việt Bắc to organize this campaign. It was the first campaign after the Hà-Nam-Ninh campaign ended over two months earlier. The 312th Brigade had not participated in the Quang Trung campaign but stayed to protect their base, so they had spend some time reinforcing and training themselves before receiving the task of advancing to the Northwest, where they took charge of the primary direction of Nghĩa Lộ while the 148th Regiment in Sơn La assumed responsibility for the coordinative direction of Bình Lư, Phong Thổ.

In an order dated September 5 to the 312th Brigade, Việt Bắc Interzone, and Northwest Front, Võ Nguyên Giáp stated that French troops, the majority of whom were puppet troops, were dispersedly arranged and had low fighting spirit. Besides, their supplies and reinforcements were mostly carried by air. It is noticeable that the French furthered the consolidation of some of their positions outside their fortifications in Nghĩa Lộ, the gateway to the Northwest, and took control of the local residents and economic bases. In this situation, the Vietnamese Headquarters decided on the goals of this campaign, which were destroying part of the enemy force, developing guerilla war, annihilating bandits, expanding revolutionary zones behind the enemy lines, and protecting local crops. In terms of the mode of operation, Võ Nguyên Giáp stressed that Vietnamese troops must take advantage of the element of surprise in annihilating enemy fortifications and have a plan to attack enemy retreats and reinforcements by road and air. Their combat plan must be made at the same time as the plan for helping local armed forces develop guerrilla warfare and expand revolutionary bases. He also reminded the 312th Brigade High Command to absolutely keep secrets to take advantage of the element of surprise, make thorough preparations in terms of logistics, strictly obey the policy on mobilization among the people and quislings, and avoid subjectivism among cadres.

The 312th Brigade soon faced unfavorable situations. Having detected the 312th Brigade when they arrived in Yên Bái on September 18, Salan ordered his troops in Nghĩa Lộ to be ready for combat. Meanwhile, signs of subjectivism soon appeared among Vietnamese soldiers, especially after their successful attacks on some French fortifications on the way to Nghĩa Lộ. Lê Trọng Tấn later wrote, "As commanders, we weren't flexible enough to deal with subjectivism among cadres. I myself didn't inspect the situation before ordering to fire."

That explained why the Vietnamese attacks on Ca Vịnh, Bản Tủ, and some other positions were not successful. It was mainly due to Vietnamese units' preparations had not met the requirements of an offensive on an entrenched fortification. When reaching Nghĩa Lộ, the 141st Regiment should have answered the question of whether they would attack Pú

Chạng, a fort in a high position from where French troops took control of the whole group of fortifications, or Nghĩa Lộ Subdivision, where French troops were concentrated and where the French Headquarters was located.

Lê Trọng Tấn wrote:

> After careful consideration, we decided to attack Nghĩa Lộ Subdivision because the Pú Chạng fort would not exist once the French Headquarters and main forces were destroyed. We had not expected that the French would rely on the height of Pú Chạng (or Nghĩa Lộ fort) and artillery to hold their ground. This one-sided mistake had negative impact on the 141st Regiment's combat plan.

Consequently, the two attacks on Nghĩa Lộ on the nights of October 2 and 4 failed. French troops ran away from small positions to concentrate around Nghĩa Lộ, where they cooperated with three reinforcement parachute battalions, supported by aircraft, counter-attacked the Vietnamese.

After over ten days of fighting both in primary direction of the 312th Brigade and in the secondary direction of the 141st Regiment, Vietnamese troops killed about 1,000 and captured over 200 French troops, confiscated more than 200 guns, and expanded the liberated zone from Quang Huy to the Ca Vịnh-Ba Khe-Sài Lương area and one from Phong thổ to the Bình Lư-Than Uyên area. However, the Vietnamese brigade also suffered heavy casualies. Regarding the 141st Regiment alone, about 300 soldiers including a battalion chief were killed, about 900 wounded, and 80 lost. About 100 rifles and 10 light machine-guns were not found.

After listening to Lê Trọng Tấn's report on the Lý Thường Kiệt campaign, Võ Nguyên Giáp commented that the brigade was right in their choice of the direction of attack and flexible in their response to French reinforcement paratroops. However, they should have had a detailed plan to proactively cope with subjectivism among their soldiers and difficulties in logistics in a campaign which was carried out far from their base like this. In addition, the advisory and logistical agencies of the General Headquarters should have worked out some way to help the 312th Brigade in this campaign.

Later in his memoirs, Salan appreciated the supporting role of the French air force, particularly the parachute reinforcement force, in this campaign. He wrote, "The 312th Brigade failed to concentrate its two regiments in Nghĩa Lộ as it had expected, because it had to cope with our reinforcement paratroops." After being informed of French casualties in the Nghĩa Lộ battlefield, he admitted, "It was a heavy loss that made us think about the fierceness of battles."

Apart from dealing with the issue of rescuing Nghĩa Lộ in the Northwest campaign, Salan had to cope with the unrest in the Red River Delta while de Lattre was in France. The Quang Trung campaign had caused disadvantages to the French in many parts of the Red River Delta. However, the Northwest campaign launched by Vietnamese troops after that attracted only three French parachute battalions for a short time. Therefore, during the two weeks in late September and early October, the French had conditions to concentrate their mobile forces and launch successive mopping-up operations with a view to annihilating the 42nd Regiment, destroying the Tiên-Duyên-Hưng guerilla base, improving the situation in their occupied delta area, and especially forcing local youth

Chapter Six: DETERMINATION TO HOLD THE OFFENSIVE

to join their army.¹ With such a large force, the French caused many difficulties to the Vietnamese struggle movement in the area, though they had not achieved their main goals. As Võ Nguyên Giáp later commented, in the second half of 1951, the French won great victories, which they had not ever before, on the front behind their lines.

Having heard of the French plot to mop up and pacify their temporarily-occupied areas and realized possible difficulties and complicated developments in the areas behind the French lines and the risk of guerilla zones and bases being narrowed, Commander-in-chief Võ Nguyên Giáp proposed to the Politburo a line of action in the new context. Before the Politburo convened the Second Plenum of the Party Central Committee to discuss the issues related to the areas behind the French lines, Võ Nguyên Giáp assigned the 3rd Interzone to conduct a guerilla operation for a month (from late

---

1. According to statistics of the Strategic Summarization Board under the Central Military Commission, during the Citron (Lemon) and *Mandarine* (Tangerine) mopping-up operations in Hưng Yên and Thái Bình from late September to early October 1951, the French mobilized over four mobile regiments (including about 15–18 infantry battalions), one mechanized battalion, four 105-mm artillery battalions, one sapper battalion, and thirty ships and boats. Meanwhile, in Central Việt Nam, the French used a maximum of three infantry battalions and one artillery battalion in a period from two to ten days for their mopping-up operations in Phong Điền, Quảng Điền, and Cam Lộ. In the South, only 3–4 infantry battalions with 30–65 amphibious vehicles were mobilized for raids in Cao Lãnh, Cái Bè, Đồng Tháp Mười, and Sa Đéc for a period from two to four days. Regarding the fierceness of these raids, in the Meduse raid in Thụy Anh, Thái Bình, the French captured 8,000 young men and destroyed three-fourths of fighting villages; in the Citron raid in southern Thanh Miện, they arrested 2,600 civilians and set up more 17 garrisons; in the Mandarine raid in Thái Bình, they captured 8,000 and killed 2, civilians and looted two-thirds of local buffaloes and cows.

493

September to late October) with a view to resisting French raids (mainly in the Hà-Nam-Ninh area) and preventing French troops from expanding raids to Hòa Bình and Nho Quan. He also assigned the 316th Brigade to cooperate and direct local armed forces in the midlands to promote guerilla war in Bắc Ninh and especially in Bắc Giang.

After those operations finished, the Second Plenum of the Party Central Committee took place from September 27 to October 5, 1951, to discuss the direction of fighting in the areas behind the enemy lines. At the meeting, Võ Nguyên Giáp suggested dividing these areas into the temporarily-occupied and guerrilla zones. The division was based on the particular condition and situation of each zone and especially the differences in the balance of power between the two warring sides, which laid the foundation for the definition of appropriate struggle guidelines and tasks for each zone. The guerilla focused on armed struggle with a view to developing into a guerilla base while the temporarily-occupied zone gave priority to economic and political struggle. The Commander-in-chief emphasized the flexibility in applying the aforementioned guidelines and tasks, since there was no clear boundary between the two zones due to continuous changes in the balance of power between the two warring sides.

This dry season, the French Headquarters had mobilized seven mobile regiments and was promoting conscription for the establishment of a puppet army. With over 20 out of more than 160 well-equipped infantry battalions in hand, de Lattre could conduct operations to seize the strategic initiative at any time. What the Vietnamese Headquarters was most concerned about was the question of what they should do to keep and promote their strategic initiative and

Chapter Six: DETERMINATION TO HOLD THE OFFENSIVE

to make offensive operations to draw French mobile forces. At that time, making offensives to draw French mobile forces seemed to be the best strategic solution for Vietnamese forces as it would not only help to destroy French forces but also improve the worsening situation in the occupied zone. This strategic problem remained unsolved until early October 1951.

Due to difficulties in choosing the direction of attack, it was not until mid October that the Vietnamese General Staff could finalize the winter-spring combat plan to be submitted to the General Military Commission. At the Politburo meeting held on October 19 for the discussion of the direction for the campaign in the dry season of 1951, Võ Nguyên Giáp reported that after the Hà-Nam-Ninh campaign, the French, with the support from the United States, strengthened their Northern defense line,[1] conducted more than ten raids in their occupied areas throughout the country, and developed the puppet army. It was estimated that they would continue to strengthen their defense lines, carry out raids in both the occupied and guerrilla zones and prepare for large-scale raids in the Vietnamese liberated zones in order to expand their occupied zone. Therefore, General Giáp reminded Vietnamese forces to remain vigilant over the Hòa Bình-Thanh Hóa direction and particularly the Thái Nguyên-Lạng Sơn one. On the Vietnamese side, all the five infantry brigades and three independent regiments had been strengthened, and their tactical and technical knowledge and skills had been improved but unequally. There was concern about the enemy's newly-built fortifications and fighting

---

1. From northern Hà Đông (close to the 9th Route) to Sơn Tây, Việt Trì, Lục Nam, Đông Triều, Quảng Yên, and Tiên Yên.

in the daytime among cadres. There was still a shortage of grenades, bayonets, and explosive. Winter was coming but blankets were still insufficient. Regarding the direction of the campaign in the dry season of 1951, after analyzing advantages and disadvantages of each direction in the Northern battlefield,[1] Võ Nguyên Giáp suggested launching the campaign in the Hữu Ngạn (right river bank)-3rd Interzone direction, in coordination with forces in the midlands, Bình-Trị-Thiên area, and Tả Ngạn (left river bank), with a view to annihilating enemy forces, promoting guerilla war, courting the people's support, and destroying the puppet army.

On November 9 and 10, the Central Military Commission held a meeting to discuss the implementation of the dry season plan, which had been approved by the Politburo. After analyzing the situations of both warring sides, the Central Military Commission concluded that in order to implement the combat guideline of Vietnamese regular forces in the North proposed by the Central Party Committee at its

---

1. In the Northwest direction, French troops (the majority of whom were puppet troops) were dispersedly arranged and their fortifications were not strengthened. When attacked, they might quickly withdraw, so the Vietnamese could not use their big forces to annihilate big enemy forces. In the midland direction, the French defense line was the strongest. Given the narrow terrain in the area behind the French lines and poorly-equipped troops, the Vietnamese could hardly launch mobile battles or attack French fortifications. In the Northeast direction, French troops were arranged into a defense line, but their fortifications were quite solid, the transportation system was not conducive to supplies, and the people's bases were weak. In the Hữu Ngạn-3rd Interzone direction, the French fortifications were still weak and far away from their bases; the battlefield was large and conducive for both attacks on fortifications and mobile battles. However, the terrain was divided by many rivers, so it was hard for troop movement and supply transportation. If the French attacked Hòa Bình, the Vietnamese would have good chance to kill them.

Chapter Six: DETERMINATION TO HOLD THE OFFENSIVE

Second Plenum, they needed to implement the guideline of mobile guerilla war, which was most appropriate to the present situation.

Regarding the specific combat techniques in the areas behind the French lines, the meeting judged that in the Hữu Ngạn-3rd Interzone, the French were disposed thinly but solidly outside, loosely but thickly outside. So it would be hard to attack them both from the front and back. Therefore, it was advisable for the Vietnamese to launch guerilla attacks which were small in size but sure of victory.

Although the combat plan had been approved by the Politburo, General Giáp had not felt secure because two Vietnamese brigades would have to dispose their troops in a large area in the 3rd Interzone, so it would be hard for them to kill many enemy troops. What would happen if the six Vietnamese brigades did not win any decisive victory? But November had come and there was no better way, so this plan was the only choice for Vietnamese troops.

On the night of November 14, no sooner had Head of the General Department of Politics Nguyễn Chí Thanh, who was assigned to organize a Party committee to direct the campaign in the 3rd Interzone, and Vice Head of the Operational Department Đỗ Đức Kiên set off for the delta when they heard that the French had launched a large-scale operation in the Chợ Bến-Hòa Bình direction. A strategic event occurred in the combat of wits and power between the Vietnamese and French commands. That the French would attack the liberated zone of Hòa Bình had been predicted and presented by General Giáp in his report at the Politburo meeting held one month earlier. This operation was later revealed in Salan's memoirs to have originated from a letter from Paris.

After his trips for seeking aids, de Lattre returned to Sài Gòn on October 11. Shortly afterwards, a large-scale parade was held to welcome General Joseph Lawton Collins, who served as American Army Chief of Staff from 1949 to 1953, to Sài Gòn. De Lattre directly hosted this welcome ceremony in return for the considerate treatment he received from the American government during his stay in New York and Washington. After this ceremony, he hoped to receive more military aids from the United States. After Collins left Sài Gòn, Salan noticed many changes in de Lattre. The death of his son and the recurrence of his cancer seemed to make him tired and depressed. He frequently showed concern over the coming dry season and the operations of his opponent.

In early November, de Lattre flew to the North to commend and encourage the French air force and combat units in Nghĩa Lộ, inspect the building of defense lines, and urge the organization of more puppet units and the foundation of mobile divisions. He expected that nothing would happen before these big projects were completed, when he could decide whether to attack the Việt Minh zone or cope with the operations launched by his opponent. On the afternoon of November 4, de Lattre received a letter from Paris which urged him to launch an offensive and achieve a military victory. At first, he thought it was not appropriate. After a second thought, however, he found that a military victory would facilitate the French Congress's approval of the 1952–1953 military budget and realize his need for reinforcement and financial support from the French government.

Salan and de Linarès were summoned to discuss with de Lattre about the implementation of Paris's plan. In which direction would the offensive be made, Thanh Hóa or Lạng

Chapter Six: DETERMINATION TO HOLD THE OFFENSIVE

Sơn? While de Lattre proposed an attack on Lạng Sơn to take revenge for the French expeditionary army, de Linarès suggested attacking Hòa Bình, capital of the Mường region, to prevent Vietnamese troops from attacking the Đáy River defense line and separating the Red River Delta from Việt Bắc. De Linarès's suggestion was accepted and then tasks were assigned. De Linarès was entrusted with task of launching the Tulip operation in the direction of Chợ Bến to cover the hole between Hòa Bình and Phủ Lý. Salan was in charge of directly commanding a great operation called Hoa Sen (lotus) to occupy the Hòa Bình-Đà River-6th Route.

On November 10, the Swallow radio station and the press in Hà Nội and Sài Gòn told the news that the Tulip operation had ended successfully and that Vietnamese troops had been totally defeated. Four days later, a French army including fifteen infantry, three parachute, two armored, and two sapper battalions and two naval units were divided into two "wings" to attack Hòa Bình. The northern wing from Sơn Tây-Trung Hà followed the road and waterway to Đá Chông and Tu Vũ Hamlets, while the southern one from Xuân Mai followed the 6th Route to Hòa Bình Town. The targets along the Đà River and the 6th Route were defeated by French troops so quickly that General Jean Marchand later wrote, "The French could occupy a large mountainous area along the Đà River stretching to as far as Hòa Bình without fighting." At that time, Western reporters who were urged by de Lattre to follow the operation made headlines on front pages like "The Hòa Bình operation is a big gamble and a short gun of de Lattre's at the enemy's heart." On November 15, de Lattre announced in a press conference in Hà Nội that he had caught Việt Minh. The following day, he and Salan flew to Hòa Bình to encourage their troops and warn them of the coming task. De Lattre said, "The hard time is coming. You must get ready for a fight against Việt Minh troops." Four days later, he returned to France for his cancer treatment.

After hearing that French troops had launched an attack in the Chợ Bến-Hòa Bình direction, the Vietnamese General Headquarters was overwhelmed by a bustling atmosphere. It was strange that everyone there became excited when Hòa Bình, an area of strategic significance, was invaded and the Việt Bắc base was isolated from the plain area. It was because their concern over the strategic direction of attack over the last months had been eased. Immediately, General Giáp called Head of the General Department of Politics Nguyễn Chí Thanh back and suggested Chief of the General Staff Hoàng Văn Thái consider a change in the direction of attack in accordance with the new situation. The next morning, he convened a Central Military Commission meeting. Before the meeting started, he excitedly repeated President Hồ Chí Minh's comment on the French offensive on Hòa Bình. The President wrote, "Formerly we had to lure them out. Now they've presented themselves for us to strike. It's a good chance for us." Then Giáp added, "It's true that de Lattre has given us a golden chance to kill his troops and improve the current situation in the temporarily-occupied zone."

So what should be done to take advantage of de Lattre's strategic mistake? Hoàng Văn Thái reported two different opinions among the staff members. Most of them agreed on the launching of an operation in the Hòa Bình direction because the battlefield was suitable with Vietnamese troops' fortes. There, they could easily surround and divide enemy troops, move around, and receive supplies from the nearby rear. They suggested conducting the operation soon, before the French reinforced their defense system. Some people argued that they should not launch the operation in that direction for fear that the French might have set a trap there to lure Vietnamese regular forces.

The meeting came to a conclusion that de Lattre wanted to regain the initiative. With this offensive, he wanted to exert a political impact on Paris and Washington caused more difficulties to Vietnamese troops. However, that he moved a great force out of the bunker defense line and established a long, unplanned one in the mountainous and forested battlefield gave Vietnamese forces a good chance to open a large-scale operation, annihilate French troops in the main direction, and promote the struggle in the areas behind the enemy lines. Finally, the Central Military Commission agreed to propose to the Politburo and President Hồ Chí Minh the plan of launching an operation in the Hòa Bình direction. In a letter dated November 15 to President Hồ Chí Minh, General Secretary Trường Chinh, and other members of the Party Central Committee, Võ Nguyên Giáp reported that the Vietnamese Headquarters had predicted an operation by French troops but underestimated its feasibility. They had also planned to change the direction of attack in case it occurred. Specifically, they would focus forces to annihilate French troops in the Hòa Bình battlefield and promote guerilla war. Hòa Bình was the important political center of the Mường community, so the liberation of this province would be of military, political, and economic significance. Besides, that part of the French mobile force was moved out of their bunker defense line would facilitate the development of the guerilla war in particular and the struggle in the temporarily-occupied plain areas in general.

While waiting for an official decision from the Politburo, the logistical board sent its staff to southern Phú Thọ to do research and set up a depot system; the advisory board convened a meeting to assign preliminary tasks to the 308th, 312th, and 316th Brigades and Việt Bắc Interzone, and asked the 312th Brigade being in the Northwest to quickly move southwards and prepare the battlefield, protect the supply base and logistical transportation route, and send a unit to Hòa Bình who would cooperate with local soldiers in Phú Thọ to closely follow, disturb, and grind down the enemy's strength.

On November 18, the Central Military Commission held an official meeting to evaluate the current situation and check the preliminary preparations made by the General Headquarters' agencies. It was judged that Vietnamese troops would have a better chance to annihilate enemy troops in this battlefield than in the previous ones. It was also stressed that Vietnamese troops should take advantage of the enemy's weaknesses to step up guerilla war in the enemy-occupied areas and expand their revolutionary bases in the areas behind the enemy lines. If Vietnamese troops operated actively both inside and outside the enemy-occupied areas and cooperated well with each other, they would make the most use of this chance to grind down the enemy's strength, promote guerilla war, and failed the enemy's plot of occupying and reinforcing the areas behind their lines. To realize this plan, the Central Military Commission sent Head of the Operational Department Hà Văn Lâu to the 320th and 304th Brigades and the 3rd Interzone Command to disseminate the policy of establishing the Provisional Steering Committee led

Chapter Six: DETERMINATION TO HOLD THE OFFENSIVE

by Commander and Political Commissar of the 320th Brigade Văn Tiến Dũng. This committee was tasked to mobilize forces to closely follow and annihilate enemy troops along the 6th Route, maintain the people's spirit and bases, and promote military activities in Chợ Bến. The Campaign Party Committee highlighted the importance of taking time to annihilate enemy troops and crush their plan to take control of Hòa Bình. At that time, the French were strengthening their defense lines. If the Vietnamese did not speed up their activities, they would encounter more difficulties. Moreover, if they were subjective and were not active, flexible, and proactive in fighting against enemy troops, they would miss this golden chance. One of the problems that Vietnamese troops should solve immediately was related to logistics. Specifically, it was necessary to promptly change the direction of developing the depot system from the Bắc Ninh-Bắc Giang-Phú Thọ area to the Đà River-6th Route area, covering the "white-belt" areas such as Trung Hà on the 89th, 87th, and 21st Routes.

Hoàng Văn Thái and Nguyễn Chí Thanh set off as soon as the meeting ended.

On November 20, 1951, the General Headquarters issued the 1st Combat Order, assigning tasks to brigades in the midland and Hòa Bình Front directions. The order clearly stated the guidelines of the General Headquarters[1]—taking

---

1. The 312th Brigade would spread its activities from Hòa Bình Town to Trung Hà, along the Đà River; the 316th Brigade and 246th Regiment would coordinate with local soldiers in Bắc Ninh and Bắc Giang to launch guerilla war; the 176th Regiment would be stationed in Lạng Sơn and Lộc Bình to prevent French troops from attacking the 4th Route; the 308th Brigade would be stationed in Phú Thọ to continue its military training and get ready to fight.

time to annihilate enemy troops and liberate Hòa Bình and taking advantage of the enemy's weaknesses to promote guerilla war, develop revolutionary bases, and fail the enemy's plan to exploit Vietnamese human and material resources in their temporarily-occupied areas.

The 312th Brigade achieved the first feat of arms in this dry season. On November 24, the brigade had just arrived in Phục Cổ (Yên Lập, Phú Thọ) when it received the news that a French battalion had just left the Northwest for Thu Cúc, Lai Đồng, to destroy local crops and drive local residents into their temporarily-occupied zone. Head of the 312th Brigade Lê Trọng Tấn reported the situation to Lê Chí Thanh and was allowed by the latter to carry out an offensive against this battalion. Fifty French troops were captured in this offensive.

On November 30, Võ Nguyên Giáp went to the Campaign Headquarter based in Đồng Lương, Cẩm Khê, Phú Thọ, to attend a Campaign Party Committee meeting held on the following day to approve the combat plan. It was reported by Vietnamese scouts that the French had strengthened their occupied zone and divided it into two subzones: the Hòa Bình-6th Route subzone and the Đà River subzone. Their two defense lines were established in La Phù-Đan Thê and Tu Vũ-Núi Chẹ. The Campaign Party Committee realized that the Tu Vũ-Núi Chẹ defense line was weaker because it was isolated from the Sơn Tây and Trung Hà bases. To rescue or support it, French reinforcements had to follow the 87th Route or a waterway along the Đà River. The Tu Vũ and Núi Chẹ forts were closely related to each other. Núi Chẹ served as the fire-power battlefield and logistical base of Tu Vũ while Tu Vũ served as a screen for Núi Chẹ. However, they were separated by the river. Therefore, the

Chapter Six: DETERMINATION TO HOLD THE OFFENSIVE

Campaign Party Committee decided focus forces to open an attack on the Đà River defense line with Tu Vũ and Núi Chẹ being the first targets and annihilate enemy reinforcements both on land and on the river. Meanwhile, the guerilla war in the areas behind the enemy lines was actively promoted. The fortification-attacking and reinforcement-annihilating tactics was also applied in the Hòa Bình-Đà River-6th Route battlefield. Vietnamese troops were directed to finish the battle within one night and get ready to fight the following day. They were also ordered to get prepared to fight against French reinforcements of different arms and take every opportunity to annihilate them at night.

Another meeting was held the following day to disseminate to cadres involved in the campaign the Campaign Party Committee's combat instructions as follows:

The 308th Brigade was ordered to attack Tu Vũ and French reinforcements on land and on the Đà River from Tu Vũ to Hòa Bình. The 102nd Regiment was stationed in Cổ Tiết, Phú Thọ, to cooperated with local armed forces to get prepared to prevent French troops from invading Hạc Trì, Lâm Thao, Hưng Hóa; therefore, the task of attacking Tu Vũ was assigned to the 88th Regiment.

The 312th Brigade was in charge of attacking Núi Chẹ and coordinating with the 308th Brigade to attack Tu Vũ, destroying French reinforcements in the Sơn Tây-Đá Chông-Trung Hà direction. The 312th Brigade assigned its 209th Regiment to attack Núi Chẹ.

The 304th Brigade was responsible for stopping French forces in Hòa Bình Town and attacking French troops on the 6th Route.

Although the 88th Regiment (of the 308th Brigade) failed to destroy the Chùa Cao fortification in the previous campaign, it was still considered to be experienced in attacking reinforcements, so it was assigned to start this campaign with its attack on Tu Vũ, an important position controlled by a battalion and a detachment of three tanks on the left bank of the Đà River. After the meeting, General Giáp had a private talk with Chief of the 88th Regiment Thái Dũng and Political Commissar Đặng Quốc Bảo. He said:

> The Campaign Party Committee had considered carefully before assigning this task to you. We believe that you can do it. Remember that you have to win this battle at any cost. There will be lots of difficulties and you have to be determined to overcome them. Once you have, you'll become much stronger.

An unexpected event occurred to the first battle. The 209th Regiment was given an unscheduled task, so it could not attack Núi Chẹ while the 88th Regiment attacked Tu Vũ as planned. The Vietnamese Headquarters immediately reinforced the 88th Regiment with a battalion from the 36th Regiment and ordered artillery to repress French artillery in Núi Chẹ to cover the 88th Regiment during its attack on Tu Vũ. For the late arrive of mountain artillery, the Tu Vũ battle did not start until 2 am on December 11, 1951. After many hours of waiting, the late attack still took French troops by surprise. But they fought back fiercely with the support of artillery fire-power from Núi Chẹ which formed a fire fence stopping Vietnamese troops' advance. The battle got fierce right from the beginning and did not end until dawn. A small number of French troops fled to an ait in the middle of the river. The battle was reported to be successful, but the death-toll of the 88th Regiment was rather high, mainly due to French artillery.[1] After this battle, General Giáp had a an inspection trip to the newly-liberated area of Tu Vũ. He said to Hoàng Văn Thái and Nam Hà, Chief of Staff of the 88th Regiment that, it was necessary to draw lessons from this battle for the following ones in the midland and plain areas. In a letter dated December 10, General Giáp praised the soldiers of the 88th Regiment and encouraged them to learn from this battle to gain more victories in the autumn-winter campaign, contributing to crushing the enemy's plot.

Only when the conference for a preliminary summing-up of the first phase took place could the 88th Regiment understand why the 209th Regiment of the 312th Brigade had not attacked Núi Chẹ as planned. Two days before the campaign started, an unexpected event occurred and led to a change in the combat plan to match the new situation. On the afternoon of December 8, the 209th Regiment was promptly preparing for its attack on Núi Chẹ when it was ordered to cope with a French mopping-up operation in Ninh Mít, where the Sơn Tây Provincial Party Committee was based. (The 312th Brigade Headquarters was also based in Dốc Bộp, Ninh Mít.) Chief of the 312th Brigade Lê Trọng Tấn immediately ordered the 209th Regiment to cross the river before 2 am on December 9. When the regiment arrived in Ninh Mít, men were sent out on reconnaissance. The regiment was ordered to get ready to resist the French raid and to attack Núi Chẹ as planned. After receiving the news that the 4th Mobile Regiment of the French army was launching an operation code-named Jasmine in the southern Ba Vì direction, General Giáp ordered the 312th

---

1. Salan later wrote in his memoirs that the French artillery fired 5,000 shells to support "a defense battle which deserves to be one of the greatest events in the military history of France."

Brigade to coordinate with local forces to get ready to fight against French troops heading Chúc Village from Núi Chẹ and Sơn Tây Town. The battle between the 209th and 141st Regiment of the Vietnamese army and the 1st Parachute Battalion and the 4th Mobile Regiment of the French army with the support of French artillery from Đá Chông and Núi Chẹ started at 7 am on December 9. After four days of fighting in tense conditions (both the Headquarters of the 312th Brigade and 209th Regiment were within the range of French artillery), Vietnamese troops destroyed the 1st and 5th Parachute Battalions, one battalion, and one mechanized platoon. The French Headquarters was forced to end this raid and withdrew most of its troops to Trung Hà and the rest to Núi Chẹ. On December 15, the 312th Brigade received a congratulatory letter from General Giáp for its achievement in southern Ba Vì.

The news of Vietnamese troops' victories in Tu vũ and Ninh Mít came nearly at the same time as that of the 320th Brigade's deep penetration into the area behind the French lines in Kim Sơn, Phát Diệm. After receiving the 320th Brigade's report on the outcome of its fighting from December 9–15 (thousands of enemy troops belonging to the battalions of the North African Regiment and the 1st and 18th puppet battalions were killed), General Giáp wrote a letter to praise the cadres and soldiers of the 320th Brigade and thank the Catholic community in Phát Diệm for having supported Việt Minh soldiers. It was also reported at that time that on December 9–10, Salan approved de Linarès's proposal to send two parachute battalions to Phát Diệm to cope with the Vietnamese forces who had penetrated into this Catholic region. De Linarès and a French colonel immediately flew to

Nam Định. There he ordered the colonel to stay to direct the combat and then flew to Tông, Sơn Tây, to listen to Colonel Dodelier, commander of the Đà River subzone, report on the failure of the 1st Battalion in Tu Vũ.

Having cooperated in a timely manner with the front battlefield, the 98th and 174th of the 316th Brigade in the midland direction promptly penetrated into the area behind the French lines in Bắc Ninh, destroyed the Thừa fortification (Lang Tài), annihilated French reinforcements, and threatened the Đuống bridge and Gia Lâm Town. Thừa was the first fortification in the French newly-established bunker system to be destroyed by Vietnamese troops. The northern Red River Delta was also under threat, so Salan had to mobilized some battalions from the Northeast to protect northern Hà Nội and the 1st and 4th Mobile Regiments from Hòa Bình to cope with the 316th Brigade in Bắc Ninh. On December 21, the Vietnamese Headquarters ordered the 102nd Regiment of the 308th Brigade to cross the Đà River and cooperate with the 312th Brigade in the Ba Trại-Đồng Tâm area to attack the 1st and 4th Mobile Regiments. However, Vietnamese troops were disposed far from the route and had not understood the enemy situation, so they could annihilate only a small number of French troops and missed the change to launch a large-scale battle of movement on the 89th Route.

Apart from the target of destroying some French fortifications in the main direction of the Hòa Bình-Đà River-6th Route, the Vietnamese Headquarters found it possible to annihilate French troops in southern Ba Vì and thus ordered the 312th Brigade to send three of its battalions to Dốc Bốp, Giáp Thượng, and the 66th Regiment of the 304th Brigade from the south of the 6th Route to the Bài Stream to get ready for combat. The Vietnamese Headquarters also directed the further launching of attacks on the enemy's supply convoys on the Đà River and 6th Route to restrict their supply and reinforcement capacities and then cut off their communications on these routes. In a letter to Vietnamese units, General Giáp encouraged them to promote their tradition and experience in ambushing and attacking enemy troops moving on land and on the river gained from the dry season of 1947, fighting with the spirit and determination to turn the Đà River into the Lô River and the 6th Route into the 4th Route. The staff of the Vietnamese Headquarters noticed that General Giáp still listened to the report on Hòa Bình Town and seemed not to pay any attention to a group of fortifications being built and consolidated by the French in the town.

On both banks of the Đà River, the 84th Battalion of the 308th Brigade and the 16th Battalion of the 312th Brigade continued to ambush French canoes from Trung Hà and Hòa Bình in order to crush the French plot to maintain this most important waterway. After the 84th Battalion's ambush in Đoan Hạ and the 16th Battalion's battle in Lạc Song, this waterway was likely to be blocked. To cope with this risk, the French sent the 1st and 4th Mobile Regiments, which had been mobilized to Bắc Ninh, to southern Ba Vì to protect the Đà River defense line. Meanwhile, the Vietnamese Headquarters urged the units of the 304th Brigade on the 6th Route to continuously ambush the enemy's supply convoys, putting this waterway under frequent threat.

After five days of fighting, the Vietnamese Headquarters decided to end the first phase of the campaign. That day, the Central Military Commission convened a meeting to sum up the phase. After assessing the outcomes of the phase,[1] General Giáp judged that the Vietnamese victories in Tu Vũ, Ba Vì, and the 6th Route had shaken the enemy's defense system, threatened their supply route on the Đà River, and directly affected their plan to control Hòa Bình. Their failures in Phát Diệm and Trung Du showed that they had been taken by surprise and had responded to the Vietnamese attacks confusedly. These failures also meant that the French suffered a shortage of troops to respond to the simultaneous attacks conducted by Vietnamese forces both in the primary and coordinative battlefields, both inside and outside the French defense lines.

At a meeting held on December 15 in preparation for the second phase, General Giáp repeated the Central Military Commission meeting's comments on the first phase, reviewed Vietnamese forces and capacities, and then clearly stated the policy of taking advantage of time to conduct immediate and continuous activities simultaneously in the 6th Route, Ba Vì, and the Đà River to grind down the enemy's strength, attract their mobile forces, facilitate the coordination between battlefields, and promote guerilla war in the areas behind the enemy lines. He also emphasized the importance of supporting local soldiers in the 6th Route and Sơn Tây. The fortification-attacking and reinforcement-annihilating tactics was still applied in this phase. It was realized in ambushes, surprise attacks, acts of sabotage, deep attacks into the areas behind the enemy lines, attacks on small fortifications and

---

1. In the North Vietnamese battlefield, Vietnamese troops destroyed 23 companies, most of whom were European and African. In the Đà River- 6th Route battlefield alone, ten élite French companies were killed from December 10-14.

reinforcements, battles of movement to annihilate enemy troops in their mopping-up operations and patrols, and attacks on large fortifications and reinforcements.

While Vietnamese troops were promptly preparing for the second phase, on December 17, their Headquarters was moved to a new position in the south of Giếng Đá, nearly ten kilometers to the south of Tu Vũ. This new location was still in Yên Lập District, Phú Thọ Province.

Later, in his memoirs, Salan admitted that the French Headquarters faced a worsening situation, both in France and Indochina, both in the front battlefield and in their temporarily-occupied areas. Therefore, they had to narrow the Hòa Bình-Đà River front to cope with the coming attacks by Vietnamese troops.

De Lattre's letter dated December 16 revealed his grief and fatigue in his last days.[1] Meanwhile, Jean Letourneau, Minister of the Associated States for the French Government, was criticized for his state budget plan for Indochina War, which took many French lives. There appeared the opinion among the French Congress that the burden of Indochina should be shifted to the United Nation. To maintain the spirit of French troops before the bad news, Salan invited Bảo Đại to Hòa Bình to meet and encourage French officers and troops here.

During these days, the French supply and reinforcement routes in the Hòa Bình battlefield were still being threatened.

---

1. This was his last letter to Salan. Due to his worsening health, the French government appointed Salan as Acting Commander-in-chief of the French expeditionary army in Indochina on January 1, 1952. Ten days later, on January 11, de Lattre died and was honored posthumously as Marshal of the French Republic.

Within the first ten days of December, the 304th Brigade destroyed four supply and reinforcement convoys, sixty armored vehicles, and three companies on the 6th and 21st Routes. After the French naval force's "intolerable" losses in ships and boats on the waterway, especially after the 36th Regiment's ambush on December 22 which sank a French transportation convoy on the Lạc Song-Đồng Việt river section, Salan decided to stop using the waterway for transport and rely totally on the 6th Route from Hà Nội to Hòa Bình via Hà Đông and Xuân Mai. So Vietnamese troops, as the Western press put it, succeeded in cutting off the "wet gullet" of the French army.

The outcomes of the Vietnamese army's activities, which were small in size but regular and smooth, in the second phase in the Ba Vì-Chợ Bến direction, especially those of the 326th and 320th Brigades in Bắc Ninh and Bắc Giang and on the right bank of the Red River, proved the effectiveness and creativity of the Vietnamese Headquarters' policy on the combined operation between the front battlefield and the areas behind the enemy lines. The waterway was blocked; the French groups of fortifications in Hòa Bình Town was isolated and relied only on the 6th Route for supplies and reinforcements. Besides, Vietnamese troops' simultaneous activities in late 1951 forced the French not only to shuttle their 1st and 4th Mobile Regiments between the two battlefields (one at the front and the other in the areas behind the French lines) but also to involve the 3rd and 7th Mobile Regiments from the plain area in this campaign. Salan later admitted that the French Headquarters became confused in the face of the situation which was turning unfavorable to French troops. During the last days of 1951, while Salan was looking toward a peaceful Christmas and a happy New Year's Day, Vietnamese troops made successive attacks everywhere, even on unexpected fortifications like Đá Chông. He revealed later that in the stuffy atmosphere of the New Year's Eve, a piece of news sowed in him an infinite sadness: Lieutenant Henri Leclerc was killed on the night of January 3, 1952, in a violent attack by Vietnamese troops in Ninh Bình.

It was a strange coincidence that the sons of two French commanders-in-chief, Leclerc and de Lattres, lost their lives in the Đáy River.

Before entering the third phase, General Giáp provided a detailed analysis of the French situation in the three areas in the main battlefield.[1] He said that Vietnamese troops had favorable conditions when fighting in the Hòa Bình-6th Route, but the enemy situation might change and become complicated sooner than expected. In addition, Vietnamese troops would have to deal with difficulties in supply. Therefore, the Vietnamese Headquarters decided to move southwards and choose the Hòa Bình-6th Route direction as the primary one and the Núi Chẹ-Đá Chông and northern Ba Vì directions as the supporting ones. The general task of Vietnamese troops in the third phase was to grind down the enemy's strength and attract and contain their forces, so that the Vietnamese battlefields in the coordinate directions and in the areas behind the enemy lines could develop favorably. The issue of liberating land had not been mentioned. The fortification-attacking and reinforcement-annihilating tactics was still applied in this phase, but it was required to be applied flexibly.

---

1. They included the Bãi Bằng-Yên Lệ (from southern Ba Vì to the Đà River, close to Hòa Bình and the 6th Route), Núi Chẹ-Đá Chông (northern Ba Vì), and Hòa Bình-6th Route areas.

Chapter Six: DETERMINATION TO HOLD THE OFFENSIVE

Upon realizing the important role of coordinative battlefields in this phase, Hoàng Văn Thái was sent to the Vietnamese General Headquarters by the Campaign Party Committee to report the situation to President Hồ Chí Minh and the Party Central Committee. He was also assigned to take charge of the direction of coordinative battlefields. When giving Thái this task, General Giáp stressed that the midland and right-bank battlefields had to actively cooperate with the main battlefield and get prepared to resist French mopping-up operations. Meanwhile, the left-bank battlefield needed further support. The 320th Brigade should send a regiment to this battlefield to help soldiers there launch a guerilla war and overcome difficulties, especially those in weaponry.

Before this phase, General Giáp was most concerned about how to minimize Vietnamese troops' loss caused by French artillery. Since the 18th Route campaign, the French had used artillery as their main trick to stop Vietnamese troops' advance. He raised this matter for the advisory board to consider. The suggested launching an assault on the French artillery positions in Hòa Bình. This task was then given to the 41st Company of the 36th Regiment, which gained experience from the attack on Cẩm Lý in the previous year. With support from other battalions of the 36th Regiment, the 41st Company made prompt and specific preparations for this attack. The 36th Regiment Command enthusiastically helped this company with preparation for a week, so that the battle could end after an hour. Before setting of, Head of the 41st Company Chu Tấn read aloud General Giáp's encouragement letter, which ended with these words: "I do believe that you will satisfactorily complete this task." On the night of January 7, 1952, 40 brave soldiers—neatly equipped, well prepared mentally and technically and tactically, commanded by Chu Tấn, and supported by other units—excellently fulfilled the given task, destroying four 105-mm guns, annihilating one French company, and seizing the commanding officer of the French artillery.

While the opening attack stroke the French with consternation, the following attacks on the Pheo (by the 102nd Regiment of the 308th Brigade) and Đầm Huống (by the 66th Regiment of the 304th Brigade) positions were not successful. Pheo was an important position on the 6th Route, about six kilometers north of Hòa Bình Town. If this fortification had been destroyed, the group of the French fortifications in the town would have been isolated and Vietnamese troops would have had chance to carry out large attacks and change the face of the campaign. Therefore, the attack on Pheo was considered the main one in the opening night of the third phase and was assigned to the 102nd Regiment, which was experienced in attacking fortifications. But why wasn't it successful?

In his memoirs titled *Trưởng thành trong chiến đấu* (literally: Growing up in Combat), Head of the 308th Brigade Vương Thừa Vũ explained the reason for this failure. He wrote:

> After victories, especially successive ones, people will get so drunk on them that they may become subjective and underestimate their enemy. Then they can see their anxiety but not their stubborn resistance. They can see their own advantages but not their own disadvantages. Before the battle, Pheo was said to be strong but could be easily defeated by the Capital Regiment. This judgment was right, but it was then followed by mistakes in the preparation for it.

Chapter Six: DETERMINATION TO HOLD THE OFFENSIVE

After a review of the battle, we concluded that we had not followed the tactics of attacking from different directions and making the most use of the tactical value of the terrain. Due to our subjectivism and carelessness in investigating and the enemy's situation, we came to a wrong assessment of the enemy. It is just like we had a wrong copy of the puzzle right from the beginning and so failed to solve it later.

In the letter sent to the Head and Party Committee of the 102nd Regiment on January 10, General Giáp wrote:

> In your first battle in Ba Trại, you didn't fulfill your task, missing the chance to kill enemy troops. In your second battle on the 6th Route, you once again failed, exerting bad impact on the development of the operation. Why was such an élite unit like you so bad this time while others were successful?
>
> Is it because your officers and soldiers were not brave enough? No, it isn't. Is it because your officers and soldiers were not prepared in terms of tactic and technique as well as they had been before? No. Is it because the battlefield and the task this time were too difficult? No.
>
> In my opinion, the officers were too complacent about their abilities that they disregard the task and become subjective and careless in planning and supervising the implementation of their plan. This is the main reason for the failure.

General Giáp also said that the Vietnamese Headquarters should take partial responsibility for the failure of the Pheo battle. Specifically, they were so confident of the brigade's tradition and the regiment's capacity and experience in attacking fortifications that they were careless in supervising and directing their agencies to follow and help the 102nd Regiment in this important battle. They had paid more attention to the 36th Regiment's attack on the French artillery in Hòa Bình Town since it was a new task and Vietnamese soldiers had to penetrate deep into the town. Therefore, the 36th Regiment was better prepared and thus satisfactorily fulfilled the task.

The failure of the attack on Pheo led to the failure of the plan of attacking French reinforcements in the third phase. According to international war reporters, however, the French troops in the Hòa Bình battlefield had fallen into a bad situation. General Salan later admitted in his memoirs that the fighting method used by Vietnamese troops both on the 6th Route and in the assault on the French artillery in Hòa Bình Town was tremendously effective. In fact, the battle during the night of the 7th to the 8th made Colonel Clement, commander of the French troops in Hòa Bình, feel tired and pessimistic. The sending of one commando parachute battalion to the town was just an immediate solution. He also admitted that French troops failed to cope with two battles at the same time. While in Hòa Bình Vietnamese troops kept attacking French positions, forcing the French Headquarters to send more mobile forces to rescue and then suffer heavy losses, in the French temporarily-occupied zone the 316th and 320th Brigades coordinated with local forces to incessantly sabotage the French rear stretching from the Red River Delta to the midlands. On the French side, the 1st, 3rd, 4th, and 7th Mobile Regiments had to change their areas of operation frequently. No sooner had they been mobilized from Hòa Bình to the inner defense line for rescue than they were ordered to immediately move from the midland and delta areas to the 6th Route. General de Linarès frankly admitted to General Salan that such prolonged pressure and troop

Chapter Six: DETERMINATION TO HOLD THE OFFENSIVE

mobilization were intolerable. The latter found it necessary to narrow the range of French garrisons to create more reserve forces which could be quickly turned into mobile forces to carry out operations on the 6th Route and then in the delta, where the 316th and 320th Brigades were ceaselessly causing French troops heavy losses.

According to General Salan's observation, Vietnamese troops were aiming at not only the 6th Route but also an airport in Hòa Bình Town in order to prevent the French air supply route. The protection of the 6th Route alone involved the participation of 16 French battalions. It was "an intolerable thing when the French troops were getting stunted, unsystematic, and incompetent to undertake simultaneously different tasks awaiting inside their defense lines." It resulted in General Salan's decision made on January 17 to withdraw all French troops from the Hòa Bình-6th Route battlefield, first narrowing their occupied zone in the Đà River direction, making step-by-step preparations, and then secretly and quickly withdrawing their entire force of more than 20 thousand troops to the inner bunker defense line. Regarding to this decision, Salan said, "Hòa Bình has fulfilled its task, and there is no reason for me to maintain this position." The French had highly appreciated the important role of Hòa Bình when making an attack on it in mid November, but now they decided to run away from the entire Đà River-6th Route area for the reason that Hòa Bình was no longer significant strategically, politically, or militarily.

This plan started with the withdrawal of all French fortifications from the Đà River subdivision to Hòa Bình and the 6th Route and the shift from offensive to defense with a view to protecting this route from being cut off by

Vietnamese troops. Another important thing that should be done immediately was the replacement of the commander of the Hòa Bình subdivision. Ducourneau was ordered to replace Clement, who was said to have been so "confused and demoralized." Because the Hòa Bình airport had been occupied by Vietnamese troops, preventing all aircraft from taking off, Ducourneau had to parachute to a location close to the French Headquarters on January 17. Colonel Gilles was assigned to plan and direct the withdrawal of French troops from Hòa Bình. During the first three weeks of February, French army facilities were transferred to Hà Nội via the 6th Route safely and smoothly. On February 10, Salan held a meeting to make an announcement in order to deceive the Vietnamese. When he was asked about the prospect of the war in Indochina, he said to reporters, "We have controlled Hòa Bình and we have no intention to let them kick us out of that place." Later, Salan revealed that this utterance made the reporters confused about the French Headquarters' intention (to withdraw). Then he explained, "I had to keep secrets to avoid a clash with Vietnamese brigades and I would certainly have to pay a heavy price for this." During a week starting from mid February to the date of withdrawal, the French conducted continuous mopping-up operations the area between Pheo Hamlet and Bến Ngọc to create a corridor connecting their 6th Route defense line with Hòa Bình Town. To limit the Vietnamese ambushes for road and bridge destruction, over ten French battalions supported by artillery were ordered to occupy some heights on the Ao Trạch-Hàm Voi road section. As the French press commented, the French made every effort and used every measure to "revitalize the 6th Route." On the late afternoon of February 22, the French withdrawal plan, which was codenamed Amarante, started with the movement of five battalions from Hòa Bình Town to the right bank of the Đà River.[1]

On the Vietnamese side, in early January 1952, the Chief of the General Staff sent a letter from the rear to convey President Hồ Chí Minh and the Party Central Committee's opinions on the direction of the coming activities. The letter read:

> The Party Central Committee and President Hồ Chí Minh approve the Campaign Headquarters' policy on the third phase and emphasize that:
>
> First, it is basically our military failure after the French attack on Hòa Bình. We've temporarily lost Hòa Bình, but that we've recovered the areas behind the enemy lines is a great victory.
>
> Second, our activities for the time being should aim at sabotaging the enemy's transport routes and containing and surrounding Hòa Bình. We should attack only when there are favorable conditions. Otherwise, let our troops rest and avoid using many forces in battles of attrition which may tire them.
>
> Last, it is not necessary to start this phase in January 1952. If possible, we can prolong it to keep our regular forces in this direction, creating favorable conditions for the consolidation of our areas behind the enemy lines. President Hồ Chí Minh also recommends that we should make a plan to develop our military and political positions in case of the enemy's withdrawal from Hòa Bình.

---

1. Hòa Bình Town was formerly situated on the left bank of the Đà River, by Mount Ba Vành. According to the Amarante plan, after crossing the river, French troops would pass different positions on their way, including Bến Ngọc, Pheo Hamlet, Đồng Bến, Ao Trạch, Đèo Kẽm, Mộ Thôn, and Xuân Mai.

Apparently, the Party Central Committee and President Hồ Chí Minh had also predicted the withdrawal of French troops. Thus the policy proposed by the Campaign Headquarters accorded with the direction from the Party Central Committee and President Hồ Chí Minh. According to this policy, Vietnamese regular forces had launched small but varied attacks to annihilate enemy troops in Hòa Bình Town and on the 6th Route since early January. Having learned from the experience gained in the battle on the 7th, several days later, a commando team of the 36th Regiment secretly penetrated deep into the town and destroyed French aircraft on the airport with explosive charges. To threaten the French supply lines by land and by air, Vietnamese troops launched ambushes aiming at their supply convoys, surrounded the town, frequently sabotaged and disturbed French troops on the 6th Route, and took control of the airport with artillery. All these activities contributed to the isolation of the French group of fortifications in the town. On average, Vietnamese troops made a small- or medium-size attack, annihilated part of French forces, and destroyed several motorized vehicles (sometimes including an aircraft) every three days.

After three weeks of small-size operation, on January 27 or the Lunar New Year's Day, the Vietnamese Headquarters decided to end the third phase.

On January 30, after reviewing the two months of operation, General Giáp assessed the enemy's situation and predicted their coming plan. He said:

> Despite their efforts, the French were increasingly confused and passive in responding to our attacks. Obviously, they had been surprised by our strong attacks on both fronts for quite a long time. They faced numerous difficulties

and failures in response: they were forced to leave their Đà River defense line; Hòa Bình Town was strongly attacked and surrounded; the 6th Route was attacked and cut off; the areas behind their lines were threatened; a great number of their troops, especially in Hòa Bình, Bắc Ninh, Thái Bình, and Nam Định were annihilated.

Their situation was made worse by new difficulties, including the death of General de Lattre, the crisis of the French cabinet,[1] and the rise of Tunisian people's revolutionary movement. Letourneau and Valluy had to immediately fly to Việt Nam to investigate the situation and find solutions to cope with it.

The French are curently stuck between the requirements of the battlefields and the military and political demands.

As a general trend, they will have to withdraw from Hòa Bình, whether they liked it or not. At present, there is a lot of evidence that they are withdrawing or trying to make a quick retreat. However, they are likely to hold on to Hòa Bình for a short time because they still have difficulties in the organization of a retreat or some political reasons, or they realize that we still have some weaknesses that prevent us from destroying them right now.

On February 1, in an order to Vietnamese units, General Giáp clearly stated that they should try to hinder the withdrawal of French troops because the slower it was, the more challenges they would have to face both on the main front and in the areas behind their lines. He also emphasized that Vietnamese troops should seek

---

1. In late January and early February 1952, the Pleven cabinet collapsed and René Pleven was succeeded by Edgar Faure. This was the 16th cabinet of France since the French returned to Indochina. However, the Faure cabinet only lasted for three weeks and Edgar Faure was succeeded by Antoine Pinay.

opportunities to crush this plan of withdrawal, so that the French could expose their weaknesses and thus easily be destroyed by Vietnamese troops.

According to the plan proposed by the Advisory Board, two-thirds of each Vietnamese unit would enter the period of consolidation and reorganization, but they should be ready to fight (and cooperate with reinforcements to annihilate enemies when the chance came). The rest would continue fighting to grind down the enemy's strength little by little, surround and make surprise attacks on the town to destroy roads and bridges, and promote the propaganda and mobilization among enemy troops. Once having detected French troops withdrawing, Vietnamese troops should promptly ambushed to destroy part of them. It was clearly stated in the Vietnamese Headquarters' order that Vietnamese brigades should check carefully their plan, especially their fire-power battlefield and accesses to attack and pursue enemy troops. After ten days of consolidation and reorganization, if the French did not withdraw, Vietnamese forces would promote their activities to fail their plan of withdrawal. They were also reminded to remain vigilant over the enemy's surprise acts.

At midnight on February 22, the staff of the Vietnamese Headquarters heard the repeated sounds of cannons. Then through telephone, they were informed that the French had started their withdrawal. The 36th Regiment, which was surrounding the town, was the first Vietnamese unit to attack the French troops when their last detachments were crossing the river. The withdrawal was found late. It was not until 1 am on February 23 that the scouts of the 36th Regiment detected the bright light of French headlights in Bến Mới and the sound of French canoes and vehicles moving. French troops were gradually withdrawing from their outer positions into the town. When the 36th Regiment attacked the town, it was empty and French troops, supported by artillery and aircraft, were crossing the river. Most of them had arrived at the right bank of the river. They were concentrating their air force fire-power and artillery to create a fire line to support the withdrawal, but the 36th Regiment was still determined to approach the left bank to attack the French troops who were about to cross the river. By 1:30 pm that day, the last French troops had arrived at the right bank of the Đà River.

The Hòa Bình campaign ended, failing de Lattre and the French Headquarters' plan to regain the initiative. The Vietnamese army and people completed the strategic task set for the 1951–1952 dry season. General Giáp returned to the base with satisfaction about the outcome of the campaign and concern about the coming difficulties confronting the Vietnamese soldiers and people in the areas behind the enemy lines, especially in the Red River Delta. Thousands of French troops returned to their temporarily-occupied zone, which had become unfavorable to them over the past two months.

He found that the Vietnamese army and people would have to struggle more violently in the coming spring-summer days to maintain and develop their position and strength in the areas behind the enemy lines in the face of the enemy's plot to conduct mopping-up operations.

During his journey back to the Việt Bắc base, he revealed his initial but cherished thoughts about the two months of fighting to Vice Head of the Operational Department Đỗ Đức Kiên for the latter to note down in preparation for the coming summary conference. They were new ideas of strategic guidance, fighting methodology, and command organization.

In terms of strategic guidance, over the past six years, the coordination between the front battlefield and the battlefield in the areas behind the enemy lines had been so close and effective as that in the Hòa Bình campaign. It not only facilitated Vietnamese forces to grind down the enemy's strength and force them to confusedly and passively mobilize their mobile regiments to cope with Vietnamese forces in both battlefields, but also created favorable conditions for Vietnamese people and army in the areas behind the French lines to promote guerrilla warfare while restoring, consolidating, and expanding their guerilla areas and bases. The three spring-summer campaigns held successively in the midland and plain regions and Hòa Bình confirmed an issue of strategic significance, that is, the mountainous and forested battlefield not only facilitated Vietnamese troops to restrict French troops' advantages in weapons, techniques, and reinforcement mobilization, but also enabled them to promote their fighting strengths to annihilate enemy troops and make changes of strategic significance.

In terms of fighting methodology, it was the first time the French had used the form of defense with a group of fortified positions in Indochina in a battlefield they chose themselves. The Vietnamese found that they were still unable to attack where French troops were the strongest, so they decided to isolate the group of French fortifications in Hòa Bình Town while launching strong attacks on the 6th Route and the Đà River. With this tactics, they avoided the strong point and attacked the weak point of the enemy when the latter was controlling a vast mountainous and forested area isolated from their base in the delta. This fighting method helped Vietnamese troops annihilate French troops and dug deeply into the latter's difficulties in logistics and troop mobilization in their shortage of force. New, unique, and effective fighting methods appeared not only in big attacks but also in ambushes on the road and river launched by Vietnamese troops. They not only considerably deteriorated the enemy's power in artillery fire-power and air force, but also greatly contributed to isolating and threatening the French group of fortifications.

In terms of command organization, the Hòa Bình campaign brought the Vietnamese General Headquarters' bodies new experience in organizing a large-scale campaign in a place far away from their rear, especially that in logistical organization. Before the campaign took place, none of them had expected to gain such valuable experience from the two months of fighting.

The Hòa Bình campaign was actually a large-scale and comprehensive rehearsal for the 1953–1954 winter-spring and Điện Biên Phủ campaigns, which were commanded by Commander-in-chief Võ Nguyên Giáp in cooperation with the advisory, political, and logistical bodies, and ended successfully two years later.

Maintaining the Struggle in Areas Behind the Enemy Lines

On April 1, 1952, General Salan officially became the sixth Commander-in-chief of the French expeditionary army and also the sixth opponent of General Giáp. Western press was not surprised by the fact that after the French troops' withdrawal from Hòa Bình, particularly after Salan officially became the Commander-in-chief, he seemed to be unsatisfied with Western reporters' comments on the Hòa Bình campign which he considered as "washing their dirty linen to public."

De Lattre had died already, but the operation to Hòa Bình remained a long-lasting subject for French press and generals. They saw the French attack on Hòa Bình as a big strategic mistake of the French Headquarters which was described as "a high-risk gamble in the 100-day operation." According to Bernard Fall, author of *Street without Joy*, the fact that the French concentrated their strategic mobile forces in Hòa Bình created loop-holes in other battlefields. However, the most embarrassing thing was that although the French Headquarters was aware of the "high-risk gamble," they continued to take it only because of bitterness and pressure. As a result, not only their plan to control Hòa Bình was foiled, but also their "safe rear" in the vast Red River Delta was destroyed completely. The fighting method applied by Vietnamese troops on the two fronts was a great shock that made the French confused and so-called "intolerable" by the press.

The centre of the criticism was the new French commander-in-chief. However, he did not take that criticism for the reason that he had no choice. Through the Swallow Radio of the French expeditionary army and Hà Nội and Sài Gòn press, the Vietnamese soon saw the conflicting reactions to the event of Hòa Bình after the withdrawal of French troops from the other side.

The Advisory Board of the Vietnamese General Headquarters had known General Salan well since the dry season of 1947, when he directed the French operation to Việt Bắc. He and American General Westmoreland had some things in common, especially in the assessment of the situation on both sides (both tried to persuade others to accept that the French had won and the Vietnamese had lost) after each operation of strategic significance.

In a press conference on the afternoon of February 24, 1952, when being asked about the French withdrawal from Hòa Bình, Salan stressed that it was the French who proactively withdrew from the Đà River-Hòa Bình-6th Route area instead of being forced to do so as others might think. He also drew public attention to the Vietnamese weak points by clearly stating that having seen French troops attack Hòa Bình, General Giáp wanted to launch an offenive to destroy them. However, he failed and his troops were able to isolate Hòa Bình and push French troops out of it. He also claimed that Vietnamese troops suffered a loss was three or four times as much as French troops, and that this result made Vietnamese troops too tired to make any more attack before the rainy season. He added that it would be a good chance for him to direct his troops to return to the Red River Delta, which had been abandoned by the French for their lack of forces.

These statements were made 20 years before Salan started to write his memoirs. It should be noted that he appeared more truthful in his memoirs. Regarding the number of casualties suffered by the French, he admitted that about 3,300 French troops were killed during the three months of fighting in Hòa Bình. In the withdrawal alone, 350 more troops were killed. He also concluded that the French had paid a heavy price for de Lattre's gamble. At that time he did not explain why he had stated that the occupation of Hòa Bình was a victory of strategic significance, but 20 years later he admitted that the withdrawal from Hòa Bình was a big strategic mistake since the French left had to leave an important position that they had occupied.

On the Vietnamese side, before the campaign ended, General Giáp reminded Vice Head of the Operational Department Đỗ Đức Kiên to keep watch on the situation in the Red River Delta, because the withdrawal of about 20,000 French troops to the inner defense line would cause difficulties to the Vietnamese people and army in the areas behind the French lines.

On February 25, General Giáp was arranged to visit the French group of fortifications. It was the first time he had appeared in the town and visited some of the French positions on the 6th Route which Vietnamese troops had failed to eliminate such as Đồng Bến and Pheo. Regarding this visit, he later recalled:

> In front of me appeared a new form of defense used by the French in the mountainous and forested area. It is totally different from their previous fortifications. When attacking any fortification of the system, our troops would be shot from different directions, sometimes from all the four directions. This partly accounted for our failure in the Pheo battle.

During the days following the victory of the Hòa Bình campaign, General Giáp did not expect that he would have chance to learn more about this new defense form of the French army when researching the Him Lam entrenched fortification in the Mường Thanh field over two years later, in the spring-summer of 1954. At this moment, Vietnamese regular forces were not able to cope with it in Hòa Bình Town. They should assess their victory at its true worth and draw useful lessons from the three consecutive months of fighting.

Chapter Six: DETERMINATION TO HOLD THE OFFENSIVE

On February 27, in the Order of the Day delivered in the recently-liberated Hòa Bình Town, General Giáp clearly stated the significance of the victory of the campaign. He said:

> It failed de Lattre's plan to regain the initiative and occupy the strategic position of Hòa Bình in order to cut off the North-South route and oppress the Mường community. It also considerably thwarted the enemy's strategic plan to pacify the areas behind their lines, use the Vietnamese to eliminate the Vietnamese, and use the war to raise the war in the Red River Delta.

Regarding the areas behind the enemy lines alone, he said to the leadership of the 3rd Interzone:

> It was really hard for us to solve such problems as the enemy's regional and armed administration, small- and large-scale mopping-up operations, white belts, concentration camps, and troop mobilization. Now we can solve them all quite easily. The combat ability of our local troops, militiamen, and guerilla has improved quite a lot; guerilla bases have been expanded quite fast in many localities.[1]

He also called his soldiers to draw experience from the Hòa Bình campaign while identifying the enemy's new plot in the areas behind their lines and trying to crush it. He required Vietnamese armed forces to coordinate with Vietnamese people to to form a united bloc, promote guerrilla warfare, and get prepared to cope with the enemy's mopping-up operations. Several days later, on February 29, 1952, in his speech delivered at a meeting held to instruct the summarization of the campaign, General Giáp analyzed the significance of the Hòa Bình campaign. He also added

---

1. Letter sent to Lê Thanh Nghị and Văn Tiến Dũng on January 22, 1952.

that this victory was not a complete one because many Vietnamese units missed opportunities to grind down the enemy's strength.[1] He said:

> We cannot say that "We have ground down much of the enemy's strength and successfully completed our task," because we shall be considered complacent if we make such an utterance. With the spirit of a revolutionary militant, we should admit that we have made many mistakes and thus failed to fulfill our task.... In this campaign, some units have won big victories while others have won small ones. But generally speaking, we have won a big victory. We could have won a bigger one if we hadn't made such mistakes.... We should simultaneously acknowledge the significance of the campaign and realize our mistakes to correct them. We should also avoid ourselves from being pessimistic as well as subjective and complacent.

Sine the leaders of some Vietnamese brigades had to direct and command their soldiers to fight in the areas behind the enemy lines, the summary conference was not held until early April. It was among carefully-prepared summary conferences for the appearance of new lessons on the coordination between the battlefields in front of and behind the enemy lines. Fighting the enemy in both battlefields with the close cooperation between the inside and outside of the enemy lines was an important guideline proposed by the Party Central Committee and implemented quite satisfactorily by Vietnamese troops. It was also the

---

1. According to the report by General Giáp, on the main front alone, Vietnamese forces missed opportunities to destroy the 4th Mobile Regiment in Ba Vì, two parachute battalions in Ba Trại, and the 1st Mobile Regiment mobilized to rescue the 600th peak.

main content of General Giáp's report at the conference.[1] He said:

> In the previous campaigns, we combined two battlefields, but our combat forces behind the enemy lines were mostly made up of local armed ones. There were times when regular troops were involved, but they were small in number and operated for a short time only. Therefore, the cooperation between the two battlefields was weak.

Regarding the Central Military Commission's weaknesses, he said:

> ... Before the enemy attacked Hòa Bình, the direction of the areas behind the enemy lines in general and that of the guerilla war in particular was not good. We did not keep a close watch on the situation, especially that of the enemy. Consequently, when the enemy attacked Hòa Bình, we only knew that there were loop-holes in the areas behind the enemy lines, but we didn't know exactly where they were. So our assessment and analysis of the situation was not thorough enough; our plan, especially that for our regular units to the areas behind the enemy lines, was not detailed enough. These weaknesses were overcome later.

He also pointed out that the French aimed to caused Vietnamese troops many difficulties when launching the attack on Hòa Bình, but they also revealed their weaknesses, especially in the areas behind their lines, in this attack. This time, Vietnamese troops had to fight in both battlefields and promote the close coordination between the two battlefields. If they had only attacked French troops in the

---

1. The report had five parts: 1- Experience in campaign direction; 2- Main experience in fighting tactics; 3- Main experience in political encouragement and ideological leadership; 4- The manners and thought of Vietnamese soldiers; 5- Conclusion.

front battlefield, the latter would have concentrated their forces to cope with the former and thus the former would have hardly taken advantage of the latter's loop-holes. On the contrary, if Vietnamese troops had only attacked French troops in the back battlefield, the latter would have mobilized their forces to counter-attack the former. As a result, Vietnamese troops would have hardly win and the remaining French troops in the front battlefield would have been quickly consolidated.

The French formerly thought that Vietnamese troops could only attack in one direction. This time, Vietnamese troops attacked in different directions and Vietnamese regular forces were sent to the areas behind the French lines. It took the French by surprise.

Implementing the Party Central Committee's guideline "fighting the enemy on both fronts," right from the beginning, the Central Military Commission prepared the combat plan for the front battlefield and directed the development of the guerilla war into the areas behind the enemy lines. Having a thorough grasp of the Party Central Committee's spirit, the Central Military Commission courageously sent Vietnamese regular forces to the areas behind the enemy lines and then set up machines for a united command of all armed forces. It also proposed to the Party Central Committee the establishment of steering boards for a united direction of the struggle in all aspects in each area behind the enemy lines.

General Giáp also presented experience in the direction of the coordination between the two battlefields as follows:

On the one hand, the grasp and direction of the non-fighting situation has a great impact on that of the fighting situation, so the situation should be closely followed during the non-fighting time.

On the other hand, it is necessary to send regular forces to the areas behind the enemy lines in order to fight the enemy in both battlefields and promote the close cooperation between these two battlefields. With right instructions, Vietnamese regular forces can stand firmly in the areas behind the enemy lines and win the enemy, even though they are not supported by combat forces in front of the enemy lines.

In reply to some attendees' question about the maintenance of fighting in the areas behind the enemy lines after the victory of the Hòa Bình campaign, General Giáp clearly stated that the Central Military Commission decided to leave the 316th and 320th Brigades in these areas to continue their activities such as annihilating enemy troops, maintaining the guerilla struggle movement, reinforce guerilla zones and bases, and especially help local people get prepared to cope with the enemy's mopping-up operations. It was estimated that after their failure in the Hòa Bình campaign and in the face of their disadvantages in the delta over the past months, the French Headquarters would launch large-scale mopping-up operations to improve their situation and continue their unfinished plan of Vietnamization. General Giáp confirmed that the areas behind the French lines would soon become a violent battlefield which alternated with mopping-up operations launched by French troops and anti-mopping-up ones launched by Vietnamese troops to keep and reinforce their newly-gained strategic position.

General Giáp ordered the Southern battlefields to support the areas behind the enemy lines in the Red River Delta one in the coming fight. He stressed the importance of the area behind the enemy lines south of the 4th Zone, which was a narrow and thinly-populated battlefield but played an important role in the strategic cooperation between Northern and Southern battlefields, as well as that between the Vietnamese, Cambodian, and Lao battlefields. After years of hardships, a Vietnamese regular brigade was established and soon became a vanguard in Central Việt Nam. General Giáp was very satisfied with the transformation of the 325th Brigade in the Bình-Trị-Thiên battlefield. In late 1951, when it had not received new military equipment, the 325th Brigade carried out an offensive which lasted for days in the areas behind the enemy lines in cooperation with the Hòa Bình battlefield to annihilate enemy troops, liberate some occupied areas in Bố Trạch District (Quảng Bình Province), and improve the Vietnamese situation in the north of Central Việt Nam. At the Vietnamese Headquarters, General Giáp received a report by Head of the 325th Brigade Trần Quý Hai on the brigade's initial activities. The 95th Regiment[1] of the 325th Brigade cooperated with local forces in Quảng Bình Province to kill thousands of enemy troops, leveled nearly 20 enemy posts, and liberated many communes and villages with a total population of nearly ten thousand people in Bố Trạch District. After the Hòa Bình campaign ended, the 325th Brigade received new equipment. It continued to launch offensives in the districts of Gio Linh and Quảng Trạch to expand the guerilla zones and bases in the battlefield in the areas behind the enemy lines. General Giáp highly appreciated the brigade's activities in the Bình-Trị-Thiên

---

1. Other regiments of the 325th Brigade were operating in the battlefield south of the 4th Zone or marching to Việt Bắc to receive new equipment, so most activities in the areas behind the French lines in Quảng Bình Province were conducted by the 95th Regiment and local armed forces.

Chapter Six: DETERMINATION TO HOLD THE OFFENSIVE

battlefield during and after the Hòa Bình campaign. He later recalled:

> In the summer of 1952, the 325th Brigade and the local armed forces in the Bình-Trị-Thiên battlefield made a great progress, putting an end to the dark days of this battlefield. The combined operations of the Bình-Trị-Thiên battlefields and others in the areas behind the French lines were indispensable for coping with French troops' destructive offensives on our regular units in these areas in North Việt Nam.

Salan was sometimes attracted by the Bình-Trị-Thiên battlefield in March, but his biggest concern remained the Red River Delta. As estimated by many French journalists, the organization of violet mopping-up operations to improve the French position in the areas behind their lines had become an urgent strategic demand to Salan, an event that would certainly happen.

Genreral Giáp had foreseen this, so when the Hòa Bình campaign was developing into its third phase, he thought about ways to maintain the struggle in the areas behind the enemy lines and protect newly-established guerrilla zones and bases in the Red River Delta. In a letter sent to the 3rd Interzone on January 22, he wrote:

> Victories of the guerrilla war over the past time are partly thanks to the progress of local armed forces and the support of local people, and mainly thanks to the enemy's weaknesses and the combined operations and support of regular forces.
>
> Besides this progress, there are still many weaknesses that should be immediately overcome. For example, the political bases have not kept pace with military victories; there is still a big gap between our local troops, militiamen, and guerilla and our regular troops.

Regarding the direction for guiding the struggle in the areas behind the French lines after the Hòa Bình campaign, General Giáp repeated the spirit of the Second Party Central Committee Conference on the three main tasks in these areas (public relations, propaganda among enemy troops, and guerilla war development). He also highlighted the relationship between these three tasks in the development and consolidation of the struggle movement. The task of Vietnamese troops at that time was to maintain and promoted the guerilla war. General Giáp stressed that the maintenance and promotion of the guerilla war aimed to reinforce the recently-gained victories and cope with difficulties in the future. At present, the key issue of the guerrilla war development is the guerrilla bases, the most important contents of which were the development and reinforcement of political bases (including Party bases and mass organizations), the development and strengthening of commune militiamen and guerillas, and the propaganda among enemy troops.

As soon as the first signs of the French withdrawal from the Hòa Bình battlefield were detected, in a decree titled *"Nhiệm vụ phá âm mưu mới của địch ở địch hậu"* (literally: "The Task of Crushing the Enemy's New Plot in the Areas Behind Their Lines") dated February 21, General Giáp mentioned the questions of what should be done and how to implement the guideline of combining two fronts and the three big tasks in the areas behind the enemy lines in the new context. After an analysis of difficulties confronting French troops during months of coping with Vietnamese troops on both fronts,[1] General Giáp anticipated French troops' activities after their withdrawal from Hòa Bình such as launching operations to recue some positions, reoccupy some important ones, and support areas under violent attacks by Vietnamese troops, and organizing large-scale mopping-up operations on Vietnamese guerilla bases. He assigned specific tasks to Vietnamese forces—maintaining and developing the guerilla war and mobilizing the people to struggle against the enemy, especially along the important routes (such as the 1st, 5th, 6th, and 21st Routes). He asserted that only by promoting the establishment of political bases and the guerrilla war could the Vietnamese take the initiative in foiling their enemy's plot of launching raids and policy of using the Vietnamese to fight against the Vietnamese and using the war the raise the war, as well as consolidating Vietnamese guerilla bases. Then he further analyzed French troops' strengths and weaknesses and gave instructions on the preparation for coping with their mopping-up operations, command organization, force use, and ways of fighting and preventing damages to the people.

Along with this decree, the Staff of the Vietnamese General Headquarters also sent military zones and provinces a reference document titled *"Mấy ý kiến về kế hoạch phát triển và củng cố các vùng du kích và căn cứ du kích, chuẩn bị chống giặc càn quét"* (literally: "Some Ideas on the Plan of Developing and Strengthening Guerilla

---

1. French troops' difficulties included the shortage of troops, the mental impairment after their failure in the Hòa Bình campaign and the death of de Lattre, the considerable destruction of their pacification system in the areas behind their lines, the growth of Vietnamese forces, and the stronger struggle movement of local people.

Zones and Bases and Preparing for the Fight against the Enemy's Raids").

Thus, before the end of the Hòa Bình campaign, the Vietnamese Headquarters had taken a step ahead in preparing for the next battle in the areas behind the French lines. In his letters and decrees to the delta, General Giáp always highlighted the importance of making Vietnamese people and soldiers in these areas well aware of their enemy's coming plot in order to prevent them from becoming complacent and subjective and so underestimating their enemy.

Besides directing the Vietnamese General Headquarters' bodies to closely follow and help units to conduct the summarization of the campaign and reinforce their troops, General Giáp spent a lot of time keeping watch on and directing the struggle of the Vietnamese people and soldiers in the areas behind the French lines. The newly-received shipments of aid, a puppet army being urgently built, the adjustment of forces, and the mobilization of troops from the Central Highlands to the North showed that the French were preparing for a new plot. After the withdrawal of tens of thousands of French troops from the Hòa Bình battlefield to the inner bunker defense line, the fighting in the areas behind the French lines would certainly become extremely violent. From the realities of the Quang Trung and Hòa Bình campaigns, General Giáp instructed the advisory body to consider and submit to the Party Central Committee the proposal of reorganizing the battlefield in the Red River Delta to fit the commanding and directing abilities of Vietnamese commanders, especially in the condition that the delta was becoming more and more important to both sides in the North Vietnamese battlefield and in the context as the

Chapter Six: DETERMINATION TO HOLD THE OFFENSIVE

Secretariat of the Party Central Committee pointed out in its decree dated January 26, 1952, that "Many good chances are still waiting for the Vietnamese in the areas behind the enemy lines. The French were very confused. But they're still strong and they can launch large-scale mopping-up operations on our guerilla zones and bases."[1]

The 3rd Interzone soon had a thorough grasp of the Party Central Committee's policy on maintaining and developing the guerilla war, coping with the enemy's mopping-up operations, and protecting the people's achievements in their struggle in the areas behind the enemy lines. Therefore, at the conference held in February 1952, the 3rd Interzone Party Committee proposed many specific measures to perfect Party committees at all levels and authorities at grassroots level, reinforce mass organizations, develop militia and guerilla forces, and especially promote the united leadership of guerilla zones and bases which had been recently established and expanded. The prompt application of Party and State policies, especially those on the temporary division and allotment of land to tillers, tax reduction, moratory campaign for poor peasants, and land-reclaiming and mass-education encouragement, had soon brought practical benefits to the population, most of whom were peasants.

In preparation for the fight against French troops' mopping-up operations, with the assistance of the regular units assigned to stay in the areas behind the French lines after the Hòa Bình campaign, the development of local armed forces, the building and strengthening of combat villages, and

---

1. Communist Party of Việt Nam: *Văn kiện Đảng toàn tập* (literally: The Complete Collection of Party Documents), op. cit., vol. 13, p. 23.

the dissemination of a united plan for fighting the enemy and protecting localities to all forces were conducted urgently. Never before had the plans for fighting against enemy raids been implemented so perfectly with such an uninterrupted disposition of the local people's war as they were in the summer of 1952. According to the general plan of the entire interzone, all localities were quickly involved in the organization and reinforcement of the system of combat trenches, underground hideouts, shelters for wounded soldiers, and local logistical bases. The destruction of routes where enemy tanks might run on was implemented on a large scale according to the combined operation plan for the three arms of troops in each area. The combat plan was complemented, perfected, and implemented urgently, creating favorable conditions for local people and armed forces get ready to fight the enemy.

Thanks to the intensified communication between the Vietnamese General Headquarters and the 3rd Interzone Command, all activities of French troops were studied and analyzed carefully so that Vietnamese commanders at all levels would not be taken by surprise by any of their mopping-up operations. A lot of news and events grasped by the Vietnamese General Headquarters at that time were later justified by General Salan in his memoirs.

General Salan was anxious to improve the bad situation of French troops in the Red River Delta. Apart from previous small-scaled operations like the *Crachin* (Drizzle) and *Ouragan* (Hurricane) operations, the French launched a large-scale operation called *Amphibie* (Amphibious) just three weeks after their withdrawal from Hòa Bình to the delta. This operation, which started on March 10 and was commanded by General Berchoux, involved the participation of four mobile regiments (the 1st, 2nd, 4th, and 7th), two artillery battalions, and one motorized battalion. It targeted at the Vietnamese guerilla bases in Lý Nhân and Bình Lục (Hà Nam Province). French troops surrounded each area to annihilate the 64th Regular Regiment and the local battalion. Having been well prepared mentally, organizationally, and tactically, the regiment and local armed force proactively fought against the enemy. While the regular troops continuously made massive attacks, the local troops cooperated with guerilla and militiamen operated extensively, particularly on the 62nd Route. The 1st Route, interprovincial route, and Red River dyke were continuously sabotaged by Vietnamese troops, contributing to limit the operation of enemy vehicles.

After ten days of fighting, the French failed to reach their goal and suffered heavy casualties. They concentrated more forces and on March 23 promptly changed their direction of attack to the southwest of Thái Bình Province. There they launched mopping-up operations in a large area of about 700 square kilometers with a view to eliminating the Thái Ninh-Kiến Xương-Tiến Hải-Vũ Tiên interdistrict guerilla zones and bases. The French Headquarters expected that with a great force,[1] the second operation (named *Mercure* or Mercury in English) of French troops from different directions would drive Vietnamese troops into the area of Tiến Hải, a coastal district south of Thái Bình Province, and annihilate simultaneously the Party Committee and Command of the

---

1. It included about 20 battalions of five regular regiments (the 1st, 2nd, 3rd, 4th, and 7th Regiments), 2 motorized battalions, 3 artillery battalions, about 500 motorized vehicles, over 42 warships and canoes, and some parachute units. It was under the direct command of General de Linarès.

320th Brigade as well as the 48th and 52nd Regular Regiments, thus removing a great "red spot" in the land of Thái Bình.

General Giáp and the Staff paid special attention to this operation of French troops. The operation area was located near many great rivers (including the Diêm Hộ, Trà Lý, Đào, and Red River) with the sea in the east, the entrance to which was blocked by the Arromanches aircraft carrier as well as many French warships and canoes. Due to the large scale of the French operation, both regiments of the 320th Brigade and local troops fell into French troops' mopping-up area,[1] despite their proactive preparations for the fight. In that situation, after analyzing the enemy's forces and dispositions on both banks of the Red River, General Giáp and the Staff directed the 320th Brigade to break the siege and reach Nam Định, where they would cooperate with the 304th Brigade to fight against the enemy outside their defense line. He also ordered the 57th Regiment of the 304th Brigade in Nam Định to promptly attack the enemy to share fire with Vietnamese troops on the left bank of the Red River.

In southern Thái Bình, the 320th Brigade proactively sent a unit to the north of the province to attack the enemy's weak spot behind their formation, and left another one in the siege to cooperate with local troops, militiamen, and guerillas to fight against the enemy here. The organization of combat was promptly implemented at the same time as the evacuation of local people, the dispersion of local cattle, and the dismantlement of local houses to prevent them from being destroyed by French troops. The combat of wits

---

1. The 52nd Regiment was in Thụy Anh, Thái Ninh; the 46th Regiment 46, in Tiền Hải, Kiến Xương; the 320th Infantry Brigade and the Guard Battalion, in Lưu Phương, six kilometers south of Tiền Hải.

Chapter Six: DETERMINATION TO HOLD THE OFFENSIVE

and forces between Vietnamese and French troops took place violently in the area of southern Thái Bình Province, especially in communes where Vietnamese regular or local troops were disposed. In combat villages, Vietnamese troops held on to the pockets of resistance combined with spike and dynamite traps to stop and annihilate enemy troops step by step. In many places, French troops failed to enter villages, despite having fired thousands of cannon shots and launched many offensives.

During French troops' mopping-up operation, they were incessantly strained and annihilated by Vietnamese troops, who had launched successive attacks on different scales. Vietnamese regular battalions not only directly fought against French troops but also took advantage of their weaknesses to guide the local people out of the raided areas in order to safeguard them. After destroying the Nguyễn bridge on the 10th Route, a Vietnamese regular unit headed the north of the Trà Lý River and tried to attack the formation of French troops at their back.

On the first few days of the operation, the 320th Brigade Headquarters stayed in Lưu Phương, within the French siege. French aircraft took turns to bomb this area. In this expeditious situation, the Standing Party Committee of the 320th Brigade at the meeting held on March 28 and hosted by Party Secretary Văn Tiến Dũng stated that, French troops were implementing their plan of encirclement and would possibly arrived at their rendezvous in La Cao, Phố Trình, and Đồng Châu in a few days. The 48th and 52nd Regiments were assigned to promptly order their battalions to escape from the French siege that night. As suggested by General Giáp, Commander and Political Commissar of the 320th

Brigade Văn Tiến Dũng and part of the 320th Brigade Headquarters were helped by local people to cross the Red River to Nam Định. After reaching an agreement with the 57th Regiment of the 304th Brigade on the combined combat plan, the 320th Brigade Headquarters returned to the Tiên-Duyên-Hưng guerilla base in northern Thái Bình Province to keep watch of, direct, and command Vietnamese forces in different directions.

After 29 days of fighting, the 48th Regiment, together with about ten thousand local people, took advantage of the ebb-tide to escape from the French siege on the 10th Route and Diêm Hộ River to get to Thụy Anh. It was not until dawn that the leading unit of the regiment arrived at Bích Du Hamlet. The others had to stop and prepare for battle to protect the local people in the Bích Du-Sơn Thọ-Vọng Hải area. It was a narrow area south of Diêm Điền, with the 39th Route in the front that made it easy for French troops to attack with motorized vehicles and the sea at the back where French canoes and warships were patrolling and blocking and might land troops to support the ground forces at any time.

The one-day battle of the 48th Regiment drove back seven attacks on Bích Du Village launched by the 3rd Mobile Regiment, which was supported by a battalion of the 4th Mobile Regiment and some armored tanks. It was a violent battle because the French had advantages in military power and geographical condition. It was written in *Lịch sử kháng chiến chống Pháp của Liên khu 3* (literally: History of the Anti-French Resistance War of the 3rd Interzone) that, "After a day of fighting in the excellent spirit of bravery, on the night of March 30, the 48th Regiment took wounded soldiers and local people to Thụy Anh via the Diêm Điền estuary.

Chapter Six: DETERMINATION TO HOLD THE OFFENSIVE

No sooner had the Vietnamese General Headquarters' staff received the report on the combat results from the 302nd Brigades than the Swallow Radio of the French expeditionary army started the rumor that the 302nd Brigade had been destroyed and General Dũng had been killed. Having heard this, General Giáp smiled and said, "I'm relieved to know that Dũng and the brigade had crossed the Red River and got to our base in Hưng Nhân, Thái Bình."

During April and the remaining months of the summer following the Mercure operation, the French army continuously launched large-scale mopping-up operations,[1] besides medium- and small-size ones, in the Red River Delta. They caused many difficulties and damages to Vietnamese forces, typically the 98th Regiment during the former's three successive operations in mid April 1952. After a week of fighting within the French siege, the regiment killed nearly one thousand French troops, but it also suffered heavy losses with about 600 dead and wounded, including its political commissar and chief of staff. Its failure resulted from its lack of experience in coping with enemy raids and its acceptance to fight within the enemy siege in unfavorable conditions. It showed the failure of the policy of involving a regiment in a battle in a flat area where the enemy had advantages in military power as well as aircraft and artillery fire-power. It also showed the failure of the policy of organizing a large-

---

1. They included there mopping-up operations, involving six mobile regiments, in Thuận Thành and Quế Võ, where the 98th Vietnamese Regiment was stationed; one, involving four mobile regiments, aiming at the 42nd Vietnamese Regiment, called the "Ghost Regiment" by the French, in the north of the Luộc River; one, involving eight battalions, in Phú Xuyên, Ứng Hòa, and Kim Bảng to eliminate the 46th Vietnamese Regiment; and one, involving ten battalions, in Duy Tiên and Lý Nhân.

scale operation to overcome enemy raids when the troops had become exhausted after a week of non-stop fighting. The loss of the regiment had been the biggest ever one of the Vietnamese regular army in the areas behind the French lines in the summer of 1952.

Since the French started their first raids after the Hòa Bình campaign, the Vietnamese General Headquarters' Staff and battlefield messengers had help General Giáp study the developments of the struggle in the areas behind the French lines and gradually draw conclusions on the laws of French troops' raids and Vietnamese troops' anti-raid fights. This helped to find the answer to the question of strategic significance that "Why did the French fail to achieve the goal set for their raids, despite certain difficulties and damages they had caused to Vietnamese forces?" As General Giáp later wrote, the large-scale operations in the Red River Delta were held by the French in a classical style. Their biggest weakness was their inability to identify specific targets, because Vietnamese forces were dispersedly allocated and flexible. So they had to choose a vast area, create a large siege, and scan when tightening it. Their artillery, tanks, gunboats, aircraft were unable to find targets on empty fields or in thatched houses behind bamboo fences to show off their destructive power. With such a huge combat force, the French had to spend a lot of time tightening their siege and hunting for Vietnamese soldiers and guerillas, despite they were not stopped or attacked by the latter. Thanks to this, Vietnamese forces had enough time to escape from the area if they wished to avoid a fight unfavorable to them. Furthermore, despite their advantage in numbers, the French could hardly cover all gaps within such a large blockade, especially at night,

Chapter Six: DETERMINATION TO HOLD THE OFFENSIVE

to prevent small Vietnamese neatly-equipped units from escaping from it on foot.

On April 22, at the Third Plenum of the Party Central Committee, General Secretary Trường Chinh reconfirmed the Party's policy of waging a protracted resistance war against French colonialism. Commander-in-chief Võ Nguyên Giáp delivered a report titled *"Mấy nét chính về tình hình và nhiệm vụ quân sự hiện nay"* (literally: "Some Main Features of the Current Military Situation and Tasks"), in which he analyzed the face of the battlefield from the Border campaign in 1950 to the summer of 1952 and the immediate tasks of the armed forces throughout the country, especially in the regular troop re-organization and re-education campaign which was being implemented in the rear and in the fight against French raids in the areas behind the French lines. Political re-education, together with Party rectification, was a key task of the Vietnamese regular army at that time. This issue was addressed in a separate part of the report by General Giáp. The development of the guerilla war and the maintenance of the struggle in the areas behind the enemy lines were also significant issues presented in his report. Regarding these issues, he said:

> Fighting behind the enemy lines is one of the most important tasks of Vietnamese forces in order to crush the enemy's plot of strengthening their temporarily-occupied areas, feeding war with war, and using Vietnamese people to fight against Vietnamese people. Only by speeding up the struggle in the areas behind the enemy lines can we protect our free areas, mobilize our human and material resources in areas behind the enemy lines, and build up military forces to launch a general counter-offensive.
>
> To develop the guerilla war and uphold the struggle in the areas behind the enemy lines, our immediate task is

to maintain our resistance against enemy raids, because raids and resistance against them are currently the primary forms of fighting between us and the enemy in these areas. Only by fulfilling this task can we reinforce and develop our guerilla bases. In return, strengthened guerilla bases will facilitate our resistance against the enemy's raids.[1]

General Giáp emphasized that the struggle in the areas behind the French lines was an all-people and comprehensive one which demanded united direction for the combination of military activities and political and economic tasks and that of armed and semi-armed forces' activities and the people's struggle movement. It also required the simplification and unification of the steering apparatus, the improvement of the working style, and the reinforcement of cadres for the enhancement of leadership in the areas behind the enemy lines.

As a contribution to the education of the Vietnamese people and army about the Party's strategic policy in the areas behind the French lines, after this plenum, General Giáp had an article titled *"Giữ vững và đẩy mạnh phong trào đấu tranh trong vùng sau lưng địch ở Bắc Bộ"* (literally: "Maintaining and Promoting the Struggle Movement in the Areas Behind the Enemy Lines in North Việt Nam") published in the 56th issue of the newspaper *Nhân dân* (literally: The People) on May 1, 1952. In this article, he explained clearly why it was necessary to promote the struggle in the areas behind the French lines, the current situation of these areas in North Việt Nam, as well as the advantages and difficulties confronting Vietnamese people and army in maintaining and promoting this struggle.

---

1. Communist Party of Việt Nam: *Văn kiện Đảng toàn tập* (literally: The Complete Collection of Party Documents), op. cit., vol. 13, p. 112.

To implement the Party Central Committee's Third Plenum's resolution on strengthening the Vietnamese leadership in the areas behind the French lines, General Giáp also signed a decree on the establishment of the Red River Left Bank Zone, which lay between the Red River and the 5th Route and covered such provinces as Thái Bình, Hải Dương, Hưng Yên, and Hải Kiến (Hải Phòng and Kiến An at that time). He also gave instructions on the competence and responsibilities of the High Command of the Left Bank.[1]

To opportunely encourage the Vietnamese people and army and rectify their activities in the areas behind the French lines in the Red River Delta, on June 10, General Giáp sent a telegram to Vietnamese combat units and localities, summarizing and evaluating the past situation and giving them instructions on the direction of operation before the dry season.

After repeating the enemy's strategic plot in the areas behind their lines after the Hòa Bình campaign, General Giáp highlighted the Vietnamese people's victories over the French such as grinding down the enemy's strength (up to tens of thousands troops), strengthening bases both politically and militarily, and gaining more experience from challenges. He

---

1. The Party Central Committee appointed Đỗ Mười as Zone Party Committee Secretary cum Political Commissar of the Red River Left Bank Zone, Nguyễn Khai as Commander, Dương Hữu Miên as Deputy Commander, and Đặng Tính as Deputy Political Commissar. Due to the fierce and continuous struggle of the Vietnamese people and army against the enemy's mopping-up operations, the Left Bank Zone was not officially separated from the 3rd Interzone to become an independent political, economic, and military unit until July 1, though it was supposed to start its independent operation in June according to the decision on its establishment and the instruction on its tasks released in May.

also stated that the French were also successful to some extent since they had eliminate part of the Vietnamese regular army (some Vietnamese units in the midland battlefield suffered heavy losses and therefore had to leave the battlefield for reorganization), reoccupied some positions, narrowed Vietnamese bases, and conscripted a great number of Vietnamese youngsters into their army. However, they failed to re-establish their puppet government apparatus (puppet officials and spies). General Giáp also presented factors that restricted the Vietnamese people's success in their struggle in the areas behind the French lines in the last summer. These factors included the Vietnamese people's incomplete grasp of the tactical ideology and leadership of the guerilla war and especially their mistakes in the resistance against the enemy's raids. Particularly in terms of ideology, many cadres were still eager for big successes and unaware of the importance of self-training and building up great victories from small ones; many others made wrong assessments of the enemy, either underestimating them or overestimating them (and thus avoiding fighting against them).

General Giáp also pointed out Vietnamese cadres' shortcomings in the direction of tactics, the unity in command and leadership, and the review of experience.

He predicted that the French would launch more mopping-up operations on different scales in the coming time, especially in the Left Bank. So he said:

> We should be determined to crush the enemy's mopping-up operations and prevent them from realizing their wicked plot. Particularly, it is necessary to prepare regularly and actively for raid resistance. Only by dealing them successive death-blows during their mopping-up operations can we

Chapter Six: DETERMINATION TO HOLD THE OFFENSIVE

reduce these operations gradually, deprive the enemy of the ability to launch more, and change the form of fighting between us the the enemy.

To implement this policy, General Giáp proposed tasks that should be done immediately during the remaining time of the summer action plan (up to the end of September). They included destroying completely roads in the guerilla bases and zones, developing all forms of the guerilla war, preparing a plan for raid resistance, combining military activities and public propaganda and education about economic protection, and having plans to protect dykes and rice and helping local people with crops, especially in areas frequently persecuted by the enemy.

Two days later, on June 12, 1952, General Giáp issued an instruction titled *"Tình hình ta, địch ở Bắc Bộ và nhiệm vụ giữ vững cuốc đấu tranh sau lưng địch, tích cực chuẩn bị chống càn quét"* (literally: "Our Situation and the Enemy's in North Việt Nam and the Tasks of Maintaining the Struggle in the Areas Behind the Enemy Lines and Actively Preparing for Raid Resistance"),[1] giving specific instructions on the contents presented in the telegram. This instruction was just a preliminary summing-up of the activities of the Vietnamese people and army in the North over the last four months. In it, General Giáp also defined the directions and tasks to be done by the Vietnamese people and army in the remaining

---

1. The decree included the following contents: 1- Assessment of the Vietnamese and French situations; 2- Thorough Grasp of the Tactical Ideology and Leadership of the Guerilla War; 3- The unification of leadership and command and the simplification of departments and troops; 4- the reinforcement of public relations; 5- The issue of supplies; 6- The summer action plan.

time before the dry season in order to fail the enemy's plot of launching raids and pacifying North Việt Nam. He also provided a detailed analysis of two emerging issues as follows:

On the one hand, the Vietnamese had many great advantages in the areas behind the French lines at that time. To fully promote all of these advantages, they had to immediately correct their existing mistakes.

On the other hand, a full grasp of the strategic ideology and sound leadership in the guerilla war were the important prerequisites for proactively and successively coping with an enemy who had advantages in troop strength and firepower, grinding down their strength, failing their plot, and strengthening Vietnamese forces.

As for the 5th Interzone alone, on May 16, General Giáp sent a secret telegram to Nguyễn Chánh, giving his assessments of the situation and opinions about the force building and combat of the interzone. He emphasized the task of establishing bases in the areas behind the enemy lines. Specifically, he reminded the interzone to continue to build revolutionary bases in the north of the Central Highlands, which was considered as the primary direction and the link between Đác-pếch and Komplong; avoid animated activities and focus on the establishment and consolidation of the bases in the south of Central Highlands; attach special importance to cities such as Đà Nẵng, Đà Lạt, and Nha Trang and reorganize liaison committees in Đà Nẵng and Đà Lạt; and pay attention to agitation and propagada among enemy troops.

To promptly prepare for the coming dry season, the Vietnamese regular brigades actively participated in the

Chapter Six: DETERMINATION TO HOLD THE OFFENSIVE

campaign for political and military re-education. General Giáp closely followed the re-education courses organized by the General Headquarters during the summer months. At the Third Plenum of the Party Central Committee, General Giáp reported on the importance of the political and military re-education for the regular army in that summer. He said:

> After the Border campaign, our regular troops in North Việt Nam were reorganized and given chance to learn from the experience of the Chinese liberation army. They also participated in many re-educational courses in 1951. Thanks to these, they have made great progresses, gained many victories in campaigns, and held the initiative in the North Vietnamese battlefield.
>
> However, our army is still young and inexperienced. Therefore, there still exist many phenomena which are incompatible with the nature of the Vietnamese People's Army.[1]

In the face of this situation, the re-education of troops should be grounded on politics and applied first to cadres. It was necessary to turn the Vietnamese army into a revolutionary one and an invincible one of the people.

At a re-educational class held by the Party Central Committee in mid June, General Giáp addressed many issues related to the Vietnamese people and army's thought and awareness of the situation and their tasks when the resistance war had entered its seventh year and when the Vietnamese were fighting fiercely against the French to complete their task of preparing for the shift to a general counter-offensive. In his speech titled *"Cần hiểu sâu hơn*

---

1. Communist Party of Việt Nam: *Văn kiện Đảng toàn tập* (literally: The Complete Collection of Party Documents), op cit., vol. 13, pp. 113–114.

nữa phương châm trường kỳ kháng chiến, tự lực cánh sinh" (literally: "The Necessity of Having a Deeper Understanding of the Guideline of Protracted Resistance and Self-reliance"), he mentioned three points of view that were important to the awareness and thought of Vietnamese cadres and branches at that time.[1]

After analyzing the characteristics of the Vietnamese resistance war against French colonialism, he cited the facts of the Vietnamese struggle over the past five or six years to prove the rightness of the Party's guideline of protracted resistance war and self-reliance, analyzed the policy of conducting a people's war and relying on the people to do so, and confirmed the conditions for the success of that guideline and policy. Regarding the point of view that the resistance was protracted but it had a time limit, General Giáp recalled the incorrect awareness of Vietnamese cadres during the 1949–1950 period and the rectification of the Party Central Committee stated in the instruction released in July 1950 and in its conferences after the Second National Party Congress. He said:

> The idea of quick fight and quick victory and that of dependence are currently criticized. Generally, they no longer exit systematically in the Party. However, such ideas still remain and thus may affect our resistance. No sooner had we recognized the incorrectness of the idea of quick fight and quick victory than the reality of the battlefield proved the rightness of a protracted resistance war. During the

---

1. These matters included: 1- It was necessary to fully understand the characteristics of the resistance war; 2- The resistance war was protracted, but it had a time limit; 3- It was important to actively mobilize the masses in order to foster them and build up forces, and make careful preparations for the shift to a general counter-offensive.

Chapter Six: DETERMINATION TO HOLD THE OFFENSIVE

years of 1950 and 1951, the French made a lot of effort and the Americans interfered more actively. Therefore, although we won many victories and had many new advantages, we faced many new difficulties, especially economic ones in the areas behind the enemy lines. In the face of the French army's power, the Americans' interference, and our own difficulties, many of our cadres made successive mistakes and changed their minds, from the wish to launch quick fights for quick victories to the concern about the time limit of the resistance war. So we have to fight against not only the remnants of the idea of quick fights and quick victories, but also the idea of an unlimited resistance war that may affect the people's belief in the final victory.

After his explanation and confirmation of the Vietnamese army's increasing power and the enemy's decreasing strength through battles and his analysis of the influence of the American interference on the Vietnamese resistance war, General Giáp analyzed deeply the tasks of actively mobilizing the masses and fostering and building up forces in preparation for a general counter-offensive. He firmly stated that these were the focal tasks at the time, and addressed some specific issues related to them. He specified that in order to awaken the masses, Vietnamese cadres should be patient when carrying out propaganda and educational activities, so that they could improve the masses' awareness of the rightness of the resistance war and promote their political advantages. They should bring benefits to the masses; otherwise, all the propaganda and educational activities would become vain efforts and fail to reach their goals. To conclude his explanation, General Giáp said:

> At present, we are making every effort to prepare for the general counter-offensive. The focal task in this course of preparation is to build up forces. To do it, we should rely on

the people, trust the people, and encourage the people to actively participate in the resistance and production.

After four months of instructing the Vietnamese people and army to resist the enemy's mopping-up operations, really maintain and promote the struggle in the areas behind the enemy lines before the next campaign, force the enemy to disperse their forces to cope with Vietnamese ones, and create conditions for the battlefield in the areas behind the enemy lines to share fire with the front battlefield in the campaigns launched by the Vietnamese regular army, in July 1952, General Giáp suggested the Party Central Committee hold a conference on the guerila war in North Việt Nam. Some military, civil, political, and Party cadres in the areas behind the enemy lines from the Bình-Trị-Thiên area southwards were also summoned to this conference to learn from others' experience. The conference aimed to summarize the experience in resisting the enemy's raids and concretize the main points mentioned in the Central Military Commission on the issue of maintaining the struggle in the areas behind the enemy lines and actively preparing for the resistance against the enemy's raids. In the opening report, General Giáp set the specific goals and contents of the conference as follows:

Firstly, the conference would summarize the experience in resisting the enemy's mopping-up operations, with the focus put on the tactical one, and clearly state the role of local soldiers, militiamen, and guerillas.

Secondly, the conference would hold discussions to understand the situations of both warring sides and have a full grasp of the tasks and ideas of maintaining the struggle in the areas behind the enemy lines, promoting the guerila

Chapter Six: DETERMINATION TO HOLD THE OFFENSIVE

war, and continuing preparations for the resistance against the enemy's raids.

Lastly, the conference would touch upon and solve some particular issues such as the unity in command, the personnel organization, and the supply work. It would also make a preliminary summing-up of the main experience in public relations, Party work, and economic work in the areas behind the enemy lines.

Besides the report on the process of realizing the policy of using the guerilla war as the primary combat tactics and the war of movement as the secondary one during the past strategic period as the basis of the lessons on the maintenance and promotion of the guerilla war to a high level, General Giáp also delivered an important report on raid resistance tactics.

After reviewing the development of the aggressive war of French colonialism, the increasingly large raids launched by French troops, and the increasingly arduous anti-raid resistance of the Vietnamese people and army, General Giáp concluded that launching raids and resisting raids were the main forms of fighting between the Vietnamese and French armies. Only by successfully resisting the enemy's raids could the Vietnamese maintain and boost the guerilla war and their struggle in the areas behind the enemy lines, protect their human and material resources, annihilate and subdue the enemy forces, as well as preserve and build up their forces for the effective combination of the two battlefields in front of and behind the enemy lines. It was the developmental law of the struggle in the areas behind the enemy lines in the Vietnamese battlefield in general and in the North Vietnamese battlefield in particular. General Giáp based himself on some typical mopping-up operations of French troops (including one in the southeast of Thái Bình Province, one in the north of the Đuống River, and one in the north of the Luộc River) for his analysis of the characteristics, strengths, and weaknesses of their mopping-up tactics. After drawing some general lessons (relying on the people, thoroughly understanding the idea of the guerilla war, and getting ready for combat), he analyzed both successful and unsuccessful experience in giving instruction and resisting raids. In addition, he pointed out a number of urgent issues such as the tactics for each Vietnamese arm in fighting against enemy troops in villages, the dispersion and concentration of troops, as well as the coordination between regular troops and local troops, militiamen, and guerillas.

After a month of working promptly and effervescently with democratic and straightforward discussions, all participants were well aware of the importance and necessity of the armed struggle in the areas behind the enemy lines, the idea of the guerilla war and the guiding principle of raid resistance, and the contents of united leadership. They also clarified and solved a number of specific issues on the Party policies in localities, and reported the situation of the local struggle to the Party Central Committee so that the later could have a thorough grasp of the situation in the areas behind the enemy lines and have timely instructions.

General Giáp also reminded Vietnamese cadres to fully grasp the focal points of the resolution, have plans for its gradual implementation, and apply it to the right subject and in the right situation. At the closing ceremony of the conference, he officially launched the emulation movement to kill the enemy and achieve feats among the Vietnamese people and army in the areas behind the enemy lines in the Red River Delta. Participants in this movement were encouraged to kill as many enemy troops and confiscate as many enemy weapons as possible; safeguard the people's lives and properties, actively participate in production, and protect crops and youngsters and cadres; develop and reinforce revolutionary bases in the temporarily-occupy areas as well as guerilla zones and bases; and promote propaganda among puppet troops and destroy the puppet administration.

In the exciting atmosphere of the farewell moment, General Giáp strongly believed that the prospect of the combination of the battlefields in front of and behind the enemy lines would bring about more new achievements in the coming campaign.

Changing the Attack Direction to the Northwest Mountainous Battlefield

The war in Việt Nam had entered the last months of the seventh year and the sixth commander-in-chief of the French expeditionary army had been sent to Việt Nam. What would be the best solution for Paris at that time? General Salan complained that he took up the post in unfavorable conditions, and his memoirs later revealed that he had been right in doing so.

First of all, he did it when Paris was "disabled and discouraged."

Having heard of the coming meeting of the National Defense Committee, General Salan promptly ordered Chief of Staff Ala to return to France to reflect the concern of the Headquarters of the French expeditionary army about the troop strength. When de Lattre returned to France the previous year, he "borrowed" the French Ministry of War 20,000 troops and promised to "pay his debt" by the summer of 1952. Now the deadline had come. No sooner had he arrived in Paris than General Ala went to see the Military Secretary of President Vincent Auriol to confide that the puppet army was still weak. He said that if he returned part of the Euro-African expeditionary army to France, then the French Ministry of War would have to narrow France's controlled zone in Việt Nam. This would discourage France's puppet administrations in the Indochinese countries since the French expeditionary army would be foreseen to leave forever. Ala conveyed straightforwardly and publicly to many members of the French Government what he had been told by Salan. He said, "The Commander-in-chief cannot accept that France has decided to give up when the balance of power is favorable to the French army." To the indifference of many figures in the French leadership in Paris, Ala returned to Sài Gòn and reported to Salan on the suspicious and depressed attitudes of the French Government. According to him, Paris wanted to end the war soon.

But Salan was not discouraged. In late July, he flew back to France and met every member of the French Government to persuade them to believe in the "historical mission" of the French expeditionary army. What he got in return was the deep division in the French Government and the application of "an immediate solution" proposed and stressed by President Auriol, Prime Minister Pinay, and Minister of National Defense Pleven. The press reflected the French people's complaint about the consequences of the French involvement in Indochina—the loss of dignity, tax increase,

Chapter Six: DETERMINATION TO HOLD THE OFFENSIVE

and sorrow. Having heard that the White House and Pentagon had paid 40 percent of the French cost of war in Indochina, the progressive Americans raised their voices to require their government to let the Vietnamese mind their own business. In early September, Salan returned to Việt Nam without any results or promises from his government. He still had to return the borrowed number of troops to France before the dry season. The only consolation he received from the French Government was the Legion of Honor awarded on August 20. According to the press, it was just a tranquilizer from President Auriol to French Commander-in-chief Salan.

Despite the indifference of his government, Salan still had a source of hope and encouragement, that is, the military and financial aids from the American Government.[1] The 150th American aid ship had arrived in Sài Gòn and the 200th one was estimated to come in October. With the American aids, the French would have conditions to develop their puppet army and make up for the shortage of troop strength. The promising meeting with Bảo Đại in May, the replacement of Prime Minister of the State of Việt Nam Trần Văn Hữu with Nguyễn Văn Tâm, who promised to "determinedly promote the war," the promotion of Nguyễn Văn Hinh to the military rank of Lieutenant General, the appointment of a French colonel as chief of the military office in the Bảo Đại government, and the settlement of contradictions between religious sects and the Bình Xuyên army were all seeds of hope for Salan. That the Vietnamese reduced their

---

1. Salan later revealed that within 17 months (from mid 1950 to early 1952), the American Government provided the French army with 120,000 tons of military equipment including 178 airplanes, 170 ships and canoes of different kinds, and many tanks and others.

pressure in the areas behind the French lines, especially in the midlands, alone eased his anxiety during the remaining time of the rainy season.

With his knowledge of Việt Nam and the Vietnamese army,[1] and in his new position, Salan found it necessary and possible to study more deeply his opponents to have effective measures to cope with them in the coming dry season. He later revealed that he assigned a group of French military officers to do this task based on some documents confiscated from his opponents. The research results were recorded honestly in his memoirs. Accordingly, the Vietnamese army originated from the Vietnamese people, so it was organically related to the people and inherited their best qualities. It was the main force of the regime. Its combat brigades were established to fulfill their functions—leveling the French posts and annihilating the French mobile regiments in the war of movement. They were also suitable for the guerilla war and the task of propaganda for the satisfactory launching of the war of movement and the battlefield-based war. The Vietnamese Headquarters attached special importance to the preparation, supplementation, and development of spearheads to maintain the continuity of their campaigns. The Vietnamese army was currently strong but plain. They all came from rural families, were accustomed to hard labor, and could stand hardships. They had undergone trials. This army was led by thousands of Party cells, so it was encouraged with a profound hatred of the enemy. The Party work had penetrated into the smallest units and was the determinant

---

1. Salan used to be chief of the Đình Lập post in Lạng Sơn Province during the 1920s, and confront the Vietnamese not only in the battlefield but also in negotiations in the wake of the August Revolution.

of the army's spirit and will. It was noticeable that all the levels of the army were supported politically and militarily to together complete their tasks according to the principle of "bravely destroying enemy troops, continuously fighting, incessantly promoting public relations, and unanimously enhancing the unity between superiors and inferiors, between Party members and non-Party members." From the research results, he concluded that the Vietnamese Headquarters paid much attention to quality and efficiency. Based on the realities of combat, they incessantly improved their war machine and enhance the fighting spirit, heroism, bravery, hatred for enemies, and trust in victory according to Marxism. They ceaselessly cultivated a spirit of perseverance and a simple style at high level among their troops, and incessantly improved techniques and studied tactics. They gained power in attack by making careful calculations based on the principle "taking the strong to fight against the weak," according to the ratio five, seven, or ten against one. In Salan's opinion, Vietnamese infantry soldiers were the creepiest opponents that the French had ever confronted. This made him worried when the dry season was coming. It was because these soldiers, under the command of good leaders and with improved fighting tactics, would promote their fire-power and combat superiority up to three times once they attacked the French defense system.

He cited a report delivered by General Giáp at a conference. In this report, General Giáp criticized his cadres for being subjective and complacent, so the combat results, which would have been better, were restricted. Salan wrote that this criticism was conveyed to all Party cells, who would strictly review their educational work, withdraw lessons of experience, and apply them immediately in their following combat tasks. Soldiers who could dress their own wounds were incomparable tools of combat.

After comparing the combat forces of both side before the dry season, Salan concluded that the Vietnamese had the advantages in numbers (310,000 compared to 260,000 troops), but he wrote that "Mr. Giáp has no air force or motorized vehicles, which are important in the comparison of combat forces." While he was staying in Hà Nội to study his opponent, he urged the French intelligence to closely follow every move and combat policy of the Vietnamese army. He thought that General Giáp must have made a new combat plan in the past quiet months. He admitted that the Second Bureau had not provided any useful information since "the opponents have changed their codes, which means that they are about to rush into a new period of what is so-called a 'general counter-offensive' by Mr. Giáp. He wants to extend the war throughout Indochina."

Then according to Salan, it was not until late September that the French detected changes in the activities of the Vietnamese army. It was reported that about 20,000 conscripted laborers had been gathered. There was a sharp rise in the transportation across the Red River in Yên Bái, together with an increase in the shifts of radios. "It is obvious that the Việt Minh army attaches special importance to Sơn La in the Black Thai land and to Sam Neua in the middle section of the Mã River, the gateway to northern Laos," Salan wrote. On October 4, General de Linarès ordered to give the alert and reinforce reconnaissance across the Northwest (*Tây Bắc* in Vietnamese) area, especially the right bank of the Đà River. On October 5, General Salan flew to Sài Gòn to receive

Chapter Six: DETERMINATION TO HOLD THE OFFENSIVE

French Minister of War Pierre de Chevigné, after having ordered de Linarès to keep contact with and send timely reports to the General Headquarters. He confirmed that the Northwest was obviously under threat and this concern, as he admitted later, became clear to the Headquarters of the French expeditionary army.

On the Vietnamese side, during the last days of the Hòa Bình campaign, Chief of the General Staff Hoàng Văn Thái heard of the death of General de Lattre, the temporary replacement of de Lattre by Salan, and the withdrawal of French troops from the Hòa Bình battlefield. He also heard his staff talk about de Lattre and the French Headquarters. They said that the French press was criticizing de Lattre for having ordered the attack on Hòa Bình and then left it to his inferiors. That action of irresponsibility attested to his words in the capital city of Italy a few days earlier that he had done all what he could,[1] his task had been accomplished, the apparatus had operated stably, and it was then the turn of inferior officers. The also talked about the event that before taking troops to attack Hòa Bình, de Lattre heard that the negotiation for the cessation of hostilities in North Korea had started. He immediately "threatened" that if Paris negotiated with the Việt Minh in Indochina, he would return the post of commander-in-chief to the French Government. As a celebrated general in the Second World War, de Lattre was considered the most aggressive commander-in-chief who

---

1. For example, he had livened up the spirit of the expeditionary force, used his personal prestige in the relation with the United States for aid reinforcement, quickly arranged troops for Bảo Đại, established defense lines so as to maintain the Red River Delta, and, above all, gradually Vietnamized the war.

believed the most in the potential of the Indochina War, in which France could not lose with the adequate aid from the United States. This aid was considered the leading prerequisite for his determination to pursue the war to the end. It was said that if de Lattre had still been alive, he might not have withdrawn French troops to the defense line so soon. The talk led to an unanswered question: "What else could de Lattre had done apart from using more ammunition than Salan did if he had not been dead?"

Regarding the coming situation, the Vietnamese staff predicted that the French might not attack the free zone in 1952, especially when the command of the French army went to Salan, who had been considered by the press and the French Ministry of War in Paris as a general who "always waits for his opponent to attack first before fighting." General Giáp told Thái to suggest his staff withdraw useful lessons from the last campaign to apply to the coming dry season. As for himself, General Giáp found opportunities to study and learn more about the French army as well as the strengths and weaknesses of the Vietnamese army from the Border campaign to the summer of 1952. The Vietnamese formerly considered modern military equipment as the strength, as well as spirit as the weakness, of their enemy. Now they could see more clearly the strength of their enemy as a professional army. The French army was really good at defense. In the Đông Khê battle, they could resist two Vietnamese regular regiments in 52 consecutive hours with fewer than three companies. The Pheo post in the Hòa Bình campaign was considered by French military expert as a model of fortification-based defense organization. The French army could draw timely lessons from their failures. The withdrawal

Chapter Six: DETERMINATION TO HOLD THE OFFENSIVE

of French troops in Cao Bằng was completely different from that in Hòa Bình, though they both took place in the mountainous area. Recent talks had focused on the mental degradation of French troops in the Border campaign. Still it would be unfair not to mention their violent resistance during the Vietnamese attacks on their fortifications, in some of which the last French troops dropped their weapons only when they had ran out of bullets.

On their side, the Vietnamese had realized the weaknesses of their revolutionary army, which merely included infantry soldiers, when they launched a large-scale attack in the plains, where the enemy could make the best use of their modern weapons, technology, and high mobility. The Vietnamese did not intend to overcome their weaknesses by putting emphasis on quantity over quality. The development of their army in terms of quantity had reached the limit. The self-supporting economy did not allow them to increase troops. However, they needed to maintain their initiative in the Northern battlefield. The plains and midlands were not favorable for their big campaigns in the coming dry season. The main attack direction of their regular forces in the 1952–1953 autumn-winter period would be the mountainous battlefield. In as early as March 1952, the Central Military Committee decided to launch a big campaign in the Northwest, the only mountainous area still under the French control in North Việt Nam.

So it was not until that dry season, about four or five years after he directed the establishment of the first secret political and armed bases in the area of special significance which he often called "Western Việt Nam," that General Giáp had opportunity to take the army to the Northwest.

At that time, the comparison between the Vietnamese and French combat forces allowed him to launch a campaign which involved the participation of many brigades. The war had gone through seven years, but the Northwest battlefield remained unfamiliar to several Vietnamese regular brigades. The troop movement to the Northwest was also a surprise to some cadres and soldiers of the Vietnamese regular army who were longing to liberate their hometowns in the plains.

According to the assessment of the Staff of the Vietnamese General Headquarters, the Northwest battlefield was the place where the French would reveal their weaknesses and which was far away from the rear of the resistance. So the supplies of the campaign must be transported from Việt Bắc and the 3rd and 4th Interzones. Therefore, no sooner had the Hòa Bình campaign ended than advance parties as well as logistical and sapper missions, one after another, secretly set off to investigate the enemy situation and study transport and supply routes. The annihilation of bandits was also promoted. In May, the General Department of Logistics started their preparation for the battlefield. A Party committee for the campaign was established, and an executive board of three people was also founded to instruct the opening of roads and the preparation for the campaign.[1] The Vietnamese had predicted their difficulties in transporting supplies with manpower and primitive vehicles for a protracted

---

1. The Party committee for the campaign was comprised of Võ Nguyên Giáp, Hoàng Văn Thái, Nguyễn Chí Thanh, and Trần Đăng Ninh. The executive board in charge of logistics included Đặng Kim Giang (Vice Head of the General Department of Logistics), Hoàng Văn Tiến (Member of the 3rd Interzone Party Committee), and Nguyễn Văn Thân (Member of the 4th Interzone Party Committee).

Chapter Six: DETERMINATION TO HOLD THE OFFENSIVE

campaign in a large mountainous battlefield which had a scattered population, poor economy, and restricted on-site food mobilization. It was the first time that the Vietnamese Government had issued temporary regulations on the mobilization of conscripted laborers and the establishment of provincial boards of conscripted laborers to mobilize manpower for the front line.

News from the army intelligence gradually complemented what bodies had learnt about the direction of the coming campaign, especially about the enemy and requirements for logistical organization. To keep the campaign's direction a secret, the advisory body changed the encryption law and organized boisterous diversionary marches in the midlands and plains. Besides, the repair of the road to the Northwest was implemented first in the place far away from the enemy and stopped at the left bank of the Red River. It would be continued in the directions of attack when the campaign started. Thanks to the diversionary marches of the Vietnamese army, the French could not figure out the primary attack direction of the Vietnamese regular brigades in the coming dry season, especially the advance of the 304th and 320th Brigades into the areas behind the French lines, until the last ten days of September, or a few weeks before the start of the campaign. It was reported that the French Headquarters had adjusted the troop disposition in their temporarily-occupied zone and deployed some mobile regiments which would be ready to rescue key positions in the areas behind their lines, especially in the midlands and at the Đáy River defense line. Meanwhile, Vietnamese regular brigades were urgently preparing for their march to the Northwest.

With four big fields of Điện Biên, Nghĩa Lộ, Than Uyên, and Quang Huy, the Northwest area was twice as large as the Red River Delta. It had a population of 400,000 people, most of whom were Thái, Mèo, Mường, Dao, and Tày while some were Vietnamese. The French made it an autonomous area which was comprised of four subdivisions of Nghĩa Lộ, Sơn La, Đà River, Lai Châu and one independent subzones of Tuần Giáo. While Nghĩa Lộ Subdivision was the strongest screen of the whole area in terms of combat force and terrain for the French; it was a pedal pad for the Vietnamese army to penetrate deep into the area.

The French combat force in the Northwest area was comprised of five Thái infantry battalions, three Euro-African mobile battalions, forty-three odd puppet infantry companies, and eleven 75-mm and 105-mm cannons. The enemy troops were divided into 144 entrenched fortifications, 40 of which were of one-company size while the rest were of one-platoon size each. Except for some positions like Nghĩa Lộ, Gia Hội, and Cửa Nhì (belonging to Nghĩa Lộ Subdivision) with improved fortifications and underground tunnels, other positions only had cursory fortifications. In some places, enemy troops were garrisoned right in the local houses which were over ten kilometers away from one another. The terrain was full of obstacles, which made it easy for the enemy troops to be isolated and hard for them to assist each other. Besides, they had to rely on the airway, which was more or less 300 kilometers away from the plain bases, for supplies and reinforcements

It was originally estimated in the combat plan prepared by the Vietnamese staff that the campaign would undergo two or three phases. In the first phase, Vietnamese troops would focus on destroying Nghĩa Lộ Subdivision (the screen of the Northwest area), creating a springboard for a further westward movement. At the same time, they would concentrate on annihilating Phù Yên Subzone, expanding the offensive to the Đà River, opening the transport routes, and creating favorable conditions for their attack toward Sơn La. After Nghĩa Lộ was liberated, if there had not been favorable conditions for the attack on Sơn La, Vietnamese troops would be divided into two armies: one would head Cò Nòi from Tạ Khoa, cut the 41st Route, and then expand southward; meanwhile, the other would head Mộc Châu from Vạn Yên, attack northward from the southeast, and then coordinate with a small part of soldiers who were tasked to create a diversion to operate deep in the areas behind the enemy lines, mobilize the masses, and establish the people's bases. After liberating southeastern Sơn La, the Vietnamese army was reinforced before entering the third phase to liberate the whole province. It was a new point in this combat plan that Vietnamese troops created a diversion in the east, deep in the areas behind the enemy lines. It reflected the application of the experience in combining two battlefields, one in front of and one behind the enemy lines, from the Hòa Bình campaign. Despite its smaller scale, this campaign forced the French forces to cope with the Vietnamese ones in both battlefields simultaneously. On the overall scale, the campaign involved the combination of the 304th and 320th Brigades in the Red River Delta and Vietnamese forces in the Northwest battlefield.

The campaign cadres' conference was held from September 6–9. Its participants included not only commanding officers of regular regiments and brigades but also leaders of Việt

Bắc Interzone, the 3rd and 4th Interzones, and the Northwest battlefield. In the opening report, General Giáp summarized the situation after the Hòa Bình campaign, the tasks assigned by the Party Central Committee and President Hồ Chí Minh for this dry season, and the fundamentals for the whole Vietnamese army and people to accomplish these tasks. After that, participants discussed in groups a document titled *"Chủ trương tác chiến ở chiến trường Tây Bắc"* (literally: The Combat Policy in the Northwest Battlefield"), which had been drafted by the advisory department and approved by Commander-in-chief Võ Nguyên Giáp.

After an analysis of the enemy situation, the document ended with the following conclusions:

> From the analysis of the situation of enemy troops in the Northwest, we can find that they are weak but quickly changeable, especially in Nghĩa Lộ Subdivision. However, if we know how to make use of their changes and grasp the opportunity to eliminate their reinforcements, we can destroy Nghĩa Lộ and thus open the gateway to the Northwest. Then, there may be greater changes in the enemy. We should quickly grasp the opportunity to quickly extend our offensive into the center of the enemy.

Regarding the Vietnamese situation, after pointing out the improvements of Vietnamese soldiers after several summer months' organizational reinforcement and troop reorganization, the document directed the participants' attention to the situation of the people in the Northwest. It also explained why courting popularity was considered as one of the objectives of the campaign and why the Campaign Headquarters issued the Ten Disciplines, most of which were those on public relations, in the Northwest campaign. It wrote:

Chapter Six: DETERMINATION TO HOLD THE OFFENSIVE

Our people are generally good; however, due to our mistakes and the enemy's previous terrors, most of them have lost contact with us or their bases have broken down. We have recently got in touch again with some bases in Nghĩa Lộ, Phù Yên, and Quỳnh Nhai. Nevertheless, most of our bases are located in mountainous areas, have not been expanded to the plains but have been mainly situated near the temporarily-occupied areas, and have not been developed into the areas behind the enemy lines. There's hardly any bases in Sơn La and Lai Châu.

Regarding the combat policies, plans, and guidelines for the two phases,[1] as well as the task assignment and force arrangement, the Commander-in-chief explained in the document that the tactics used by the Vietnamese army were to encircle fortifications and eliminate reinforcements, and to eliminate reinforcements and destroy fortifications. Their actions would take place in this order: encircling enemy fortifications, waiting for enemy reinforcements, eliminating them, and attacking enemy fortifications. Among these actions, encircling and waiting for enemy reinforcements were the most difficult. The document emphasized that Vietnamese cadres had to educate soldiers, open classes to teach them techniques in fortifications, air defense, anti-artillery defense, disguise, and diversion. Regarding the strategies and campaign, the document addressed the issue of defending the rear during the campaign. Because they focused their regular soldiers for long-term fighting in a mountainous battlefield far away from the rear, which meant

---

1. Vietnamese troops were tasked to eliminate Nghĩa Lộ Subdivision and simultaneously penetrate into the areas of Phù Yên and Quỳnh Nhai, where they would coordinate with local soldiers to restrain the enemy, in the first phase. In the second phase, they were tasked to liberate Sơn La.

losing part of their mobility, the French might take advantage of this to destroy their rear.[1]

In the document, General Giáp suggested different possible situations, especially in the first phase, for Vietnamese cadres to discuss democratically and prepare plans to tackle. The most noticeable of these suggested situations was when their troop operation was detected by the enemy, who would then immediately increase reinforcements (most possibly paratroops), or withdraw to form big positions, building defense fortifications or occupying more heights around these big positions. In such a situation, General Giáp suggested Vietnamese troops take advantage of the opportunity to attack enemy reinforcements or create favorable conditions for this attack. In special situations, however, they were suggested to attack large fortified positions and attack to an extent which enabled them to launch a mobile attack, pursue the enemy, or compel the latter to respond.

The conference was going on when President Hồ Chí Minh visited and encouraged the cadres. The story of his visiting the conference despite hard weather conditions became a practical and profound lesson of determination for each Vietnamese cadre in this campaign. In their reminiscences, both Vương Thừa Vũ and Lê Trọng Tấn, two brigade chiefs, recalled memorable details about this chance of meeting the President. Tấn wrote:

> Seeing rows of forest trees stirring in the rain, we all felt worried about his health. We looked down the path flooded

---

[1]. To implement the plan for defending the rear, Commander-in-chief Võ nguyên Giáp approved the plan proposed by the advisory body. According to it, two battalions of the 246th and 238th Regiments were disposed in Thái Nguyên; the 176th Regiment of the 316th Brigade, one battalion of the 246th Regiment, and two more regiments which were being built, in Phú Thọ.

Chapter Six: DETERMINATION TO HOLD THE OFFENSIVE

with water at the foot of the hill. Dimly looming in the rain was the shape of a black umbrella. Văn and Thanh ran out. It's him, Uncle Hồ! He was holding an umbrella in one hand and a stick in the other; his feet were covered with mud. He stepped over the flowing gutter and entered the meeting hall. Through the wet shirt his thin shoulders was seen to rise. I was moved to tears.

Everyone sat quietly. He said, "Today it's raining heavily and streams are being flooded. When I reached a swift-flowing stream, I saw some compatriots waiting for the water to recede to pass. I thought that I would have to go immediately so as to save your time. I and some others were determined to take off our clothes and use sticks for support to pass the stream. Having seen me manage to pass the stream, the compatriots were also determined to do the same. That is a lesson for you. With a strong determination, you can do everything, including appealing to others to have the same determination as you do."

From the story of passing the stream, Hồ Chí Minh encouraged Vietnamese cadres to have determination to accomplish the assigned tasks in the coming campaign. He said:

> When having an advantage, you should be determined to take it. When confronting a difficulty, you should be determined to overcome it. If you are not determined to take an advantage, it may become a difficulty. If you are determined to overcome a difficulty, it may become an advantage.

Then he had private talks with some cadres of the Vietnamese regular units who would take part in the campaign. He encouraged Chief of Brigade Lê Trọng Tấn, who had met difficulties in the Lý Thường Kiệt campaign the previous year, and Chief of Regiment Vũ Yên, who had missed the opportunity to kill enemy troops in Ba Trại and failed to destroy the Pheo post in the Hòa Bình campaign. After hearing the staff promise to determinedly accomplish the assigned tasks in this campaign, he intimately shook hands with each of them. The determination of the Party Central Committee had become that of the whole army.

After four days of heated discussions, on September 9, General Giáp delivered a report on the results of the conference.[1] He combined the results of discussions about the situation and tasks with answers to the questions raised by the cadres during discussions, such as the question "Which target is more important to attack, on-site troops or mobile troops?" and that about the tasks and possibility of courting popularity. Many issues relating to the combat policy for each phase of the campaign were also addressed, such as the issue of attacking enemy fortifications and reinforcements, the policy of marching to Sơn La right after eliminating Nghĩa Lộ Subdivision and Phù Yên Subzone, and solutions to possible situations. In his answers, General Giáp emphasized the importance of making the best use of conditions for an assured victory and the determination to promote all capabilities to overcome difficulties in transportation as well as food and ammunition supply, tackle the immaturity of the people's bases, enhance the possibility to annihilate enemy troops most of whom were local puppet troops, and keep

---

1. The report, entitled "*Quyết tâm đánh thắng trong chiến dịch Tây Bắc*" (literally: "The Determination to Win in the Northwest Campaign"), included five parts: 1-The significance and objectives of the campaign; 2- Combat policies of the Central Military Committee; 3- Combat guidelines; 4- Conditions for an assured victory and difficulties to overcome; 5- Some notices in directing the campaign.

silent about the marches and preparations for combat. To conclude the report, he said:

> In this campaign, we should be determined to build up the manner of actively annihilating and bravely fighting against enemy troops, looking for enemy troops to defeat, and keeping on fighting after winning one battle. We should not miss any chance and look for and create opportunities to eliminate enemy troops. The more difficulties we meet, the more active and determined we become in eliminating enemy troops. It is the manner of a revolutionary army. Many units of our army have raised high that manner, while many others still have shortcomings. To foster that manner, we should have determination to oppose to the attitude of hesitation and lack of determination which were revealed in some of the battles in the Hòa Bình campaign.
>
> The Central Military Committee hopes that at the summing-up conference held after the campaign, we can come to the following conclusions:
>
> 1- We have accomplished all the tasks and completely won the campaign.
>
> 2- We have realized the teachings of President Hồ Chí Minh and kept our promise to him.
>
> 3- We have promoted the manner of actively annihilating and bravely fighting against enemy troops.
>
> Whether we can make such conclusions depends on our efforts.

After the conference, the advisory body sent to all units an instruction titled *"Chỉ thị về nhiệm vụ chiến đấu ở Nghĩa Lộ và Sơn La"* (literally: "Instruction on the Combat Tasks in Nghĩa Lộ and Sơn La"), which provided a summary of the general situation, tasks in the dry season of 1952, conditions for task completion, disciplines to be observed by all levels when carrying out combat tasks, and finally basic tactical requirements. This had been the main content of the conference, and was generalized by General Giáp for the purpose of orienting the actions of brigades and interzones. This instruction was issued at the same time as Hồ Chí Minh's *"Lời kêu gọi toàn quân thi đua lập công"* (literally: "Appeal to the Whole Army to Emulate for Feats") to receive his awards. To encourage the whole army to accomplish the tasks assigned by the President, General Giáp explained the criteria for each individual and unit (especially regiments) and then called upon the whole army to determinedly and bravely overcome hardships and difficulties to annihilate the enemy.

Before setting off to the Northwest, General Giáp sent a letter or telegram to nationwide battles, informing them of the latest news about the enemy situation, assessments of their own situation, and anticipations of possible situations. He also reconfirmed the task of building and promoting the combined operation of units and localities in the dry season.

Regarding the Southern battlefield, he emphasized the importance of maintaining the guerilla war, defending and developing the guerilla bases, and pinning the enemy down and preventing them from bringing troops to the North.

As for the 5th Interzone, in his letter dated September 15 to Nguyễn Chánh, he informed that the French were promptly developing the local force in the Central Highlands in order to withdraw gradually the Euro-African regular force to other battlefields. He mentioned the current drawbacks of the 5th Interzone (such as cumbersome organization, poor health, and limited combat quality) and instructed the interzone to streamline its organization, increase its regular troops, and develop local forces. Regarding instructions for the areas behind the enemy lines, he stressed the necessity of making a plan for the building a long-term base south of the Central Highlands. After French troops had landed in northern Quảng Nam and launched a large-scale mopping-up operation in Thừa Thiên, General Giáp sent a telegram to the 5th Interzone Command on September 26. In this telegram, he clearly stated the enemy's plot to fortify the Central battlefield and concentrate their forces to cope with the Vietnamese army in the main battlefield. He instructed the 5th Interzone to promote its activities in favorable directions (such as southern Đà Nẵng and northern Central Highlands) to attract enemy forces. He also instructed the interzone to develop revolutionary bases among the ethnic minorities in western Phan Thiết, closely follow the situations of Khánh Hòa and Ninh Thuận to make timely changes to the direction of struggle, and combine legal and illegal forms of struggle to promote the struggle movement. He also reminded the interzone to base its plan for coordinating with the main battlefield on its own military and economic conditions without indisposition.

Then he reminded leaders of the Bình-Trị-Thiên battlefield to prevent themselves from keeping the idea of "big fights and big victories." Each combat unit here should have the size of a battalion. The involvement of two battalions or an entire regiment in one combat unit should be made only when there were favorable conditions. He also called their attention to the task of directing the guerilla war, the preparation for enemy raid resistance, and first and foremost the plan for harvest protection.

Regarding the activities of Vietnamese forces in the areas behind the enemy lines in the Red River Delta, General Giáp sent a telegram to the 304th and 320th Brigades, the Red Bank Command, and the 3rd Interzone. According to him, each brigade should assign only one or two of its regiments to combine with the interzones' armed forces to continue their small-scale activities in accordance with the agreed plan. The remaining regiments should stay in the mobile areas outside the free zone, continuing their military and political re-educational programs, consolidating their organizations, and getting ready for coordination when the conditions were favorable. The chance would come when enemy forces were attracted to the main direction and when they were likely to bring their mobile troops to the free zone, which would weaken their rear. About ten days later, having detected the new symptoms of the enemy, General Giáp emphasized the possibility that the enemy might launch a mopping-up operation in the Red River Delta, and thus reminded the Vietnamese brigades to cooperate with localities to get ready for combat and prevent themselves from the idea of subjectivism.

As for Việt Bắc Interzone alone, from the judgment of the possibility that the French might threaten the resistance rear when the Vietnamese regular brigades moved to the Northwest, General Giáp gave specific instructions on the action direction for the forces in the interzone. In *"Chỉ thị hoạt động thu-đông 1952"* (literally: "Instructions for the 1952 Autumn-Winter Activities") sent to the Việt Bắc Interzone Command on September 16, he judged that when the campaign started, one part of the French mobile troops (especially paratroopers) and one part of

Chapter Six: DETERMINATION TO HOLD THE OFFENSIVE

the French air force in the North might be attracted to the main direction. Then, the battlefield behind the enemy lines in the midlands would be more advantageous for us, but only to some extent because the majority of the French mobile forces would remain strong. He estimated that the French might launch an operation which involved from one to two mobile regiments to the free zone in the direction of Thái Nguyên and especially Phú Thọ. In that situation, they might cause the Vietnamese rear difficulties, but their temporarily-occupied areas would reveal more weaknesses. In order to combine with Vietnamese regular soldiers in the main battlefield, Việt Bắc Interzone should be prepared to fight against French troops in several battlefields, not only in the French army's temporarily-occupied areas but also in the direction of their operations which might destroy the free zone. In the French army's temporarily-occupied areas, the Vietnamese army should reinforce their activities to constraint French troops and combine with the main battlefield to promote the guerilla war and resist the French mopping-up operations. They should also have a thorough grasp of the idea of guerilla war and the principles of raid resistance proposed at the Conference on Guerilla War held in July in order to crush the political and economic plots of the French in their temporarily-occupied areas. In the directions in which French troops might attack (like Phú Thọ, Thái Nguyên, Bắc Giang, and Lạng Sơn), the Vietnamese should urgently complete the plan of combining the forces of the Campaign Headquarters, interzones, and localities while getting ready to resist French troops when the latter launched attacks on the Vietnamese resistance rear.[1] On the other hand, they should continue the plan of consolidating their bases in the borders areas (such as Lao-Hà, Lạng Sơn, and Móng Cái) and determinedly preventing the bandits' acts of sabotage.

On October 2, General Giáp set off to the Northwest battlefield.

It was not until this dry season that he had the chance to return to this battlefield, after his trip to the Lao-Hà battlefield from Tiên Kiên Commune (Phú Thọ Province) with Bằng Giang during the first few days of the national resistance war. He had not forgotten his recommendations in the letter to the Westward soldiers in early 1947. As early as the dry season of that year, the first dry season of the national resistance war, the French expanded their temporarily-occupied areas in western Việt Nam to the right bank of the Red River, along with their offensive operation in Việt Bắc. As a result, the whole mountainous area that stretches along the border line from northeast to northwest was tightly locked. Had it not been for the Westward units' efforts in overcoming days of hardship and deprivation to hold on to the local land and people, the Vietnamese brigades would not have been able to reach the Northwest that day. General Giáp was sad when thinking of

---

1. According to the plan to protect the Vietnamese resistance rear, when the Vietnamese regular brigades marched to the Northwest, one battalion of the 246th Regiment was disposed in southern Thái Nguyên Town while one another was arranged to stay in the free zone of Phú Thọ and combine with local forces to get ready for the fight against French troops. The 238th Regiment of Việt Bắc Interzone rotated their activities the areas behind the enemy lines in Bắc Ninh and Bắc Giang. When the French army had not attacked yet, local soldiers and regular regiments, especially the newly-founded units, in Thái Nguyên and Phú Thọ continued with the training program.

Chapter Six: DETERMINATION TO HOLD THE OFFENSIVE

his soldiers who had lost their lives in deprivation and his compatriots in this immense mountainous region who had not ever seen the national flag or enjoyed the atmosphere of independence and freedom though the Autumn Revolution ended over seven years earlier.

On October 4, General Giáp stopped over at a place north of Yên Bái Town where Vietnamese troops gathered for the campaign and where Vietnamese unit cadres received orders, were informed of battlefield disciplines, and joined discussions for the final agreement upon tactical issues. At the conference held on the evening of October 7, General Giáp summarized the preparations made for the campaign from the previous campaign cadres' conference and confirmed the unshakeable determination of the Party Central Committee and the Central Military Commission. He reminded Vietnamese cadres to thoroughly grasp all the tactical requirements set for this campaign, recognize the differences in attacking fortifications and reinforcements between this campaign and the previous campaigns, and learn how to command troops to gain victory over an enemy who was well prepared in a mountainous and forested battlefield. He also reminded them to make timely and sufficient preparations, especially after their troops had crossed the river and entered the French occupied areas. Since the campaign was launched in a battlefield which was far from the resistance rear, required long marches, was featured with dangerous terrain and hard weather conditions possibly resulting in difficulties in supply transportation, and was subject to swift changes, Vietnamese troops were required to remain determined during the campaign, especially in difficult situations. He firmly stated that no matter how dangerous the situation might be, the

Central Military Commission would be determined to lead the whole army to overcome all obstacles and difficulties, fully realizing all the intentions of the Party Central Committee and keeping promises to the Central Party Committee, President Hồ Chí Minh, the people, and the army.

Regarding the issue of maintaining determination, General Giáp cited some stories from the advisory body's reports during the days of preparation for the campaign. It was the story of the Northwest units' spirit and results of fighting against bandits during the past months, paving the way for the units who were tasked to launch the campaign. It was the story of a reconnaissance unit which had arrived in the area of Nghĩa Lộ about three month earlier overcoming all daily difficulties to fulfill their task—keeping the campaign directions secret—for months. It was the story of the emulation spirit in supporting the front line among the people in Yên Bái and Phú Thọ. They had mobilized tens of ferry-boats and 400 basket boats, getting ready to take soldiers and conscripted laborers across the river. All those facts were examples for Vietnamese cadres and soldiers to follow and to strengthen their determination to overcome all difficulties to accomplish their tasks. He particularly highlighted the spirit of self-motivation of many cadres who went out in the rain and got close to enemy posts for field reconnaissance. Among them was Chief of Brigade Vương Thừa Vũ. That time, he led a group of Vietnamese cadres during a field trip to Nghĩa Lộ to get information of the terrain and enemy situation in preparation for the battlefield. They finally reached the destination after having walked five or six consecutive days and nights and crossed the 60-km outer belt of the area. General Giáp had heard Vũ talk about his days' imprisonment in Nghĩa Lộ, so

Chapter Six: DETERMINATION TO HOLD THE OFFENSIVE

he easily understood why the latter got so excited when his brigade was assigned to attack it. This town was the place where over 200 political prisoners had been kept and where so many Party members had lost their lives after days of being cruelly tortured. Among these Party members were the 13 comrades who had joined Vũ to carry out the prison-break in March 1945. Unfortunately, they failed to escape and was shot dead by warders. Their bodies were thrown out on a ground full of wild guava trees south of Pú Chạng hill, which was later turned into a military airport.

Also in this place did General Giáp listen to Bằng Giang's report and give more instructions on the preparation and operation directions to some Vietnamese regular units in the Northwest. During their discussion on the direction and guideline of the campaign at the campaign cadres' conference held in September, cadres of units and localities unanimously agreed with General Giáp's judgment that Vietnamese troops' activities deep in the areas behind the enemy lines played an especially important role in this campaign. These activities would force the enemy to disperse their troops to cope with Vietnamese regulars in both directions (Nghĩa Lộ and Phù Yên in the front and a vast mountainous area, stretching from the right bank of the Red River to the other side of the Red River, at the back). Besides, the Vietnamese units who penetrated deep into the areas behind the enemy lines would take the chance to court popularity, build up the people's political bases, carry out armed activities to grind down the enemy's strength, and cooperate with Vietnamese regular forces in the front.

In his telegram to the 910th Battalion—a unit which had cooperated with the 148th Regiment to gain many achievements in wiping out bandits during the preparation for the Northwest campaign and was operating independently along the Đà River, General Giáp its three tasks in cooperation with the coming campaign. These tasks are: 1- Courting popularity and consolidating and expanding political bases; 2- Developing the guerilla war, widening bases, and establishing local armed forces; 3- Making a plan for grinding down part of the enemy's strength.

He emphasized the guideline of "small fighting and assured victory." He also firmly stated that armed activities should go together with public propaganda and organization, and that there should be plans to resolve logistical issues and not to over-rely on supplies from the rear.

On the way to the battlefield, General Giáp frequently received additional reports on the situation ahead, as well as those from the technical radio station on the enemy's activities across the country. In early October, de Linarès ordered to give the alert throughout the Northwest and assigned reconnaissance planes to fly along the Đà River and the Nghĩa Lộ-Than Uyên route. It was reported that the French Headquarters had been moved from Nghĩa Lộ Subdivision to Pú Chạng. After reinforcing Nghĩa Lộ with one company, the French were urgently strengthening their defense system. General Giáp instructed Thái to re-check the situation, because it might be the sign of the French having discovered the attack directions of Vietnamese troops. Then Vietnamese troops were ordered to promptly complete all preparations for the campaign so that it could start on schedule.

Before crossing the Red River, General Giáp sent a letter to President Hồ Chí Minh, General Secretary Trường Chinh, and the Politburo in the rear on October 11 to report on the situation. Accordingly, there had not much change in the enemy situation. On the Vietnamese side, all activities to stimulate the army's determination had been fully implemented and the detailed combat plan had exerted a good impact on their determination. A specific issue was also mentioned in the letter, that is, the preparation for the soldiers' river crossing. "Thanks to the close cooperation of local cadres and people, our soldiers were equipped with sufficient means to cross the river," he wrote. He judged that there still remained the possibility that the enemy might attack Phú Thọ or Thái Nguyên, but he believed that they would withdraw after the attack. It was planned that after the first phase of the campaign, a Vietnamese regiment would be sent to Phú Thọ, which was more likely to be attacked by the enemy.

On October 12, General Giáp with his escort passed the Red River.

On arriving at the Campaign Headquarters based in Khe Lóng near the 13th Route, he learned that Vũ and the field reconnaissance group of the 308th Brigade in Nghĩa Lộ had not returned. Political Commissar Song Hào further reported that, the Chief of the 36th Regiment was waylaid by French troops at the Ca Vịnh stream when he was on the way back after finishing the reconnaissance of Cửa Nhì. After being retaliated, the French troops ran away. Having heard that a French company had been assigned to catch Vietnamese reconnaissance groups early in Khâu Vác, the 308th Brigade tasked a battalion to immediately set off to rescue the group. However, no news about them had been received yet. In the direction of the 312th Brigade, Chief of Regiment Hoàng Cầm met with French troops on his reconnaissance. He was injured, and two other scouts were killed. Therefore, the French might have smelt out Vietnamese regular forces. The Vietnamese advisory body was concentrating on watching and checking information about the French. If the French sent troops to block Vietnamese troops on Khâu Vác pass, it would be very difficult for the Vietnamese army to go along the only path to the main direction of Nghĩa Lộ.

Luckily, the worst situation did not happen because the 308th Brigade reported that its chief and reconnaissance groups on both directions had returned safely the following day. It was not true that a French company had been waiting to catch Vietnamese reconnaissance groups early on Khâu Vác pass. Due to the fact that the time to research the French situation was longer than expected, tactical plans were being urgently prepared by Vietnamese units. By this time, Vietnamese soldiers had crossed the Thao River safety and were marching toward the gathering places. During the first few days, they learnt how the jungle rain in the Northwest was. The "out-of-season" rains might make streams deep and paths slippery, which affected the soldiers' marching speed even though they had taken advantage of daylight to march without fear of French planes. After continual jungle rains came dry and sunny days of October.

On October 14, the campaign began with a series of small battles aiming at some positions in the outer circle of the gateway to Nghĩa Lộ,[1] paving the way for the first key battle of

---

1. The 141st Regiment of the 132nd Brigade eliminated Sài Lương; the 98th Regiment of the 316th Brigade eliminated Bản Trại; the 174th Regiment of the 316th Brigade eliminated Ca Vịnh and Ba Khe. French troops ran away from many posts such as Thượng Bằng La, Đồng Bồ, Khe Địa, Gốc Báng, Vạn Yên, and Bản Muồng.

Chapter Six: DETERMINATION TO HOLD THE OFFENSIVE

the campaign. In the previous campaigns, Vietnamese troops often began with big battles, which attracted French troops and shook their defense system right in the beginning. In this campaign, the combat mode of the Vietnamese army was different. It was known through foreign press that after the Lý Thường Kiệt campaign of the 312th Brigade, General Salan in particular, as well as the French Headquarters of the French expeditionary army in the North and Northwest in general, still thought that the Vietnamese army could hardly "return to Nghĩa Lộ." They still believed that the Vietnamese army would still attack the midlands and plains that dry season. Therefore, the small battles in the beginning of the campaign did not draw much attention of the French Headquarters to the Northwest direction. As said by General Giáp, the French had not "seen the stature of this offensive" yet. It was known that having listened to de Linarès report on French troops' skirmish with the Vietnamese, on October 15, General Salan still instructed the commander of French troops in North Việt Nam "not to immediately send a parachute battalion to Gia Hội or Tú Lệ and to take actions only after seeing how the Vietnamese army's activities develop."[1] But the instruction arrived when de Linarès had sent a parachute battalion to Tú Lệ with the task to proceed to the Red River to sound out the Vietnamese situation. This proved that the French had not known that the Northwest was the main attack direction of the Vietnamese regular brigades and that Nghĩa Lộ was the first big target of attack. Hardly had the French paratroops started to march eastward to do their task when shots were heard in Nghĩa Lộ, about 30 kilometers southeast of Tú Lệ. On October 19, the French paratroops had just got out of

---

1. This detail was revealed in Salan's memoirs nearly 20 years later.

Tú Lệ and walked about seven or eight kilometers when they encountered the 165th Regiment coming from Gia Hội. The paratroops were immediately ordered to stop proceeding to the Red River and return to Tú Lệ.

In the main direction of Nghĩa Lộ, on the night of October 16, the 308th Brigade had passed Khâu Vác and reached the Nghĩa Lộ valley. When being asked why the brigade had reached the gathering place and approached the target late, its chief reported that it had stopped raining four days earlier, but they had made incorrect calculations of the marching speed and failed to predict terrain difficulties. The following morning, French reconnaissance planes from Khâu Vác, Nậm Mười, and Bản Hợp kept prying into Nghĩa Lộ. Chief of Regiment Vũ Yên reported that the French had discovered their phone line. The Chief of the 308th Brigade asked the Staff of the campaign if the French had worked out the main attack direction of Vietnamese regular brigades. Having received the answer, he felt secure to keep supervising and speeding up the preparation. He also proposed to General Giáp an early attack on Pú Chạng. After knowing that there had been enough conditions for a guaranteed victory, General Giáp approved the proposal. He even felt more secure after learning that the 267th Company, accompanied by Vice Chief of Regiment Hùng Sinh, were getting close to Pú Chạng. All preparations were promptly made.

At 4:30 pm, mortars started aiming at Nghĩa Lộ Town to constrain enemy cannons so that Vietnamese troops could get closer to Pú Chạng. At 5:10 pm, the attack on Pú Chạng (or Nghĩa Lộ hill) began. Two hours later, Vice Chief of Brigade Cao Văn Khánh reported that Vietnamese troops had occupied all fortifications and were looking for the enemy's underground tunnels. Vũ soon realized that the 102nd Regiment might finish Pú Chạng earlier than expected, so he suggested the 88th Regiment attack Nghĩa Lộ Subdivision before dawn. This was also an unplanned decision. General Giáp asked about the certainty of success and get the guarantee from Vũ, so he approved the decision. He also praised it as "a flexible decision." At about 8:30 pm, no sooner had Vietnamese troops started their attack on Nghĩa Lộ Subdivision than they learned that about 100 enemy troops in Pú Chạng, including Major Tirillon as commander of the subdivision and about ten captains and lieutenants, came and surrendered to the Vietnamese army. The attack on Nghĩa Lộ Subdivision ended before dawn, exactly as estimated by Vũ. Thus the first big battle of the campaign was successful. Meanwhile, in the Southeast direction, the 36th Regiment had defeated Cửa Nhì and the 174th Regiment had eliminated Ba Khe. The Yên Bái-Nghĩa Lộ route was finally opened after having been closed for five years. The way leading to the heart of the Northwest area was widely opened.

In his congratulatory letter sent to the 102nd and 88th Regiments on October 18, General Giáp wrote:

> The two battles in Pú Chạng and Nghĩa Lộ prove that you, cadres and soldiers, made sufficient preparations, grasped opportunities to attack, and promoted the spirit of fighting bravely and strongly as well as the close coordination between different arms. Thanks to these, you were able to annihilate the enemy completely and quickly.

The first phase of the campaign ended with satisfactory results. Besides two major positions of Nghĩa Lộ and Phù Yên, the Vietnamese army eliminated a great number of minor positions along the routes between the Red and Đà Rivers.

Around 1,500 French troops, including most of commanding officers of Nghĩa Lộ Subdivision and Phù Yên Subzone, were killed or arrested. Thousands of guns, including two 150-mm howitzers, and thousands of bullets of different kinds were collected. A large area, including Văn Chấn and Than Uyên Districts (Yên Bái Province), Phù Yên District and part of Mường La District (Sơn La Province), and part of Quỳnh Nhai District (Lai Châu Province), was liberated. The face of the battlefield changed radically. The entire outer defense line of the French army, which stretched from the right bank of the Thao River to the left bank of the Đà River and from Vạn Yên (Sơn La Province) to Quỳnh Nhai (Lai Châu Province) was smashed. Lai Châu and especially Sơn La were under a direct threat.

It is noticeable that in the first phase of the campaign, there was a Vietnamese unit which managed to destroy completely a French reinforcement battalion in a strengthened fortification before dusk, regardless of the latter's non-artillery fire-power. And there was another one which pursued French troops for many consecutive days along a stretch of road of nearly 100 kilometers on the mountainous and forested terrain. Different combat tactics were used in the first phase, including attacking fortifications, attacking reinforcements, and pursuing enemy troops for many days. In terms of objectives, the first phase focused on launching offensives, creating diversions southeast of Lai Châu, widening the liberated zone, directly threatening Tuần Giáo, and clearing the westward road. In his report at the campaign cadres' conference held on September 11, General Giáp presented an analysis of the progresses and strengths of Vietnamese cadres and soldiers, as well as their shortcomings

Chapter Six: DETERMINATION TO HOLD THE OFFENSIVE

that restricted their achievements in the first phase. The most serious shortcoming was the disobedience of time disciplines, especially in marching to the gathering location (the unit in charge of attacking French reinforcements was half a day late and that in charge of attacking Nghĩa Lộ was two days late). The other shortcomings included loosely encircling enemy troops and so giving them chance to escape, such as in the battles of Sài Lương, Gia Hội, and Ca Vịnh; being quick in breaking through the enemy's outer defense line but prolonging the fight deep in the enemy's occupied areas, resulting in heavy casualties; and being inactive or perfunctory in pursuing and searching for enemy troops.

For French troops, the first phase of the campaign was a big surprise. At first, they were so subjective that they made wrong predictions of the Vietnamese situation, so they were confused in coping with Vietnamese troops. Only after Nghĩa Lộ Subdivision was destroyed did the French Headquarters realized that the Northwest was the main attack direction of Vietnamese regular brigades in the dry season. Later, in his memoirs, Salan revealed how the French Headquarters reacted in such a passive situation. On the night of October 17, he was attending a party held by Minister Letourneau to welcome Minister de Chevigné when General Salan heard that Nghĩa Lộ was under attack. That night, he was overwhelmed by worry. The following morning, he and the two ministers flew to Hà Nội. At noon, they arrived in Gia Lâm and met de Linarès, who had flown from the Northwest. Seeing the three guests from Sài Gòn, de Linarès immediately uttered, "It's all over!" Later Salan wrote:

> The truth of that tragic night all was exposed to me that night. I had strongly believed in the resistance ability of our

fulcra. But this time, Giáp and the Vietnamese Headquarters had put all the 308th Brigade's efforts into their attacks on the two posts, first the high one and then the low one. The other directions were just diversionary ones. At midnight, the attack on the peak of the mountain ended and the death sentence to Nghĩa Lộ was approved.

After being told about the battle, I thought that the loss of Nghĩa Lộ Subdivision was a painful blow to us, but it was not a decisive one. It was just the start of a game of chess. It was our turn to take actions. I wouldn't let Giáp win the next battle. I decided to withdraw all our posts—the fortifications that had become the easy preys of the three warring brigades of the opponent—and promptly take all the combat forces from the middle section of the Đà River to Nà Sản.

Salan sent a telegram to Bigia, commander of a parachute battalion, who was said to be very familiar with the terrain because he had operated in this area since 1947. Salan ordered this major to immediately take his battalion and all the troops stationed in the posts along the way to Nà Sản.[1] After giving the order, Salan and the two ministers flew to Nghĩa Lộ. From the plane, the could see the fortification in ruins. The plane changed the direction and landed in Nà Sản.

---

1. According to a battlefield reporter, Salan did not expect that his order would bring disaster to Bigia's battalion. Although they were supported by the troops in Mường Chén and air force, the French paratroops who could survive after weeks of running away from Tú Lệ and return to Nà Sản were just ones who had become exhausted with soil and terrestrial leeches all over their bodies and were trembling with fear and because of a malaria. Salan alone was relieved after learning that Bigia and some paratroops had returned safely. In his memoirs, he wrote, "Paris won't forgive me if I let a parachute battalion eliminated." The surviving paratroops were unable to continue to fight, so they were immediately taken to Hà Nội.

Chapter Six: DETERMINATION TO HOLD THE OFFENSIVE

There, Salan gave Gilles and Vaudrey instructions on what should be done to immediately turn the Nà Sản valley into a solid "dyke to prevent waves," stopping the Vietnamese army from penetrating deeper into the Thai region, and a springboard and a base for the French army's march. General Ala and General Debernardi[1] were ordered to set up an airlift to tackle all issues relating to the air force's troop rotation, supply, and fire-power reinforcement to the group of fortifications. Nà Sản had to stand firm because it was said to be a matter of life and death for the French army at that time. Salan's orders were later recorded in a document in which he stressed that the purpose of the Vietnamese army in the Northwest campaign was to regain the Thai region and then penetrate into Laos, and that the French army was to crush this political plot.

Salan also stressed the necessity of building around Nà Sản airport a group of fortifications which was strong enough to stand cannons and resist any attack. From Nà Sản, the French would launch operations to fight against Vietnamese brigades and at this fortification, they would be ready to "welcome" any attack.

It was 2 am on October 20. Salan had arrived in Hà Nội when he heard that the 6th Battalion led by Bigia in Tú Lệ was under attack. He immediately flew to the Northwest to urge Bigia to find ways to withdraw toward the Sơn La-Nà Sản direction. At the same time, he ordered the French unit at the

---

1. Colonel Gilles was tasked to build Nà Sản into a group of fortifications and command the Sơn La front, specifically the defense line along the Đà River from Mường Sài to Mộc Châu, preventing the Vietnamese army from crossing the river. Major Vaudrey was second in command in Nà Sản.

Mường Chén post to support the paratroops when the latter went by and ordered Vaudrey to lead a puppet battalion from Sơn La to cross the Đà River in Tạ Bú to receive Bigia. In the face of the worsening situation, Salan urgently flew back to Hà Nội, where he and Ala discussed the sending of more French troops to the Northwest for rescue[1] and the launching of the Lorraine operation to the Phú Thọ-Đoan Hùng area to destroy the rear of the campaign and force the Vietnamese to mobilize all their forces from the Northwest to protect the rear.[2]

During these days, at the Vietnamese Headquarters, the departments were busy following the situation and directing the preparation for the next phase of the campaign.

On October 31, General Giáp sent a document to the departments of the Vietnamese Headquarters to give his comments on the first phase of the campaign. He wrote:

> During a combat, it is important to have a thorough grasp of all possible situations and give timely instructions suitable for them. Compared to the Hòa Bình campaign, we were not good at grasping situations this time. For example, enemy troops parachuted in Tú Lệ on October 16, but we could not discover it before October 18; the enemy reinforced Sơn La with three battalions, but we did not know it until

---

1. Before the second phase of the campaign, the French increased their troop strength in the Northwest to 16 battalions and 32 companies, and organized the Northwest area into the battlefields of Lai Châu and Sơn La.
2. Departing on October 29, the 1st and 3rd Mobile Regiments of the French army, together with two armored vehicle groups, crossed the Đà River in Trung Hà and marched to Lâm Thao, Phú Thọ. They cooperated with the 2nd and 4th Mobile Regiments and paratroops to occupy Phủ Đoan. The center of their search was the T-junction of the Lô River, the Chảy River, and Đoan Hùng.

two or three days later; we did not know anything about the withdrawal of enemy troops from Than Uyên, either. In general, we were late in grasping the enemy's situation, especially their mobile forces.

In terms of command, the Central Military Commission this time determinedly supervised and sped up units to launch an early attack on Pú Chạng. As a result, we finished Pú Chạng and Nghĩa Lộ within one night, and soldiers were encouraged to fight in the daytime. In general, forces were used properly and no mistakes were made in command. However, we were unable to predict that the enemy would abandon Than Uyên and Ít Ong. The pursuit of the remnants of the enemy army after battles was paid much attention to, so we have basically swept all enemy troops from Nghĩa Lộ and Phù Yên so far. Nevertheless, we were still slow in grasping the situation of our units after a fight. It took some units five to seven days to know the exact numbers of their casualties. If the fight had been complicated, they could have more difficulties in grasping their troop strength.

The late supply also had negative impacts on the spirit and health of soldiers. So it was impossible to complete the reorganization of units five days after each battle as required.

The Central Military Commission had predicted difficulties in supplying a battlefield which was far from the rear, so the major mistakes in supply in the first phase belonged to the Campaign Headquarters. They failed to implement the transport plan, which affected the kitchen situation of the soldiers. In the first phase, a Vietnamese unit had to take soup while pursuing enemy troops. The road to the Northwest had been widened. However, to get the soldiers well-prepared to enter the second phase, General Giáp stressed the necessity of ensuring the rice supply to them. The transport route across Khâu Vác pass from Mậu A was secret and seldom threatened by enemy aircraft, but it was very dangerous. So it often failed to meet its daily transport target. Having heard of this situation, Head of the Logistical Department Trần Đăng Ninh, who was supervising and speeding up the transport route from the rear, immediately went to the Headquarters. The staff offered to stop all military activities and mobilize all soldiers to return to the depot on the right bank of the Red River to collect rice. Each trip lasted about ten days. A special meeting on rice-related issues was held at the Headquarters and chaired by General Giáp. The meeting decided to dissolve the transport routes of Khâu Vác and Sài Lương. Transport forces were then moved to the 13th Route; a transport route from Âu Lâu to Gia Phù was established; the Thu Cúc-Quang Huy-Tống Cao transport route was also urgently reinforced. Simultaneously, the transport route from Tống Cao to Suối Cao was organized and prepared to be linked with that on the 41st Route in Cò Nòi; a transport route to Vạn Yên was opened and connected with that on the 41st Route in Xôm Lồm to receive rice supplies from Thanh Hóa. The Campaign Headquarters reinforced the rear with Đàm Quang Trung and Trần Văn Quang and nearly 30 cadres for the organization and command of the 41st Route. Despite difficulties, the on-site food mobilization was also addressed in the meeting.[1] At the end of the meeting, General Giáp happily said, "So we've done what General Secretary Trường Chinh had said before we set off for the campaign, 'Be clever! Don't let the rice general block our way.'"

After the meeting, some stretches of the road such as the Suối Rút-Mộc Hạ-Xôm Lồm and Yên Bái-Ba Khe-Tống Cao-

---

1. In this campaign, the people in the Northwest provided the Vietnamese army with 1,140 tons of rice, 40 tons of meat, and 150,000 working days.

Chapter Six: DETERMINATION TO HOLD THE OFFENSIVE

Gia Phù stretches were urgently repaired by sappers. Besides over 50 motorized vehicles, the carrying bicycles which were invented by the conscripted laborers in Thanh Hóa were used for the first time to replace carrying poles, increasing the amount of transported supplies up to five to ten times. Thus the supply issue was basically solved before the start of the second phase.

To prepare for the second phase, the Campaign Headquarters particularly attached importance to the cooperative role of Bằng Giang's unit, which was in charge of launching diversionary offensives in southern Lai Châu-northern Sơn La direction.

In his order sent to the Northwest Interzone Command and the 312th Brigade Command on October 22, General Giáp ordered the 165th Regiment to cooperate with the 910th Battalion, the 148th Regiment, and local soldiers in Yên Bái, Than Uyên, Văn Bàn, and Lai Châu to "take advantage of the enemy's weaknesses to eliminate part of their strength, court popularity, launch the guerrilla war, expand the base area of Quỳnh Nhai, liberate and fortify Quỳnh Nhai into a firm foothold, develop into the directions of Luân Châu, Thuận Châu, and Tuần Giáo, and liberate Điện Biên Phủ in combination with the forces in the Nghĩa Lộ-Sơn La direction."

In his letter sent to the units which were tasked to penetrate into the enemy rear, especially those in the Quỳnh Nhai-Tuần Giáo-Điện Biên Phủ direction, the General Giáp pointed out advantages and disadvantages that they might encounter while carrying out this significant military-political policy of the Party Central Committee. Major disadvantages included difficulties in supply, weak revolutionary bases among the local population, language barriers, and unfamiliar local customs. In addition, the puppet army was mainly comprised of local men, who were familiar with the local terrain and thus could easily flee away, which made it hard for Vietnamese troops to completely annihilate them. General Giáp emphasized the combat guideline of penetrating units. Politically, they should attach importance to courting popularity and establishing political bases for a firm foothold. Militarily, they should develop the guerilla war, observe the principle "stead fight and assured victory, complete annihilation, and no fighting in case of unassured victory," and incessantly combine the task of conducting military combats with that of fortifying political bases.

On November 9, the Campaign Headquarters was running a meeting in preparation for the second phase when they heard that enemy troops were marching to Phú Thọ. In his report at the meeting, General Giáp judged that in order to save their defense line on the right bank of the Đà River, which might be crushed by the Vietnamese army, after their severe failure on the left bank, the enemy concentrated their mobile troops and launched an attack on Phú Thọ for the purpose of disturbing the Vietnamese rear and attracting Vietnamese troops back there. As the enemy had sent reinforcements to the Northwest and part of their mobile forces to Phú Thọ, the areas behind their lines in the plains, which were formerly fortified and strictly guarded by them, then revealed many weaknesses.

In the face of this situation, the Central Military Commission was determined to continue the march to the Northwest and concentrated troops to launch another offensive on Mộc Châu, on the right bank of the Đà River,

Chapter Six: DETERMINATION TO HOLD THE OFFENSIVE

despite the enemy's attack on Phú Thọ and their disturbance of the Vietnamese rear. In Phú Thọ, the Vietnamese advocated the enhancement of activities and guidance to constrain and annihilate the enemy. In the plains, they actively operated to take advantage of the enemy's weaknesses and to combine with Tây Bắc and Phú Thọ.

Regarding the Northwest battlefield, the Central Military Commission was determined to focus forces to annihilate the 3rd Battalion and the 1st Moroccan Regiment of the French army in Bản Hoa and wipe out Mộc Châu while making arrangements for fighting against enemy reinforcements or paratroops from Cò Nòi in the second phase.[1] Further developments would depend on specific situations.

In the order sent to units, the Vietnamese Campaign Headquarters particularly emphasized the importance of blocking the roads to prevent the 3rd Battalion and the 1st Moroccan Regiment from fleeing to Mường Lụm, Mộc Châu, or the 41st Route. In his appeal to Vietnamese troops for further marching to the Northwest, General Giáp also emphasized the requests for tight encirclement, complete annihilation, and pursuit to the last.

Because of the combat characteristics of the second phase (in which situations might happen quickly and the Vietnamese army would have many chances to eliminate enemy troops), the Vietnamese Campaign Headquarters gave soldiers specific instructions on river-crossing, marching,

---

1. The 312th Brigade was tasked to annihilate the 3rd Battalion, the 1st Moroccan Regiment, and the position of Ba Lay of the French army; the 316th Brigade was assigned to destroy Mộc Châu; the 308th Brigade was ordered to destroy Mường Lụm. All these units were also ordered to get ready to attack enemy reinforcements.

approaching, encircling, and pursuing enemy troops; and at the same time emphasized the positive, mobile, and flexible spirit in eliminating the enemy with resolution and avoiding relying on orders from the superiors.

Together with the determination to get soldiers across the Đà River to penetrate into and liberate the Northwest, the Central Military Commission assigned the 36th Regiment 36 to cooperate with the 176th Regiment and local armed forces to fight against the enemy in the areas of Phú Thọ, Yên Bái, and Tuyên Quang (with Phú Thọ and southern Tuyên Quang being the focal directions), grinding down part of the enemy's strength and crushing their plot to penetrating deep into the Vietnamese rear. Vũ Hiển, Vice Chief of the 351st Brigade, was put in charge of this battlefield.

It was later revealed that General Salan put much hope in the Lorraine operation in the Phú Thọ-Yên Bái direction. The French army marched into an area which they regarded as "the vital base of the opponent." What surprised them during the first few days was that they had to confront the units of the 176th and 246th Regiments and local armed forces. The Vietnamese forces sank enemy ships in the river; stopped and attacked the enemy landing in Vĩnh Lại and Ngọc Tháp; waylaid enemy troops in Lâm Thao, Phù Ninh, Thanh Ba, and Đoàn Hùng; and made an ambush in Phú Hộ. After five days of rummaging Đoan Hùng, on November 14, the enemy launched a mopping-up operation in Phù Hiên, Yên Bái. The same day, the French Headquarters received the news that the 36th Regiment of the Veitnamese army was going to the midlands from the Northwest. There were several factors accounting for General Salan's order withdraw French troops on the afternoon of November 15. The demand for supply

Chapter Six: DETERMINATION TO HOLD THE OFFENSIVE

transport through the airway for thirty thousand troops did not enable a prolonged march which had gone through two weeks with daily annihilated combat forces. One more regular regiment from the Northwest to Phú Thọ meant more losses to the French army while the movement of four mobile regiments from the plains revealed weaknesses of the inner bunker defense line. The French troops had not expected that no sooner had they been ordered by General Salan to withdraw than the 36th Regiment arrived in Phú Thọ and promptly deployed their combat formation in the Chân Mộng-Trạm Thản area on the 2nd Route. Of the two withdrawing armies, the one from Phủ Đoan to Việt Trì via the 2nd Route passed the ambushed battlefield of the 36th Regiment.

The battle in Chân Mộng happened severely from the noon till the night of November 17. It was reported that the French withdrawal was going on slowly on a road full of holes of sabotage like the frets of a piano when the Vietnamese regular army, with short-sleeved olive-green coats and disguised palm-leaf hats on, suddenly appeared as if they had been from the heaven. Being ambushed unexpectedly, the marching formation of the French troops was cut and the 4th Mobile Regiment, under the direct command of the 2nd Legionary Battalion, had to face the 36th Regiment. Together with over 40 vehicles, including 17 tanks and armored vehicles, the legionary battalion was supposedly eliminated. Then, the French withdrawal was slowed down due to the continuous pursuits and attacks of Vietnamese troops in Năng Yên, Phú Hộ, Nậu Phó, Phú Lộc, Mai Đình and Thanh Mại. Consequently, it took the two French armies six days to arrive in Việt Trì and Trung Hà. As for the 1st Mobile

Regiment, hardly had they arrived in Ngọc Tháp when they were picked up by an aircraft to reinforce Nà Sàn.

Shortly after that, General Salan held a press conference and claimed that all the French units involved in the Lorraine operation had arrived in Hà Nội and the victory of the operation had kept the Northwest area out of threat for a certain period of time. However, it was later firmly stated by war correspondents, as well as some French generals and historians, that it was just "a march in a vacuum," which was both costly and useless because it did not help to slow down the Vietnamese army's advance in the Western battlefield.

From mid November, in the areas behind the French lines in the Red River Delta, when the French mobile regiments were attracted to the Lorraine operation, the 304th and 320th Brigades of the Vietnamese army had further promoted their activities in Hà Nam, Nam Định, and Thái Bình, leveling many places, ambushing the 2nd Mobile Regiment during the latter's mopping-up operation, destroying nearly twenty vehicles, sinking three ships in the river, and killing thousands of enemy troops.

In the Northwest battlefield, on the nights of November 18 and 19, the 312th Brigade attacked Bản Hoa and Ba Lay, completely eliminating the 3rd Moroccan Battalion and one puppet company and seizing the chief of the battalion. Meanwhile, the 308th Brigade assailed Hát Tiểu and Mường Lụm and the 316th Brigade attacked Mộc Châu. The battle in Mộc Châu was the second key battle of the campaign, because it was considered as the French army's shield on the 6th Route to prevent Vietnamese troops from penetrating into the Northwest from the southeast. During the night of the

19th to the 20th of November, the 174th Regiment completely eliminated this important group of fortifications, killed and caught alive more than 350 enemy troops (including Chief of Battalion Vincent), and gained one 94-mm gun and over 500 ones of other types. The remaining French troops on the 41st Route from Mộc Châu to Sơn La (totaling about four battalions) were ordered to withdraw to Nà Sản.

In his congratulatory letter sent to the victorious unit in Mộc Châu, General Giáp clearly stated, "This victory proves that you have made a great progress after the re-educational course and the first phase of the campaign, and have actively overcome difficulties to successfully implement the order and complete the task with great determination."

By that time, the diversionary army had formed two directions of attack: one attacked Tuần Giáo and Luân Châu, and then penetrated deeper to completely annihilate the 58th Battalion of the puppet army and liberate Điện Biên Phủ; the other attacked Thuận Châu and pursue enemy troops to as far as Sơn La. On November 18, the enemy in Sơn La urriedly retreated to Nà Sản. The Vietnamese army simultaneously pursued enemy troops and rummaged for puppet officers in Sơn La Town, catching almost 500 remnants of enemy troops and over 100 puppet officers. The diversionary army completed their task, killing and capturing 1,400 enemy troops, liberating a large area including six districts and one town[1] with a total area of 3,000 square kilometers and a population of 100,000 people, and smashing the enemy defense line in southern Lai Châu.

---

1. They included the districts of Than Uyên, Quỳnh Nhai, Tuần Giáo, Mường La, and Thuận Châu and the town of Sơn La.

On November 23, the second phase of the campaign came to an end. In this phase, the Vietnamese army annihilated about 3,000 enemy troops, including one legionary battalion, one puppet battalion, the majority of the 55th, 56th, and 58th Puppet Battalions, and part of two parachute battalions; and liberated completely Sơn La Province (except Nà Sản) and part of the important land of Lai Châu Province. The remaining positions of the enemy along the Mã River were under serious threat, which forced the enemy to run away. Many local remnants of the enemy hiding in the forests were being pursued.

When the second phase of the campaign ended, most of the remaining enemy troops in the Northwest had flocked to Lai Châu and Nà Sản, two big groups of fortifications left in the vast Northwest area. The enemy force remained great in size (about 36 to 38 companies). It included some legionary and North African units which was relatively intact and had been sent here from the plains. The French Headquarters decided to concentrate and send their combat troops to Nà Sản, and urgently build it into a strong group of fortifications to prevent the Vietnamese army from penetrating deep into the western direction. They quickly built up a series of nearly 30 company-size fortifications and field-works around the airport, the command post, and fire-power battlefield. Materials were repeatedly transported by air from the plains to Nà Sản.

With the spirit of promptly preparing for the new phase of the campaign and not letting the enemy have time to fortify their defense line in Nà Sản, on November 30, the Central Military Commission convened a meeting of campaign staff. In his report at the meeting, General Giáp presented an

Chapter Six: DETERMINATION TO HOLD THE OFFENSIVE

analysis of the victories of the second phase in the main and cooperative battlefields. Then he said:

> Since the end of the first phase, we have overcome difficulties which seemed unsurpassable, thanks to our sustained determination. Therefore, the biggest lesson of the second phase is that of maintaining determination; the victory of the second phase is that of maintaining determination.

After analyzing the enemy situation in the group of fortifications in Nà Sản, the Central Military Commission realized that the strength of the enemy lay in their large number of troops, which were arranged into different groups of fortifications and so could support one another and were supported by artillery and aircraft fire-power. However, the enemy also revealed weaknesses. Among them, the fortifications were still field-based and isolated; the supply relied completely on the airway; the troops were still mentally affected by their previous failures. The Central Military Commission decided to focus forces for the launching of the third phase with a view to annihilating the enemy in Nà Sản and gaining a complete victory for the campaign. Regarding the combat guideline of the third phase, General Giáp said:

> The Central Military Commission was not forced to determinedly launch an offensive on Nà Sản. Instead, we are totally proactive in making such a decision. We have analyzed our situation and that of the enemy, and found that we have conditions to eliminate the enemy and win them in Nà Sản.

Then he stressed that in order to successfully implement the "steady fight and steady advance" guideline, Vietnamese troops should attack weak positions first and strong ones later, the surroundings first and the center later; collect enough information about their own situation and that of the enemy, and make sufficient preparations in terms of ideology and organization; and keep fighting.

To implement the afore-mentioned guideline, in the beginning of the third phase, the Vietnamese Campaign Headquarters decided to concentrate forces (including units experienced in attacking fortifications) to break through the surrounding fortifications, create access, and control the enemy's artillery battlefield and airport, preparing conditions to develop into the center of the group of fortifications and destroy them all. These fortifications were assessed by the Vietnamese to be not as strong as those in Nghĩa Lộ, Mộc Châu, and Pú Chạng.

On the night of November 30, the Vietnamese army began the third phase with two attacks on the 173rd height (Pú Hồng) and Bản Hời. After nearly two hours of fighting, two battalions of the 308th Brigade eliminated one reinforcement company of the 1st Mobile Regiment in Pú Hồng and seized the commanding officer of the fortification. Meanwhile, one battalion of the 312th Brigade annihilated an enemy company in Bản Hời. The following day, the enemy launched many offensives with the support of aircraft and artillery on the 173rd height, dislodging Vietnamese troops from Pú Hồng and taking control of this position.

On the night of December 1, the 209th Regiment attacked Bản Vây, the main fortification of those in southern Nà Sản, being occupied by two legionary companies. In the meantime, the 174th Regiment, which had been reinforced with one battalion of the 308th Brigade, attacked Nà Xi. Both attacks did not succeed. At dawn, the enemy strafed the formation of Vietnamese troops with aircraft and artillery to relieve the

Chapter Six: DETERMINATION TO HOLD THE OFFENSIVE

fortifications. The following day, they sent two reinforcement battalions to Nà Sản.

That Vietnamese troops had been tired after long days of fighting (especially pursuing enemy troops) in unfavorable weather conditions and difficulties in supply was not the main reason for their failures in the battles. Their determination to fight and eliminate the enemy was still strong. However, their failures mainly resulted from their inexperience in dealing with the enemy's new defense disposition. It was the first time the Vietnamese army had attacked an uninterrupted defense system in which fortifications closely supported one another. It was obvious that Vietnamese troops needed further practice to be able to eliminate such a defense system as that in Nà Sản.

The Northwest campaign gained great victories but ended after several last unsuccessful battles. In order to promptly stabilize the soldiers' mentality before they undertook new tasks, on December 10, the Vietnamese Headquarters convened a conference right in the command post in Tạ Khoa. In his report at the conference, General Giáp stated that it was not a preliminary summing-up conference or a summing-up one. It just aimed to confirm the significance of and reasons for the victory of the campaign, and to reach an agreement on the issue of whether to attack Nà Sản or not.

General Giáp affirmed the significant victories of the Vietnamese army and people across the country in the past two months: killing over 6,000 enemy troops and seizing over 7,000 ones. In the Northwest battlefield alone, they succeeded in releasing 250,000 people. This particular victory was important for the building of the great national unity, which laid the firm foundation for the long-term resistance war. In addition, an area of 28,500 square kilometers in the

Northwest which extended from the right bank of the Thao River, via the Đà River, to the 270-km stretch of the 41st Route stretching from Mộc Châu to Pa Ham (except Nà Sản and some positions along the Mã River) was liberated. This victory laid the foundation for the establishment of a new revolutionary base: the Northwest one. From then on, whether the situation might be favorable or not, the Việt Bắc and Northwest bases would be a guarantee for the long-term resistance war of the Vietnamese people and army, and would exert influence on the Lao revolution. In the areas behind the enemy lines, the guerrilla war was incessantly promoted in the plains. The struggle in these areas was extremely fierce during the year. It can be said during the previous months, the Vietnamese army and people successfully maintained an important part of the victories they had gained in the Hòa Bình campaign.

Regarding the five reasons for victories,[1] General Giáp highlighted the Vietnamese soldiers' progress in technique and tactics shown in marching, river-crossing, attacking heights, and pursuing enemy troops; as well as those in thinking and manners which helped to maintain their determination from the beginning to the end and promote their spirit of actively eliminating the enemy and bravely fighting and standing hardships.

Regarding the attack on the group of fortifications in Nà Sản, General Giáp mentioned three issues: Why was there the policy of attacking Nà Sản? Why was there a suspension

---

1. 1- The leadership of the Party Central Committee, the Government, and President Hồ Chí Minh; 2- The leadership of the Central Military Commission; 3- The progress of Vietnamese cadres and soldiers in all aspects; 4- The people's spirit of sacrifice and support to the front line; 5- The enemy's mistakes in command.

on the attack? What the situation would develop after the suspended attack?

The policy of attacking Nà Sản was based on the evaluations of the enemy's strengths (the large number of troops arranged into groups of fortifications, supported by artillery and air force) and weaknesses (weak fortifications, isolated positions, difficult supply, and feeble spirit). Regarding the Vietnamese side, the Vietnamese army managed to overcome difficulties in troop strength and supply, thanks to their efforts. They still had the advantage over their enemy in terms of troop strength and spirit. With the guideline of sufficient preparation and assured victory, the Central Military Commission considered the attack on Nà Sản not as a merely simple one to be finished to end the second phase. It was a combat phase of the campaign which was not less, but more, important than the previous ones. Therefore, it was necessary for Vietnamese cadres to be fully aware of themselves and the enemy, make new preparations in thinking and organizations, and understand the new fighting method, which was different from that in the two previous phases.

The Central Military Commission decided to suspend the attack on Nà Sản after realizing that after the two battles, the enemy forces there were reinforced with more troops and artillery, their defense line was strengthened, and their spirit was heightened, though their weaknesses remained unchanged. Meanwhile, after some battles on the periphery of Nà Sản, the Vietnamese combat forces suffered new casualties and bad health. In addition, there would be difficulties in the prompt supplementation of troops for the next series of attacks on fortifications. Therefore, although most of the Vietnamese cadres and soldiers were still eager to fight, some began feeling fearful of the enemy. The Central Military Commission was not sure of their victory in the attack on Nà Sản. Furthermore, their newly-liberated areas were very large, but they had not been fortified. These led to the Central Military Commission's decision to suspend the attack on Nà Sản and change to the task of consolidating the Northwest base to maintain their newly-gained victories.

The French plot was probably to fortify Nà Sản and then attack some places in the newly-liberated areas. However, the situation had changed by then. If French troops returned to the newly liberated areas, they would encounter many difficulties. To cope with this plot and to strengthen and expand their victories in the autumn-winter of 1952, the Vietnamese people and army had to, first and foremost, actively court popularity and fortify the Northwest base, especially the newly-liberated areas.

General Giáp emphasized the need for a thorough understanding of the significance of fortifying the revolutionary base, which laid the foundation for the implementation of the four main tasks, which included promoting propaganda and education among the population for the building of the people's bases, mobilizing and organizing the people to increase production, building up local armed and semi-armed forces, and heightening the people's vigilance over the return of the enemy.

On December 12, General Giáp ordered some Vietnamese units[1] to stay and penetrate further westward with the mission

---

1. These units were comprised of two regiments of 141 and 98 and battalion 88 of regiment 176 commanded by the Commander of brigade 312 Lê Trọng Tấn.

of developing military activities in the direction of the Mã River as a contribution to strengthening the newly-liberated areas. Specifically they were tasked to grind down part of the enemy's strength, court popularity, and liberate part of the land in the Mã River area if possible.

In his speech at the conference on the program for fortifying the newly-liberated areas, General Giáp emphasized the demand for a thorough grasp of the Central policy on keeping in close contact with local people, training local cadres, and actively fortifying the Northwest revolutionary base. He analyzed that it was "an important and heavy task" which required Vietnamese cadres at all levels to be fully aware of favorable and unfavorable conditions, as well as major and central tasks. He particularly emphasized the demand for a full awareness of the Central guidelines in the policy of mobilizing ethnic minorities. The guidelines includes patience, caution, certainty, and that of constantly improving of the people's awareness and leading them to proper struggle without any specific tendency (either leftism or rightism). Regarding the cultivation and training of local cadres, he said, "The Party Central Committee and Government instruct us to focus on cultivating and training local cadres in the mobilization of ethnic minorities. I particularly emphasize this issue, because it was a key issue and also a serious weakness of ours."

Regarding the tasks of improving working manners, keeping in close contact with local people, and fighting against bureaucracy, General Giáp cited some lively stories such as those of Sơn Hà (Quảng Ngãi Province), Lào Cai, and the recent campaign, from which he drew useful lessons of experience in mobilizing the public. He said:

> We should keep in close contact with people; listen to their opinions; make them trust, esteem, and love us as taught

by President Hồ Chí Minh; respect local cadres, patiently educate and persuade them, and always grasp the local situation for practical work plans.

With confidential words and personal experience in the years of revolutionary mobilization in the Cao-Bắc-Lạng base during the period of preparing for the armed uprising, he disseminated the operational orientations to local cadres as well as those who had been dispatched to the Northwest base to participate in the fortification of this base. He also strengthened their belief in the victory of the coming tough tasks.

On December 16, 1952, General Giáp left the Northwest battlefield for the General Headquarters.

In the Lao Battlefield

The similarity between de Lattre and Salan was that both always tried to make their feats of arms known to as many people as possible. De Lattre did it after "the feat on the 18th Route" and so did Salan after having set up "a dyke" in Nà Sản. The mere difference seemed to lie in the ways they did it. De Lattre needed a group of correspondents whereas Salan invited guests to visit the dyke right on the spot. Salan invited ten guests in the last week of December 1952. His guests were of various ranks[1] and almost all of them were invited to visit Nà Sản.

---

1. They included Mac Mahon, Minister of Australian Air Force and Navy; Alexandre Parodi, General Secretary of the French Presidency; Jacques Foccart, Advisor and Vice Chairman of the National Defense Committee of the French Union; André Montel (Minister of French Air Force; Luce (Editor-in-chief of the *Times* and *Life* magazines; Heath, American Ambassador; Boegner, head of all Catholic churches in France; Jean Lacouture, reporter of the *World* newspaper; General Lechères, Chairman of the Council of Chiefs of Staff; General Clark, American Commander in South Korea; and Alphonse Juin, French Marshal.

Each guest was invited for some purpose. The Ministry of Air Force had told Salan that "the attack on a bush also requires a squadron of bombers." He invited Montel to show the latter that Nà Sản could not have existed without the air force and to receive the latter's promise to help. The French Congress was still considering the budget for national defense. Salan invited Foccart to show the latter that the countries associated with France could not win this war without an increase in the budget. However, there were also guests who did not do what they had been supposed to do. One of them was Jean Lacouture, a young reporter from the *World* newspaper. He openly revealed his thoughts about the source of the Vietnamese power and factors that led to the victories of President Hồ Chí Minh's army. It is easy to understand why Salan was not satisfied with this young man.

There were also close guests (such as Foccart and Lechères) who made Salan feel free to reveal the worry of the French Headquarters when the year 1952 had ended and the war had entered a new year. The French Commander-in-chief said to Foccart that the year 1952 was "a long year when we had to suffer heavy losses for being attacked continuously . . . . The year 1953 has started with some omens showing that the French will cope with new difficulties."According to Salan's statistics, within only two and a half months in late 1952, about 4,000 French officers and soldiers were killed, wounded, and lost. The lost French troops in the Euro-African forces were only replaced by perfunctory phases of reinforcement from Paris. When being asked about the French troop strength at the end of 1952 and the budget plan for 1953, Salan said that soldiers from associated countries accounted for 58 percent of the total French troop strength of 401,000. In 1952, the United States provided the French army with 110 billion francs in cash and military equipment worth 90 billion francs. France was expected to spend 370 billion francs on the war, which means over one billion a day, mostly for the French expeditionary army because all the expenses for the troops from the associated countries were covered by the United States. Salan honestly said to Foccart and Lechères:

> Việt Minh troops are as tough as leeches. They have driven French troops into a miserable situation in the Northwest and is about to do the same in the Central Highlands. If Giáp had attacked the Northwest and the Central Highlands or Laos simultaneously, I would have met great troubles because I did not have any mobile force left to rescue them.

Among the guests, Juin was much expected by Salan. This man with an influential voice could make Paris pay more attention to Indochina. But Salan was soon disappointed: while this man had achieved great feats of arms in Italy during the Second World War, he was so unfamiliar with this enigmatic tropical battlefield. Later in his memoirs, Salan wrote:

> He was a great strategist who was used to commanding great brigades in battlefields where transport axes were always available in the rear, where his army did not have to worry about violent ambushes, and where they might encounter the fierce strength of the air force but not unexpected disasters that seemed to have fallen down from the sky. The war in Indochina was completely different. The terrain here was extremely odd with thick forests in the plains, swampy areas, and salty waters. Anyway, fighting here was less difficult since we could avoid the seemingly-endless ambushes. The road system was destroyed partly,

if not completely, so there were only difficult-to-pass paths left. I intended to explain to him that all those realities had become unendurable to Westerners, but then I realized that he was only worried that the Indochina War was lessening France's prestige in Europe and that he alone was so unfamiliar with our concerns.

Salan also disclosed that he had invited Juin to Nà Sản to introduce to this man the dyke and its role, and to inform him of some similar groups of fortifications which were under construction in Upper Laos. But Juin showed an indifferent attitude and said, "Be careful with the 'porcupine strategy.' We should remember Stalingrad. Nà Sản 'went for a good price' due to the Vietnamese army's mistakes, but they realized their mistakes in a timely manner, stopped, and finally retreated."

There was one guest who did not disappoint Salan. It was American General Clark, who came on the landfall of the 300th American aid ship together with the consent to send six Packett C119 airplanes, which were needed to transport vehicles to the French bases being built in Upper Laos. Before leaving, the American general said to Salan that, the American base in Tokyo was near Hà Nội and Sài Gòn and was able to satisfy what the French army's need for Indochina because this was their joint battle. Unlike Juin, Clark encouraged Salan to reinforce defense in Upper Laos as required by the King. So excited, Salan sped up the construction of defense buildings, not only in Luang Prabang and Vientiane but also in Siang Khouang and Plain of Jars.

While Salan was really worried about Upper Laos, the Staff of the Vietnamese General Headquarters was instructed by General Giáp to investigate the situation to prepare for a campaign which would be launched before the rainy season with Sam Neua as the target of attack.

This instruction did not result only from the viewpoint that Indochina was basically a battlefield or from the current efforts of French troops in fortifying Upper Laos. The combat alliance between Laos and Việt Nam had gained new steps of development in the new conditions, especially from the end of 1950.

In August of 1950, the Congress of Delegates of the National United Front of Laos (also called the Congress of Neo Laos Itsala Delegates), which involved the participation of more than 100 delegates,[1] issued a 12-article political program which aimed to unite all resistance forces in Laos and strengthen the solidarity with Việt Nam and Cambodia. Prince Souphanouvong was appointed as Chairman of the Front, as well as President and Prime Minister of the Lao Resistance Government. Since then, the combat alliance between Laos and Việt Nam had been enhanced. Shortly after the Second National Delegate Congress of the Communist Party of Việt Nam, the Việt Nam-Laos-Cambodia alliance was established; the relations among the three Indochinese countries gained new steps of development. President Hồ Chí Minh and the Standing Central Committee were especially

---

1. The congress took place in Gò Tre, Thổ Ngòi (Ngòi Là) Hamlet, Mỹ Bằng (Mỹ Lâm) Commune, Yên Sơn district, Tuyên Quang Province, in the revolutionary base of Việt Bắc. After the congress, in late 1950, President Souphanouvong and the Lao Resistance Government moved to Đá Bàn Hamlet at the foot of Mount Là (also in Mỹ Lâm Commune). Shortly afterwards, President Hồ Chí Minh came to Đá Bàn to visit President Souphanouvong and the Lao Government. Vestiges of the meeting hall floor, the house floor of Prince Souphanouvong, and that of Kaysone Phomvihane can still be seen nowadays in Thổ Ngòi.

interested in leading the thinking of Vietnamese cadres who had relations with Laos. Attending the conference held by the Việt Nam-Laos-Cambodia Liaison Committee in September 1952 on the issue of combined operation in the new stage, President Hồ Chí Minh had a talk with cadres of the three countries. He said that Việt Nam, Laos, and Cambodia were brothers under the same roof, and that the Vietnamese people and government would make every effort to help the Lao and Cambodian fronts, governments, and peoples unconditionally. He used the word "help" since he could not find a more suitable one. According to him, Việt Nam was not helping Laos and Cambodia, but it was doing an international mission.

One of the Vietnamese and Lao leaders' concerns in this stage was the building of a Lao revolutionary base in Upper Laos. Sam Neua—a Lao province which borders on Sơn La in the Northwest and Thanh Hóa in the 4th Interzone—had been chosen by leaders of the two countries as the target of liberation when the opportunity came. The opportunity was after the Vietnamese army had liberated eight-tenths of the Northwest, including Sơn La Province. Since the Northwest campaign ended earlier than expected, leading to a change in the face of the battlefield which was favorable to the Vietnamese side, the westward road was widened. In mid December, on the way from the Northwest back to the base, General Giáp thought of taking advantage of the time before the rainy season to send Vietnamese regular troops to Laos to help the people here liberate part of the land in Upper Laos and expand the Lao Resistance Government's foothold in an area which was contiguous to the newly-liberated Northwest area, according to the discussions between leaders of the two countries.

General Giáp had discussed with Nguyễn Chí Thanh and the Central Military Commission the dispatch of Vietnamese troops to Sam Neua. The Staff was ordered to officially investigate the French situation in Upper Laos and submit the results to the Central Military Commission.

It was worth noticing that the French had established a group of 11 fortifications with a total troop strength of three battalions in Sam Neua.

A review of the fighting process of Vietnamese regular troops from the dry season of 1950 revealed that, a battlefield in the mountainous and forested area created more favorable conditions for the Vietnamese army to win than one in the plains. But since the dry season of 1951, the appearance of groups of fortifications in Hòa Bình and then Nà Sản had posed a new challenge to their advance. Salan considered the groups of fortifications as a tactical defense measure and a dyke which helped the French expeditionary army stop the opponent. Therefore, it was a must for the Staff of the Vietnamese General Headquarters to urgently investigate this significant defense measure to defeat it, especially after the Northwest campaign and the battle in Nà Sản.

The Vietnamese regulars' growth in terms of equipment, tactics, and techniques enabled them to destroy from wooden and soil positions in the early stage to cemented and steeled blockhouses, from individual fortifications each occupied by one regiment or brigade to a group of fortifications occupied by more than one brigade like Đông Khê. After "saying goodbye" to spears and getting support of artillery, in the last dry season, a Vietnamese regular regiment attacked an individual position of a solid fortification occupied a French battalion in the mountainous and forested battlefield and eliminated it within a night. The test of the Vietnamese regular army's strength in the third phase of the Northwest campaign revealed that, with a group of fortifications equipped with a big army including mobile forces which could offer on-site rescue and supported by an airport, an artillery battlefield, and air forces, the French could not only cope with any artillery-supported attack by Vietnamese troops but also restrain Vietnamese regular regiments right in the mountainous and forested terrain, which was supposedly favorable to them.

The battles on the periphery of Nà Sản proved that Vietnamese troops were not capable of attacking the enemy's infantry and coping with their tanks, artillery, and aircraft at the same time. In the meantime, they lacked the support of artillery and anti-aircraft fire-power, so they were unable to constrain the fire-power of the group of fortifications itself in order to prolong the battle in the daytime and nighttime. Obviously, it would take them much time to be able to annihilate a group of fortifications like Nà Sản. First of all, they should spend time investigating this new defense measure to figure out a way of fighting that corresponded with their limited equipment.

According to General Giáp's instructions, at the end of February 1953, the Staff summoned some cadres of the 308th and 312th Brigades to together investigate the French group of fortifications. After nearly ten days of investigation, the Staff drew initial conclusions about the strong and weak points of the group of fortifications. These initial conclusions were further complemented and perfected with the results of the comparison of the French group of fortifications in Nà Sản and that in Sam Neua. Also in February of 1953,

General Giáp anticipated and proposed to the Party Central Committee the coming attack on Upper Laos.

In the letter sent to President Hồ Chí Minh, General Secretary Trường Chinh, and the Politburo on February 3, 1953, General Giáp reported on the recent open meeting of the Central Military Commission. The meeting discussed if the Vietnamese army should launch a campaign before the dry season or focus on preparing for the autumn-winter campaign, and what difficulties they would encounter if they launched a campaign in Upper Laos and what they should do to overcome these difficulties.

The Central Military Commission realized that if the Vietnamese army launched a campaign in Upper Laos, they would earn some benefits. First, they would be able to grind down part of the enemy's strength (estimated 2,000 to 3,000 troops). Second, they would help to build a small base for the Lao revolution. Third, they would force the enemy to disperse forces among the plains, Nà Sản, Lai Châu, Luang Prabang, and Vientiane. Thus, the enemy would be unable to send more reinforcements to the Northwest (which would create favorable conditions for the Vietnamese army to launch the autumn-winter campaign) or focus mobile forces in the plains (which would create conditions for the guerrilla war in the Red River Delta to develop). Last, Vietnamese troops would have a chance to practise attacking a small-size group of fortifications like that in Sam Neua before attacking a big-size one like that in Nà Sản.

To launch a campaign in Upper Laos (specifically Sam Neua), it was necessary to resolve some difficulties, especially those in transporting supplies (on a road which was twice as long as that in the battle of Nà Sản). If the Politburo determined

Chapter Six: DETERMINATION TO HOLD THE OFFENSIVE

to launch the campaign, the Central Military Commission would study on how to overcome those difficulties. The letter of the Central Military Commission sent to the Politburo ended with the following sentences: "In general, we propose to launch the campaign. There might be difficulties, but we are able to overcome. We would like to report this to you in advance for your consideration."

After discussing with leaders of the Lao Party for the last time, the Vietnamese Politburo approved the proposal of the Central Military Commission. The bodies of the Ministry of National Defense promptly set off to make preparations for the battlefield. General Giáp understood the thoughts of logistical officers when they participated in this campaign. This time, they would have to overcome more difficulties to meet the requirement of mobilizing about 3,500 tons of rice. At the meeting of the Central Military Commission, Head of the Logistical Department Trần Đăng Ninh reported that in order to serve soldiers in the coming campaign in Sam Neua, the two departments in charge of military supplies and transportation had to set up a system of storehouses along the over-600-km route from Lạng Sơn via Suối Rút, Mộc Châu, and Sốp Hao to Sam Neua. Sappers would destroy the waterfall in the upper section of the Mã River so that supplies could be transported by basket boat from Sốp Hao to Sam Neua. Besides conscripted laborers, cars, bicycles, and horses were also utilized. Lao people were also mobilized to provide soldiers with on-site food.

The meeting of campaign staff held in March focused on discussing the ways to attack the group of fortresses. By this time, the Staff had gained initial results of the examination of the French defense measure in Sam Neua. The French established a group of 11 fortifications in the centre of Hua Phan. Because of topographical conditions, the formation of the group of fortifications was based on length; its periphery was thin and revealed many weak spots, especially in the south. The biggest difficulty confronting the French here was that their supplies and reinforcements were transported completely by air, but the airport was far from the central base. Once the airport was dominated, they would be on the verge of annihilation.

In his concluding report, General Giáp presented the Central policy, the objectives of the campaign, as well as advantages and disadvantages confronting the Vietnamese army. Then he delved into analyzing the strengths and weaknesses of the French group of fortifications, ways to attack it, and some specific tactical issues. They included ways to overcome enemy strengths in fire-power; ways to deal with enemy artillery, aircraft, and troops counter-attacking in the daytime; the issue of continuous fighting; and command-related issues such as having a thorough grasp of soldiers, the arrangement of a fire-power battlefield, and the guarantee of communication. Regarding the task of continuing preparations for soldiers, General Giáp emphasized the direction for the satisfaction completion of the military re-educational program, specifically the tactical rehearsal on attacking the group of fortifications. Politically, soldiers should be well-prepared tactically and technically. The bodies of the General Headquarter and other related units should promptly make preparations for the campaign in the set direction.

In the report sent to the Politburo, General Giáp judged that after the Northwest campaign, the French incessantly strengthened fortifications and intensified combat forces to the Northwest. By then, 21 out of 105 French battalions, including 17 out of 33 mobile battalions, in North Việt Nam had been sent to the Northwest. Nà Sản alone had been reinforced with two battalions of the 7th Mobile Regiment, so the combat force here had increased to 15 infantry battalions and 3 artillery ones. French troops were often ordered to march in the direction of Sơn La and down to Chiềng Đông and Yên Châu; French aircraft and raiders were ordered to intensify their activities on the Vạn Mai-Suối Rút and Chợ Bờ-Suối Rút routes to explore and obstruct the Vietnamese preparations, which were thought to aim at the group of fortifications in Nà Sản. In the Northern plains, the French continued their mopping-up campaigns to stabilize the situation.

General Giáp anticipated that Vietnamese soldiers would cope with three to six French infantry battalions in Sam Neua, so he suggested that six to seven Vietnamese infantry regiments should be gathered here. Artillery fire-power should be reinforced as well. The cooperative directions should be actively involved in the campaign with Sam Neua to disperse the French mobile forces and aircraft. Regarding the preparations for soldiers, General Giáp mentioned tactical thinking as an important content in his report.

With regard to the preparation for the battlefield, the Vietnamese reconnaissance groups were reported to have approached Sam Neua and completed the arrangement of observatories. The Vietnamese Headquarters had understood the situation of French troops in Laos in general and in each area in particular. Particularly in Sam Neua, they had grasped the major characteristics of the terrain, the situation of the

French forces, and the arrangement of their fortifications. However, they were still unclear about the detailed disposition of the French troops and fire-power. Regarding the preparation of supplies, one of the emerging issues in the preparation of this campaign, General Giáp remarked that thanks to the experience in the Northwest campaign and the close guidelines and supervision, a majority of the plan had been completed despite limited time. It was estimated that there would still be difficulties from the middle line to the front line, but they could be overcome. Another favorable condition was that in many directions of the campaign, officials of the Lao Government kept accompanying Vietnamese soldiers to cooperate and help with the organization and mobilization of human and material resources for the campaign.

During the days of rehearsal, while Vietnamese soldiers were thinking about the group of fortifications in Nà Sản, the Vietnamese Staff was considering a diversionary plan which aimed to create a diversion in the enemy judgment about the Vietnamese army's attack direction. However, the Staff did not exclude the possibility that the enemy might discover that the group of fortifications in Sam Neua was under threat. They estimated two situations that might happen once the attack direction was discovered: the enemy would reinforce Siang Khouang with one to two battalions and Sam Neua with one to three battalions and turn Sam Neua into a big group of fortifications, or they would withdraw from Sam Neua. Both situations would be hard for the Vietnamese army to cope with.

On March 22-23, 1953, the 308th and 312th Brigades departed for the battlefield. Before the departure day, the political department held a class for soldiers to learn from

Chapter Six: DETERMINATION TO HOLD THE OFFENSIVE

President Hồ Chí Minh's encouragement letter. Because of the nature and characteristics of this campaign, the President encouraged the soldiers to overcome difficulties, emulate in eliminating the enemy, fight in Laos as courageously as they would do in Việt Nam, raise high the international spirit, respect the sovereignty as well as customs and practices of Laos, and esteem the Lao people.[1]

Vietnamese troops gradually penetrated into the Northwest. By that time, they had known that their coming target of attack was in Laos. They no longer thought that they would attack Nà Sản as they had expected several days earlier.

In early April, General Giáp set off for the battlefield. The Campaign Headquarters comprised Võ Nguyên Giáp, Hoàng Văn Thái, Nguyễn Chí Thanh, and Trần Đăng Ninh. In this campaign, Nguyễn Khang, a member of the Party Central Committee who was in charge of the Vietnamese army's affairs in Laos, was assigned to accompany the Campaign Headquarters. Lao members of the Campaign Headquarters included General Secretary of the Lao People's Revolutionary Party Kaysone Phomvihane, Prime Minister of the Lao Resistance Government Souphanouvong, the then Deputy Minister of National Defense, and the then Secretary of Sam Neua Provincial Party Committee. Chinese advisors did not join this campaign because it took place outside the Vietnamese borders.

Along the way, the military intelligence team of the Vietnamese Headquarters in the front line always reported to General Giáp that the Swallow radio sometimes spread

---

1. *Hồ Chí Minh toàn tập* (literally: Hồ Chí Minh's Complete Works), op cit., vol. 7, p. 64.

the news that the Vietnamese army was going to attack the Northwest and Upper Laos with Siang Khouang, Sam Neua, or Nà Sản as the target; and sometimes announced that they would probably attack Upper Laos in two directions: one from Mộc Châu to Sam Neua and the other from Điện Biên to Luang Prabang. Thus, the French had discovered that the Vietnamese army was marching westward, but they were still unclear about the specific directions of the campaign. French airplanes severely attacked the Hòa Bình-Suối Rút, Tạ Khoa-Quang Huy, and Kỳ Sơn-Bản Ban-Siang Khouang routes. It was reported that the French Headquarters called the troops who had just marched to Yên Châu and Cò Nòi back to Nà Sản, and provided this group of fortifications with more food and ammunition. Vietnamese troops secretly crossed the Mã River without the enemy's knowledge. Their diversionary activities had worked well.

On April 7, a member of the Vietnamese Staff brought General Giáp's report to the rear before the General left the middle line in Mộc Châu for Laos. General Giáp reported to President Hồ Chí Minh and the Politburo results of the staff meeting held on April 5–6 to check the preparations for the campaign and disseminate the plan for the last time before soldiers set off. According to the plan, the Vietnamese army would grasp every opportunity to annihilate the enemy and also get ready to attack enemy reinforcements to Sam Neua. In the first phase, they would try to eliminate some important peripheral heights within one night. In the second phase, they would penetrate deep into the battlefield and destroy big posts in the town. Then, they would eliminate the remaining positions, pursue the remnants of enemy troops, and assign a unit to expand the victory if possible. In case the enemy sent reinforcements, any of their decisions would be based on the specific situation. They would not fight if they were not sure of success. A unit of the 312th and 316th would create a diversion and prepare for the attack on the enemy on the Nà Sản-Cò Nòi route. They would also get ready to move along the 6th Route to Hòa Bình if the enemy sent paratroops there. On the night of April 9, four lightly-equipped battalions would depart from Mộc Châu and arrive at the targeted area before the morning of April 15 with the tasks of controlling the Mường Sầm airport and field to prevent enemy paratroops and blocking Route 6B to prevent the enemy from withdrawing to Siang Khouang. On the night of April 10, the majority of the remaining units would set off. The campaign was estimated to start on the night of April 17. According to the plan, two regiments of the 304th Brigade were in charge of Siang Khouang and the 148th Regiment was responsible for Điện Biên Phủ; the cooperative battlefields were set in the Right Bank and midlands. The 5th Zone would promote operations in mid April if there were not any obstacles. Regarding supplies, the amount of rice from the middle line (the Mã River banks) was sufficient for use by soldiers in 20 days, starting from April 15. There were difficulties on the 60-km route from the middle line to the front line, but they could be overcome.

At this time, the enemy were hurriedly reinforcing combat forces and consolidating fortifications to deal with the Vietnamese army in Upper Laos, though they had not figured out the latter's specific attack directions. During the last week of March, General Salan flew to Luang Prabang or the Plain of Jars almost everyday to instruct the reinforcement of the defense system and two airports. Sam Neua was a concern for the French Headquarters. Although, General de Linarès had supervised and sped up the strengthening of the group of fortifications for many days, General Salan still felt insecure. On April 5, Lieutenant-colonel Maleplate, commanding officer of Sầm Nưa, was summoned to Hà Nội to report the situation and get instructions to deal with the possibility that the group of fortifications might be attacked. A week later, he reported that eight Vietnamese battalions were heading Sam Neua.[1] From Hà Nội, Salan ordered a withdrawal of all French troops from Sam Neua to the Plain of Jars on the afternoon of April 12. The withdrawal was supported by the air force and raiders.

The Vietnamese Campaign Headquarters heard of the enemy withdrawal when their leading unit was still about ten kilometers from Sam Neua. General Giáp immediately ordered Vietnamese troops to pursue the enemy. On April 13, the ordered was delivered to the troops with his words of encouragement. He said, "The enemy has fled away from Sam Neua. Sam Neua has been liberated. However, in order to help our Lao friends fortify their revolutionary base, we have to eliminate the enemy at all costs."

Afterwards, telegrams from the Vietnamese Campaign Headquarters were continuously sent to regiments and brigades, urging units to pursue and annihilate enemy troops, first and foremost lightly-equipped ones. According to the first two telegrams dated April 13, the enemy had

---

1. According to *Từ Đồng Quan đến Điện Biên* (literally: From Đồng Quan to Điện Biên) by General Lê Trọng Tấn, the attack direction was revealed when one guide of the Vietnamese reconnaissance platoon's surrendered to the enemy. Later, on April 12, one cadre of the platoon was arrested by the enemy in Sam Neua.

Chapter Six: DETERMINATION TO HOLD THE OFFENSIVE

completely withdrawn from Sam Neua on the night of April 12. The enemy was predicted to reach Mường Hàm on April 13 and Mường Peun on April 14. One part of them might go to Mường Hiểm. General Giáp ordered Hùng Sinh and the 102nd Regiment to immediately start pursuing enemy troops day and night. They were ordered to depart from Khang Thọ to the main road in Nà Thông, past Sam Neua, and finally towards the Bản Ban-Siang Khouang direction. In the meantime, Vũ Yên and the 308th Brigade were ordered to immediately go along the main road, past Sam Neua, and towards the Mường Hàm-Mường Peun-Bản Ban-Siang Khouang direction.

General Giáp reminded units to bring along radio transmitter and report every two hours. Along the way of pursuing enemy troops, they were required to investigate the enemy situation and watch out for enemy mines.

It was calculated that the first Vietnamese units departed from Sam Neua at about 5 pm on April 13, so they were eight hours slower than the last French unit and nineteen hours slower than the leading one.

Shortly after the liberation of Sam Neua, the Lao Resistance Government made a statement:

> The liberation of Sam Neua is a great victory in the hard resistance war of Lao people.... We have not only gained an important tactical area but also eliminated a great number of enemy troops. The liberation of Sam Neua has created favorable conditions to widen the revolutionary base of Lao people.

In a consultation held on the morning of April 14, the Central Military Commission assessed that although having

633

withdrawn from Sam Neua, the enemy could hardly keep its strength intact. It was a long way from Sam Neua to Bản Ban (it took them at least five days to go from Sam Neua to Bản Ban); they were closely pursued by Vietnamese troops; they were demoralized and inexperienced. Therefore, they would be easily disintegrated and eliminated. The enemy was forced to withdraw from an important position in their western defense line, which made the group of fortifications in Nà Sản more isolated and put the positions of Siang Khouang and Luang Prabang under more direct threat. Although the Vietnamese army had not attacked Sam Neua, they opened the gateway to Upper Laos and fortified their free areas in the Northwest, Hòa Bình, and Thanh Hóa, thanks to the enemy withdrawal. In addition, the Lao Resistance Government managed to built up a revolutionary base which was almost as large as the Northwest and was connected to the free areas in Việt Nam, creating favorable conditions to promote the Lao revolution to a new stage.

From the night of April 13, the races between Vietnamese troops, who were highly spirited and determined to pursue and annihilate the enemy but unfamiliar with the local terrain and language, and French troops, who were demoralized but familiar with the local terrain and supported by reconnaissance aircraft, had taken place on the roads of Upper Laos. Also from that night, the Vietnamese intelligence had detected various sources of information transmitted in the air, mostly in the French and Lao languages. With the assistance of some Lao cadres, Vietnamese intelligence officers could finally gather necessary information of the enemy situation from such a mixture of sounds. They could realize orders from Hà Nội,

Chapter Six: DETERMINATION TO HOLD THE OFFENSIVE

orders from Lieutenant-colonel Manplate, calls for help from French troops who were being closely followed by Vietnamese troops, and calls from French airborne raiders. In a panic, enemy troops spoke directly to each other without using slangs or codes. Vietnamese staff collected information and demonstrated it on a map every hour, forming a miniature of the enemy retreat, which was going on quickly on a road of hundreds of kilometers. Although the miniature showed the moves of French troops more clearly than those of Vietnamese troops, it still provided General Giáp with a foundation to send telegrams to Vietnamese units which were pursuing the enemy in each stretch of the road. In many telegrams, he gave soldiers instructions on how to ask local people about the enemy's retreat directions so that they could take shortcuts and wait in front for the enemy, how to solve the issue of provisions on the spot, and how to mobilize local horses to catch up with the enemy.

The Vietnamese Campaign Headquarters was continuously updated with news on the situation of their soldiers in all directions. The first news was received on April 13. That night, Vietnamese soldiers met the last enemy unit, and the French lackey government in Sam Neua together with 40 Lao puppet troops were all arrested in Mường Hàm. Next came the news of the 48th Regiment's annihilation of two French battalions in Nà Noọng on the morning of April 14. After this victory, the regiment sent two battalions to continue pursuing the enemy without waiting for a new order. Some units of the 156th and 165th Regiments also proactively pursued the enemy. The 79th Battalion of the 102nd Regiment and the 209th Company of the 88th Regiment determinedly pursued the enemy in a 24-km stretch of road from Hứa Mường southwards, despite their failure to receive supplies and their small troop strength.

Orders from the Vietnamese Campaign Headquarters were regularly recorded in the command post's diary. Here is an extract of it:

> April 15. Telegram to Khánh and the 209th Regiment:
>
> "Encourage our men that one more step may help eliminate one more enemy troop. Don't miss any opportunity for having sympathized with their tiredness."
>
> On the morning of April 16, it was reported by the enemy radio that many enemy units had been closely pursued and routed in the Hứa Mường-Mường Lập-Tam La area.
>
> 11:50 am, April 16. Telegram to Kiên[1] and Khánh:
>
> "We don't have a thorough grasp of the situation. You should catch up with Hùng Sinh's unit, bringing along radio transmitters to urge the units, grasp the situation, and receive notifications and instructions."
>
> 9 pm, April 16. Telegram to Kiên and Khánh:
>
> "Pursue the enemy to the last and wipe them out completely. Don't let any of them escape. Determination will result in victory. Hesitation means not complying with orders and not completing the tasks of pursuing and raiding remnant troops. Try to catch up with the previous unit."
>
> The enemy radio disclosed that clashes occurred continuously in many directions on the evening of April 16 to the morning of April 17. Calls for help were heard

---

1. Đỗ Đức Kiên, Head of the Campaign Operations Section, was assigned to accompany the 308th Brigade as envoy of the Headquarters. Other names written in the telegram belonged to commanding officers of brigades and regiments.

Chapter Six: DETERMINATION TO HOLD THE OFFENSIVE

everywhere. The voice of Lieutenant-colonel Manplate was hardly heard.[1]

April 17. Telegram to Lâm, Khánh, Kiên, and minor sections of the 209th and 102nd Regiments:

"The enemy plans to withdraw to Bản Ban along the Mường Lạp-Tam La route. After passing Tam La for about 20 kilometers over to Sóp Ó, there will be two ways to go. One way directly leads to Bản Ban in 35 kilometers. The other leads to Mường Pek, the 7th Route (after two days walking), and finally to Khang Khay. The enemy may turn to Mường Hiểm (there is a 40-km road connecting Mường Lạp with Mường Hiểm). They may also go to Mường Hiểm from Tam La and then follow the 7th Route from Mường Hiểm to Sốp Khao, Mường Xén, Bản Hang, and finally the Plain of Jars. If they go in the Mường Péc and Mường Hiểm directions, they can avoid our soldiers coming from the south, especially from Noọng Hét, which had just been annihilated on the night of April 16. You should ask war prisoners and local people for the enemy's marching directions. At Tam La, you can send two companies and a regimental officer with radios to Mường Hiểm if you are unclear about the enemy's marching directions. The rest keeps following the shortest way to Bản Ban to meet other soldiers[2] and together discuss ways to expand the results of the campaign. All cadres should fully understand the significance of pursuing the enemy to the last and completely eliminating them for the joint victory, and that of building up soldiers to maintain their determination to overcome all difficulties and complete all tasks. You are tired, but enemies

---

1. It was later known that Manplate and about 200 troops of the 1st Lao Puppet Battalion were taken to shelters to wait for helicopters. They could not return to the Plain of Jars until the end of the campaign.
2. They included regular units of the Lao Liberation Army and those of the Vietnamese Voluntary Army who had operated in Laos earlier.

are much more miserable. Some of you may be hungry now, but you will suffer much more casualties should you attack enemy fortifications. Wish you all a complete victory."

April 17. Telegram to Khánh and the minor sections of the 209th and 102nd Regiments:

"Try to catch Lieutenant-colonel Manplate. The enemy has withdrawn and Manplate has disappeared. You have to pursue him till the end. At Tam La, you should find out which way enemy troops have run before moving on. Wait until remnant troops return to kill. In case you don't know which direction enemy troops have run, take the shortest way to Bản Ban and then return. Fight any enemy troops you meet on the way back. Now, our slogan is 'Kill the enemy to the last and seize Manplate.' I know you are all tired, but enemies are much more tired. I send to you my best regards and wish you successful pursuits."

April 17. Telegram to the 98th Regiment:

"The enemy is still in Mường Hiểm. An unverified source reveals that the retreating units and Manplate turned into Mường Hiểm on April 16. Detach a minor battalion to promptly march over Sa Thoue near Mường Kout and find a shortcut to Sốp Cốp. Should the enemy retreat to Luang Prabang, pursue them. The majority of you should move long Mương Hiểm road, killing any enemy you meet on the road, and get to Sốp Cốp. We have favorable conditions to pursue the enemy because they will have become exhausted and demoralized by then."

April 17. The first telegram to the 304th Brigade[1]:

"On the morning of April 17, our troops arrived in Tam La (136 kilometers away from Sam Neua) and eliminated

---

1. The 304th Brigade was tasked to block the enemy on the 7th Route from running to Bản Ban and Siang Khouang.

most of enemy troops there. Our troops are still pursuing the rest. The rest, including one battalion and Manplate, have arrived in Sốp Ó (29 kilometers away from Tam La) and got exhausted. From there, they may go straight to Bản Ban (35 kilometers away) or turn into Mường Pek and keep on moving for two days to reach the 7th Route leading to Khang Khay to avoid our troops. The enemy may send one battalion to the north to pick up the retreating units in Bản Ban or Khang Khay, but the number and avenue are unknown. So you should order soldiers to immediately march to Bản Ban. You can detach one company to go first and try to get there tonight to stop the retreating troops, and simultaneously send another company to the Mường Pek three-way junction in case they go that way. Base yourselves on the particular conditions to decide whether to fight or pass the enemy troops who come to pick up the retreating ones. Strict orders, hard urges, and timely arrival will result in victory. Slowness will lead to a failure to fulfill the duty".

The second telegram to the 304th Brigade the same day:

"Instruct the 9th or 66th Regiment to detach one company to Bản Ban to stop the enemy. Can the 57th Regiment send one unit to the north of the Plain of Jars? Keep reporting the soldiers' itinerary and the whole brigade's position. Take any opportunity the expand our combat results."

April 18. Telegram sent to the 308th Brigade:

"Your central mission is to urge soldiers to pursue and eliminate all enemy troops. The order from the Headquarters is to pursue enemy troops to the last and wipe them out completely. Tell cadres that determination will lead to a complete victory and hesitation means disobedience of the order and incompletion of the duty. Cadres in charge of ideological issues should raise high the determination to pursue and kill enemy troops, clarify the significance of the complete elimination of enemy troops, and prevent the ideas of complacence and task underestimation from emerging among the army."

April 18. The first telegram to 304th Brigade:

"Detach the 66th Regiment to attack Noọng Hét immediately and pursue the enemy if they withdraw.[1] Both battalions of the 9th Regiment quickly march in, detaching one section to encircle Bản Ban and the rest to block retreating troops from Sam Neua to Bản Ban and those from Sam Neua to Bản Hiểm. After eliminating Noọng Hét, the 66th Regiment quickly moves to Sam Neua to reinforce the 9th Regiment. Meanwhile, the 57th Regiment promotes operations in Siang Khouang to help eliminate the enemy retreating from Sam Neua."

The second telegram to the 304th Brigade the same day:

"Your main task now is to coordinate with Lao units to prevent the enemy from retreating to Bản Ban and Khang Khay, so that they can come in time to eliminate the enemy. This task is decisive to the campaign. You will have to take the responsibility if you fail to accomplish it. The Party Central Committee will make a specific plan based on this spirit. Send troops to Bản Ban immediately and try to eliminate Noọng Hét as soon as possible to send more troops there. Urgently supervise and speed up units responsible for blocking the enemy."

April 19. The first telegram to Khánh and the 209th Regiment:

"Lao units arrived in Bản Ban on April 17, but their specific disposition has not been reported. Send troops to the north of the 7th Route to annihilate the enemy there. One or two parachute companies were sent to pick up remnant troops in northern Phanaphao. They will arrive in Bản Yai tonight and follow the small road to the 7th Route at the crossroads

---

1. Thus, the news that Noọng Hét was eliminated on April 16 was false.

Chapter Six: DETERMINATION TO HOLD THE OFFENSIVE

north of Bản Lèo (three kilometers away) tomorrow. They will be picked up in Trấn Ninh in the late afternoon and taken back to Khang Khay. Try to eliminate them."

The second telegram to Khánh and the 209th Regiment the same day:

"Remnant troops will be picked up by a parachute company in Sóp Hao and Lác Bona and then by cars coming from Khang Khay. Apart from one company left behind, all the troops in Bản Ban, including those of the 9th Regiment, immediately march to Mường Pek, Lác Bona, and Sốp Hao today to block all the ways down from the north and get ready to fight against retreating troops and cars coming from Khang Khay. Whether we can eliminate the whole enemy depends on today's battle. Encourage our soldiers to try their best."

April 19. Telegram sent to the 304th Brigade:

"Your main task now is to coordinate with the main direction to eliminate retreating troops between Bản Ban and Hứa Mường. If we are late, the enemy will escape. Order the 9th Regiment to detach two companies to go ahead of others and march as quickly as possible to Bản Ban to encircle the enemy there and stop those from Khang Khay. Other companies move toward Hứa Mường to block the enemy there. After eliminating Noọng Hét, leave one section there for fortification. Meanwhile, the 66th Regiment and one battalion of the 9th Regiment quickly march to Bản Ban. There are three ways to go from Bản Ban to Hứa Mường: by the old 6th Route, the new 6th Route, and Mường Khao Road. Try to figure out which way the enemy troops in Bản Ban go to pick up the retreating ones, and follow that way. The 57th Regiment takes this opportunity to immediately attack Siang Khouang and then sends one reinforcement battalion to the area between Khang Khay and Bản Ban. After settling Bản Ban, the Brigade Command quickly leaves for Bản

Ban. Encourage soldiers to overcome tiredness and hunger to determinedly complete the task."

On April 20, the pursuit on the about-270-km stretch of road basically came to an end. In the main direction, most of the enemy troops retreating from Sam Neua and from posts along the road were annihilated. In the direction of the 7th Route, after Noọng Hét was eliminated, the enemy hurriedly retreated from Bản Ban and Siang Khouang.

To promote the victory in the Sam Neua-7th Route-Siang Khouang direction, General Giáp ordered the 148th Regiment to promptly march to fight against enemy troops in the direction of the Nậm Hu River. Simultaneously, he ordered the 98th Regiment to separate itself from the combat formation of the main direction of Sam Neua, and move to northern Luang Prabang to cooperate with the 148th Regiment, under general command of Bằng Giang, to grind down part of the enemy strength in Pakseng, Mường Sung, and Mường Ngòi. In the favorable face of the Upper Laos battlefield, within one week from April 21–27, Vietnamese troops eliminated Mường Ngòi, Bản Sẻ, Pakseng, and Nậm Bắc. Meanwhile, a Vietnamese army moved along Mường Von and Mường Sủi to threaten the Lao capital, forcing Salan to hurriedly send the 1st Mobile Regime to defend Luang Prabang. Together with the military victory of expanding the revolutionary base of Nậm Hu, the Vietnamese army succeeded in applying the ten regulations on policies, political campaigns, and courting the people's support for the Lao Resistance Government.

Commander-in-chief Võ Nguyên Giáp dispatched Chief of the General Staff Hoàng Văn Thái to the 304th Brigade in the cooperative direction to communicate the new task. In the letter sent to Lê Chưởng, Hoàng Minh Thảo, and the

Chapter Six: DETERMINATION TO HOLD THE OFFENSIVE

304th Brigade, General Giáp praised the brigade and the conscripted laborers of Nghệ An for having overcome lots of difficulties while operating relatively independently in a foreign battlefield for the first time and completed all their tasks there. After acknowledging the efforts of Vietnamese cadres, soldiers, and conscripted laborers, General Giáp pointed out their shortcomings.

Firstly, regarding the tactical instruction, due to defects in the tactics of encirclement in Bản Ban, Vietnamese troops let their enemies escape though they had arrived there the day before. This failure was repeated in Siang Khouang.

Secondly, regarding the assessment of the enemy situation, signs of subjectivism were found among the Vietnamese army. Consequently, they failed to recognize the enemy scheme to preserve the Plain of Jars. They also failed to realize that the enemy had reinforced their troops in the Plain of Jars, so they decided to surround and prepare to attack it.

Finally, cadres did not have a full grasp of their units, so their reports were not regular and specific enough.

General Giáp also gave instructions on the 304th Brigade's direction of operation in the coming time as follows:

Firstly, although the 304th Brigade had won a great victory over their enemy, General Giáp still reminded them to be fully aware of the enemy's plot as well as their new disadvantages in terms of weather conditions and supplies if their operations should be prolonged. The liberated areas were very large, but the public knowledge was still poor, there was still a great number of remnant enemy troops and spies left, and the enemy force had been reinforced. Therefore, they should remain vigilant, prevent themselves from being subjective and underestimating the enemy, and watch out for dangers and weaknesses to avoid any mishaps.

Secondly, they should detach only small units to march westwards to cooperate with the forces in Luang Prabang when required.

Thirdly, in order to preserve the victory, they should organize the troop withdrawal exactly at the scheduled time and guarantee its secrecy. While their troops were still in localities, they should mobilized them to help local people consolidate the liberated areas, which was also a key task in reinforcing the recent victory.

Fourthly, in ideological leadership, it was necessary to make soldiers feel heartened without being subjective or underestimating the enemy. Specifically, it was vital to make them be aware of the general victory of the campaign, the efforts of the units, their shortcomings in eliminating the enemy strength, and their own defects so as to avoid two possible tendencies: either feeling pessimistic or feeling subjective and underestimating the enemy.

Finally, it was necessary to comply with policies for conscripted laborers.

The Campaign Headquarters estimated that Vietnamese troops would stop pursuing remnant troops and expanding their victory on April 30. Most of Vietnamese regulars would return to their country. Only three regiments and four battalions would stay in Laos to help the local people fortify their liberated areas. In mid May, there were only two battalions of the 98th Regiment left in Sam Neua, one battalion in the Nậm Hu River valley, and two battalions of

Chapter Six: DETERMINATION TO HOLD THE OFFENSIVE

the 304th Brigade in Siang Khouang. About 15 companies of the Vietnamese voluntary army continued to stay and operate as required by the Lao Resistance Government.

General Giáp remarked that the face of the Upper Laos changed in the wake of the victory in Sam Neua. He emphasized the importance of mobilizing the people and cultivating the Pathet Lao armed forces in fortifying and extending the victory in Sam Neua. Regarding the cultivation of the Lao revolutionary forces for new victories, he highlighted the ideological rectification among Vietnamese cadres and soldiers so that they were fully aware of the Party's position on the Lao revolution. Specifically, it was necessary to make all Vietnamese cadres and soldiers understand that they should fight for the sake of both Vietnamese and Lao revolutionary causes, and that the Lao revolution was mainly undertaken by Lao people, who were believed to become a powerful force.

In the meeting with the Civil Affairs Committee of the Communist Party of Việt Nam in Upper Laos on May 6 about the preparation for and practice of the campaign, the Central Military Committee remarked that during the preparation for the campaign, the Civil Affairs Committee cooperated with the General Department of Politics to prepare policy-related issues and arrange cadres for the campaign. At the end of the campaign, the Civil Affairs Committee was ordered to help the Lao Resistance Government fortify the liberated areas and organize the "Việt Nam-Laos Solidarity Week" in localities.

According to Prince Souphanouvong's suggestion, the "Việt Nam-Laos Solidarity Week" started with a victory-honoring ceremony held by both Vietnamese and Lao armies in the liberated town of Sam Neua. At the ceremony, Prince Souphanouvong said that the liberated Sam Neua was the result of the Lao people's years of fighting against aggressors. It was also the result of the solidarity of the Vietnamese and Lao nations, as well as that of the unconditional support of the Vietnamese people and army for the Lao people in the fight against the common enemy.

While the Vietnamese people and army were preparing for the campaign to be launched in the dry season of 1953, General Salan was in his "gloomiest days." He had not thought that the French army's failure in the Upper Laos would put an end to his military career in Indochina.

On the way back to Việt Bắc, General Giáp heard of changes being made in the leadership of the French expeditionary army.

Chapter Seven

THE FINAL EFFORTS OF FRANCE AND THE UNITED STATES

The Seventh Commander-in-chief of the French Expeditionary Army

On May 19, the Swallow radio and the press in Hà Nội and Sài Gòn told the news that General Henri Navarre, the new commander-in-chief of the French expeditionary army, had just landed on the Tân Sơn Nhất airport. It was disclosed by reporters that the former commander-in-chief was not in Sài Gòn to receive his successor. Two days later, on May 21, General Navarre and Minister Letourneau flew to Hà Nội. The new commander-in-chief was thought to be reserved, but he looked excited when seeing his old friend, General de Linarès.

The appearance of General Navarre in Sài Gòn verified that General Salan was replaced. Thus, General Navarre officially became the seventh commander-in-chief of the French expeditionary army and the seventh opponent of General Giáp in Indochina. It was revealed that not only Salan but most of the high-ranking military officers under General de Lattre's command were also recalled and replaced.

According to the press in Sài Gòn and Hà Nội, Navarre had been trained in intelligence and had held the post of Chief of Staff of the Central European Infantry of the North Atlantic Treaty Organization (NATO). Bodet, a former air force commander, was appointed to become Navarre's Second-in-command. Lauzin, a former pilot, replaced Chassin and became Air Commander. Gambiez, former commander of the southern Red River Delta battle, took the place of Ala as Chief of Staff of the French Headquarters. He had studied the experience of the American army and allied forces in North Korea, and was appraised to be successful and experienced in pacification. General René Cogny replaced de Linarès and became Commander of Tonkin (North Việt Nam). He had commanded a number of mopping-up operations in the Left Bank and had been awarded the third star.

Among the new high-ranking military officers of the French expeditionary army, many had worked with the American and European armies and sent to North Korea for study; many others had become acquainted with the Indochinese battlefield and experienced in pacification. The new French command and the possible increase in the American aid for the French expeditionary army were obviously remarkable changes to the situation in Việt Nam when the North Korea war was about to end.

At that time, the Vietnamese General Staff paid their attention mostly on the new strategic designs and combat plans of the Headquarters of the French expeditionary army to help the Central Military Commission in investigating the situation, reviewing the general face of the battlefield in the first six months of the year, and preparing the course of action for the coming dry season.

Chapter Seven: THE FINAL EFFORTS OF FRANCE AND THE UNITED STATES

On June 27, General Giáp sent a report to the Politburo. He wrote:

> In the first six months of the year, we won a great victory in Upper Laos and a number of successes throughout Việt Nam. Although they had suffered heavy losses and many of their regulars had been sent to Upper Laos, they enemy expanded their occupied areas in the Northern plains, encroached and separated our bases in the Central and Southern regions, and actively implemented their plot to pacify and blockade villages and plunder our human and material resources. Moreover, they also sent reinforcements from the Central and Southern regions to the North.

Based on the realities of the Upper Laos campaign and the estimated course of action for the coming dry season, General Giáp came to the following judgment:

> Thanks to the Government's establishment of the Front-line Logistical Council in the early year, progresses were made in front-line logistics, as well as in the coordination between the Ministry of National Defense and other ministries and localities. However, the organization of the Front-line Logistical Council had not been strengthened, and unions of vessels and bicycles had not been developed and consolidated. Another big weakness was that the repair of roads and bridges had not been paid enough attention to. This restricted transportation, caused difficulties in front-line logistics, required more support from local people, and affected the army's marches. In the coming time, we should attach importance to the perfection of the organization of the Front-line Logistical Council, the consolidation of unions of vessels and bicycles, the construction and repair of roads and bridges, the improvement of cadres' knowledge of new policies, and the concentration of all efforts for the on-time and full implementation of the scheduled program.

649

While the staff continued learning about the new commander-in-chief of the French expeditionary army and the new combat plan of the French Headquarters, other units of the Vietnamese General Headquarters kept implementing their summer plan, preparing for the eight dry season of the resistance war.

Regarding force building, the political education was aimed at strengthening the class standpoint among soldiers, increasing the political-ideological power, and supporting the people's struggle for the implementation of the Party's land policy. Meanwhile, the military training was aimed at improving soldiers' combat capacities in large-scale operations with enemy troops in solid fortifications or groups of fortifications as the main target. The military training policy for this dry season was designed clearly, as the outcome of the lessons withdrawn from the unsuccessful attack on the group of fortifications in Nà Sản and the failure to attack that in Sam Neua. Along with his investigation into the campaign direction for front-line regulars, General Giáp also thought about measures to maintain the struggle in the areas behind the enemy lines with the Red River Delta being the main point.

During 1952, with nearly 100 small- and large-scale mopping-up operations in their temporarily-occupied areas and the insidious activities of the groups they founded to pacify the areas and call Vietnamese civilians and soldiers to surrender, the enemy caused a lot of difficulties to the struggle of Vietnamese people and army in these areas throughout the country, especially in the Northern plains. Although their coming scheme and plan were still unknown, the appearance of French high-ranking military officers in the French command such as Cogny and Gambiez showed that there were still many great challenges to the struggle of the Vietnamese people and army in the areas behind the enemy lines.

Thanks to the assistance of Chinese comrades, in late September 1953, the staff of the Vietnamese General Headquarters grasped the major contents of the Navarre plan, a strategic one proposed by the French Headquarters. It was planned to be implemented over two phases equivalent to two dry seasons and completed within 18 months. It was later recorded in General Navarre's books titled *L'Agonie de l'Indochine* (literally: The Agony of Indochina) and *Le temps des vérités* (literally: The Time of Truths).[1]

According to this plan, during the 1953-1954 dry season, the French army would be on the defensive from the 18th parallel of latitude northwards and try to avoid big battles. On the contrary, from the 18th parallel southwards, they would launch offensives to pacify Central Việt Nam and southern Indochina and to exploit both human and material resources. They highlighted the task of eliminating the 5th Interzone.

After gaining the advantage in mobile forces, from the autumn of 1954, they would start to launch offensives in North Việt Nam in order to create favorable military conditions to win the war.

When the plan had not been approved by Paris-based National Defense Council, General Navarre intended

---

1. Henri Navarre: *L'Agonie de l'Indochine* (literally: The Agony of Indochina), Plon, Paris, 1956; *Le temps des vérités* (literally: The Time of Truths), Plon, Paris, 1979.

to boost the building of forces, especially mobile ones, which would be used as tools to realize his plan. Within two years, he planned to increase the Indochinese puppet army from 168,000 troops to 280,000 troops and build up 122 battalions (including 108 in Việt Nam and 14 in Laos and Cambodia) which were tasked to eliminate Vietnamese local soldiers, destroy revolutionary bases in the French-controlled areas, and participate in the development of strategic mobile forces. He also planned to build a powerful strategic mobile army as the main reserve whose main targets were Vietnamese regular brigades. It was scheduled that from August 1953 to March 1955, seven strategic mobile divisions, including six infantry divisions (24 mobile regiments) and one airborne divisions (3 mobile regiments), would be established. Accordingly, the strategic reserve was increased to 27 mobile regiments, including 12 local regiments and 15 Euro-African ones.

Due to limited reinforcements from Paris, General Navarre had to follow the tracks of his predecessors, developing local troops to overcome troop shortages. Specifically, he replaced Euro-African troops with local ones as General Salan had done. In order to apply this measure, he found it necessary to destroy Vietnamese guerilla bases and armed forces in the French-controlled areas. After these areas had been "cleaned," low-quality troops (puppet ones) would be brought in. To have enough low-quality troops to occupy these areas and replace quality troops, who would be gathered for the building of a strategic mobile army, the French had to launch a pacification campaign to conscript local men into their army. Therefore, the conscription of local men for the development of the puppet army was closely associated with the severe mopping-up operations in the French temporarily-occupied areas.

The Central Military Commission made a move ahead of the enemy in the temporarily-occupied areas. Having foreseen new difficulties that Vietnamese people and army in the areas behind the enemy lines would have to confront, General Giáp proposed a conference to be held in early October 1953. Participants in this conference included not only Vietnamese cadres in the areas behinds the enemy lines in the North but also representatives of the 4th and 5th Interzones, South Việt Nam, and the Party Central Committee and Government. In the opening address, General Giáp clearly stated that the conference aimed to not only increase participants' awareness of the guidelines of the struggle but also find solutions to a number of specific matters (such as how to fight against the enemy's mopping-up operations, build district-level armed forces and commune-level guerilla forces, fight against conscription, prevent villages from being herded, and crush the enemy's pacification plot). Beside the issue of armed struggle, the conference also tacked some other issues such as the implementation of the Party's policies on land and agricultural taxation. It firmly stated that the struggle in the areas behind the enemy lines must involve the concerted strength of all forces.

The conference was directed by General Giáp. It was more comprehensive than the one held in July 1952, but it still focused on the direction of the armed struggle. In the closing speech, General Giáp said that the conference had achieved its highest result—improving the participants' trust in the Party policies and spirit of implementing them in the areas behind the enemy lines. He firmly stated that the people were the root of all tasks, and that armed struggle was the main form of struggle in the areas behind the enemy lines. Once the Vietnamese had thoroughly grasped these principles, they would be able to crush the enemy's plot in the guerilla bases, guerilla areas, and temporarily-occupied areas.

One of the most noticeable actions of the French army under the command of General Navarre during the summer was the spreading of spies and the parachuting of bandits into the Northwest who would cooperate with local reactionaries to disturb the Vietnamese resistance rear and act as informers for bombers. In mid July, for example, French paratroops launched a surprise attack on a Vietnamese unit garrisoned near Lạng Sơn Town. Therefore, the need of safeguarding the Vietnamese revolutionary rear had become more urgent. In the instruction dated August 1, 1953, General Giáp clearly stated:

> When the war develops and expands to a large scale, it requires closer cooperation between the frontline and the rear. The task of reinforcing and defending the rear becomes heavier and more urgent. Only when this task is fulfilled can the logistics for the front line be ensured.

He reminded all the military, civil, political, and Party organizations to continue militarizing daily activities, have plans to consolidate political bases and guard against evildoers, keep secrets, strengthen local armed forces, and get ready to fight against enemy troops attacking the Vietnamese rear in order to protect bodies, bridges, roads, depots, and production facilities in each locality.

In the instruction on the coming military policy sent to the battlefield of the 5th Interzone, which included the Central Highlands strategic area and the Quảng Nam-Quảng Ngãi-

Bình Định-Phú Yên free zone, on September 28, 1953, General Giáp analyzed the situations of both warring sides and the next plan of the French expeditionary army. Then he highlighted the necessity of preparing for a phase of strong activities in the northern Central Highlands in the spring of 1954 to cooperate with the battlefield in the North to grind down part of the enemy strength, promote the guerilla war, widen existing bases, and build a base in the northern Central Highlands which would be linked with Lower Laos and western Quảng Ngãi. Two months later, after having a thorough grasp of the enemy's plot to launch offensives from the west and from the coast to occupy the free zone of the 5th Interzone, General Giáp predicted three possibilities and presented them in his report to the Politburo on November 27, 1953. According to him, the enemy might firstly expand their occupied areas in southern Quảng Nam Province, so that they could rejoin the 14th Route and break off the communication between the 5th Interzone and Lower Laos and that between the 5th Interzone and the Bình-Trị-Thiên area. Secondly, they might occupy the 19th Route (from An Khê to Quy Nhơn) and expand the scope of their control in the south of the 5th Interzone. Lastly, they might increase their acts of sabotage in the coastal region to expand the scope of their attack.

Based on the afore-mentioned predictions, the Central Military Commission decided to actively and boldly develop the struggle movement in the Central Highlands, first and foremost the north of this region, while actively consolidating the current free zone. The development of the struggle movement in the Central Highlands was regarded as the first important task while the consolidation of the free zone was considered as the second one. General Giáp firmly stated that only by developing the struggle movement in the Central Highlands could the Vietnamese people and army gain the most important strategic zone in the South. If this zone remained under the control of the French army, it would be very difficult for the Vietnamese people and army to change the face of the South. He also affirmed that the development of the struggle movement in the Central Highlands would enable the Vietnamese people and army to maintain their existing free zone and expand it to the west. Further more, in the present context, the task of strengthening the free zone was still an important one. The maintenance of the free zone would facilitate the development of revolutionary bases in the Central Highlands. Aware of this, the Central Military Commission proposed the active reinforcement of the 5th Interzone's armed forces in both quantity and quality, the drastic development of the struggle movement in the Central Highlands (first and foremost the northern area) and Lower Laos to grind down part of the enemy strength, the westward expansion of revolutionary bases, the strengthening of the corridor in the northern Central Highlands to link the 5th Interzone with Lower Laos, and the crushing of the enemy plot to fortify their occupied areas in the Central Highlands and expand them to the coast.

The afore-mentioned strategic policy and combat plan were then approved by the Politburo. Realities later proved that this was among strategic surprises to General Navarre. During the preparation for the winter-spring campaign, General Giáp took a step ahead of General Navarre. It was a significant step that determined the fate of the French large-scale offensive named *Atlante*, which aimed to eliminate the free zone of the 5th Interzone.

Chapter Seven: THE FINAL EFFORTS OF FRANCE AND THE UNITED STATES

Since he took office, General Navarre had stated several times that he would take the initiative in attacking. And he did so actually.

The first offensive of the French army, named *Hirondelle* (Swallow), was directly commanded by Cogny and targeted at a Vietnamese depot north of Lạng Sơn Town on July 17. The troop deployment for it was initially disguised as a troop parade in Hà Nội to celebrate the French National Day (July 14) which involved the concentration of French aircraft and paratroops. The French company-level commanding officers were only informed of the attack plan and tasks an hour before the aircraft took off. In short, the plan was kept secret to the very end. The outcome of this offensive announced by French reporters was different from that announced by the Swallow radio. According to these reporters, the two French parachute battalions were afraid of being ambushed, so they did not dare to enter the cave and could destroy only a small amount of food and several vans parking on the roadsides. Then they hurriedly withdrew at 1 pm that day for fear that they might encounter disadvantages if they should stay any longer. It was obvious that they had been confused in investigating their opponent's troop strength and transportation, which resulted in their failure in this offensive.

General Navarre's second blow was the operation named *Camargue*,[1] which took place in the Hải Lăng-Phong Điền

---

1. Camargue is the name of a marshy area in the lower section of the Rhone River. The Camargue operation was led by a general, two colonels, and four lieutenant-colonels. It involved the participation of 4 infantry mobile regiments, 2 parachute battalions, 3 armored squads, 1 assault squadron, 2 artillery regiments, 12 warships, 160 amphibious vehicles, 60 airplanes of different kinds. It took place on a 15-km-long and 3-m-wide muddy stretch of road along the Vân Trình canal with the Tân An-Mỹ Thủy coast on the east.

area in Thừa Thiên Huế Province. The operation aimed to annihilate the 95th Regiment of the Vietnamese army and clear the Quảng Trị-Đà Nẵng route axis. It involved such a large combat force that it was considered as one of the biggest campaigns in Indochina. It was initially thought that the 95th Regiment would hardly escape the blockade with armored vehicles on the west and infantry troops and amphibious vehicles on the east. However, the French vehicles took turns to fall into ambushes prepared by the soldiers-in-black of the 95th Regiment, which had penetrated into the areas behind the French lines and conducted undercover activities here for two years. The 95th Regiment took advantage of the spaces between canals in the southwest to escape the blockade. After 36 hours, the operation was defeated and forced to end.

Over two months later, in the middle of October, General Navarre launched the *Mouette* (Seagull) operation—his third blow—in the southwest of Ninh Bình Province. This operation involved the participation of 32 battalions and aimed to search and annihilate the 320th Brigade. Simultaneously, a part of the brigade was tasked to launch another operation named *Le Pélican* (Pelican) and supported by naval troops who would land on the Thanh Hóa coast to prevent the 304th Brigade from penetrating into the south of the delta. While it was spread among the populace in Paris that General Navarre had gained the initiative in attacking, on October 27, 1953, the rightist newspaper *Le Monde* (The World) released an article with disastrous comments. The article read:

> Many Government members know clearly that the news about the fighting situation in Việt Nam which have been released for recent weeks is not true. Those excessive propaganda words are only aimed at creating favorable

conditions for the French army to lend money from the United States. It is because the French army has suffered heavy losses for the past 20 days. If losses keep increasing, the reinforcements will be just enough to compensate for the lost troops.

On November 7, 1953, General Giáp sent a congratulatory letter to the 320th Brigade in the wake of their victory in southern Ninh Bình. He wrote:

> Despite the great numbers of French élite troops, infantry units, vehicles, and air forces mobilized in this battle, you have bravely fought and overcome all difficulties. You've missed no chance to grind down the enemy strength, forcing them to withdraw from our free zone. This is our first great victory in the Northern battlefield in the early autumn-winter combat season. It proves that you've made progress after the recent phase of political re-education. The Politburo has decided to award the entire brigade a Military Medal.

The staff of the Vietnamese General Headquarters could not help being surprised by some of the initial acts of the new French commander-in-chief. In mid August, General Navarre withdrew six French battalions from Nà Sản to the Red River Delta. Northwest was scheduled to be the strategic direction and Nà Sản was planned to be one of the targets of attack in this dry season. The withdrawal of French troops from Nà Sản not only meant that the French strategic mobile army was reinforced with two mobile regiments, but it also affected the Vietnamese General Headquarters' plan for the dry season since their scheduled target of attack (Nà Sản) no longer existed. After the French withdrawal, there were only two positions left in the Northern mountainous and forested battlefield—Lai Châu and Hải Ninh. These two targets were not so important that they would bring about any great changes to the face of the Northern battlefield if they were eliminated. So the greatest concern of the Vietnamese General Headquarters at that time was the question of what should be the next strategic direction of attack for Vietnamese regular brigades in this dry season.

In the draft of the strategic combat direction prepared in late August, after the French withdrawal from Nà Sản, the Central Military Commission judged that the enemy plotted to reinforce their combat forces and concentrate more mobile troops to pacify and occupy the delta and then gain the initiative. It was among General Navarre's outstanding activities at that time. The Vietnamese army had not gained the advantage over the enemy in troop strength in the battlefield in general or in the main direction of a campaign in the delta in particular. So what should they do to crush the enemy's plot and create favorable conditions for a large-scale offensive in the delta? To answer this question, the Vietnamese staff suggested the Central Military Commission speed up the struggle in the areas behind the enemy lines, choose appropriate modes of operation for Vietnamese regulars to grind down the enemy strength in the delta little by little and support the struggle of the Vietnamese people and soldiers in the areas behind the enemy lines, reinforce armed forces and have plans to get soldiers ready to fight against the enemy if the latter should attack the free zone, and enhance operations in the Northwest (Lai Châu), Upper Laos, and other battlefields to disperse the enemy forces.

Regarding the use of forces in the 1953-1954 winter-spring combat season, the Vietnamese staff proposed the dispatch of the 316th Brigade to the Northwest and Upper

Laos, the participation of two or three regular brigades (besides local troops) in the midland battlefield, the use of two brigades (including the force in the Left Bank-3rd Interzone area behind the enemy lines), and the mobilization of two regular regiments of the 5th Interzone in the Central Highlands.

This proposal was approved by the Central Military Commission and would be presented at the Politburo conference held in October. In the short term, in his secret telegram sent to localities and units after the French withdrawal from Nà Sản, General Giáp highlighted the French plot to concentrate great combat forces in the delta and remind localities to enhance the direction of the struggle in the areas behind the enemy lines, develop the guerilla war extensively, get ready to resist the enemy's mopping-up operations and plot to propagandize and call the people to surrender, and get prepared to fight against the enemy to protect the free zone.

The First Strategic Moves on the Threshold of the Dry Season

In early October 1953, General Giáp attended the Politburo meeting on the 1953–1954 winter-spring combat plan. The meeting was held in Tín Keo and was chaired by President Hồ Chí Minh. Tín Keo Village in Lục Giã Commune, Chợ Chu District, Thái Nguyên Province, and many other places in the revolutionary base of Việt Bắc have gone down in the history of the anti-French resistance war. At that time, however, no one knew that what was decided in that remote mountain village of the Dao people at the foot of Mount Hồng would determine the fate of the strategic plan which was approved by the French Defense Council at the Matignon Palace three months earlier, put an end to General Navarre's military career, and led to the denouement of French invasion and American intervention in Indochina.

At the beginning of the conference, General Giáp delivered a report on the face of the battlefield after the Sam Neua campaign, the new French commander-in-chief, the major contents of the next strategic plan of the French Headquarters, and General Navarre's initial moves, including the withdrawal of French troops from Nà Sản and noticeably the urgent construction of a strategic mobile army in the Red River Delta.

Understanding the thoughts of General Giáp, who was going to deal with the ever biggest mobile army in the past nine years of the resistance war, President Hồ Chí Minh raised his fist and said, "The enemy builds up a mobile bloc to create power. We don't fear it. We shall force them to disperse their troops and that power will be no more."

He then opened his fist with the fingers pointing to different directions. His hand and his way of expression reminded the others of an image that he used six or seven years earlier. In the dry season of 1947, thousands of French soldiers fiercely attacked the Việt Bắc revolutionary base with a pincer movement. Hồ Chí Minh used the image of an umbrella when talking to some cadres of the Vietnamese General Headquarters. He analyzed that the enemy intended to close the pincers and gather troops in the Chợ Đồn-Đài Thị area in order to form an umbrella covering the center of the safe zone. Then they would fold the umbrella and attack simultaneously from the upper and downer sides in order to catch the revolutionary commanders. He affirmed that the enemy power was concentrated only at the pincers, and that the umbrella would become a ragged one when the pincers had been broken. As a matter of fact, the enemy had to pull back after the Vietnamese army conducted a strong attack in the Lô River-2nd Route direction and defeated completely the weaker pincer in the west. This dry season, the President's outstretched hand implied the combat direction of the entire Vietnamese army—neutralizing the French strategic mobile bloc, which was regarded by the French Headquarters as their main tool to successfully realize the Navarre plan.

In his report on the next strategic direction of the Central Military Commission, General Giáp said that in order to maintain and promote the initiative, the Central Military Commission proposed the cooperation between local armed forces and a part of the regular army. They would launch offensives on important strategic positions where the enemy forces were weak to grind down the enemy strength, liberate the land, and force the enemy to disperse troops to cope with them. With continuous and large-scale operations, they would simultaneously deepen the enemy's basic contradiction between gathering and dispersing troops and gradually create new favorable conditions. When the chance came, they would quickly concentrate forces, mainly including regular ones, to grind down an important part of the enemy strength and change the face of the war.

Specifically, the 316th Brigade would annihilate the enemy in Lai Châu and liberate the entire Northwest zone. Then the brigade would cooperate with the 148th Regiment (the regular force of the Northwest zone), Vietnamese voluntary soldiers, and Lao liberation troops to liberate Phonsaly Province in Upper Laos.

Meanwhile, in the Central and Lower Laos, the 66th Regiment (of the 304th Brigade) and the 101st Regiment (of the 325th Brigade) would cooperate with Lao troops to widen the liberated areas, break the Vientiane-Ngang Mountain Pass "forbidden line," and unblock the corridor to penetrate deep into southern Laos.

Two regular regiments of the 5th Interzone would expand the liberated areas north of the Central Highlands, crushing the enemy's plot to threaten and occupy the free zone of the 5th Interzone.

Local armed forces would cooperate with the 320th Brigade and the regular regiments of the 3rd Interzone to speed up the guerilla war, consume the enemy, narrow their occupied areas in the Red River Delta, destroy the means of transport and battlefields in the areas behind the enemy lines to contain the enemy and restrict their support for the mountainous directions which were under attack the Vietnamese army, and enhance the timely cooperation with regular brigades in the font line.

The remaining regular brigades, including the 351st Air Assault Brigade, would be secretly billeted in mobile bases in the midlands, and prepared for fighting against the enemy when the latter attacked the Vietnamese free zone and moving to other battlefields for combat.

The afore-mentioned combat plan showed the thorough grasp of the guideline of temporarily avoiding strong positions and attacking weak ones proposed at the conference of the Party Central Committee which was held at the beginning of the year. This plan was aimed at grinding down an important part of the enemy strength and

Chapter Seven: THE FINAL EFFORTS OF FRANCE AND THE UNITED STATES

creating conditions and chances for a victory that would change the face of the war. To achieve this goal, during the implementation of the plan, the Vietnamese army should be fully aware of the Politburo's principle of being active, proactive, mobile, and flexible.

To answer President Hồ Chí Minh's question about the enemy's possible reactions in the Northwest primary direction and the possibility of attracting enemy troops in the cooperative directions, General Giáp presented some possibilities. In the primary direction, the enemy might withdraw from Lai Châu (and then the Northwest would be liberated entirely), send reinforcements to the Northwest to defend it, or attack the free zone as they had done in the 1950 Border campaign and the 1952 Northwest campaign to attract Vietnamese troops. Battlefields in the other directions all revealed weak points of the enemy, but they were all important to them. Therefore, the enemy would not abandon them, especially when it was reported that the French and Lao governments were about to sign an association treaty. The defense of Laos might be addressed by General Navarre.

At the end of the conference, President Hồ Chí Minh instructed the Central Military Commission to make a long-term and comprehensive plan to cope with the enemy in the battlefields throughout the country, as well as one to promote the guerilla war in the Red River Delta. Regarding the course of action for this dry season, he instructed the Central Military Commission to take the Northwest as the primary direction and the other directions as cooperative ones. However, the primary direction might subject to changes in actual operation. Military usage should be multiform.

665

After the strategic directions were defined, all preparations for the battlefield were promptly conducted. Preparations for the primary direction focused on three aspects: wiping out bandits, repairing roads and bridges, and building logistical stations. General Giáp particularly highlighted the repair of roads and bridges, and suggested the Government should allow it to be started right after the Sam Neua victory. Without roads, there would be no big battles. This idea had been thoroughly grasped by the Vietnamese staff and logistical department.

On November 14, the 316th Brigade took orders to go into battle. Their immediate tasks were liberating Lai Châu and cooperating with Lao troops to liberate Phonsaly. In the combat order sent to the 316th Brigade, General Giáp reminded them to watch for bandits along the way and closely follow the enemy situation that might change quickly. Should the enemy withdraw, they would have to pursue them immediately.

On November 19, a conference to disseminate the winter-spring plan was held in a location near the military base of the Vietnamese General Headquarters. For many battlefield cadres, the General Headquarters in Chợ Chu was like their home. This year, the participants asked each other why the conference was held so late. Everyone welcome the newly-appointed Chief of the General Staff Văn Tiến Dũng, who attended this conference with the echo of the victory battle in southwestern Ninh Bình, defeating the French army's Mouette operation. As usual, the representatives of the General Headquarters' departments and offices took advantage of this opportunity to ask the delegates about their professional skills in this winter-spring campaign. "The guests," especially commanders of distant battlefields, were always willing to answer these questions so that they could all together complete the tasks.

On the afternoon of November 20, the conference became excited the news that the French paratroops had occupied the Mường Thanh field in Điện Biên Phủ. It was a new occurrence, but it was not beyond the Vietnamese General Headquarters' expectation. In the Politburo meeting held in Tỉn Keo Village a few weeks earlier, General Giáp answered to President Hồ Chí Minh's question about the enemy's possible reaction by predicting that the enemy might send more troops to the Northwest. That prediction turned into reality when only one Vietnamese brigade (the 316th Brigade) had gone into battle. A supplementary order from the Commander-in-chief was sent to the 316th Brigade when it was on the way to the battlefield. According to this order, besides the tasks stated in the previous order, the 316th Brigade and the 148th Regiment were assigned to investigate and thoroughly grasp the enemy situation in Lai Châu and Điện Biên Phủ and send timely reports to the General Headquarters; crush the enemy plot to reinforce Điện Biên Phủ and break off the connection between Điên Biên Phủ and Lai Châu and that between Điện Biên Phủ and Upper Laos; and immediately pursue the enemy if they withdrew from Điện Biên Phủ to Upper Laos.

The Political Commissar of the 316th Brigade, Chu Huy Mân, left the conference early to catch up with the soldiers. Before his leaving, General Giáp told him to supervise and speed up the march, so that the soldiers could arrive in time to surround and annihilate the enemy and liberate Lai Châu. He also reminded the soldiers to block the Lai Châu-Điện

Biên Phủ route. He predicted that a big battle might take place in Điện Biên Phủ.

On the morning of November 23, Giáp, Dũng, and Thái had a working session with Hoàng Sâm, Lê Quảng Ba, and Bằng Giang—commanders in charge of not only the battlefield in the Northwest but also those in Laos. In this session, they exchanged ideas and reached an agreement on the evaluation of the situation and the next combat direction. That afternoon, the conference to disseminate the winter-spring plan ended, so that cadres could popularize it to their units and start the preparations for the dry season. In his closing report, General Giáp delivered his judgments of the enemy situation in the primary direction. According to him, although the specific time and location were still unknown, the landing of French paratroops in Điện Biên Phủ was not a surprise to the Vietnamese General Headquarters. (They had predicted that the enemy would send reinforcements there if the Northwest was under threat.) Thus, the French had to cope passively with the threat from the Vietnamese. Specifically, they had to send part of their mobile forces to Điện Biên Phủ to support the Northwest, defend Upper Laos, and crush the offensive plan of the Vietnamese army. Then they might keep both Điện Biên Phủ and Lai Châu. Should they be threatened by the Vietnamese army, they would concentrate in either position, but more likely in Điện Biên Phủ. If they were under greater threat, they would send more reinforcements there and turn it into a group of fortifications, or they would withdraw.

No matter what would happen, the landing of French paratroops in Điện Biên Phủ was basically beneficial to the Vietnamese side. It revealed the enemy contradiction between occupying land and concentrating forces and that between occupying the mountainous battlefield and reinforcing the plain one.

On November 25, General Giáp approved and signed the instruction *"Tích cực chuẩn bị sẵn sàng đánh địch bảo vệ vùng tự do"* (literally: "Actively Preparing for Fighting against the Enemy to Defend the Free Zone") sent to interzones. The instruction repeated the enemy plot to concentrate over 40 mobile battalions in the Red River Delta, and predicted that the enemy might send part of their mobile forces to the direction where Vietnamese troops were actively operating and simultaneously detach 15 to 18 battalions to penetrate into the free zone from the direction where Vietnamese troops revealed weaknesses to sabotage the combat plan, human and material resources for the campaign, and mass mobilization of the Vietnamese side. Specific instructions on the course of action and on the preparation for the campaign were also given to Vietnamese regular and local armed forces, so that they would be ready to fight and defend the free zone.

On November 26, the front mission of the Vietnamese General Headquarters set off for the Northwest. The mission included Vice Chief of the General Staff Hoàng Văn Thái,[1] Vice Head of the General Department of Politics Lê Liêm, Vice Head of the General Department of Logistics Đặng Kim Giang, Vice Head of the Combat Department Đỗ Đức Kiên, and Chinese consultant Mei Jiasheng. General Giáp assigned Thái to get prepared for the possibility that the enemy withdrew to Upper Laos via Tây Trang, besides the

---

1. In November 1953, Commander and Political Commissar of the 320th Brigade Văn Tiến Dũng was appointed to become Chief of the General Staff.

tasks of directing the 316th Brigade to liberate Lai Châu and cooperating with the 148th Regiment and Lao armed forces to liberate Phonsaly. The mission was also ordered to promptly investigate the battlefield and prepare a plan for the offensive against the enemy in Điện Biên Phủ.

By that time, commanding officers of battlefields had received orders and promptly set off. Regarding the 5th Interzone, General Giáp found it necessary to have more discussion with its Commander and Political Commissar, Nguyễn Chánh. In October, the 5th Interzone was informed by the General Headquarters that the enemy might attack the free coastal provinces, and that two of its regular regiments would be detached to expand the liberated areas in the north of the Central Highlands while the others would stay and cooperate with local soldiers to fight against the enemy and defend the free zone. Both Giáp and Chánh realized the importance of discussion for a high level of unanimity within the Interzone Party Committee regarding the Central strategic direction, which was based on the policy of sending regular forces to the Central Highlands as the best strategic measure for crushing the enemy plot to eliminate the Nam-Ngãi-Bình-Phú area[1] and for defending the free zone. Giáp handed to Chánh the project titled *"Tình hình địch, ta ở Liên khu 5, chủ trương tác chiến và kế hoạch công tác quân sự của ta sắp tới ở Liên khu 5"* (literally: "The Vietnamese and French Situations and the Vietnamese Combat Policy and Military Plan for the Coming Time in the 5th Interzone"),

---

1. It included Quảng Nam, Quảng Ngãi, Bình Định, and Phú Yên. These were four provinces in the free zone of the 5th Interzone during the anti-French resistance war. General Navarre's Atlante offensive plan was aimed at occupying these provinces.

which was submitted to and approved by the Politburo on November 27. The project firmly stated the 5th Interzone's strategic guidelines: actively and bravely developing into the Central Highlands, firstly in the north, and continuously strengthening the present free zone.

Realities showed that the early days of December 1953 were unforgettable days to both Vietnamese and French commanders. It was when the two sides "got closer and closer to each other" after choosing Điện Biên Phủ as a strategic battlefield.

On the French side, according to daily reports sent by Vietnamese reconnaissance officers in Điện Biên Phủ that the French Headquarters continued parachuting troops, weapons, and other material means into the Mường Thanh field. The main airport was repaired and reused. The villages close to the field was eliminated. Local houses were dismantled for timbers for the construction of fortifications. There were signs of a group of fortifications which was much bigger than that in Nà Sản being built on the Mường Thanh field. It was later known that on December 3, General Navarre decided to build a strong group of fortifications in Điện Biên Phủ. In his book *"Le temps des vérités* (literally: The Time of Truths), Navarre presented many political, military, and economic reasons for his choice of the Mường Thanh field. Among these reasons, this 144-square-km field was alleged to be an ideal place for the task of defending Upper Laos. Lai Châu, Vientiane, and Luang Prabang were all incomparable to it. Along with the selection of Điện Biên Phủ as the strategic battlefield, Navarre named the occupation army here the "Operational Group of the Northwest," and appointed Colonel Christian de Castries to replace General Gilles in commanding this army. He also ordered General Cogny, commander of the French army in northern Indochina, to concentrate all human and material resources to defend Điện Biên Phủ at any cost. The same day, he decided to move all the garrison in Lai Châu to Điện Biên Phủ. This operation was named "Pollux." It took place at the same time as the other two named "Régate" and "Ardèche," which started from Điện Biên Phủ and Luang Prabang. They would meet at Sốp Nao and create a corridor including a number of fortifications along the Nậm Hu River in order to prevent the Điện Biên Phủ group of fortifications from being isolated and to create a safe corridor for any troop withdrawal from Điện Biên Phủ to Upper Laos.

On the Vietnamese side, after General Navarre sent troops to Điện Biên Phủ, the Northwest was further confirmed as the primary strategic direction as determined in the winter-spring plan. General Giáp directed the staff to modify the plan in accordance with the actual happenings at that time: the French were promptly promptly reinforcing Điện Biên Phủ while the Vietnamese were preparing for their attack on the group of fortifications in the Mường Thanh field. On December 6, 1953, General Giáp sent a report titled *"Phương án tác chiến mùa xuân"* (literally: "The Spring Combat Project") to the Politburo. After analyzing the possibility of the French reinforcing Điện Biên Phủ with about ten battalions and turning it into a big group of fortifications and the possibility of their withdrawal, he stated that whether the French would withdraw or reinforce Điện Biên Phủ was still uncertain since there were still signs of their reinforcement. But once great numbers of Vietnamese regulars had been concentrated there and the French had been attacked in Middle and Lower Laos, the latter would have to made the decision. To complete

Chapter Seven: THE FINAL EFFORTS OF FRANCE AND THE UNITED STATES

the tasks of annihilating the enemy and liberating Lai Châu, Phonsaly, and Luang Prabang in the winter-spring campaign, the Vietnamese army was ordered to make preparations with regard to the possibility that the enemy promoted the establishment of a group of fortifications.

In the face of the increase of French occupation troops in Điện Biên Phủ, the Vietnamese General Headquarters ordered the 312th Brigade (garrisoned in the Yên Bái-Phú Thọ area) and the 351st Artillery Assault Brigade (billeted in the north of Tuyên Quang Town) to get ready to set off for the Northwest. After receiving the order to set off several days earlier, the 308th Brigade crossed the Red River with the task of closely following all the enemy activities in the Mường Thanh field. It particularly detached the 36th Regiment to take a shortcut to Pom Lót and get ready to block the enemy withdrawing from Điện Biên Phủ to Upper Laos via the Tây Trang mountain pass. It should be noted that by that time the Vietnamese General Headquarters had not heard of the so-called "strategic corridor" along the Nậm Hu River, which linked Điện Biên Phủ with Luang Prabang, or General Navarre's plan for any troop withdrawal along this corridor when necessary. General Giáp dispatched Vice Chief of the General Staff Hoàng Văn Thái to the front and Chief of the 308th Brigade Vương Thừa Vũ to Pom Lót because he had missed the chance to attack a group of fortifications (in Sam Neua) and he did not want to miss it this time. The Vietnamese regular brigades had set off for the battlefield. Which battlefield would become the strategic direction of attack when the dry season went and the rainy season came should the enemy withdraw from Điện Biên Phủ? General Navarre had not expected that the 36th Regiment's station established on December 21 in Pom Lót, a small move actually, would exert such a great effect—containing the enemy at the Mường Thanh field. This station contributed to the failure of a French plan for withdrawal from the Mường Thanh field to Upper Laos via the Tây Trang mountain pass.

In late December, it was reported by Hoàng Sâm and Trần Quý Hải from the Lao battlefield that the 66th Regiment of the 304th Brigade and the 18th and 101st Regiments of the 325th Brigade had opportunely cooperated with the Northwest primary direction to launch strong offensives against enemy troops in Central and Lower Laos. These battlefields revealed the enemy's weaknesses, but they were so important that the enemy could not abandon.

After the Kham He and Banaphao victories in Central Laos, on December 21-22, the Vietnamese army progressed to the Mekong river, liberating Tha Khet and annihilating some enemy positions on the 9th Route. Confronting the risk of "Indochina being divided into halves" as put by the rightist newspapers in Paris, General Navarre immediately detach four mobile battalions in the Red River Delta and one occupation battalion in the South to cooperate with the forces in Central Laos to organize a group of fortifications including ten battalions in Seno.

By that time, the Vietnamese General Headquarters had not received any information about their army's operations in Lower Laos. But the staff reported on a call by the French from Lower Laos to their headquarters in Sài Gòn, informing that they had detected "abnormal signs" in Lower Laos. It was known to the Vietnamese General Headquarters that those signs were the 325th Brigade's perilous strokes. Implementing the General Headquarters' policy, the 325th Brigade detached a battalion to southern Laos to coordinate with the battlefields nationwide, especially that in the 5th Interzone, to launch an offensive in the north of the Central Highlands. The 436th Battalion, which was good at launching ambushes, assaults, and mobile battles, was entrusted with this task. Vice Chief of the 101st Regiment Lê Kích and Vice Political Commissar of the 101st Regiment Nguyễn Minh Đức were appointed as chief and commissar of this battalion respectively. Preparations for the battalion were directed meticulously by the General Headquarters. Troops were reinforced; military equipment and especially means of communication were supplemented; and an advance party was sent to the Việt Nam-Laos border area to ask the local people and administration for support and food supplies for the battalion during their march from Nghệ An southwards. After two months of marching along the Trường Sơn mountain range, the battalion finally arrived in the Việt Nam-Laos border area in Quảng Nam Province and then crossed the river to Attapeu. During the night of the 29th to the 30th of January 1954, the battalion launched an attack on Pui, the first battle in Laos, completely annihilating the French assault company in Pui Village, liberating Attapeu Town, and killing and arresting over 50 French troops. Taking advantage of the French weaknesses, the battalion cooperated with the Lao armed forces in Lower Laos to launch the guerilla war in many places in the Bolaven Plateau. The battalion's offensive was so unpredictable that General Navarre had to immediately detach three mobile battalions of the 51st Regiment which had been newly built in Cambodia and a parachute battalion in North Việt Nam to reinforce Pakse. Hence, after the Red River Delta and Điện Biên Phủ, Central and Lower Laos became the third troop-gathering place of the French army.

On the occasion of the seventh anniversary of the National Resistance Day and the ninth anniversary of the foundation of the Vietnamese People's Army, from the General Headquarters in Việt Bắc, General Giáp sent out the "Order of the Day" to encourage the whole army to enter the campaign. The "Order of the Day" promoted the army's determination to crush the Navarre plan in the cooperative battlefields such as the Central Highlands and the Red River Delta and especially in the strategic battlefield of Điện Biên Phủ.

In the early days of the New Year, what was called the "Atlante dream"[1] by the French press and mentioned in the Navarre plan from the beginning, was implemented in the battlefield. The first step, Aréthuse, started on January 20, 1954. While 22 French infantry and parachute battalions and some artillery, motorized, sapper, and transport units were moving to Tuy Hòa, Phú Yên, General Blanc was informed that many French and puppet stations on the 14th Route had been eliminated, Kon Tum Town was being "overwhelmed," Pleiku had been assaulted, and the 19th Route was being seriously threatened. Head of the Operational Department reported to General Giáp that Nguyễn Chánh and the leadership of the 5th Interzone had seriously complied with the Central policy, detaching regular forces to launch an offensive in the north

---

1. It was revealed later that Atlante was a plan for the occupation of the free zone of the 5th Interzone. It included three steps. The first step, called Aréthuse, was aimed at occupying Tuy Hòa in Phú Yên Province; the second one, Axelle, was targeted at occupying Quy Nhơn and Bồng Sơn; the last one, Attilat, was aimed at linking Bồng Sơn to Quảng Nam, completing the whole operation. After the failure of the plan of occupying the Nam-Ngãi-Bình-Phú area, the Western press satirized that Atlante failed because the dream was too big and heavy.

Chapter Seven: THE FINAL EFFORTS OF FRANCE AND THE UNITED STATES

of the Central Highlands. General Giáp got excited when he heard that the Vietnamese forces in the battlefields in the Central Highlands and Lower Laos had opened fire (on the 26th and 31st of January 1954 respectively) in cooperation with the primary battlefield according to the plan.[1]

A few days after the Vietnamese army opened fire in the Central Highlands battlefield, General Navarre realized the risk of losing such a large area which stretched from the Quảng Nam-Quảng Ngãi coastal area to the Việt Nam-Laos border area and Bolaven Plateau. Unable to pursue the Atlante plan, General Navarre ordered General Blanc to withdraw the 100th Mobile Regime and two parachute battalions from the 5th Interzone and send the 11th and 21st Mobile Regiments to the Central Highlands to rescue General de Beaufort. Two more groups of fortifications were established in Pleiku and An Khê. Thus, not only Aréthuse, which was called satirically by the French press as the first-born child of Atlante, died prematurely, but General Navarre's "strategically mobile bag" shrank by tens of battalions. With nearly 30 French and puppet battalions being pinned down in the south of the Central Highlands, the mountainous and forested battlefield became Navarre's fourth troop-gathering place.

Regarding the battlefield behind the enemy lines, the summary report of the Vietnamese staff showed that the resolution of the conference of the Vietnamese cadres in the areas behind the enemy lines held in early October 1953 had gradually proved its effect since the early dry season, especially in the Red River Delta battlefield. There, since mid

---

1. According to the initial plan, the Điện Biên Phủ front would open fire on the afternoon of January 20. It was then postponed to January 25 and finally to January 26, 1954.

December, the Vietnamese regular forces, including units which had been listed as "annihilated" by the French Staff, had promoted their operations and opportunely cooperated with the front line. That the 320th Brigade had penetrated deep into the areas behind the enemy lines and launched strong attacks on the Đáy River defense line encouraged the 42nd, 46th, and 50th Regiments to develop their activities extensively, from the Sơn Tây midland area to the Thái Bình coastal area and around Hà Đông, close to the center of Hà Nội. The 5th Route, the life-line of hundreds of thousands of French expeditionary troops in North Việt Nam, was under frequent threat, hindering the transportation of French reinforcements to the battlefields. In the areas behind the enemy lines in Central Việt Nam, during the last months of 1953, Vietnamese troops recorded outstanding achievements such as overturning tens of trains and annihilating nearly 200 French posts and watch-towers. Later, General Navarre himself admitted that the power of the guerilla war forced the French to delay many mopping-up operations which had been schedule to be launched along the Central coastal region. In the Southern battlefield, after the 11th Mobile Regiment, the only mobile regiment, had been sent to the Central Highlands, the remaining French troops had to shrink to defend the important positions. It was a good opportunity for the Vietnamese to develop the guerilla war and force the French and puppet troops to leave thousands of posts and watch-towers. General Navarre confessed that the "decay" increased so rapidly that he did not think about the occupation of the free zone of the 9th Interzone as planned.

Basically, the first phase of the 1953–1954 winter-spring campaign ended successfully in early January 1954. Thanks to alternate and concomitant offensives in the directions which revealed the enemy weaknesses, the Vietnamese forces annihilated thousands of enemy troops, liberated many strategic areas, and excellently fulfilled the task assigned to the whole Vietnamese army by President Hồ Chí Minh—forcing General Navarre to disperse the French mobile bloc, which was considered as the main tool to implement his 18-month strategic plan. Over half of the French mobile forces (23 out of 44 battalions) which General Navarre mustered in the Red River Delta were divided and sent to the battlefields in the Northern and Central regions of Việt Nam, as well as those in the Central and Lower regions of Laos. The remaining 20 French battalions failed to promote their mobile capacity because they were distributed across the Red River Delta to defend strategic roads, seaports, military ports, as well as military, political, and economic centers.

General Giáp realized that there was still one uncompleted task in the first phase. At that time, the whole Vietnamese army was preparing for the elimination of the "bristling porcupine" in the Mường Thanh field, so they had not had opportunities and conditions to cooperate with Lao forces to liberate Phonsaly and northernmost Laos. A "strategic corridor" reinforced by six French battalions had been established along the Nậm Hu River. That so-called "defense line" had not been set as a target of the Vietnamese forces.

While monitoring and directing the operation of the whole army, the staff of the Vietnamese General Headquarters assisted General Giáp in preparing for the implementation of the combat plan for the next phase with Điện Biên Phủ being the key battlefield. The military project for the 1953–1954 and 1954–1955 winter-spring campaigns was a comprehensive one. It focused on the tasks of promoting struggle both in the North and South, supporting Laos and Cambodia, building forces and military infrastructure in battlefields (especially roads in the Northwest direction), and reorganizing and strengthening the directing body. In the military project, General Giáp presented an analysis of General Navarre's strategic plan and then clearly stated that whether the enemy could realize this plan was another matter. According to him, the enemy was suffering their first failures in the areas behind the enemy lines in the North, southwestern Ninh Bình, and Lai Châu, so they would have to passively disperse their forces to the Northwest of Việt Nam and to Central Laos. However, the Vietnamese should heighten vigilance and make all efforts in order to crush the enemy plot.

Based on the afore-mentioned situation of both sides, the Central Military Commission proposed the strategic policy and combat plan for the 1953-1954 winter-spring campaign with a view to liberating the Red River Delta. Accordingly, the Vietnamese army should promote the guerilla war in the areas behind the enemy lines and operations in the battlefields in South Việt Nam, Laos, and Cambodia to force the enemy to further disperse their forces and drive them into a passive situation; actively and proactively annihilate the enemy strength and weaken them little by little; actively reinforce and develop their troops and simultaneously diminish the enemy's puppet troop and material resources in the areas behind the enemy lines; and thoroughly grasp and comply with the strategic guideline of first and foremost liberating the Northwest and Central Highlands and threatening the South to create favorable conditions for the liberation of the North.

Chapter Seven: THE FINAL EFFORTS OF FRANCE AND THE UNITED STATES

The 1954–1955 military plan and the policy of launching the Điện Biên Phủ campaign were approved simultaneously. On December 20, the Điện Biên Phủ Campaign Party Committee[1] was established; the 312th and 351st Brigades, including the 105-mm Howitzer Regiment and the 37-mm Antiair-craft Artillery Regiment, took the order to set off. At the end of December 1953, before going to the front, General Giáp sent a letter of encouragement to the training course for conscripted laborers participating in the Điện Biên Phủ campaign, released the "Five Disciplines in the Battlefield," and sent a telegram to encourage the cadres and soldiers of the 320th Brigade, who were penetrating deep into the areas behind the enemy lines and cooperating with the main battlefield.

To the Front with the Whole Nation

On January 5, 1954, General Giáp set off for the battlefield with the determination to annihilate the Điện Biên Phủ group of fortifications and crush the Navarre plan. His departure was unforeseen by the highest representatives of Paris in Indochina, including High Commissioner Maurice Dejean. It was later revealed that Dejean sent a telegram to Paris that day to inform that according to the commander-in-chief of the French expeditionary army, the Vietnamese Headquarters did not dare to participate in the Điện Biên Phủ battle. The French thought that the Vietnamese army under the leadership of General Giáp had never dealt with such a fierce offensive before. If the Vietnamese army attacked the Mường Thanh valley, a severe battle would take place. However, the French had many chances to win it.

---

1. It included Võ Nguyên Giáp as secretary and Hoàng Văn Thái, Lê Liên, and Đặng Kim Giang as members.

It is true that Điện Biên Phủ was the largest battle in the anti-French resistance war, but it was not as "dreadful" as Dejean had said. Vietnamese leaders also acknowledged that it had been the biggest challenge to the Vietnamese people and army in the battle of wits and power against leaders of the French expeditionary army. Therefore, President Hồ Chí Minh gave General Giáp careful recommendations before the latter's leaving. The President said that it was an important battle and thus instructed General Giáp to fight only when he was certain of victory. His advice reflected the operational guideline defined by the Party Central Committee at its conference held in early 1953. Accordingly, the Vietnamese liberation war was a long-term one which was mainly based on self-reliance. Therefore, it required the Vietnamese to prevent themselves from being subjective, underestimating the enemy, losing patience, and engaging in hazardous activities. If they took risks once and suffered losses, the catastrophe would be immeasurable. Their battlefield was narrow and their forces were small, so they should win the battle, otherwise they would not be able to continue their resistance war.

General Giáp set off, bearing in mind President Hồ Chí Minh's recommendations and the Party Central Committee's instructions.

He was accompanied by Head of the Operational Department Trần Văn Quang, Head of the Intelligence Department Lê Trọng Nghĩa, Head of the Information Department Hoàng Đạo Thúy, Vice Head of the Security Department Phạm Kiệt, and Head of the Chinese Advisory Delegation Wei Guoqing. According to Phạm Kiệt's narration, before leaving, General Giáp cheerfully said to everybody, "It

Chapter Seven: THE FINAL EFFORTS OF FRANCE AND THE UNITED STATES

will be the most comfortable ever journey this time. We shall travel by car, though it is just a cranky one, so the journey will not be as hard as the previous ones."

On the way to the battlefield, they kept talking about three significant issues: the Vietnamese army's task of eliminating the group of fortifications to boost the resistance war, things they should do to cope with the French withdrawal from Điện Biên Phủ if this should happen in order not to miss the target of attack, and the fighting method they should apply to annihilate such a group of fortifications as Điện Biên Phủ.

The fortification group was the latest form of defense in the Indochinese battlefield, which had been used in the Hòa Bình campaign in 1951, as well as in the Plain of Jars and Nà Sản in 1952 and early 1953. At that time, the Vietnamese troops' combat capacity was still limited, so in late 1951 General Giáp did not let them attack the group of fortifications in Hòa Bình Town. Instead, he ordered them to fight against the enemy's mobile forces on the 6th Route and the Đà River, and launch an offensive in the areas behind the enemy lines in North Việt Nam. In the last phase of the Northwest campaign, enemy troops concentrated in the group of fortifications in Nà Sản. After launching several attacks on the periphery of Nà Sản, the Vietnamese army succeeded in grinding down part of the enemy strength. However, they also suffered some losses, so General Giáp ordered them to stop the offensive against the group of fortifications. In the development of the revolutionary war, it was an indispensable strategic requirement for the Vietnamese army to crush the enemy's latest form of defense during the last years of the resistance war, since it would bring about a turning-point to the Vietnamese course of armed struggle for national liberation. However, the Vietnamese army missed the chance to annihilate the French group of fortifications in Sam Neua in the summer of 1953. The French troops withdrew before the Vietnamese army reached there, so they had to change to pursuing the French troops instead of attacking the group of fortifications. After the Sam Neua campaign, all the political and military re-educational courses were aimed at preparing for Vietnamese regular soldiers mentally, ideologically, technically, and tactically, so that they could launch a large-scale offensive against a group of fortifications. On the threshold of the 1953-1954 winter-spring campaign, the Vietnamese regular brigades were ready to confront a group of fortifications as directed by the General Headquarters. General Giáp wrote later that having realized the possibility of the French reinforcing Điện Biên Phủ and turning it into a group of fortifications, the Party Central Committee immediately decided to grasp the opportunity to eliminate it.

General Giáp kept observing the situation along the way to the battlefield to see if the enemy withdrew from Điện Biên Phủ. At each stop, he often reminded the front military intelligence to watch for any abnormal signals that revealed the enemy withdrawal. Although the enemy strength in Điện Biên Phủ had rose to nine or ten battalions, what had happened in Hòa Bình, Nà Sản, and recently Lai Châu showed that the enemy was able to organize large-scale withdrawals. They could launch a quick airborne withdrawal. Within five days, six battalions could be transported from Nà Sản to the delta by air. Otherwise, they could make a sortie through the 36th Regiment's station in Pom Lót to Laos. If the enemy withdrawal from Điện Biên Phủ succeeded, the Vietnamese army would lose the strategic offensive target of this dry season and their winter-spring plan would be considerably affected.

After nine years of fighting and construction, the Vietnamese regular army included only six infantry brigades, one sapper-artillery brigade, one 105-mm howitzer regiment, and one 37-mm anti-aircraft artillery regiment. To realize the Central determination to eliminate the Điện Biên Phủ group of fortifications, the Vietnamese General Headquarters sent the majority of the regular army to the Northwest for a battle which was not allowed to fail as President Hồ Chí Minh said.

It was the first time the Vietnamese army had conducted an assault on such a strong group of fortifications which was much better equipped than that in Nà Sản, not to mention the possibility of reinforcement. They would confront tens of thousands of enemy troops on an over-100-square-kilometer-wide flat field, which was chosen by the enemy and which would promote the enemy's maximal strength of aircraft, tanks, cannons, and counter-attack and rescue forces. That is why General Giáp was always concerned about the fighting method in this battle of strategic significance. The chosen method should guarantee that the Vietnamese army could not only win the battle and grind down an important part of the enemy's élite forces but also preserve their regular brigades—the spearheads of the resistance war.

On the way to the front, General Giáp listened to daily reports on the operation of Vietnamese regular brigades and the preparation of coordinative battlefields.

The 320th Brigade was the first Vietnamese unit to confront de Castries several months earlier, when this colonel followed the Mouette operation to southwestern Ninh Bình. The 320th Brigade crushed the operation right in front of Vice President of the United States of America Nixon, who was present in Ghềnh to monitor the battlefield. While the other brigades were marching to the Northwest to "have a dialogue" with de Castries and more than a ten thousand French troops in the Điện Biên Phủ group of fortifications, the 320th Brigade penetrated deeper into the flooded rice areas to attack the Đáy River defense line—an action of "further decaying the useful delta areas" as later called by General Navarre. For this special task, the 320th Brigade was the first Vietnamese brigade to receive General Giáp's letter of encouragement before the whole Vietnamese army enter the second phase of the winter-spring campaign. The telegram read, "Your duty was very heavy. With your accomplishment of this task, you have made a great contribution to the general victory and created favorable conditions for new victories in the coming time."

In the Central battlefield, the 325th Brigade had no conditions to conduct concentrated operations. At the conference to disseminate the combat plan held in mid November, Chief of the 325th Brigade Trần Quý Hai was tasked to organize and direct the Front D (Central and Lower Laos), which functioned as an important strategic direction in central Indochina and revealed the enemy's weaknesses. While the 101st Regiment (insufficient) of the 325th Brigade and the 66th Regiment of the 304th Brigade attacked the enemy in Central Laos, the 436th Battalion of the 101st Regiment, directly commanded by Lê Kích, conducted a perilous offensive in southernmost Laos. To contain the enemy and coordinate with Front D, the 18th Regiment dispersed itself

Chapter Seven: THE FINAL EFFORTS OF FRANCE AND THE UNITED STATES

into sections which then penetrated into the areas behind the enemy lines to promote the guerilla war. Their main activity was conducting attacks along the 1st Route in the Bình-Trị-Thiên area. The 95th Regiment, which had just crushed the Camargue operation in the Hải Lăng-Phong Điền area in Thừa Thiên Province, was dispatched to Nghệ An to act as a reserve force of the Vietnamese General Headquarters and defend the free zone of the 4th Interzone.

On the way to the front, General Giáp dropped in Phú Thọ to visit the 304th Brigade. Perhaps he did not know that there were still widespread and inclusive discussions about an anecdote relating to a two-month operation among the cadres and soldiers of 304th Brigade. While they were all being billeted in Thanh Hóa and impatiently waiting for the troop dispatch order, the 66th Regiment was ordered to coordinate with another regiment in Central Laos. Next, the 9th and 57th Regiments took orders to march to the Northwest as soon as they heard that General Navarre had sent troops to the Mường Thanh field. They were excited to set off. Unpredictably, when they were 15 kilometers away from Mộc Châu, they were ordered to turn right at the Xốm Lồm three-way crossroads and follow the Quang Huy-Thu Cúc-Lai Đồng route to Phú Thọ. It was not until they passed the Chí Thủ wharf on December 25 that Chief of Staff Nam Long revealed that the past over-one-month operation was just a strategic diversion. On the occasion of his visit on the evening of January 5, 1954, General Giáp ordered the 304th Brigade to immediately dispatch the 57th Regiment to the Northwest. Meanwhile, the 9th Regiment was tasked to stay to defend the revolutionary base and get ready to set off when ordered. Thus, like those of the 325th Brigade, the regiments of the 304th operated in different areas which were far from each other.

When he reached the Yên Bái-Phú Thọ area, General Giáp learned that the 312th Brigade had left for the Northwest. So he did not have the chance to listen to the confidences they had while waiting for the orders to set off. These confidences were later reported in the brigade's chronicle. The brigade was thought to have marched to the delta. In fact, they were still hiding in the forests in the areas of Đại Phạm, Quang Nhiễu, and Lương Bằng in northern Phú Thọ. They had equipped themselves with necessary things like guns, ammunition, needles and threads, tiger oils, dried fishes, and fish sauce. They had been waiting for the order to set off. Finally, the order came on December 20, 1953, like the sunlight that dispelled the clouds of anxiety. All the units were eager to depart for the battlefield.

The 316th and 308th Brigades confronted the Điện Biên Phủ group of fortifications earlier than the others. After liberating Lai Châu, the 316th Brigade coordinated with the 308th Brigade to surround the Mường Thanh field. They had witnessed the construction of the group of fortifications since the beginning. They were tasked not to lose the target at any cost. That explained why they had soon established a station at the Việt Nam-Laos borders. If the 308th Brigade had marched straight to Điện Biên Phủ from the revolutionary base as a united bloc, the 316th Brigade would not have had such a favorable condition. When Political Commissar Chu Huy Mân left the conference held in Việt Bắc to disseminate the combat plan for the battlefield, the three regiments of the 316th Brigade were still being in three different directions. After the Sam Neua campaign, the 98th Regiment stayed to

Chapter Seven: THE FINAL EFFORTS OF FRANCE AND THE UNITED STATES

help Lao people and militants reinforce the liberated zones before moving to Sơn La to prepare for the autumn-winter campaign. The 176th Regiment stayed in the Northwest, where they were tasked to abolish bandits along the Đà River and support the plan of repairing roads and bridges until they received the order to take part in the campaign for the liberation of Lai Châu. It can be said that the 98th and 176th Regiments participated in four successive campaigns in the Western battlefield, including Northwest, Sam Neua, Lai Châu, and Điện Biên Phủ. The 174th Regiment was seemingly luckier as they were sent to Thanh Hóa for the re-educational course at the end of the Sam Neua campaign before taking orders to return to the brigade formation for the task of liberating Lai Châu.

In comparison to seasoned infantry brigades, the two anti-aircraft artillery and howitzer regiments of the 351st Brigade were considered as "new recruits." They had little experience in both arms and operations, especially combined ones. The 367th Anti-aircraft Artillery Regiment was tasked to eliminate French planes to support their companion-in-arms on the ground. However, the 37-mm batteries under the command of Vice Chief of the 367th Regiment Nguyễn Quang Bích had been trained only by shooting flying balloons. Only when they arrived in the Điện Biên Phủ battlefield did the artillerymen learn about the shapes and technical features of each kind of French aircraft by observing the Mường Thanh airport with binoculars or directly watching the planes flying up and down in the sky of Điện Biên Phủ. For the reason of secrecy, the anti-aircraft guns were only allowed to fire a few days before the opening of the campaign. These anti-aircraft guns were a great surprise for not only the Điện

Biên Phủ-based French troops but also the French delegates to the workshop held in mid April 2004 in Hà Nội on the occasion of the 50th anniversary of the Điện Biên Phủ victory. People could not help feeling astonished to learn that the 45th Howitzer Regiment, also known as Tất Thắng (Sure-to-win) Regiment, had the same situation on the threshold of the dry season. In the training course held in the summer of 1953, the 105-mm howitzer units learned how to attack enemy troops in fortifications and enemy regulars in combined operations. At the end of the course, they were allowed to shoot some real bullets, but there was no "subjects" for combined rehearsal. Before the dry season started, General Giáp presented the regiment a baldachin embroidered with eight golden words "*Ẩn lặng như tờ, đánh mạnh như sét*" (literally: "Hide as quietly as the grave, fight as violently as the lightning"). The military and political re-education courses had ended and the dry season had come, but the Vietnamese troops still "hid as quietly as the grave" in the Bắc Mục old forest by the 2nd Route running from Tuyên Quang to Hà Giang. They became impatient, especially after learning about the victories in Central Laos and southwestern Ninh Bình. A poem expressing the feelings of the artillerymen appeared in the wall newspaper of the 45th Howitzer Regiment. The poem read:

> *Chiến dịch thu đông đã đến rồi.*
> *Trung đoàn Tất Thắng vẫn nằm chơi!*
> *Sao không cơ động linh hoạt nhỉ?*
> *Chiến dịch thu đông đã đến rồi.*
>
> (The autumn-winter campaign has come.
> Tất Thắng Regiment remains unoccupied!

Chapter Seven: THE FINAL EFFORTS OF FRANCE AND THE UNITED STATES

Why don't we promote mobility and flexibility?
The autumn-winter campaign has come.)[1]

In his meeting with Political Commissar of the 351st Brigade Phạm Ngọc Mậu, General Giáp praised the soldiers for their legitimate question. However, he also reminded Mậu to make the soldiers thoroughly grasp the spirit of the General Headquarters' instruction: "Keeping the strong firepower secret will spring surprises on the enemy. Howitzers should be used in the right time and place for the achievement of appropriate victories."

General Giáp did not mention anything about the task of the 45th Regiment during the conference to disseminate the combat plan held in mid November 1953. Political Commissar of the 351st Brigade Phạm Ngọc Mậu, Chief of the 45th Regiment Hữu Mỹ, and Political Commissar of the 45th Regiment Nam Thắng were called for a private meeting with General Giáp. The meeting resulted in the resolution released by the 351st Brigade on December 11. The resolution read:

> The 45th Regiment should absolutely keep the combat plan secret, have confidence in the seniors, get ready to fight against the enemy to defend the free zone or move to the Northwest or the delta, and take advantage of the time to continue technical training courses and preparations for fight.

---

1. President Hồ Chí Minh awarded the 45th Regiment, formerly known as the 50th Regiment, the title *Tất Thắng* for their achievements in Nam Định City during the early days of the resistance war. The strategic principles of activeness, proactiveness, mobility, and flexibility were set by the Politburo before the whole Vietnamese army entered the 1953-1954 dry season, and were then thoroughly grasped by the soldiers. The composer intentionally repeated the words "mobility" and "flexibility" in this poem.

Having thoroughly grasped the resolution, cadres and soldiers of the 45th Regiment continued to "hide as quietly as the grave." They only carried out some diversionary activities, using bamboo-made and black-painted cannons in feigned operations around some towns in Thái Nguyên, Tuyên Quang, or Phú Thọ.

The departure day finally came. On December 21, "the flock of elephants"[1] left the Tuyên Quang revolutionary base for the Northwest. When assigning tasks to commanders of the 351st Brigade and the 45th and 367th Regiments, General Giáp warned that the heavy guns would meet difficulties in their first battle. He reminded the commanders to guarantee the absolute security and secrecy of the operation. He also emphasized that once they had taken the troops, cars, and guns to the battlefield safely, they would gain 60 percent of the victory.

The secrecy of "the flock of elephants"[1] was extremely important because until the firing day, the 105-mm howitzers and 37-mm anti-aircraft guns of the Vietnamese army were unknown to the French army. The results of the campaign later revealed that one of the reasons for the French failure was that they could not find out the right answer for Vietnamese artillery. The appearance of "the flock of elephants" was a secret to the enemy, but a special event and a great source of encouragement to Vietnamese people. They were glad to see these "elephants" on the road and were willing to let them pass. Whenever the "elephants" stopped for a while along the road, people would come to touch them and encouraged them to accomplish their task of hitting the enemy stations. The

---

1. This phase referred to the convoy of cars and cannons.

Chapter Seven: THE FINAL EFFORTS OF FRANCE AND THE UNITED STATES

Vietnamese General Headquarters had ordered the restoration and opening of roads for soldiers, conscripted laborers, and particularly these "elephants" to travel on. Ground forces, including those carrying small cannons on their shoulders, could travel on narrow paths, while these "elephants" required roads which were wide enough (about 8–12 meters) and moderately slopping. At sharp bends, artillerymen had to move the guns from carriers and push them.

During the journey to the front that dry season, General Giáp was extremely pleased with the achievements gained by soldiers, voluntary youths, conscripted laborers, and especially the 151st Sapper Regiment, which spearheaded the building and promotion of the tradition of "opening the road to victory." This regiment set off on November 7. It was tasked to repair and widen the road running from Tạ Khoa to Cò Nòi and then from Cò Nòi to Tuần Giáo, open the 86-km road connecting Tuần Giáo with Điện Biên in December, and finally restore and widen the Tạ Khoa-Điện Biên Phủ route with 76 narrow bends. The combination between sappers and artillery was reflected in an especially urgent task—the sappers opened the road in time for the howitzer and anti-aircraft artillery regiments to arrive at the troop-gathering place near Tuần Giáo safely in early January 1954. Next, the remaining 86-km road running from Tuần Giáo to Điện Biên should be reinforced and widened in time for artillery to arrive at the front from the troop-gathering place safely. It was an important and urgent task that was waiting for the sappers ahead.

During consecutive months working on the road, the 151st Regiment had to cope with harsh weather conditions and the enemy bombings. The French staff knew clearly that the long-distance transportation of supplies was one of the biggest difficulties of the Vietnamese army, so they focused digging deeper into this difficulty. The mountain passes of Pha Đinh and Lũng Lô, the Cò Nòi three-way crossroads, and the Tạ Khoa wharf were the targets of their bombings. Besides blow-up bombs and delayed-action bombs, they also used jump mines, butterfly bombs, and iron spikes to obstruct the Vietnamese conscripted laborers and vehicles. When General Giáp arrived at the Cò Nòi three-way crossroads, the junction of the 13th and 41st Routes, he felt as if he had reached the front. He later wrote, "The roads had disappeared under bomb craters . . . Even the surrounding mountains and hills were covered in red . . . The Cò Nòi three-way crossroads became a frontier passage that anyone to the front had to cross."

While the car was crossing the crossroads, General Giáp was informed that the terrain here changed every day. The observation team had to draw up the map more or less ten times.

"Without that road, this campaign would not have taken place." This statement of General Giáp after the victory day was his overall acknowledgment of the achievements of the 151st Sapper Regiment and other road workers during the Điện Biên Phủ campaign. Seen on such roads were the images of not only soldiers and voluntary youths but also conscripted laborers who were called "inexhaustible ants" by the French press. It was among the outstanding features of the overall picture of "all the nation to the front." General Giáp later recalled:

> People travelled up and down as if they were going on a pilgrimage. There were conscripted laborers from the Việt Bắc base, Northwest, 3rd and 4th Zones. There were units of

Chapter Seven: THE FINAL EFFORTS OF FRANCE AND THE UNITED STATES

infantry, sappers, and vehicles, and ensembles. There were conscripted women carrying laden loads of rice cheerfully crossing the rivers on fragile bamboo-made or tree-trunk bridges. There were conscripted men silently driving "baby elephants" like the wind on roads. This seemingly limitless picture was embellished with images of pack horses led by the Mông people going down from the highlands and conscripted women from different minority groups such as Tày, Nùng, Thái and Dao carrying papooses on their shoulders or backs. Sometimes, singing was heard from the groups of conscripted laborers, by a young woman from the delta or a young man from the 4th Zone. The singing encouraged them to overcome the increasing difficulties awaiting ahead.

The rice transported to the front those days was the fruit of not only the Vietnamese peasants who were bravely rising in the rear of the resistance but also those who were tenaciously fighting against the enemy in the temporarily-occupied areas to protect crops, cattle, and farming tools to produce and bring rice through the enemy posts and the "white belt" to the free zones. During the transportation from the rear to the front, the rice was not only once imbued with the blood of conscripted laborers in the rain of enemy bombs.

On January 12, 1954, General Giáp and his entourage arrived in Tuần Giáo. He immediately asked Chief of Staff Hoàng Văn Thái, "Will the enemy withdraw from Điện Biên Phủ?"

Obviously, General Giáp was obsessed by that question during the one-week journey to the font. Thái replied, "Perhaps not. They're still reinforcing the fortifications."

General Giáp was released after hearing the reply, especially after he was informed that the two artillery regiments had arrived in Tuần Giáo safely. He reminded Thái to quickly set the 312th Brigade into the blockage formation. They had to contain the enemy in Điện Biên to assure that the script of Nà Sản would not repeated there. Shortly afterwards, he listened to Thái's report.

Thanks to a wide-open map of the enemy group of fortifications, General Giáp had the first chance to clearly visualize the hollow-terrain of Mường Thanh and the dense disposition of enemy positions there. Although there were some contiguous heights in the east, Vietnamese troops would have to cross wide fields to approach the central area from all the four directions, especially the west. According to Thái's report, their most difficult task at that time was to complete the expansion of the Tuần Giáo-Điện Biên route. Once this task had been done, cannons could be brought into the battlefield and the campaign could start. The advance party of the General Headquarters and the cadres of brigades all suggested that they should start the campaign early when the enemy had not established a firm foothold, otherwise the enemy would continue reinforcing their group of fortifications until they became too strong to eliminate. They were also afraid that if the campaign was prolonged, they would have to deal with increasing problems related to troop strength, casualties, and especially supplies.

That afternoon, General Giáp moved on to the 15th kilometer on the Tuần Giáo-Điện Biên Phủ route. The Western landscape was impressive, but the General was being too overwhelmed by emerging questions that he did not notice it. Without a road for cannons to get into the battlefield, an early attack was impossible. The French continued reinforcing their defense system while the Vietnamese needed more time

Chapter Seven: THE FINAL EFFORTS OF FRANCE AND THE UNITED STATES

to restore bridges and widen the over-80-km road from the troop-gathering place to the front. How long would it take the Vietnamese to complete this task? The Vietnamese staff estimated five days. Suppose the estimation was correct, what the French could do within nearly a week to strengthen their defensive? How was their reinforcement capacity? By that time, gunshots had not been heard from the cooperative battlefields of Lower Laos and Central Highlands.[1]

The car stopped at Thẩm Púa, where the Front Headquarters of the Vietnamese army was temporarily based. Officers of the General Headquarters had stayed there for a month and were busy preparing for combat.

There was not much time left, so General Giáp immediately consulted with the Campaign Party Committee about the combat plan. The project had been prepared by the staff and some consultants. Members of the Campaign Party Committee including Hoàng Văn Thái, Lê Liêm, and Đặng Kim Giang attended this consultation. As it had been reported by Thái, all participants opined that if they launched an early attack on the enemy when the latter was on the defensive and had not had time to reinforce their fortifications, they would possibly win victory within a few days. In terms of fighting method, they suggested the use of all their forces, which would simultaneously attack the enemy from all directions in combination with howitzers and anti-aircraft guns. The offensive campaign would start with a fierce artillery strike on the enemy artillery and aircraft at the airport. Then spearheads of the ground forces would penetrate into the

---

1. The Central Highlands battlefield opened fire on January 26; the Lower Laos battlefield, on January 31.

group of fortifications and divide it. Meanwhile, the main spearheads from the west and southwest would assault the headquarters and information center of the enemy, make a mess in the center of their defense system, and launch an inside-out attack, in combination with the outside-in attack by other spearheads, to eliminate all the enemy troops within three nights and two days. Thus, the daytime battles would take place with alternate Vietnamese and French troops, so the French artillery and aircraft would find it hard to hit the Vietnamese formation without hurting their own one.

After listening to the report, General Giáp wondered if it would be too dangerous and if they would be sure of victory. He did not believe that they could mobilize all their forces to annihilate tens of thousands of enemy troops in the group of fortifications within two or three days. Then he discussed the issue with Head of the Chinese Advisory Delegation. Wei Guoqing had listened to Mei Jiasheng's report on the situation and agreed with him on the idea of an early campaign. He also believed in the victory of the Vietnamese army. After listening to General Giáp, he said that they should attack when the enemy had not established a firm foothold. He also thought that if they delayed the offensive, they would miss the chance to annihilate the enemy since the enemy fortifications had become too strong to eliminate.

Although he did not believe in the victory of a quick offensive, General Giáp had no reasons to turn down a project which had been prepared by the majority of the Campaign Party Committee and approved by all the Chinese consultants. Moreover, he could not either phone or send a telegram to President Hồ Chí Minh for his instructions on such a top-secret issue. To avoid wasting time, he finally agreed with the

Campaign Party Committee to hold a meeting to disseminate the combat plan to units for timely preparations.

Afterwards, through Western publications and especially the two books of reminiscences written by General Navarre, researchers collected more information on the preparations made by the two generals on the threshold of the Điện Biên Phủ campaign.

General Navarre did not expect that Paris would send an envoy to Sài Gòn to convey its message to him right on the day his troops landed on the Mường Thanh field. According to this envoy, France could not afford the recent operations of the French expeditionary army and General Navarre should adjust his plan to "cut his coat to suit his cloth." Paris wanted to let the Vietnamese army know that although they could not be defeated, they would not be able to send the French army home. The best solution for both warring sides should be a negotiation. Paris also suggested a negotiation between the two warring sides as the best solution to the present situation. Paris also warned that General Navarre should not expect any more reinforcement from France, and that it would be too late to be sorry if he kept using forces as he used to.

Objectively speaking, Navarre was a confident general. Although he had to take over a "contaminated legacy" from Salan, he had never thought of stepping down. It might be because he could not step down when he had been praised to the sky by the Paris and Sài Gòn press in the wake of his 18-month plan being approved by the Council of National Defense. It also might be that his superiority complex prevented him from resigning from office.

On December 3, General Navarre decided to build Điện Biên Phủ into a group of fortifications to fight against the opponent. Without the public support from Paris, he was backed by the United States. So he had gathered enough spiritual and material elements to realize his determination. During the implementation of this plan, General Navarre anticipated three posibilities.

Firstly, the Vietnamese regular brigades had moved to the Northwest, so the pressure in the delta which had weighed upon him since the beginning of the dry season had lessened. He had been worried that the Vietnamese army would march towards the delta.

Secondly, if the Vietnamese army withdrew instead of attacking the "invincible" group of fortifications once they had approached it, it would be a good chance for the French army. When the dry season went and the rainy season came, the Vietnamese army would not have the chance to launch a strategic attack. Then the French Headquarters would deliberately implement their policy of occupying the four free provinces of the 5th Interzone and preparing for the second step of the Navarre plan.

Finally, if the Vietnamese army was brave enough to strike the iron and steel pillboxes of the group of fortifications, then the French generals under the command of General Navarre would gain what they had expected. They all believed that their army would pulverize the Vietnamese army.

According to the book *La bataille de Dien Bien Phu* (literally: The Battle of Điện Biên Phủ) written by Jules Roy, while General Giáp was considering the operational guideline of the campaign, in Sài Gòn, General Navarre was reviewing the defense plan that he approved in early December. This combat plan was considered as a guide for the French army in defending the group of fortifications. It included four steps as follows:

In the first step, the French army would promote their operations on the ground and in the air to hinder and slow down the opponent's transfer of troops to the Northwest. Specifically, they would make raids on the main routes from Yên Bái and Thanh Hóa to the Northwest and actively obstruct the opponent's logistical system.

In the second step, the opponent would be directly approaching the group of fortifications (it was estimated to take six to ten days). The French army would use aircraft and artillery to dislodge the opponents from the approached positions.

In the third step, if the opponent launched an assault, which was estimated to last a few days, the French army would counter-attack using both fire-power and assault forces to force their opponent to pay a high price before suspending the assault.

In the last step, after the opponent's withdrawal, they would expand their victory and continue to cause the opponent more losses during the retreat.

The airlift connecting Hà Nội and Hải Phòng with Điện Biên Phủ allowed a great number of American DC3 transport planes to land on the Mường Thanh airport. These planes carried around 200 to 300 tons of building materials for the construction of fortifications and the reinforcement of the defense system every day. Besides, the C119 transport planes steered by American pilots parachuted about 100 to 150 tons of military supplies every morning. French commanders estimated that they needed 70 tons of supplies in normal combat conditions and 90 tons in fierce ones to maintain the fighting capacity of their troops.

Based on the anticipation of the opponent's limited capacity to prolong the battles, they only prepared provision for use in ten days, fuel in eight days, and ammunition in six to nine days.

General Navarre believed that with his words of encouragement at the Christmas party held in de Castries' bunker in the previous year, with the large quantities of means and materials being transported to Điện Biên Phủ, and with an approved defense plan, the Điện Biên Phủ group of fortifications would stand firm. With his maximal efforts during the last days of January, General Navarre believed that he would win the Điện Biên Phủ battle in order to end the fight "in a draw" as he revealed in his book *Le temps des vérités* (literally: The Time of Truths) 25 years later.[1] That explained why General Navarre kept focusing on the Atlante plan which was aimed at occupying the Nam-Ngãi-Bình-Phú free zone of the 5th Interzone though he had assigned Cogny to closely follow the situation of Điện Biên Phủ and he was still overwhelmed by unanswered questions about the opponent's capacity in attacking the group of fortifications in the Mường Thanh field.

The days of January 1954 witnessed the silent combat of wits between the two generals from adverse fronts during

---

1. According to Navarre, the French lost in the first phase of the winter-spring campaign (during the last months of 1953 and January 1954) after Giáp's continuous actions. In the second phase, or the Điện Biên Phủ campaign, Navarre determined to win in both Điện Biên Phủ and the 5th Interzone to gain the 1-1 score.

their step-by-step approach to a strategic chess board—the Điện Biên Phủ chess board. On the French side, military officers who were responsible for the fate of the group of fortifications such as Cogny and de Castries had several times firmly said to delegations from Sài Gòn, Paris, and Washington that victory was within their grasp because they had gathered weapons and other materials which were more than enough for them to crush their opponent.

On the Vietnamese side, General Giáp had reasons to take precautions against an opponent who had excessive confidence in the American power to defend Điện Biên Phủ at any cost. During the last two weeks of January 1954, he experienced sleepless nights in the Nà Tấu-based command post considering every step of the campaign. As the person who was responsible to the whole Vietnamese Party, people, and army, he had to find out the answer to the question of how to win this strategic battle.

What was the best move?

At that time, the ultimate result of the combat between the commanders-in-chief of the two adverse armies in the Mường Thanh field remained unknown.

Twelve Unforgettable Days

Western reporters, especially battlefield-based ones who had followed General Navarre to Điện Biên Phủ, all thought that his mood in late 1953 and early 1954 was like a thermometer which alternated between high and low temperatures, since he was undecided about leaving or staying in the Mường Thanh field.

On December 3, he ignored Paris's advice and decided to build a group of fortifications to exchange fire with his opponent in the Northwest with the determination to defend Điện Biên Phủ at any cost. A reliable officer of good lineage was appointed from the delta to Điện Biên Phủ to command the group of fortifications. He was de Castries, who had taken part in the Indochinese battlefield three times, under the command of Leclerc, de Lattre, and finally Navarre. A number of experienced and talented lieutenant colonels were also dispatched there. Within a few days in mid December, some fortifications were promptly established; the troop strength increased from six to ten ground battalions; four artillery companies with sixteen 105-mm guns were reinforced. On December 18, the first tanks which had been disassembled and transported there by aircraft were reassembled and started to travel up and down on the Mường Thanh field. It was reported to General Navarre that a meeting was held on the spot to discuss artillery-related issues. After analyzing the situations of both warring sides, all participants of the meeting came to the conclusion that, "France has no reasons to fear the Vietnamese artillery." While the porcupine of Điện Biên Phủ was ruffling up its quills, the French commanders under General Navarre were all waiting for their opponent's attack.

The 308th Brigade was told to arrive in Tạ Khoa on December 15 and in Điện Biên Phủ nine days later. It was also told that both the 312th and 351st Brigades had set off for the battlefield. It turned out that not only the 316th Brigade but also three other brigades of the Vietnamese army would gather together around the Mường Thanh hollow. As it was said by well-informed Western reporters, only a few days after deciding to accept the challenge to fight, Navarre's "nervous thermometer" sometimes dropped extremely low.

It explained why in late December he ordered the French commander of the French army in Upper Laos to rely on the results of the "twin operations"[1] to "transplant" six battalions along the Nậm Hu River and establish a corridor to support the French troops withdrawing from Điện Biên Phủ to Upper Laos when necessary. Initially, General Cogny strongly opposed General Navarre's intention to withdraw troops from Mường Thanh in case of emergency. Outwardly he explained that he wanted to fight against the opponent, but inwardly he harbored another scheme. Điện Biên Phủ had played the role of "an infected boil" and had attracted the "revolutionary spearheads,"[2] releasing the delta from pressure. According to Cogny, the group of fortifications should complete its functions: breaking off the revolutionary spearheads and wiping out the Vietnamese regular brigades. He said that it would be alarming for his "useful delta" if the Vietnamese forces left Điện Biên Phủ for the plains. Cogny's opposition to the French withdrawal and his and de Castries' determination to fight against the Vietnamese army pushed Navarre into a dilemma. His hesitance over the choice between staying in and leaving Mường Thanh was clearly shown during the last week of December 1953. At the Christmas party held in de Castries's bunker on the night of December 24, he loudly encouraged his army to be determined to fight against the opponent. He alleged that the

---

1. They were the Régate and Ardèche operations of French troops to Sốp Nao from Điện Biên Phủ and Luang Prabang respectively. They were aimed at surveying the possibility of establishing a communication line between Northwest Việt Nam and Upper Laos. The results of these operations led to the establishment of a "strategic corridor" linking Điện Biên Phủ and Luang Prabang.
2. This phase refers to the Vietnamese regular brigades.

Vietnamese army did not have artillery and that they did not have enough provisions to prolong the battle. However, a week later, on December 31, he secretly ordered his inferiors to prepare for a withdrawal from Điện Biên Phủ at any required time. Therefore, General Giáp's worry about the possibility of losing the target again after the French withdrawal from Điện Biên Phủ to Upper Laos was understandable. As it was later commented by Western reporters, however, General Navarre had not known that he no longer had any chance to withdraw. After Navarre's withdrawal plan leaked out, they predicted that in late December and early January, the piece of wax would dry and Navarre would not be able to knead it any longer.[1] Then, whether he wanted it or not, he would be forced to stop at the "historical rendezvous" in the combat of wits between him and General Giáp in the Điện Biên Phủ campaign. The opponent's blockade had been formed around the Mường Thanh field and was being gradually tightened.

On the morning of January 14, 1954, at the Thẩm Púa-based command post, General Giáp disseminated the combat plan approved by the Party Central Committee and assigned combat tasks to units. In the first step of this combat plan, the Vietnamese ground and artillery forces would attack Mường Thanh from the west and penetrate deep into its center in order to quickly annihilate enemy troops here and in western and northwestern fortifications. In the second step, they would eliminate the remaining enemy troops in the east-northeast and in the south simultaneously or successively. The combat was scheduled to last three nights and two days. The cannons were expected to be dragged into the battlefield

---

1. It means that the opponent's blockade would become too tight for the French troops to escape to Laos.

on the afternoon of January 19, before the combat started at 5 pm on January 20, 1945.

In the concluding report of the conference, General Giáp emphasized the multi-sided significance of this campaign and reminded the brigades of their tasks in different directions.[1] He also highlighted the Vietnamese army's advantages regarding the troop strength, results of the preparation of the campaign, and especially infrastructure and logistics. Then he required the cadres and soldiers to heighten their determination, especially in case the enemy situation changed, and reminded them to exactly evaluate the enemy's efforts and reactions, realize their own difficulties and have measures to overcome them, and avoid themselves from being subjective. He pointed out that it had been their biggest campaign so far, and that they would unavoidably meet tactical difficulties (such as those in dominating the battlefield, conducting combined operations, fighting continuously, organizing anti-aircraft and anti-artillery battles, and ensuring the timely and appropriate command in complicated situations, especially in the central area). He stressed their immediate task—focusing all forces to bring the cannons into the battlefield. According to his explanation, they should use human power instead of tractors to keep these cannons secret until the fire-opening hour.

---

1. The 308th Brigade was tasked to assault the center of Mường Thanh (including the areas of Mường Thanh and Nà Noọng) from the west and southwest. The 312th Brigade was assigned to decimate the hills of Độc Lập, Bản Kéo, and Căng Na. It was also tasked to eliminate enemy troops in the airport area (including the 105th, 106th, 203rd, 204th, 205th, 206th, 207th, 303rd, and 309th heights). The 316th Brigade (except one regiment) was responsible for annihilating enemy troops in Zone A and cooperating with the forces in the main direction to defeat those in the center of Mường Thanh. The 45th and 367th Artillery Regiments were tasked to support the ground forces during the campaign.

The conference was filled with an exciting atmosphere, especially after the participation of 105-mm howitzers and 37-mm anti-aircraft guns was disclosed. All participants showed their confidence in these "newcomers." All units expressed their determination to complete the tasks of fighting, building roads, and pulling cannons into the battlefield. No proposal for any change to the assigned tasks was heard. To make ideological preparations for the cadres, however, General Giáp said, "The enemy situation is quite stable now, but it might be subject to changes in the future. Therefore, we should closely follow the enemy situation in order to have timely solutions to any change."

In his commanding style, General Giáp made a habit of encouraging his inferiors to speak out the difficulties they might encounter during their implementation of the tasks assigned by him and to suggest solutions to overcome these difficulties. It is noticeable that in this conference, no one, including even those responsible for the main attack direction, made any suggestions on possible difficulties. They only asked for more information about their tasks. The brigade commanders including Vương Thừa Vũ, who would command the 308th Brigade to penetrate into the enemy headquarters in the center of Mường Thanh, made no suggestions to their superior. General Giáp found it an abnormal phenomenon. Later in his memoirs, he wrote:

> It was not until ten years later, on the occasion of the anniversary of the Điện Biên Phủ victory, that some brigade commanders revealed their thoughts at that time. Only then did I know that some of them found the tasks so heavy. They were afraid that they would not be able to solve the problems of wounded soldiers and supplies while conducting successive assaults if the battle was prolonged.

However, in the exciting atmosphere of the task-assigning conference, no one dared to speak out their concerns. It was such a profound lesson internal democracy.

As for General Giáp, although he had appointed tasks to the units, he had not been fully confident in the victory of the quick-assault combat plan. He told Vice Head of the Frontier Reconnaissance Section Cao Pha to keep track on the enemy situation, especially their troop and fortification reinforcement, and to report to him twice a day. He particularly required Cao Pha to focus on the west of Mường Thanh, the main attack direction of the Vietnamese army toward the center of the group of fortifications. Besides, he revealed to Chief of the Secretariat Nguyễn Văn Hiếu his thoughts, asked the latter to closely monitor and carefully consider the situation. He also reminded Hiếu to exchange ideas on the situation with him when necessary.

After the movement of the Headquarters from the 15th kilometer to the 62nd kilometer inside an old forest of Nà Tấu Village, the officials alternately visited the units to supervise their preparations for the combat, especially those for the cannon-pulling task. General Giáp spent a lot of time monitoring the enemy situation in the Mường Thanh field with binoculars from a peak behind the command post. The key to the quick-assault plan was the time. With each day passing by, the enemy fortifications became more solid. The Vietnamese army had to race against their enemy to prevent the latter from reinforcing troops and fortifications. General Giáp wondered if the time spent on pulling cannons would "support" the quick-assault plan. He inspected the 15-km-long and 3-m-wide road which had been finished before the deadline by the 308th Brigade. It was located on a difficult terrain with numerous high slopes and deep abysses. He wondered if Vietnamese troops could successfully drag the cannons into the battlefield within three days as scheduled.

Having been frequently updated on the cannon-pulling progress, General Giáp found that Vietnamese troops would encounter more and more difficulties, and that it would take more time to finish this task. Due to the Vietnamese staff's inexperience, the road for pulling cannons in reality was much different from the one drawn on the map, in terms of length and slope. The highest slope was estimated to be 30 or 40 degree, but it was in fact up to 60 degrees. It was scheduled that Vietnamese troops would stop the tractors at the entrance of the Na Nham forest and used human power to drag cannons from there to the battlefield to avoid being detected by the enemy. Having found that it would take longer to drag cannons into the battlefield (and thus the cannons would not be settled in the battlefield on the 19th day as scheduled), General Giáp discussed with consultant Wei Guoqing about the changes in the enemy situation and the difficulties in pulling cannons. Then both agreed to postpone opening fire until January 25 and at the same time allowed tractors to reach Nà Ten. Thus the time spent on pulling cannons by hand would be reduced by three days. Shortly after that, Wei sent a telegram to Beijing to report on the reasons for his agreement with Vietnamese cadres on the five-day postponement of the fire-opening day. On January 21, the Chinese Central Military Commission sent Wei a telegram. According to this telegram, they unanimously approved the postponement plan and reminded Wei to use forces to separate and decimate the enemy part by part instead of using equal forces on all fronts. Time flew and the fire-opening day was coming near. However, Vietnamese troops were reported to be unable to complete the task on schedule despite their extreme efforts. Later General Hoàng Văn Thái recalled:

> On January 23, I went to the 351st and 312th Brigades to examine their preparations for combat and especially to grasp the cannon-pulling progress... The campaign would start in two days. However, not all the cannons had been settled in the battlefield, despite the fact that the ground, artillery, and sapper units had put all of their efforts in building and disguising roads, pulling cannons, and ensuring the safety of both humans and cannons. It was scheduled that twelve cannons would be taken to the north of the battlefield, but only six had arrived at the battlefield by that time while the other six were still on the way. Only a small quantity of bullets had been transported to the battlefield. Bullets were heavy and the road was sloping.

During the consultation held on the afternoon of January 23, Thái not only reported on the cannon-pulling progress but also summarized the enemy situation on the Mường Thanh field. According to reports from front scouts and brigades' intelligence, the enemy had increased their combat forces to over ten battalions and was incessantly reinforcing their defense system. Regarding their fire-power, apart from twenty-four 105-mm howitzers, four 155-mm howitzers, and twenty 120-mm mortars, some tanks had been reassembled. The newly-set barbed-wire fences and minefields were very wide, up to hundreds of meters wide in some places. The Độc Lập height in the north was no longer an outpost, but it had been developed into a group of fortifications and was being guarded by an Euro-African battalion. The northwestern Mường Thanh field was considered a weak spot of the enemy in January, but a series of fortifications had been built there, to the west of the airport. The Na Căng fortification had been fortified. According to the statements of French war prisoners, those northern fortifications were particularly important to the whole group. They not only served as screens on northern roads but also guaranteed the standard height and length required for the safety of the northwest-southeast single-axis airway in the airspace of the Mường Thanh field. In the south, the Hồng Cúm fortification had been developed into a group of fortifications, equipped with an airport and an infantry battlefield ready to support the central subdivision. The enemy was strongest in the east. There they could rely on heights to prolong their defensive battles against the 316th Brigade's offensives.

On January 23rd, General Giáp received a call from Vice Head of the Security Department Phạm Kiệt. Kiệt reported that some cannons had not arrived at the battlefield. He also noted that the big cannons were not only occupying a large area but also lying uncovered in the battlefield, so they would be easily detected and destroyed by enemy artillery and aircraft. In addition, the artillerymen had not known how to use these cannons flexibly to support the ground forces during the battle. General Giáp immediately phoned Lê Trọng Tấn to ask him about the preparation of the 312th Brigade. Tấn told Giáp that he was examining how to organize the combat in order to concurrently break through the three defensive lines of the enemy from the north, pass the hills of Độc Lập, Bản Kéo, and Căng Na, reach the airport, and finally penetrate into the enemy headquarters. Then he said, "Despite difficulties, we promise to accomplish the task." Obviously, the 312th Brigade needed support from higher

Chapter Seven: THE FINAL EFFORTS OF FRANCE AND THE UNITED STATES

authorities. General Giáp then sent Vice Head of the Military Intelligence Department Cao Pha to the 312th Brigade. Giáp said to him, "We have not thoroughly grasped the enemy situation in the center, so you will go there and closely follow our ground forces. Catch enemy troops and question them for information wherever our ground forces develop to help Tấn strike deep into the enemy center." After investigating the situation in the west, the main attack direction of the campaign, the operational staff reported that the 308th Brigade did not meet any fortifications on heights as the 316th Brigade in the east or the 312th Brigade in the north had. However, the soldiers had no shelters. In addition, they would have to not only attack newly-established fortifications on large fields surrounded by barbed wires and minefields but also cope with the opponent's ground forces supported by tanks, artillery, and air forces on a flat battlefield. Chief of the Secretariat Nguyễn Văn Hiếu said that by then, the political-ideological work had only focused on how to improve the determination among the army instead of finding solutions to problems relating to operational organization, command, and practice. This explained for the occurrence that an infantry regiment commander offered to return part of the reinforcement cannons because he had received too many of them and had failed to manage them well in combined operations.

All these realities were then reported to the Chinese Advisory Delegation by the Vietnamese operational staff. After receiving the telegram from Beijing on January 21, Wei gradually found it impossible to defeat the groups of fortifications by quick assaults. On January 24, after being updated on the enemy situation and the cannon-pulling progress, he sent a telegram to Beijing to propose a revision of the combat plan. The telegram read, "The entire 312th Brigade is involved in pulling cannons, but they have moved only twelve kilometers after six days. The soldiers have got exhausted, but all the cannons have not been taken to the battlefield as scheduled."

As it was an important issue, Wei had to wait for a reply from Beijing and continue considering it the following days before he could mention it to Giáp. As for Giáp, after 11 days thinking it over and especially after one sleepless night on January 25, he made a decision which he later called the hardest one in his military career.

As early as in the conference to disseminate the combat plan held on January 14 in Thẩm Púa, General Giáp realized that it was risky to launch quick assaults and that they did not ensure victory, because the Vietnamese army was not qualified enough to eliminate the groups of fortifications within two days and three nights by massive attacks. Over the past ten days, he had kept thinking about what President Hồ Chí Minh told him before his departure and what General Secretary Trường Chinh said at the Party Central Committee conference last January. Accordingly, they should not fight if they were not sure of victory. The daily happenings in the Mường Thanh field and the ideas of such officers as Lê Trọng Tấn, Phạm Kiệt, and Nguyễn Văn Hiếu contributed to fortifying his thought: they could not win by quick assaults. On January 24, an unexpected incident happened: a solider of the 312th Brigade was captured. Concurrently, the Vietnamese reconnaissance radio caught the news which was being communicated among the enemies that the Vietnamese army would open fire at 5 pm on January 25. Initially, the

Chapter Seven: THE FINAL EFFORTS OF FRANCE AND THE UNITED STATES

arrested soldier was thought to leak the information after being tortured by the enemy. It was later revealed that it was the false of the front logistics radio. Since the fire-opening time had been disclosed, General Giáp decided to postpone it until the afternoon of January 26 to put the enemy off the scent and have more time for careful consideration before making the final decision—changing the operational method from quick attack to firm attack.

On the morning of January 26, General Giáp was seen to have a wisp of mugwort, which overgrew around the command post and helped reduce headache, tied to his head. It was doctor Trịnh Văn Khiêm who told physician Thùy to do so after learning that General Giáp had experienced one sleepless night.

That morning, General Giáp, still with the mugwort on the head, and his assistant, Hoàng Minh Phương, came to see Wei Guoqing. Then he spoke out what he had thought over the past ten days. He pointed out the tactical difficulties that Vietnamese soldiers had not managed to overcome; asserted that quick attacks would not ensure victory; and finally proposed the postponement of the offensive, the withdrawal of troops back to the troop-gathering place, and the re-preparation for combat according to the firm-attack guideline.

How did Wei easily agree with Giáp after a half-an-hour discussion? Like Giáp, Wei had experienced many days considering the enemy situation and realized that it would be impossible for the Vietnamese to win the enemy by quick attacks. However, he had to wait for instructions from Beijing before talking to Giáp. Then, when Giáp, who was directly responsible for the result of the campaign, came and proactively proposed a change to the operational method, he found a congenial companion and so immediately approved the proposal. He also promised to persuade other members in his delegation to accept it.

What Giáp had to do then was to persuade other members of the Campaign Party Committee to reach a consensus with a view to ensuring the complete victory of the campaign. The Campaign Party Committee meeting was summoned on the morning of January 26.

The participants of the meeting were his intimate comrades. They had been standing side by side with him since the early days of the Liberation Army or at least since the beginning of the resistance. He believed that with the spirit of "giving priority to the common interest," it was indispensable for them to together discuss the issues of how to realize President Hồ Chí Minh's instructions, how to win the final victory in this campaign, and how to minimize damages to their soldiers.

At the conference, General Giáp recalled the Party Central Committee's constant determination to annihilate the enemy groups of fortifications with a view to creating a new step of development for the resistance war. He also told the others what he had thought over the past twelve days about the changes in the enemy situation and the tactical difficulties confronting Vietnamese soldiers, and then emphasized the necessity of changing the operational method for an assured victory.

The participants raised their voices, one after the other. At first, there was opposition to Giáp's proposal among them. Over the past twelve days, they had directed the preparations for the campaign as instructed at the conference held on January 14. All preparations, both ideologically and organizationally, had been almost completed. Political Commissar of the 312th Brigade Trần Độ had even held a solemn ceremony to hand a flag embroidered with four Vietnamese words *"Quyết chiến quyết thắng"* (literally: "Determined to fight and win") to the vanguard. The soldiers were all eager to start the campaign. The campaign postponement and the troop withdrawal would possibly cause spiritual uneasiness among them.

The discussion had lasted quite a long time before this question was raised by General Giáp, "Will quick assaults ensure a 100-percent victory?" No reply was received. Then, General Giáp repeated President Hồ Chí Minh's instructions and the spirit of the Fourth Plenum of the Party Central Committee, and stressed the responsibility to the result of the campaign. Ultimately, they all agreed that they should not stick to an operational method which did not ensure a 100-percent victory just because they were afraid of confronting difficulties caused by any change to the operational guideline or a prolonged campaign. Difficulties would arise if the campaign had not been well prepared. They all admitted that the modification of the operational guideline required a great determination and required a thorough grasp of the Central guideline—they had to win at any cost.

At the end of the meeting, General Giáp concluded that the determination to change the operational method required all front branches and levels to adjust their thoughts and actions in accordance with the new situation. The Campaign Party Committee promised to report the situation to the Party Central Committee and suggest the latter encourage the rear to cooperate with the front to overcome all potential difficulties and win over the enemy.

Only at the challenging and decisive moments like those on that unforgettable day in the Điện Biên Phủ battlefield that the revolutionary virtue and the disciplinary and organizational consciousness of a people's army officer who had been educated and trained by the Party were shown fully and clearly. It was not an easy task to pull tens of cannons back to the point of departure and take tens of thousands of officers and militants who were highly-spirited and eager to fight and kill the enemy back to the troop-gathering place. At those challenging moments, all the officers who were in charge of political-ideological affairs went to units and complete their task of disseminating the change among the whole army. It was a masterstroke of the Campaign Party Committee at a special time in the Điện Biên Phủ campaign.

After the meeting, General Giáp dispatched an officer to drive a jeep and take his urgent letter to the rear. In the letter, he informed President Hồ Chí Minh and the Politburo about the change to the operational method.

The following day, January 27, Wei Guoqing received a telegram from Beijing. According to this telegram, the proposal for a change to the operational method was approved by Beijing. That day, Vietnamese soldiers were pulling the cannons back to the troop-gathering place and the 308th Brigade was marching at lightening speed towards Upper Laos.

Meanwhile, the French leaders in Paris, Sài Gòn, and Hà Nội were making every effort to find out the best ways to fortify the groups of fortifications.

Chapter Seven: THE FINAL EFFORTS OF FRANCE AND THE UNITED STATES

Cogny felt anxious whenever he received news about the Vietnamese army's preparation for the campaign. On January 15, he reported a lot of news to de Castries after his inspection tour to the groups of fortification, such as that the Vietnamese cannons had arrived in Tuần Giáo (enclosed with his complaint about their air forces' failure to prevent these cannons during the several-hundred-kilometer road), that over 20 Vietnamese infantry battalions accompanied by 37-40-mm anti-aircraft guns with the shooting ranges of 1,800-3,000 meters had been had reached the battlefield, and that the 57th Regiment of the 304th Brigade had set off, increasing the Vietnamese combat strength to 28 battalions. Cogny also told de Castries what he had firmly said to Navarre that there was no chance to implement the withdrawal plan and that they should let the garrison in Điện Biên Phủ lose their lives for having made a sortie through the blockade to Upper Laos. In summary, they should stay and get ready for combat.

During this period, Paris sent Deputy Minister of Associated States Marc Jacket to Việt Nam to investigate the situation. Within a week, this envoy, together with Navarre and Cogny, flew to Điện Biên Phủ twice. Navarre, Cogny, and de Castries, who were directly responsible for the battles, tried their best to assure the French Government's representative of the solidity of the groups of fortifications. Cogny reported that on his trip to Điện Biên Phủ on January 15, he assigned Lieutenant-colonel Langlais to organize the training courses and maneuvers with real bullets in the field, so that the two parachute battalions of the reserve force would be well-prepared for any counter-attack to reoccupy any target from the opponent. Ten tanks for this task had been sent there from Hà Nội. To fortify the west and southwest of the airport and the Headquarters, Cogny order de Castries to set up more slanting barded-wire fences, which overlapped like an anti-wave dyke hundreds of meters wide.

On January 22, after hearing that the Vietnamese army might start their attack on the night from the 25th to the 26th, Deputy Minister Marc Jacket, accompanied by Navarre and Cogny, flew to Điện Biên Phủ. He did not pay much attention to the military welcome etiquette or even the party with champagne, beefsteak, and salad that he received. He told the driver to take him to the northernmost and north-easternmost positions of the groups of fortifications: Gabrielle and Béatrice (Độc Lập and Him Lam hills respectively). He asked about the defensive capacity of each position, the counter-attack plan, and the artillery-withstanding capacity of bunkers. Jacket had been an air force reserve officer, so he knew that the Mường Thanh airport and the airspace of the whole region would be under threat if these two positions were annihilated. At Him Lam, Lieutenant-colonel Gaucher tried to convince his visitor of the artillery-withstanding capacity of the five-meter-thick trench covers, which were made of soil and wood. In terms of troop strength, "Please don't be worry, mister Deputy Minister. A seasoned battalion of the 13th Legionary Semi-brigade have been garrisoned on three hills." In the bunker of Lieutenant-colonel Piroth, Jacket was told that this artillery commander of the groups of fortresses could order all the cannons of the groups of fortifications to fire anywhere he wanted just by waving his hand, and that the 155-mm cannons could even annihilate any artillery battlefield set up behind the mountains. Jacket was assured many times that Vietnamese artillery would not be able to withstand French artillery under the command of

Piroth. After hearing that the Vietnamese army was about to take action, whenever the mist on the mountains lifted every morning, Piroth would get on a reconnaissance plan, flying many times over Mường Thanh and taking photos of suspected positions. In the three subdivisions of the groups of fortresses, French soldiers were put on the alert.

At the party held on January 25, Jacket questioned Navarre about the upcoming battle. The latter assured his guest that the French occupation of Điện Biên Phủ had stopped the only way to Laos. He said that if the Vietnamese army dared to assault, there would be two possibilities: they might attack the groups of fortifications with all their forces, or they might use part of their troop strength to neutralize the groups of fortifications and spend the over ten remaining battalions attacking Upper Laos. He stated that in both cases, the French artillery would decimate all the Vietnamese offensive forces and cannons, while the Nậm Hu River defense line would stop the Vietnamese army as soon as the latter had crossed the Việt Nam-Laos border. Navarre repeated the conclusion made at the conference on artillery that General Giáp could not arrange cannons behind the mountains due to the long distance or on the slopes as they could easily be wiped out by French artillery after their first shooting. The remaining short-range cannons, namely mortars, were not capable of backing the ground forces.

During those days, after some contacts with the French officers, the war reporters all felt that these officers were seemingly over-optimistic about the outcome of the upcoming battle.

On arriving in Hà Nội on January 15, Cogny told the *United Press* reporters that the French wished that the Điện

Biên Phủ clash would take place soon. He added that they would be disturbed by the Vietnamese cannons for a while, but they would then force these cannons to keep silent. He stated that if General Giáp wanted to move his combat forces to Laos without any obstacles, he would have to attack Điện Biên Phủ. Cogny finally assured that the French would defeat General Giáp to stop him from further risky strategic intentions.

As for the French Commander-in-chief, although he was still sometimes inconsistent in evaluating the situation, during their visit to Điện Biên Phủ on January 22, Navarre not only told Jacket that he would win the battle but also anticipated that he might deploy troops from Mường Thanh to Tuần Giáo if possible. Two days earlier, no sooner had he heard that the Vietnamese army would attack the groups of fortifications than he ordered the start of the Atlante operation, which was aimed at the Tuy Hòa-Phú Yên area. Meanwhile, Colonel de Castries, commander of the Điện Biên Phủ groups of fortifications, ordered planes to scatter leaflets on the roads and had his words of challenge conveyed to the Vietnamese army by radio such as "You've come here already. What are you still waiting for? Attack us, otherwise you're just cowards," and "We're ready. Show up if you think you're stronger."

These leaflets with provoking words were put on Giáp's table every day, but none of them could affect him. While his gentle but extremely courageous soldiers silently replied to de Castries, "Just wait," he spent sleepless nights thinking and finally made an unforgettable decision. Accordingly, he refused to apply the human-sea attack, which did not suit the conditions of the Vietnamese battlefield, and discussed

Chapter Seven: THE FINAL EFFORTS OF FRANCE AND THE UNITED STATES

with other members of the Campaign Party Committee for another operational method which guaranteed victory.

The Vietnamese army's repeated postponements of firing was an incomprehensible question to the French. It was later revealed that a French civil-military delegation led by Marc Jacket was present in Điện Biên Phủ on January 26, 1954. At about 4 pm that day, Navarre said to Jacket under his breath, "We anticipate that they will fire tonight. I'm responsible for safeguarding your delegation. I don't want you to be in danger."

At 16:45, the plane took off and headed the delta, leaving thousands of French troops on the Mường Thanh field, ready to fight. In the bunker, Colonel de Castries and the staff were in a state of anxious suspense waiting for the opening shots from the Vietnamese army. The bunker was filled with cigarette fumes. But that night passed by peacefully. The Vietnamese army was such an enigmatic opponent.

The next morning, Jacket, at the Metropole Hotel in Hà Nội, phoned Navarre, still in Hà Nội, to ask about the situation in Điện Biên Phủ. The latter replied that he had received a short telegram from Colonel de Castries. The telegram read, "There's nothing to report. They haven't attacked yet."

The reporters who had closely followed the fighting situation in Điện Biên Phủ spent a lot of time discussing the possible reasons for the postponement at that time, especially on the afternoon of January 26. Some said the truth while some others intentionally falsified it. Among the people who knew the truth were two French journalists named Boudarel and Caviglioli, who later became historians. Nearly 30 years after the Điện Biên Phủ battle, on April 8, 1983, they narrated this even in an article on the French newspaper *Le Nouvel Observateur* (literally: The New Observer) with a relatively sensational title, "How General Giáp nearly failed in the Điện Biên Phủ battle?" They commented that the combat plan approved on January 14 was a crazy risk. That plan had led to the failure of Nà Sản and would not suit the large-scale campaign this time. They wrote that General Giáp gave up the plan since he had learned from the experience of the Nà Sản battle in December 1952, a small-scale Điện Biên Phủ battle. The plan reflected the human-sea attack that had been applied by the Chinese army in the North Korea war. Though being a great commander, General Giáp was modest enough to realize that Điện Biên Phủ was a strong fortress which should not be underestimated. If he had not been a great general, he would not have admitted his mistake or dared to diverge from a theory. If he had not been a great politician, he would not have disobeyed or displeased such a strong friend as China.

It was just the wording style of Western journalists. But it should be admitted that Boudarel was right when he used the word "nearly" in this case. It reflected the boundary between two options: accepting or refusing a fighting method which was incompatible with the real situation of Việt Nam in general and that of Điện Biên Phủ in particular. Giáp refused to accept it because it did not reflect President Hồ Chí Minh's instructions and thus it did not ensure complete victory. For him, the best method was one that suited the situations of both warring armies and the balance of power on the Mường Thanh field. More specifically, it should minimize the possible damages to the Vietnamese army and guarantee a 100-percent victory.

Chapter Seven: THE FINAL EFFORTS OF FRANCE AND THE UNITED STATES

Obviously the happenings and results of the battle proved that, the road from working out the best operational guideline to setting up the *"Quyết chiến quyết thắng"* (Determined to fight and win) flag atop the French commander's bunker was full of obstacles and challenges that few people had anticipated and that the Vietnamese army had to overcome to gain the final victory.

Chapter Eight

THE FINAL STRATEGIC MOVE

Preparation for a Decisive Battle

The Campaign Party Committee's meeting had just ended. While Chief of Staff Hoàng Văn Thái was transferring the commands to infantry brigades, Commander-in-chief Võ Nguyên Giáp was directly giving commands to artillerymen by telephone. Political Commissar of the 351st Brigade Phạm Ngọc Mậu listened to his words thinking that—as he revealed later on—"these words do my heart good."

General Giáp said that the determination to annihilate the group of fortifications was unchanged but the fighting method was changed, hence they had to prepare again. That afternoon, Vietnamese soldiers were ordered to immediately pull the cannons back to the troop-gathering place. The cannon-pulling task was regarded as a combat task.

Without an explanation on the phone, General Giáp believed that his subordinates still completely obeyed the commands despite existing doubts.

Right after that, the 308th Brigade was assigned a very important task. Due to time limitations, General Giáp also

Chapter Eight: THE FINAL STRATEGIC MOVE

transmitted it to the brigade through the phone. Receiving the phone was Chief of the 308th Brigade Vương Thừa Vũ, who had learned General Giáp's strategic proposal earlier, at the conference held last November to disseminate the winter-spring combat plan. Thus, it did not take him much time to thoroughly grasp his superior's briefly-expressed command. General Giáp said:

> At exactly 4 o'clock this afternoon, your brigade will change the direction to Luang Prabang and annihilate the enemy there to widen the liberated area. Keep in touch via radio and come back immediately on request. Decide by yourselves the size of combat troops. Depend on the local people to solve logistical issues.

Then the whole brigade led by Vũ set off.

With a little roasted rice and nearly haft a kilogram of reserve rice per person, tens of thousands of soldiers departed for Luang Prabang just one hour after receiving the command. The unknown terrain, unprepared battlefield, unidentified enemy situation, and communication barrier due to different languages were fully acknowledged by General Giáp, but he still believed in Vũ, who always lived and fought with an immutable principle that "military orders are like mountains." That afternoon, however, General Giáp assigned Vice Head of the Front-line Logistical Department Nguyễn Thanh Bình to dispatch some logistical officers to run after the 308th Brigade and help them mobilize on-site food. Nobody in the General Headquarters could forget the famous words by General Secretary Trường Chinh, "Without the 'Rice General,' all commanders have to give up."

The combat targets of the 308th Brigade in that speedy operation were about 20 French brigades along the Nậm

727

Hu River in Upper Laos. After dropping troops into Điện Biên Phủ and being determined to exchange fire with the Vietnamese army, in early December 1953, General Navarre ordered Crevoco, commander of the French army in Laos, to cooperate with the French forces in the Mường Thanh field to organize the twin operations named Régate and Ardèche to Sốp Nao from Điện Biên Phủ and Luang Prabang respectively, creating a defense line guarded by six battalions sent from Mường Khoa to Luang Prabang. The Régate and Ardèche operations mainly served a withdrawal plan which aimed to make a strategic passageway for the French army to safely retreat to Upper Laos in case of emergency. With the sending of the 308th Brigade to Upper Laos, General Giáp could kill many birds with one stone. Firstly, he could complete the task proposed in the winter-spring plan that was to help Laos widen the liberated area from Phonsaly to Luang Prabang. Secondly, he could satisfy the strategic requirement of the campaign that was to destroy the bridge connecting Điện Biên Phủ with Luang Prabang, isolating the group of fortifications, and preventing the enemy's withdrawal. Finally, he could turn the tables on the enemy, luring their aircraft to fight in the west and creating favorable conditions for Vietnamese soldiers in Điện Biên Phủ to pull the cannons out of the battlefield and prepare for a new operational guideline.

A week before the Lunar New Year or *Tết* holiday of 1945, after the Campaign Headquarters was moved from Nà Tấu to Mường Phăng, General Giáp both directed the preparation for the campaign cadres conference and spent much time supervising the cannon-pulling work. He understood that pulling cannons out of the battlefield was much harder than pulling them in. Fortunately, the cadres and soldiers had gained some experience in this task. Moreover, this task was also facilitated by the presence of the 308th Brigade in Upper Laos, which attracted the enemy aircraft to the west. Therefore, the noise of the enemy aircraft was absent from the sky of Điện Biên Phủ during those days. Before dawn on the first day of the new year, the cannons had arrived at the entrance of the forest, at the 62nd kilometer of the 41st Route, before it was pulled to the troop-gathering place. Like other cadres in the Campaign Headquarters, General Giáp could breath a sign of relief. The soldiers made a masterstroke within a weak in early spring.

Shortly afterwards, a specially good piece of news came right on the *Tết* holiday. An urgent letter dated February 3 was sent from the rear. President Hồ Chí Minh and the Politburo agreed that the Campaign Party Committee's decision to change the fighting method was absolutely right. The Central Government promised to encourage the people in the rear to devote all their strength to supporting the front line to achieve total victory in this important campaign.

Those stressful days of supervising the cannon-pulling work had passed already. The repeated comings of good news made General Giáp very happy. He came to the shack where Wei Guoqing was staying to give the latter New Year's greetings. He also shared with Wei the good news that President Hồ Chí Minh and the Politburo had agreed on the new operational guideline, and that the 308th Brigade was pursuing the enemy on the other side of the Việt Nam-Laos border.

On the fifth day of the lunar new year, the 45th Howitzer Regiment and the 367th Anti-aircraft Artillery Regiment warmly welcomed General Giáp to the troop-gathering place. He informed them that in the first morning of the lunar new year, the 757th Mountain Artillery Company fired the first shot and achieved victory in the early spring—setting one Moran aircraft on fire and damaging some others parking on the Mường Thanh airport. Then he praised the howitzer and anti-airplane artillery regiments for having completed the task of moving the cannons to the battlefield and then moving them back to the troop-gathering place. In order for the artillerymen to complete the next combat task, he recommended them to courageously fight, actively annihilate the enemy, totally obey the orders from the seniors, tightly cooperate with the infantry, try to learn new techniques and shoot the targets accurately, protect weapons, and save ammunition. He emphasized that the cadres should follow the soldiers, share joys and sorrows with them, and set good examples for them. He also said that the most important task at that time was to well prepare the firing elements and battlefield equipment and ensure the safety of artillerymen when the occupation of the artillery battlefield took place.

It was revealed later that the combat preparation and effectiveness of Vietnamese howitzers and anti-aircraft artillery at the first battle were beyond the imagination of not only General Navarre but also many French artillery experts. More than one time, the French confirmed that Vietnamese artilleries could not be placed in an effective firing position on that side of the mountain. They believed that the Vietnamese artilleries would be immediately "locked" by theirs once the first shell had come out of the cannon barrel, and that the Vietnamese side could not have enough shells to prolong the battle. That was the reason why the French army went from

Chapter Eight: THE FINAL STRATEGIC MOVE

one surprise to another, not only in the first battles of the campaign but throughout the whole campaign.

The Campaign Cadres Conference was held on the morning of the fifth day of the lunar new year (or February 7). It was mainly aimed at reaching an agreement on the thought and perception of the fighting method of and the preparation for the campaign. In the battlefields throughout the country at that time, from the front-line battlefield to the battlefields in the areas behind the enemy lines, people were doing their best to share fire with the focused one. In the face of the enemy group of fortifications which was being strengthened in the Mường Thanh field, the Vietnamese army was establishing and fortifying a blockade around them.

At the beginning of his report delivered at the conference, General Giáp brought happiness to everybody by saying, "Today, our conference is opened in the spring when we have achieved many victories in the battlefields. On behalf of the Central Military Commission, I wish all cadres and soldiers health and more victories in the new year."

He briefed the victories gained by the Vietnamese army in the first phase of the winter-spring plan in the Northwest, the 5th Interzone, the Bình-Trị-Thiên area, the South, the rear area, the Northern delta, as well as Laos and Cambodia. He also clarified the Central military guideline that was to strengthen and spread the winter-spring victories. Then he gave a detailed analysis of the operational guideline of the Điện Biên Phủ campaign. The Vietnamese army was formerly instructed to quickly fight and gain victory, but he later decided to change this operational guideline and plan and the artillery battlefield in the awake of changes in the enemy situation. This change was grounded on the principle "only fighting when being sure to win" that he had thoroughly grasped.

After proposing a three-phase plan for the campaign[1] and pointing out the advantages and disadvantages of the new fighting method,[2] General Giáp analyzed how to prepare for the campaign. First of all, a mobile road, a fortified battlefield for howitzers, and an artillery fire plan should be made ready for the artillery. Second, a battlefield for infantry forces to besiege and attack the enemy should be prepared as well. Third, preparations should be made to promote soldiers' health, tactics, techniques, political thought, and determination. Last but not least, supplies should be well prepared and the enemy situation should be closely monitored.

The conference ended with a happy spring party attended by the ensemble of the General Department of Politics and one who had just come back from the World Festival of Youth and Students held in Bucharest.

Right after the conference, the guideline of "making full preparations but still making use of time" was thoroughly

---

1. According to this plan, the campaign would undergo three phases: 1- actively completing all preparations; 2- besieging and controlling the airport and wearing out and annihilating every part of the enemy strength; 3- conducting an all-out offensive to eliminate all the enemy army.
2. Regarding disadvantages, the enemy might be reinforced, the campaign might last long, and the Vietnamese soldiers might get exhausted and suffer a shortage of supplies. In terms of advantages, the new fighting method was compatible with the combat principle and level of Vietnamese soldiers. Moreover, the Vietnamese army would have conditions to attack the biggest weakness of the enemy to deepen the latter's difficulty in supply, and to promote their initiative in preparation and in the choice of the time and target of attack. In addition, the operations in the major battlefield could facilitate those in other battlefields in annihilating enemy troops.

grasped among the army and all preparations were promptly made. Vice Head of the General Department of Logistics Đặng Kim Giang was in charge of supervising and speeding up the transportation of supplies from the intermediate area to the front line, directing the mobilization of food on the spot, and promoting the self-supported movement among units, especially during the days when the supply was delayed and the soldiers encountered difficulties in daily life. Vice Head of the General Department of Politics Lê Liêm was entrusted with the responsibility of going to units every day to inspect and supervise the political-ideological work to make sure that the new operational guideline was thoroughly grasped by them. Head of the Operational Department Trần Văn Quang was responsible for directing the technical and tactical training which focused on the infantry-artillery combination. Learning from the experience of the Chinese consultants, the front-line operational department offered cadres a training course on how to establish a battlefield for attacking and besieging the enemy. Chief of Staff Hoàng Văn Thái was assigned to direct the preparation for a road for pulling cannons and the establishment of an artillery battlefield—quite new tasks for Vietnamese soldiers. It was an advantage for the combat preparation in the entire battlefield at that time, especially for the artillery, that the Vietnamese had quite a detailed map of Điện Biên Phủ. After the soldiers of the 62nd Company of the 426th Battalion found a 1:25,000 scale map in an enemy-parachuted package, the campaign staff immediately had it taken to the rear, where it was made into 300 copies in good paper and delivered to units which were preparing for combat according to the new operational guideline.

In mid February, a huge construction site was formed around the Điện Biên basin stretching from west to southeast. It served the building of mobile roads and bridges for artillery tractors, artillery battlefields, and battlefields for attack and besiegement. Tens of thousands of soldiers experienced days of sweat and even blood for the completion of six big road axes with a total length of over 70 kilometers, fortified artillery battlefields, and a system of trenches surrounding the enemy group of fortifications towards the Mường Thanh field. During the construction of the mobile road system and the battlefield system for infantry and artillery, the Vietnamese soldiers absolutely kept secrets and thus the enemy was almost ignorant of what was going on around their group of fortifications. That explained why tens of thousands of enemy troops were taken by surprise on the day Vietnamese heavy artilleries fired to open the campaign.

After more than two weeks directing the prompt preparation for the campaign, on February 20, the Campaign Headquarters held a campaign cadres conference to find solutions to some remaining problems and especially to make the operational guideline, tactics, and techniques thoroughly grasped by the whole army. The conference discussed the detailed fighting method for each coming combat phase in order to satisfactorily implement the policy of besieging and controlling the airport, limiting and destroying the enemy's airborne supply routes, wearing out and annihilating every part of the enemy strength, deepening their difficulties and weaknesses, and gradually facilitating the transition to an all-out offensive. The Front Party Committee directed the conference to in-depth discussions for answers to cadres' questions about the enemy's reinforcement capacity and ways to help soldiers recover from fatigue caused by the prolonged campaign.

In the summary report delivered on February 22, General Giáp once again affirmed the rightness of the "steady fight and steady advance" guideline and provided answers to the remaining questions about the tactical and technical thought and the command organization. He also proposed the direction and the detailed operating method compatible with the afore-mentioned operational guideline.[1] Besides, he required the cadres to have high determination, maintain armed forces for continuous fighting, ensure the close combination between infantry and artillery and that between artillery units, and establish the battlefields as required. Finally, due to the characteristics of a great campaign, big workloads, and time limitations, General Giáp reminded the cadres to thoroughly grasp the main items of their tasks, distinguish urgent tasks from non-urgent ones, and make a clear assignment of tasks and regularly supervise the implementation of these tasks, especially the focal ones.

In early March, when the preparation entered the final phase, the 308th Brigade returned to Điện Biên Phủ. The advisory, political, and logistical departments dispatched officers to examine situations and help the units prepare for the combat. Through the report of the 308th Brigade's

---

1. 1- Control the airport to limit and then destroy the enemy's airborne supply routes; 2- Develop small and frequent activities of the infantry and artillery (such as ambushing the enemy's airport, artillery battlefields, command post, and warehouses and wounding their troops); 3- Actively wear out and annihilate enemy troops during their attacks on Vietnamese battlefields; 4- Annihilate some enemy outposts; 5- Develop a really entrenched attack battlefield.

command, the Campaign Headquarters was well informed of the brigade's activities during the last month in the Lao battlefield.

After leaving Điện Biên Phủ, the 308th Brigade formed two armies moving in two directions, Mường Khoa and Luang Prabang. On January 29, 1954, when one army arrived in Sốp Nao, they were informed by the General Headquarters that the enemy had discovered their changing the direction to the west and thus had started to withdraw from Mường Khoa. Immediately the brigade switched to pursuing these troops along an over-200-km stretch of road. On February 13, after receiving the report that the brigade was only 20 kilometers from Luang Prabang, General Giáp ordered the brigade to stop to help Lao people fortify the newly-liberated area and then hurriedly came back to Điện Biên Phủ. After half of month marching at lightening speech and and about a week continuously fighting against the enemy during the march, the brigade annihilated nearly 20 enemy companies along the Mường May-Mường Khoa-Mường La and Nậm Bạc-Pác U routes. A very large liberated area was established in Laos, facilitating the 148th Regiment to liberate Phonsaly. The group of fortifications in Điện Biên Phủ was totally isolated in the Northwestern area. In the face of Luang Prabang being under threat, the French Command hastily send air forces to Upper Laos. The 7th Mobile Regiment and some separate units were sent from the Northern delta of Việt Nam to the group of fortifications in Luang Prabang, and a group of fortifications was built in Mường Sài. Once again, the strategic mobile bloc built by General Navarre seriously decreased in number before Vietnamese soldiers opened fire in the Điện Biên Phủ battlefield. The fact that the 308th Brigade changed their direction to the west, collapsed the "strategic corridor" connecting Upper Laos with the Northwest of Việt Nam, and then quickly came back to Điện Biên Phủ was beyond General Navarre's imagination. Later on, Jules Roy, author of the book *La bataille de <u>Diên Biên Phu</u>* (literally: The Battle of Điện Biên Phủ), wrote, "The 308th Brigade's sudden march toward Laos surprised the (French) strategists. They could not be stopped by anyone but the units who had been assigned to bar their way and fight against them. But how can these unit catch them up?"

Not until the beginning of March did General Navarre realize that the road from the Northwest to Upper Laos was still undefended, so not only separate units but also an entire local brigade could pass it easily. He also realized that the "iron" brigade's return to the battlefield proved that the Vietnamese army had not given up the intention of attacking the group of fortifications as Cogny and de Castries thought. In the combat of wits and forces, the French generals were once again taken by surprise.

The congratulatory letter dated March 10, 1954, came when the 308th Brigade had returned to their base west of the Mường Thanh field and was preparing for a new battle. In this letter General Giáp wrote:

> In the latest mobile battle, you have shown the determination to annihilate the enemy. In the coming battle against the enemy fortifications, you should cultivate and enhance your determination to defeat the enemy. Recently, you have achieved a great victory with few casualties and almost undamaged forces. The cadres and soldiers have been further trained in the combat practice. This time, I hope you will maintain and enhance the determination to

annihilate the enemy, thoroughly grasp the "steady fight and steady advance" guideline, maintain and enhance the spirit of incessantly and enduringly fighting, and bravely fight to annihilate more and more enemy troops.

When the combat preparation in Điện Biên Phủ entered the "sprint" stage, the victory news from the many cooperative battlefields continuously came, encouraging the main battlefield in time. After the "Upper Laos event," General Navarre returned the air forces to Điện Biên Phủ. No sooner had the Northwest sky was refilled with the aircraft's noise than the people and soldiers of Hải Phòng and Hà Nội opportunely attacked two airports, Cát Bi and Gia Lâm respectively, destroying many cargo and combat airplanes including large-sized cargo airplanes and one B26 bomber which had just been reinforced by the United States. As it was written in General Giáp's congratulatory letter, the two surprise attacks on the airports had a tremendous impact on the enemy's airborne operations and supplies, creating favorable conditions for the Vietnamese army to gain more victories in the battlefields nationwide. Several days later, General Giáp was informed of two attacks on the Nha Trang air base and Tân Sơn Nhất airport that destroyed millions of liters of petrol and hundreds of tons of bombs. Vietnamese people throughout the country were sharing fire with Điện Biên.

All activities of the Vietnamese soldiers and people in battlefields, from the cooperative to the major ones, challenged the French generals to new strategy-related problems. By then, the French generals had not reached an agreement on the Vietnamese capacity before the power of the fortification group in Điện Biên Phủ. While de Castries and Cogny longed for the battle and believed in victory, Navarre could not stop doubting the defensive capacity of the French army. He was still suspicious about the counter-artillery efficiency of the French artillery under the command of Lieutenant-colonel Pirot. The 155-mm howitzers of the French army had not destroyed any of the Vietnamese artillery which had opened fire at the group of fortifications by then. He was also dubious about the capacity of the air forces, because they had not detected certainly any of the Vietnamese artillery battlefields. Meanwhile, General Giáp had won the logistical battle. With groups of conscripted laborers, he had done his best to overcome logistical difficulties.

On March 12, General Cogny took a flight to Điện Biên Phủ. Having heard that Béatrice (or Him Lam hill) was being besieged, he wanted to re-examine its ability to withstand any offensive by the Vietnamese army. How should a counter-attack be conducted if it was the first to be attacked? Cogny spent much time directly inspecting the two parachute battalions and asked Langlais to give a detailed presentation of the proposed counter-attack to re-seize this group of fortifications. After several hours with de Castries watching a combat rehearse directed by Langlais, Cogny felt assured about the rescue capacity of reserve paratroops. As the evening wore on, Cogny shook hands firmly with the others and got on the airplane. Suddenly, shells came out of nowhere and blew up in the airport. Cogny's airplane took off while a Moran nearby burnt up and another was hit on the left side and broken into halves. That unforgettable moment was also a specific milestone that Cogny was the last French high-ranking official to Điện Biên Phủ till the day the group of fortifications there was wiped out.

After the inspection, both Cogny and de Castries felt more assured about the power of the fortification group and they had reasons to have such a belief. Before the battle took place in mid March, the French had spent over 100 days building and strengthening their defense system in the Mường Thanh basin. The French troop strength in the group of fortifications had increased to about 12,000 soldiers belonging to 12 battalions and 7 infantry companies. Most of these units were élite ones from the French expeditionary army. In comparison to Nà Sản, Điện Biên Phủ was equipped with a doubled combat force and and much stronger fire-power. Apart from one 155-mm howitzer company, two 105-mm howitzer battalions, and two 120-mm mortar battalions, the enemy was also supported by fire-power including ten 18-ton tanks and seven fighters, which were permanent in the Mường Thanh airport.[1] According to the defensive plan, the French Command would sent two thirds of their fighters and all their cargo planes in Indochina to Điện Biên Phủ if the group of fortifications there was attacked.

The group of fortifications in Điện Biên Phủ was divided into three divisions which could support each other. It included nine subgroups or "resistance centers" as called by the French. Each resistance center was occupied by one battalion. The northern division included two resistance centers, namely Độc Lập hill (known as Gabrielle by the French) blocking the Lai Châu-Mường Thanh route and Him Lam hill (known as Béatrice by the French) blocking the Tuần Giáo-Mường Thanh route. To the northwest of the fortification group lay the Bản Kéo resistance center (known

---

1. The permanent air force in the Mường Thanh airport included seven fighters, five reconnaissance planes, four cargo planes, and one helicopter.

Chapter Eight: THE FINAL STRATEGIC MOVE

as Anne Marie by the French). Although it did not belong to the northern division, it combined with those on the Độc Lập and Him Lam hills to create a shield for the central division from northeast to northwest. The central division, the most important one, included six resistance centers supporting each other. It was equipped with five occupation battalions and three mobile ones. The French command post, information center, main airport, and fire-power and logistical bases were situated there. The heights in the east, especially including A1, C1, D1, and E1, were organized into a range of bases which served as a screen for the central division. The southern division, Hồng Cúm or Isabelle as called by the French, was equipped with a reserve airport and an artillery battlefield. It was responsible for protecting the fortification group from the south and blocking the route from Điện Biên Phủ to Upper Laos. Each resistance center was provided with mortars of different sizes, flame-throwers, and different types of straight-shooting guns. These weapons were organized into an independent system of fire-power which could defend its resistance center and the fortifications nearby. Apart from the fire-power disposed in each resistance center, the enemy artillery from the two fire-power bases in the central and southern (Hồng Cúm) divisions, could support each other and the attacked fortifications.

The group of fortifications, equipped with the Mường Thành and Hồng Cúm airports, was connected with Hà Nội and Hải Phòng by an airlift. This airlift was the only communication and reinforcement line which linked Điện Biên Phủ with the source of supplies in the delta.

Regarding the balance of power between the two warring armies in the Mường Thanh field, the Vietnamese army had more infantry battalions than the French army (27 to 12), but the number of soldiers in each Vietnamese battalion was just two thirds of that in each French counterpart and Vietnamese soldiers were more poorly equipped.[1] With regard to the artillery forces directly supporting the infantry, the Vietnamese army had more batteries (64 to 48) but fewer reserve shells than the French army. Besides, the Vietnamese army had neither tanks nor aircraft. It had only one 37-mm anti-aircraft artillery regiment to cope with the French air forces both in Điện Biên Phủ and on the transport routes from the rear to the front. According to General Giáp's assessment, the Vietnamese army was still a weak opponent in the battle against the French army in Điện Biên Phủ.

Despite these disadvantages, the Vietnamese army was the besieger who took the initiative in choosing the attack target and time, while the French army was the besieged who had to defend passively. The Vietnamese not only assessed accurately the French army's strengths, especially those in weapons and techniques, but also realized its basic weaknesses, so that they could restrict the strengths and exploit the weaknesses to gradually change the balance of power and create conditions favorable to them.

The first weakness of the French army was that its forces were large but spread out over a wide area of about 70 square kilometers. Besides, some of the French resistance centers were separated from the whole complex, so they would be easily

---

1. Before the campaign started, the Vietnamese army had nine infantry regiments (29 battalions), one 75-mm mountain artillery regiment (24 batteries), two 105-mm howitzer battalions (24 batteries), four 120-mm mortar companies (16 batteries), one 37-mm anti-aircraft artillery regiment (24 batteries), and two sapper battalions.

isolated. They especially included Gabrielle in the north and Isabelle in the south. In addition, the ground reinforcement forces were limited and mobilized from very far places, so they would be easily stopped by Vietnamese fire-power. In each division, each fortification was in an isolated position and had to depend on the fire-power in a nearby position and rescue forces from afar. The Vietnamese army could exploit that disposition to apply the "steady fight" principle and focus its fire-power to annihilate each chosen target.

The second weakness, which was also the most basic one, of the French army was that its group of fortifications was established in an isolated position in a vast mountainous area within the Vietnamese free region, several hundred kilometers as the crow flies from the delta. So it had to depend on the aircraft for supplies and reinforcements. When the airports were disabled and the Vietnamese anti-aircraft artillery operated effectively, the airspace and controlled area of the fortification group would be narrowed. Consequently, the source of supplies and reinforcements was prone to restriction and severance, and the fortification group would face material shortages and worn-out and demoralized forces.

The "steady fight and steady advance" guideline allowed the Vietnamese army to gradually establish and develop a battlefield system to besiege, isolate, and attack the enemy; concentrate its forces and fire-power in each battle against the enemy subgroups of fortifications, first of all those in the north, paving the way for its forces to advance to the Mường Thanh field; and control and destroy the airports to limit and sever the enemy source of supplies and reinforcements. This fighting method was compatible with the level of Vietnamese soldiers.

"Peeling"

At a scientific workshop held in April 2004 in Hà Nội on the occasion of the 50th anniversary of the Điện Biên Phủ victory, a participant compared the three outer subgroups of fortifications in the north as a pyramid and a helmet of the fortification group. In the first phase, General Giáp entrusted his soldiers with the task of annihilating the three targets of Him Lam, Độc Lập hill, and Bản Kéo. It meant to take away the helmet and facilitate Vietnamese soldiers' offensive against the French nerve-center in the fortification group. The task of attacking Him Lam, Độc Lập hill, and Bản Kéo was assigned to the 141st and 209th Regiments of the 312th Brigade, the 88th Regiment of the 308th Brigade and the 165th Regiment of the 312th Brigade, and the 36th Regiment of the 308th Brigade respectively. Hence, in the first phase, the entire 312th Brigade was on mission. Beside the task of giving fire-power support to ground forces, the 105-mm howitzer soldiers were responsible for controlling the enemy artillery and launching surprise attacks on the two airports and the command post of the fortification group. The 316th Brigade created a diversion with a small force to lure enemy troops to the east. The 57th Regiment of the 304th Infantry Brigade was in charge of controlling the enemy artillery in Hồng Cúm. The 367th Regiment was assigned to get ready to attack enemy aircraft and protect the sky.

On March 12, after listening to the reports of Vice Chief of the 367th Regiment Nguyễn Quang Bích and Chiefs of the Anti-aircraft Artillery Battalions Trịnh Duy Hậu and Vũ Thanh Giang, General Giáp directly assigned the combat tasks to the anti-aircraft artillerymen. Accordingly, the 367th Regiment was in charge of fighting against the enemy air

Chapter Eight: THE FINAL STRATEGIC MOVE

forces. Specifically, it was assigned to ensure the safety of the 312th Brigade, who were responsible for the main direction, from the place of departure to the place of attack; protect the ground artillery battlefield stretching from Nà Lời to Hồng Cúm; and prepare for the force development towards the east and northwest of the Mường Thanh field. The 818th Anti-aircraft Machine-gun Company of the 383rd Battalion alone was ordered to dispose two groups, one in eastern Mường Thanh and the other in northeastern Hồng Cúm, to contribute to safeguarding the combat formation of the 316th Brigade and the 57th Regiment of the 304th Brigade. It should make the French air forces scared of the Vietnamese anti-aircraft artillery.

The following morning, General Giáp phoned Chief of the 367th Regiment Nguyễn Hữu Mỹ to remind the latter that the fire-power attack that afternoon should be fierce, surprising, and accurate. He also accepted the regiment's suggestion to carry out a trial fire of howitzers at Him Lam for calibration when required.

It was the first battle of the anti-aircraft artillerymen and howitzer soldiers, so they received special care from the Campaign Headquarters.

Initially, there was an idea that in the first battle the Vietnamese army should launched an offensive against both Him Lam and Độc Lập hill and finish it within one night before attacking Bản Kéo. After consideration, however, the Campaign Headquarters realized that it was necessary to focus all fire-power to secure victory in the first battle. Therefore, they decided to attack the targets in succession. The campaign would start with an offensive against the Him Lam resistance center, then the Độc Lập hill, and finally Bản

Kéo. In the first phase, the Vietnamese army was tasked to annihilate part of the enemy strength, narrow their occupied area, develop towards the field, and continue to tighten the siege around the central division. General Giáp directed the staff of the campaign to strictly supervise the preparation, especially that for the opening battle.

The results of reconnaissance and the statements of the prisoners revealed that right in the opening battle, soldiers of the 312th Regiment had to cope with a strong target. The Him Lam resistance center was comprised of three fortifications and supported by multi-layered fire-power. These fortifications were separated by 100-to-200-m-long fences and minefields. There were trenches and on-the-spot counter-attack forces in each fortification. Moreover, each fortification was protected by a legionary battalion from the 13th Semi-brigade, a famous unit in the Second World War. Besides the fire-power of the fortification subgroup (including guns with object-finders), Him Lam would be supported by artillery from Mường Thanh and Hồng Cúm and counter-attack forces from Mường Thanh. It reminded General Giáp of the subgroup of fortifications in Pheo in the Hòa Bình campaign in late 1951. They both had round shape and consisted of three fortifications which could support each other and operate independently. In addition, both were guarded by a legionary battalion each and were supported by artillery from afar. However, Him Lam was much stronger than Pheo, because it belonged to a group of nearly ten subgroups of fortifications which could support each other with fire-power. Its basic weakness was its being a rather isolated resistance center in the northeast. Although a mobile road had been built, the infantry and tanks had to cross a distance of about 2.5 kilometers from Mường Thanh to Him Lam for rescue.

According to a captured sub-lieutenant, both American and French military officers who had visited Him Lam assessed that it was a perfect defensive architecture. He said that it was not a normal position but a real fort, and advised the Vietnamese army not to touch it.

The French had reasons to believe in the viability of Him Lam. They had spent hundreds of days preparing and fortifying the battlefield and got ready to wait for the Vietnamese offensive, which they knew would happen soon. Therefore, General Giáp often reminded Chief of the 312th Brigade Lê Trọng Tấn to inspect carefully all preparations for the campaign. Particularly, the 141st Regiment, which undertook the main direction, had to cross the Nậm Rốn River to approach the 1st and 2nd fortifications. Special attention should be paid to the preparation for the gate-opening stage. Gates should be opened as quickly as possibly to limit casualties. According to the plan, the safeguarding of the assault-launching battlefield and controlling the enemy artillery would be undertaken by campaign-level artillery. The 312th Brigade had to well organize a fire-power battlefield for battalions and regiments. An assault against the French nerve-center required the participation of experienced cadres and soldiers and the reinforcement of grenades. It was aimed at separating and annihilating targets, one by one, including the French command post and information center. There should be a plan for fighting French ground forces and tanks coming from Mường Thanh for rescue and counter-attack.

Later on, it was revealed by Western newspapers that Navarre and Cogny had not known any details of the

Vietnamese combat preparation when they went to the group of fortifications for inspection on March 3. A week later, however, on his inspection visit there on March 12, Cogny learned that Him Lam was the Vietnamese army's next attack target. The French started to react viciously. Having discovered a system of trenches from the assault-launching position at the edge of the forest to the field and towards their fortifications, the French immediately mobilized infantry and bulldozers, supported by tanks, to bury mines in these trenches and then fill them up. Afterwards, they used artilleries to fire and aircraft to bomb the distance from the assault-launching line to the edge of the forest. At night, they used searchlights, patrols, and watchtowers to prevent the penetration of Vietnamese reconnaissance soldiers. There were casualties in the battles for trench protection as well as in the investigations for information about the enemy situation inside the fortifications.

The Vietnamese side decided to keep secrets about heavy artilleries until the time of firing on the afternoon of March 13. However, before the campaign began, the situation changed and required a flexible reaction. At about 11 am, it was reported that two French tanks leading an infantry brigade were fighting to occupy the assault-launching line of the 312th Brigade. Almost simultaneously, General Giáp received phones from Lê Trọng Tấn and Đào Văn Trường requesting to have howitzers stop the enemy and protect the assault-launching line. To turn the tables, General Giáp ordered an early fire to both protect the 312th Brigade's battlefield and have a trial fire for calibrating fire-power elements. Đào Văn Trường gladly reported the firing results of the 806th Howitzer Company. Except for two trial shoots,

Chapter Eight: THE FINAL STRATEGIC MOVE

the 18 following shoots hit the targets, destroying many trenches and bunkers. One shell hit the enemy commander's bunker, destroying a haft underground blockhouse. The enemy troops who came from Mường Thanh to sabotage Vietnamese trenches and their two tanks had to run away. The first series of firing from cannons made Vietnamese infantry truly believe in their howitzers, which appeared on the battlefield for the first time.

The French were surprised not only by the presence of Vietnamese heavy artilleries but also by a fact which was beyond their imagination that Vietnamese soldiers could dispose artilleries in the positions they had not expected. About the heavy artillery disposition at the first battle in accordance with the "dispersed fire-arms and concentrated fire-power" guideline, General Giáp later wrote that Vietnamese artilleries were located on the hillside, opposite to Mường Thanh, but they were well disguised and supported by false battlefields. Therefore, the enemy found it hard to launch counter-artillery battles or use aircraft to bomb these artilleries effectively. Though dispersed, they still concentrated on set targets during combat.

The use of heavy artilleries and the combination of infantry and artillery in a large-scale battle were quite new to Vietnamese cadres at brigade level and below, but they still believed in the young artillerymen. Lê Trọng Tấn said that it was the first time he had learned about artillery tactics. The soldiers said that in such a rugged artillery battlefield that required them to fire from a higher place to a lower one, after watching the results of only one trial shoot from each company and calibrating a series of crossfire, they could fire for effect. Although they still respected the tactical and

749

technical principles of artillery, they did not let themselves be bound with theory.

The heavy artilleries had been revealed earlier than scheduled, but they were still a great blow to the French. At first, they did not believe that the Vietnamese could drag the artillery up to such a suitable spot. Then after the first few shells, they were dazed by the "masterly shooting skills" of the Vietnamese artillerymen.[1] The assault-launching battlefield was protected. At 3 pm, the 312th Brigade fully covered the battlefield and prepared for the opening battle of the campaign.

As the Vietnamese Headquarters had expected, two main-attack battalions of the 141st Regiment met difficulties in crossing the river because the French artillery had destroyed the underground bridge. Despite casualties, the Vietnamese soldiers succeeded in occupying the starting point for attack on time. In late afternoon, fog became more and more dense. To ensure artillery adjustment, the commanding officer decided to fire early. At about 5 pm, 40 artilleries and mortars of different sizes simultaneously fired at Him Lam, the central division, the Mường Thanh airport, Hồng Cúm, and the French artillery battlefields. Every member in the Vietnamese Headquarter had attentively followed the battlefield situation from the beginning. General Giáp also kept a constant contact with Tấn directly by telephone.

The 130th Battalion's attack on the 3rd fortification was smoothly made. Vietnamese soldiers quickly penetrated into the area to separate and complicate the French defense

---

1. P. Grawin: *J'étais mé dein à Dien Bien Phu* (literally: I was a Doctor in Điện Biên Phủ), France Empire, Paris, 1955.

formation. At the same time, the spearhead advanced up the hill and decimated the command of the fortification. The combat ended an hour later. Regarding the attack on the 2nd fortification, the 428th Battalion met difficulties right from the outer line. However, they calmly fired at point-blank range to limit the French army's dangerous fire spots, and were determined to rush forwards and break through the area. Step by step, they penetrated deep into the entrenched fortification. The hand-to-hand battle happened violently. Finally, Vietnamese soldiers annihilated the remaining French troops who were stubbornly holding on to the northwestern peak to wait for reinforcements. After two hours of fighting, the 428th Battalion occupied the 2nd fortification. However, it was not until the attack on the 1st fortification took place that the expected fierceness of the opening phase was proved. The 1st peak was the highest one in Him Lam where the headquarters of the fortification subgroup was located, so it was strengthened by densely-disposed fortified positions, obstacles, and fire-power. The door-opening breakthrough battle of the 11th Phủ Thông Battalion happened fiercely right at the beginning. Then it gradually became advantageous to the Vietnamese side. Having detected the French underground gun emplacements and ambushed mobile firing-posts, the Vietnamese immediately changed their fire-power plan and reinforced their breakthrough forces. As the way to the fortification was opened, Vietnamese soldiers staged an impetuous advance and separated the enemy. They both fought and called for the enemy's surrender. After further 15 minutes of fighting in the fortification's nerve-center, the 11th Phủ Thông Battalion completely annihilate the 1st fortification and excellently accomplished their assigned task.

At about 11 pm, the Chief of the 312th Brigade reported to the Campaign Headquarters that his soldiers had successfully wiped out the Him Lam subgroup of fortifications. He suggested that the Campaign Headquarters should allow a French wounded officer to return to Mường Thanh and ask de Castries to send ambulances to Him Lam to collect dead bodies and receive the injured. General Giáp accepted his suggestion and reminded him that this humanitarian act should be accompanied by vigilance. So General Giáp ordered him to immediately reorganize the soldiers and get them ready for any counter-attack.

This humanitarian act, however, was distorted by the French officials in Hà Nội, Sài Gòn, and Paris. They told the press that the Vietnamese army had asked for a cease-fire and the request was accepted by the French Headquarters. Jules Ruy did not believe in such a thing. Later on, he asked General Giáp about it. General Giáp gently answered, "Actually there was no fire-cease on March 14, after the failure of Him Lam. For humanitarian reasons, we unilaterally allowed the command of the fortification group to get their wounded soldiers back."

The books *La bataille de Dien Bien Phu* (literally: The Battle of Điện Biên Phủ) and *Pourquoi Dien Bien Phu?* (literally: Why Điện Biên Phủ?)[1] revealed more about what really happened at the French command post in the central division right on the first night of the campaign. Although the Vietnamese attack had been predicted and expected by the French, what happened was still a great surprise to them.

---

1. Jules Roy: *La bataille de Dien Bien Phu* (literally: The Battle of Điện Biên Phủ), Julliard, Paris, 1963; *Pourquoi Dien Bien Phu?* (literally: Why Điện Biên Phủ?), Pierre Rocolle, Flammarion, Paris, 1968.

Chapter Eight: THE FINAL STRATEGIC MOVE

They were surprised by the Vietnamese capability to wipe out such a powerful fortification as Béatrice and especially by the Vietnamese fire-power. At the beginning, Lieutenant-colonel Langlais witnessed "a dark night strongly shaken by a huge fire-storm which hit the heart of the fortification group." Right after the first series of preparatory shoots, the commander and vice commander of the Him Lam fortification subgroup lost their lives. Lieutenant-colonel Gaucher, commander of the central division, suffered the same fate shortly afterwards. At that time, the French leaders could not figure out where those "dazzling lightning and rabidly roaring fires" had come from. After being appointed the new commander of the central division, Langlais asked for fire-power reinforcement for Him Lam, but Piroth's artilleries had been heavily damaged by Vietnamese artilleries.

At the French surgical station, "the sick-rooms were full of wounded soldiers, as many as 150 people, and the charnel-house was overloaded with dead bodies after the central division was hit by the opponent's artilleries." De Castries draw the first conclusion, "The counter-attack forces with only two reserve battalions were not enough to support Béatrice. Twenty-four 105-mm cannons were obviously too few." This conclusion was completely contrary to the refusal which was made by Cogny and de Castries ten days before. When General Navarre visited and asked if they needed more troops and fire-power, they both refused. To explain for this refusal, they said, "We should not let General Giáp see so many forces in the fortification group, otherwise he will not dare to attack."

It was reported that after the first attack by the Vietnamese army, on the morning of March 14, General Navarre with his gang flew back to Hà Nội while Cogny hurriedly sent de Castries the 5th Parachute Battalion. It was the second time this parachute battalion had appeared in Mường Thanh. Due to the presence of Vietnamese anti-aircraft guns, the French troops were parachuted from an altitude and thus were scattered over a large area, so they could not be gathered until midnight. The decimated battalion was immediately replaced by a new one, so the number of French forces returned to 12 battalions.

According to the plan, Vietnamese soldiers would annihilate enemy troops on the Độc Lập hill on the night of March 14. The fortification subgroup here was built in mid December 1953 to block the Điện Biên-Lai Châu route and defend the northern airspace of the Mường Thanh airport. Located about 4 kilometers from the east of the central division, this isolated fortification subgroup was built into two resistance lines. Its new garrison was equipped with new weapons and supplemented with a 120-mm mortar company. The warlike 5th Algerian Battalion (with four companies) was entrusted with the task of guarding this dangerous position. Moreover, Lieutenant-colonel Piroth, who commanded the French artillery of the fortification group had promised to assist the battalion with fire-power as much as he could so that this fortification subgroup could stand still. Therefore, it was judged to be a powerful subgroup of fortifications by the Vietnamese Campaign Headquarters.

The command of the 308th Vietnamese Brigade was commissioned to direct the attack on the subgroup of fortifications on the Độc Lập hill. The 165th Regiment of the 312th Brigade was entrusted with the task of launching a breakthrough attack on the fortification subgroup from the southeast, the main attack direction, while the 88th Regiment of the 308th Brigade was responsible for the attack from the northeast.

After the battle in the previous night, mountain artilleries and mortars had to be moved up from Him Lam to strengthen the fire-power for the attack on the Độc Lập hill. Because of heavy rains, however, these weapons came late, so the shooting time was delayed until there was enough fire-power. While awaiting, Chief of the 308th Brigade Vương Thừa Vũ asked to throw howitzers into the French fortifications in order to destroy strengthened positions and threaten the enemy's morale. After each wave of howitzers from the Vietnamese side, the French artillery from Mường Thanh fired back to block the assault-launching trenches of Vietnamese soldiers. Having seen that Vietnamese soldiers stopped attacking at midnight, the French side thought that the battle would not go on any more as Vietnamese attackers might have been crushed by their artilleries. However, the battle did not really start until 3 am on March 15, when the Vietnamese side finished arranging mountain artilleries and mortars. Once again the French side was taken by surprise when the Vietnamese mortars of different sizes were fired at the same time. Jean Pouget recorded, "Just three minutes later, the commanding bunker of Gabrielle, which had been considered as the most solid position and a model for the whole fortification, collapsed because of the Vietnamese army's firing."[1] When the fire changed its direction, the spearhead of the 165th Regiment immediately made a thrust at the entrenched fortification, wiped out the mortar battlefield,

---

1. Jean Pouget: *Nous étions à Dien Bien Phu* (literally: We were in Điện Biên Phủ), Presses de la Cité, Paris, 1964.

and then attacked the enemy headquarters. Meanwhile, other units assaulted the fortifications to separate the enemy and support the spearhead by killing all the enemy troops around the headquarters. In the northeast, after realizing that they had opened the wrong gate, Vietnamese soldiers immediately changed the direction. The assault unit rushed straight towards the enemy headquarters and coordinated with the vanguard of the 165th Regiment to annihilate the enemy commanders in the bunker. At the same time, the Vietnamese soldiers behind separated the enemy and fought over each part of the trenches. The battle ended when the morning was just dawning, after three hours of fire exchange. The 5th Algerian Battalion was eliminated.

According to Jean Ponget, Langlais had prepared a counter-attack plan to rescue the Độc Lập hill and directed two parachute battalions to rehearse it in early March. However, it was 6 am already when the three French tanks leading the counter-attack troops passed Anne Marie (or Bản Kéo). The Vietnamese army had occupied Khe Phai and the 477th height already. So the French counter-attack troops were stopped when they were just 400 meters from Gabrielle (or Độc Lập). When Độc Lập was eliminated, the French counter-attack troops also ended their task. They had neither regained the fortification nor backed the remaining forces. At 11 am, the last tank in the rescue army returned to the central division. The French central headquarters was covered with mournful and gloomy atmosphere. Lieutenant-colonel Piroth, commander of the French artillery, had just committed suicide with a grenade in the bunker.

Unlike his announcement, Piroth failed to implement his counter-attack plan. According to Jules Ruy, he felt helpless

Chapter Eight: THE FINAL STRATEGIC MOVE

right in the first battle. He lost belief in himself when his artilleries were destroyed by Vietnamese artilleries. When Béatrice (or Him Lam) was eliminated, Piroth cried in front of Langlais. After Gabrielle (or Độc Lập) fell into the hands of the Vietnamese army, Piroth skipped his meals and then killed himself. He paid a heavy price for his bombastic statement that he would silence the opponent's artilleries right after their first shots.

After the two fortifications in the north and northeast were eliminated, Anne Marie (or Bản Kéo), especially the 1st and 2nd Anne Marie (or Bản Kéo) fortifications to the northwest of Bản Kéo hill, became a suddenly weak position. The fact that the two powerful fortification subgroups of Béatrice and Gabrielle were annihilated within two consecutive days and that the French counter-attack by tanks was repelled were beyond the resistance of the Thai troops of the 3rd Battalion in Bản Kéo. These troops knew that it would be their turn to face the Vietnamese army "in fear and worry for the feeling that the waves of desperation caused by Vietnamese attacks were spreading over Điện Biên Phủ. They were apprehensive of a fire-power attack and assaults by the Vietnamese army," as admitted later by Major Thimonnier, commander of the 3rd Battalion.

After the Độc Lập battle, as suggested by the Vietnamese Campaign Headquarters, Political Commissar of the 308th Brigade Lê Quang Đạo[1] discussed with the command of the 36th Regiment about the utilization of agitation and propaganda among enemy troops to

---

1. Because of illness, Song Hào did not take part in the campaign. He was temporarily replaced by Head of the Propaganda and Education Department Lê Quang Đạo.

eliminate Bản Kéo. As for the Thai soldiers, they were very surprised that the Vietnamese army did not continue the attack though Vietnamese mortars were still hitting the French fortification. Instead of the Vietnamese infantry's attacks, they only saw leaflets scattered in the streets; heard appeals for surrender in the Thai, French, and Vietnamese languages from a loud-speaker; and found a large picture at the foot of Bản Kéo hill which called upon them to come back to their hometowns. The Thai soldiers at the 1st and 2nd Bản Kéo fortifications found the Vietnamese army's appeals suitable with their thoughts and they knew what to do to avoid the same fate as the legionary soldiers a few nights before.

On March 17, many Thai soldiers gathered in front of the French command post and asked for provisions and permission to return to their hometowns. In the face of the soldiers' aggressiveness, Major Thimonnier had to show a conciliatory attitude, reporting the situation to the central headquarters and asking for their permission to withdraw troops to the Mường Thanh airport. No sooner had the order was given did the Thai soldiers found it a good chance to "escape from the cage." They did not obey their commander's order but stormed towards the loudspeaker where the 36th Vietnamese Regiment and local soldiers were awaiting. French artilleries were fired from Mường Thanh to block them, but Vietnamese artilleries opportunely retaliated against the French artillery battlefield to back their withdrawal. After occupying the two high positions in Bản Kéo, the Vietnamese army quickly turned them into observatories and mortar battlefields which directly headed towards the Mường Thanh center and airport.

Chapter Eight: THE FINAL STRATEGIC MOVE

On the morning of March 17th, the news that Vietnamese soldiers had occupied two positions in Bản Kéo thanks to agitation and propaganda among enemy troops was spread to the Vietnamese Headquarters in Mường Phăng, where the meeting for a preliminary summing-up of the first phase of the campaign was going on. The meeting was then covered with excitement. In this atmosphere, General Giáp announced a break and shook hands with Vương Thừa Vũ. He said, "Welcome the vanguard, who excellently fulfilled the tasks at both Độc Lập and Bản Kéo though having just returned from the western battlefield."

After only five days, Vietnamese soldiers won a resounding victory, successfully completing their tasks, opening the northern gate to the French group of fortifications, and facilitating their advance to the Mường Thanh field to get close to the enemy and prepare for the next battles.

In the concluding report presented at the preliminary summing-up meeting, General Giáp said:

> With our victories in the Him Lam and Độc Lập battle, we have annihilated the two most élite battalions of the enemy, destroyed the two most fortified positions in their defense system in Điện Biên Phủ, broke their peripheral line, and exposed their nerve-center in the north and northeast. The enemy has suffered heavy losses—the main parts of their peripheral line were broken, the northern division and part of the central division were eliminated, and the airport, the heart of the whole group of fortifications, was controlled by us.
>
> With these two victorious battles, we have gained great achievements. The enemy has suffered a heavy failure, but their forces are still strong and are trying to fight against us. We should be well aware of the balance of power

between us and the enemy to avoid being subjective and underestimating the enemy and to maintain our determination in the next severe battles.

After analyzing some phenomena which showed the incomplete understanding of the "steady fight and steady advance" guideline among some Vietnamese cadres, General Giáp proposed some immediate missions for the Vietnamese army, such as quickly approaching and besieging the enemy, continuing their control of the airport, actively wearing out and decimating enemy forces, gaining an absolute advantage over the enemy in terms of human- and fire-power, and creating favorable conditions for the Vietnamese army to enter the third phase. Specifically, the Vietnamese army was tasked to continue building battlefields to quickly keep the enemy within a range that would enabled their artilleries of different sizes to promote their fire-power and to separate the southern division from the central one, attack the peripheral fortifications, fight against the enemy counter-attacks, control the airport more effectively with the less use of bullets, and strengthen their small activities. Of these five tasks, the building of powerful battlefields was the most important.

After mentioning the Vietnamese army's shortcomings in building battlefields in the first phase of the campaign, General Giáp emphasized,

> Building battlefields is a matter of great significance. A battlefield which is built solidly and in accordance with the size and standard required will ensure the effective implementation of the "steady fight and steady advance" guideline and maintain high determination among soldiers.

Chapter Eight: THE FINAL STRATEGIC MOVE

To help Vietnamese soldiers fulfill their tasks in the next phase, General Giáp gave units specific requirements,[1] the most important of which was to maintain and raise determination to a higher level. To meet this requirement, General Giáp reminded units to avoid three following things: the incomplete understanding of the "steady fight and steady advance" guideline, the lack of resilience in fighting and the idea of subjectivism and underestimating the enemy, and bureaucracy and formalism.

At the end of the report, on behalf of the Central Military Commission, General Giáp praised all units for their contributions to the first success of the campaign. Then he excitedly said:

> It is our great honor to receive a *"Quyết chiến quyết thắng"* ("Determined to fight and win") flag from President Hồ Chí Minh. It will be passed from brigade to brigade during the campaign. After considering the brigades' achievements over the past time, the Central Military Commission decided to give the flag to the 351st Brigade. Other bridges should follow the 351st Bridge's example, and try to promote infantry tactics and techniques without depending on artillery in order to fulfill the tasks and get the flag. All units and arms should compete with each other to achieve feats, raise high and firmly hold the flag, and win the absolute victory for this campaign.

Besides, General Giáp sent artillerymen a congratulatory letter. It read, "In the past phase, you have fulfilled your tasks by successfully cooperating with ground forces and

---

1. 1- Maintaining and raising determination to a higher level; 2- Building solid battlefields according to the requirements and standards; 3- Promoting the close combination between infantry and artillery; 4- Maintaining forces for continuous fighting.

frightened the enemy. You have become experienced after your first battle. You should make more efforts. Wish you more success."

The following afternoon, Head of the General Department of Politics Lê Liêm reported to General Giáp that the 351st Brigade had passed the flag to the 806th Howitzer Brigade, who fired the first shot at Him Lam, opening the historical campaign.

Thanks to the French press later, the Vietnamese knew how French soldiers had been shocked and worried about damages caused by Vietnamese soldiers' first attack. French Prime Minister Laniel made a statement that summarized the common feeling of French soldiers during the days in mid March, which changed from being superior to the opponent to being extremely pessimistic and frightened.

After the first two battles, de Castries phoned Cogny to express his worry about being eliminated in the next attack. He was especially concerned about the fate of the Mường Thanh airport, because the two fortifications to defend the northern airspace had been lost and Vietnamese artilleries on the two northern peaks of Bản Kéo were pointing at the airport. He wondered if his remaining forces could stand their ground firmly in pride or make a sortie through the siege to escape. After being reinforced with two parachute battalions, especially after Bigeard's 6th Parachute Battalion landed and was immediately taken to the eastern heights, de Castries informed Cogny that the soldiers' spirits had been lifted up.

On the morning of March 14, Cogny was informed that Béatrice had been lost. He was taken by surprise and

Chapter Eight: THE FINAL STRATEGIC MOVE

wondered why such a solid position, which was protected by an élite legionary battalion, could collapse so quickly. When Gabrielle fell, he was not shocked any more but still wondered why Piroth's 155-mm artillery company had failed to retaliate effectively. An idea suddenly appeared in his mind at midday on March 17, when he was flying in Điện Biên's sky. He wondered if he should parachute troops into the Mường Thanh field to raise the French soldiers' spirits, help them correct mistakes, and force de Castries to make a move. Then he wondered if he should let himself, the Commander of Tonkin, be captured by the Vietnamese army when people were afraid that Điện Biên Phủ was about to fall. Finally, he persuaded himself that Điện Biên Phủ was not his business but Navarre's.

Meanwhile, Navarre was being in a special situation. Seeing that the Vietnamese army did not attack Điện Biên Phủ on March 12, he assumed that they had reached their limits and had been "out of breath." He thought it was high time for his army to carry out the second step of the Atlante plan to gain the initiative in combat by attacking the coastal free zone of the 5th Interzone. Unexpectedly, the Vietnamese army launched an offensive, opening the Điện Biên Phủ campaign, the following afternoon. On the morning of March 14, Navarre hurriedly flew to Hà Nội, but no effective plan was made by him. The only thing he did was blame French air forces for having failed to support the group of fortifications. Colonel Nicole said that they should not be blamed as they were also planning to venture a landing on the Mường Thanh airport at night to take wounded soldiers to Hà Nội. He added that French air forces were encountering difficulties because the Americans had threatened to take their technicians home for fear of insecurity after the Vietnamese attacks on the Cát Bi and Gia Lâm airports. In such a situation, Navarre only knew to inform Paris that Điện Biên Phủ was in danger and that the Vietnamese army was tightening their siege around the resistance centers. Then he phoned the French staff in Sài Gòn and urged them to produce artificial rains to prevent the Vietnamese army's activities. Finally, he had no choice but to send an artillery battalion, which was participating in the second step of the Atlante plan in the south of Central Việt Nam, to rescue Điện Biên Phủ.

For the remaining tens of thousands of French soldiers in Điện Biện Phủ, a new fear was creeping closer. The trenches of the Vietnamese attack forces were gradually encroaching on the group of fortifications, meter by meter, as Jules Roy later wrote, and the French knew that the Vietnamese victory was at the edge of their hoe and shovel blades.

The happenings accorded with General Giáp's evaluations on the enemy situation in Điện Biên Phủ after the first phase. On his letter, dated March 19, to President Hồ Chí Minh, General Secretary Trường Chinh, and the Politburo, he wrote:

> The enemy has suffered heavy losses. They have lost troops and control of the northern division; their airport has been almost dominated; their air forces have been heavily damaged. For the last two days, their air counter-attacks have become stronger. Outwardly they are trying to hide their failures, but inwardly they are really worried about the fate of Điện Biên Phủ. This campaign is much related to the situation of Indochina and the coming diplomatic struggle. Therefore, we all predict that the French will use all their abilities and the American imperialists will actively support them. As a result, the next phase will be extremely fierce and severe.

Chapter Eight: THE FINAL STRATEGIC MOVE

The Vietnamese Headquarters analyzed and realized that the enemy failures in the first phase exposed the fortification group's weak points. The French army was on the verge of losing the airport—a very important support and the only link between Điện Biên Phủ and their delta bases. Frozen local air forces, restricted supplies and reinforcements, and wounded soldiers stuck in the emergency station exerted a negative impact on the spirits of French soldiers in Điện Biên Phủ. However, General Giáp was still convinced that French forces were still strong and that Vietnamese forces had not gained the absolute advantage. Over the past days, the French had promptly made up for their losses in terms of troops and weapons. In the second phase, the Vietnamese army was still a weak opponent in the battle against the French army. So the Vietnamese army was reminded to be fully aware of the balance of power between them and their enemy to avoid being subjective and underestimating the enemy and maintain their determination in the coming severe phase.

It was judged that after the first phase, the French forces in Điện Biên Phủ would still be reinforced with both troops and weapons and would try to consolidate the remaining fortifications, defend the airport, and enhance the bandits' activities to disturb the direct rear of the campaign. French Chief of the General Staff Paul Ely's trip to Washington showed that the American imperialists might promote their aids to the French expeditionary army to rescue Điện Biên Phủ. Therefore, the Vietnamese army should promptly overcome their shortcomings in the previous phase, consolidate their achievements, choose appropriate combat tactics, and gradually gain an advantage over the enemy in terms of human- and fire-power to win victory.

General Giáp had a personal meeting with Lê Trọng Tấn and Trần Độ. The 312th Brigade involved all of its three regiments in the first phase of the campaign. Their obvious improvements in attacking fortifications and achievements in both battles were highly appreciated by the Campaign Headquarters. However, they still revealed some weaknesses. After the personal meeting, on March 21, General Giáp sent a letter to the 312th Brigade's command, confirming their achievements and pointing out two main shortcomings they should promptly overcome. On the one hand, the inspection of preparations for the combat was not conducted carefully. Consequently, none of the assault-launching positions were made to the standards, resulting in increased casualties. On the other hand, the investigation of the troop situation and the ideological work after the battles were not carried out promptly, so reports on the fighting situation were submitted to the Campaign Headquarters late.

On this occasion, General Giáp also proposed a plan for the advisory, political, and logistical departments to consolidate and develop the achievements of the Vietnamese army. This plan was based on the Central Military Commission's policy on promoting the role of these three departments in leading Vietnamese units to complete victory.

April—The Touchstone

While in the first phase the Vietnamese army faced separate subgroups of fortifications such as Him Lam and Độc Lập hill, in the second one they had to confront the central division. It was a complex of about 40 fortifications which were divided into four connected resistance centers and occupied by tens of thousands of French soldiers. The resistance centers

Chapter Eight: THE FINAL STRATEGIC MOVE

of Huguet and Claudine were located on the right side of the Nậm Rốn River, in a flat field. They were comprised of about 20 fortifications surrounding the Mường Thanh airport and stretching from the northwest to the south of the French Headquarters area. The resistance centers of Eliane and Dominique were situated on the left side of the river. They also consisted of about 20 fortifications and controlled the central division. Among these fortifications, A1 (or Eliane 1 as called by the French) was extremely powerful. It took control of a large area along the 41st Route and Nậm Rốn River, spreading from the south to the east of the central division. While Huguet was important to the existence of the airport, Eliane served as a shield which would decide the fate of the central division, especially that of the command post of the fortification group.

As mentioned in the Vietnamese Campaign Headquarters' report on March 17, the first important task in the preparation for the second phase was to build an assault and siege battlefields. According to the combat plan and strategic requirements for the second phase, the assault and siege battlefield system included two lines of trenches: an axis line and an infantry one. The axis line formed a big circle surrounding the central division. It ran from southern Độc Lập hill; passed Bản Kéo, Pe Nọi, Nậm Bó, Bản Mé, Bản Cò My, the Nậm Rốn River, Bản Ten, Bản Bánh, and Him Lam; and was finally linked to the axis road south of Độc Lập hill. The infantry line started from the unit stations at the forest gates, ran across the field, crossed the axis line, and finally headed towards the attack targets in the second phase.[1]

---

1. They included the 106th fortification in the northwest of the airport (which would be attacked by the 308th Brigade); the subgroup of D, E1, and 105th fortifications (by the 312th Brigade); and the Eliane subgroup of fortifications (by the 316th Brigade).

In his letter, dated March 20, to the Vietnamese soldiers in Điện Biên Phủ, General Giáp explained the reasons for building the assault and siege battlefield. According to him, the battlefield was constructed to restrict the three biggest strengths of the French army (reinforcement capacity, fire-power, and air forces), create favorable conditions for Vietnamese soldiers to approach and control the French nerve-center with fire-power, and enable them to operate in a large area without being threatened by the French straight-shooting artilleries. He pointed out the tactical and technical requirements for the battlefield, and required Vietnamese soldiers to determinedly fight against the enemy counter-attacks and protect the battlefield. As for Vietnamese commanding officers at all levels, he required them to make thorough plans for battlefield construction and force distribution and set appropriate timetables for soldiers. He also stressed that cadres ought to check the battlefields themselves.

After about ten days of hard working and tenaciously fighting against the French counter-attacks which aimed to sabotage the Vietnamese battlefield, the Vietnamese army finally completed a large battlefield which included a 100-km line of trenches and tens of thousands of underground hideouts surrounding the central division. All the French positions, including the Mường Thanh airport and the French command post, were within the range of Vietnamese mortars. It was the Vietnamese assault and siege battlefield that cracked down the original structure of the fortification group by separating the southern division from the central one. It enabled the Vietnamese army, though the weaker side, to fight against tens of thousands of enemy troops in a new form of war, the battlefield-based one, which took place on the flat terrain of the Mường Thanh valley.

Later, when talking about the trench-based war in Điện Biên Phủ, the Western (including French) generals and historians often compared the Vietnamese trench system to a classical one which dates back to the early 20th century and is introduced in a French textbook on infantry. They found similarities between these two systems. For example, both enabled their creators to gradually encroach on their opponents' battlefields and disabled these opponents (defenders) from being reinforced with troops and weaponry. After attack battlefields were established, they would launch offensives against their opponents. However, the Western generals and historians could not figure out the differences between the two trench systems in terms of their purposes and characteristics. For instance, the trench system in Điện Biên Phủ was built by a weak attacker in the fight against a strong defender. It not only reflected the use of a classical trench-based war form in a new context, but it also manifested the creative application of the Sino-Korean allied troops' experience to the specific conditions of Việt Nam in general and Điện Biên Phủ in particular. Only with an incessantly-developed trench system could the Vietnamese army preserve its forces in the fight against the French army—a stronger opponent, keep French troops in fixed positions, fail any of the French withdrawal plans, dig deeply into the basic weakness of the French group of fortifications—being completely isolated in the vast Northwest battlefield, make an attack on the fortification group's "stomach" as put by the cadres and soldiers of the 308th Brigade, and finally switch to an all-out offensive against the French army. General

Giáp later put it, "This huge, rapidly-expanding loop would determine the fate of the steel porcupine of Điện Biên Phủ."

Before starting the second phase, General Giáp directed the staff to separate the 9th Regiment from the combat formation of the campaign and to send more forces from the midlands to Lai Châu and Sơn La to boost the extermination of bandits, defend and stabilize the direct rear of the campaign, and repair the supply transportation roads before the rainy season came. He did not forget to send his congratulatory letter to the armed forces on the 5th Route for having strongly fought against the enemy on this life-line, annihilated an important part of their strength, attracted their mobile forces, and interrupted their transportation of ammunition from Hải Phòng to Hà Nội and other fronts.

The second phase was scheduled to start in late March, when the Vietnamese army had been completely reorganized and had basically completed the assault and siege battlefield. On March 27, the campaign cadres were summoned to a meeting by the Campaign Headquarters to learn about the combat plan for the second phase. In his report at the meeting, General Giáp made an assessment of the Vietnamese army's achievements after ten days of working and fighting. He acknowledged that the newly-build battlefield had almost neutralized the enemy's fierce bombardments and, more importantly, tightened the stranglehold on the enemy and created favorable conditions for the Vietnamese army to approach and assault them.

The Central Military Commission decided to concentrate all Vietnamese troops and fire-power to annihilate the eastern area of Điện Biên Phủ in the second phase to grind down an important part of the enemy strength (including some mobile units), occupy part of the enemy's artillery battlefield, and take control of all the eastern heights and turn them into Vietnamese battlefields to threaten the Mường Thanh area.

As analyzed by General Giáp, the second phase was much different from the first one. While the first phase featured Vietnamese attacks on separate resistance centers and battalions, one by one, the second one was targeted at a system of heights comprised of many resistance centers and occupied by many Euro-African battalions. Therefore, the second phase was considered to be the largest ever offensive on fortifications launched by the Vietnamese army. It was a decisive battle. If the Vietnamese army won it, they would have favorable conditions to switch to a genera offensive to gain complete victory. Due to the complexity and importance of this battle, a careful organization of fighting and a detailed and systematic organization of commanding are required. As a result, Vietnamese commanding officers at all levels were required to study and inspect these two activities carefully.

After assigning tasks to units,[1] General Giáp specified that

---

1. The 312th Brigade was tasked to occupy the fortifications E (Dominique 1), D1 (Dominique 2), and D2 (Dominique 3) . It was also tasked to annihilate the French artillery battlefield on the 210th peak and the mobile troops from the 5th Puppet Parachute Battalion stationed there. The 316th Brigade (with an absent regiment) was assigned to defeat A1 (Eliane 2), C1 (Eliane 1), and C2 (Eliane 4). It was also assigned to cooperate with other brigades to eliminate the 6th Parachute Battalion. The 308th Brigade was entrusted with the task of exterminate the eastern part of the French central division, including the 2nd Thai Battalion and an artillery battlefield there. It was also ordered to coordinate with the 316th Brigade to eliminate the 6th Parachute Battalion, restrain the enemy in the west of Mường Thanh with fire-power, assault the 106th and 311th (Francoise) fortifications with small units, and fight against enemy paratroops in the west and block reinforcements from Hồng Cúm (Isabella). The 57th Regiment of the 304th Brigade was

the success of this phase would prove the Vietnamese army's great advance, from defeating enemy battalions successively to defeating them simultaneously in one battle against enemy fortifications. Lastly, he requested Vietnamese commanding officers at all levels to be determined, bold, and fast in order not to lose any chance to annihilate the enemy.

After the meeting, General Giáp had a personal meeting with commanders of the two regiments which were responsible for the two most important targets, Nguyễn Hữu An as commander of the 174th Regiment and Vũ Lăng as commander of the 98th Regiment. He asked them about difficulties that might arise in the coming battle and about the time estimated to complete the tasks. Finally, the three men together discussed how to meet the requirements of the coming battle, including the request for fire-power reinforcement raised by Vũ Lăng.

Before the second phase started, General Giáp sent a letter to all Party members to encourage them to take part in the campaign. He called upon everyone to set good examples of bravery in fighting, especially in tough moments. In the letter sent to cadres and soldiers all over the front the same day, he repeated the purposes of the attacks on the eastern heights, confirmed conditions for success, pointed out the difficulties that should be overcome, and encouraged

---

ordered to restrain enemy artillery from Hồng Cúm (Isabella), block reinforcements from there, and defeat paratroops around there. The 45th Howitzer Regiment of the 351st Brigade was tasked to support Vietnamese ground forces' attacks on E, D1, D2, C1, C2, and A1, as well as control and restrain enemy artillery from Mường Thanh and Hồng Cúm (Isabella); meanwhile, the 367th Anti-aircraft Artillery Regiment was assigned to support Vietnamese ground forces and howitzers during the combat.

everybody to determinedly fight to cause the enemy heavy losses and create all necessary conditions to eliminate all enemy troops in Điện Biên Phủ.

The second phase started at 18:30 on March 30. While some units completed their tasks quickly and easily,[1] some others met difficulties right from the beginning, especially in the attack on the A1 fortification.[2] Because the telephone line was broken by fire-power, the 174th Regiment did not receive the attack order. In this situation, Nguyễn Hữu An flexibly ordered his troops to open fire. However, the regiment was half an hour later than other Vietnamese units. By that time, the enemy had recovered and concentrated their fire-power to block Vietnamese troops from the front line, so they caused the Vietnamese army many losses right in the gate-opening step. When the reserve battalion of the 174th Regiment joined the battle, other Vietnamese regiments had completed their tasks. So the French troops had conditions to concentrate their fire-power to rescue A1. By midnight, the Vietnamese army had only occupied

---

1. The 98th Regiment (of the 316th Brigade) had defeated C1 (Eliane 1) in just 45 minutes with few casualties before preparing for the next attack on C2 (Eliane 4). E1 (Dominique 1) suffered the same fate after over an hour of resistance. The 209th Regiment (of the 312th Brigade) was ordered to attack D2 (Dominique 6) after finishing D1 (Dominique 2).
2. Three changes had been made by the French army to the eastern heights before the campaign started. Firstly, Euro-African troops had been sent to Dominique 1 (E1) to replace Thai troops there. Secondly, Eliane 2 (A1) had been reinforced with a legionary parachute company. The French army turned the bunkers available here into a dangerous firing point to control a wide area below. Lastly, most of the French mobile counter-attack forces (three battalions including the newly-sent 6th Parachute Battalion under the command of Bigeard) focused on the task of conducting counter-attacks to rescue the eastern heights, especially A1.

the eastern half of the hill. The French troops tried to rely on artillery reinforcement and especially the firing point located behind the mound atop the hill to last the battle until the next morning, when they planned to launch a counter-attack to regain the lost half of the hill.

After the advantages gained at the beginning of the phase, the situation gradually became complicated. After occupying C1, the 215th Battalion of the 98th Regiment started to change troops, which not only prevented them from attacking C2 but also caused them severe damages. It was because troops gathered when the enemy's artillery counter-attack took place. The terrain was narrow and there were not enough trenches and hideouts. Consequently, there was an increase in the number of casualties on the Vietnamese side. Simultaneously, the attack on C2 was not only postponed but also blocked by enemy fire-power. As a result, the 215th Battalion had to return to C1. Similarly, the 130th Battalion of the 209th Regiment failed to attack D2 after occupying D1. The later it got, the stronger the enemy fire-power became. Obviously, the struggle in the heart of the fortification group was much fiercer than that on the periphery.

In summary, after a night of fighting, Vietnamese units completed an important part of the task set for the second phase. The 174th Regiment in particular was unable to complete their task, though they had been reinforced with a reserve battalion. The Vietnamese Headquarters decided to replace the 174th Regiment with another unit which would resume the attack on A1, a defense height of strategic significance of the enemy. The 102nd Regiment of the 308th Brigade, one of the reserve forces of the campaign, was entrusted with this task. Other Vietnamese units which were occupying E,

Chapter Eight: THE FINAL STRATEGIC MOVE

D1, and C1 were commanded to quickly consolidate their defense battlefields and get ready to fight against enemy counter-attacks in the morning. General Giáp also ordered Vietnamese units in the west to boost their operations to share fire with those in the east. Specifically, the 88th and 36th Regiments (of the 308th Brigade) were entrusted with the task of eliminating the 106th and 311th fortifications in the west of Mường Thanh; the 165th Regiment (of the 312th Brigade), defeating the 105th fortification; the artillery, menacing the airport and oppressing enemy artillery battlefields.

The battles against French counter-attacks had taken place fiercely since the early morning of March 31. A legionary battalion which had followed tanks from Hồng Cúm (Isabelle) to take part in the counter-attack was repelled by the 57th Regiment. On the hill D1, the 209th Regiment rolled back many enemy counter-attacks despite their limited troops. That D1 stood firm forced the enemy to withdraw the Thai company which was occupying D3 (Dominique 5) and the artillery battlefield at the 210th fortification nearby. On the hill C1, the 98th Regiment succeeded in repulsing second counter-attacks made by nearly two French parachute battalion, one of which was the 6th Battalion commanded by Bigeard.

The battle on A1 was still the fiercest one. The handover of information on the situation and the combat task between the 174th and 102nd Regiments was carried out quickly on March 31. However, due to the rain, the 102nd Regiment had to walk along the axis trench line flooded with water to get to the east of the field. Consequently, it was not until the nightfall that the battle took place. The 102nd Regiment also met with the strong resistance of enemy fire-power from the

775

mound atop the hill as the 174th Regiment had previously. Although the struggle had lasted all night long, Vietnamese troops were still unable to approach the defense bunker. In such an urgent situation, Chief of the 102nd Regiment Hùng Sinh directly commanded the battle and brought the last battalion into it the following day. However, the 102nd Regiment's attacks were all blocked by enemy fire-power and they had to retreat to the eastern side of the hill. After four days and nights of continuous fighting, there were only about 50 Vietnamese gunmen left on A1. Meanwhile, the mound atop the hill remained unsolved.

Regarding the fighting situation in the west, General was reported that Vietnamese troops had successfully forced the 311th fortification, also known as Nà Noọng or Francoise by the French, to surrender. Particularly, the 36th Regiment had completely eliminated the 106th fortification, also known as Huguette 7 by the French, in the northwest of Mường Thanh airport by surrounding and encroaching. The 243rd Company (of the 11th Phủ Thông Battalion of the 312th Brigade) under the command of Hà Văn Noạ had excellently completed their task on the E hill. The soldiers took advantage of the gaps between the E and D hills, penetrating deep into the enemy's defense battlefield and attacking parachute units and an artillery battlefield at the 210th fortification between the 41st Route and the Nậm Rốn River before moving towards the river. They repelled a lot of counter-attacks made by an enemy force which was much stronger. Though suffering heavy losses, they succeeded in draining the enemy's force, harassing the center of their defense system, forcing them to react by dispersing their troops, and giving timely assistance to Vietnamese attacks on the western heights. What was noticeable in the area of Hồng Cúm (or Isabella) was that Chief of Staff of the 304th Brigade Nam Long and the 57th Regiment's command proactively promoted the movement of seizing enemy supplies parachuted to overcome the shortage of ammunition and complete the combat task. The amount of ammunition gained every day amounted to hundreds of bullets, peaking four hundred 105-mm cannon-balls and mortar-bullets of different kinds. This created favorable conditions for the Vietnamese artillery to suppress the French artillery battlefields and support the Vietnamese ground forces in the east.

Before holding a consultation to assess the outcomes of the second phase, General Giáp reminded Hoàng Văn Thái to instruct units to immediately do several tasks.

Firstly, the High Command of the 308th Brigade should instruct the 36th Regiment to promptly draw lessons of experience from the attack on the 106th fortification. It was the first time the surround-and-encroach tactics had been applied by Vietnamese troops in the battle. This creative fighting method was compatible with the "stead fight and steady advance" guideline. It helped to narrow effectively the French-occupied area and reduced casualties on the Vietnamese side. So it should be disseminated among Vietnamese units.

Secondly, the 243rd Company should be awarded a second-class military medal for their achievements in the battle, and the 11th Battalion should be instructed to keep contact with and support this battalion.

Finally, the 304th Brigade should be praised for having launched the movement of winning the ammunition supplies parachuted by the enemy. Simultaneously, Chief of Staff Nam Long should be reminded to contact the High Command of the 351st Brigade to transfer these ammunition supplies to Vietnamese artillery battlefields in accordance with the tasks and fire-power plans of artillery units.

Regarding the second phase of the campaign, the Vietnamese Headquarters judged that the commanding officers who were in charge of the attack on A1 were unable to accomplish their tasks, maybe because they had not fully grasped the situation of enemy troops and that of their own troops or had met some difficulty. General Giáp found it necessary to have personal meetings with chiefs of the 174th and 102nd Regiments, as well as some chiefs of battalions, to learn more about the actual situation and have discussions with them to work out the best fighting method before the preliminary summing-up meeting took place. In the short term, attacks should be suspended and fortifications should be consolidated, so that the Vietnamese army could maintain the eastern half of the A1 hill under their control. Besides, the majority of Vietnamese forces should be withdrawn from battlefields for reorganization and consolidation, so that they could get themselves ready for the next battles.

Once again, the question of how to fight the enemy returned to General Giáp's mind. He raised it at the Headquarters for everyone to think and solve together. They should find out a fighting method which would suit the contemporary situation and their soldiers' health conditions and qualifications, dig deep into the enemy's weaknesses and restrict their strengths, reduce casualties on the Vietnamese side, and gradually drive the enemy into the state of being certainly eliminated.

Chapter Eight: THE FINAL STRATEGIC MOVE

Hùng Sinh and Nguyễn Hữu An showed up at the command post on the morning of April 5. Both of them looked tired with deeply sunken eyes but eager to deliver reports immediately. General Giáp told them to take a bath, have a rest, and eat something to regain their health before seeing him again in the afternoon. Through the conversation with General Giáp that afternoon, the two chiefs of regiments knew that the enemy had encountered a lot of difficulties related to troop strength during the days of coping with Vietnamese attacks on the eastern heights. The question was why Vietnamese troops had failed to occupy A1. Sinh and An reported to General Giáp about the mound atop hill. Vietnamese troops were unable to get close to the entrance of the bunker there because they were blocked by enemy artilleries. Furthermore, the enemy force on the hill had an advantage over the Vietnamese one in terms of human- and fire-power since they were supported by ground forces and tanks from the south and mobile paratroops from the east.

Thus, the Vietnamese failure on the hill A1 was due to many factors. First of all, the Vietnamese soldiers there opened fire half an hour later than other units. By that time, the French artillery had recovered and concentrated all their fire-power to block Vietnamese troops right from the outer line. As a result, Vietnamese forces suffered heavy losses on the way to the target. Later, during their assault, Vietnamese troops encountered the enemy's firing points right in the bunker. This bunker had not ever been mentioned in the reconnaissance report or combat plan. Finally, French reinforcements were not intercepted effectively, so Vietnamese soldiers were not supported during their attack. General Giáp directed the Chief of Staff to gather more opinions from the cadres and soldiers attending the preliminary summing-up conference, based on which an appropriate fighting method for the next phase might be built.

General Giáp was particularly concerned about the number of troops and their health conditions after the second phase of the campaign. The early rains were followed by hot and muggy days, and the atmosphere on the front became sultry and suffocating. Both the health and the number of troops were going down. The western units, who were fighting in the trench-based battlefield in the middle of the Mường Thanh field, suffered the most. In such situation, the improvement of the soldiers' living conditions during the rainy season should be closely directed. The careless management of soldiers were still found among some commanding officers, so their soldiers still had to live and fight in miserable conditions. General Giáp reminded Lê Quang Đạo to work out a solution to quickly bring the living conditions of the 308th Brigade back to normal and then disseminate the experience throughout the front. It was really an ideological and perceptional struggle which was aimed at raising the commanders' responsibility for their troops' living conditions. There was also an opinions that fighting itself was not a normal activity, so there cannot be normal living conditions on the front. It should be asserted that the soldiers had fought for over half a year and thus what used to be seen abnormal had turned normal. Accordingly, their living conditions should be normalized to suit the long-lasting combat conditions. General Giáp also suggested Đặng Kim Giang, head of logistics, order the medical troops to see and ask the local elderly about the weather in Mường Thanh in order to prepare prophylactics for the coming summer.

Through telephone conversations with doctors Tôn Thất Tùng and Vũ Văn Cẩn, General Giáp learned that approximately 67 percent of the wounded soldiers were slightly injured. Expectedly by the end of April, around 5,000 sick and slightly injured soldiers would be returned to their units. Doctor Tôn Thất Tùng added that the medical troops, especially those at surgical stations, were overcoming all difficulties and dealing with exceedingly huge workloads to cure as many wounded soldiers as possible. For example, there were only six doctors and twenty nurses at the medical station in Tuần Giáo, but the number of wounded soldiers there amounted to seven hundred. Due to the lack of personnel, shifts could not be arranged and the medical soldiers, especially those in the operating-room, were constantly tired. However, their spirit of serving wounded soldiers was admirable.

Rice and ammunition supplies were badly affected by rains and floods. Observing the supply chart, General Giáp found that the input of rice into the storehouse was sometimes less than one ton. He spent several days meeting with Đặng Kim Giang and some other key logistical officers. They discussed sending some officers to local bases to supervise and urge the transportation of supplies. At the same time, General Giáp sent a letter to all organizations involved in the campaign, from conscripted laborers to medical officers and staff, nurses, cooks, and voluntary youths, to encourage them to try their best to overcome all challenges and win the complete victory.

A conference was held from April 6-8 to make a preliminary summing-up of the second phase of the campaign. In his concluding report, General Giáp delivered his assessment of the phase. According to him, the Vietnamese army killed over two thousand French troops, including one battalion and nine companies. They also occupied four out of five fortifications in the eastern area, which was of great significance since it directly safeguarded the French Headquarters, and took control of the northern and western parts of the Mường Thanh field, and got closer to the airport. He concluded that the Vietnamese army had accomplished a great part of the task set out for the second phase. However, the task as a whole had not been fully completed due to the failures of some units.

Later, General Giáp claimed that the Party Central Committee's determination to defeat the group of fortifications remained unchanged. He also disseminated the combat guideline for the next phase, pointed out the conditions for the Vietnamese to gain an assured victory and difficulties to overcome,[1] and proposed specific tasks that should be done for the coming phase.

Firstly, the Vietnamese army should continue building the assault-and-siege battlefield, further tighten the siege to disconnect the enemy from supplies and reinforcements, threaten the center of the fortification group more strongly, and crack down the connection between Mường Thanh and Hồng Cúm (or Isabella).

Secondly, all Vietnamese soldiers should be fully aware that the building of the assault-and-siege battlefield was

---

1. Conditions for an assured victory included the superiority in human- and fire-power; battlefield-related advantages gained after the two phases; and the determination of the whole Party, army, and people. Difficulties included the sagging morale of cadres and soldiers; the declining health of soldiers, especially when the rainy season was coming; and some problems relating to fighting in the center of the fortification group.

also a combat task. Therefore, they should remain ready and determined to fight against any enemy counter-attacks and defend the battlefield. At the same time, they should promote other activities, such as shooting enemy aircraft and controlling the airspace of Điện Biên Phủ day and night, controlling and then destroying completely the airport, restricting and then disconnecting the enemy from supplies and reinforcements, organizing small units with various types of fire-power and launching battles of attrition against the enemy throughout the battlefield, and continuing to defeat some enemy positions (with reference to the 308th Brigade's experience gained from their attack on the 106th fortification).

Thirdly, the Vietnamese should reorganize their forces and enhance their fighting capacity (by adding more troops, rearranging commanding officers, and, most importantly, strengthening the determination and morale of soldiers).

Fourthly, the summarization and dissemination of fighting experience and the review of strengths and weaknesses should be conducted simultaneously among the army.

Finally, the soldiers' provisions and living conditions should be improved; their numbers and health conditions should be maintained.

A new way had been opened after the three days' conference. If the combat guideline which had been disseminated in the conference was the right remedy prescribed by the Campaign Headquarters, then one of the main medicines in that remedy was the neutralization of the Mường Thanh airport. Despite the absence of airplanes, the airport remained a protected landing spot for paratroops and a main spot for receiving supplies and reinforcements sent every day. General Giáp showed everybody the necessity of cutting off this "stomach" (of the French army), which was considered to be the enemy's most basic weakness.

On April 16, the High Command of the 308th Brigade received a written order from General Giáp. According to it, the brigade was ordered to concentrate forces to annihilate the 105th fortification (to the north of the airport) and keep it as a springboard to control and destroy the northern part of the airport. The brigade was also ordered to use small units to surround and encroach on the 206th and 311th fortifications (to the west and southwest of the airport respectively) and then eliminate them. The written order emphasized the importance of this battle to the development of the campaign and thus required the brigade to comprehensively understand their responsibility and make all efforts to win it.

The 105th fortification was eliminated on April 18; the 206th fortification suffered the same fate four days later. The Vietnamese army applied the surround-and-encroach tactics to both fortifications. On the night of April 22, the 206th fortification was defeated by the 36th Vietnamese Regiment so quickly that it remained mysterious to de Castries (after he was taken prisoner). He could not make it clear when and how the 206th fortification was overpowered. On the morning of April 23, enemy troops in Mường Thanh still transported supplies to the 206th fortification. Only when they were stopped by Vietnamese troops at this fortification did they know that it had fallen. The attack on the 206th fortification was considered the most typical example of the surround-

and-encroach tactic. After the fall of the 105th, 106th, and 206th fortifications, the entire northern and northwestern parts of the airport were threatened. Meanwhile, the two trench lines of the Vietnamese army from the east and west were still heading to the airport. The struggle to control the airport became fiercer and fiercer. Eventually, on April 22, the airport was cut into halves, creating a turning-point which was considered "the worst ever seen in the battle of Điện Biên Phủ" by the Western press.

The battlefield of Điện Biên Phủ wore a new face during the second half of April. Although there were no large-scale battles, the small ones were still very fierce. Every hour, every day, from every direction, Vietnamese combat trenches were like unstoppable drills heading to the remaining fortifications of the French army. Realizing the threat of being strangled, the French army reacted fiercely. Barbed wires and minefields were thickened. Violent counter-attacks were carried out every day to fill Vietnamese trenches and keep Vietnamese troops away from their positions. On the contrary, the Vietnamese army not only spread the surrounding battlefields and resolutely fought against French counter-attacks, but also enhanced the launching of sniping movement. The encouragement letter from General Giáp to all soldiers of the campaign raised a competition to hunt French troops among Vietnamese gunners. The combination between Vietnamese anti-aircraft artillery units, who were determined to destroy enemy planes and force the latter to parachute supplies at great altitudes, and Vietnamese infantry units, who were entrusted with the task of fighting the enemy to seize the latter's supplies, was naturally established. French troops were parachuted from very high above, more and more of them fell into Vietnamese battlefields.[1] Later on, General Giáp wrote in his memoir:

> At the command post, I received daily reports on the number of enemy troops killed by our snipers, as well as the amount of food and weaponry we had gained from enemy paratroops. I thought that the enemy was tasting the most bitter blows by us. Actually, we were gaining victories with few casualties and little ammunition. The trophies had different impacts on the campaign. They would push the enemy into an increasingly miserable situation, bring us what we needed, make us become stronger in the fight against the enemy, and save us a lot of time and effort in transporting supplies on fire roads.

With various and creative activities during the second half of April, the Vietnamese army continued to complete their tasks in the second phase, creating favorable conditions for the next one. The French army reacted violently to reoccupy the airport. However, their counter-attacks to reoccupy the resistance center of Hughette deprived themselves of their last interception units.

On these days, the Front Party Committee received the April 19 Politburo Conference Resolution titled *"Tiếp tục thấu triệt phương châm đánh chắc tiến chắc, đề cao quyết tâm, tích cực giành toàn thắng cho Chiến dịch Điện Biên Phủ"* (literally: "Continue to Comprehend the 'Steady Fight and Steady Advance" Guideline, Raise High the Determination, and Actively Fight for the Final Victory of the Điện Biên Phủ

---

1. A preliminary summary of a small phase in April showed that the 57th Regiment (of the 304th Brigade) killed over two hundred enemy troops and gained approximately six hundred 105-mm gun-balls, three thousand 81-mm and 120-mm mortar bullets, tons of ammunition of other types, and tens of tons of food and medicine and even dried blood.

Campaign"). After complimenting on the achievements made by the Vietnamese army in the past two phases, analyzing the reasons and limitations of those achievements, and repeating the significance of the Điện Biên Phủ campaign, the resolution clearly stated that the Party committees and members at all levels should be fully aware of the victories gained by the Vietnamese army during the last two phases of the campaign, the then abilities of Vietnamese people and soldiers, and the difficulties confronting the Vietnamese army in terms of ideology, tactics, and logistics. These difficulties were partly caused by the French army, who were also fully aware of the relation between this campaign and the fate of their invasion. With the American support, the French army was trying to resist Vietnamese attacks and maintain their remaining fortifications. These difficulties could be overcome by the Vietnamese army. In addition, the Vietnamese Party committees and members at all levels were also recommended to strive to overcome the rightist deviationism; reinforce and raise high their determination and responsibility to the people, the army, and the Party; determinedly remedy their shortcomings, continue to improve their understanding of the "steady fight and steady advance" guideline; actively save the time; absolutely obey orders; and try to overcome all difficulties to fulfill their duties and gain the complete victory for the campaign. Finally, the Resolution called upon the whole nation, Party, and Government of Việt Nam to try their best to support the Điện Biên Phủ Campaign and do all necessary to gain the absolute victory.[1]

On the same day, General Giáp received a letter from General Secretary Trường Chinh. According to the letter,

---

1. Communist Party of Việt Nam: *Văn kiện Đảng toàn tập* (literally: The Complete Collection of Party Documents), op cit., vol. 15, p. 88.

the Politburo agreed with the situation evaluation and operational guideline of the Front Party Committee. The letter also provided an analysis of the French plot and American interference, and revealed that the Politburo was urging the Logistics Board and localities to mobilize human and material resources to meet the demand of the front and help Vietnamese soldiers to win the complete victory.

Regarding the Party's care and leadership towards frontline soldiers in the 1953-1954 winter-spring campaign in general and the Điện Biên Phủ campaign in particular, General Giáp later wrote:

> Since the beginning of the campaign, the Party and Government had focused on leading the army and people to the successful implementation of the winter-spring attack plan. The Party and Government had never refused any request of the front line, even a very difficult one. The special care from the Party, Government, and people to Điện Biên Phủ made us more responsible.

The Politburo's resolution and Trường Chinh's letter not only gave the direction to the whole army but also supported them throughout the front on the threshold of the final decisive phase of the campaign.

Time for Action

In late April, the French army was driven into an area of approximately one square kilometer—a situation which was described as "intolerable" by General de Castries.[1]

---

1. In late April, de Castries, commander of the group of fortifications in Điện Biên Phủ, was promoted to the rank of major-general; Langlais, colonel; Bigeard, lieutenant-colonel.

Chapter Eight: THE FINAL STRATEGIC MOVE

The Vietnamese control of the airport and airspace caused the French army many supply- and reinforcement-related problems. The legionary parachute battalion named 2BEP, with about 400 troops, was the only untouched battalion of the French army in the group of fortifications. It was occupying the C hill. According to Jules Roy, most of the French battalions suffered heavy losses and each of them had only one-fourth of troops left. Therefore, the reoccupation of the lost fortifications, including the 206th fortification close to the airport, was almost impossible. Even the existence of the whole group of fortifications was counted by days. General Cogni said to General Navarre that he could not drive more parachute battalions to the death. On May 1, there were only enough food for three days, nearly three hundred 155-mm gun-balls, about fourteen thousand 105-mm gun-balls, and five thousand 120-mm mortar bullets left in the fortification group. Meanwhile, Langlais and Bigeard were ordered by de Castries to strengthen their defense and wait for reinforcements.

However, the French forces in Điện Biên Phủ did not know that all plans for reinforcement from outside could hardly come true for many reasons.[1] At the same time, the

---

1. After the failure of the first withdrawal plan, three others were successively worked out by the French Headquarters. The first plan, named *Opération Vautour*, was proposed by the Americans to meet the request for rescue made by the French Chief of the General Staff in late March 1954. According to this plan, B29 airplanes from American air bases in the Philippines would bomb Điện Biên Phủ. This plan was not realized, not only because it was not approved by the British Prime Minister (Britain was waiting for the outcomes of the Geneva conference) but also because the bombardment would cause damages to both warring sides as Vietnamese troops had got close to French fortifications. The second plan, *Opération Condor*, was reported to de Castries on April 14. According to

Vietnamese army was promptly preparing for the final phase of the campaign.

While directing the preparation for the third phase, General Giáp paid much attention to abnormal phenomena that appeared among some cadres during the Vietnamese attacks on the eastern heights, such as being fearful of hardship and making sacrifices, disobeying orders, and abandoning tasks in the middle of the battle. He mentioned those negative phenomena in his letter to President Hồ Chí Minh and the Politburo. At the conference held on April 19, the Politburo issued a resolution which clearly stated that all Vietnamese soldiers in Điện Biên Phủ had to try their best to overcome the rightist deviationism, reinforce and heighten their determination and sense of responsibility, absolutely obey orders, and overcome all difficulties to win the complete victory.

After receiving this resolution, General Giáp summoned all the brigade Party committee secretaries and cadres in charge of the advisory, political, and logistical affairs of the campaign to a meeting. It was not a normal meeting, but it was actually a political training course which lasted for three

---

this plan, about six battalions under the command of Creveco would cross the Việt Nam-Laos border from Nậm Bạc in Upper Laos and cooperate with three or four airborne battalions in Mường Nhạ to attack Tây Trang (scheduled for April 27) and reach the Mường Thanh field to support the French soldiers in the fortification group to break through the Vietnamese siege and escape to Upper Laos. The plan was not realized, either. When Creveco was about 50 kilometers away from Điện Biên Phủ, he heard that the French troops in Mường Thanh was between the horns of a dilemma, so he decided to withdraw. Accordingly, the sending troops to Mường Nhạ did not take place. The third plan, *Opération Albatros*, suffered the same fate as its two predecessors.

days (April 27–29). In this training course, all participants were required to conduct criticism and self-criticism with a view to overcoming the rightist deviationism and some other negative phenomena which had appeared among the people who were most responsible for the result of the Điện Biên Phủ campaign.

Most of the cadres who participated in the meeting held at the Vietnamese command post in Mường Phăng on the morning of April 27 were those who had stood side by side with General Giáp since the early days of the Vietnamese army. That day, as a person who took the highest responsibility for the result of the campaign to the Vietnamese Party, people, and army, General Giáp sincerely told his companions-in-arms all what he needed to say with the spirit of putting the common interests of the nation above all else, as taught by President Hồ Chí Minh ten years earlier, when he instructed the establishment of the Việt Nam Propaganda and Liberation Army. On April 29, General Giáp delivered a summary report on the results of the political training course. This report not only summarized the contents of self-criticism of each participant but also addressed some ideological problems among Vietnamese cadres which hindered the whole army's advance to the complete victory. At the same time, the report pointed out the directions and solutions to these problems in order to bring about a deep change in ideology and politics before the third phase of the campaign started.

Later on, General Giáp assessed this training course as successful since it strengthened all participants' belief in the victory of the campaign. It was considered as one of the biggest successes of the political work in the history of the Vietnamese army.

Preparations for the third phase were made considerately by the advisory, political, and logistical departments of the campaign. The last meeting before the start of the third phase showed that the depots of the campaign had never been so full. Gone were the days when Vietnamese soldiers had to suffer the shortages of food and ammunition. They were now equipped with enough food and ammunition for the coming battles. The enemy was still parachuting supplies and the task of winning these supplies was still being done by the 57th Regiment every day. Two more artillery battalions would join this phase. Troops had been added to the combat units. The 9th Regiment had completed the task of eliminating bandits and had returned to the combat formation of the 304th Brigade in Điện Biên Phủ. The cooperative battlefields were still promoting their operations. The armed forces in the Red River delta were still operating strongly and effectively on the strategic 1st and 5th Routes. Meanwhile, the enemy forces were incessantly being dispersed. Navarre had only one parachute battalion left in Điện Biên Phủ. The possibility of Điện Biên Phủ receiving reinforcements had never been so low since the beginning of the campaign.

On the threshold of the third phase, General Giáp ordered the 312th and 308th Brigades to make attacks on some fortifications in the west and east in order to inflict further damages on the enemy and minimize the enemy-occupied area in order to create favorable conditions for the final battle.[1] He also stressed the 312th Brigade's uncompleted task

---

1. The 312th Brigade was tasked to destroy some eastern fortifications, namely 505, 505A, 506, 507, and 508, and get close to the Nậm Rốn River; the 308th Brigade was ordered to eliminate two western fortifications, 311A and 311B; the 304th Brigade was commissioned to put a stranglehold on

in the second phase, which was destroying A1, C1, and C2. Chief of the 316th Brigade Lê Quảng Ba was excited to take the task. He confided to General Giáp that since the 174th and 102nd Regiments failed to eliminate A1, he had been obsessed by this fortification for a month. It was told that he had met the locals to ask them about the so-call "tunnel" on the hill. This tunnel was built by the Japanese to protect them from the aircraft of Allied forces. Then it was covered with a layer of soil and turned into a solid bunker by the French. He also heard the story about a young soldier in Bắc Ninh who used a special tactic to fight underground. Later, he discussed it with Chu Huy Mân and both reached an agreement on the way to fight A1 before proposing it to their superiors. In mid April, while drafting the tasks for brigades, General Giáp and General Thái listened to Lê Quảng Ba's report on the solid bunker atop A1 and then suggested digging a tunnel leading to the center of the hill and bringing a great explosive charge there through this tunnel. The tunnel was expected to be completed in half a month. Chief of the Sapper Regiment Phạm Hoàng promised to send technical officers to the 316th Brigade to help with digging the tunnel and fetch enough explosive for the brigade. The sappers had a collection of some bombs which had not been defused. After approving the plan for attacking A1, General Giáp reminded Chief of the 316th Brigade Lê Quảng Ba to dig a trench line along the 41st Route, which was sandwiched between A1 and A3, to sever the enemy from reinforcements and prevent them from launching counter-attacks. He emphasized that the 174th

Hồng Cúm, block the route from Hồng Cúm to Tây Trang, destroy the C area of Hồng Cúm, and assault the enemy's artillery battlefield; the 305th was entrusted with the task of supporting Vietnamese infantry's assaults and resisting the enemy's counter-attacks.

Regiment should attack only when the tunnel through A1 and the trench line severing A1 from A3 had been completed.

Although the tunnel and trench line had not been finished by May 1 for some reasons, General Giáp still decided to start the third phase as planned.

At 6 pm, the nearly-one-hour preparatory artillery battle ended and all Vietnamese ground forces simultaneously opened fire. General Giáp and General Thái were in a trench to follow the operations of all Vietnamese combat units. Applying the 36th Regiment's surround-and-encroach tactics, the 88th Regiment managed to occupy 311A in half an hour. After eliminating C1 at midnight, the 98th Regiment in the east promptly reinforced the battlefield and got ready to resist any French counter-attacks. Thus after more than one month of struggling against the French army to take control of this fortification, the Vietnamese army ultimately won. After C1 fell, the French did not have enough strength to launch a counter-attack. Near the Nậm Rốn River, the 209th Regiment had destroyed 505 and 505A before dawn. The Dominique resistance center was completely exterminated. In the south, due to the pressure of the 57th Regiment, the French troops had to run away from the C area of the Hồng Cúm resistance center. Right in the first night of the third phase, the French-occupied area was significantly narrowed. Apart from the sound of the gun-fire in a desperate attempt to support the French troops in the eastern area, no counter-attack was made by the French army.

It was later revealed that General Navarre flew to Hà Nội on the morning of May 2. He did not agree with Cogni's suggestion to make a raid on the Vietnamese rear in an attempt to improve the situation in Điện Biên Phủ, because there were

Chapter Eight: THE FINAL STRATEGIC MOVE

not enough troops for this plan and he found little chance to improve the situation in Mường Thanh. He realized that the group of fortifications in Điện Biên Phủ could not survive until the Geneva conference on Indochina started, so he decided to leave the wounded soldiers behind and allow the others to break through the Vietnamese siege and escape to Upper Laos. De Castries was entitled to decide the time and method for this withdrawal plan. The last withdrawal plan, *Opération Albatros*, was made. According to it, a battalion would parachute into Mường Thanh to rescue the garrison there and then, with the support of two other battalions which would be deployed in Nậm Nưa, Mường Nhạ, anh Nậm Hợp, try to approach the west. After reporting this plan to de Castries (on May 4), the commanders of the fortification group convened a meeting where they decided to use reinforcement forces to replace the current ones and strengthen A1—the mainstay of the group of fortifications. Simultaneously, they decided to reorganize their combat forces and make a sortie on the night of May 7. At the meeting, many participants argued that only ten percent of the over 5,000 remaining French troops were still able to fight and escape. However, these troops were said to be unable to run as far as ten kilometers. Although there was a low possibility that the French troops would survive the sortie, there was no other way out for them. According to many Western journalists and historians, when the withdrawal plan was reported to de Castries and a battalion was parachuted into Mường Thanh, the group of fortifications had been narrowed by nearly one kilometer per side and therefore had become a space full of challenges to all the pilots who were tasked to parachute supplies and reinforcements, however good they might be. The group of fortifications was lying at the point of death.

On May 6, the advisory department of the Vietnamese Headquarters reported to General Giáp that the tunnel thought A1 had been completed and the explosive was being moved in. Nearly 30 Vietnamese sappers had worked on this tunnel in the range of French guns and grenades for over half a month. They had overcome all seemingly unsurpassable difficulties, such as the shortage of light and oxygen, to dig the tunnel in the right direction, keep secrets the combat intention, and get ready to fight enemy troops at the mouth of the tunnel.

At noon that day, General Giáp climbed up the mountain behind the command post. There he used binoculars to watch the battlefield for the last time before deciding to launch the general offensive. The battlefields of the two warring sides were so close to each other that it was hard to recognize the boundary between them. Head of the Military Intelligence Department Cao Pha tried to assist General Giáp in this. Vietnamese combat trenches were only about 500 meters away from de Castries' command post. Then there was news from the east that all preparations for the attack on A1 had been completed. General Giáp realized that it was time for the Vietnamese army to launch the final battle against the enemy before the opening of the Geneva conference.

On May 6, an artillery round for preparation started at 8 pm and lasted nearly one hour with the participation of a missile battalion, aiming mainly at the two peaks A1 and C2, and the 310th fortification, which was considered the eye of the central division. The advisory department had earlier reported to General Giáp that an about-1,000-kilogram explosive charge would create a great explosion which functioned as an order for the whole battlefield that night.

Vietnamese soldiers at the assault-launching positions had been ordered to be cautious of the shock waves and flashes from A1. However, at about 8:30 pm, the explosive charge only made a bang with smoke rising high, creating the feeling of a mild earthquake in some seconds. A French officer, an insider, later recalled:

> Everybody heard a thunder-like noise which shook the land in the center of the hill. The peal of thunder soon spread widely. The ground suddenly rose up like the lid of a boiler. The heat spread out and blocks of soil, each of which must have weighed more than one ton, blending with streams of fire were flung into the air. The top of the Elaine hill suddenly disappeared as if it had been destroyed by a volcano. Blocks of soil, pieces of human bodies, as well as pieces of metal, stones, and concrete dropped repeatedly."[1]

Shortly after the explosion, the soldiers of the 174 Vietnamese Regiment assaulted the fortification from the southwest and southeast. Being repressed by a pair of pincers, the remaining soldiers in the fortification resisted fiercely in the hope that reinforcements would come soon. According to a source of news, about 100 French troops in the central division were mobilized to counter-attack, but none of them could cross the section of trench line between A1 and A3. This normal trench line, which had been dug by the 316th Brigade before the 174th Regiment entered the third phase of the campaign, proved very useful at that time. Without reinforcements, the resistance of the French troops on A1 increasingly weakened. However, the battle did not end until five hours after the reserve company of the 174th

---

1. Erwan Bergot: *170 jours de Dien Bien Phu* (literally: 170 Days in Điện Biên Phủ), Presses de la Cité, Paris, 1979.

Regiment joined it. Meanwhile, shots were still heard from the eastern heights since the French troops on C2 were still resisting fiercely. The 98th Regiment's battle stopped at 9:30 am on May 7, after the 316th Brigade was ordered to fire at A1 with cannons and fire continuously 200 howitzer bullets at C2 to directly support the 98th Regiment. After nearly 40 days of fighting fiercely, the Vietnamese army finally eliminated the last two heights, completing the last task of the second phase. After taking control of the eastern shield of the central division, the Vietnamese army made a critical change to the fighting situation: the whole central division, including de Castrie's command post, was completely within the range of Vietnamese fire-power. The time to toll the knell of the group of fortifications had come.

To explain the reason why the French could not realize their intention of making a sortie to Upper Laos, Erwan Bergot, author of *170 jours de Dien Bien Phu* (literally: 170 Days in Điện Biên Phủ), told the story of Lieutenant-colonel Bigeard, one of the most enthusiastic officers in the commanding ranks of the French army in Điện Biên Phủ.

> That morning, he refused to leave Điện Biên Phủ in order to direct the paratroops to make a sortie to Laos. He could not choose any one for this bloody task. All battalions were killed, one by one. Like a sinking torpedoed warship, the group of fortifications in Điện Biên Phủ was suffering constant waves of Vietnamese attacks that were coming from different directions. The thrusts were increasingly extended and Điện Biên Phủ sank within two hours.

French generals in Hà Nội tried to support their accomplices in the Mường Thanh valley to keep their lives to the last breath. They used aircraft to drop bombs into the

Vietnamese battlefields. The Beaufort four-barrel gun of the central division was still continuously strafing at the Mường Thanh bridge to support the French troops in the 507th, 508th, and 509th fortifications. However, many symptoms of changes were seen in the central division. Some French soldiers left the fortifications and surrendered to the Vietnamese army; some others threw their weapons into the Nậm Rốn River. Vietnamese radio transmitters caught the news that Cogny had directly ordered Langlais to try to implement part of the withdrawal plan named *Opération Albatros* in the southern division, and that Mường Thanh had required Hà Nội to maintain food supplies and stop ammunition ones for Điện Biên Phủ.

The Vietnamese staff ordered Vương Thừa Vũ in the west and Lê Chưởng and Nam Long in the south to tighten the blockade on the fortification group to prevent French troops, especially the over 1,000 troops in Hồng Cúm, from making a sortie. The Vietnamese artillery brigade was commanded to gather fire-power to help the 209th Regiment quickly eliminate the fortifications near the Nậm Rốn River and pave the way for Vietnamese troops to cross the bridge and infiltrate into the French Headquarters.

After 15 hours of fighting, Vietnamese troops took control of the 507th and 508th fortifications before launching an attack on the 509th fortification, the last fortification to protect the Mường Thanh bridge. At the same time, symptoms of chaos were found inside the remaining fortifications. More and more white flags were seen at the fortifications, including those being occupied by Euro-African troops. The Vietnamese Campaign Headquarters judged that French troops were disintegrating and the time had come. General

Giáp ordered the Vietnamese army to grab this opportunity to switch to a general offensive against the central division without waiting till the nightfall. "The 312th Brigade from the east assaults the central division; the 308th Brigade from the west approaches the French Headquarters. Strongly attack and tightly surround the enemy. Don't let de Castries or any other enemy troops escape."

General Giáp did not leave the war room during the third phase of the campaign. The Vietnamese command post was overwhelmed by urgent but exciting atmosphere. News from Vietnamese watch towers came every few minutes. Vietnamese soldiers were getting closer and closer to the final target. The first unit of the 312th Briagade had successfully passed the Mường Thanh bridge while a unit of the 308th Brigade had crossed the airport and was heading to the French Headquarters area. At around 3 pm, it was reported that French troops at many fortifications had stopped fighting and were going out to surrender. Most noticeable was the report from the 312th Brigade: all the French officers in the Epervier command post, including General de Castries and his staff, had surrendered. No sooner had he received this news than General Giáp phoned Tấn to ask him about the capture of the French command. He warned Tấn that the French might fraudulently exchange de Castries for another one. In order to help Tấn recognize this French general, General Giáp appointed an officer to bring a photo of him to Tấn.

Hoàng Văn Thái continued keeping an eye on the fighting situation in all directions. He kept reminding all Vietnamese combat units to maintain their fighting positions, prevent themselves from neglecting their tasks, and well organize the

Chapter Eight: THE FINAL STRATEGIC MOVE

leading of French prisoners to the assembling place. He also reminded the 304th Brigade to tighten the siege before the nightfall. At the same time, Lê Liêm and Đặng Kim Giang appointed officers to deal with a range of problems arising after the Vietnamese occupation of French fortifications, such as taking care of wounded soldiers and martyrs, collecting war booty, and cleaning up the battlefield. Receiving tens of thousands of enemy troops had been thought of before, but it was still a new task for the Vietnamese army at that moment. In the short term, the Vietnamese army had to prepare food and shelters for these troops and give first aid to the wounded with limited medical conditions. Thus the victory brought about not only surprises but also interesting worries to the Vietnamese army.

After a long wait, the telephone rang. General Giáp directly received the call from Chief of the 312th Brigade Lê Trọng Tấn. He was relieved to hear that de Castries and his staff were caught and were all standing in front of Tấn. De Castries was seen with a swagger-stick and a red cap on.

Chief of the Secretariat Nguyễn Văn Hiếu was ordered to sent a newly-drafted telegram to the rear to report the news to President Hồ Chí Minh, the Party Central Committee, and the Government. The President must have been looking forward to it.

After the phone talk with the Chief of the 312th Brigade, General Giáp immediately called Chief of Staff of the 304th Brigade Nam Long. Once again he ordered Nam Long to tighten the siege, use surrender appeals to the enemy and firepower to threaten them, and consolidate the key positions in Tây Trang. He particularly reminded the brigade to watch out for the enemy making a sortie at night.

Then General Giáp officially informed Chinese consultant Wei Guoqing and his company of the news before returning to his tent. He had another sleepless night that day, not because of his worry about the fighting method like the January 25 night, but because of his review of all the happenings in the past 56 days. Many of his fellows had fallen down for this historical moment, which created an advantage for Phạm Văn Đồng and the Vietnamese delegation in the Geneva conference on the following day. The international imperialists and reactionaries, especially American imperialists, were still hatching many malicious plots. When one failed, another would be made. "Which should be the next attack target after Điện Biên Phủ, Upper Laos or the Red River delta?" he wondered. For half a year, the Mường Thanh field had been ploughed up by the enemy. It was time to clear up the battlefield and bring the green back to the field.

At midnight, General Thái came to see General Giáp. From the south division, Lê Chưởng reported that the over one thousand French troops, included their commander, in Hồng Cúm had been caught. General Thái asked General Giáp to pass a newly-drafted order which would be sent to regiments. This order regulated each unit's sphere of control in the areas where the enemy had surrendered, as well as their tasks before leaving the battlefield. In the short term, they were tasked to patrol and block the airspace to prevent any enemy bombardment, and satisfactorily solve the issues related to the wounded, martyrs, prisoners of war, and defeatists. Also on the night of May 7, a special announcement was drafted, approved, and delivered to the whole people. It read, "At exactly 10 pm on May 7, our army decimated all the enemy troops in Điện Biên Phủ. The great Điện Biên Phủ campaign gained the complete victory."

The Vietnamese informed the French that the latter could collect their wounded soldiers by plane, so it was the first time warplanes had not appeared in the airspace of Điện Biên. After persistent rainy days, the sky over Mường Thanh was clear and peaceful on the morning of May 9. General Giáp took advantage of the good weather to inspect the battlefield. He paid special attention to different arrangements of the French in fortifications, gave comments on the fighting methods of Vietnamese units, and drew out some causes of their causalities. When he visited Him Lam—the northeastern gateway to Điện Biên, he reminisced about the Pheo fortification in the Hòa Bình campaign and Jacques' words before the campaign started. Jacques was partially right when he said Him Lam was an inviolable target and when he advised the Vietnamese "not to touch Béatrice." The French chose a very good area with three hills which created a three-leg tripod to organize their defense. General Giáp himself examined a gun emplacement. There, a powerful light machine-gun with an infrared telescope helped users to detect the object at night as well as observe a large area. Soon he realized that Vietnamese combat trenches in the assault-launching battlefield were still narrow and had not met prescribed standards. It was one of the reasons why the 209th Vietnamese Regiment had suffered so many casualties. Standing by the combat trenches where the first battle took place two months earlier, he suddenly recalled his March 21 letter sent to the command of the 312th Brigade. The letter blamed the officers for not directly checking the construction of the assault-launching battlefield.

The car took General Giáp and some other officers along the 41st Route from Him Lam to Mường Thanh. The field was flat, spreading to the foot of the southern mountain range. In stead of the green color of rice, this large red-soil area was full of broken vehicles, planes, parachutes, trenches, and blockhouses with layers of barbed wires. It would take Vietnamese soldiers a lot of time and effort to clean up the battlefield, fill up hundreds of kilometers of trenches, and remove a great amount of barbed wires and mines to bring the green back to the field.

The car left the 41st Route for the Nậm Rốn River. General Giáp asked to stop the car. This river bank was where the brave 243rd Company under the command of Hà Văn Nọa made a thrust on the fortification group from the east, killed many enemies, disturbed their defense area between the 41st Route and the left bank of the Nậm Rốn River, and excellently completed their task. Although the company's remaining force was just equal to a squad, they could still repel the counter-attack of the French with a much stronger combat force. Hà Văn Nọa and nearly the whole company courageously lied down after the last bullets were fired.

When the car ran over the Mường Thanh bridge, Vice Chief of the 308th Brigade Cao Văn Khánh guided General Giáp and his company to visit command bunker of General de Castries in the middle of the field. The bunker outstood with many curved iron bars and sandbags. There, de Castries had received many noisy compliments on the solidity of the group of fortifications from many American and French top-notch officials. And there, de Castries, as revealed by foreign journalists, still had enough time to correct his dress before stepping out. At the sight of the soldiers of the 312th

Vietnamese Brigade who first approached the entrance of the bunker, he said, "Don't shoot me!"

As soon as the soldiers made a safe way through the minefields, the visitors climbed up A1. On the way to the hill, an officer showed General Giáp the French trench line which caused heavy damages to the 102nd Regiment when they replaced the 174th Regiment. General Giáp also easily realized the trench line between A1 and A3 which he had asked Vietnamese soldiers to complete at any cost before the 174th Regiment opened fire in the third phase of the campaign. Looking westwards from the top of A1, General Giáp had an overview of the fierce battlefield without gun-fire. From this position, one could easily identify each blockhouse and each gun emplacement in the central division. The French had good grounds for regarding A1 as the key to and the shield of the fortification group.

General Giáp was taken to a bunker under a high mound which was considered as the guardian of A1. The Vietnamese explosive charge had left a funnel-shaped hole on the surface of the hill, paving the way for Vietnamese soldiers to eliminate this final powerful target. As the locals said, this solid bunker was upgraded from a wine cellar. The bunker was equipped with an ideal firing position, and was covered with a solid layer of bricks and cement, as well as a thick layer of soil which could stand howitzer and mortar fire-power. This explained why the French troops disappeared into the deep trenches running backwards whenever Vietnamese soldiers attacked, so that their artilleries could fire at the top of the shelter to hinder Vietnamese solders' advance. Each inch of soil there bore the stamps of fierce battles. Thousands of Vietnamese soldiers and officers had lain down on this historical hill.

The car took General Giáp and his company back to the command bunker of General de Castries after their visit to the devastated Long Nhai Village with more than 400 villagers killed by French bombers. At nightfall, Cao Văn Khánh invited General Giáp to spend a night at the head office of the Điện Biên over-taking board placed right inside the bunker. That night, General Giáp wrote a letter to the wounded soldiers in Điện Biên Phủ and the residents in the Northwest Zone, and listened to a report on the preparation for the victory celebration. All the tiredness resulted from the battlefield trip seemed to disappear when he was informed of President Hồ Chí Minh's letter. The President praised all the soldiers, conscripted laborers, voluntary youths, and local people in the Northwest for their glorious victory in Điện Biện Phủ. He also reminded the whole army and people that the victory was just a start. At the end of the letter, he promised to award those who had recorded special credits.

Lying on bed, General Giáp thought of the President's words in the letter, "Though the victory is great, it is just a start." The President had foreseen and firmly stated that the forthcoming struggle was still long. Many years later, General Giáp wrote, "Such words came from no one else but President Hồ Chí Minh."

On May 13, the victory celebration was officially held on a large ground to the east of the Mường Phăng Headquarters. Participants included representatives of the local authorities and residents. The celebration also involved the participation of representatives of all the campaign units, including the leading sapper unit who had "paid the way for the victory," the artillery unit who had been honored to fire the first battery salvo to start the campaign, the infantry unit who had won the Him Lam victory and opened the northeastern gateway to the fortification group, the unit who had bravely dug trenches across the airport and persistently struggled with the enemy over every inch of soil, the unit who had confronted the enemy for months on the eastern heights, the artillery unit who had shot down the most warplanes in Mường Thanh, and the infantry unit who had attacked the command bunker and captured de Castries and his staff. Each unit had its own achievements, but they were all proud of their contributions to the victory of the whole army and people in this campaign.

The chiefs of two companies, one infantry and one anti-aircraft artillery, were honored to hoist the *"Quyết chiến quyết thắng"* ("Determined to fight and win") flag on behalf of the whole army. A minute's silence in memory was touching. Many participants could not hold back their tears when thinking of their companions-in-arms who had laid down their lives and thus were absent from this celebration.

On behalf of the Campaign Headquarters, Lê Liêm read President Hồ Chí Minh's congratulatory letter. The whole army silently listened to every of his words. Over the past few years, the President had closely followed every of their footsteps in all battlefields. Every soldier and every unit in the historical land of Điện Biên had made a contribution to the complete victory of the campaign as a birthday gift to him.

General Giáp began the Order of the Day at the victory celebration with the following words:

> By order of the Government and President Hồ Chí Minh, I officially commend the whole Vietnamese People's Army, including officers and soldiers of all infantry, sapper, and artillery units, on your great achievements as contributions to the glorious victory of the Điện Biên Phủ campaign. I

bow in deep respect to the memory of those who laid down their lives for this historical victory.

Then General Giáp analyzed the enormous stature and strategic significance of the Điện Biên Phủ victory as well as the great progress of the whole army. This progress was a strong base for the Vietnamese army to win more and greater victories.

As for the reasons, he clearly pointed out that this victory resulted from the sound leadership of the Party Central Committee, the Government, and President Hồ Chí Minh; the fighting spirit and determination of all the officers and soldiers in Điện Biên Phủ; the great support of the conscripted laborers, voluntary youths, and people in the Northwest and in the rear; and the efficient cooperation of other battlefields throughout the country and the Cambodian and Lao armies.

As a commander-in-chief, General Giáp ordered the whole army to be fully aware of the great significance of the Điện Biên Phủ Victory, be vigilant over any wicked scheme of French colonialists and American interferers, prevent themselves from being subjective and underestimating the enemy, determinedly fight against any new plot of the enemy, learn from the valuable experience of the Điện Biên Phủ campaign, and actively combat to develop the victory of the Điện Biên Phủ campaign in particular and that of the winter-spring campaign in general to achieve more victories.

After reviewing all units, he returned to the rostrum and announced, "I am honored to hand over the flag from President Hồ Chí Minh to the officers and soldiers of the Điện Biên Phủ front."

On behalf of the whole army, Đàm Quang Trung as Vice

Chapter Eight: THE FINAL STRATEGIC MOVE

Chief of the 312th Brigade, who had fought the opening battle of the campaign, and six soldiers with great achievements stepped onto the rostrum to receive the flag in the acclamations resounding all over the Mường Thanh forest. When handing the flag over to them, General Giáp said, "Under this flag, I call upon all of you, officers and soldiers, to bravely advance, for national independence, for the land of farmers, and for the peace in Indochina and in the world."

That night, in a meeting with heads of the three departments of the Ministry of National Defense and chiefs of brigades, General Giáp directly gave all units the task of preparing for the moving of troops out of the battlefield.[1] It was the first time General Giáp had mentioned the issue of liberating the Red River delta to the whole army since the nine-year resistance ended.

In late May, General Giáp returned to Việt Bắc base. After shaking his hands and welcoming him back from Điện Biên Phủ, President Hồ Chí Minh reminded his confidential fellow of the words which were written in his letter a few weeks before. He said, "Our people still have to fight against American imperialists."

---

1. Mountain artillery units followed brigades to the midlands and plains. Howitzer regiments returned to Tuyên Quang and Phú Thọ to consolidate and develop the army there. Anti-aircraft artillery soldiers were deployed to Việt Bắc base. The 308th Brigade was sent to Thái Nguyên and Bắc Giang while the 312th Brigade was dispatched to Vĩnh Xuyên and Phúc Yên. The regiments of the 304th Brigade were entrusted with different tasks: the 66th Regiment was ordered to stay in Central Laos, the 57th Regiment was sent to Sơn Tây and Hà Đông, and the 9th Regiment was dispatched to Nam Định and Ninh Bình. The 316th Brigade stayed behind to clean up the battlefield before moving to Thanh Hóa. One of its regiment, however, stayed behind to help the local people consolidate the liberated area.

809

General Giáp reported to the President on the moving of troops to prescribed areas and on the first activities of soldiers in the midlands and plains after the Điện Biên Phủ campaign. The President said that the situation was changing quickly and becoming complicated. Then he emphasized the necessity of closely following American imperialists' scheme during the Geneva conference for the correct assessment of the situation and the definition of tasks in the new context. He also informed that the Party Central Committee planned to hold a meeting the following month.

In late June, Ngô Đình Diệm was reportedly taken to Sài Gòn by American imperialists. A foreign radio station despisingly said that "the war-horse with the surname Ngô had been saddled and shoed by the American President." This partly explained why the Geneva conference was making no headway. It was reported that Chinese Minister of Foreign Affairs Zhou Enlai had returned to China from Geneva and had asked to meet Vietnamese leaders. The Vietnamese Politburo sent General Giáp and President Hồ Chí Minh to Liuzhou (Nanning, China) to meet Zhou Enlai.

During the three days from July 3–5, the two parties exchanged ideas and discussed how to continue the struggle at the Geneva conference. After meeting Zhou Enlai in Liuzhou, Giáp understood why both the Soviet Union and China had advised Việt Nam not to promote military activities in both regions. Both countries hoped that a "quiet atmosphere" would contribute to an agreement to be reach at the Geneva conference. Zhou described the happenings at the Geneva conference, the stubbornness of the Laniel government, and the headstrong standpoint of American imperialists. According to Zhou, the world needed peace at that moment. Therefore, he advised Việt Nam to allow for the temporary demarcation to court a legal base for a general election which would unify the nation. In the past, French colonists insisted on taking the 18th parallel of latitude as the temporary line of demarcation. Due to Việt Nam's violent opposition, however, France, Britain, and the United States agreed to take the 17th parallel of latitude instead. About this moment, General Giáp later wrote, "Uncle Hồ and we were very surprised. We had to scan the map closely to find out the small river of Bến Hải in northern Quảng Trị".

President Hồ Chí Minh said, "With reference to both armies in the current battlefield, the 13th parallel of latitude is reasonable while the 17th one is unacceptable to us. At least, it should be the 16th parallel of latitude."

He assigned Giáp to make assessments of the prospect of the Geneva conference and present them at the coming conference of the Party Central Committee.

On the train back to Việt Nam from Nanning, General Giáp said to President Hồ, "Apart from the remaining fifty thousand soldiers, France also gets support from the United States. Therefore, the chance to unify Việt Nam is very small."

The Sixth Open Conference of the Central Committee of the Việt Nam Labor Party lasted for four days (July 15–18, 1954). After listening to and discussing the reports of President Hồ Chí Minh, General Secretary Trường Chinh, and Commander-in-chief Võ Nguyên Giáp,[1] the whole

---

1. The reports were titled *"Tình hình mới, nhiệm vụ mới"* (literally: "New Situation, New Tasks"), *"Để hoàn thành nhiệm vụ và đẩy mạnh công tác trước mắt"* (literally: "For the Completion of the Tasks and the Promotion of the Imminent Work"), and *"Sự tiến triển của Hội nghị Giơnevơ"* (literally: "The Progress of the Geneva Conference") respectively.

conference agreed to end the war and restore peace in Việt Nam.

On July 20, 1954, the Geneva Accords were signed. Two days later, General Giáp ordered a cease-fire all over the country. In the summary report at the conference on summing up the Điện Biên Phủ campaign, he said:

> Our army's duty will become heavier and heavier. The cease-fire is only the first step to peace restoration. Peace has not been restored and our country has not been completely independent and united. Therefore, we must strengthen our forces, improve our fighting spirit, continue political re-education, and maintain the study of tactics and techniques in order to support the whole nation's political struggle for peace maintenance as well as for national unification, independence, and democracy.

The 308th Brigade was entrusted with the task of taking over Hà Nội. Chief of the 308th Brigade Vương Thừa Vũ, who deserved the most to be given credits for the past 60-day combat, was appointed as Chairman of the Hà Nội Military Administrative Committee.

On November 10, 1954, General Giáp came back to Hà Nội. He had been away from Hà Nội for 2,882 days. On his return, he was still burdened with military tasks as the liberation had got just halfway.

Concluding Chapter

PORTRAIT OF A GENERAL

When this book was still in manuscript, a friend of mine read the Concluding Chapter. He asked me why I collected a large number of documents by foreign researchers and never used their comments on General Võ Nguyên Giáp. Truly, foreign journalists, historians, generals, and politicians always show their esteem and admiration when talking about him. Many beautiful words have been used to describe him as "a person who contributed to changing the flow of history," "a legendary general," and "a person who knocked down the giants." All these comments are true and they all express foreign researchers' appreciation to Việt Nam and General Võ Nguyên Giáp, particularly through the two wars of the Vietnamese people. However, I asked myself whether we should only evaluate General Võ Nguyên Giáp's talent as a commander-in-chief from the angle of foreign researchers. His talent and righteousness is the result of his obedience to President Hồ Chí Minh's teachings which are "to place the interests of the people and the country above all" and the six virtues of a general—wisdom, faithfulness, courage, benevolence, uprightness, and loyalty.[1] President Hồ Chí Minh's teachings are not only valuable to generals but also teach revolutionary cadres. Actually, General Võ Nguyên Giáp has applied these teachings not only in the command of troops, but also to various aspects of his revolutionary life and daily life. Therefore, it is important we learn from the example of General Võ Nguyên Giáp, and apply this to building the army in particular and developing the country in general.

With such thinking, I would like to introduce a portrait of General Võ Nguyên Giáp as a person of great talent, righteousness, and generosity on macroscopic scale as well as in specific things, from my knowledge accumulated in many years of working in the staff of the Vietnamese General Headquarters and from my research of foreign and domestic documents. I hope that I can make a small contribution to research works on General Giáp in the future.

It is common knowledge that Võ Nguyên Giáp was commissioned to command the Vietnamese army when the country was on the "eve" of great changes. The rapid development of the political movement during the pre-uprising days and the subsequent rising of the whole

---

1. In a speech at the Fifth Military Conference (in August 1948), when mentioning the mission of a general, President Hồ Chí Minh put forward six points. They were *wisdom* (to have a clear-sighted mind to think of all things and to make good judgment on the enemy), *faithfulness* (to make somebody believe in oneself, or self-confidence but not arrogance), *courage* (to be enterprising and ready to face challenges), *benevolence* (to have love for inferiors and to share joys and sorrows with inferiors), *uprightness* (not to be greedy for wealth, for feminine beauty, and for fame and not to cling to life and fear death), and *loyalty* (to be loyal to the country, the people, the revolution, and the Party).

Vietnamese people in the August Revolution were favorable political and moral conditions for Võ Nguyên Giáp. He was able to develop his skills and spirit as a commander-in-chief when the country changed from an armed uprising looking to seize power, to a revolutionary war defending the government.

When entrusting Võ Nguyên Giáp with the task of organizing the Việt Nam Propaganda and Liberation Army, Hồ Chí Minh only told him a few brief and basic words on the line of action and the moral principles of a general. Empty-handed, lacking the necessary knowledge and experience in organizing and commanding military activities, as well as material and technical facilities, Võ Nguyên Giáp and his new-born army rushed into the revolution and picked up military lessons from the battlefield.

When the August 1945 Revolution succeeded, Võ Nguyên Giáp, being responsible for national security and defense, had gained some initial experience in guerilla war and the training of primary-level military cadres from the Anti-Japanese Politico-military School. Facing the urgent request to defend the country after the Vietnamese seized power, a number of cadres under the command of General Võ Nguyên Giáp in the Việt Nam Propaganda and Liberation Army had to act as commanders of platoons and march southwards or as leaders of bases from the 16th parallel of latitude northwards. During the 16 months of monitoring and directing the local resistance in the South and preparing to confront the French expeditionary army, facing the potential of a nationwide war, Commander-in-chief Võ Nguyên Giáp entered the nationwide resistance with new experience gained from the battles in South Việt Nam, the south of Central Việt Nam,

815

the Central Highlands, the Northwest, Lạng Sơn, and Hải Phòng. At that time, his army was essentially a guerrilla army with enthusiastic young people who had recently joined. Although the troop strength reached approximately 80,000, with numerous battalions and regiments, equipment and facilities were very rudimentary and cadres of all levels and soldiers lacked fighting experience.

There were two wars of resistance by the Vietnamese people. The first Vietnamese revolutionary army seemed to start from scratch and still remains unknown to many foreign journalists, historians, statesmen, and generals. They wondered how a new-born revolutionary armed force, under the leadership of a history teacher having never participated in any military training course, could confront the modernly-equipped French expeditionary army and defeat it in the earth-shaking battle of Điện Biên Phủ.

Foreigners, on the one hand, highly appreciate the talent of Võ Nguyên Giáp as a commander-in-chief. On the other hand, though, they want to find his key to success, especially in the nine-year war of resistance and the Điện Biên Phủ victory.

As Senior Lieutenant-general Trần Văn Trà says, it requires many "open, sophisticated, and impartial" research works to "decipher" Võ Nguyên Giáp's military talent. It is even more difficult to study his command of the Vietnamese army in the first war of resistance, when soldiers had almost no military knowledge and he was forced to give them specific instructions in almost everything.

For this reason, I personally find it more difficult to write the Concluding Chapter than to describe historical happenings, as I have done in the previous hundreds of pages.

A Politician First, a Military commander Later

In *La Grande Encyclopédie* (The Great Encyclopedia), published in 1987, Commander-in-chief Võ Nguyên Giáp was defined first as a politician and then a military commander in Việt Nam. To the Vietnamese, this definition reflects Võ Nguyên Giáp having been imbued with Hồ Chí Minh's military thinking since the early 1940. It particularly shows his thorough grasp of the relations between political and military affairs, the people and the army, troops and weapons, fighting spirit and technical equipment. Hồ Chí Minh emphasized the idea "troops first, weapons later" right on the day he first met Võ Nguyên Giáp.

During the anti-French resistance war, most Vietnamese military commanders began their revolutionary life with political activities. When they joined the army, most of them had become Party members. At that time, they joined military activities for the Party's political purposes—liberating the nation and unifying the country. Võ Nguyên Giáp was a typical example. He had been a Party member and a politician for years before he undertook to lead the Vietnamese army.

During the years of mass political mobilization, or the "fire-making period" as called by Hồ Chí Minh, Võ Nguyên Giáp wandered up hill and down dale, enlightening the people in the provinces of Cao Bằng, Bắc Cạn, and Lạng Sơn as to the revolution. Thanks to this, he had a better understanding of the revolutionary role of the masses. Among the people enlightened by him, many later became local leaders or members of the Liberation Army. The element of "people" was an indispensable part of his military and revolutionary thought.

It was only when the revolution get a footing in the population that Hồ Chí Minh entrusted Võ Nguyên Giáp with the task of organizing the Liberation Army. He told Giáp that if the army relied on the people, then it would not be defeated by any enemy. Therefore, it is true to say that the mettle of Võ Nguyên Giáp is first and foremost that of a politician who is fully aware of the role of the masse in the revolutionary cause, the relations between the military activities and political targets of the Party, and the close relationship between the armed forces and the masses. At the very beginning of its establishment, the small army was told by him that all military activities should aim to develop the political movement among the population and should never cause any damage to it. It was also instructed on what it should and should not do to maintain its close relationship with the people. During the preparation for an armed uprising, all of its activities were to serve the political goal of mobilizing the whole population to fight French and Japanese troops and liberate the nation. Although the pre-uprising period only lasted nearly half a year, the slogan "Enlarge the pond for the fish to swim freely," initiated by the General Committee of Việt Minh, helped the Liberation Army understand the importance of the public political environment to its existence, development, and operation. Võ Nguyên Giáp's writings about the 1940–1945 period, such as *"Khu giải phóng"* ("The Liberated Zone") and *"Kinh nghiệm Việt Minh ở Việt Bắc"* ("The Experience of Việt Minh in Việt Bắc") show his special attention to mass politics during the process of public political mobilization for an armed uprising for power to take place.

After the General Uprising, Việt Nam seized power, but the newly-established government was under the pressure of different enemies, from different directions. In this context, Võ Nguyên Giáp continued building political bases among the population, so that the revolution could get a footing in and gain support from the people. He persistently sent armed propaganda teams to the Northwest after the establishment of the revolutionary government to set up political bases among the local people. He also suggested the command of the 5th Zone battlefield send some armed units to the enemy-controlled areas in the south of Central Việt Nam to promote propaganda and court the local people's support. In addition, he attached special importance to directing the struggle to maintain and develop political and armed bases in the areas behind the enemy line during the anti-French resistance war. They included the areas of the ethnic minorities in the Central Highlands, the northeast and northwest of North Việt Nam, and Upper Laos, as well as those of the Catholic community in the south of the Red River. All these strategic measures showed Võ Nguyên Giáp's concern about political bases among the people before and during the war. Whenever the Vietnamese army launched its campaign in or near a populous area, it always attached special importance to courting the local people's support. When the campaign took place in a special populated area, such as the Northwest, Upper Laos, or Hà-Nam-Ninh area, military orders were always enclosed with regulations on public relations. Therefore, when Vietnamese troops arrived in the Catholic area of Phát Diệm (in Ninh Bình Province), the local people soon realized their good nature, which was opposite to what they had been told by reactionary lackeys, and they were willing to support the war of resistance. After each campaign, General Giáp always instructed the army to consolidate the newly-liberated area, safeguard the local people, watch for the return of the enemy, promptly stabilize the socio-political life of the locality, and improve the local people's living standards.

There Vietnamese people and army has traditionally enjoyed a close relationship which is manifested not only in wartime but also in peacetime. It results not only from the leadership and education of the Party and political organizations in the Việt Minh Front, but also from Võ Nguyên Giáp's interest in guiding Party organizations and political system in the army to keep the discipline of public relations. The second factor is significant for maintaining and strengthening the people-army unity in the struggle for national independence. That explains why Vietnamese soldiers, under the leadership of Commander-in-chief Võ Nguyên Giáp, won the people's support on the front line as well in the rear. Thanks to Võ Nguyên Giáp, they were imbued with Hồ Chí Minh's teachings: popular politics was an indispensable mainstay of the revolutionary army—the people's army—in any of its military activity.

In the military relations with neighboring countries (Laos, Cambodia, and China) during the anti-French resistance war, Commander-in-chief Võ Nguyên Giáp always paid attention to the principles of diplomatic politics—equality, friendship, and respect for the noble international spirit. Facing the different opinions on combat policies between the Vietnamese High Command and the Chinese consultants (such as the issue of whether to attack Đông Khê or Cao Bằng in the opening battle of the Border campaign, the launching of the Hòa Bình and Sam Neua campaigns, and the fighting method in the Điện Biên Phủ campaign), he discussed with and persuaded the Chinese consultants to court their approval and, at the same time, defend the Vietnamese people's independence and self-control, without displeasing them. That is the reason why French historian Georges Boudarel considers him a great politician and a brilliant military commander. Besides, he always reminded Vietnamese voluntary soldiers and the Party's Civil Affairs Committee in Laos to heighten the pure international spirit, struggle against Pooh-Bah's style of work, help Laos train its cadres (so that they could shoulder the tasks of the Lao revolution, help Lao people fight against the enemy, and contribute to improving their living standards.

Regarding the position and effect of the popular political force, Võ Nguyên Giáp said in his lecture on the Party's military policy that, "The popular political force is the foundation of the building and development of all forces of the revolution, armed uprising, and revolutionary war. It is also the solid mainstay of the people's armed force in combat.

The success of Commander-in-chief Võ Nguyên Giáp in more than 30 years of commanding the Vietnamese army was, first and foremost, the success of a politician who supported the idea that military activities should serve the Party's target of national liberation. It was also the success of the idea that the whole people's power determines the success of a revolutionary cause, and of a military commander who frequently reminded his troops of the important role of the masses and took interest in maintaining and developing the close relationship between the army and the people so that the army could gain support from the masses, whether the army was on the front line or in the rear, in wartime or in peacetime.

Lawyer Vũ Đình Hòe, a patriotic intellectual who had joined the revolutionary government from the early days, mentioned another political aspect of Nguyên Giáp. Vũ Đình Hòe is two years younger than Võ Nguyên Giáp. Both of them were members of the First National Assembly. In the first government, Vũ Đình Hòe was Minister of Education, and then Minister of Justice. In an interview by the *Văn Nghệ* (Letters and Arts) newspaper about Võ Nguyên Giáp in late 2005, he said:

> Hồ Chí Mính's strategically military-political thought and infinite compassion were absorbed by Commander-in-chief Võ Nguyên Giáp—his best and closest student.
>
> Võ Nguyên Giáp learned from Hồ Chí Minh the method of dialectical materialism. The understanding and application of this method prevented him from falling into empty theories, dogmatism, and leftist deviation.
>
> I personally think that Võ Nguyên Giáp kept following Hồ Chí Minh's spirit of national unity for a great cause and for humanity. That explains why he was loved and trusted by the whole army. Until the present day, Võ Nguyên Giáp has been loved, esteemed, and admired by the intellectual circle, the whole nation, and the whole world.

When writing about the two wars of resistance by Vietnamese people and the Vietnamese People's Army, foreign historians usually take interest in the political quality in Võ Nguyên Giáp. Jean Lacouture—writer, journalist, and war correspondent—is a typical example. He was first seen in Việt Nam in the early days of the revolutionary government, and was among the first guests of Võ Nguyên Giáp after the General Uprising. The negotiation between Việt Nam and France had began by then, but it was still in secret. Lacouture's first works on Hồ Chí Minh and Võ Nguyên Giáp were soon released, such as *Võ Nguyên Giáp—A Portrait* and *Survey of an Author*.

Having listened to Võ Nguyên Giáp talk about his determination to fight for national independence as the political target of the resistance war by Vietnamese people in his first meeting with this commander-in-chief, Lacouture remarked that Giáp mentioned "independence" as an ultimate request and stated that the Việt Minh would launch a war if this request was not satisfied. Then Giáp firmly stated, "We don't allow ourselves to stop in the face of any sacrifice, violence. or destruction." The way he stressed this statement made a strong impression on Lacouture. For this journalist, Giáp was not only a politician but also a fighter of a powerful movement.

In his first meeting with General Philippe Leclerc in March 1946, Võ Nguyên Giáp mentioned again the political target of the Vietnamese war for national liberation. He said, "I am a communist fighting for the independence of our country." Of course, at that time, the commander-in-chief of the French expeditionary army could not fully understand the significant statement by Võ Nguyên Giáp, a politician who assumed the military missions of the Vietnamese revolutionary government. His will, determination, and national spirit were clearly manifested in these words.

At the conference held in Đà Lạt, Jean Lacouture had another opportunity to "learn about politician Võ Nguyên Giáp." Afterwards, he wrote:

> At the conference, he showed his eloquence in strongly denouncing the war being conducted by the French expeditionary units in South Việt Nam. His debates with Pierre Messmer, who later became French Minister of

823

National Defense, were very severe. Võ Nguyên Giáp, however, moderated his words and always sought mutual understanding from the French side during the negotiations.

The pity is that the French at that time intentionally refused to perceive it and so did not create conditions for the mutual understanding between Việt Nam and France, as Former President de Gaulle admitted in his letter dated February 8, 1966 to President Hồ Chí Minh.[1] Jean Lacouture wrote, "Võ Nguyên Giáp gave me a long interview on the evening of the closing day of the conference. After that, he insisted on reading my notes and carefully edited my writing in French—the language he loves and masters."

Jean Lacouture also revealed a detail which was considered as a discovery about the goodwill of Võ Nguyên Giáp. Although the meeting in Đà Lạt was unsuccessful, as J. Lacutuya revealed, Giáp suggested him using the phrase "cordial disagreement" (originally: *"le désaccord cordial"*) to describe the Đà Lạt meeting. His ability as a politician and his uncompromising political view were expressed in each statement. When being asked why Võ Nguyên Giáp was then called "a snow-covered volcano," Jean Lacouture wrote:

> That image reflects a blend of burning zeal and cold verdicts making up the strength of this man. It is necessary to describe his talent and passion. He looks small in the uniform, but he has the head of a lion and the forehead of a thinker. He uses violence as the material for building a nation.

---

1. Twelve years after the defeat of the French expeditionary army in Điện Biên Phủ, Former French President Charles de Gaulle sent a letter to President Hồ Chí Minh. In the letter he wrote, "After the Second World War, had there been a better mutual understanding between the French and Vietnamese, we could have avoided the disastrous upheavals in our country as can be seen today."

For international friends, especially the Africans sharing the same plight, "lion Võ Nguyên Giáp" gave them affectionate political feelings. The governments and peoples of many African countries admire Võ Nguyên Giáp not only for his art of war in the past but also for his interest in the relationship and cooperation between Africa and Việt Nam. Foreign press had numerous articles about the meeting between General Võ Nguyên Giáp and representatives of 23 African countries, who arrived in Hà Nội to attend the Việt Nam-Africa Seminar in May 2003. At the meeting, regarding the cooperation between Việt Nam and Africa, Võ Nguyên Giáp said:

> The cooperation has developed, but the development has not corresponded with the great potentials of both sides. Therefore, both sides have to make more efforts to promote that relationship. I hope that the Việt Nam-Africa cooperation will be promoted not only in agriculture but also in science and technology. The Việt Nam-Africa unity, based on the cooperation with developed and progressive countries, will gradually catch up with other developed countries in the world.

Võ Nguyên Giáp also introduced to African delegates a lesson of experience which contributed to the victory of the Vietnamese revolution. The lesson is reflected in President Hồ Chí Minh's slogan "Unity, unity, great unity – Success, success, great success."

Võ Nguyên Giáp's visits to Africa left deep impressions on the local people. Algerian people, especially young ones, still remember the statement he made at the welcome meeting held on the occasion of his visit to Algeria. "Imperialists are bad students; they are unable to acquire the lessons of history," said he. Algerian people were very interested in this statement, because it reminded them of a significant event in 1954. The French expeditionary army waged an aggressive war in North Africa that year, shortly after their defeat in Điện Biên Phủ. Eight years later, in 1962, they had to sign the Évian Accords and withdrew from Algeria.

Also at the meeting in Algiers, the capital city of Algeria, Võ Nguyên Giáp mentioned another reason leading to the success of the Vietnamese cause of national liberation. It was national spirit or the factor of people. Several years later, Võ Nguyên Giáp received an Indian senior military delegation, headed by Air Chief Marshal Om Prakash Mehra, to Việt Nam. He thanked Indian people for their support to Việt Nam in the cause of national liberation and responded to the Air Chief Marshal's praise, Võ Nguyên Giáp said, "As for our generals, however talented they might be, they would not have gained such achievements without a sound and lucid command, a heroic nation, and a brave army."

These words were targeted at international friends and those sharing the same plight with Vietnamese people in the third world. Võ Nguyên Giáp also did not miss any opportunity to explain to Westerners, including those who had been Việt Nam's enemies, that for the last tens of centuries, both friends and enemies have underestimated the national spirit and strength of Vietnamese people.

On June 23, 1997, Võ Nguyên Giáp received an American high-ranking military delegation headed by Former American Secretary of Defense McNamara. At the meeting, a member of the delegation asked him, "Which general did you most highly evaluate during the thirty years' war?" He said that it was the Vietnamese people who had defeated American imperialists, and that any other generals were just drops of water in the ocean, however great their merits might be. So the most highly-evaluated general for him was the people. Like General Leclerc, General McNamara and his company could not fully understand the profound statement made by Võ Nguyên Giáp, a veteran politician and the number-one military commander in Việt Nam.

The "Ego" in the Relation with the Collective

In *The Sunday Times* magazine issued on November 12, 1972, James Fox wrote, "It is a mistake to separate him (Võ Nguyên Giáp) from the framework of collective leadership."

During his life as a commander-in-chief, Võ Nguyên Giáp always respected, observed, and obey to the leadership of the Standing Committee (later known as the Politburo), the Party Central Committee, the Government, and President Hồ Chí Minh. He always put the interests of the country above all, actively and proactively proposed new policies and strategies to his superiors, and gathered up his mind and talent to best implement them once they had been approved. Whenever speaking in front of Vietnamese generals and soldiers about the reasons for the success of a policy, strategy, or campaign, he often mentioned the leadership of the Party Central Committee and Hồ Chí Minh before the collective direction of the Central Military Commission. His "ego" had never appeared in his periodic summary reports or achievement reports after each campaign, even when he himself was obviously the first determinant of the success, such as the case of changing the operational guideline in the Border or Điện Biên Phủ campaign.

When he was entrusted with the task of organizing the Việt Nam Propaganda and Liberation Army, the first determinant of success Hồ Chí Minh told him was the leadership of the Party (and then the strength of the masses). Although the members of the Party cell of the Việt Nam Propaganda and Liberation Army had limited limitary knowledge at that time, Võ Nguyên Giáp still discussed the attack targets and fighting methods in the battles of Phay Khắt and Nà Ngần with them.

When guiding the whole country to prepare for the resistance period in late 1946, he also based himself on the resolution of the military conference held on October 19 in Nguyễn Du Street (Hà Nội) and presided over by General Secretary Trường Chinh. Having agreed with Trường Chinh that "the possibility of détente is reducing while that of a large-scale conflict is increasing," especially after the unsuccessful coup d'état by French troops in July 1946 and the unsuccessful negotiations in Fontainebleau, and having received the approval from the Standing Committee, Commander-in-chief Võ Nguyên Giáp based himself on the situation of battlefields to direct the division of war zones, arrange cadres and forces, and prepare a suitable plan for each strategic area. Once the resolution of the Nguyễn Du military conference was adopted, the preparation was implemented from Đà Nẵng northwards. In Hà Nội, for example, Võ Nguyên Giáp gave Vương Thừa Vũ and Hoàng Văn Thái specific instructions on preparing for combat in accordance with the spirit of General Secretary Trường Chinh's instruction, "Not to allow the event of Hải Phòng to be repeated in the capital." The time of attack in Hà Nội and in the whole country proposed by Võ Nguyên Giáp was adopted by the Standing Committee at the final meeting held on December 18 in Vạn Phúc. Commander-in-chief Võ Nguyên Giáp supplied concrete guidance on the preparation for the historical moment on the evening of December 19 in Hà Nội, as well as in the whole country.

The changing of the combat plan in the dry season of 1947 was a great decision. It was made when the situation of the battlefield was urgently changing and when Võ Nguyên Giáp had realized that the French army's operations in different directions throughout Việt Bắc base were much different from the Vietnamese predictions. With reference to the French army's operations in the six provinces of Việt Bắc, the broken front in early 1947, and the practical experience of an armed unit operating in an enemy-controlled area in the south of Bắc Ninh Province, Commander-in-chief Võ Nguyên Giáp proposed the deployment of troops into three battlefields and the changing of the fighting method to President Hồ Chí Minh and the Standing Committee. Due to timely changes to the combat plan, the Vietnamese army could turn the tables on the enemy, switching from the passive to the active and winning the final victory in the Việt Bắc campaign.

Launching the guerilla war was a long-term strategic policy of the Party during the war for national liberation. However, it took Võ Nguyên Giáp a lot of time and effort to find out the way to successfully implement this strategic policy. The "independent company-concentrated battalion" guideline reflects the Vietnamese art of war. Bearing the stamp of Võ Nguyên Giáp, it was soon approved by President Hồ Chí Minh and General Secretary Trường Chinh. Võ Nguyên Giáp boldly proposed the dispersion of one-third of Vietnamese regulars for the promotion of guerilla war. It was a daring strategic method that reflected Võ Nguyên Giáp's intelligence, clear-headedness, sense of responsibility, venturesome spirit, and determination to satisfactorily implement the strategic policy proposed by the Party Central Committee in early 1948.

After the first large-scale campaign was launched by Vietnamese regulars, Võ Nguyên Giáp always proposed the campaign direction for each dry season and got approval from President Hồ Chí Minh and the Standing Committee. In his project for each campaign, he always mentioned both advantages and disadvantages, and suggested the Party Central Committee and the Government direct all levels and branches to perform tasks relating to military affairs such as building roads and mobilizing human and material resources to the front. He also commanded the three military departments of the General Headquarters to proactively solve problems that could be overcome by the Ministry of National Defense and not to rely on any other ministries.

Besides making arrangements to ensure the regular communication between the front and the rear during the campaign, Võ Nguyên Giáp would write letters or dispatch cadres to see Hồ Chí Minh and the Standing Committee (later known as the Politburo) to report situations and ask for instructions. Although he was entitled to make decisions at the front, he would still send timely reports to his superiors to seek their support to his decisions, especially those on important issues such as the changing of the operational guideline in the Điện Biên Phủ campaign.

In summary, in his relations with the Party Central Committee and the Standing Committee (later known as the Politburo), Võ Nguyên Giáp would promote his proactiveness in proposing policies, asking for instructions, and conducting group discussions for unanimity. Once his proposals had become resolutions, he would determinedly, proactively, and creatively implement them.

Võ Nguyên Giáp also had a sincere respect for other leaders at the same level in the Central Military Commission and the Front Party Committee. Even in case of emergency, he would still find chance to exchange and discuss his opinions with other members of the Central Military Commission or the Front Party Committee to seek their agreement on important issues, such as the changing of the first attack target in the Border campaign and the withdrawal of troops when confronting difficulties in the last phase of the Trần Hưng Đạo or Hoàng Hoa Thám campaign or after several attacks on Nà Sản in the third phase of the Northwest campaign. Most typical was the changing of the operational guideline in the Điện Biên Phủ campaign. Although he was Secretary of the Central Military Commission and the Front Party Committee, he was not the final decision-maker that time. Although he had soon realized the infeasibility of this operation guideline, he did not show his opposition to this operational guideline, because it had been decided by all the others, including Chinese consultants, before he arrived at the front. It was not until January 26, 1954, after 12 days and 12 nights thinking and observing the preparations made by the Vietnamese army and changes in the enemy situation, that he had good grounds for confirming the infeasibility of the "quick fight" operational guideline. With the spirit of "putting the interests of the country above all," the sense of responsibility for the outcome of this significant campaign, and the respect for collective leadership, Võ Nguyên Giáp persuaded the others and finally gained their agreement on his new operational guideline, which would ensure the success of the campaign.

In an interview in the *Tiền phong* (Vanguard) newspaper, Senior Lieutenant-general Trần Văn Trà praised Võ Nguyên Giáp for his generosity and tolerance. In his opinion, Võ Nguyên Giáp always based his decisions on the vital principle of winning victory with minimal sacrifices by generals and soldiers.

As his subordinate, I always heard him talk about the good and right points of his comrades. I had never heard him account for any problems within the scope of his responsibility. He always tried to fulfill any tasks given by the revolution and he did it all well.

In his article published in the *Đại đoàn kết* (Great Unity) newspaper in August 2001, General Đoàn Huyên wrote:

> While struggling to solve controversial problems arising in leading the revolution, Võ Nguyên Giáp always adopted the rightest attitude and held the view that constructive struggle was for unity. Therefore, he always kept calm and restrained himself. He had never let the interests of the revolution controlled or affected by any individual interests.

Võ Nguyên Giáp attributed the success of any strategic policy or campaign to the contributions by the whole army and people. He held the view that history was made by the masses. When talking about a feat of arms, he had never forgotten to mention his subordinate generals and soldiers who directly faced the enemy on the front; the sappers, conscript laborers, and voluntary youths who sweated and bled to ensure the safety of food and ammunition supplies to the front; the artists of the firing-line ensemble; as well as the doctors and nurses who spent sleepless nights treating and taking care of wounded soldiers. After each successful campaign, he would commend the achievements of combined operations, encouraged and consoled wounded and sick soldiers, and gave thanks to local people for their food supplies to the front. Võ Nguyên Giáp told writers not to forget anybody involved when they wrote about feats of arms. A feat of arms does not belong to the soldier alone; it belongs to the whole people.

"A Great Commander-in-chief"

For American General William Westmoreland, Võ Nguyên Giáp was "a great commander-in-chief." Western generals and historians have made similar comments in different ways of expression.

Truly, Võ Nguyên Giáp was the military commander of the Vietnamese people's war and the Vietnamese People's Army. He was also the pioneer in applying Hồ Chí Minh's military thought to the Vietnamese struggle for national independence. Many Vietnamese patriotic personalities and generals have voiced their opinions of Võ Nguyên Giáp. Vũ Đình Hòe said:

> So far, I have not fully understood the great career of Võ Nguyên Giáp yet. I have only seen clearly that under the direct leadership of Hồ Chí Minh in great campaigns, Võ Nguyên Giáp, as Commander-in-chief of the Vietnamese People's Army, commanded the whole army to turn the tables on French colonialists and American imperialists.
>
> The thought of a history teacher and that of a lawyer[1] made important contributions to his talent in analyzing the

---

1. Vũ Đình Hòe meant that General Võ Nguyên Giáp was a graduate in law.

situations of our troops and the enemy, the development of battlefields, and foreign affairs.

The thought of Võ Nguyên Giáp was developed on the foundation of Hồ Chí Minh's thought and reached a special height, which had rarely been seen, in commanding campaigns of different sizes and in politically directing the whole army.

Võ Nguyên Giáp not only focused on analyzing the general, but also paid special attention to analyzing the most typical parts in the general in order to find out the best solutions or the best fighting methods (such as the "firm fight and firm advance" tactic in the Điện Biên Phủ campaign). This helped to shorten time to the great victory of Điện Biên Phủ in particular and the two resistance wars by Vietnamese people in general, reduced the number of casualties, and reached the height of humanism.

Shortly, through the two resistance wars, I personally think that Võ Nguyên Giáp surpassed his great French and American opponents in terms of military-political thoughts.

Under the leadership of Commander-in-chief Võ Nguyên Giáp during the 30 years' war for national liberation, Vietnamese generals have their own opinions of their superior. Although they worked in different places (some worked in the General Headquarters while others directly commanded troops on the front) and expressed their opinions from different angles of view, they all converged at one point—Võ Nguyên Giáp's art of war.

Senior Lieutenant-general Trần Văn Trà said:

> Võ Nguyên Giáp's visionary, sharp, and original ideas on military strategies and tactics in the two Vietnamese wars against French colonialism and American imperialism should be researched openly, meticulously, and impartially

by historians. Personally, I have never ever found any of his mistakes in military strategies and tactics during the two wars. I have only found his master moves in encircling and attacking the enemy.

In an interview by the *Quốc tế* (International) newspaper in August 2011, Senior Lieutenant-general Hoàng Minh Thảo said:

> Võ Nguyên Giáp is a military master. He always found out original and creative ways of fighting, which both ensured the highest victory for campaigns and minimized casualties. He was a preeminent commander-in-chief. During the two wars, he always showed himself a general who was bold enough to fight any battle, determined to win victory, and creative in fighting. He penetrated his subordinate generals and soldiers with the whole nation and Party's determination to win, so that they would turn this determination into action in the battlefield.

Many generals who had worked in the staff of the General Headquarters and directly assisted Võ Nguyên Giáp in designing and implementing combat plans often talked with each other about their all-powerful commander. They all thought that his guidance had always followed up the realities of the battlefield. Although he had a deep understanding of the force-using theory, he did not apply it mechanically to commanding the battle. From the realities of the battlefield, he attached much importance to public discussions with other members of the General Headquarters to find out the best ways of fighting. In many cases, especially in some campaigns of great strategic significance, he proposed ways of fighting which were different from those of the majority. He always closely followed the situations of the enemy and Vietnamese troops on the front in order to make lucid, cautious, and timely decisions. He was a good commander not only in a guerrilla war, but also in a regular one involving various arms. Particularly, he cleverly combined the guerilla war in the enemy-occupied areas with the regular war by regular brigades.

General Đoàn Huyên also found a military theorist in Võ Nguyên Giáp. He said, "He was not only an excellent commander, but also a leading military theorist of Việt Nam in the Hồ Chí Minh era. It is an outstanding feature of Võ Nguyên Giáp."

Having learned from the feats of arms and lessons of experience from the realities of the revolutionary war, been imbued with the thought of Hồ Chí Minh, inherited the military tradition of the nation, and selectively and creatively acquired the Eastern and Western military quintessence, General Võ Nguyên Giáp made great contributions to developing the military science and art of Việt Nam in the new era, leaving a valuable military legacy to the generations of today and tomorrow.

A Man of Humanism

General Võ Nguyên Giáp often showed great care to the people, not only in great deeds but also in small acts. For example, he wrote some lines of condolence at the death of Văn Cao, who he considered an outstanding musician. He sent a letter of thanks to the people in a mountainous commune in Nguyên Bình District, Cao Bằng Province, who had supported the revolution during its early days. Although the letter was written in normal paper, it conveyed his deep sentiments towards the local people. It was then placed in a mirror frame and hung on a wall in the office of the Commune People's Committee. He also sent a brief letter to doctor Nguyễn Thúc Mậu being in Lạng Sơn in April 1947 and telephoned doctor Tôn Thất Tùng being in Điện Biên in April 1954 to encourage doctors and nurses to overcome all difficulties and hardships to cure wounded and sick soldiers. Over half a century had passed, but he still remembered excellent soldiers in the anti-French resistance war. Nguyễn Quốc Trị was among the army heroes commended at the First Festival of Heroes and Model Workers held in 1952. He also received the title *"Nhanh như sóc, mạnh như hổ"* ("As swift as an arrow, as strong as a lion) from General Võ Nguyên Giáp for his nimbleness and courage in the Tu Vũ battle in the Hòa Bình campaign. When his family built a house in memory of him, they asked General Võ Nguyên Giáp to write them some words and he agreed. The page with his brief lines and signature was then enlarged, placed in a mirror frame, and hung solemnly on a wall in the memorial house.

Võ Nguyên Giáp not only cared about Vietnamese people, but he also showed interest in other peoples in the world. That year he received the president of an African country. At the guest's request, he conveyed to the people of this country a message which was Hồ Chí Minh's slogan *"Đoàn kết, đoàn kết, đại đoàn kết; thành công, thành công, đại thành công"* ("Unity, unity, great unity; success, success, great success"). He also recommended the young people in this country to incessantly study to develop the country.

There are still many other stories of humanism in Võ Nguyên Giáp, which is the topic for discussion by war veterans, his companions-in-arms, during their meetings. In their eyes, Võ Nguyên Giáp is a general of benevolence.

People show their love and admiration for General Võ Nguyên Giáp in different ways. For instance, some want to call him "the eldest brother of the army" as Hồ Chí Minh did. Foreigners admire him for different reasons. French historian Jean Lacouture, for example, was impressed by his appearance at their first meeting. In his first visit to Indochina, Jean Lacouture met Võ Nguyên Giáp, who was then Vietnamese Minister of the Interior, and was strongly impressed by the appearance of this 35-year-old minister. In his book *Võ Nguyên Giáp—A portrait*, Jean Lacouture wrote:

> His lively eyes are alight with special attraction. One will easily get bewildered by his face. It shows that he is not easy to be subdued or convinced to give up his objectives. He is really one of the embodiments of the revolution—following both socialism and patriotism, being both romantic and scientific. He has bright eyes and ebullient gestures. His voice is sometimes emotional, sometimes humorous. No Vietnamese has left such a strong impression on me.

Indian, Cuban, and African people showed warm feelings towards General Võ Nguyên Giáp. Local people would give him a warm welcome when he visited their countries. In the streets, they would ebulliently shout, "Việt Nam! Hồ Chí Minh! Giáp!" Leaders of these countries considered him a great friend of theirs and the representative of a country close to the third world.

The Việt Nam-Africa Seminar was attended by 23 delegations from Africa. On behalf of these delegations, K. Angola, a Namibian minister, paid a visit to General Giáp. He sincerely revealed that during their struggle for national liberation, Namibian leaders always brought along with them General Võ Nguyên Giáp's books on the revolutionary struggle. He also spent much time studying and evaluating the Vietnamese revolution's great contributions to the African struggle for national liberation. Among these contributions was the Điện Biên Phủ victory, which is attached to name of General Võ Nguyên Giáp.

An Indian high-ranking military delegation, headed by Air Chief Marshal Om Prakash Mehra, paid a visit to Việt Nam in February 1989. In this visit, Air Chief Marshal Om Prakash Mehra expressed his desire to see Commander-in-chief Võ Nguyên Giáp. It was reported that on the afternoon of February 22, Air Chief Marshal Mehra went to the car to receive and embrace General Giáp as representative of the Vietnamese Government. He sincerely said to General Giáp, "Dear Sir Commander-in-chief,[4] I had a premonition several days ago that I would meet you. And now, we are honored to see you here. Honestly speaking, meeting you is one of my aspirations in this visit."

He also revealed that *Điện Biên Phủ* had become a favorite book of many Indian generals, and that Indian people had talked much about Việt Nam, Hồ Chí Minh, Điện Biên, and Võ Nguyên Giáp. Air Chief Marshal Mehra was lavish with his praise for the victory of "Điện Biên Phủ in the air." He said, "When Việt Nam crushed American strategic airstrikes, downed tens of B52 flying fortresses, arrested many American pilots, and created a "Điện Biên Phủ in the air" in the sky of Hà Nội, I was really amazed and overwhelmed with admiration. I personally think that it is an unparalleled exploit of air battles in the 20th century."

Air Chief Marshal Mehra affirmed that the success of the Vietnamese people's resistance war would surely be praised by the world as the mankind's greatest struggle for independence and freedom. "I personally think that in Asia, you are not only the most excellent tactical commander but also the most brilliant strategic commander. You are a general of legends," said he.

The meeting between the two military commanders was longer than expected. At the farewell moment, Air Chief Marshal Mehra held Võ Nguyên Giáp's hands for a while and repeated his previous words from the bottom of his heart. "I have seen you already and I still hold that you will be a general of legends forever," said he.

Air Chief Marshal Mehra's manner of address is coincident with the thought of Senior Lieutenant-general Trần Văn Trà. The latter said, "I think we should not call Võ Nguyên Giáp 'General.' It is not wrong to address him by this title, but it does not express his role as the eldest brother of the whole Vietnamese army and his relation with it. I prefer to call him 'Commander-in-chief' or 'brother Văn.'"

"Commander-in-chief" is a formal way of address. During the two resistance wars by the Vietnamese people, under the leadership of the Politburo, Võ Nguyên Giáp held the posts of Secretary of the Central Military Committee and Commander-in-chief, commanding all political commissars, commanders, and generals. Therefore, I personally think that if we need a formal title to address him, "Commander-in-chief" should be the best choice. Hồ Chí Minh is the highest commander-in-chief of the Vietnamese revolution for national liberation; Võ Nguyên Giáp is the commander-in-chief of the Vietnamese People's Army.

Meanwhile, "brother Văn" is an informal way of addressing him. It reflects his role in the army and his relations with the whole army and the circles of intellectuals, writers, and artists.

Perhaps, being loved and respected by almost the whole army is his greatest happiness. In other words, his nearly absolute prestige remained unchanged to his last breath.

Numerous well-known intellectuals and artists hold Võ Nguyên Giáp in high esteem. Among them are Professor Tôn Thất Tùng, doctor Phạm Ngọc Thạch, and musician Lưu Hữu Phước.

Many generals said that humanism in his commanding style was one of the main reasons why he was loved by the whole army. General Hoàng Minh Thảo said, "The Commander-in-chief never accepted any victory at the expense of his soldiers' lives resulting from any random or incautious decisions. Never did he do so. His commanding style stemmed from his heart and was imbued with humanism."

He had been seen several times staying up all night or shedding tears after listening to reports on death-tolls in some battles. It was the urgent and severe moments that helped him find out the answer to difficult puzzles and stay calm to deal with all situations of the campaign most cleverly, so that all requirements of the campaign could be met and casualties could be reduced. Obviously humanism had penetrated deep into his soul since the early moments of the combats of wits and forces against the enemy during the campaign.

General Đồng Sỹ Nguyên, commander of Trường Sơn soldiers, still remember his visit with Võ Nguyên Giáp to the ATP[1] area on Trường Sơn Road in early 1973. During

---

1. ATP is the code name of a group of three important positions on Trường Sơn Road. It is made up by the first letters of these place-names—A-shaped turning, Tà Lê tunnel, and Phu La Nhích mountain pass. They were most severely attacked by the American air force for consecutive days.

the trip, General Võ Nguyên Giáp thoroughly asked about the transportation on the road, the operation of enemy air forces, and Vietnamese casualties. In his memoirs that night General Nguyên wrote, "His tears for the soldiers who laid down their lives in this area are imbued with humanism and will stay forever in my mind."

General Trần Văn Trà also talked about humanism reflected in the Commander-in-chief's sense of responsibility and love for soldiers. He wrote:

> Võ Nguyên Giáp was a commander-in-chief who felt hurt with every of the soldier's woulds and regretted every of the soldier's drops of blood. In the role of a commander-in-chief, he always abided by one of the vital principles of a just war—winning victory with minimal sacrifices.
>
> Brother Văn patiently and determinedly struggled for that vital principle throughout his military career. For this reason, he was given the honor to be called "the eldest brother of the Vietnamese army."

As a teacher, Võ Nguyên Giáp is loved and respected by his students at Thăng Long School. In their annual meetings, they keep talking about their teacher with great respect and admiration. On the occasion of the Teachers' Day in 2002, Trần Văn Lan, one of Võ Nguyên Giáp's students in the 1934–1935 school year, wrote, "My teacher is very gentle. He never reprimanded his students."

I left Thăng Long School and said good bye to my beloved teacher for 63 years. Whenever I think of the old school or hear about my teacher in the newspaper or on radio, I reminisce about the image of an intellectual with bright eyes, fair complexion, and unhurried gait. He was strict but tolerate and generous.

He taught me many lessons on patriotism and national pride through the subject of history. The best of all, however, were those on proper behaviors.

In 2005, on the occasion of his 95th birthday anniversary, a group of veterans, cadres, teachers from Mỹ Đức District, Hà Đông Town (in present-day Hà Nội) came to wish him good health and longevity. The group leader, on behalf of the group, said:

> Dear General,
>
> Yesterday, when we heard the news that we would come to the capital to meet the General, we all washed up to purify our bodies and souls.

His simple and sincere words showed the love and respect of soldiers under his command. The group offered Võ Nguyên Giáp wall hangings embroidered with a poem in praise of his virtue and talent as the eldest brother of the army.

I shall end this book with the comments by General Trần Văn Trà and Hoàng Minh Thảo. "Võ Nguyên Giáp has become an eminent historical personage in the national liberation movement against old colonialism and neo-colonialism in Việt Nam and in the world during the 20th century. At the same time, Võ Nguyên Giáp is one of the brilliant faces of Vietnamese culture" Trần Văn Trà said.

Meanwhile, General Hoàng Minh Thảo wrote, "The image of Võ Nguyên Giáp in an old suit, with an old felt hat on and a pistol on the side, remains bright beside those of cannons, missiles, fighter planes, fleets, army doctors, veterans, young soldiers, and millions of young people on the economic and cultural fronts across Việt Nam."

**CÔNG TY TNHH MỘT THÀNH VIÊN
NHÀ XUẤT BẢN THẾ GIỚI**

Trụ sở chính: 46 Trần Hưng Đạo, Hà Nội
Tel: 0084. 4. 38253841 – Fax: 0084. 4. 38269578
Chi nhánh: Số 7 Nguyễn Thị Minh Khai, Quận 1, TP Hồ Chí Minh
Tel: 0084. 8. 38220102
Email: thegioi@thegioipublishers.vn
Website: www.thegioipublishers.vn

TỔNG TƯ LỆNH
ĐẠI TƯỚNG VÕ NGUYÊN GIÁP

Chịu trách nhiệm xuất bản:
Trần Đoàn Lâm

Biên tập: **Quách Ngọc Anh**
Hiệu đính: **Garima Stephen**
Trình bày: **Trần Hiếu**
Bìa: **Trung Dũng**

In 720 bản, khổ 14 x 20,5 cm tại Trung tâm Chế bản & In – Công ty THHN MTV Nhà xuất bản Thế Giới. Giấy xác nhận ĐKKHXB số: 547-2014/CXB/05-48/ThG. Theo quyết định xuất bản số: 258/QĐ-ThG cấp ngày 13 tháng 11 năm 2014. In xong và nộp lưu chiểu quý IV năm 2014.